Human Perspectives *in the* Internet Society
Culture, Psychology *and* Gender

WIT*PRESS*

WIT Press publishes leading books in Science and Technology.
Visit our website for the current list of titles.
www.witpress.com

WITeLibrary

Home of the Transactions of the Wessex Institute, the WIT electronic-library provides the international scientific community with immediate and permanent access to individual papers presented at WIT conferences. Visit the WIT eLibrary at www.witpress.com.

FIRST INTERNATIONAL CONFERENCE ON

HUMAN PERSPECTIVES *IN THE* INTERNET SOCIETY

CULTURE, PSYCHOLOGY *AND* GENDER

CONFERENCE CHAIRMEN

K. Morgan
University of Bergen, Norway

C.A. Brebbia
Wessex Institute of Technology, UK

Organised by
Wessex Institute of Technology, UK
The University of Bergen, Norway
and
The University of Cádiz, Spain

Human Perspectives
in the
Internet Society
Culture, Psychology *and* Gender

Editors

K. Morgan
University of Bergen, Norway

C.A. Brebbia
Wessex Institute of Technology, UK

J. Sanchez
University of Cadiz, Spain

A. Voiskounsky
Moscow State University, Russia

K. Morgan
University of Bergen, Norway

C.A. Brebbia
Wessex Institute of Technology, UK

J. Sanchez
University of Cadiz, Spain

A. Voiskounsky
Moscow State University, Russia

Published by

WIT Press
Ashurst Lodge, Ashurst, Southampton, SO40 7AA, UK
Tel: 44 (0) 238 029 3223; Fax: 44 (0) 238 029 2853
E-Mail: witpress@witpress.com
http://www.witpress.com

For USA, Canada and Mexico

WIT Press
25 Bridge Street, Billerica, MA 01821, USA
Tel: 978 667 5841; Fax: 978 667 7582
E-Mail: infousa@witpress.com
http://www.witpress.com

British Library Cataloguing-in-Publication Data

A Catalogue record for this book is available
from the British Library

ISBN: 1-85312-726-4
ISSN: 1742-5069

The texts of the papers in this volume were set individually by the authors or under their supervision. Only minor corrections to the text may have been carried out by the publisher.

Reprinted 2005 by Lightning Source, Milton Keynes, UK.

Preface

Over the past 30 years Information and Communications Technology (ICT) has become a pervasive part of all aspects of modern life. Even the most superficial observation shows the impact of this technology being felt throughout industry, commerce, education, entertainment and society. Much literature and effort has been devoted to documenting and understanding the technical aspects of these developments whilst in contrast relatively less attention has been given to their human consequences.

This book attempts to redress some of this imbalance by bringing together leading authorities from around the world to present the current state of research and understanding into the social, psychological and cultural impact of the new technologies. Contributions cover the whole range of perspectives from changes in social norms through to an examination of the complex issues involved with gender representation within the new communication mediums. This book will be of value both to newcomers to this area and also to established authorities interested in the current state of this important domain.

The Editors
2004

Contents

Section 8: Gender stereotypes

Section 9: Cyber society norms and values

Section 10: Threats and challenges to diversity

Section 1
Understanding online behaviour

Predicting and understanding student attitudes and behaviour in e-learning

K. Morgan
Department of Information Science and Media Studies,
University of Bergen, Norway

Abstract

This paper will review personality theory with respect to technology use with a special emphasis on education and educational technology. The paper summarises some of the major personality and learning theories and details much of the research which has been conducted in this area. Major emphasis is placed on work which has adopted the Myers-Briggs Type Inventory (MBTI) and the latter part of the paper concentrates on describing research which has used the MBTI in computer based education. The paper concludes with a summary and suggestions for future work using personality theory in educational technology.
Keywords: personality, student attitudes, e-learning

1 Introduction

The idea of looking at personality as a factor in human computer interaction is not new. Van Muylwijk et al. [48] was among the first to recognise that personality traits would have a major impact on both behavior and attitudes when using technology. This idea of looking at personality and interaction styles was followed up by both Van der Veer et al. [46] and Singleton [44]. Van der Veer proposed a more general approach where various personality factors would have some affect on attitudes towards and use of the system. In contrast Singleton proposed intelligence as a single factor which he believed would predict the degree of success in using computer systems and in having positive attitudes towards computer systems. Later investigations into the role of personality included a series of experimental studies by Van Hoe et al. [47] who attempted to look at the role of personality and preferences for menu characteristics and Weil et al. [49] who tried to find links to computer phobia. Neither Van-Hoe or Weil were successful in their attempts to find links between

Human Perspectives in the Internet Society: Culture, Psychology and Gender, K. Morgan, J. Sanchez, C. A. Brebbia & A Voiskounsky (Editors) © 2004 WIT Press, www.witpress.com, ISBN 1-85312-726-4

personality styles and computer use or attitudes. This may have been because they were simply looking at more high level personality factors or that the tasks they selected were so far removed from day to day experience that classical personality theory was overwhelmed by system characteristics. By the early 1990's computer systems had advanced enough to allow for computer mediated communication which permitted more naturalistic communication styles. It is not therefore surprising that when Adrianson and Hjelmquist [1] investigated the role of extroversion in computer mediated communication he found significant differences connected with the extroversion factor but that these were much weaker than in normal face to face communication. We must again recognise that in the early 1990's although CMC provided naturalistic communication it did not support video or audio conferencing except in rare research settings.

2 Personality factors in educational technology

Much of the potential for successful use of personality factors within technology lies within the area of educational information technology. For example, Arnone et al. [2] proposed that curiosity would be the major factor in deciding how effective a student would find a computer based teaching environment. More recently others [5,35] have proposed that it would be the teachers personality factors that would be most influential in the success of pedagogical information systems. While there appears to be little doubt among researchers that personality factors are of great importance in determining the successful use of information technology in educational settings [7, 24, 5, 22, 43] comparatively little work has actually been reported in the general personality literature. Those studies which have been reported either have looked at abnormal and pathological computer users [16] who are hopefully not representative of a general student body or have reported finding no differences in personality between predicted groups of users [9]. Those studies that have reported finding differences have usually concentrated on the most negative areas of information technology use, such as gender imbalance [23], the role of personality in repetitive strain injury [34] or the personality factors involved in computer based stress [32,25].

2.1 Current personality measures

Throughout the study of the mind various types of personality have been proposed, ranging from the "humours" proposed by the early Greek philosophers to the personality factors investigated by psychologists in the 20th century [28, 13, 14]. Although different personality theorists have used different terms to describe the important (non-cognitive) dimensions of personality, more recent research has isolated 5 broad dimensions of personality, which are often called "The Big Five". One frequently cited organisation of these Big Five is Goldberg's FFI [18, 19, 20] where the Big Five are associated with the following types: Extraversion, Agreeableness, Conscientiousness, Emotional Stability and Openness. In contrast to these formal descriptive types the less discriminatory measures derived from Jung's [30] personality theory are called the Myers-

Human Perspectives in the Internet Society: Culture, Psychology and Gender, K. Morgan, J. Sanchez, C. A. Brebbia & A Voiskounsky (Editors) © 2004 WIT Press, www.witpress.com, ISBN 1-85312-726-4

Briggs Type Inventory (MBTI). Within the MBTI 'The Big Five' are associated with the following types: Extraversion vs. Introversion, Feeling vs. Thinking, Judging vs. Perception and Intuition vs. Sensing.

2.2 The Myers-Briggs personality type inventory (MBTI) in education.

The history of the use of the Myers-Briggs Type Inventory within education is relatively long. As early as the late 1960's Richek [42] had proposed that the MBTI might be a suitable instrument to determine the best teachers with regard to teaching style and material presentation to students. Although the history of the MBTI within education is long it took some considerable time for it to gain widespread support. Early evaluations compared the MBTI and other personality measures such as Cattell's 16PF [6] in the role of predicting successful learning styles and grade point averages [12] and although researchers such as Lorr [36] had problems recognising the usefulness of the MBTI on the whole by the early 1990's there was growing support and recognition for both the validity and reliability of the MBTI in education [40,4]. Since that time although there have been some studies which raised concerns that the MBTI was being taken out of context from Jungian theory [17] and that it might not truly reflect unconscious desires [3] it has been found to be one of the best predictors for many aspects of education and educational technology [12, 26].

2.3 Learning styles

As early as the mid 1970's researchers in education were investigating the possible links between Carl Jung's typology of conscious functioning [30] and general learning styles amongst students. Early results from studies such as Millott and Cranney [39] found significant links between the MBTI types INP (Introversion, iNtuition, Perception) and learning style differences in reading comprehension. Later work by Lyons [37] proposed that teaching styles matched the teacher's own learning style and factors identified by the teachers MBTI scores. Following Lyons proposal Provost and Anchors [41] reported the importance for the teacher to match their teaching style to the preferences of the students learning styles as determined by the MBTI. Indeed, work by Jensen [27] showed that there was a strong link between the students MBTI type and their preferred and most effective learning style. However, it took nearly another decade before researchers could define specific MBTI types to students preferred learning styles. One of the first researchers to investigate this area was Drummond [11] who proposed that there were strong links and overlaps between the MBTI type of a student and their preferred Gregoric Style Delineator (GSD) [11]. By the mid 1990's researchers had begun to specify the actual learning styles preferred by specific MBTI types such as Harasym et al.'s [21] work with the GSD such that MBTI type SJ (Sensing, Judging) had a marked preference for GSD learning styles of a concrete sequential nature. In contrast MBTI types NP (iNtuition, Perception) preferred concrete random GSD learning styles and MBTI type T (Thinking) showed a marked preference for GSD learning style of abstract sequential. Finally MBTI types F (Feeling) preferred GSD learning styles of an abstract random nature. In terms of MBTI types and group

Human Perspectives in the Internet Society: Culture, Psychology and Gender, K. Morgan, J. Sanchez, C. A. Brebbia & A Voiskounsky (Editors) © 2004 WIT Press, www.witpress.com, ISBN 1-85312-726-4

interactions the work of Johnson [29] showed that MBTI type T's (Thinking) liked learning environments with competition to other students, MBTI types F preferred learning groups which focused on accommodation, MBTI types E (Extraversion) preferred group working where individuals collaborated and finally MBTI types I preferred group activities where conflicts were avoided. These findings are of major importance when we take students and force them to use computer supported collaborative environments. It is therefore vital to gain further understanding of the consequences in terms of student satisfaction performance and effectiveness of putting students with different MBTI types into one common environment.

2.4 MBTI in subject study prediction

Most modern research with the MBTI has not focused on trying to identify the MBTI type of the highest scoring students, since we have already recognised that this may simply be a result of the learning style imposed in that particular educational environment. It is known that the students communication when working in groups is strongly predicted by MBTI scores [31] and this may have a direct link to findings that have shown that students in non typical learning situations, for example, TV presentation of lectures or other distance learning settings do best if they have an MBTI type N profile [10]. Indeed it has been known since the late 1980's [33] that non standard teaching environments such as distance learning settings or computer based teaching (CBT) give preference to different MBTI types and different learning styles than traditional learning settings. For example, early experiments reported finding that students with MBTI type S performed better on computer based teaching systems than N types [33]. However, we must realise that these early CBT systems did not involve a distance component and that these findings may well have changed as the nature of computer based teaching and learning environments have changed (modern computer based teaching systems place an emphasis on collaboration). The overall activity and types of interactions undertaken by a group are known to be under the influence of MBTI types such that the overall combined MBTI types of the individuals in a group accurately describe and predict that groups behaviour [45]. This means that it is possible for an educator to accurately gauge the overall MBTI types of a particular cohort of students before formal educational practices begin. The potential for allowing modification of teaching style or learning environment to match individual MBTI types or even group MBTI types is enormous. For example, when controlled studies are performed where professors deliberately teach in the manner matching their student MBTI scores, student satisfaction ratings and overall grade performance are significantly enhanced [41, 8, 38, 15].

3 Summary and conclusions

In this paper we have summarised some of the important research in the area of personality and the use of technology with a particular emphasis on the role of personality in education and especially with regards to educational technology.

Human Perspectives in the Internet Society: Culture, Psychology and Gender, K. Morgan, J. Sanchez, C. A. Brebbia & A Voiskounsky (Editors) © 2004 WIT Press, www.witpress.com, ISBN 1-85312-726-4

In our own research which builds upon this literature we have investigated the possible link between MBTI types and the attitudes and behaviour of students using computer supported collaborative learning environments. We have found statistically significant differences between the major personality factors in terms of the use of the learning environment and attitudes towards the various components of the online collaborative learning system. Based on our findings we strongly support the idea that the MBTI can provide a useful tool in configuring such online learning environments to student's personalities and preferred learning styles. Of the MBTI types investigated in our own work the dimensions of Extrovert/Introvert and Sensor/Intuitive appear to be most promising as major predicting factors in learning styles and system component preferences. These can be summarised such that Extrovert-Introvert dimension determines the primary learning and interacting style, while the Sensing-Intuitive dimension predicts the use or avoidance of certain system components. The remaining dimensions Thinkers / Feelers and Judgers / Perceivers appear more related to attitudes toward group work and may reflect some previous experience within our subject population. It is to be hoped that future research will investigate methods in which MBTI type tests for Extrovert / Introvert and Sensor/ Intuitive can be directly linked to real time online changes within the collaborative learning environment to more closely match students preferred interaction styles and preferred learning tools.

References

[1] Adrianson, Lillemor; Hjelmquist, Erland *Group processes in face to face and computer mediated communication.* Behaviour and Information Technology". Jul Aug; Vol 10(4): 281 296 1991.

[2] Arnone, Marilyn P.; Grabowski, Barbara L.; Rynd, Christopher P. *Curiosity as a personality variable influencing learning in a learner controlled lesson with and without advisement.* Educational Technology Research and Development; Vol 42(1): 5 20 1994.

[3] Barbuto, John E. Jr. *A critique of the Myers Briggs Type Indicator and its operationalization of Carl Jung's psychological types.* Psychological Reports. Apr; Vol 80(2): 611 625 1997.

[4] Brown, Virginia L.; DeCoster, David A. *The Myers Briggs Type Indicator as a developmental measure: Implications for student learners in higher education.* Journal of College Student Development. 1991 Jul; Vol 32(4): 378 379 1991.

[5] Calvert, Sandra L. *Children's journeys through the information age.* New York, NY, USA: Mcgraw Hill. xxii, 298 pp. McGraw Hill series in developmental psychology. 1999.

[6] Cattell, R. *A guide to mental testing.* London. 1936.

[7] Clements, Douglas H. *Teaching creativity with computers.* Educational Psychology Review. Jun; Vol 7(2): 141 161 1995.

[8] Cooper, Stewart E.; Miller, John A. *MBTI learning style^teaching style discongruencies.* Educational and Psychological Measurement. Fal; Vol 51(3): 699 706 1991.

Human Perspectives in the Internet Society: Culture, Psychology and Gender, K. Morgan, J. Sanchez, C. A. Brebbia & A Voiskounsky (Editors) © 2004 WIT Press, www.witpress.com, ISBN 1-85312-726-4

[9] Davis, Dineh M. *Review of "The perpetual novice: An undervalued resource in the age of experts"*: Response to reviewer comments. Mind, Culture, and Activity; Vol 4(1): 55 56 1997.

[10] Dawson, Betty G.; Guy, Rebecca F. *Personality type and grade performance in a TV assisted course.* Journal of Psychological Type; Vol 29: 38 42 1994.

[11] Drummond, Robert J.; Stoddard, Ann H. *Learning style and personality type.* Perceptual and Motor Skills. Aug; Vol 75(1): 99 104 1992.

[12] Eison, James A.; Pollio, Howard R. *A multidimensional approach to the definition of college students' learning styles.* Journal of College Student Personnel. Sep; Vol 26(5): 434 443 1985.

[13] Eysenck, HJ. *Dimensions of personality: 16: 5 or 3? criteria for a taxonomic paradigm.* Personality and Individual Differences, 12, 773-90 1991.

[14] Eysenck, H. J. & Eysenck, S. B. G. *Personality structure and measurement.* London. 1969.

[15] Fisher, Darrell; Kent, Harry; Fraser, Barry Relationships *between teacher student interpersonal behaviour and teacher personality.* School Psychology International. May; Vol 19(2): 99 119 1998.

[16] Gackenbach, Jayne (Ed) *Psychology and the Internet: Intrapersonal, interpersonal, and transpersonal implications.* San Diego, CA, USA: Academic Press, Inc. (1998). xix, 369 pp.

[17] Garden, Anna Maria, *Unresolved issues with the Myers Briggs Type Indicator.* Journal of Psychological Type. Vol 22: 3 14 1991.

[18] Goldberg, LR. *The development of markers for the big-five factor structure.* Psychol. Assessment, 4, 26-42. 1992.

[19] Goldberg, LR *The structure of phenotypic personality traits.* Am. Psychol., 48, 26-34. 1993a.

[20] Goldberg, LR. *The structure of personality traits: vertical and horizontal aspects.* In DC Funder, RD Parke, C Tomlinson-Keasey, & K Widaman (Eds.), Studying lives through time: personality and development (pp. 169-88). Washington, D.C.: American Psychological Association. 1993b.

[21] Harasym, P. H.; Leong, E. J.; Juschka, B. B.; Lucier, G. E. *Relationship Between Myers Briggs Type Indicator and Gregorc Style Delineator.* Perceptual and Motor Skills. Jun; Vol 82(3, Pt 2): 1203 1210 1996.

[22] Harris, Roger W. *Attitudes towards end user computing: A structural equation model.* Behaviour and Information Technology. 1999 Mar Apr; Vol 18(2): 109 125 1999.

[23] Harrison, Allison W.; Rainer, R. Kelly Jr.; Hochwarter, Wayne A. *Gender differences in computing activities.* Journal of Social Behavior and Personality. Dec; Vol 12(4): 849 868 1997.

[24] Hartley, James *Learning and studying: A research perspective.* New York, NY, USA: Routledge. xii, 179 pp. 1998.

[25] Henry, John W.; Stone, Robert W. *The development and validation of computer self efficacy and outcome expectancy scales in a nonvolitional context.* Behavior Research Methods, Instruments and Computers. 1997 Nov; Vol 29(4): 519 527 1997.

[26] Jackson, Stacy L.; Parker, Christopher P.; Dipboye, Robert L. *A comparison of competing models underlying responses to the Myers Briggs Type Indicator.* Journal of Career Assessment. Win; Vol 4(1): 99 115 1996.

[27] Jensen, George H. *Learning styles.* In Provost, Judith A. (Ed); Anchors, Scott (Ed); et al. Applications of the Myers Briggs Type Indicator in higher education. (pp. 181 206). Palo Alto, CA, USA: Consulting Psychologists Press. iv, 288 pp 1987.

[28] John, OP. *The "Big Five" factor taxonomy: Dimensions of personality in the natural language and in questionnaires.* In LA Pervin (Ed.), Handbook of personality: Theory and research . New York: Guilford. 1990.

[29] Johnson, Alan K. *Conflict handling intentions and the MBTI: A construct validity study.* Journal of Psychological Type.; Vol 43: 29 39 1997.

[30] Jung, C. *1953 –1971 Collected works.* London. 1971.

[31] Kagan, Dona M.; Grandgenett, Donald J. *Personality and interaction analysis.* Research in Education. May; No 37: 13 24 1987.

[32] Kahn, Howard; Cooper, Cary L. *The potential contribution of information technology to the mental ill health, job dissatisfaction, and alcohol intake of money market dealers: An exploratory study.* International Journal of Human Computer Interaction. Oct Dec; Vol 3(4): 321 338 1991.

[33] Kern, Gary M.; Matta, Khalil F. *The influence of personality on self paced instruction.* Journal of Computer Based Instruction. Sum; Vol 15(3): 104 108 1988.

[34] Kiesler, Sara; Finholt, Tom *The mystery of RSI.* American Psychologist. Dec; Vol 43(12): 1004 1015 1988.

[35] Lieskovsky, Peter *Personality and social determinants of attitudes toward computers in university students.* Studia Psychologica. 1988; Vol 30(2): 115 124.

[36] Lorr, Maurice *An empirical evaluation of the MBTI typology.* Personality and Individual Differences.; Vol 12(11): 1141 1145 1991.

[37] Lyons, Carol A. *The relationship between prospective teachers' learning preference/style and teaching preference/style.* Educational and Psychological Research. Fal; Vol 5(4): 275 297 1985.

[38] McCutcheon, John W.; Schmidt, Charles P.; Bolden, Samuel H. *Relationships among selected personality variables, academic achievement and student teaching behavior.* Journal of Research and Development in Education. Spr; Vol 24(3): 38 44 1991.

[39] Millott, Robert; Cranney, A. Garr *Personality correlates of college reading and study skills.* Journal of Reading Behavior. Fal; Vol 8(3): 335 336 1976.

Human Perspectives in the Internet Society: Culture, Psychology and Gender, K. Morgan, J. Sanchez, C. A. Brebbia & A Voiskounsky (Editors) © 2004 WIT Press, www.witpress.com, ISBN 1-85312-726-4

[40] Murray, John B. *Review of research on the Myers Briggs Type Indicator.* Perceptual and Motor Skills. Jun; Vol 70(3, Pt 2): 1187 1202 1990.

[41] Provost, Judith A. (Ed); Anchors, Scott (Ed) *Applications of the Myers Briggs Type Indicator in higher education.* Palo Alto, CA, USA: Consulting Psychologists Press. (1987). iv, 288 pp.

[42] Richek, Herbert G. *Jung's typology and psychological adjustment in prospective teachers: A preliminary investigation.* Alberta Journal of Educational Research. Dec; Vol. 15(4): 235 243 1969.

[43] Shavinina, Larisa V.; Loarer, Even *Psychological evaluation of educational multimedia applications.* European Psychologist.; Vol 4(1): 33 44 1999.

[44] Singleton, W. T. *The mind at work*: Psychological ergonomics. Cambridge, England UK: Cambridge University Press. . xiii, 348 pp. 1989

[45] Stever, Gayle S. *Gender by type interaction effects in mass media subcultures.* Journal of Psychological Type.; Vol 32: 3 22 1995.

[46] Van der Veer, Gerrit C.; Tauber, Michael J.; Waern, Yvonne; Van Muylwijk, Bert *On the interaction between system and user characteristics.* Behaviour and Information Technology. 1985 Oct Dec; Vol 4(4): 289 308 1985.

[47] Van Hoe, Rudy; Poupeye, Karel; Vandierendonck, Andre; de Soete, Geert *Some effects of menu characteristics and user personality on performance with menu driven interfaces.* Behaviour and Information Technology. Jan Feb; Vol 9(1): 17 29 1990.

[48] Van Muylwijk, Bert; Van der Veer, Gerrit; Waern, Yvonne *On the implications of user variability in open systems: An overview of the little we know and of the lot we have to find out.* Behaviour and Information Technology. Oct Dec; Vol 2(4): 313 326 1983.

[49] Weil, Michelle M.; Rosen, Larry D.; Wugalter, Stuart E. *The etiology of computerphobia.* Computers in Human Behavior.; Vol 6(4): 361 379 1990.

The ontology of internet user interactions

J. Shires
Department of Communication, Purdue University North Central

Abstract

Internet communication, like traditional mediated communication, places a barrier between the message's sender and receiver. However, where traditional mediated communication (television, magazines) is unidirectional, internet technologies provide for one-on-one communication albeit with a high degree of mediation. The basic ontology of this interaction has yet to be fully explicated. Traditional communication theory focuses on interactions that are face-to-face while mass communication theory looks at communication situations where feedback is delayed or completely absent. Internet interactions are both interpersonal and mediated and, at the same time, are neither of these. The paper will use the framework of self- and other-informed theories of Edmund Husserl and Mikhail Bakhtin to understand how users construct "faces" for all parties involved in the internet communication interaction. In addition, the paper will use the theories of Nicolai Hartmann to discuss how this ontology is, on the one hand, stratified and, on the other hand, unified. The paper will discuss how the user actively constructs a self-identity which is then portrayed to other people involved in the interaction and how the individual deconstructs the identities of other users.

1 Introduction

". . . just as there is a sole universal nature as a self-enclosed framework of unity, so there is a sole psychic framework, a total framework of all souls, which are united not externally but internally, namely, through the intentional interpenetration which is the communalization of their lives" [2].

"The highest architectonic principle of the actual world of the performed act or deed is the concrete and architectonically valid or operative contraposition of I and the other . . . it is around these two centers that all of the concrete moments of Being are distributed and arranged" [3].

We live in a world of connections and relations. Every moment of every day we interact with others or are the object of interactions for others. Communication

Human Perspectives in the Internet Society: Culture, Psychology and Gender, K. Morgan, J. Sanchez, C. A. Brebbia & A Voiskounsky (Editors) © 2004 WIT Press, www.witpress.com, ISBN 1-85312-726-4

theory attempts to explicate these moments in order to predict or understand how human beings exchange ideas, concepts and worldviews. The most vexing phenomena that communication faces is not traditional interpersonal communication but interpersonal communication that is mediated through technology. Edmund Husserl, in the first quote above, notes that our interactions take place in a unified world of experience. But how is that world unified when both parties are separated by thousands of miles of distance? Mikhail Bakhtin, in the second quote, states that interactions bring together two contraposed positions—the self and the other. But how can two people who are not in close physical contact share a similar horizon of an event?

There is a real need in computer mediated communication (CMC) to understand both the relationship between the user and the computer and the relationships between users who employ the computer as a means of interacting with others. CMC presents a problem because it is neither truly an interpersonal nor mediated communication process but a combination of both. I believe that what is needed is an ontology of communication that encompasses all areas of communication. I refer to this ontology as a stratified dialogic model, borrowing both from the dialogic method employed by Mikhail Bakhtin and a stratified ontology employed by Nicolai Hartmann. This model focuses on the "act" or interaction in communication as opposed to just either the sender/author or the listener/receiver. The stratified dialogic model sees the act communication as a unified event consisting of several layers.

2 Bakhtin and the dialogic

2.1 Self and other

Bakhtin does not base his ontology on being *qua* being, but instead focuses on the being of the event of interaction between two concrete individuals. According to Bakhtin, the "act is truly real . . .only in its entirety" [3]. Bakhtin uses the term "act" very loosely-any thought that I have or task I undertake is labelled as an "act." I am unable to abstract anything from the interaction/act and still maintain the integrity and uniqueness of the act—I must consider the act as a unity or a whole. Acts are historical; they take place in a particular time and a defined place [3]. Each act is unique and non-repeatable [3]. What I accomplish cannot be replicated since the "unity of the event" will have changed. An individual involved in the act realizes the uniqueness of the act [3] and the value of the act. Individual acts combine both universal and particular moments—it is universal in that the individual employs values and value systems that transcend time and it is particular in relating of the situation, time, and context to the transcendental moment [3].

Within the interaction are two necessary positions: self and other [2, 3]. Both I, as a self, and the other must be viewed as concrete individuals: "Man-in-general does not exist; I exist and particular concrete others exist—my intimates, my contemporary" [3]. I must be able to strike a relationship towards the other as a subject or object; I can form this relationship only with an actual, concrete

Human Perspectives in the Internet Society: Culture, Psychology and Gender, K. Morgan, J. Sanchez, C. A. Brebbia & A Voiskounsky (Editors) © 2004 WIT Press, www.witpress.com, ISBN 1-85312-726-4

other, not a possible other [3]. The other, if a subject, will reveal a portion of herself to me—the other-for-me. If the other is an object, I will be able to see only the outside of it, superficial characteristics. I, also, retain a portion of myself that cannot be seen by the other—the I-for-myself. Dialogue is how I am able to bridge the gap between self and other. Michael Bernard-Donals writes, "dialogue begins when the self's non-coincidence with itself and with other selves requires a bridge between the I-for-myself and I-for-other" [4]. Dialogue requires an exchange of selves--the I-for-other and the other-for-me "overlap" in the interaction (see figure 1).

2.2 Dialogic relationships

Bakhtin focuses on the body as the site of overlap—it is the extension of the self into the world. The I-for-myself and the unknown component of the other can only be seen if they are embodied. If the other is a person, the unknown portion will most likely involve her thoughts and emotions. I can only know what the other chooses to show me—what she chooses to embody. Ideas and feelings can only be known to me if the other displays them for or discusses them with me—I must engage her in a dialogue. If the other is an object, there will be characteristics that I will not be able to see at the surface level—I must break it apart to see its internal compounds and characteristics. By playing up the difference between the self and the world and the mind and the body, it seems as if Bakhtin is creating a form of dualism.

Bakhtin's interest, however, does not lie in opposition but interaction [2, 3], as seen in figure 1. Bakhtin attempts to move away from an idealist position and move towards a more materialistic position [1, 2, 3]. As such, he is interested only in phenomena that appear concretely. Only the physical manifestations of the I-for-self that are embodied in the I-for-other can enter into to a dialogue with the other. Only the embodied other-for-me, likewise, can be part of interaction. This is not to say that the exchange does not have an effect on the I-for-self. Unless an idea can be demonstrated or expressed in language, it cannot become part of the world dialogue. This process, the creation of the I-for-other, is also fundamentally dialogic in that it is a relation between the I-for-self and the I-for-other [2, 3].

2.3 Bakhtin, Husserl and the other

Bakhtin expresses very clearly the debt we owe to the other for definition [2], but he focuses primarily on the "I" side of the interaction. In order to understand the other, we must turn to the writings of Husserl, particularly the *Cartesian Meditations*. Husserl, in the fifth meditation, wonders how it is that I can perceive of the other as another Ego. He states that it is my acknowledgement of "harmonious behaviour" that not only indicates that the other is an animate being but also that the other possesses a psychic (psychological) presence [8]. We understand the other is another Ego through the analogy of the other with our own behaviour [8]. I cannot bridge the gap between myself "here" and the other "there" by physically approaching the other—whenever I walk "there" it

Human Perspectives in the Internet Society: Culture, Psychology and Gender, K. Morgan, J. Sanchez, C. A. Brebbia & A Voiskounsky (Editors) © 2004 WIT Press, www.witpress.com, ISBN 1-85312-726-4

becomes "here"—but through the exchange of ideas from my own unique position "here".

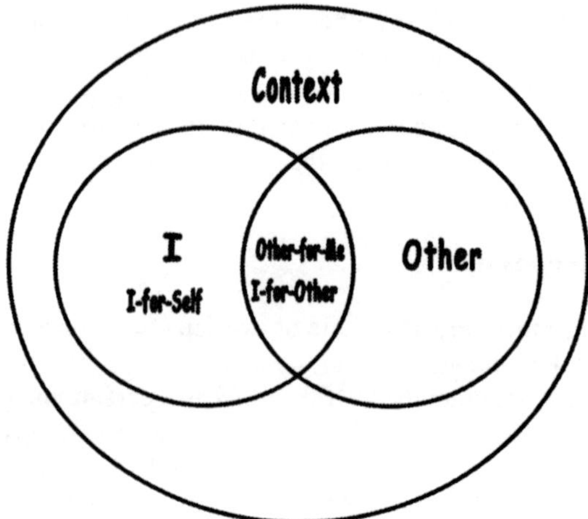

Figure 1: Basic dialogic model.

Relative of this position, Bakhtin notes that I and the other both have a surplus of vision towards each other [2]. The other can see things that I cannot—what is behind me, my face—while I can see objects and relations that the other cannot. I need the other to help me create my sense of self by giving me information that I cannot see. Reciprocally, I have a responsibility to respond or answer the other in the same manner—this is our responsibility to each other.

3 Nicolai Hartmann and ontology

3.1 Concrete individuals

Nicolai Hartmann shares many of the ontological concerns of Bakhtin. Hartmann also focuses on the concrete individual subject. Hartmann's ontology is a non-reductionist, "natural" ontology [7, 10]. He believes that we must understand being as we find it, not as we might theorise it. Like Bakhtin, Hartmann believes that only a concrete individual can enter into actual interactions. Hartmann writes, "The subject—not as a metaphysical subject in general but as empirical, actual, just how we know man—fulfils in every particular the specified conditions" [6]. Ontology, for Hartmann, is not simply a matter of developing *a priori* conditions. Instead, ontological categories are "gleaned step by step from an observation of existing realities" [7]. Any knowledge we are able to gain of ontological categories we gain "through an analysis of objects to the extent that they are intelligible to us" [7]. Hartmann believes that the categories and principles of ontology "must somehow be included in being and that,

Human Perspectives in the Internet Society: Culture, Psychology and Gender, K. Morgan, J. Sanchez, C. A. Brebbia & A Voiskounsky (Editors) © 2004 WIT Press, www.witpress.com, ISBN 1-85312-726-4

consequently, it must be possible to discover them if only a sufficiently broad basis of ontic data is supplied" [7].

Hartmann, like Bakhtin, divides individuals up into two portions—the body and the mind. While this too seems like a continuation of Descartean thought, Hartmann does not view the mind and body as independent entities: "Body and spirit, however, do not shade off into each other, and there is no continuum between them" [7]. Simply put, the psychic qualities of an individual must be embodied. The link between the bodily and the psychic can be seen in the relationship of how the body affects thought and the thought process: "In every individual, human nature starts its career with purely organic life, and only in this stratum is it directly connected with its ancestral line. Consciousness is not taken over from the consciousness of the parents, but it is formed anew. But it is formed in a very definite dependence upon the particular growing organism" [7]. Consciousness develops in the unique context of each individual's life.

3.2 Rules for strata division

The levels for strata are organized and divided by four rules [7]:

1. Categorical dependence is dependence of only the higher categories upon the lower, not conversely.
2. Although the categories of the lower stratum afford the basis for being of the higher, they are indifferent in regard to them.
3. The lower categories determine the higher ontological strata as either matter or as a basis for its being.
4. The novelty of the higher stratum is completely free in relation to the lower stratum.

The lower strata are the stronger. They are the building blocks for everything above. The higher strata use materials from the lower, but are able to combine and change these materials to create new structures. The higher strata are dependent on the lower strata—if the lower strata are not present, the higher strata cannot develop. Certain characteristics may appear in several strata. How it appears in the lower strata, however, does not predict how it will appear in the higher strata. These strata are shared by the whole of the physical world, not just mankind. Not everything in nature, though, will have all of the higher strata.

The two primary divisions, as mentioned above are the body and the mind (sometime the mind is called intellect or spirit—for purposes of simplicity I will refer to the higher strata as the mind and the intellect and the spiritual as strata of the mind). The mind is dependent on the body but the mind is not fully determined by the body. Categories that appear in the body may also appear in the mind, but the categories will not bleed from the body to the mind—the body/mind division is seen as a hard division. The body is divided up into two primary aspects—the inorganic (the lower and stronger) and the organic (the higher and freer). The mind, likewise, has two primary aspects—the intellectual (the lower) and the spiritual (the higher). It is unclear if Hartmann sees the self and other as categories within the strata themselves. I believe a more fruitful and

Human Perspectives in the Internet Society: Culture, Psychology and Gender, K. Morgan, J. Sanchez, C. A. Brebbia & A Voiskounsky (Editors) © 2004 WIT Press, www.witpress.com, ISBN 1-85312-726-4

productive way to view individuals is as monads and not as a part of the strata of the being of the world.

4 Towards an integrated ontology

4.1 Dialogic stratification

Understanding intersubjective relationships is vital to understanding the process of human communication as all interactions, even with one's self, are ultimately intersubjective. However, if ontology is stratified like Hartman suggests, how do I conceive a relationship between individuals? Does this type of ontological model show a stratification of the world with individuals as part of the natural world or does it see relationships between individuals in the world as relationships between monads?

I believe that each individual is uniquely stratified and that we share some categories or modalities based upon the context of the interaction. Individuals project a self into the world that is constructed from a dialogical relationship between the I-for-self, the other-for-me and the context. The external self, the I-for-other, is not just made up of bodily/external qualities that can be viewed, but also mind/internal qualities that are revealed through verbal or non-verbal communication. Through interaction, individuals share information about beliefs, ideas, and concepts along with psychical characteristics. Individuals do not necessarily "overlap" each other, but instead come into correlation with each other in an attempt to come to knowledge about the other (see figure 2).

4.2 Correlation

The Neo-Kantian philosopher/theologian Hermann Cohen discusses correlation in regard to both man's relationship with God and man's relationship to his fellowman [5]. We are able to "come alongside" God. We cannot merge with God, nor can we see things from His perspective. The same is true in relationships between individuals—we are contraposed to the other and can never occupy the space she occupies. We are never able to see from the position of the other. In his later writings, Bakhtin discusses the possible relations that exist in the world: relations between two objects, relations between subject and object and relations between two subjects [1]. These relations form a continuum that ranges between monologic at one pole dialogic at he other.

Relations between objects would be purely monologic. This relation is between two "things" that do not possess consciousness. Relations between two subjects would be purely dialogic. However, neither of these two poles is obtainable for the self. I neither can be an object—as mentioned above I am a subject of or for an other—nor am I able to treat the other fully as a subject—I must finalize or reify the other to some point in order to consider them an other. The positions I can take on this continuum range from treating the other as an object, treating the other as a subject with equal rights and treating the other as a Subject. These are all types of correlation and each one determines the type of

Human Perspectives in the Internet Society: Culture, Psychology and Gender, K. Morgan, J. Sanchez, C. A. Brebbia & A Voiskounsky (Editors) © 2004 WIT Press, www.witpress.com, ISBN 1-85312-726-4

perception I have of the other (see figure 2). If I completely reify the other, the other becomes an object to me. I view the other as a means as opposed to an end in herself. The type of perception I receive from this type of correlation is explanation. If I partially finalize or reify the other, I am able to treat her as a subject. This can be best understood as a form of sympathy. In order to sympathise with the other I must have knowledge of her grief or pain. I do not need to understand it, only know of it. I treat her grieving as a static "thing", I reify it into a moment of being and not a process. This type of correlation allows to perceive the other through a knowledge of her. If I only marginally finalize the other, I am able to treat her as a Subject. I am able to empathise with her grieving by treating it as an event and not an object. I see that she is in the process of becoming and changing and allow her the room to change. I am never able to completely empathise with the other since I am never able to stand in her place. I can only stand alongside her, correlate with her, and, as a result, understand her. This is the closest correlation I can achieve with the other.

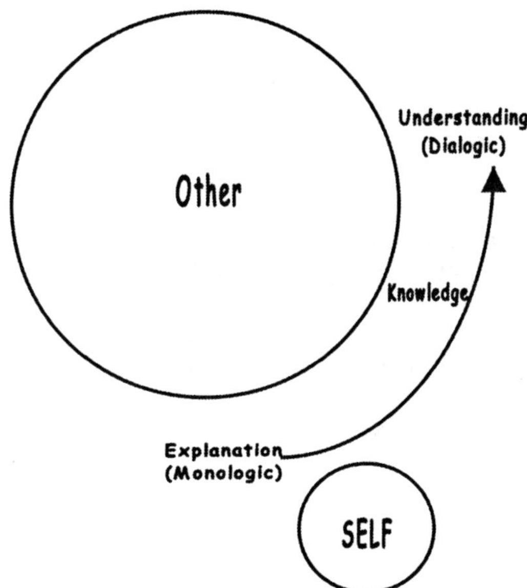

Figure 2: Correlation between self and other.

5 Users and interactions

5.1 Users, computers and software

All three types of correlations may be seen in interactions between the user and the machines and programs that they use. The type of correlation depends on the use of reification and personification by the user and the experience level of the user. Ontologically, the user is going to approach the machine through her level of experience, the context of the interaction with the computer and the ability to

Human Perspectives in the Internet Society: Culture, Psychology and Gender, K. Morgan, J. Sanchez, C. A. Brebbia & A Voiskounsky (Editors) © 2004 WIT Press, www.witpress.com, ISBN 1-85312-726-4

relate to the computer. Each interaction between the user and the computer is unique because of the experience gained by the computer. The computer is not changed by the interaction except in the most basic physical terms (wear, usage time).

I routinely teach a course in the use of technology and communication. I find that users who have little experience using computers tend to correlate to the computer through explanation. The user understands that the computer is an object but the user's lack of experience leads them to explain the computer's behaviour by relating it to human behaviour ("the computer hates me," "the program is stupid"). While at first glance it may seem that the novice user is personifying the computer and trying to relate to it dialogically. What the user is actually doing is attempting to further reify computing. The user is assigning human behaviour to the computer instead of understanding the functioning of the computer. He remains at the level of explanation and does not try to engage the computer on any terms but his own.

As the user gains experience, his correlation with the computer shifts to one of knowledge. The user partially personifies and partially reifies the machine. Software packages that employ agents are aimed at these users. The software gives the illusion of personalization without actually personalizing the program towards the user. Operating systems label file folders with generic personal terms ("My Computer", "My Documents"). This level of personification is very superficial. The user is still dealing with the machine using analogous experience, although this experience now includes working with the machine. There is not yet a true personification of the computer as an individual.

Those who have the most experience with computing enter into the most dialogical correlation. These users recognise that each machine, although similar, are individuals and that each one operates slightly different. The user understands the machine as the distinct machine. The individuation shows the highest degree of actual personification.

As users become more technically savvy the need for false personification decreases and the need for adaptability increases. Novice users need to see a "reified individual" in the machine. Agents play an important role and allow the users to project (perceived) human characteristics into the machine. Novice users need the familiarity that human cognates bring. These users need to be able to relate to the machine in a reified personalised manner. As users advance in experience, the agent's role should diminish and be replaced with a transparency that allows the user to see the individuation of each machine.

5.2 Users and internet interaction

The relationship between internet users is perhaps the more pressing ontological question. How does the user view the other involved in surfing experience? There are two distinct issues that arise: the interaction between users in real time and the interaction between web site designers and those who view the sites. Each one of these has it own issues and implications.

One of the benefits of the internet is that it allows for instant communication over great distances. As speed increases, the communication becomes more

Human Perspectives in the Internet Society: Culture, Psychology and Gender, K. Morgan, J. Sanchez, C. A. Brebbia & A Voiskounsky (Editors) © 2004 WIT Press, www.witpress.com, ISBN 1-85312-726-4

seamless. Conversations take place in real time. Non-verbal information can be conveyed through the use of emoticons or plug-ins that indicate the individual user's mood and reaction. Problems can arise when there is a disconnect in the relationship between users or between a user's I-for-self and I-for-other.

First, in an ideal world, individuals would treat each other dialogically. Everyone would strive for either knowledge or understanding of the other. In practice, however, this is not the case. People attempt to use others as a means to some end. The self misuses the other by taking advantage of his surplus of vision either in context of the interaction or in the experience advantage the self holds over the other. The same is true in online communication. The difference is that since the communication is mediated, you can never be sure of who the other is. There may be large gaps in experience between one user and the other which leads to one being able to take advantage.

Second, problems can arise due to the anonymity of the internet. One user may put on a mask when communicating with others. Genders can be switched and age can become fluid. The I-for-other that the user projects may be false. While the I-for-other develops in the interaction between the I-for-self and the context of the situation, knowledge and experience of the situation allows for the more proficient user to exploit the situation. Ultimately this leads to an ethical question—how ought I view the other? Any interaction depends on the context of the situation. One of the elements within this context is value. I am answerable to the other in a dialogue. If I wear a mask, I am no longer answerable to the other. I can always claim to be somewhere or someone else. I have, in Bakhtin's words, "an alibi in being" [X].

Finally, the web site designer must keep the user in mind when she is creating an internet home. She must consider the context of the situation in which the user will be surfing—what is the user looking for, what level of user am I attempting to attract and how should I respond to the other? The designer must answer the user before he finds the web site. She must answer him by anticipating his needs and his context.

6 Conclusion

Ontology must be a consideration when dealing with technology and individuals. It is only through understanding the user, the context of the communicative situation and the relation or correlation that the I of the user can strike toward the other that we can see both the promise and pitfalls of technology. We must conceive of being as active and stratified which allows for the user to change and build off of experience. Further investigation needs to look at the three correlations and the actual experience of the user.

References

[1] Bakhtin, M.M., trans. V.W. McGee, eds. C Emerson & M. Holquist, *Speech Genres and Other Late Essays*, University of Texas Press, Austin, 1986.

Human Perspectives in the Internet Society: Culture, Psychology and Gender, K. Morgan, J. Sanchez, C. A. Brebbia & A Voiskounsky (Editors) © 2004 WIT Press, www.witpress.com, ISBN 1-85312-726-4

[2] Bakhtin, M.M., trans. V. Liapunov, eds. M. Holquist & V. Liapunov, *Art and Answerability*, University of Texas Press, Austin, 1990.

[3] Bakhtin, M.M., trans. V. Liapunov, eds. V. Liapunov & M. Holquist, *Toward the Philosophy of the Act*, University of Texas Press, Austin, 1993.

[4] Bernard-Donals, M.F., *Mikhail Bakhtin Between Phenomenology and Marxism*, Cambridge University Press, 1994.

[5] Cohen, H., trans. S. Kaplan, *Religion of Reason*, Scholars Press, Atlanta, Georgia, 1995.

[6] Hartmann, N., trans. S Coit, *Ethics*, George Allen & Unwin LTD, London, 1932.

[7] Hartmann, N., trans. R.C. Kuhn, *New Ways of Ontology*, Henry Regency Company, Chicago, 1953.

[8] Husserl, E., trans. D. Cairns, *Cartesian Meditations*, Martinus Nijhoff, The Hague, 1969.

[9] Husserl, E., trans. D. Carr, *The Crisis of European Sciences and Transcendental Phenomenology*, Northwestern University Press, Evanston, 1970.

[10] Siitunen, A., *Problems of Aporetics*, Suomalainen Tiedeakatemis, Helsinki, 1989.

Human Perspectives in the Internet Society: Culture, Psychology and Gender, K. Morgan, J. Sanchez, C. A. Brebbia & A Voiskounsky (Editors) © 2004 WIT Press, www.witpress.com, ISBN 1-85312-726-4

The neuropsychology of Human Computer Interaction (HCI)

M. Brosnan
University of Bath, Bath, BA2 7AY, UK

Abstract

This paper proposes that biological factors such as the organisation of the brain and (relatedly) exposure to prenatal hormones affect how successfully individuals use technology. The paper outlines a neuropsychological perspective upon the computer culture. It suggests that the computer culture can be characterised as dominated by the processes associated with the left hemisphere to the exclusion of the processes associated with the right hemisphere. This exclusion is argued to reflect male brain organisation to a greater degree than female brain organisation. This provides a biologically based account of why gender differences emerge within HCI. Two preliminary studies examine the relationship between exposure to prenatal testosterone and computer-related abilities and anxieties. Significant relationships are found and the implications discussed.

1 Introduction

For many psychologists, at least, HCI represents an application of cognitive psychological theory to the design and appropriation of technology. Cognitive psychological theory has traditionally been concerned with modelling and accounting for reasoning and rationality. Recent theorising, however, has emphasised the role of emotion within cognitive psychology and how emotion impacts and interacts with traditional notions of reasoning. Additionally, since the 1990s the emergence of neuroscience has had a significant impact upon cognitive psychology, integrating into a cognitive neuropsychology. This has given rise to an emerging body of research which focuses upon affective aspects of HCI. In crude neuropsychological terms, traditional HCI can be seen as accounting for the traditional cognitive psychological theory represented by the

Human Perspectives in the Internet Society: Culture, Psychology and Gender, K. Morgan, J. Sanchez, C. A. Brebbia & A Voiskounsky (Editors) © 2004 WIT Press, www.witpress.com, ISBN 1-85312-726-4

'logical, rational, sequential' left hemisphere of the brain whereas emotional, creative aspects of human cognition are associated with the right hemisphere of the brain. To incorporate theories of emotion and its impacts upon cognitive processing within HCI, it therefore becomes necessary to understand the neuropsychology underpinning cognition.

2 Basic neuropsychology

The human brain has two hemispheres, the left and the right. A great deal of evidence suggests that the left and right hemispheres primarily sub serve different cognitive functions, termed 'lateralised' and described below:

LEFT HEMISPHERE	RIGHT HEMISPHERE
Verbal competence	Nonverbal, visual-spatial
Sequential	Simultaneous (parallel)
Logical analytical	Gestalt
Rational	Emotional
Scientific	Artistic
Western thought	Eastern thought

Obviously this is a crude characterisation of the hemispheres but it summarises a large body of literature (see [1]). As a species we are left hemisphere dominant as this is where language processing primarily occurs (with the possible exception of a small proportion of left handers: see [2]). The two hemispheres are linked by the 'corpus callosum' which allows information to be integrated between the two hemispheres. In humans, it is possible to severe the corpus collosum, termed a 'commissurotomy', which is a surgical procedure used to alleviate the symptoms of epilepsy. By and large the sequential, analytical, logical abilities are lateralised to the left hemisphere, which underpin scientific principles, at least within Western cultures.

Sex differences

Science generally is male dominated, and the disciplines that educate those who contribute to the design and development of technology are no exception.

Human Perspectives in the Internet Society: Culture, Psychology and Gender, K. Morgan, J. Sanchez, C. A. Brebbia & A Voiskounsky (Editors) © 2004 WIT Press, www.witpress.com, ISBN 1-85312-726-4

This male domination occurs from the undergraduate level through to the professoriate (2.5% are female in the UK) and Fellowship of the Royal Society (3.6% are female). When females do select Science, there is a tendency to select life sciences, such as Biology, and particularly Social Science, such as Psychology [3,4]. This could be explained in neuropsychological terms, were males to be more left hemisphere dominant than females. This presupposes that there are indeed sex differences in the cognitive processing associated with each hemisphere. By and large, the literature is consistent in identifying males as having superior visual-spatial ability (associated with the right hemisphere) and females having superior language abilities (associated with the left hemisphere: see [5,6]).

The neuropsychological explanation for these differences in cognition is that males are more lateralised than females [7]. Levy found that while language was distributed over both hemispheres in females, language was confined to the left hemisphere in males. Thus, females have an advantage in language as both hemispheres of the brain contribute to language processing. Conversely, males have an advantage in visual-spatial processing as the right hemisphere is specialised for this processing. Females have lower visual-spatial performance as the processing capacity of the right hemisphere is shared between language and visual-spatial processing. Meta analyses confirm that males are more lateralised than females supporting the reality of sex differences in cognition and brain organization [8,9]. Males depend on their left hemispheres for the tasks listed for the left hemisphere above and their right hemispheres for tasks listed for the right hemisphere above, whereas females have more distributed functioning over both hemispheres.

Clearly, there are variations within each sex as well as between the sexes. Sanders et al. suggest that prenatal testosterone can account for such variations. Prenatal hormones have been shown to exhibit long lasting organisational effects on the brain [10]. Typically, males are exposed to higher levels of prenatal testosterone than females. The effect of this greater exposure is to enhance the development of aspects of the right hemisphere while handicapping the development of the same aspects of the left hemisphere [11]. Thus, males are more lateralised (reducing their language abilities but increasing their spatial abilities) as a result of higher exposure to prenatal testosterone. Within each sex there is also variability in exposure to prenatal testosterone, such that females exposed to relatively higher levels of testosterone will demonstrate a cognitive pattern similar to that of males, and males exposed to relatively higher levels of testosterone will have an 'extreme male brain'.

3 Extreme male brains

Left hand side, excellent systematising but to the detriment of empathising visual spatial abilities underpin what Baron-Cohen [12,13,14,15] terms 'systematising', that is an intuitive everyday understanding of how things work: The understanding the properties of physical objects, including their causal impact on other objects. Systematising is independent from what Baron-Cohen terms

Human Perspectives in the Internet Society: Culture, Psychology and Gender, K. Morgan, J. Sanchez, C. A. Brebbia & A Voiskounsky (Editors) © 2004 WIT Press, www.witpress.com, ISBN 1-85312-726-4

'empathising', that is an intuitive everyday understanding of how people work: The understanding of how actions are caused by mental/ intentional states of others. Systematising and empathising represent the essential sex difference [13] and are naturally developing forms of knowledge not explicitly taught and acquired universally. Thus Systematising skills are different from academic skills as they are found in children prior to formal education although the principles derived from systematising are developed within disciplines such as Mathematics, Computer Science and Physics. Baron-Cohen conceives of a continuum from systematising through to empathising upon which males are more proficient in systematising and females are more proficient in empathising, thereby providing a theoretical account for the male domination of Science. Extreme systematising with minimal empathising skills however epitomise the developmental disorder of Autism/ Asperger Syndrome. Baron-Cohen et al. [16] have found that experts (i.e. professors) in these fields demonstrate a similar level as individuals with Asperger Syndrome on the assessments for Asperger Syndrome. Whilst individuals with autism/ Asperger Syndrome have deficits in language and communication, visual-spatial abilities can exceed normal levels [17,18]. In this way, Scientists, including computer Scientists are conceived of as being towards the far end of a distribution of skills:

Extreme male brain	Extreme female brain

Autism--Asperger Syndrome--Computer Scientists--Males--Females--???

Computer Scientists share their place on the continuum with physicists, mathematicians, engineers etc. A disorder of being too empathising with little systematising skills is also theorised but yet to be identified [13].

The critical feature is limited empathising skills in computer scientists. Empathising centres on the concept of Theory of Mind (ToM). ToM is the capacity to think how others think (e.g. John thinks that Mary thinks) that differs from one's own perspective. This capacity is crucial for design, if the principle of design is to design for others. Baron-Cohen's work identifies that computer science attract those who have excellent systematising skills but with a cost to the abilities in thinking how others would perceive the situation (or task). Thus those who are best placed to develop new technology are least able to develop technology for 'the other', that is anyone who does not share a cognitive profile similar to their own. This is not primarily an arrogance that dismisses other style of interaction as being inferior but the manifestation of a biological system that favours systematising at a cost of empathising.

4 Sex differences and brains

Sanders et al. [19] conclude that even when studies do not find sex differences described above, the insignificant trends are in the predicted direction. The authors suggest that it may be variations in testosterone that underpin the very

Human Perspectives in the Internet Society: Culture, Psychology and Gender, K. Morgan, J. Sanchez, C. A. Brebbia & A Voiskounsky (Editors) © 2004 WIT Press, www.witpress.com, ISBN 1-85312-726-4

nature of sex differences. This hypothesis has received a great deal of attention recently as an accessible index of prenatal testosterone has been developed namely dividing the length of the index finger (next to the thumb, called 2D) by the length of the ring finger (next to the little finger, termed 4D). The 2D/4D ratio is then calculated by dividing the former length by the latter length. There is a genetic reason why this ratio relates to prenatal testosterone exposure. The HOX gene family is required for the growth and patterning of digits and the differentiation of the genital bud. Hoxd and Hoxa genes are strongly expressed in the gonads and are also required for the growth and differentiation of digits. This sharing of causal factors in digit and gonad differentiation allows patterns of digit formation to be a marker for prenatal sex hormone concentration [20]. Digit length is fixed in utero and relative digit lengths remains constant through development and is constant across ethnicities [21]. The digit ratio is sexually dimorphic with males having a mean of 0.98, i.e. 4D longer than 2D and females having a mean of 1.00 (2D and 4D the same length). This pattern is set before the age of 2 and remains constant over the life span [20].

Three independent studies have shown the digit ratio is negatively correlated with mental rotation abilities that are associated with the right hemisphere and in which males out perform females (see [19]). Inexplicably, however, this relationship has only been significant for males, not females, An extreme male digit ratio has also been identified in (again mostly male) children with autism (0.94) suggesting prenatal testosterone as a contributory factor in the aetiology of autism [22]. Identifying Asperger Syndrome-typical cognitive profiles in computer scientists does not necessarily imply that all computer scientists as sub clinically Asperger Syndrome. Such a characterisation, however, does share many overlaps with the descriptions of the computer culture.

5 Sex differences and the computer culture

The sex differences described above are epitomised by the repeated finding of sex differences within the computer culture. Turkle and Pappert [23] characterise a computer culture in which programmers and educators privilege an intellectual method that is sequential, logical, rational (consistent with that described above as typical of the left hemisphere). The authors argue that this characterises males preferred programming style to a great extent than females' programming style. Turkle and Pappert cite evidence for alternative intellectual methods, constructing theories by arranging and rearranging, negotiating and renegotiating that are potentially equally viable strategies but are not legitimated by the computer culture. Turkle and Pappert report that frequently female students are forced to use particular strategies with which they are not comfortable. Grundy [24] concurs arguing that there is a pure, abstract form of strategic thinking that is deemed to be prestigious within the computer culture in which males get intensely involved. More distributed, integrated, less abstract strategies, more typically preferred by females, are not privileged. Turkle and Pappert argue for an 'epistemological pluralism' within the computer culture, that is acceptance of the validity f multiple ways of knowing and thinking.

Human Perspectives in the Internet Society: Culture, Psychology and Gender, K. Morgan, J. Sanchez, C. A. Brebbia & A Voiskounsky (Editors) © 2004 WIT Press, www.witpress.com, ISBN 1-85312-726-4

Finding the a computer system unnatural whether as a programmer or user increases the sense that the technology has lower perceived usefulness and lower perceived ease of use as well as a lower perceived fun factor. As a consequence, females have been shown to have more negative attitudes towards technology and more anxiety concerning technology [25]. These factors have been identified as affecting the acceptance of technology [26]. Davis draws upon psychological theory to propose a Technology Acceptance Model that provides a theoretical framework for understanding and predicting intentions to use technology. The recent inclusion of computer anxiety into this model represents an update to incorporate affective response [27]. Thus, an examination of computer anxiety represents an inclusion of emotional factors with a theoretical account of how technology is used.

6 Sex differences and computer anxiety

Computer anxiety is a real phenomenon [28] predicting whether computers are used or not and if so, to what extent [29]. A vast array of professions has been surveyed, typically revealing that between 25% and 50% of employees register as computer anxious (see [25]). The expectation that computer anxiety would be a phenomenon that applied to older people who missed out on computers in their education has proved false. Research within the educational system has identified that computer anxiety is prevalent in comparable proportions of students from 6 to 24 years of age [30,31]. For both adults and children, the most consistent finding is that females report higher levels of computer anxiety than males (see [25] for a review).

A male-dominated computer culture has been identified as one of the causes of computer anxiety in females. A great deal of research has identified that both boys and girls perceive computing to be genderised, that is, more gender-appropriate for boys than girls [see 25 for a review]. This has largely been discussed in terms of the social factors influencing technology usage, epitomised by the correlations between psychological gender and computer-related abilities [25]. Sandra Bem [32] conceived of 2 independent dimension to psychological gender, masculinity and femininity. Masculinity has been found to vary positively with computer-related perceptions and abilities whereas femininity has been found to vary negatively with computer-related perceptions and abilities [33,34]. Although the gender variables described by Bem were theorised to be cultural in nature, recent research has identified significant relationships with digit ratio [35]. This signifies a relationship between exposure to prenatal testosterone and self reported psychological gender. The correlates of psychological gender with computer anxiety, attitudes and abilities may therefore be indicative of a relationship between prenatal testosterone and computer-related performance.

Preliminary investigations

The hypothesis is that, for the reasons outlined above, success within the computer culture will be predicted (at least in part) by exposure to

Human Perspectives in the Internet Society: Culture, Psychology and Gender, K. Morgan, J. Sanchez, C. A. Brebbia & A Voiskounsky (Editors) © 2004 WIT Press, www.witpress.com, ISBN 1-85312-726-4

prenatal testosterone. Two preliminary investigations examine this possibility, relating digit ratio with JAVA programming ability and computer anxiety.

7 Study 1: JAVA programming

At the University of Bath, we have a Masters course in Human Communication and computing, jointly run by the departments of Psychology and Computer Science. Students undertake a range of courses in the first semester, including JAVA programming and Communication Theory (in addition to research methods). The hypothesis under investigation is that digit ratio will negatively correlate with JAVA programming scores (a higher digit ratio indicates less exposure to prenatal testosterone). There were no correlations with Communication Theory marks.

23 Masters students (18 males) were sampled. Both sexes had a mean digit ratio of 0.98 and there were no significant differences in JAVA marks between males and females. The correlation between digit ratio and JAVA mark was significant, however: r= -0.56, p=0.003.

8 Study 2: computer anxiety

The relationship to computer anxiety was then analysed with the hypothesis that digit ratio would positively correlate with computer anxiety (less testosterone related to more anxiety).

161 undergraduate students (71 males) were sampled. Again both sexes had a mean digit ratio of 0.98. There was a significant difference in computer anxiety, with females registering as more anxious than males (t=2.55, p=0.012). Consequently the correlations between digit ratio and computer anxiety were conducted separately for each sex.. For males, there was a significant positive correlation (r=.24, p=.02) and for females there was a significant negative correlation (r=-.22, p=0.019).

9 Conclusions of studies

The findings are clearly preliminary (and larger scale studies are already underway). However the findings are consistent with theory to suggest that exposure to prenatal testosterone, as indexed though digit ratio, has a significant impact upon multiple aspects of HCI. It is interesting that with this academic sample, both studies identify females as having the male-typical digit ratio mean. For both sexes greater testosterone exposure related to better JAVA marks, consistent with prediction. Great testosterone also related to less computer anxiety – but for males only. For females the opposite pattern was true, more exposure to testosterone related to greater computer anxiety (opposite to prediction). As prenatal testosterone is theorised to affect brain organisation, it is crucial to incorporate a neuropsychological perspective into HCI. The results are consistent with theory, for males at least, with further examination of the relationships for females required.

Human Perspectives in the Internet Society: Culture, Psychology and Gender, K. Morgan, J. Sanchez, C. A. Brebbia & A Voiskounsky (Editors) © 2004 WIT Press, www.witpress.com, ISBN 1-85312-726-4

10 Futures: evolution or revolution?

The functioning of the left hemisphere has traditionally characterised both cognitive psychology and its application to HCI. The functioning associated with the right hemisphere needs to be incorporated. Within neuropsychology the two hemispheres are linked by the corpus collosum. As an appropriate metaphor to apply to the future, HCI has had a commissurotomy and designers and the design process should represent the corpus collosum to allow the processing associated with the right hemisphere to impact upon HCI.

The question then becomes, how does this happen? Traditional computer scientists are unable to undertake this task. If these skills are genetically predetermined, it is unclear how useful tuition in these skills would be. Those with high theory of mind or empathising skills are not drawn to the academic disciplines that would develop the requisite skills to fully partake in the design process. This emphasises the role of the designer as the corpus collosum, bridging between the user and the programmer, between the salient right hemisphere aspects of processing and the left hemisphere computer culture. So the perfect designer would be motivated to apply themselves in a sequential, logical, rational manner as required but able to appreciate the perspective of other users. This role is crucial as theory would suggest that the traditional programmer is unable to do this. This represents an evolutionary step in HCI: Evolving an affect sensitive perspective out of traditional HCI. Computer Science courses could be developed to attract non-traditional entrants, such as those able to appreciate the differing perspectives of others (possibly through recruiting more females). This develops Turkle and Pappert's [23] call for epistemological pluralism, acceptance of multiple ways of knowing and thinking, within the computer culture. In the past this has happened by orienting the course to business applications, for example. What is required, however, is an educative process true to the theory and principle of programming but with the opportunity not to program. Computer Science without programming may seem an anathema to some, but an informed designer should be able to co-ordinate the programming requirements with the usability requirements. The key to motivating such individuals to focus their talents within HCI is to focus on 'Design'. Selection for such courses should be based up salient factors such as Theory of Mind and empathising as well as systematising – by the submission of a photocopy of both hands! So, for example a candidate with a high systematising ability and a digit ratio of 1.0 may constitute, at a theoretical level at least, as ideal candidate. Currently, however, such a high digit ratio correlates with a lower JAVA programming score, resulting in a less successful candidate (at least in this aspect of the course).

At the heart of the system will still be based on a programming language derived from the traditional computer culture. This therefore represents a short-term measure with limited possibilities. The revolutionary approach is to involve multiple perspectives in the development of new languages based upon new technologies, for example thinking beyond silicon-based systems. Already, though, I am importing a software/hardware distinction from the old paradigm to

Human Perspectives in the Internet Society: Culture, Psychology and Gender, K. Morgan, J. Sanchez, C. A. Brebbia & A Voiskounsky (Editors) © 2004 WIT Press, www.witpress.com, ISBN 1-85312-726-4

the new. If DNA-based technology is to develop in the future, for example, this would be entirely consistent with applying a biologically based understanding to current HCI. There are still issues to clarify, not least sex differences in the relationship between brain organisation and HCI. A better understanding of the neuropsychology of humans will lead to enhanced HCI research and development.

References

[1] Ivry, R. and Robertson, L. (1995) *The two sides to perception.* Bradford Books.

[2] McCarthy, R. and Warrington, E. (1990) *Cognitive Neuropsychology: A clinical Introduction.* Academic Press.

[3] Brosnan, M. (1998) The implications for academic attainment of perceived gender-appropriateness upon spatial task performance. *British Journal of Educational Psychology*, 68, 203-215.

[4] Mellor, F. (2001) Gender and communication through Multimedia. *Public Understand. Sci.* 10, 271-29.

[5] Halpern, D. F. (2000). *Sex differences in cognitive abilities.* (3rd ed.). Mahwah, NJ: Lawrence Erlbaum Associates.

[6] Maccoby, E. E., & Jacklin, C. N. (1974). *The psychology of sex differences,* Stanford, CA: Stanford University Press.

[7] Levy, J. (1969). Possible basis for the evolution of lateral specialization of the human brain. *Nature, 224,* 612-615.

[8] Hahn, W. K. (1987). Cerebral lateralization of function: From infancy through childhood. *Psychological Bulletin, 101,* 376-392.

[9] Sanders, G., & Wright, M. (1997). Sexual orientation differences in cerebral asymmetry and in the performance of sexually dimorphic cognitive and motor tasks. *Archives of Sexual Behavior, 26,* 463-480.

[10] Collaer, M. L., & Hines, M. (1995) Human behavioral sex differences: A role for gonadal hormones during early development? *Psychological Bulletin,* 118, 55-107.

[11] Geschwind, N., & Galaburda, A. M. (1985) Cerebral lateralization. I. A hypothesis and a program for research. *Archives of Neurology* 13, 428-495.

[12] Baron-Cohen, S. (2002) The extreme male brain theory of autism. *Trends in Cognitive Sciences* 6(6), 248-254.

[13] Baron-Cohen, S. (2003) The Essential Sex Difference. Men, women and the extreme male brain. London: Allen Lane.

[14] Baron-Cohen S. et al. (2001) The Autism Spectrum Quotient (AQ): evidence from Asperger Syndrome/High Functioning Autism, Males and Females, Scientists and Mathematicians. *Journal of Autism and Developmental Disorders* 31(1), 5-17.

[15] Baron-Cohen, S., Wheelwright, S. and Spong, A. (2001) Are intuitive physics and intuitive psychology independent? A test with children with

Human Perspectives in the Internet Society: Culture, Psychology and Gender, K. Morgan, J. Sanchez, C. A. Brebbia & A Voiskounsky (Editors) © 2004 WIT Press, www.witpress.com, ISBN 1-85312-726-4

Asperger Syndrome. *Journal of Developmental and Learning Disorders*, 5, 47-78.

[16] Baron-Cohen, S., Wheelwright, S., Stone, V. and Rutherford, M. (1999) A mathematician, a physicist and a computer scientist with Asperger syndrome: performance on folk psychology and folk physics tests. *Neurocase* 5, 475-483.

[17] Frith, U. (1997) The neurocognitive basis of autism. *Trends in Cognitive Sciences* 1, 73-77.

[18] Happe, F. (1999) Cognitive deficit or cognitive style? *Trends in Cognitive Sciences* 3, 216-222.

[19] Sanders, G., Sjodin, M. and de Chastelaine, M. (2002) On the Elusive Nature of Sex Differences in Cognition: Hormonal Influences Contributing to Within-Sex Variation. *Archives of Sexual Behavior, 31:* 145-152, 2002.

[20] Manning, J.T., Scutt, D., Wilson, J., & Lewis-Jones, D.I. (1998) The ratio of 2nd to 4th digit length: a predictor of sperm numbers and concentrations of testosterone, luteinizing hormone and oestrogen *Human Reproduction* 13, 3000-3004.

[21] Lippa, R.A. (2003) Are 2D:4D finger length ratios related to sexual orientation? Yes for men, no for women. *Journal of Personality and Social psychology* 85(1), 179-188.

[22] Manning, J.T., Baron-Cohen, S., Wheelwright, S. and Sanders, G. (2001) The 2nd to 4th digit ratio and autism *Developmental Medicine & Child Neurology* 43, 160-164.

[23] Turkle, S. and Pappert, S. (1990) Epistemological pluralism: syles and voices within the computer culture. *Signs*, Autumn, 128-157.

[24] Grundy, F. (1994) women in the computing workplace: some impressions. In A. Adams and J. Owen (eds) *Women, work and computerisation: breaking old boundaries – building new forms*. Amsterdam: North-Holland.

[25] Brosnan, M. J. (1998) *Technophobia: the psychological impact of information technology*. London: Routledge.

[26] Davis, F., Bagozzi, R. and Warshaw, P. (1989) User acceptance of computer technology: a comparison of two theoretical models. *Management Science*, 35(8), 982-1003.

[27] Venkatesh, V. (2000) Determinants of perceived ease of use: Integrating control, intrinsic motivation, and emotion into the Technology Acceptance Model. Informations Systems research, 11(4), 342-365.

[28] Moldafsky, N. and Kwon, I. (1994) Attributes affecting computer aided decision making – a literature survey. *Computers in Human Behavior*, 10(3), 299-323.

[29] Scott, C. and Rockwell, S. (1997) The effect of communication, writing and technology apprehension on likelihood to use new communication technologies. *Communication Education*, 46(1), 44-62.

Human Perspectives in the Internet Society: Culture, Psychology and Gender, K. Morgan, J. Sanchez, C. A. Brebbia & A Voiskounsky (Editors) © 2004 WIT Press, www.witpress.com, ISBN 1-85312-726-4

[30] Brosnan, M. (1998) The role of psychological gender in the computer-related attitudes and attainments of primary school children (aged 6-11). *Computers and Education*, 30(3/4), 203-208.

[31] Brosnan, M. (1998) The impact of psychological gender, gender-related perceptions, significant others and the introducer of technology upon computer anxiety in students. *Journal of Educational Computing Research*, 18(1), 63-78.

[32] Bem, S.L. (1974) The Measurement of Psychological Androgyny. *Journal of Consulting and Clinical Psychology*, 42, 155-162.

[33] Weil, M. M., Rosen, L. D. & Sears, D.C. (1987) The Computerphobia Reduction Program. Year 1. Program Development and Preliminary Results. *Behavior Research Methods, Instruments and Computers*, 19, 180-184.

[34] Brosnan, M. and Davidson, M. (1996) Psychological Gender Issues in Computing. *Journal of Gender, Work and Organisation*, 3(1), 13-25.

[35] Csatho, A. et al. (2003) Sex role identity related to the ratio of second to fourth digit length in women. Biological Psychology, 62, 147-156.

Human Perspectives in the Internet Society: Culture, Psychology and Gender, K. Morgan, J. Sanchez, C. A. Brebbia & A Voiskounsky (Editors) © 2004 WIT Press, www.witpress.com, ISBN 1-85312-726-4

Current problems of moral research and education in the IT environment

A. Voiskounsky
Moscow State University after M.V.Lomonosov, Russia
Moscow City University of Psychology & Education, Russia

Abstract

Prevention of computer crime includes two types of action: first, enhancement of computer security, and second, moral education adjusted to the IT environments. The latter is the main theme of the paper. Research on moral conduct in the IT environment is currently being carried out under the heading of cyberethics. New trends in cyberethics are discussed, aimed at reducing harmful effects of adolescents' uncontrollable misuse of computers and the Internet. One of the reasons of this misuse is inability of younger generations to transfer rules of moral conduct to the new (virtual) environments. To reduce the number of newcomers to hackers/carders/crackers/phreakers' communities, world-wide educational courses for adolescents are urgently needed. The objective of these educational programs need to be the development of flexible decision making in moral situations, including those inherent of the IT environments. The programs and training sessions need to be internationally approved and realized, since computer crime is trans-national. It is proposed that the theoretical background of this educational program might be the Kohlberg's stage theory of moral development, which was worked out within the field of developmental psychology. Fieldwork research is needed, aimed at finding out the specifics of moral views of computer-savvy adolescents in different countries, and at working out programs of moral education which would fit the new environments.
Keywords: cyberethics, education, moral, psychology, computer crime, stages of moral development, Internet.

Human Perspectives in the Internet Society: Culture, Psychology and Gender, K. Morgan, J. Sanchez, C. A. Brebbia & A Voiskounsky (Editors) © 2004 WIT Press, www.witpress.com, ISBN 1-85312-726-4

1 Introduction

Ethics is one of the oldest fields of knowledge; in its development it has undertaken changing views on the origin and functions of moral behavior. Ethics has usually been investigated and taught within philosophy; on the contrary, philosophy could be sometimes found within ethics. No matter what are the "correct", or "true" relationships between the two fields, it's well known that both ethics and philosophy have always been inseparable of certain elements of law. Less known perhaps, that both can hardly been separated from individual and group psychology, too.

Law is beyond the theme of this paper, but for the following point. Although ethics and law overlap, usually the matching is only partial. The reason is that whenever any new practical ethical issue emerges, the estimation of it as legal does not necessarily imply the estimation of it as moral, and vice versa; these two categories only rarely coincide. Human psychology takes the most part of responsibility for this discrepancy. This responsibility will be discussed in more details, taken the new issues in practical applications of ethics, namely the so-called cyberethics.

Cyberethics is usually meant as rules of ethical (i.e., right, lawful, and just) behavior in online environments. It should not be confused to legal, the latter being heavily and often fiercely discussed in the field. Cyberethics is largely dependent on universal ethical laws, and at the same time it is in many ways special and peculiar. As Barger puts it in [1], "I do not believe that computer ethics are qualitatively different from medical ethics or legal ethics or any other kind of professional ethics. I do, however, believe that the nature of the computer and its operation gives certain dilemmas in computing a unique character".

2 Current research on cyberethics: a brief review

Cyberethics goes far beyond the "netiquette" rules worked out at the earlier period of the Internet use. Nowadays, cyberethics refers to both communicative (including chat rooms, web forums, live journal and weblog discussions, guestrooms' and newsgroups' exchanges, etc.) and non-communicative services, including collaborative work, online games, shopping and bargaining, shared cognitive actions, etc. Peculiarity of the current stage of the cyberethics is not yet fully realized. Most published sources display complicated issues of computer ethics which deal with, and mostly restrict with crime, safety and security, privacy and civil liberties, porn, harassment and fraud, children protection from Internet damages and identity theft, hacking/carding/phreaking and software pirating, right/left extremism and hacktivism, blackmailing and disseminating junk email, plagiarism and "digital divide", spoofing, flaming and trolling, etc. (Grodzinsky [2]; Langford [3]; Rotenberg [4]; Spinello and Tavani [5]; Whine [6]). For example, Mason and colleagues [7] distinguish four cyberethical issues: accessibility, accuracy, privacy, and property. New issues arose recently dealing with cyberspace-related rights Lastowka and Hunter [8], and with the ethics of

Human Perspectives in the Internet Society: Culture, Psychology and Gender, K. Morgan, J. Sanchez, C. A. Brebbia & A Voiskounsky (Editors) © 2004 WIT Press, www.witpress.com, ISBN 1-85312-726-4

human research on the Internet (Bruckman [9]; Frankel and Siang [10]; Hudson and Bruckman [11]).

Much the same issues one will find at the available bibliographical/program web sources (cyberethics.cbi.msstate.edu/biblio/, www.cpsr.org/program/ethics/, etc.). As a supplement to universal moral rules, codes of professional ethics have been worked out and are systematically updated. It is worth mentioning the codes of professional ethical conduct (Jamal and Bowie [12]; Rest and Narvaez [13]), particularly in the computer science and information management field (Cronan and Kreie [14]; Grodzinsky [2]; Mason et al. [7]; Panteli [15]). Besides, the ACM Code of Ethics and Professional Conduct (http://www.acm.org/ constitution/code.html) is a useful source and is widely discussed, as well as the APA ethical code which was recently revised (http://www.apa.org/ethics/).

Important as they are, cyberethical issues and professional ethical codes have already been thoroughly discussed within the professional community. Moreover, useful empirical research has been done in the field. For example, illegal computer-related behaviors (ranging from illegal copying of licensed software pieces to changing/stealing data in other persons' computers) are widely spread and often initiated by middle/high-school students: surveys held recently in San Diego, CA make it evident (McGuire et al. [16]). Ruf and Thomas [17] investigated the likelihood that university students would cheat, dependent on certain IT-related cases (copying spreadsheets, illegally sharing access to an electronic textbook, downloading and selling music CDs, copying computer programs) and on gaining varying awards (i.e., moderate or higher than moderate). Not a surprise, differing factors are shown to influence selectively the university students' ethical/unethical behavior. Close to this is the conclusion made by Cronan and Kreie [14]: various combinations of legal or professional (i.e., codes of conduct) factors, or factors referring to personal beliefs and attributes (religious values, morals, experience, etc.), and to social environments impact processes of ethical decision making in the IT environment.

Culture specifics is believed to represent a valuable factor. Specific religious beliefs widely common in India (namely, belief in cyclic processes of personal birth and subsequent rebirth) are shown to influence significantly the likelihood of software piracy and deterioration of privacy in the IT field (Debnath and Bhal [18]). Research held in Korea within an adult sample demonstrated that moral judgment is dependent on Ss' age, sex, and position in administrative hierarchy (Kim [19]).

Attitudes towards the computer/Internet abuse may vary greatly dependent on certain cultural backgrounds, too (Voiskounsky et al. [20]). Nevertheless, attitudes towards software license infringement, or use of viruses, or misuse of corporate computing resources are shown to be significantly different among professionals belonging to nine cultures; an important finding is that representatives of no nation (out of the nine investigated) might be characterized as holders of perverted, or totally opposite moral attitudes, compared to what is believed to be correct in Great Britain or in the USA (Whitman et al. [21]). Ang and Lo [22] found that the attitudes towards illegal copying of software pieces

Human Perspectives in the Internet Society: Culture, Psychology and Gender, K. Morgan, J. Sanchez, C. A. Brebbia & A Voiskounsky (Editors) © 2004 WIT Press, www.witpress.com, ISBN 1-85312-726-4

depend upon three major factors, namely: (1) perceived personal gain (e.g., social acceptance, favour, repay of debt, etc.), (2) altruism, and (3) perceived negative consequences – if the illegacy is out.

2.1 The Internet misuse within the hackers' communities

Besides attitudes, we believe that the actual level of knowledge in the area of cyberethics is of great importance, too. Let us take for example the activities characteristic for hackers/crackers/carders/phreakers/hacktivists (Sterling [23]; Taylor [24]). This underground population, though strongly differing in intentions, in methods used, in publicity, etc. is very special for a discussion of the cyberethics issues. Indeed, each protection device that is installed to prevent crime turns out to be rapidly confronted by circumventing techniques. Unsolicited intrusions into distant computers and databases, provocations of web-servers' denials of service, spoofing, dissemination of computer viruses happen more and more often. Thus, the hackers' population and the hackers' qualification is ever growing; the same is believed to be true with the harm resulting from their improper actions.

There are different classifications of those who cause computer crime; we are going to mention only few of them. According to the one, we are recommended to distinguish the following subgroups: professional criminals or "cyberwar" terrorists, white collar criminals, disgruntled employees, and teenager hackers (Nicholson et. al. [25]; Shinder and Tittel [26]). Rodgers [27] classifies subgroups of hackers dependent on their expertise, areas of interests (software, hardware, cell phones, the Internet, etc.) and behaviour patterns: he differentiates tool kit/newbies, cyber-punks, internals, coders, old guard hackers, professional criminals, and cyber-terrorists. Obviously, there are no exact borders between them. In full correspondence with the reality, both classification schemes include children and teenagers. The least qualified newcomers (often children or adolescents) to the hackers' underground are known as newbies, or wannabes. Every day wannabes enter this population, reasoning that hacking is a fashionable hobby or a profitable occupation. Newbies start with the simplest tasks just for fun, then some of them turn to more advanced tasks and gradually become either qualified crackers/carders, or else professionals in computer security; the majority of those who go on doing only elementary hacking tasks soon enough leave the population of hackers (Voiskounsky and Smyslova [28]).

One might suppose that the great amount, if not the majority of computer hacking/cracking/phreaking episodes in which middle/high school or college students are actors, stem from the fact that they are often unable to prognosticate the effects of their actions, and thus are simply unaware of the consequences - damaging, illegal, and at least unethical. Had the children/adolescent newbies knew of the harmful results, or could they foresee the problems they cause, many of them would never again use the cracking "vandalware". "Mild and usually unintentional forms of deviance are the result of carelessness, playful mischief, immaturity, or simple ignorance" (Suler and Philips [29]). Being unaware does not always mean being ignorant, indifferent, or non-curious; taken children and adolescents, it often means psychological inability to transfer well-known

Human Perspectives in the Internet Society: Culture, Psychology and Gender, K. Morgan, J. Sanchez, C. A. Brebbia & A Voiskounsky (Editors) © 2004 WIT Press, www.witpress.com, ISBN 1-85312-726-4

behavioral patterns into new situations. No wonder, in the cyberspace one usually finds oneself in peculiarly unfamiliar situations; this is equally correct for grown-ups and for children or adolescents.

3 A new direction of research in cyberethics

We are approaching the essence of this paper. It might be phrased in the following way. Decisions on some of the new cyberspace-related problems would not be based on exclusively ethical ground; traditional cyberethics seems to be insufficient. Instead, decision making needs to be based on data gained in developmental psychology and education. Thus, the newest trend within cyberethics is its overlap with psychology.

Each coin has two sides. Failing to transfer norms of ethical behavior into the cyberspace and thus “innocently” committing cybercrime, children and adolescents at the same time often become victims of deceiptors, paedophiles and/or manipulators: they use to inform strangers about personal data, meet grown-up “friends” face-to-face and undergo sexual harassment, etc. The use of connected computers for communication, work, cognition, and gaming brings new educational and ethical dilemmas and problems to parents and educators – problems in the area in which caregivers, teachers and school principals usually lack training. The use of the Internet by K-12 students states technical, legal, organizational and ethical (or cyberethical) problems – this time overlapping psychological ones.

The world-wide community of the Internet users as well as non-users should work hard to teach new generations the essentials of the cyberethics. The latter is certainly based on traditional moral and should extend the moral norms into IT-related environment. Not that computer crime would perish, but at least the recruitment of “newbies” and wannabes might be reduced. This challenge is worth trying. Importantly, some theoretical models of ethical behavior stress the importance of the so-called "ethical sensitivity", that is, the ability to distinguish ethical or unethical behavior (Bommer et. al [30]; Wortuba [31]). The factors influencing the discrimination between ethical or unethical are shown to vary from case to case (Cronan and Kreie [14]). An ability to recognize ethical issues and to assess ethical/unethical alternatives is dependent on one's priority structure of values (Wortuba [31]).

3.1 Organizational support for research in new areas of the cyberethics

Facing the new challenge, concerned educators, IT and justice experts, and parents express their concern. Books by Schwartau on the theme [32] got a bestseller status; this fact might be taken as a signal of concern. Several organizations and associations (www.cybercitizenpartners.org, www.cybersmart.org/, www.internetwatch.org.uk/, www.staysafeonline.info, disney.go.com/cybersafety/, etc.) claimed readiness to consult every interested person or group on the newest issues of cyberethics. Enthusiasts worked out recommendations for safe use of the Web by children and adolescents: for

Human Perspectives in the Internet Society: Culture, Psychology and Gender, K. Morgan, J. Sanchez, C. A. Brebbia & A Voiskounsky (Editors) © 2004 WIT Press, www.witpress.com, ISBN 1-85312-726-4

example, a SUSI project, or Safer Use of Services on the Internet (www.besafeonline.org/) has recently started in Scotland. More ambitious project Cybercitizen Awareness Program (www.cybercitizenpartners.org) is supported by the U.S. Department of Justice and the Information Technology Association of America. Within this project, several US-wide conferences have been held. Different governmental sources have worked out and compiled plenty of useful recommendations for children, for parents and for educators (www.cybercrime.gov/rules/cybercitizen.htm, www.usdoj.gov/criminal/cybercrime/, etc.).

In attempts to ensure security and to make web-navigations of K-12 students as safe as possible, the abovementioned web-pages and books refer exclusively to the traditional cyberethics. In an effort to prevent or obstruct improper/unethical use of computers the usually proposed measures are such as: enhanced security, prompt and fair reporting, tough sanctions, etc. All this is only one side of the coin. The other is in minimizing harm caused by K-12 students. To minimize harm, an educational program is urgently needed: children and adolescents need to be taught the likely unethical consequences of uncontrollable use of information and communication technologies.

3.2 New educational issues

Every high-school student of the coming generations needs to be the recipient of the would-be educational program; the advanced course should be taught to the most experienced computer/Internet users, including owners of homepages, hackers, gamers, winners of local and national competitions of high-school age programmers, creative software developers, etc. Such a program need to be international, since there are no borders in the cyberspace. Moreover, only a limited amount of "web-targets" are popular among hackers, including mostly the US-located web-sites and web-pages. These include the US Department of Defense, and the major world-known companies, especially those operating in the IT field. To secure the "web-targets" it's preferable to combine computer security measures (firewalls, etc.) and the educational measures. The latter might help in reducing the number of wannabes and "newbies", i.e. the newcomers to the hackers/carders/crackers/phreakers community.

The educational courses need to be based on psychological data describing stages of moral development during childhood and adolescence (and the adult age, too). The most sophisticated theory that proved its value is that introduced by Kohlberg in [33] and partly modified and developed by his followers (Turiel [34]). The Kohlberg's stages include pre-traditional moral, traditional moral, and post-traditional moral (each stage is subdivided into two substages). Necessary corrections need to be made that stem from the Lefebvre's differentiation of ethical principles inherent for a democratic and for a totalitarian society (Lefebvre [35]). This correction might be useful since totalitarian-type moral views and attitudes (as Lefebvre found) survive long enough after the transfer to the democratic social system. To make it more evident, we might remind that an Israeli hacker of certainly Russian origin was recently arrested in Israel (Shachtman [36]).

Human Perspectives in the Internet Society: Culture, Psychology and Gender, K. Morgan, J. Sanchez, C. A. Brebbia & A Voiskounsky (Editors) © 2004 WIT Press, www.witpress.com, ISBN 1-85312-726-4

It is unlikely to come upon the highest stages of moral development testing children's and adolescents' judgments. It is true, however, that many adults never reach the highest stage of moral judgments throughout their life. It seems even less probable that teenagers be mature enough to base their judgments on independent moral system of post-traditional value. It is widely believed (irrespectively of whether the belief is true) that when online, the majority of children and adolescents stay on a lower stage of moral development than in real life. The possible explanation lies in the anonymity of the Internet-mediated contacts. For example, rather few teenagers would steal a wallet from someone's pocket; at the same time many of them are eager to purchase goods – and especially services – using stolen card numbers. Thus, to adapt the adolescents' system of moral judgments to the Internet anonymity is a challenge. Traditional books on cyberethics miss this challenge. New books and educational courses have all the chances to meet the challenge: in these sources, we believe, cyberethics will overlap developmental psychology.

References

[1] Barger, R.N., *Is computer ethics unique in relation to other fields of ethics?*, 2001. www.nd.edu/~rbarger/ce-unique.html.

[2] Grodzinsky, F.S., The development of the 'ethical' ICT professional and the vision of an ethical on-line society: how far have we come and where are we going? *ACM SIGCAS Computers and Society*. **30 (1)**, pp. 3–7, 2000.

[3] Langford, D., (ed.). *Internet Ethics,* Houndmills et al.: Macmillan Press, 2000.

[4] Rotenberg, M., Protecting Human Dignity in the Digital Age, *Infoethics 2000. Ethical, legal and Societal Challenges of Cyberspace. Third International Congress. UNESCO Headquarters, Paris, France, 13-15 November, 2000. Final Report and Proceedings.* webworld.unesco.org/infoethics2000/report_151100.html#rotenberg.

[5] Spinello, R.A. & Tavani, H.T., (eds.). *Readings in CyberEthics,* Jones and Bartlett Publ., 2001.

[6] Whine, M., Far right extremists on the Internet, *Cybercrime: Law Enforcement, Security and Surveillance in the Information Age*, eds. D. Thomas & B. Loader, L. & N.Y.: Routledge, pp. 234-250, 2000.

[7] Mason, R.O., Mason, F.M. & Culnan, M.J., *Ethics of Information Management*, Thousand Oaks, CA: Sage Publ., 1995.

[8] Lastowka, F.G. & Hunter, D., The Laws of the Virtual Worlds. *California Law Review*, 2003, http://ssrn.com/abstract=402860.

[9] Bruckman, A., *Studying the Amateur Artist: A Perspective on Disguising Data Collected in Human Subjects Research on the Internet*, 2002. www.nyu.edu/projects/nissenbaum/ethics_bru_full.html.

Human Perspectives in the Internet Society: Culture, Psychology and Gender, K. Morgan, J. Sanchez, C. A. Brebbia & A Voiskounsky (Editors) © 2004 WIT Press, www.witpress.com, ISBN 1-85312-726-4

[10] Frankel, M.S. & Siang, S., *Ethical and Legal Aspects of Human Subjects Research on the Internet: A Report of a Workshop June 10-11, 1999.* American Association for the Advancement of Science (AAAS), 1999. www.aaas.org/spp/dspp/sfrl/projects/intres/report.pdf.

[11] Hudson, J.M. & Bruckman, A., "Go Away": Participant Objections to Being Studied and the Ethics of Chatroom Research. *The Information Society*, **20(2)**, pp. 127-139, 2004.

[12] Jamal, K. & Bowie, N.E., Theoretical Considerations for a Meaningful Code of Professional Ethics. *Journal of Business Ethics*, **14**, pp. 703-714, 1995.

[13] Rest, J.R. & Narvaez, D., *Moral Development in the Professions: Psychology and Applied Ethics,* Mahwah, N.J.: Lawrence Erlbaum, 1994.

[14] Cronan, T. P. & Kreie, J. Making ethical decisions. *Communications of the ACM,* **43(12)**, pp. 66-71, 2000.

[15] Panteli, A., Code Confidential: Codes of Practice for Computing Professionals. *ACM SIGCAS Computers & Society,* **32(6)**, 2003. www.computersandsociety.org/AccessController/sigcas/subpage/sub_page.cfm?article=844&page_number_nb=1.

[16] McGuire, Sh., D'Amico, E., Tomlinson, K. & Brown, S., Teenagers self-reported motivations for participating in computer crime, *8th International Conference on Motivation (Workshop on Achievement and Task Motivation). Abstracts,* Moscow, pp. 72-73, 2002.

[17] Ruf, B.M. & Thomas, S.B., *Unethical decision-making with computer usage in a university environment*, 2003. http://aaahq.org/AM2003/EthicsSymposium/Session%205a3.pdf.

[18] Debnath, N. & Bhal, K.T., Religious belief and pragmatic ethical framework as predictors of ethical behavior, eds. F. Sudweeks & Ch. Ess, *Cultural Attitudes towards Technology and Communication.* Proceedings of the 3rd International Conference (Montreal, Canada, 12-15 July, 2002), pp. 409-420, 2002.

[19] Kim, K.H., A study of the conduct of Korean IT participants in ethical decision making, eds. C.-H. Chung, C.-K. Kim, W. Kim, T.-W. Ling & K.-H. Song, Web and Communication Technologies and Internet-Related Social Issues – HSI 2003. Proc., Second International Conference on Human.Society@Internet (Seoul, Korea, June 2003). *Lecture Notes in Computer Science*, **2713**, Berlin et al.: Springer, pp. 64-74, 2003.

[20] Voiskounsky, A.E., Babaeva, J.D. & Smyslova, O.V., Attitudes towards computer hacking in Russia, eds. D. Thomas & B. Loader, *Cybercrime: Law Enforcement, Security and Surveillance in the Information Age,* L. & N.Y.: Routledge, pp. 56-84, 2000.

[21] Whitman, M.E., Townsend, A.M. & Hendrickson, A.R., Cross-national differences in computer-use ethics: A nine-country study. *Journal of International Business Studies*, **30(4)**, pp. 673-687, 1999. http://copenhagen.jibs.net/Archive/1999/30_4_99_673.pdf.

[22] Ang, A.Y. & Lo, B.W.N., *Software piracy attitudes of tertiary students in Australia*, 2001. www.hkcs.org.hk/searcccd/ed11_aa.htm.

Human Perspectives in the Internet Society: Culture, Psychology and Gender, K. Morgan, J. Sanchez, C. A. Brebbia & A Voiskounsky (Editors) © 2004 WIT Press, www.witpress.com, ISBN 1-85312-726-4

[23] Sterling, B., *The Hacker Crackdown: Law and Disorder on the Electronic Frontier,* London: Penguin, 1992.

[24] Taylor, P., *Hackers. Crime in the Digital Sublime*, London: Routledge, 2002.

[25] Nicholson, L.J., Shebar, T.F. & Weinberg, M.R., Computer crimes. *American Criminal Law Review*, 2000. www.albany.edu/acc/courses/acc680.spring2001/curtin101.ppt.

[26] Shinder, D.L. & Tittel, E., *Scene of the Cybercrime: Computer Forensics Handbook,* Syngress Media Inc., 2002.

[27] Rodgers, M., A *new hackers' taxonomy,* Dept. of Psychology, University of Manitoba, 1999. www.mts.net/~mkr/hacker.doc.

[28] Voiskounsky, A.E. & Smyslova, O.V., Flow-Based Model of Computer Hackers' Motivation. *CyberPsychology & Behavior*, **6(3)**, pp. 171-180, 2003.

[29] Suler, J.R. & Phillips, W., The Bad Boys of Cyberspace: Deviant Behavior in Multimedia Chat Communities. *CyberPsychology and Behavior*, 1, 275-294, 1998. www.rider.edu/~suler/psycyber/badboys.html.

[30] Bommer, M., Gratto, C., Gravander, J., & Tuttle, M., A Behavioral Model of Ethical and Unethical Decision Making. *Journal of Business Ethics,* **6**, pp. 265-280, 1987.

[31] Wortuba, T.R., A Comprehensive Framework for the Analysis of Ethical Behavior, with a Focus on Sales Organizations. *Journal of Personal Selling and Sales Management,* **10(1)**, pp. 29-42, 1990.

[32] Schwartau, W., *Internet & Computer Ethics for Kids (and Parents&Teachers Who Haven't Got a Clue)*, Inter-Pact, 2001.

[33] Kohlberg, L., *The Meaning and Measurement of Moral Development*, Clark Univ. Press, 1981.

[34] Turiel, E., *The Development of Social Knowledge: Morality and Convention,* Cambridge Univ. Press, 1983.

[35] Lefebvre, V.A., *Algebra of Conscience*, Dordrecht, Holland: Reidel, 1982.

[36] Shachtman, N., Sex sites sick of getting screwed. *Wired,* September 13, 2003. www.wired.com/news/business/0,1367,60423,00.html.

Human Perspectives in the Internet Society: Culture, Psychology and Gender, K. Morgan, J. Sanchez, C. A. Brebbia & A Voiskounsky (Editors) © 2004 WIT Press, www.witpress.com, ISBN 1-85312-726-4

Why do people publish weblogs? An online survey of weblog authors in Japan

A. Miura[1] & K. Yamashita[2]
[1]*Department of Psychology, Kobe Gakuin University, Japan*
[2]*School of Network and Information, Senshu University, Japan*

Abstract

This research was conducted to examine the psychological profiles of people who publish their weblogs on the Internet. Weblogs can be defined as on-line sites, not owned by major corporations, which are frequently updated by one or more people. Weblogs provide an opportunity to develop communication with other Internet users. We categorize weblogs into two types, according to their style and content. The weblog form, in which the authors have a powerful desire to share their knowledge and provide information, is termed the "informative weblog". The other weblog form, in which the authors have powerful need for self-disclosure and the resulting interactions, is termed the "diary-like weblog". In this study, we conducted an online survey of 1,142 weblog authors to examine the current weblog situation in Japan. We obtained two hypotheses from the results, as to why weblog authors are motivated to continue weblogging.
Keywords: diary-like weblog, informative weblog, online diary, questionnaire, survey.

1 Overview

We conducted an online survey of weblog authors, known as webloggers in Japan. Weblogs, also known as blog, are now one of the most popular personal content sites on the World Wide Web (WWW). Weblogs have gone from being a marginal activity of Internet enthusiasts, to being squarely mainstream. Weblogs are frequently updated (at least once a day, or more times in some cases) and are characterized by their communication-oriented content.

In Japan, before the emergence of weblogs, a similar trend, known as online diaries, was popular with Internet users. From the inception of personal websites

Human Perspectives in the Internet Society: Culture, Psychology and Gender, K. Morgan, J. Sanchez, C. A. Brebbia & A Voiskounsky (Editors) © 2004 WIT Press, www.witpress.com, ISBN 1-85312-726-4

around 1994, many websites contained "diary" sections. With the rapid and widespread growth of the web, online diary authors began to form their own communities and to develop some original tools for online diaries, causing them to become more popular than ever. Moreover, since around 2000, many Internet service providers have begun to offer users free Web services for online diaries. Even Internet users with little HTML knowledge or skills, could easily become an online diary author. In other words, before weblogs appeared on the web, there were many active online diary authors and communities.

Early in 2001, weblog tools developed in U.S. were introduced to Japan and caught the attention of enormous numbers of Internet users. Even Internet users, who had no interest in online diaries, became intrigued with weblogs. Together, online diaries and weblogs have become extremely popular.

1.1 Online diaries

People can transmit personal information in various forms over the web. The most popular form is to create and publish personal websites or homepages. On personal homepages, there are two main types of content, self-description, and interaction with others. Online diaries are like a junction of these two types.

Kawaura et al [1] investigated the situation of online diary authors. They conducted a survey of 337 online diary authors, examined the reasons they maintained their online diaries, and the role of online diaries as computer-mediated communication (CMC) systems. They regard online diaries as a venue for self-description in public spaces. According to the survey results, they suggested that personal online diaries were a realization of the authors' desire for self-description and also fulfilled their need for communication with others. In addition, the path analysis results confirmed the causal relationship that the psychological need for self-disclosure had a significant effect on the authors' intention to maintain their online diaries. In other words, most online diaries can be defined as content on a personal website that allows the participation of others and establishes personal communication between the author and others.

Table 1: Basic diary types.

Orientation	Expression content	
	Fact	Sentiment
Self	Memoir	(Narrowly defined) diary
Relationship	Journal	Open diary

Cited from Kawaura *et al* [1].

Kawaura *et al* [1] divided online diaries into 4 types, based on two dimensions (Table 1). One dimension is its content expression (fact or sentiment), and another is its orientation (self or reader). The four types of online diaries are memoirs (fact and self-oriented), journals (fact and reader-oriented), narrowly defined diaries (sentiment and self-oriented), and open diaries (sentiment and reader oriented). The results of their survey confirmed the

Human Perspectives in the Internet Society: Culture, Psychology and Gender, K. Morgan, J. Sanchez, C. A. Brebbia & A Voiskounsky (Editors) © 2004 WIT Press, www.witpress.com, ISBN 1-85312-726-4

validity of this categorization and revealed that the ratio of each type was almost equal. (The ratio of narrowly defined diaries was slightly lower than for the others. Other studies about online diaries confirmed the validity of this categorization (e.g. Murata [2], Sugawara and Narukami [3]).

1.2 Online diaries versus weblogs

It has been more than 5 years since Kawaura et al's survey [1] was conducted. Since then, the Internet has matured greatly as a communication medium. Following this trend, weblogs have become increasingly popular amongst Japanese Internet users. Weblogs are websites that contain periodic, reverse chronologically ordered posts. Authors add new topics (i.e. some information or hyperlinks to information sources) to their weblogs daily. Readers are allowed to comment on the posted topics freely, and often anonymously. A participatory online community between authors and readers in weblog sites emerged.

Many academic researchers and Internet users are now debating whether weblog and online diaries can be regarded as the same personal website content or not. For example, some people discriminate between the two and define online diaries as content that includes private and immediate topics, whereas they define weblogs as content that includes the authors' opinions or comments about social news and events. Others focus their attention on weblog modules, such as trackback, which enhances personal communication between the authors and readers. Trackback enables authors to automatically notify another weblogs about new entries. A link to their site will appear in that weblog's list of trackback pings, inviting visitors to visit their weblog. Depending on the absence or presence of these modules, many researchers argue that weblogs are novelties, and not the same as existing online diaries. However, most of existing tools or services for online diaries have modules that enhance personal communication. Some weblogs published, using a Movable Type weblog tool, address highly private and immediate topics.

Consequently, we believe that there are no fundamental differences between online diaries and weblogs. Online diaries and weblogs both have individual authors who record and publish their personal and social experiences and comments. There may be differences in the authors' motivations between online diaries and weblogs. As suggested in Kawaura et al's study [1], authors of online diaries have a strong need for self-disclosure and the resulting mutual exchanges with readers. On the other hand, weblog authors who want to share their knowledge with others, have not yet been investigated. We believe that it will be valuable to study the psychological profiles of people who publish their weblogs on the Internet.

As described above, there are no substantial differences between online diaries and weblogs. But we need to define a given continuous index that can readily identify weblog-like and online diary-like features. This will enable us to examine the differences in the various psychological profiles and motivations of online diary/weblog authors. We also need to explore some changes in the ratio of the four types (Kawaura *et al* [1]) that are caused by weblog imports, and the consequent increase in authors.

Human Perspectives in the Internet Society: Culture, Psychology and Gender, K. Morgan, J. Sanchez, C. A. Brebbia & A Voiskounsky (Editors) © 2004 WIT Press, www.witpress.com, ISBN 1-85312-726-4

1.3 Redefinition of weblogs

In this study, we will refer to online diaries and weblogs together as "weblogs". We redefine weblogs as widespread content, which can satisfy the authors' desire for both self-description and interaction with others. One form of weblog, in which the authors have a powerful need to share knowledge by providing information, is called the "informative weblog". The other, in which the authors have a powerful need for self-disclosure and the resulting interactions, is called the "diary-like weblog." Furthermore we will try to define an appropriate continuous index that can readily identify informative and diary-like weblogs. By categorizing weblog authors using this weblog index, the causal relationship between their psychological profiles and motivations for maintaining the weblog will become more apparent. It will also lead to a more lucid understanding of the role of weblogs as personal websites.

Based on previous studies of online diaries and actual weblog conditions, we conducted an online survey of weblog authors in Japan. In this paper, we will give an outline of the survey and examine the present situation surrounding weblogs and their authors.

2 Method

2.1 Respondents

The respondents in this study were people who had kept and published some sort of weblog on the Internet. The subjects were Internet users who used the Internet service named "Hatena" (URL: http://WWW.hatena.ne.jp). Hatena has provided a free service for weblogs called the "Hatena diary" (URL: http://d.hatena.ne.jp) since March 2003, and has the most registered users in Japan. By January 2004, the total number of hatena diary users (authors and readers) reached 2.02 million (Netratings [4]). The Hatena diary mainly provides support for making diary-like weblog content, but it also has various functions for making informative weblog content, such as automatic hyperlinks of keywords or categorization of specific topic content. Weblog authors who use the Hatena diary service can publish either diary-like or informative weblogs, according to their preference.

2.2 Procedure

With the collaboration of Hatena Co., Ltd., we sent e-mail to all of the subjects on March 1, 2004, requesting them to take part in the survey. They were asked to access the website address listed in the e-mail, and fill in the survey form posted there (URL: http://www.team1mile.com/asarin/research/04survey/survey.html). The replies were then automatically stored in our CSV-format data files. At the beginning of the survey, the number of weblogs on the Hatena diary was 28,541. The website for the survey was accessible from March 1 to 14, 2004.

2.3 Questionnaire

The questionnaire contained more than 100 questions related to weblogs, such as reasons for keeping weblogs, the advantages/benefits of weblogs, individual personality, demographic traits, and psychological variables such as public/private self-consciousness).

3 Results

3.1 Outline of respondents

The total number of responses was 1,434, of which 1,142 were considered valid after eliminating incomplete questionnaires, illegible replies, and duplicate responses. The demographic traits of the respondents are listed below:

There were 783 males (68.6%) and 359 females (31.4%). The respondents fell into the following age categories: teenage, 119 (10.4%); twenties, 602 (52.7%); thirties, 339 (29.7%); forties, 67 (5.9%); over fifty, 15 (1.3%). The distribution of the respondents was almost the same as that of the hatena diary register. This also suggests that these respondents would be good representatives of weblog authors as a whole.

Respondents were divided into 3 groups based on the year they began their weblog; the first generation (before 1999), 250 (21.9%); the middle generation (2000-2002), 314 (27.5%); the later generation (after 2003), 578 (50.6%). Table 2 shows the anonymity levels of the respondents, (anonymous, using a screen name unrelated to their real name, using a screen name related to their real name, and using real name), as weblog authors by generation, group, and gender. In all generation groups, female authors tried to protect their anonymity more than male authors, particularly in the middle generation. This generation coincides with the appearance and popularization of free Web services for online diaries.

Table 2: Anonymity of weblog authors by generation group and gender (%).

Anonymity	First generation		Middle generation		Later generation	
	Male	Female	Male	Female	Male	Female
Anonymous	3.7	5.8	4.6	3.4	7.8	9.1
Screen name unrelated	44.8	59.8	46.9	73.7	49.5	61.0
Screen name related	34.4	21.8	32.1	20.3	30.0	22.7
Real name	17.2	12.6	16.3	2.5	12.7	7.1
Respondents	*163*	*87*	*196*	*118*	*424*	*154*

3.2 Weblog types

The respondents' weblogs were categorized into four types, based on the responses for two items. We asked the respondents, "Why do you think you

Human Perspectives in the Internet Society: Culture, Psychology and Gender, K. Morgan, J. Sanchez, C. A. Brebbia & A Voiskounsky (Editors) © 2004 WIT Press, www.witpress.com, ISBN 1-85312-726-4

publish a weblog?". They were asked to select one of the five answers; 1) keeping notes of everyday occurrences for myself, 2) offering information I pick up daily to others, 3) letting people know me better as a person, 4) understanding myself better, and 5) no particular reason. These answers corresponded to the weblog types, memoirs, journals, open diaries, and narrowly defined diaries, respectively. We then asked the respondents to select one from the four types.

Table 3: The ratio of each weblog types (%).

	Kawaura *et al* [1]	Reason question	Direct selection
Memoir	24.4	47.4	24.3
Journal	24.1	18.7	19.4
Narrowly defined diary	14.3	11.9	22.1
Open diary	23.1	9.9	34.3
No reason	13.1	12.1	----

Table 3 summarizes the ratio of each weblog type, categorized based on each of two questions from this study and comparing the answers to that of Kawaura *et al* [1]. In the first question, the existence of all four types was confirmed, and nearly half of respondents selected "keeping notes of everyday occurrences for myself." In the case of the second question, the existence of all four types was also confirmed.

3.3 Motivations of weblog authors: diary-like and informative

Five items were chosen to objectively determine the motivations of the weblog authors, (self-description and interaction with others, or knowledge sharing by providing information): 1) recording units of each weblog (topic or date), 2) content of each weblog (social/public or private), 3) necessity for any category (no or yes), 4) necessity for reference to other weblogs (no or yes), and 5) necessity for author's profile for easy understanding (no or yes). Respondents were asked to rate each item on a five-point scale. The scores for each of these five items were summed up and used as the weblog index score. Gender differences were average scores on the weblog index. Male respondents had a significantly higher score (M=14.37) than female (M=12.94), which suggests that male weblog authors are more interested in knowledge sharing than female authors.

According to the score distribution of the weblog index, the respondents were divided into 3 groups, high, middle, and low informative (Table 4). Then, the average scores of the various questionnaire items related to the weblog were compared. Though the frequency of updating the weblogs was significantly higher in the high informative group than the other groups, both the amount of time spent updating their weblog and the volume of text per update were not significantly different among the groups. There was no significant difference among the groups in mental stress and their intention for continuing to weblog.

Human Perspectives in the Internet Society: Culture, Psychology and Gender, K. Morgan, J. Sanchez, C. A. Brebbia & A Voiskounsky (Editors) © 2004 WIT Press, www.witpress.com, ISBN 1-85312-726-4

Table 4: Weblog index and distribution.

Group	Score	Frequency
High informative	Over 15	373
Middle informative	12 to 14	424
Low informative	Under 11	345

Table 5: Ratio of perceived interest of readers (%).

Interested in	High	Middle	Low
Information	26.0	39.1	59.4
Personality	74.0	60.9	40.6

Table 6: Ratio of their own interest in other weblogs (%).

Interested in	High	Middle	Low
Information	35.7	39.1	57.4
Personality	64.3	60.9	42.6

To compare the interest of the respondents in the weblog content, along with the weblog index, we calculated the ratio of the perceived reader interest in their own weblogs (Table 5) and the ratio of their own interest in other weblogs (Table 6) by groups. The respondents in the high informative group believed that their readers were interested in the information on their weblogs, whereas the people in the low informative group believed that their readers were interested in their personality traits, not included their weblogs. As shown in Table 6, a similar trend was found in their own interest in other weblogs. These results suggest that the weblog index used in this study was valid for discriminating the motivations of weblog authors, informative or diary-like.

4 Discussion

In this study, we were interested in the psychological profiles of people who publish their weblogs on the Internet, and conducted an online survey. Results from preliminary data analysis clarified the differences in weblog behaviour by gender or generation group and suggested that the weblog index used in this study was valid for discriminating the motivations of weblog authors, informative or diary-like.

Based on the results of the Kawaura et al's previous study [1] and our survey, we propose two hypotheses to discover why weblog authors were motivated to continue publishing their weblogs. By testing these two hypotheses, we will be able to clarify the relationship between individual personality, psychological variables and the various behaviours of weblog authors. In diary-like weblog authors, the higher their self-consciousness was, or the more positive emotional feedback they received from their readers, the higher they valued their weblogs, increasing their gratification levels and strengthening their intention to

Human Perspectives in the Internet Society: Culture, Psychology and Gender, K. Morgan, J. Sanchez, C. A. Brebbia & A Voiskounsky (Editors) © 2004 WIT Press, www.witpress.com, ISBN 1-85312-726-4

continue their weblogs. On the other hand, in case of informative weblog authors, the more significant their information was, or the more comments or additional information they received, the more they valued their weblogs, increasing their gratification levels and strengthening their intention to continue their weblogs. We will construct a causal model for continuing publishing weblogs by structural equation modelling, based on this data.

In recent years a new-found weblog content has rapidly combined with existing online diaries to provide a new style of online communities, centering on personal websites in Japan. This could lead to a more integrative understanding of personal behaviour on the web, that will assist in the construction of a new model, with a view to exposing the behaviours of weblog authors.

References

[1] Kawaura, Y., Kawakami Y., and Yamashita, K., Keeping a diary in cyberspace, *Japanese Psychological Research*, **40**, pp. 234 245, 1998.

[2] Murata, K., Psychological gratification from communication in online diary, Graduation thesis in the School of Human Sciences, Osaka University, 2003 (in Japanese, unpublished).

[3] Sugawara, K. and Narukami, Behaviours in online diary, Graduation thesis in the Faculty of Liberal Arts, University of the Sacred Heart, 2004 (in Japanese, unpublished).

[4] Netratings, csp.netratings.co.jp/nnr/PDF/227_2004release_j_final.pdf (in Japanese).

Human Perspectives in the Internet Society: Culture, Psychology and Gender, K. Morgan, J. Sanchez, C. A. Brebbia & A Voiskounsky (Editors) © 2004 WIT Press, www.witpress.com, ISBN 1-85312-726-4

Interacting with virtual lecturers: outcomes from introducing streamed video into the classroom

C. D. Smith[1], A. M. Morley[1], H. E. Whiteley[1], L. Hodgson[2] & K. Williams[2]
[1]*Learning and Literacy Research Unit, Department of Psychology, University of Central Lancashire, United Kingdom*
[2]*Learning and Literacy Research Unit, Department of Psychology, University of Central Lancashire, United Kingdom*

Abstract

Streamed video is being introduced into higher education on an increasing scale. The technology may allow remote students to participate synchronously, when the video is streamed live, or asynchronously, when it is most convenient for them. This paper reports the outcomes from a project to introduce and evaluate asynchronously streamed video into undergraduate psychology modules within three online lectures. Each author separately adapted an existing lecture for video streaming. The resulting uses of video streaming varied somewhat between the authors and will be compared. Hence, one reported outcome is the differing perspectives taken by the authors on the uses to which video streaming could be put and the use they actually made of streamed video. A second outcome is to report the authors' views of the process of creating video streamed lectures, especially in terms of time, ease of use, pedagogy and the development of expertise. Two of the video streamed lectures were part of a second year undergraduate psychology module. The third lecture was part of a third year module on the psychology of reading. Outcomes are also reported in terms of student usage of and feedback on the asynchronous material, in particular how it affected interaction with staff relative to other online and traditionally-delivered lectures. A final reported outcome is to compare the examination performance of students in terms of marks for questions based on the video streamed lectures and marks for questions based on the other methods of delivery. Recommendations are made for the scope, limitations and aspects of good practice for the use of video streaming as a teaching method. Future plans to extend the method are also discussed.

Keywords: videostreaming; streamed video; interactive video; learning; teaching; asynchronous learning; distance learning.

Human Perspectives in the Internet Society: Culture, Psychology and Gender, K. Morgan, J. Sanchez, C. A. Brebbia & A Voiskounsky (Editors) © 2004 WIT Press, www.witpress.com, ISBN 1-85312-726-4

1 Introduction

This paper does not describe a research project as such. It describes a teaching project, where streamed video was introduced into the curriculum and attempts were made to apply research methodology within the project as much as was possible, in order to assess its impact on student use of and learning from the videostreamed materials.

The use of 'streaming' digital video as a teaching and learning resource is rapidly becoming an attractive option for many educators as an innovation expanding the range of learning resources available to students by moving away from static text-and-graphic resources towards a video-rich learning environment. This environment can offer images, interactivity and integration with other resources. It can integrate, *inter alia*, still and moving images, live or recorded lectures, locally produced video, web resources and synchronous and asynchronous communication tools.

Streamed video is a new technique, which is attracting attention in the HE community. It is already widely used in a few universities. For example the University of Cincinnati offers six complete courses and over 400 individual items of instructional material and events via videostreaming [1]. It sees videostreaming as successfully replacing the classroom and as drawing the wider learning community and the university closer together. At the University of Western Australia videostreaming has given over 6000 students access to recordings of over 1800 lectures [2]. 50000 hits have been recorded to date – 60% of which came from off campus Another example of using streamed video comes from the School of Psychology at the University of Sydney, where lectures have been delivered both synchronously and asynchronously by DVT (Digital Video Taping) - streamed video by another name [3].

2 Advantages of using streamed video

2.1 The advantages of replacing a lecture with streamed video are that:

A lecture which is sent live by streamed video (synchronous transmission) to students at a remote location offers little compared to a live face-to-face lecture or a televised lecture. The only obvious advantage of synchronous streamed video is that it can reach any PC on a network, which, given access rights to the network, could mean any PC anywhere.

Asynchronous transmission, however, offers significant advantages for students and staff. For students, the advantages are:

- The lecture is available at any time via the internet or the university network
- Students have control over when, where and how they watch the lecture – 'how' meaning that they control the sequence, duration and repetition of the video clips which make up the lecture. Learner control allows the student to adopt their preferred mode of learning at their preferred time and in their preferred location

Human Perspectives in the Internet Society: Culture, Psychology and Gender, K. Morgan, J. Sanchez, C. A. Brebbia & A Voiskounsky (Editors) © 2004 WIT Press, www.witpress.com, ISBN 1-85312-726-4

- Students also have control over access to any supplementary materials which accompany the lecture, e.g. graphics, text, references, Internet links, etc.

These points correlate positively with students' attitudes to distance learning [4] and to learning styles [5,6].

For staff, the advantages are:

- A lecture can usually be easily edited, updated and amended, because it consists of many short clips of video and many small files to provide the supplementary text, graphics, etc.
- self-assessment questions and feedback can be included: the feedback can provide links to the relevant part of the lecture
- in theory, replacing lectures with recorded versions reduces staff workload: in practice, the time spent preparing and updating the lecture may be considerable - depending on familiarity with the medium and the availability of technical support, etc.
- using streamed video reduces demand on scarce teaching resources such as large lecture theatres.

2.2 Disadvantages of using streamed video

There are few disadvantages associated with streamed video, but arguably:

- it makes the student experience more remote and impersonal and less 'connected', even compared to being in a large audience for a live lecture
- as mentioned above, using streamed video may involve the lecturer in more work, depending on how it is done
- it requires technical support
- Some lectures may be less effective as streamed video.
- The effectiveness of the medium for learning has not been fully evaluated.

3 Evaluation

The introduction of any major new teaching technique needs to be carefully evaluated in terms of what it is intended to offer and whether there are any drawbacks. The key criterion is the effect of the new technique on student learning, i.e. on whether the learning outcomes are met as well as or better than existing or alternative modes of delivery. This is often very difficult to assess adequately. Assessment may consist of no more than student and/or staff feedback on the experience of using the new technique, rather than directly assessing student performance. As far as can be ascertained from their websites, the University of Cincinnati seems to have adopted videostreaming widely without first evaluating it, while the University of Western Australia seems to regard the number of hits on its website as an indicator of the success of its streamed video. Neither approach is necessarily incorrect, but neither is really an evaluation.

Human Perspectives in the Internet Society: Culture, Psychology and Gender, K. Morgan, J. Sanchez, C. A. Brebbia & A Voiskounsky (Editors) © 2004 WIT Press, www.witpress.com, ISBN 1-85312-726-4

The School of Psychology at the University of Sydney has adopted a more systematic approach to evaluating the effectiveness of streamed video (using a sample of 11 students), by comparing it to live face-to-face lectures (n = 186) and to live video-conferenced lectures (n = 24) (White et al., 2004). Both live modes were perceived as being significantly more satisfactory, but the opportunity to rewind the video was valued by the streamed video sample. Student examination and coursework performance were not measured, nor are any views of staff reported.

The study reported in this paper is a fuller evaluation of the use of streamed video for teaching and learning. It reports this from three angles:

1. The staff experience in creating and using streamed video within psychology modules
2. The student experience of using streamed video materials
3. The effects of learning from streamed video materials on student performance.

3.1 Preparation of the materials

In the academic year 2002-03 a lecture on the psychology of creative behaviour was chosen as suitable for videostreaming. The lecture is part of a second year module (PS2400 Cognitive Psychology), which is a compulsory module for BSc. Psychology students and for other students wishing to obtain eligibility for membership of the British Psychological Society. The module regularly attracts more than 150 students and, if current recruitment patterns continue, will attract over 200 in future.

The first step was to edit the existing notes for the lecture into about 20 short pieces, each of which had a heading. The 26 'soundbites' were then recorded in the LDU – using as many takes as necessary. A text summary of each video clip was also prepared and added below the clip, in order to both summarise the point being made in the clip and to enable anyone without hearing, speakers, headphones or a soundcard to make sense of the clip.

The process of preparing the material was not lengthy, while it took about 90 minutes to film 40 minutes of video. Note that the lecture lasts slightly less long that the standard 50 minutes – presumably because it includes no unnecessary verbiage, setting up time or other non-essential activities. Perhaps, also, the pace of delivery was faster, because of the knowledge that students can view each clip as many times as they wish and the lecturer does not need to adopt note-taking pace. This, in turn, means that videostreamed lectures recorded in this way could include more material than conventional lectures.

The video clips were assembled into a package with an introductory page, navigation aids and the text summary of each clip at the bottom. The screen is split into two with the left half containing the video of the lecture and the right half available for the full text or for any other material. A pause button allows notes to be taken at leisure from the screen.

The final version was then uploaded to the UCLan video server and links were set up from the Cognitive Psychology Website within the Department of Psychology website. Students on the course were familiar with the Cognitive

Human Perspectives in the Internet Society: Culture, Psychology and Gender, K. Morgan, J. Sanchez, C. A. Brebbia & A Voiskounsky (Editors) © 2004 WIT Press, www.witpress.com, ISBN 1-85312-726-4

Psychology Website, which contains other essential material for the PS2400 module.

Student feedback on the streamed video lecture was positive, as recorded by responses to a question on the Module Evaluation Questionnaire, which was given to students at the end of the module. However, this feedback was obtained from relatively few of students -who may have watched rather than used lecture - and it was not possible to relate the feedback to their examination performance. Accordingly, it was decided to seek funding to continue and extend the development of videostreamed material. The University of Central Lancashire's Curriculum Innovation Fund supported the current project which aimed to:

- re-shoot the existing lecture and to add more and better quality supporting material to it (CDS)
- prepare videostreamed material for another topic in the cognitive psychology module (AMM)
- add videostreamed material to an existing online version of a topic on a third level module (HEW)

Thus three items of videostreamed material were prepared for use, with the aim of:

- evaluating as fully as possible the staff and student experiences of videostreaming
- assessing whether using streamed video materials affects student performance.

4 Results

4.1 Staff experiences of creating and using the videostreamed materials

Feedback was obtained from staff involved in the project about the uses they put streamed video to. The salient points are:

- HEW used streamed video to supplement an existing online lecture by embedding an introduction to each major section, which outlined the aims, objectives and outcomes of that section. She felt this prepared the students for fuller use of the existing interactive materials. It was a useful exercise for her in learning about the need to direct students and to guide them in benefiting more from the material. Preparation and videoing took 90 minutes.
- AMM prepared a videostreamed introduction to a seminar and also used the 2002-03 lecture and added paper summaries and notes, allowing comparison to be made between the use of the material in 2002-03 and 2003-04. For him the exercise brought home the value for students of having access to and control over the materials - including access to materials not available in the library. The preparation took longer than for a standard lecture and was a useful exercise in appreciating the differences between a standard lecture (where, for example, ad libbing and adding extra points are possible) and the carefully structured and supported videostreamed lecture.

Human Perspectives in the Internet Society: Culture, Psychology and Gender, K. Morgan, J. Sanchez, C. A. Brebbia & A Voiskounsky (Editors) © 2004 WIT Press, www.witpress.com, ISBN 1-85312-726-4

- CDS re-shot the lecture used in 2002-03. Preparation and videoing took 90 minutes. The supporting materials were prepared by LH. For CDS the supporting materials transform the original videostreamed lecture - providing as much breadth and depth as students could possibly use.

4.2 Student use of the videostreamed materials

No figures are available for the number of hits on the materials, but student usage of the materials was assessed by questions on the MEQ for each module and by comparing examination performance on questions relating to the videostreamed material with that on other questions. The results were as follows:

The videoed introduction to sections within an online topic (HEW): the feedback was not specific about the use of streamed video, but the online topic itself was very well received with:

- 22 students being 'very satisfied'
- 10 students being 'satisfied' and
- 1 student being 'very dissatisfied'

A frequent comment was that the freedom to access the material at any time was greatly valued.

The examination scores revealed a significant difference between the mean scores for question on the topic containing the streamed video (58.63%) and a compulsory question (53.17) ($t = 2.28$; $df = 23$; $p = 0.032$). The mean of 58.63% was the highest for any question and the question was the most popular, but further statistical comparisons between this question and other questions were not possible, because of small numbers (students were required to answer only three questions). It should also be noted that the statistically significant result is a comparison of two different questions, either of which may have been intrinsically harder or easier than the other.

The data from the MEQs and examinations for **the videostreamed materials used by CDS and the AMM** are not available at the time of writing this paper. Detailed questions will be asked in the MEQs about the videostreaming and examination marks on questions on videostreamed topics will be compared with marks on other topics.

5 Thoughts on the experience

Many points and much food for thought have arisen from this project. They are listed below in no particular order.

- The project shows that streamed video has a range of uses within the curriculum
- It is technically feasible and reliable
- It can replace traditional lectures
- It can supplement topics delivered online
- It was not difficult or time-consuming to do, given development and technical support

Human Perspectives in the Internet Society: Culture, Psychology and Gender, K. Morgan, J. Sanchez, C. A. Brebbia & A Voiskounsky (Editors) © 2004 WIT Press, www.witpress.com, ISBN 1-85312-726-4

- In teaching terms much has been learned, which will facilitate future use of videostreaming and also impact indirectly on other teaching modes of delivery
- Student feedback is so far almost entirely positive and is usually very positive
- The availability of what is effectively a hard copy of a lecture must generally aid student learning

6 Future uses of videostreaming

Many aspects of this first substantial use of streamed video can be improved upon. It has been a learning experience for all concerned, but a worthwhile one, which we wish to build on.

The technology now seems to work well and the main need is introduce streamed video more widely and to identify further uses of it - without disrupting adversely the balance in delivery modes, which provides a full learning experience for students. For example, providing more interactivity is a priority, by, for example, linking a message board in an MLE to the videostreamed lectures - rather than making staff available when lectures were streamed to a remote site, as was done in Sydney [3].

We would also seek to evaluate the use of streamed video in greater breadth and depth. For example, we would seek to obtain better feedback from students and perhaps would identify case study examples of good practice in its use. We would continue to assess the effectiveness of learning from streamed video.

References

[1] Case study example of streamed video lectures from the University of Cincinnati. http://www.microsoft.com/windows/windows/…e/casestudies/univcincinnati/default.asp).

[2] University of Western Australia. Reports of using streamed video. http://ilectures.uwa.edu.au/ilectures~uwa.htm).

[3] White, W., Sartore, J. G., Cartwright, A. and Curthoys, I. (2004). Digital videotaping (DVT): an evaluation of an innovative mode for lecture delivery for teaching psychology. Paper presented at PLAT2004 (Psychology of Teaching and Learning) conference, Strathclyde University, UK. April.

[4] Katz, Y. J. (2002). Attitudes affecting college students' preferences for distance learning. Journal of Computer Assisted Learning, 18 (1), 2-9.

[5] Dewar, T. and Whittington, D. (2000). Online learners and their learning strategies. *Educational Computing Research*, 23 (4), 385-403.

[6] Smith, C. D., Smith, C. D. and Whiteley, H. E. (2003). Distance learning and learning styles: bridging the gap. In Proceedings of the 3rd International Conference on Technology in Teaching/Learning in Higher Education. Heidelberg, Germany. July. Pages 279-284.

Human Perspectives in the Internet Society: Culture, Psychology and Gender, K. Morgan, J. Sanchez, C. A. Brebbia & A Voiskounsky (Editors) © 2004 WIT Press, www.witpress.com, ISBN 1-85312-726-4

Differentiating computer-related addictions and high engagement

J. P. Charlton[1] & I. D. W. Danforth[2]
[1]*Bolton Institute, UK*
[2]*Stanford University, USA*

Abstract

This paper discusses the difference between computing-related addictions and high engagement in computing activities. The results of two studies are reviewed, one involving factor analysis of paper questionnaire items concerning computing in general, and one involving web-based questionnaire items concerning a Massively Multiplayer Online Role-Playing Game. Across both data sets, it is shown that items tapping euphoria, cognitive salience and tolerance appear to indicate high engagement (a high degree of non-pathological involvement) rather than addiction. It is therefore suggested that these criteria, which have been used to classify pathological gambling behaviours, should not be adapted for use in classifying pathological computing behaviours, as has sometimes been done. It is argued that, while thoughts and behaviours surrounding computing may occupy a large amount of the time of people who are highly engaged with a computing activity, this cannot be considered pathological in the absence of deleterious effects on their lives. It is shown that including these types of criteria in schemes to classify people as addicted can lead to over-estimates in the number of people who are addicted to any particular computing activity. On the other hand, it is argued that people whose behaviours lead to interpersonal conflict, who experience withdrawal symptoms when not performing an activity, whose attempts to curtail their behaviour end in relapse and reinstatement, and whose behaviours result in self-neglect can be considered to be addicted to a computing activity.
Keywords: computer addiction, computer dependence, impulse control disorders, computer attitudes, computer games, Internet, taxonomies.

Human Perspectives in the Internet Society: Culture, Psychology and Gender, K. Morgan, J. Sanchez, C. A. Brebbia & A Voiskounsky (Editors) © 2004 WIT Press, www.witpress.com, ISBN 1-85312-726-4

1 Introduction

In the past ten years much work has appeared suggesting that addiction to computing activities, particularly Internet-mediated activities, may be a cause for concern. In this paper we discuss two studies with implications for classification procedures used in some of this work. But, before considering these issues, it is worth mentioning that the very idea that computer-related addictions may exist is controversial. Here, it has been argued that using the term ‘addiction’ in connection with non-chemically-related behaviours may be seen to trivialize chemical addictions (Jaffe [14]). However, recently developed brain scanning techniques have revealed close similarities between the brain’s responses to rewards irrespective of whether these stem from ingesting substances or other behaviours (Holden [13]). Another controversy concerns terminology. The revised fourth edition of the American Psychiatric Association’s Diagnostic and Statistical Manual (DSM-IV-TR) refers to conditions where people are unable to desist from behaviours resulting in self-harm or harm to others, but which do not involve ingestion of substances, as impulse-control disorders (APA [1]). Even in connection with drug use the DSM-IV-TR uses the phrase ‘dependence’ rather than addiction because the latter has become pejorative. Nevertheless, in discussing non-substance-related behavioural phenomena, Brown [4] argued that the term ‘addiction’ is still useful, and the term is adopted here given the centrality of Brown’s work to the studies described.

Among the first people to voice a concern that people may be interacting with computers to an undesirable extent was Shotton [15] who performed a study of what she termed computer dependent individuals. She defined dependency in terms of an individual’s ‘…strong compelling desire…’ to use computers (p.5). However, in the main, the behaviour of Shotton’s dependents appeared non-pathological since they experienced few negative consequences of their behaviours, such consequences being widely accepted as critical in defining pathologically excessive behaviours (e.g. DSM-IV-TR). Similarly, Griffiths and Hunt [12] identified few negative effects of the behaviours of adolescent computer game players whom they labelled as dependent based upon criteria adapted from those in the DSM-III-R for the impulse control disorder of pathological gambling. Such a classification scheme (from DSM-IV) was also used in Young’s [17] study of Internet addiction, which was criticised by Beard and Wolf [2] on these grounds. Taking into account studies such as these, we asked whether some studies may confuse pathological behaviours with highly-zealous but non-pathological behaviours.

Many of the DSM criteria used in the above studies are reflected in Brown’s [4] criteria for behavioural addiction, and Griffiths [10] has used Brown’s criteria in discussing technological addictions. The present research focussed upon Brown’s criteria as used by Griffiths, rather than criteria adapted from the DSM’s conception of pathological gambling, because the former aim to cover all behavioural addictions and therefore represent a particularly plausible scheme for classifying computer-related behaviours.

Human Perspectives in the Internet Society: Culture, Psychology and Gender, K. Morgan, J. Sanchez, C. A. Brebbia & A Voiskounsky (Editors) © 2004 WIT Press, www.witpress.com, ISBN 1-85312-726-4

Griffiths [10] summarised four of Brown's six criteria as follows; euphoria (the activity produces a 'buzz' or a 'high'); tolerance (the activity has to be engaged in to an increasingly greater extent to acquire the same 'buzz'); withdrawal symptoms (negative emotions or physical effects are experienced on cessation of the activity); relapse and reinstatement (resumption of the activity with the same vigour after attempts to abstain). The other two criteria are multi-faceted. First, conflict can take the form of inter-personal conflict as a result of performing the activity, intra-psychic conflict where internal conflict results from one's behaviour, and finally conflicts with other activities, where behaviour involving the object of addiction is preferred over activities such as work and socialising (Griffiths [11]). Second, salience can consist of cognitive salience, where an activity dominates a person's mental life, and / or behavioural salience, where an activity dominates a person's behaviour (Brown [4]; Griffiths [10]). Brown's scheme is monothetic: an individual has to meet all six criteria for a positive classification to be made. This can be contrasted with polythetic schemes, such as those used in the previously mentioned DSM-based studies, where only a proportion of criteria have to be met for a positive classification.

Behavioural addiction can be contrasted with high engagement. The latter does not necessarily entail any lesser involvement in terms of the amount of time an individual devotes to an activity, but differs from addiction in that negative consequences are absent and in that there is no compulsion to perform the activity to alleviate dysphoria upon its discontinuation. Rather, the highly engaged person performs an activity because they find it enjoyable. High computer engagement can be a positive quality, being positively related to students' academic performance on a programming-orientated computing course (Charlton and Birkett [6]).

The two studies reviewed here sought to differentiate facets of computer-related addiction from facets of high engagement. Towards this end, the suitability of Brown's behavioural addiction criteria for classifying people as having computer-related addictions was considered. A factor analytic approach was adopted, questionnaire responses to items tapping addiction and engagement being analysed. The first study considered computing in general, collecting responses to items on a paper questionnaire. The second study replicated and extended the first. Players of a specific type of putatively addictive Massively Multiplayer Online Role-Playing Game (MMORPG) were targeted via a website, and questionnaire items were altered to refer to the game at issue. Across both studies, it was reasoned that if it is appropriate to use Brown's criteria, and related DSM criteria, in classifying computer-related addictions, an Addiction factor should load more highly than an Engagement factor upon items tapping these criteria. If this was not the case, it was envisaged that this would necessitate re-assessment of the criteria used in defining computing-related addictions. Brief attention was also paid to the possibility that a developmental process may exist whereby people pass through a stage of high engagement prior to becoming behaviourally addicted to computing activities.

Human Perspectives in the Internet Society: Culture, Psychology and Gender, K. Morgan, J. Sanchez, C. A. Brebbia & A Voiskounsky (Editors) © 2004 WIT Press, www.witpress.com, ISBN 1-85312-726-4

2 Method

Study 1 (reported more fully in Charlton [5]) involved distributing a 47 item paper questionnaire to 404 students on courses at a higher education institution in northern England (193 males and 198 females, both genders having a mean age of around 26 years and SD around 9 years). The questionnaire contained a mixture of positively and negatively phrased statements seeking to tap Brown's addiction criteria (see Table 1), other addiction-related items (e.g. 'I think that I am addicted to computing'), items tapping computer apathy-engagement (e.g. 'I would hate to go without using a computer for more than a few days') and computer comfort-anxiety (e.g. 'I find computers threatening'). The majority of these two latter types of item were taken from the Computer Apathy and Anxiety Scale (Charlton and Birkett [6] – apathy and engagement constitute opposite ends of the same continuum). All items were statements concerning computing-related behaviours and cognitions in general, rather than any specific type of computing activity. Participants responded to statements on a five-point Likert-type scale with response options ranging from Strongly Disagree to Strongly Agree. To encourage participation, students completing questionnaires were entered in a raffle for prizes totalling £60 in cash.

Table 1: Items tapping Brown's criteria for behavioural addiction (italicised and parenthesised wordings are for Study 1 and Study 2 items respectively).

A1: **Salience (cognitive);** I rarely think about *computing* (playing Asheron's Call) when I am not using a computer.

A2: **Salience (behavioural);** I never miss meals because of *my computing activities* (playing Asheron's Call).

A3: **Salience (behavioural);** I often fail to get enough sleep because of *my computing activities* (playing Asheron's Call).

A4: **Euphoria;** I often experience a buzz of excitement while *computing* (playing Asheron's Call).

A5: **Tolerance;** I tend to want to spend increasing amounts of time *using computers* (playing Asheron's Call).

A6: **Withdrawal symptoms;** When I am not *using a computer* (playing Asheron's Call), I often feel agitated.

A7: **Conflict (inter-personal);** Arguments have sometimes arisen at home because of the time I spend *on computing activities* (playing Asheron's Call).

A8: **Conflict (with other activities);** My social life has sometimes suffered because of my *computing activities* (playing Asheron's Call).

A9: **Conflict (with other activities);** *Computing activities have* (Playing Asheron's Call has) sometimes interfered with my work.

A10: **Relapse and reinstatement;** I have made unsuccessful attempts to reduce the time I spend *computing* (playing Asheron's Call).

Human Perspectives in the Internet Society: Culture, Psychology and Gender, K. Morgan, J. Sanchez, C. A. Brebbia & A Voiskounsky (Editors) © 2004 WIT Press, www.witpress.com, ISBN 1-85312-726-4

In Study 2 (described more fully in Charlton and Danforth [8]), 442 players of a MMORPG entitled Asheron's Call responded to a 29 item questionnaire placed on a website devoted to the game (http://ac.xrgaming.net). Respondents were 379 males (mean age around 29 years, SD around 9 years) and 61 females (mean age around 33 years, SD around 8 years). The questionnaire contained the same basic addiction and apathy-engagement items as in Study 1. However items were modified to be specific to Asheron's Call. The equivalent items tapping Brown's addiction criteria are shown in Table 1. In this study computer comfort-anxiety items were omitted, and participants responded on a seven-point Likert-type scale with responses ranging from Completely Disagree to Completely Agree. The number of points on the response scale was increased relative to Study 1 to produce greater variability in the data. As an incentive to take part, respondents were entered into a raffle with a prize of two months free game play (value US $26).

3 Results

In both studies scree plots from initial Principal Components Analyses were used to select the number of components present. These plots revealed three components in Study 1 and two in Study 2. Principal Axis Factoring with oblique (Direct Oblimin) rotation was then performed. For both studies these solutions are reported since factors were moderately correlated (e.g. .38 in Study 1 for the two factors of major interest and -.33 in Study 2; the latter correlation was negative because of a reversal in polarity of one factor's loadings).

The Study 1 solution accounted for 43% of item variance. Based upon the factor pattern loadings, factors were interpreted as Computer Engagement (accounting for 28% of item variance), Computer Addiction (11% of variance), and Computer Comfort (4% of variance). In Study 2, 32% of item variance was accounted for. Here factors were interpretable as Asheron's Call Addiction (25% of item variance) and (Low) Asheron's Call Engagement (7% of variance). Addiction and Engagement factor pattern loadings for the 10 items tapping Brown's behavioural addiction criteria across both studies are given in Table 2.

Table 2 shows that in both studies the Engagement factor loaded more highly than the Addiction factor upon items tapping Brown's euphoria and tolerance criteria. The same was also true for the cognitive salience item, but not the behavioural salience items. As far as the main point at issue is concerned then, both studies showed that some of the criteria previously taken as being indicative of addiction appear to be more related to high engagement (a non-pathological construct) than addiction. These criteria are subsequently referred to as peripheral criteria. Across both studies the Addiction factors loaded highly upon items tapping the remainder of Brown's criteria (withdrawal, relapse and reinstatement, behavioural salience, and conflict – both inter-personal and with other activities). Henceforth, these are referred to as core criteria.

For the most part the results of the two studies were highly similar. For example, calculation of Pearson's r coefficients across the pairs of Addiction and Engagement factors in the two studies revealed a value of $r = .96$ (df=8, P<.001

Human Perspectives in the Internet Society: Culture, Psychology and Gender, K. Morgan, J. Sanchez, C. A. Brebbia & A Voiskounsky (Editors) © 2004 WIT Press, www.witpress.com, ISBN 1-85312-726-4

one-tailed) for the Addiction loadings and of r = -.93 (df=8, P<.001 one-tailed) for the Engagement loadings (these loadings were negatively correlated because of the differences in algebraic signs of the loadings for this factor in the two studies). However, there were some minor differences. In particular, taking loadings greater than +/-.32 as high, in Study 1 both the euphoria and tolerance items were complex, with both the Engagement and Addiction factors loading highly upon them, albeit that the former factor loaded more highly. But in Study 2 the euphoria item was factor pure, only the Engagement factor loading highly.

Table 2: Factor pattern loadings for items tapping Brown's behavioural addiction criteria across the two studies.

Item	Study 1 Addiction	Study 1 Engagement	Study 2 Addiction	Study 2 Engagement
A1 Cognitive Salience	-.31	-.41	-.27	.49
A2 Behavioural Salience (meals)	-.49	-.05	-.46	-.03
A3 Behavioural Salience (sleep)	.73	-.01	.53	-.17
A4 Euphoria	.39	.43	.13	-.40
A5 Tolerance	.36	.55	.36	-.42
A6 Withdrawal	.49	.10	.62	-.07
A7 Conflict (inter-personal)	.67	-.02	.54	-.11
A8 Conflict Activities (social)	.72	-.07	.69	-.02
A9 Conflict Activities (work)	.63	-.03	.66	.06
A10 Relapse & Reinstatement	.58	-.10	.62	.08

To clarify implications for classification systems, consideration was given to frequencies of responses relevant to classification decisions. To do this, in each study the original Likert-scale responses were dichotomised for each of the 10 relevant items into those falling on the side of the response scale indicating some extent of agreement and those falling on the side indicating some extent of disagreement (mid-scale responses were excluded). Then frequencies of responses on the side of the scale consistent with an 'addicted' response were counted for each item. These frequencies are shown in Figure 1. Here it can be seen that across both studies, in the main, the peripheral criteria (the first three items represented on the figure) tended to be endorsed more frequently than the core criteria. To investigate further, the extent of joint endorsement of the peripheral and core criteria was examined. To simplify matters, people were split into those endorsing low (0 and 1) and high (2 and 3) numbers of peripheral criteria, and low (0 through 3) and high (4 through 7) numbers of core criteria. These frequencies were cast into 2 x 2 contingency tables. Inspection of frequencies indicated that students giving a high number of core responses also tended to give a high number of peripheral responses (in Study 1 54.17% of students giving a high number of core responses also gave a high number of peripheral responses, while the corresponding percentage in Study 2 was 84.62% of game players). Given that the addiction and engagement factors were correlated in both studies, these observations were not surprising (therefore chi-square test results, both of which were significant, are not presented). Nevertheless, as will be discussed, this limits the implications for classification

Human Perspectives in the Internet Society: Culture, Psychology and Gender, K. Morgan, J. Sanchez, C. A. Brebbia & A Voiskounsky (Editors) © 2004 WIT Press, www.witpress.com, ISBN 1-85312-726-4

decisions of the factor analytic findings and the finding that people generally endorsed more peripheral than core criteria.

To consider whether a developmental process may exist whereby high engagement is a precursor of addiction, McNemar's Change Tests were performed on the numbers of people endorsing a high number of peripheral items but a low number of core items compared with the numbers of people endorsing a high number of core items but a low number of peripheral items. Evidence for a developmental process would consist of the former people outnumbering the latter. In both studies such evidence existed. Thus, in Study 1 12.13% of people (n=49) fell into the first category and 2.72% fell into the second category (n=11) resulting in a value of χ^2=24.07 (df=1, P<.001), and in Study 2 49.55% of people (n=219) fell into the first category and 3.17% fell into the second category (n=14) resulting in a value of χ^2=180.36 (df=1, P<.001).

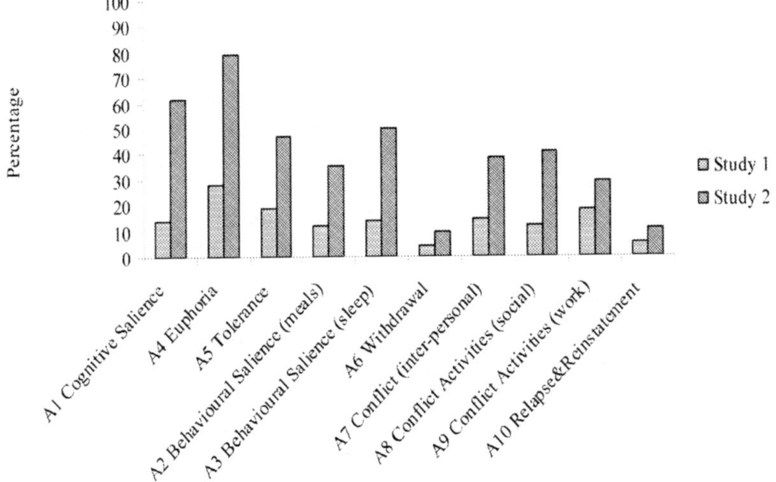

Figure 1: Frequency of endorsement of items across the two studies.

4 Discussion

The present studies show that the criteria of euphoria, tolerance and cognitive salience are not central to the definition of computer-related behavioural addictions and that it is doubtful whether they should be used in classifying people as addicted to computing–related activities. On the other hand, the criteria of relapse and reinstatement, withdrawal, behavioural salience and conflict do cluster together as a group of addiction criteria and are likely to be central in the classification of computing-related addictions. These results support some of Beard and Wolf's [2] criticisms of Young's [17] use of adapted DSM pathological gambling criteria in studying Internet addiction. Here it was argued that preoccupation with an activity (cognitive salience) and wanting to spend increasing time on it (tolerance) are not necessarily characteristics of Internet

Human Perspectives in the Internet Society: Culture, Psychology and Gender, K. Morgan, J. Sanchez, C. A. Brebbia & A Voiskounsky (Editors) © 2004 WIT Press, www.witpress.com, ISBN 1-85312-726-4

addiction, and our results support this contention. However, our results do not support Beard and Wolf's contention that the same can be said for unsuccessfully reducing a behaviour (relapse and reinstatement), and experiencing negative psychological effects when not engaging in a behaviour (withdrawal symptoms). Our findings also suggest a possible need to revise the content of some questionnaires used to study Internet addiction / impulse control problems (e.g. Brenner [3], Davis et al. [9], Morahan-Martin and Schumacher [15]), since they may contain a mixture of core and peripheral items (this is discussed at greater length in Charlton and Danforth [8]).

The implications of the studies can be clarified at a more detailed level by considering the percentages of people who could be said to be addicted / dependent under different classification schemes in the present studies and Griffiths and Hunt's [12] study (see Table 3). Looking at the first column of Table 3, note that the percentage of people classifiable as addicted based upon their endorsement of 50% of the criteria set out in each study (4 out of 8 in Griffiths and Hunt's study, and 5 out of 10 in the present two studies) is greater in our Study 2. This can be attributed to the fact that the latter study used a recruitment method (placing a message on a web site devoted to Asheron's Call) that tapped into a pool of people which was likely to contain a higher number of candidates for an addiction classification than the Griffiths and Hunt study (adolescent computer game players in a British secondary school), or our Study 1 (British higher education students). This illustrates the obvious point that one has to consider the characteristics of the population sampled when drawing conclusions as to the prevalence of any addiction.

Table 3: Percentages (and numbers) of people classifiable as addicted using various classification schemes.

Study	50% of peripheral and core criteria	50% of core criteria	All Brown criteria
Griffiths & Hunt	16.0 (62/382)	----	----
Study 1	8.4 (34/404)	8.4 (34/404)	0.0 (0/404)
Study 2	38.7 (171/442)	28.7 (127/442)	1.8 (8/442)

Other statistics (not presented for brevity) showed that in Study 1 almost two thirds of people exceeding the 50% cut-off at which an addiction classification might be made only did so because they endorsed criteria more indicative of engagement than addiction, and this rose to almost three quarters in Study 2. However, the second column of Table 3 shows that the number of people in Study 1 who would be considered addicted based upon their endorsement of 50% of the core criteria alone (all those endorsing four or more of the core criteria plus, to enable comparison and because 3.5 criteria would constitute a 50% cut-off, half of those who endorsed 3 core criteria) was exactly the same as that for a 50% cut-off involving both the peripheral and core criteria. On the other hand, the same comparison for Study 2 showed a 10 percentage point decrease in the number of people classifiable as addicted on the basis of core criteria alone. This difference across the two studies can be attributed to a greater

Human Perspectives in the Internet Society: Culture, Psychology and Gender, K. Morgan, J. Sanchez, C. A. Brebbia & A Voiskounsky (Editors) © 2004 WIT Press, www.witpress.com, ISBN 1-85312-726-4

degree of endorsement of the peripheral criteria relative to the core criteria in Study 2, the removal of the peripheral criteria from the classification scheme thereby having a greater impact in this study. Taken together, these observations show that the implications of the findings that some previously used addiction criteria signal engagement and that people meet these peripheral criteria more frequently than the remaining core criteria, are limited by the fact that people who endorse a large number of core criteria are also likely to endorse peripheral criteria. The distinction between the two types of criteria has minimal implications for the classification of such individuals: they would be classified as addicted whether or not a scheme includes peripheral criteria. However, the implications for the classification of people near the borderline of an addiction classification by virtue of their endorsement of a lower but moderate number of core criteria are greater, at least where an activity has addictive properties as in Study 2: if these people also endorse (peripheral) criteria signalling high engagement they are at risk of being erroneously classified as addicted.

Remembering that Brown [4] originally advanced a monothetic scheme, the final column of Table 3 shows that adoption of a more stringent scheme requiring endorsement of all Brown's criteria leads to a vast reduction in the number of putative addicts relative to either of the polythetic schemes.

To conclude, it seems that some criteria previously used to classify people as behaviourally addicted to computing activities are more indicative of non-pathological high engagement. Mistaking criteria signalling high engagement for addiction criteria can lead to inflated estimates of the number of people who may be addicted to an activity, particularly where polythetic classification procedures are used and an activity has addictive properties as in Study 2. The findings are also important for theory surrounding computer-related addictions in particular and behavioural addictions in general. For example, while a longitudinal study would be more definitive, the observations in both studies that the number of people endorsing a high number of peripheral items but a low number of core items was greater than the number of people endorsing a high number of core items but a low number of peripheral items suggested a possible aetiological process whereby high engagement is a precursor of behavioural addiction to computing activities.

References

[1] American Psychiatric Association, *Diagnostic and Statistical Manual of Mental Disorders (4th ed., Text Revision)*. APA: Washington, DC, 2000.

[2] Beard, K.W., & Wolf, E.M., Modification in the proposed diagnostic criteria for Internet addiction. *CyberPsychology and Behavior*, **4**, pp. 377-383, 2001.

[3] Brenner, V., Psychology of computer use: XLVII. Parameters of Internet use, abuse and addiction: The first 90 days of the Internet usage survey. *Psychological Reports*, **80**, pp. 879-882, 1997.

Human Perspectives in the Internet Society: Culture, Psychology and Gender, K. Morgan, J. Sanchez, C. A. Brebbia & A Voiskounsky (Editors) © 2004 WIT Press, www.witpress.com, ISBN 1-85312-726-4

[4] Brown, R. I. F., Gaming, gambling and other addictive play (Chapter 7). *Adult play: A reversal theory approach*, eds. J. H. Kerr & M. J. Apter, Swets & Zeitlinger: Amsterdam, pp. 101–118, 1991.

[5] Charlton, J.P., A factor-analytic investigation of computer 'addiction' and engagement. *British Journal of Psychology*, **93**, pp. 329–344, 2002.

[6] Charlton, J.P., & Birkett, P.E., The development and validation of the Computer Apathy and Anxiety Scale. *Journal of Educational Computing Research*, **13(1)**, pp. 41-59, 1995.

[7] Charlton, J.P., & Birkett, P.E., An integrative model of factors related to computing course performance. *Journal of Educational Computing Research*, **20(3)**, pp. 237-257. 1999.

[8] Charlton, J.P., & Danforth, I.D.W., Distinguishing addiction and high engagement in the context of online game playing. Manuscript submitted for publication, 2004.

[9] Davis, R.A., Flett, G.L., & Besser, A., Validation of a new scale for measuring problematic Internet use: Implications for pre-employment screening. *CyberPsychology and Behavior*, **5**, pp. 331-345, 2002.

[10] Griffiths, M.D., Behavioural addictions: An issue for everybody? *Employee Counselling Today: The Journal of Workplace Learning*, **8(3)**, pp. 19-25, 1996.

[11] Griffiths, M., Internet addiction: does it really exist? (Chapter 4). *Psychology and the Internet*, ed. J. Gackenbach, Academic Press: San Diego, pp.61-75, 1998.

[12] Griffiths, M.D., & Hunt, N., Dependence on computer games by adolescents. *Psychological Reports*, **82**, pp. 475-480, 1998.

[13] Holden, C., 'Behavioral' addictions: Do they exist? *Science*, **294**, pp. 980-982, 2001.

[14] Jaffe, J.H., Trivializing dependence. *British Journal of Addiction*, **85**, pp. 1425-1427, 1990.

[15] Morahan-Martin, J., & Schumacher, P., Incidence and correlates of pathological Internet use among college students. *Computers in Human Behavior*, **16**, pp. 13-29, 2000.

[16] Shotton, M.A., *Computer addiction? A study of computer dependency.* Taylor & Francis: London, 1989.

[17] Young, K.S., *Internet addiction: The emergence of a new clinical disorder.* Paper presented at the Annual Meeting of the American Psychological Association, Toronto, 1996.

Human Perspectives in the Internet Society: Culture, Psychology and Gender, K. Morgan, J. Sanchez, C. A. Brebbia & A Voiskounsky (Editors) © 2004 WIT Press, www.witpress.com, ISBN 1-85312-726-4

Personal competences and social structure: information management in business networks

J. Aderhold[1] & M. Meyer[2]
[1]*Innovation Research and Sustainable Resource Management,*
[2]*Chair for Organizational Behaviour,*
Faculty of Economics and Business Administration,
Chemnitz University of Technology, Germany

Abstract

We developed a procedure for exploring and describing the insufficiently investigated relationship between role expectations in the network, subjective motives, experiences and identifications, which might be employed during the iterative process of network construction. This procedure is derived from the interplay between network development, role structures, defining competence profiles and the integrated bundling in network-based value creation processes. Due to the dynamics and complexity, this unit of analysis requires (1) an intensive focus upon the notion of person-related competency and its importance in the dynamic context of networks, and (2) a method for describing and presenting subjective network constructions in as up-to-date a way as possible. We especially want to explore the mutual perception of actors within the framework of a soft factor controlling. We can gather data on context-specific personal constructs by the grid technique. Based upon the applied methods, it is possible to provide information about the relevant structures within networks, which can be used for Personal selection and competency development.
Keywords: competence, virtual business networks, information management, grid-technique, polyhedral analysis.

1 Introduction

Technological progress and the dissemination of new technologies, e.g., concerning information, communication or media, create new business opportunities especially for small and medium enterprises (SME) because of

Human Perspectives in the Internet Society: Culture, Psychology and Gender, K. Morgan, J. Sanchez, C. A. Brebbia & A Voiskounsky (Editors) © 2004 WIT Press, www.witpress.com, ISBN 1-85312-726-4

their high flexibility and their close relation to costumers [1, 2, 3]. But at the same time, this implies increasing competition [4]. The participation in networks appears to be a valuable instrument to manage both dynamics [5]. But particularly the establishment of networks – or the entry into existing ones – represents a major challenge to SME. The constitution of networks is contingent upon various conditions and involves far-reaching consequences for the single partner, the network itself and the network environment [6, 7]. However, small and the smallest enterprises cannot participate in this development – or not entirely – because of their structure and the limited resources. Consequently, present and future research has to be focused on organizational designs appropriate to enforce SME network building [8]. Above all, appropriate design principles, which allow for the maintaining of such complex and dynamic forms of cooperation, are missing.

The following proposition of a competence cells network approach reflects current tendencies in management and economic science based on the core competence concept by Prahalad and Hamel [9]. The main ideas were developed and combined with an IT-based planning and optimisation scheme. The management model that was created as a result is a modification of the concept of Extended Value Chain Management (EVCM). It enables production networks to select and focus their competences according to specific orders quickly. Furthermore, it offers various possibilities to optimize the selection process. Besides the exact representation of all flows of information and material at any time, personal and social factors, as well as economic, logistic and technical parameters, can be integrated and analysed. Especially for social factors we suggest the repertory grid method as a principal research tool. The data acquired is then used for polyhedral analysis, which will be described in detail in the end. The following insights are derived from current research within the collaboration research centre "non-hierarchical production networks", Chemnitz University of Technology.

2 The concept of linked competence cells

The concept of competence cells refers to the core competence approach of Prahalad and Hamel [9]. It relies on the assumption that economic success is due to unique, identifiable competences. These key competences represent the fertile ground of any company to create present or future products and services. Therefore they may be used directly or transformed by appropriate management measures. In general, core competences consist of technological abilities necessary to realize value creation. On the one hand, single components or aspects of those competencies are derived according to the production processes within the value chain. They can be categorized, for example, from a technical, economic, informational or activity-related point of view.

On the other hand, a given production profile can be decomposed into its components and subsequently transformed into competence cells. In this context, we emphasize that personal and social factors can't be overestimated with regard to their contribution to the frictionlessness of the production process. We assume

Human Perspectives in the Internet Society: Culture, Psychology and Gender, K. Morgan, J. Sanchez, C. A. Brebbia & A Voiskounsky (Editors) © 2004 WIT Press, www.witpress.com, ISBN 1-85312-726-4

that competence cells are defined as the smallest indivisible, economically mostly independent, specialized units that temporarily link up to other competence cells to accomplish complex tasks. Companies may provide resources by forming autonomous competence cells, which act as elementary units in value creating cooperative processes. Such competence networks enforce flexibility and temporariness, since they enable individual value chains supported by a large variety of competence cell portfolios as it is appropriate to either a given problem, a specific order or a product, for example.

The new non-hierarchical competence cell network approach faces the challenge of assuming core competences (see figure 1). It assumes that, within a given region, there are competence units, formed by a multitude of experiences, which can be interpreted as competence cells (see http://www.tu-chemnitz.de/sfb457/en/). Or from a managerial point of view: The region is scanned for potential network partners and competences are integrated through bringing them into the form of competence cells by specific management measures.

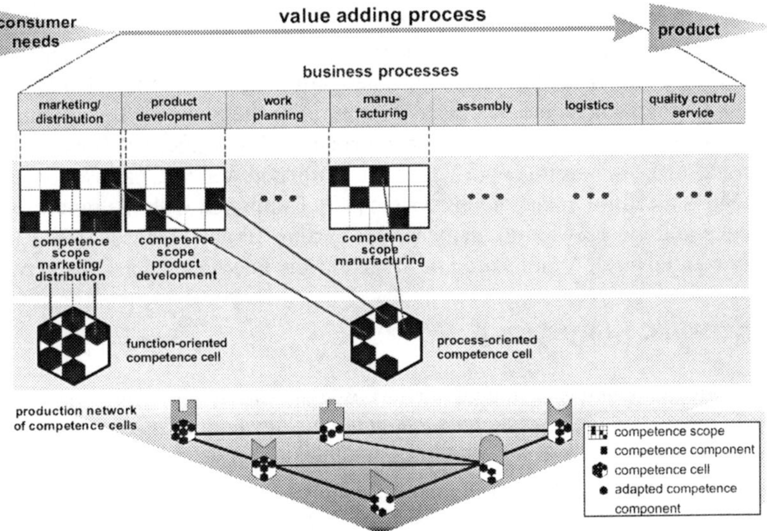

Figure 1: Relation of value adding process and types of competence cells.

This regional network potential serves to enable differently-orientated competence networks. To facilitate this project-like cooperation, it is necessary to implement a minimal amount of institutional infrastructure, such as a uniform information platform, common terms of trade, quality standards, etc. On this basis, temporary production networks can be built according to customer inquiries. The linkage may be orientated to problem solving, the specific order, production or processes. Competence cells are the basic bricks of a non-hierarchical production network. Once again, we emphasize that it is not the

Human Perspectives in the Internet Society: Culture, Psychology and Gender, K. Morgan, J. Sanchez, C. A. Brebbia & A Voiskounsky (Editors) © 2004 WIT Press, www.witpress.com, ISBN 1-85312-726-4

given entrepreneurial division that is cooperating, but only those competencies, which are selected for the production chain.

The challenge consists of creating dynamic, temporary network structures to satisfy the variety of costumer needs. The couplings originate to solve concrete problems of costumers and therefore dissolve after their accomplishment. It is assumed that the interdependencies between the single cooperation partners are homogeneous. The coordination arises by supply and demand instantaneously. This means that task-specific coordination and decision-making competences are distributed among the concerned network actors. This network design implies changes to the established system of labour division, to the dimensioning of competence cells and their linkage, to the temporal and special structure of production, to the size and equipment of production places. The introduction of mobile competence cells offering specific production possibilities may even be conceived. An overall integrating method is necessary to build and maintain non-hierarchical networks between competence cells. Incompatible information systems prevent value creation from being effective by causing high administration and coordination costs. Instruments to represent all flows of information and material exactly at any time, which would ensure appropriate reaction in case of disturbances or later-introduced customer demands, are missing. Consequently, it is necessary to centralize the planning for products and processes to ensure the continuity of informational and material flows between the single SME. Therefore, we adopt the Extended Value Chain Management (EVCM) as a central management system [10]. Combined with the repertory grid technique and the polyhedral analysis, this system allows IT-based case specific selection and overall optimisation of the workflow in competence cells networks.

3 Network competency

Inter-firm co-operations based on business networks need a suitable infrastructure. We assume that one characteristic attribute of the infrastructure in business networks is developing and cultivating informal relationships. Wenger and Snyder [11, pp. 56f] describe this "cultivation task" as a management paradox. Networks are mainly informal and self-organizing. They can be "cultivated" by special means. We can use horticulture as an analogy – plants grow best if their characteristics are respected. We need an infrastructure supporting the networks to "grow" and "take care" of them [12]. In business economics, the instrument "controlling" is used for analysing, interpreting and evaluating firm data. We would like to use this instrument for psychological purposes within a procedural framework, which will be developed in this article. Viable firms need heuristic strategies to control their targets depending on autonomous actor relationships. Therefore, business networks shall be provided the opportunities to present role expectations towards the whole system at any time. From our point of view, a controlling instrument for soft factors seems to be obligatory in order to meet the challenges derived from the above-presented arguments. We search a function-oriented social, respective relational competency that requires a different focus on the above-presented dimension

Human Perspectives in the Internet Society: Culture, Psychology and Gender, K. Morgan, J. Sanchez, C. A. Brebbia & A Voiskounsky (Editors) © 2004 WIT Press, www.witpress.com, ISBN 1-85312-726-4

depending upon the network configuration. Generally, we can understand the construct "competency" as a system of inner-psychic preconditions that reflects itself in the quality of visible action and regulates it. The notion of personal competency emphasizes the procedural quality of the inner-psychic activity. The "personal competency" represents an essential trait of the personality.

4 The role construct repertory: gaining the data

We have developed a procedure for exploring and describing the insufficiently investigated relationship between role expectations in the network, subjective motives, experiences and identifications that might be employed during the iterative process of network construction. This procedure is derived from the interplay between network development, role structures, defining competency profiles and the integrated bundling in network-based value creation processes. In particular, the dynamics and complexity of this unit of analysis requires: (1) an intensive focus on the notion of person-related competency and its importance in the dynamic context of networks, (2) and a method for describing and presenting subjective network constructions in as up-to-date a way as possible. We especially want to explore the mutual perception of actors within the framework of the soft factor controlling. Our second aim is to provide the system with the mutual assessment of the partners regarding reliability, competency, trust, etc.

Here, we present a method which has the advantages of a clinical interview on one hand and which provides data similar to data attained from a standardized interview on the other hand. The method is called "Role Construct Repertory Grid" [13]. This method allows insight into the construct system of an individual. This method is closely linked with the theory of social constructs. Up to now, the Grid method has been applied and published in very different variations [14, 15, 16].

The different methodological variants are based on a common concept. The interviewed people are asked to formulate differences between objects of their experience (elements), which are entered into a data matrix (grid) in the form of short descriptions (constructs). Finally, the interviewed people assess the elements using a given scale. A grid provides numeric data that are especially useful for comparing individuals. The data firstly describe a qualitative relationship of patterns about a person's point of view. To determine a quantitative relationship, the raw data must compute with a special kind of mathematical algorithm, such as the polyhedral analysis [17, 18]. The interviewed people directly associate patterns, which are not set in advance. Therefore, we get idiosyncratic data. The interviewed person formulates relationships, describes them ideally in his own words in a very spontaneous way. The only given structure in the grid consists of the elements. They should not only be representative but they should also be notional abstractions from reality – they stem from the environment of the interviewed persons as well as from the topic of the investigation. People, situations stemming from the network context form notional structures. The researchers ask the interviewees to

Human Perspectives in the Internet Society: Culture, Psychology and Gender, K. Morgan, J. Sanchez, C. A. Brebbia & A Voiskounsky (Editors) © 2004 WIT Press, www.witpress.com, ISBN 1-85312-726-4

formulate their subjective assessments about the given elements within a standardized research design. Then they form dimensions (construct/contrast poles) such as co-operative versus obstinate. Among the most relevant constructs, we distinguish between core constructs defining the self and core role constructs defining the relationships between the individual and other people. If an investigation is carried out within the network context, elements presenting the "self" are excluded. In a second step, the interviewees assess the elements whose dimensions are individually formed (scaling).

Self	Self (Other)	Ideal Self	NW Coordinator	NW Culture	Direct Partner	NW Culture (Future)	NW Partner (Now)	NW Partner (Future)	NW Participant (Now)	NW Participant (Future)	Person of Confidence	Enemy	Regular customer	desire customer	Competition network		
4	4	3	4	3	5	3	2	3	3	3	5	5	4	4	4	egoistically	participating
4	4	5	5	4	2	5	3	2	2	2	4	1	4	4	2	Qualification in subranges	Qualification in Multimedia
5	4	5	5	5	2	5	4	5	4	5	5	2	3	5	5	mental limits	open minded
4	3	5	5	4	3	4	4	5	4	5	5	2	5	5	5	indifferently	mental relationship
5	5	4	3	4	2	5	4	4	4	4	5	1	3	5	2	uncontrolled w isdom	Experience
3	3	3	4	5	2	4	4	4	3	4	5	1	3	4	2	are lazy	concentrate on the substantial
3	4	5	5	4	3	5	3	5	4	5	4	2	4	4	4	not sizably	to have Personality
4	4	5	5	4	3	5	3	4	4	4	5	3	4	5	5	pure Business	Creativity

Figure 2: Filled grid matrix

We assume a scale ranging from 1 to 6 – if the right pole is given a 6, this means that this pole is fully right. The same is true for the left pole (see figure 2). Finally, we receive a matrix produced by the repertory-grid-method. In a second step, all elements are assessed with regard to dimensions individually formed by the interviewee (scaling). Finally, the researchers receive a completed matrix; the personal elements can be presented as assessment spaces by means of the matrix's cell values. In the cluster analysis to be carried out, the assessed elements and constructs are compared based on their similarity. The construct pole "obstinate" contrasts the construct pole "co-operative". In the following argumentation, we do not deal with the dimensions because the argumentation would become too complex. At the end of the process, the data in the cells of the matrix can be computed and entered into a database. For example, the elements 'I ideal', 'network coordinator' and 'network culture of tomorrow' are assessed as similar elements of the person asked. Due to clarity, further interpretations based on the connection measures are not discussed here.

5 Results

An examined network has approximately 40 free cooperation partners (among others, freelancers) of different key competencies, e.g., writers, graphic artists,

Human Perspectives in the Internet Society: Culture, Psychology and Gender, K. Morgan, J. Sanchez, C. A. Brebbia & A Voiskounsky (Editors) © 2004 WIT Press, www.witpress.com, ISBN 1-85312-726-4

developers, etc., that are involved in the product development in various online projects at the same time. In addition to standardized interviews with some selected cooperation partners, we have carried out Repertory Grid interviews with particularly relevant people. The Repertory Grids were aimed at elaborating on differences and similarities between the subjective perceptions of the partners involved. Based on selected elements, which, among others, resulted from contact conversations and from interviews carried out before, constructs were extracted by means of the triad method (see above) and a main component analysis was calculated. Based on an existing data matrix consisting of elements, the charges of the variables were represented as points in the factor space by means of a factor analysis. The resulting space of points can be understood as a 'cognitive similarity room', bringing together elements and constructs that can thus be observed in their mutual interaction. The following main components analyses give an idea about the world of constructs/elements of a central person in the network. In the figure, it is recognizable that due to the position of the constructs, four dimensions are spread out. These dimensions are a first interpretation of the bi-plots, the common graphic representation of the elements and constructs (figure 3). They indicate the axes of the construct world of the person asked. Each axis symbolizes the semantic space of the constructions.

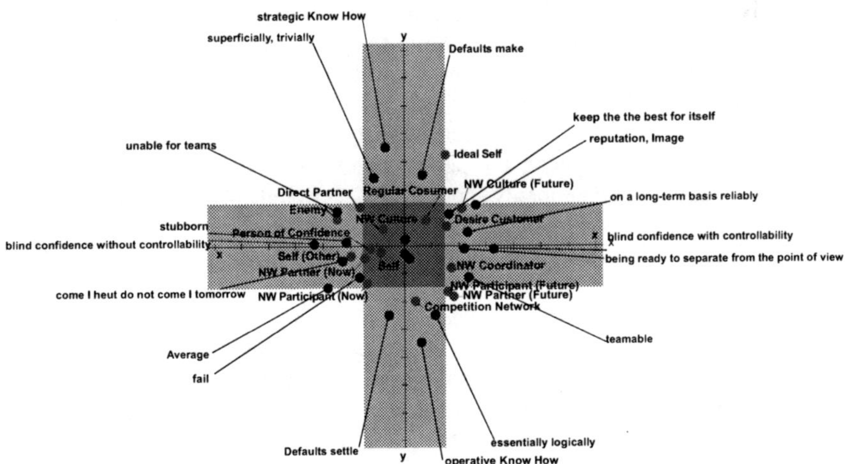

Figure 3: Illustration of the Repertory Grid result, main components analysis in the form of a bi-plot.

All constructs are more or less on one of the above-mentioned poles and show how far, i.e., with which descriptions, the associated elements are connected. Let us examine an example by means of this figure. Two dimensions (x/y-axis) are clearly presented. The dimensions can be characterized in several ways. One of these we can label with the term 'cooperation' ranges from 'team able' to 'not

Human Perspectives in the Internet Society: Culture, Psychology and Gender, K. Morgan, J. Sanchez, C. A. Brebbia & A Voiskounsky (Editors) © 2004 WIT Press, www.witpress.com, ISBN 1-85312-726-4

team able'. All elements on this axis can be connected. The relative position of the elements indicates the subjective assessment of the person asked.

For example, the element 'enemy' as well as the element 'direct partner' are on this axis near the construct 'not team able'. The 'network coordinator' and 'partner target' or 'participant (future)' are rather near the construct 'team able'. If their positions on a second dimension, called 'trust' (blind confidence without possibility of control to blind confidence with possibility of control) are compared, it becomes obvious that here the (in reality nonexistent) element 'network coordinator' is included considerably more clearly than the elements 'enemy' or 'direct partner'. Confidence in the direct partner without possibility of control therefore seems to trigger a direct association with 'not team able'.

As has already been emphasized, actors in networks are exposed to permanent uncertainties. These uncertainties are frequently covered up, often with serious consequences. A look at the evaluated Repertory Grids can show contradictory identity features. For example, the sense of community competes with the simultaneous wish to 'keep the best for itself', and thus generates identity. Confidence expectations are formulated in the same way: network participants shall be 'ready to separate from the point of view'. The other cooperation partners, however, cannot identify themselves clearly with the aims and wishes of the questioned business partners. Moreover, it can be noticed that the people asked wish for a different network culture than that existing at present. What all partners agree on is the network culture in the future. The culture should have a 'reputation, image', 'social competency' and 'sense of community', and should 'act consequent' and, 'have an overview'. However, the guide-supported expert interviews show that it is inconsistent with the existing 'culture'. Due to this premise of a latent discontent, the people involved try to keep themselves and their close environment openly and easily comprehensible, partly without considering the existing network reality.

In an inter-firm network, it is hardly possible to hire additional managers permanently in order to complete abilities needed; the development of competency gains a special importance. People acting within the network have these abilities. However, not only measures like external trainings can be the focus, but also measures to design internal structures and career development. Within networks, managers have more room for acting than in hierarchically organized firms. The related possibilities for active, self-defined action can lead to competence acquisition in the working situation if the context is formed in the right way. In order to motivate people, aspects of career development gain crucial importance because networks have a temporary and very flexible character and, thus, produce a high degree of uncertainty for the people acting in the network.

The competency to work within a network can be seen in the same way as the work in a group or team. Thus, the acquisition of competency is a development process that depends on many factors. This process leads to new requirements not only for the managers co-operating in the network but also for the employees and the management board of the participating firms. In addition, practicable supporting systems for management decisions, which allow an analysis of complex personnel structures in network, are needed.

Human Perspectives in the Internet Society: Culture, Psychology and Gender, K. Morgan, J. Sanchez, C. A. Brebbia & A Voiskounsky (Editors) © 2004 WIT Press, www.witpress.com, ISBN 1-85312-726-4

6 Conclusions

Due to the challenge to adapt to highly flexible markets, temporary, inter-organizational co-operation is of increasing importance. However, even the inner-organizational coordination between different departments tends to be inefficient or incomplete [19]. In general, the probability of failure of inter-firm co-operative arrangements is extremely high [20]. Therefore, managers as well as theorists are searching for tools and methods to create an effective co-operative design to support such complex processes. We introduced a general model to manage temporal production chains, which we have linked with a special routine to face the particularities of the partner selection within a non-hierarchical network. This routine consists of the repertory grid method to assure individual adaption to the existing points of view, which we connected in a second step with polyhedral analysis to estimate the homogeneity of selected sets of partners, which combines advantages of group psychological methods with mathematical analyses. For a further integration to the competence cell network approach, it is necessary to quantify the individual "view of the world" like a "cognitive map" [21] described by elements and pairs of constructs. The above mentioned grid-matrix serves as starting point and database. The initial idea of our approach consists of a demanded equality of elements and pairs of constructs, although they originate from person-specific interviews. As a result, we obtain a new matrix in which each representative pair of constructs only occurs once. Finally, the matrices of all competence cells are identical structures.

The actual involvement of the described attributes in network activities depends on the structure of the created distribution of the elements and constructs within the network. For example, unique attributes or competences of a certain partner won't be of interest if this partner remains isolated due to external reasons. Since the social constellations within the network change with regard to specific tasks, these conclusions drawn from repertory grid and polyhedral analysis may also vary. The polyhedral analysis takes into consideration the particularities of competence cell networks more appropriately than the usually-applied graph-based methods of empirical social research because a group/social constructional approach is used to shape relations of attributes of objects. The polyhedral analysis explores the relation or the degree of relatedness, so-called simplexes, and provides measurement values such as length of chains, connectivity or eccentricity. An appropriate identification of these simplexes allows the application of polyhedral analysis methods. This research method serves as a mathematical framework to derive further structural statements. It explores the relation between individuals and the overall network with regard to individual competencies.

Our research for an appropriate method led us to the Repertory Grid Method by Kelly [see 13] and the Polyhedral Analysis by Atkin and Casti [17]. A combination of these ideas serves to inquire into personal and socio-structural criteria (holes, connectivity and eccentricity) not only in a qualitative manner, but also to transform them so that the collected data can be inserted in the EVCM. The grid contributes images of present relational constellations, and the

Human Perspectives in the Internet Society: Culture, Psychology and Gender, K. Morgan, J. Sanchez, C. A. Brebbia & A Voiskounsky (Editors) © 2004 WIT Press, www.witpress.com, ISBN 1-85312-726-4

polyhedral analysis furnishes the algorithms to estimate social compatibility. Finally, the optimisation of value chain partnerships based on soft facts can be realized. It is furthermore possible to provide information for the partner selection and optimisation of relational structures within the network.

References

[1] Benett R., Business associations and their potential contribution to the competitiveness of SMEs. *Entrepreneurship & Regional Development.* 10: pp. 243-261, 1998.

[2] Naisbitt J., *The Global Paradox*: The Bigger the World Economy. The More Powerful its Smallest Players. Brealey: London, 1994.

[3] Scott A. J., From Silicon Valley to Hollywood. *Regional Innovation Systems*, ed. H. J. Braczyk, Ph. Cooke & M. Heidenreich. UCL Press: London, pp. 136-162, 1998.

[4] Acs, Z. J. & Audretsch, B. D., *Innovation durch kleine Unternehmen.* Edition Sigma: Berlin, 1992.

[5] Gulati, R., *Network location and learning*. Strategic Management Journal 20(5), pp. 397-421, 1999.

[6] Hogg, M. A. & Terry, D. J., Social Identity and self-categorization processes in organizational contexts. *Journal Academy of Management Review*; Vol. 25, No. 1, 2000.

[7] Ritsila, J. J., Regional differences in environments for enterprises. *Entrepreneurship & Regional Development* 11(3), pp. 187-203, 1999.

[8] Wirth S., Der kompetenzzellenbasierte Vernetzungsansatz für Produktion und Dienstleistung. *Hierarchielose regionale Produktionsnetze*, ed. Teich T. GUC: Chemnitz, pp. 1-19, 2001.

[9] Prahalad, C. K. & Hamel, G., The Core Competence of the Corporation. *Harvard Business Review* 68, 5/6, pp. 79-91, 1990.

[10] Teich, T. et al., Distributed Scheduling in Extended Value Chain Management. Procee*dings of the 12th International Conference on Flexible Automation & Intelligent Manufacturing*, eds. Sullivan et al., Dresden, Germany, July 15-17, pp. 319-328, 2002.

[11] Wenger, E. C. & Snyder, W.M., Communities of Practice. *Harvard Business manager* 4, pp.55-62, 2000.

[12] Teich, T., The Extended Value Chain Management. *DAAAM International Scientific Book*, ed. B. Katalinic, DAAAM International Vienna, 2002.

[13] Kelly, G. A., *The Psychology of Personal Constructs.* Volume One: Theory and Personality. Routhledge: London, 1991.

[14] Cassell, C. et al., Surfacing Embedded Assumptions. *European Journal of Work and Organizational Psychology*, 9(4), pp. 561-573, 2000.

[15] Easterby-Smith et al., Using repertory grids in management. *Journal of European Industrial Training*, 20 (3), pp. 2-30, 1996.

[16] Fornier, V. & Paine, R.: Change in self construction during the transition from university to employment. *Journal of Occupational and Organizational Psychology*, 67, pp. 297-314, 1994.

Human Perspectives in the Internet Society: Culture, Psychology and Gender, K. Morgan, J. Sanchez, C. A. Brebbia & A Voiskounsky (Editors) © 2004 WIT Press, www.witpress.com, ISBN 1-85312-726-4

[17] Atkin, R. & Casti, J., *Polyhedral Dynamics and Geometry of Systems*. International Institute for Applied Systems Analysis, RR-77-006, Austria, 1977.

[18] Meyer, M. et al., Optimization of Social Structure in Business Networks. *Journal of Business and Psychology*, Vol 17, No. 4, pp. 451-472, 2003.

[19] Uzzi, B., Social structure and competition in interfirm networks. *Administrative Science Quarterly* 42(1), pp. 37-70, 1977.

[20] Huggins, R., The success and failure of policy-implanted inter-firm network initiatives. *Entrepreneurship & Regional Development 12*, pp. 111-136, 2000.

[21] Brown, S., Cognitive Mapping and Repertory Grid for qualitative survey research. *Journal of Management Studies*, Vol. 29, pp. 287-307, 1992.

Human Perspectives in the Internet Society: Culture, Psychology and Gender, K. Morgan, J. Sanchez, C. A. Brebbia & A Voiskounsky (Editors) © 2004 WIT Press, www.witpress.com, ISBN 1-85312-726-4

Section 2
Personality and computer attitudes

Psychological effects of work with a helmet-mounted display

C. Pfendler & H. Widdel
FGAN - FKIE Wachtberg, Germany

Abstract

An experiment was conducted to investigate the influence of an helmet-mounted display (HMD) compared with an hand-held display (HHD) on the operator's behavior and experience. Ground vehicles and helicopters had to be detected in a computer simulation of a traffic scenario in an artificial city. The target objects were presented on HMD or HHD before appearing in the traffic scenario. Beside the performance variables detection time and detection frequency, questionnaire variables of workload and of simulator sickness have been determined by the *Belastungsverlaufstest (BLV)* and the *Simulator Sickness Questionnaire (SSQ)*. 12 subjects participated twice in the experiment with a trial duration of 140 minutes. The performance data show a consistent trend towards higher detection times and lower hit rates with the HMD. Most of the subscales of the BLV and SSQ show significantly higher scores for HMD compared with HHD.
Keywords: helmet-mounted display, hand-held display, detection task, psychological stress, performance aversion, mental fatigue, nausea, oculomotor, disorientation.

1 Helmet-mounted displays (HMD)

Helmet-mounted displays (HMD) are used with increasing tendency in civilian and military areas for all kinds of tasks, e.g., assembly work, orientation tasks, flight control. Alphanumeric and graphical information is displayed via HMDs into the operator's field of view as a virtual image regardless of the direction of gaze. The picture can be presented on eyeglasses, half transparent mirrors or visors. The used mini-displays offer in correspondence with the associated optics one or two pictures, termed as monocular or bi(n)ocular. Two separate pictures, one for each eye, can be displayed, being identical (biocular) or different

Human Perspectives in the Internet Society: Culture, Psychology and Gender, K. Morgan, J. Sanchez, C. A. Brebbia & A Voiskounsky (Editors) © 2004 WIT Press, www.witpress.com, ISBN 1-85312-726-4

(binocular). In the last case spatial perception may be produced. The picture presentation of see-through displays occurs on a half-transparent, reflecting mirror in the field of view of the operator, generating the picture at a distance from the eye of about infinite, Velger [1]. The external view can be impaired by the displayed picture itself as well as by the mirror's degree of transparency. At another type of HMDs, videodisplays present the external world on monitors, recorded by miniature cameras, which are also fixed at the helmet. The display devices can be CRTs, LCDs or laserdisplays. Laserdisplays project the picture by means of laser rays directly onto the retina of the eye. Most laserdisplays are monochrome with red light; laser color displays are still expensive and complex in construction.

2 Advantages and disadvantages of HMDs

An advantage of HMDs is that additional information, essential for the task execution, can be projected directly into the field of view. To gain this information, additional eye movements, which might detract from the external view, are not necessary. In contrast to Head-up displays (HUD) all information can be perceived permanently, even when moving the head. This makes HMDs attractive in several military areas, e.g., in the newly developed fighter aircrafts. For flight control tasks the pilot can observe the outside view as well as system information of the plane, presented on the HMD, simultaneously. In civil areas HMDs can be of benefit for assembly purposes, saving extensive search activities in large maintenance manuals. Attempts are starting to use HMDs in automotive areas, e.g., for supporting the driver in wayfinding.

Beside these advantages several disadvantages have to be considered as well. If the density of presented information is too high, the visibility of the external world might be degraded. An information flood on the HMD can focus the attention of an operator on this information, distracting from the external view, Meehan [2]. A reduced transparency of the HMD's mirror can affect the view and reduce, e.g., the perception of colors. It is considered that a high frequency of accommodations cause eye fatigue, headache, and similar discomforts up to symptoms of simulator sickness. Finally, the low wearing comfort like heavy weight of the helmet or visor resp. mirror, unbalanced center point of the system etc. lead to performance degradation and feelings of discomfort.

Several of these detrimental factors have been ascertained in empirical investigations. Rash et al [3] report visual impairments of helicopter pilots, when using the "Integrated Helmet and Display Sighting System", which allows flights at night and in bad weather. In a questionnaire 92% of the pilots stated visual problems like visual discomfort, double vision, visual afterimages, disorientation, and headache during and after the flight. Howarth and Costello [4] found motion sickness symptoms, when biocular HMDs were used. A reason for this could be a sensory conflict, when head movements are perceived by the vestibular but not by the visual system. In an experiment by Merlo et al [5] a detection task was conducted with an HMD and an hand-held display (HHD). They found that performance with the HMD decreased due to clutter effects in comparison to the HHD, when the complexity of the displayed images increased. Kooi [6] compared three HMDs with a standard monitor, using a reading and an accommodation task. Superiority was found for the standard monitor.

3 Motivation for own research

The survey of research activities shows that either questionnaire or performance data were measured. Also, the duration of task executions in most investigations was relatively short and did not take into account long-term effects. To bridge this gap, an experiment was planned and conducted, measuring performance in a detection task as well as individual experience, when using an HMD. Performance measures include detection time and hits, questionnaire measures include workload related data and variables of simulator sickness. To address long-term effects, the duration of an experimental trial was scheduled to 140 minutes. A comparison with the use of an HHD was realized as basis for interpretation of HMD results. It was postulated that performance will decrease for an HMD in comparison with an HHD, and questionnaire measures will increase.

4 Method

4.1 Participants and task

Seven male and five female subjects between 20 and 55 years participated in the experimental investigation. Preconditions to take part at the experiment were a successful accomplishment of the Ishihara test [7], measuring the color capability, and a successful testing of a sufficient acuteness of vision. Both the images of the target objects in the HMD mirror or on the HHD and the projection of the simulated traffic scenario had to be seen sharply, when eye accommodation was changing.

Figure 1: Simulated traffic scenario.

Human Perspectives in the Internet Society: Culture, Psychology and Gender, K. Morgan, J. Sanchez, C. A. Brebbia & A Voiskounsky (Editors) © 2004 WIT Press, www.witpress.com, ISBN 1-85312-726-4

The subjects had to detect ground vehicles and helicopters with a set of defined attributes for discrimination from distractor vehicles and helicopters, presented in a computer-generated dynamic traffic scenario of an artificial city, which was projected on a large screen, fig. 1. The targets to be detected were presented in different trials either on the HMD or the HHD, fig. 2. The task was characterised by homogeneous events and infrequently and irregularly appearing targets in long monitoring periods, causing monotonous task conditions.

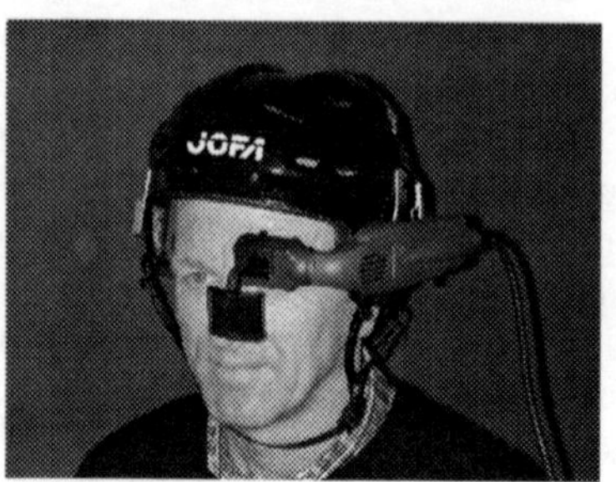

Figure 2: Helmet-mounted display (HMD) and hand-held display (HHD).

4.2 Apparatus and material

The computer-generated dynamic traffic scenario was projected in a distance of 3 m in front of the subject on a screen with a width of 1.7 m and a height of 1.3 m. An Epson EMP 9100 projector accomplished the rear projection on the screen. The target objects were displayed via a Xybernaut MA®IV on the HMD or the HHD. The semi transparent mirror of the HMD was fastened in a distance of approximately 8 cm before the left eye of the subject on a helmet, partly covering the field of view. The virtual distance of the image in the mirror was about 1 m. The HHD consisted of a 6-inch screen, which was located in front of the subject in a distance of 1 m with a screen inclination of about 75 degrees to the horizontal.

Ground vehicles differed by three shape attributes; helicopters differed by three different color combinations of their body and their skids.

The questionnaires used to measure the subjective variables were the Belastungsverlaufstest BLV (workload trend test) from Bronner and Karger [8] and the Simulator Sickness Questionnaire (SSQ) from Kennedy et al [9]. The four subscales of the BLV represent *psychological stress, psychological fitness, performance aversion,* and *fatigue.* For the experimental trials a computer-based version of the BLV developed by Pfendler and Thun [10] was used. The SSQ presents the three subscales *nausea, oculomotor, disorientation* and a *total score*, addressing 16 specific symptoms of simulator sickness.

4.3 Experimental design and statistical analysis

A 2x2x4 factorial repeated-measures design for the performance variables was used with the three factors *display, vehicle type,* and *trial section.* The factor

Human Perspectives in the Internet Society: Culture, Psychology and Gender, K. Morgan, J. Sanchez, C. A. Brebbia & A Voiskounsky (Editors) © 2004 WIT Press, www.witpress.com, ISBN 1-85312-726-4

display was varied on the two levels helmet-mounted display and hand-held display, the factor *vehicle type* on the two levels ground vehicle and helicopter, and the factor *trial section* on the four levels 1, 2, 3, and 4. A trial section is a 35 minutes partition of a trial, which lasted 140 minutes. With the first factor the influence of the HHD and the HMD, with the second factor the influence of form and color coding and with the third factor the influence of the task duration on performance was investigated. Dependent variables were the detection time and the percentage of detected targets (hits), defined as number of detected targets divided by all presented targets. For statistical analysis a 2x2x4 model of the ANOVA for three within subject factors was used (Systat [11]) followed by a Scheffé test for mean comparisons in case of significant F-statistics.

The dependent variables, representing the questionnaire measures, are composed of the subscale parameters of BLV and SSQ, which were administered before and after an experimental trial. For statistical analysis of these questionnaire variables the Wilcoxon test for paired comparisons (Sachs [12]) was used testing the difference of display dependent scores before and after the trial.

4.4 Procedure

Subjects had to complete two experimental trials at two successive days, at one day using the HMD and at the other day using the HHD. Half of the subjects started with the HMD trial and half with the HHD trial. The assignment was randomly arranged to avoid order effects. An identical traffic scenario, representing an experimental trial, lasted 140 minutes, starting and ending with the completion of the questionnaires. A detection practice of about 15 minutes preceded the experimental trial at the first day. The targets appeared in the dynamic traffic scenario 5 to 15 seconds after presentation on the HMD or the HHD. A simultaneous appearance of a target in a display and in the scenario as well as a fixed delay was prevented to avoid target cueing. Subjects had to move the cursor with a mouse on the target and press the left mouse button to document their detection.

5 Results

5.1 Performance measures

The ANOVA for the detection times with repeated measures did not show a significant main effect for the display type ($F_{1;11} = 2.258$, $p > 0.05$), but significant main effects for the vehicle type ($F_{1;11} = 7.725$; $p < 0.05$), and the trial section ($F_{3;33} = 64.123$; $p < 0.05$). I.e., the display type has no relevant effect on detection times, helicopters have shorter detection times than ground vehicles, and the Scheffé-test shows that the detection times in the first trial section are significantly longer than in the following ones. The detection times as a function of display type and trial section are depicted in figure 3.

The ANOVA for percentage of hits did not disclose significant main effects for the factors display type ($F_{1;11} = 0.55$, $p > 0.05$), and vehicle type ($F_{1;11} = 3.64$;

Human Perspectives in the Internet Society: Culture, Psychology and Gender, K. Morgan, J. Sanchez, C. A. Brebbia & A Voiskounsky (Editors) © 2004 WIT Press, www.witpress.com, ISBN 1-85312-726-4

$p > 0.05$), but for trial section ($F_{3; 33} = 3.399$; $p < 0.05$), i.e., fewer hits are found in the first section than in each other. The percentage of hits as a function of display type and trial section is depicted in figure 4.

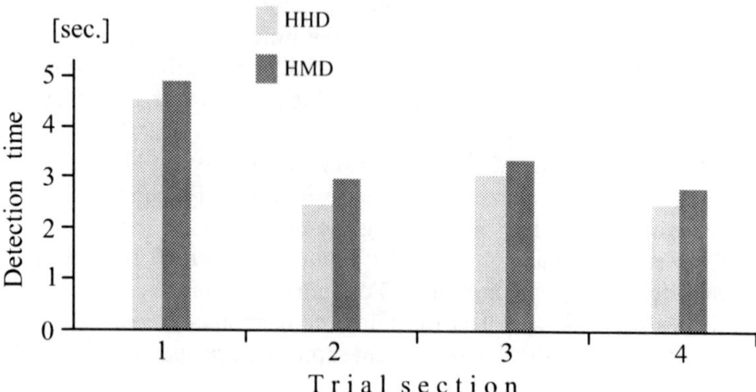

Figure 3: Means of detection times as a function of display type and trial section.

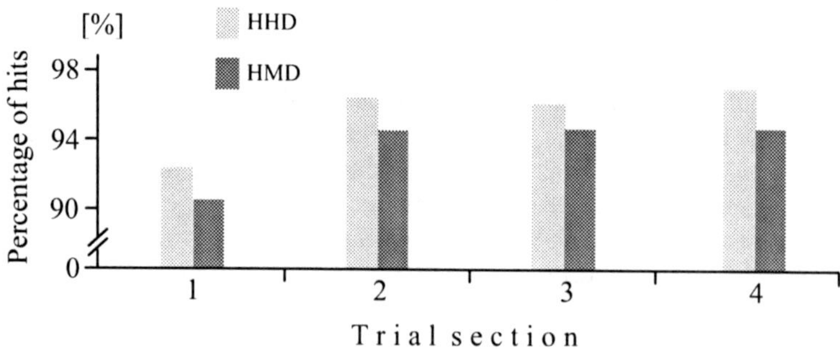

Figure 4: Means of percentage of hits as a function of display type and trial section.

5.2 Questionnaires

Analyses with Wilcoxon test did not show significant differences for the BLV subscales between HMD and HHD before an experimental trial.

When presenting the BLV after an experimental trial the subscale scores of *psychological stress* [1 < 10 = R (10; 0.05)] and *fatigue* [12 < 17 = R (12; 0.05)] are significantly higher for HMD than for HHD. HMD and HHD did not differ significantly in respect to *psychological fitness* [29.5 > 13 = R (11; 0.05)] and *performance aversion* [25 > 10 = R (10; 0.05)]. These post-test scores of the BLV subscales are depicted in figure 5.

Human Perspectives in the Internet Society: Culture, Psychology and Gender, K. Morgan, J. Sanchez, C. A. Brebbia & A Voiskounsky (Editors) © 2004 WIT Press, www.witpress.com, ISBN 1-85312-726-4

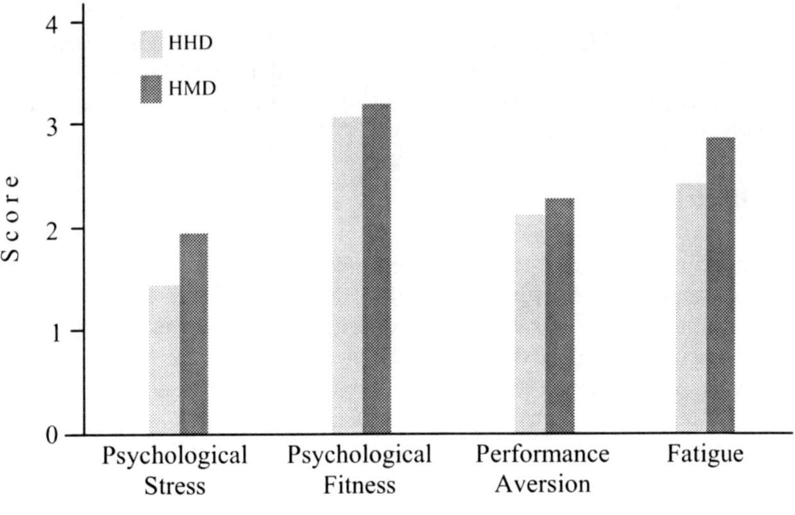

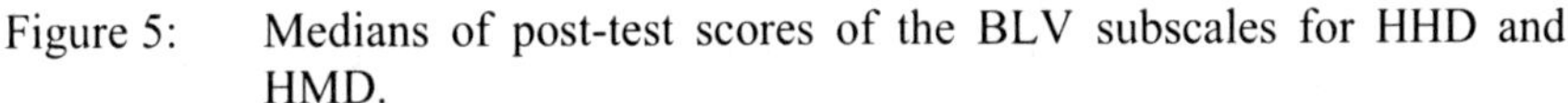

Figure 5: Medians of post-test scores of the BLV subscales for HHD and HMD.

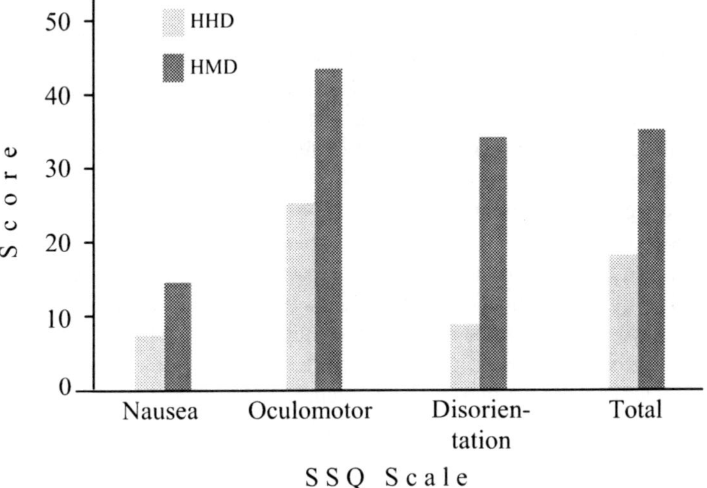

Figure 6: Medians of post-test scores of the SSQ subscales for HHD and HMD.

Analyses with Wilcoxon test did not show significant differences for the SSQ subscales between HMD and HHD before an experimental trial.

Human Perspectives in the Internet Society: Culture, Psychology and Gender, K. Morgan, J. Sanchez, C. A. Brebbia & A Voiskounsky (Editors) © 2004 WIT Press, www.witpress.com, ISBN 1-85312-726-4

When presenting the SSQ after an experimental trial all subscale scores, i.e., *nausea* [3 = 3 = R (7; 0.05)], *oculomotor* [4 < 8 = R (9; 0.05)], *disorientation* [0 < 10 = R (10; 0.05)], and *total score* [2 < 10 = R (10; 0.05)] are significantly higher for HMD than for HHD. These post-test scores for the SSQ subscales are depicted in figure 6.

6 Discussion

An increasing number of HMDs is used today in civilian and military settings, but in comparison to conventional displays, existing problem areas of workload, fatigue, simulator sickness etc. have not been empirically investigated with sufficient intensity. Therefore, the goal of the present experiment was, to investigate performance, workload related aspects, and symptoms of simulator sickness in a long-term detection task, using an HMD and an HHD.

Contrary to expectation, the HMD and the HHD did not differ significantly in respect to *detection times* and *percentage of hits*. But a consistent tendency for lower performance emerged for the HMD compared to the HHD. The absence of significant differences between hits of the HMD and HHD groups might base on the relatively long appearance duration of the targets in the traffic scenarios with the result that more than 90% of the targets had been detected. Generally, the lack of significance might be due to the small number of subjects. Also, performance differences could increase, when the task difficulty, the task complexity, and task duration increase.

The lower performance level at the first trial section compared to the following three trial sections of the experiment leads to the assumption, that learning effects were still active. A practice trial of 15 minutes before starting an experimental trial might have been too short to reach a sufficient learning level.

The HMD and HHD groups did not differ in the subscale scores of the BLV before performing the target detection task. Afterwards, the HMD group reflected a significant higher *psychological stress* and *fatigue* level than the HHD group, as postulated. This result can be explained in terms of significant higher workload, produced by the HMD use. It causes a higher psychological stress and increased fatigue of subjects, when exposed to the target detection task, because vision is impaired and must be compensated by extra efforts. An increase in workload is compensating a performance decrement, when using an HMD and may have contributed to lack of performance significance in the present study. Enhancing task difficulty by increasing task duration and complexity may show clear performance differences, because compensation is not longer possible despite increasing efforts.

The HMD and HHD groups did not differ in the subscales and total scores of the SSQ before performing the target detection task, but, in concordance with the expectation, they differed after. The use of the HMD resulted in higher scores in the subscales *nausea*, *oculomotor*, *disorientation* and the *total score* of SSQ than the use of the HHD. These findings demonstrate that simulator sickness, caused by the inconsistent feedback of visual and vestibular cues, may be another serious disadvantage of HMD usage, which also contributes to increasing workload

Human Perspectives in the Internet Society: Culture, Psychology and Gender, K. Morgan, J. Sanchez, C. A. Brebbia & A Voiskounsky (Editors) © 2004 WIT Press, www.witpress.com, ISBN 1-85312-726-4

and fatigue. The symptoms are still moderate as operator movements were limited in the present study, but it is argued, that with stronger movements a rigorous symptom increment might be expected, which could be more serious.

A side effect, not relevant to the central question of this paper, shows that detection times differ significantly, when differentiating between vehicle types. Helicopters, which vary in means of color cues, are detected faster than ground vehicles, which vary in means of shape. This finding matches the general knowledge that color-coding is superior to shape coding for tasks of search type, because of parallel processing [13].

Overall conclusion leads to the recommendation, when an application of HMDs is planned, these deteriorating psychological factors should be reflected in advance, in addition to low wearing comfort of the technical equipment. HHDs will probably be a better choice in most cases.

Future experiments should be more differentiating and involve variations in task type, task attribute, and task environment, to specify potential advantages of HMDs or to confirm the superiority of HHDs or conventional displays. Task type could be varied, e.g., as search, detection, and tracking tasks. Attributes of tasks are their difficulty and complexity as well as their duration, dynamics, and time critical aspects, which might influence the utility of specific display types. The task environment can vary, e.g., in the dimensions of monotony and information density. These interacting variables presumably lead to higher workload levels and stronger negative effects, when using HMDs compared to HHDs or other conventional displays, especially, when combined with symptoms of simulator sickness.

References

[1] Velger, M., *Helmet-Mounted Displays and Sights*, Artec House, Inc.: Norwood, MA, 1998.

[2] Meehan, J. W., *Advanced Display Technologies: What have we lost?* Volume XII: Number 3, Human Systems IAC Gateway: Wright-Patterson AFB, OH, 2001.

[3] Rash, C. E., Suggs, Ch. L., Mora, J. C., van de Pool, C., Reynolds, B. S. & Crowley, J. S., *Visual Issue Survey of AH-64 Apache Aviators (Year 2000),* USAARL Report No. 2002-02. U.S. Army Aeromedical Research Laboratory: Fort Rucker, AL, 2002.

[4] Howarth, P. A. & Costello, P. J., The Nauseogenicity of Using a Head-Mounted Display, Configured as a Personal Viewing System, for an Hour. *Proceedings of the Second FIVE International Conference Palazzo dei Congressi*, Pisa, Italy,1996.

[5] Merlo, J. L., Wickens, Ch. D. & Yeh, M., *Effect of Reliability on Cue Effectiveness and Display Signaling*, Technical Report ARL-99-4/FED-Lab-99-3, Aviation Research Lab. Institute of Aviation: Savoy, IL, 1999.

[6] Kooi; F., Visual Strain: a comparison of monitors and head-mounted displays. *SPIE Proceedings Series Vol. 2949*, The International Society for Optical Engineering (SPIE): Bellingham, WA, 1997.

Human Perspectives in the Internet Society: Culture, Psychology and Gender, K. Morgan, J. Sanchez, C. A. Brebbia & A Voiskounsky (Editors) © 2004 WIT Press, www.witpress.com, ISBN 1-85312-726-4

[7] Ishihara, S., *Tests for Colour Blindness*. Kanehara, Shuppan: Tokyo, 1974.
[8] Bronner, R. & Karger, J., Beanspruchungs-Messung in Problemlöse-Prozessen - Modifikation eines Tests zur Erfassung psychischer Beanspruchung. *Zeitschrift für Arbeits- und Organisationspsychologie,* 29, pp. 173-184, 1985.
[9] Kennedy, R. S., Berbaum, K. S. & Lilienthal, M. G., Simulator Sickness Questionnaire: An Enhanced Method for Quantifying Simulator Sickness. *The International Journal of Aviation Psychology*, 3(3), pp. 203-220, 1993.
[10] Pfendler, C. & Thun, J., *Der Belastungsverlaufstest (BLV) und seine rechnergestützte Version*. Technischer Bericht, FGAN: Wachtberg, Germany, 2001.
[11] SYSTAT, *SYSTAT 10.2*, Software Inc.: Richmond, CA, 2002.
[12] Sachs, L., *Angewandte Statistik*, Springer: Berlin,1997.
[13] Widdel, H. & Post, D.L. (eds.), *Color in electronic displays*, Plenum Press: New York and London, pp.137-138, 1992.

Human Perspectives in the Internet Society: Culture, Psychology and Gender, K. Morgan, J. Sanchez, C. A. Brebbia & A Voiskounsky (Editors) © 2004 WIT Press, www.witpress.com, ISBN 1-85312-726-4

Acceptance of an implantable data security chip to facilitate a cashless society

A. M. Young
School of Accounting and Law, RMIT University, Australia

Abstract

As the monetary system evolves new and more efficient means of payment become possible via the Internet, microchip store value cards and telecommunications. With the improved convenience and sophistication comes a greater potential for fraud and loss of privacy on a magnitude not previously possible. A logical extension of the control environment surrounding means of exchange is a permanent verification mark, which would allow unique identification and storage of personal and financial information. Chip implantation complete with global positioning satellites is a possible alternative with their increasing storage capacity, diminishing size and remote access. Successful human implantation of chips has occurred with no signs of rejection or infection. A model has been developed to test the acceptance of this new technology. The underpinnings of the model are two well researched and tested acceptance models being the Theory of Reasoned Action (TRA), Fishbein and Azjen [5], and the Technological Acceptance Model (TAM), Davis [3]. Both elements of the TAM have been adopted, those being the perception of usefulness and the perception of ease of use. The subjective norm component of the TRA is also included on the basis that the permanent and personal nature of the verification mark makes the influences of those who are important to the accountant an important explanatory variable. A perception of risk is also included as it is seen as important in such a significant and personal decision. Professionals have been surveyed to determine whether they would accept such technology into their personal lives despite changes to the risk profile including changed privacy issues. The regression analysis revealed that the developed acceptance model was more useful in predicting the acceptance of a verification mark than the previous TAM. The R Square of the developed model was 0.650 whereas the R Square of the TAM was a far less impressive 0.284.
Keywords: privacy, misuse, social control, technology acceptance.

Human Perspectives in the Internet Society: Culture, Psychology and Gender, K. Morgan, J. Sanchez, C. A. Brebbia & A Voiskounsky (Editors) © 2004 WIT Press, www.witpress.com, ISBN 1-85312-726-4

1 Introduction

Sophisticated mediums of exchange have been developed to improve convenience, save time, increase security and allow entry into the global market. Many believe that a complete switch to electronic delivery modes is a fait accompli especially for large financial payments because of their relative safety and speed. The new developing electronic value forms however have not quite succeeded in the universal acceptability required of money in this primitive sense. Some economists, model electronic money as new types of barter, some regard it as being new types of money; Green [7] refers to it as "netting arrangements".

With the advantages of convenience and speed also comes, the increased possibility of fraud, misuse and the vulnerability of confidential information. Electronically aided credit card fraud has skyrocketed, whilst electronic movement of money has reportedly stripped Russia of wealth by massive transfer of funds to offshoots of legitimate banks into America.

2 The development of mediums of exchange

The traditional textbook definition for money is that "it is a form of value generally acceptable in payments of goods and services. It ought also to serve as a unit of account and a medium for storing value effectively" Solomon [11]. The system of exchange cannot be viewed simplistically because inherent in the system is the allocation of scarce resources especially in an open global market. As economies become more sophisticated, pressure is brought to bear on the system of exchange to reflect that sophistication. Technological improvements have allowed significant advances in the sophistication of a medium of exchange.

3 Proliferation of electronic mediums of exchange

There is evidence to suggest that electronic mediums of exchange are becoming more prolific. Following on from the electronic use of credit cards, bills can now be paid by phone or via the Internet. "Although a system of networked computers is not new, the recent growth in the significance and use of internet banking has been astounding" Bollen [2].

Store value cards are also being used as a substitute to cash and some suggest that smart cards (cards that contain a silicon chip capable of storing large amounts of data) are indeed replacing cash (Ling [9]). Thirty percent of Belgium's ten million citizens use an e-cash program called Proton for purchases expected to total some five hundred million dollars annually Matlack et al [10]. E-cash is a prepaid store of cash that can be used at participating vendors via special readers.

The onslaught seems unstoppable: smart cards are invading every aspect of daily life, including cell phones, public transport, banking, building access, an advertisements even demonstrates the use of a mobile phone to purchase a bottle

Human Perspectives in the Internet Society: Culture, Psychology and Gender, K. Morgan, J. Sanchez, C. A. Brebbia & A Voiskounsky (Editors) © 2004 WIT Press, www.witpress.com, ISBN 1-85312-726-4

of soft drink or the feeding of a parking meter with the charge showing on the phone bill.

Chips continue to advance. Samsung Electronics Company, the worlds largest memory chipmaker have in 2002 developed the worlds first, two gigabyte flash memory chip which can store the equivalent of four movies. The flash memory chip can retain power even if the power is cut off. Some industry estimates suggest three billion smart cards will be in use in 2004 growing by an average of 20 per cent a year Hansen [8]. Industry analysts also think it is likely that different smart cards will converge into one super-smart card Hansen [8].

4 Verification mark

The obvious and logical control remedy is the tracking of money to the final consumer who can be traced if they are marked. What method of identification? There are various ways of individually identifying people. The uniqueness of people is a very well used area of identification, from fingerprints or eye scans to DNA. Uniqueness is an important element of control and it needs to be matched with a logical numbering system. This is possible if a person's uniqueness whether that be a fingerprint, an eye retina or other identifying feature was matched with a centralised numbering system. At a roundtable United Nations meeting, the head of Belgium's independent asylum review board put forward a plan in late 2002 that every person in the world would be fingerprinted and registered under a universal identification scheme to fight illegal immigration and people smuggling outlined at a meeting.

Without direct access to the system however then the number would have to be remembered and vendors and authorities would have to believe the number that you told them in the absence of some style of traditional identification such as a card. Alternatively a number could be applied to each individual. This technology is presently available whereby a tattoo is applied by laser beam in a manner already used to brand livestock or thousands of salmon fish, which can be branded even while they are swimming. The laser painlessly destroys the pigment of the skin but it is so extremely fine, that it is invisible to the eye. A scanner is used to read the number.

An injectable chip could store information and could be accessed from a distance. Chips like these currently exist.

Chip technology exists which can be implanted into humans as a means of identification. An example is the "VeriChip" which is a 12mm by 2.1mm radio frequency device about the size of the point of a typical ballpoint pen. The chip can be implanted via a simple procedure that could be performed in an outpatient or office setting. It requires only local anaesthesia, a tiny incision and perhaps a small adhesive bandage. Each VeriChip could contain a unique identification number and other critical data (www.adsx.com 2004). A biocompatible coating is used to keep the body from rejecting the implanted chip. As an example New Jersey surgeon, Richard Seelig, injected two of the Applied Digital Solutions chips into himself without any signs of rejection or infection.

Human Perspectives in the Internet Society: Culture, Psychology and Gender, K. Morgan, J. Sanchez, C. A. Brebbia & A Voiskounsky (Editors) © 2004 WIT Press, www.witpress.com, ISBN 1-85312-726-4

Utilising an external scanner within about a half a meter of the chip activates the passive unit. A radio frequency energy passes through the skin energizing the coil and "wakes up" the dormant VeriChip, which then emits a radio frequency signal of one hundred and twenty five kilohertz transmitting the identification number and other data contained in the VeriChip. The scanner can display the information, which can also be transmitted, via telephone or the Internet, to a compliant, secure data-storage site. Authorised personnel can then access it.

Currently Digital Solutions and other companies use a tracking bracelet or wristwatch containing the chip. The chip transmits a signal to the global positioning system, which is a network of United States navigational satellites. A person can be located within 60 seconds. Digital Solution is expecting to shortly unveil the tracking microchip, which can be embedded beneath a persons skin.

4.1 Benefits of an implantable chip

The ability to inject the chips opens up a variety of applications of human identification such as the high-security tracking of prisoners or parolees or the tracking of young children to protect against kidnapping. Terrorist could be more easily detected and perhaps prevented. Police would be more able to identify criminals.

Medical records could be included in the verification chip, preventing catastrophes such as administering drugs on an unconscious patient, which they may be allergic to.

There would also be a convenience factor; information such as driver's licence and contact details could be stored. The implantation of a chip would make it possible for all trading to occur electronically in the future and there would no longer be a need to carry cash or credit cards to the surf beach or swimming pool, eliminating the chance of it being lost or stolen as you swim or at other times. Credit card fraud could also be eliminated. If the chip were the culmination of a cashless economy, accounting for personal transactions would become easier including budgets and taxation, which may well be done centrally given all expenditure and receipts would be stored. Non-financial information would additionally be stored which would make personal management of more than just finances possible.

4.2 Problems with implanted chips

The implanting of chip does not preclude the physical interference with the chip. Another issue is privacy which has been defined by Warren and Brandeis [12] as the "the right to be let alone". So much information has been collected about individuals already and the trend is growing. Privacy is an increasing social issue. Can the controller of the increased and consolidated personal information, be trusted to use it in a manner that the community finds acceptable? Consider the assurance Toysmart.com gave to its buyers. "When you register with Toysmart.com you can rest assured that your information will never be shared with a third party". Subsequently in June 2000 Toysmart.com's assets were advertised for sale including the databases. The United States Federal trade

Human Perspectives in the Internet Society: Culture, Psychology and Gender, K. Morgan, J. Sanchez, C. A. Brebbia & A Voiskounsky (Editors) © 2004 WIT Press, www.witpress.com, ISBN 1-85312-726-4

Commissioner intervened and required the new buyer to abide by the original privacy guidelines. Recently personal information had been collected and sold for profit by an Australian business entrepreneur raising privacy issues.

Two issues arise in an effort to protect privacy, firstly the technical protection afforded to the person and secondly a person's formal protection. The encryption software sourcing from the United States have been of significant technical quality enabling information to be sent across computer networks without fear of tampering however protection is a moving target.

The United States government had curbed the export of these encryption software products via legislation before introducing amended legislation that have ended many restrictions on the export of the products. Business will inevitably pressure legislators to sacrifice security for profit as evidenced by this bipartisan group of technology companies and trade groups who argued that the existing export controls would have put the United States products at a disadvantage in the global marketplace as demand for computer-security products grew. The United States federal government are now allowing the market to decide the appropriate forms of encryption for electronic data but what of the interests of the powerless?

Is legislation sufficient to protect the privacy of the community? The Australia Card proposal in many ways raised the issue of privacy in a public forum in Australia. The community voiced their lack of support for the project via the referendum vote at that time. Many argue de facto identification numbers have been introduced via the Australian Business Number system which are unique identifiers which if not quoted have significant impact on the taxpayer. In part as a flow on from the failed Australia card project, in an attempt to protect privacy and the flow of personal data, the Australian federal Privacy act of 1988 authorised the implementation of the eleven principles developed by the Organisation for Economic Cooperation and Development in 1980.

The act was extended in December of 2000 via the Privacy Amendment (private sector) act to include most private organizations and set out how organizations should use, keep and disclose personal information. Guidelines to the National Privacy Principles where written by the Commissioner. The Privacy commission has jurisdiction over not only the Privacy act but also other related areas such as the entitlement to investigate breaches under part VIIC of the Crimes act 1914 and jurisdiction over the Data-Matching Program (Assistance and Tax) act 1990. The commissioner also has monitoring and compliance functions under the Telecommunications Act 1997 and some responsibilities under the National health Act of 1953. Can the government be relied upon to protect privacy? In many areas the lack of resources compromise good protection.

Case law in Australia has not historically been supportive of the protection of privacy. Recently however a Queensland district judge in Grosse v Purvis [2003] QDC 151 (16 June 2003), declared a preparedness to take up the challenge of the High Court to declare a tort of privacy in ABC v Lenah Game Meats Pty Ltd (2001) 208 CLR 199; 76 ALJR. The High Court Senior Judge Skoien declared that, " It is a bold step to take, as it seems, the first step in this country to hold

Human Perspectives in the Internet Society: Culture, Psychology and Gender, K. Morgan, J. Sanchez, C. A. Brebbia & A Voiskounsky (Editors) © 2004 WIT Press, www.witpress.com, ISBN 1-85312-726-4

that there can be a civil action for damages on the actionable right of an individual person to privacy. But I see it as a logical and desirable step. In My view there is such an actionable right. The district judge awarded $178,000 in damages with respect to the right of an individual person to privacy. Doctor Robert Dean stated that the courts have come under pressure to fill a void left due to the "Australian legislatures hesitancy" Dean [4].

Of the respondents of the survey undertaken for this research (details below) one third that took the opportunity to respond to the open question asking them to "identify risks that you would associate with a mark" contributed a concern for privacy related issues. In a separate survey of 523 professional qualified accountants 34% of the 141 contributed a similar concern. The following is the list of phrases used to communicate the concern:

"Unnecessary intrusion into a person's life", "privacy", "information being accumulated and assessed by third parties", "friend's family obtaining information", "failure of technology thereby creating duplication of people's records", "(perceived) lack of control over information", "discrimination – racial", "confidentiality/invasion of privacy', "a person's' history would be too easily available", "infringe personal barriers", "security of personal information", "privacy issues", "surveillance issues", "loss of anonymity" and "big brother effect"

System corruption takes on a greater magnitude with a monetary system built around implantable chip technology. The dissymmetry of power between government and individuals is also likely to increase with the introduction of a verification mark which has the potential to increase the information collected and consolidated the information into a more useable form. The concern is the control government has over the society in a way Foucault [6] describes.

5 Theory

Davis [3] explored user acceptance of computer technology in business making use of Ajzen and Fishbein's [1, 5] theory of reasoned action (TRA) as it was "an especially well-researched intention model that has proven successful in predicting and explaining behaviour across a wide variety of domains".

The Theory of Reasoned Action argues that behavioural intention measures the strengths of a person's intention to perform a specified behaviour, which in turn gives an indication of the likelihood for the person to actually undertake the specified behaviour. Behavioural intention is affected according to the Theory of Reasoned Action model by both the person's attitude towards behaviour and a person's subjective norm. Attitude towards behaviour is defined as an individual's positive or negative feelings (evaluation effect) about performing the target behaviour. The attitude towards behaviour is a result of the person's salient beliefs about the consequences of performing the behaviour multiplied by the evaluation of those consequences. Beliefs are defined as the individual's subjective probability that performing the target behaviour will result in

Human Perspectives in the Internet Society: Culture, Psychology and Gender, K. Morgan, J. Sanchez, C. A. Brebbia & A Voiskounsky (Editors) © 2004 WIT Press, www.witpress.com, ISBN 1-85312-726-4

the consequence. Therefore the attitude towards behaviour is a summation of the belief multiplied by the evaluation.

Subjective norm refers to "the person's perception that most people who are important to him think he should or should not perform the behaviour in question" (Fishbein and Ajzen [5]. A person's subjective norm is determined by the person's normative beliefs multiplied by the person's motivation to comply with the normative beliefs.

Davis [3] adapted the Theory of Reasoned Action model to tailer the model specifically for user acceptance of information systems, which he called the Technology Acceptance Model (TAM). Davis posits that two particular beliefs are of primary importance for technology acceptance behaviour. These are the perceived usefulness of the computer technology for the intended tasks and the perceived ease of use of the technology. Davis removes the subjective norm from the model completely and his explanation for this is "as Fishbein and Ajzen acknowledge, this is one of the least understood aspects of the Theory of Reasoned Action. It is difficult to disentangle direct effects of subjective norms on behaviour intention from indirect effects via attitudes towards behaviour".

This research returns to the precepts of the Theory of Reasoned Action model and includes the subjective norm component before making use of the application of the TAM in an application of the theory designed to apply to the issue of society's acceptance of a verification mark. A perception of risk is also included as it is seen as important in such a significant and personal decision from a cost benefit perspective.

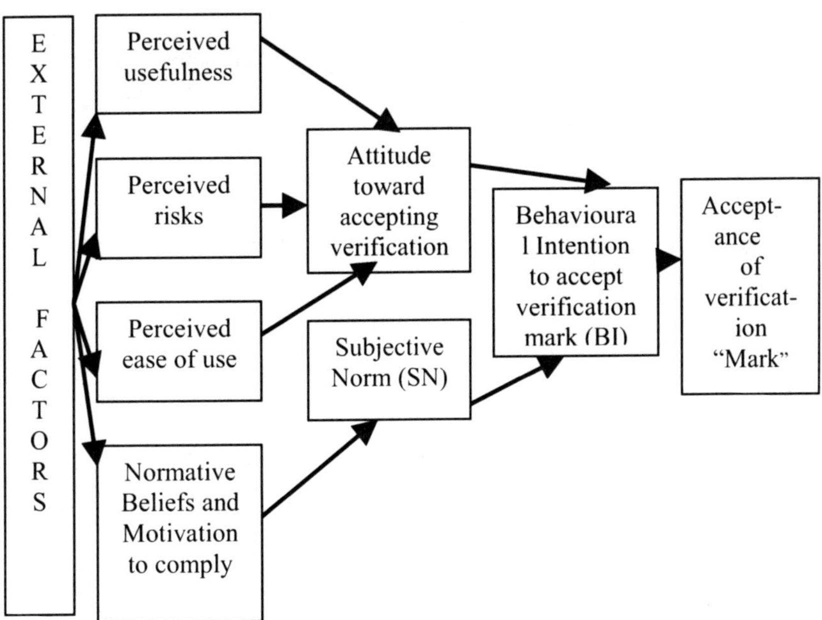

Figure 1: Verification mark acceptance model.

Human Perspectives in the Internet Society: Culture, Psychology and Gender, K. Morgan, J. Sanchez, C. A. Brebbia & A Voiskounsky (Editors) © 2004 WIT Press, www.witpress.com, ISBN 1-85312-726-4

6 Statistical analysis

H1 The Verification Mark Acceptance model is mathematically better at predicting the likely acceptance of the "mark" than the existing Technology Acceptance Model.

A survey of 32 experienced and qualified professionals was collected as a precursor to a larger sample size to contemplate relationships, which might exist in the acceptance models. The demographics of the respondents included the attachment to three particular vocational groups. The first group consisting of eleven members are professionally qualified accountants. The second group consist of those with experience and qualifications in the information technology industry (10). The final group consists of those working with both legal qualifications and work experience in the legal arena, including barristers and solicitors (11). The mean respondent's age was just above the 40 to 49 age group with representatives from the lowest group, up to the 50-59 groups, but not above. The mean average of years in the profession was between 6 and 10 years. The respondents all held senior positions or above with no assistants represented. The mean salary fell within the salary range of $60,000 to $100,000. The majority of the respondents were male.

The responses on acceptance were sought if the mark and technology was a major means of conducting transactions. Regression analysis was run for both the developed acceptance model and the existing Technology Acceptance Model. As a precursor to the regression analysis were tests for normality, along with correlation and factor analysis.

Questions where grouped into the models categories, ease of use, usefulness, normative belief and risks. There were three styles of questions relating to risk. The first style of questions dealt with the expectation of increased risks due to the associated implantible chip technology, for instance the likelihood of exaggerated privacy issues. The second style of question dealt with the diminishment of risks due to the adoption of the implantable chip. The third revolved around the faith the respondents had in technological or legal protection such as encryption software or legislative protection to protect them from resultant risks such as loss of privacy.

The final area of contemplation revolves around normative beliefs or what those who are important to the respondents feel about the issues of this technology. Three questions were asked soliciting views on wether the respondents considered those important to them would perceive the mark was easy to use, useful and risky. There were three additional questions soliciting views on wether the mark offended religious, community or family views. It was expected that if the mark offended religious views or conflicted with community or family views then there would be a negative correlation between this and acceptance. In every case the expected relationship was supported by the predicted correlation with acceptance of the technology if it was a major means of transacting.

The regression analysis of the linear relationship is important to test the performance of the two models as a predictor of acceptance. In running the

Human Perspectives in the Internet Society: Culture, Psychology and Gender, K. Morgan, J. Sanchez, C. A. Brebbia & A Voiskounsky (Editors) © 2004 WIT Press, www.witpress.com, ISBN 1-85312-726-4

regression analysis the R Square of the developed model was 0.650 showing a useful degree of fit. The R square shows the proportion of the variation in acceptance (the dependent variable), which is explained by the independent or explanatory variables, which were ease of use, usefulness, risk and subjective norm in accordance to the model. A non-ordinal figure of 1 was attached to strongly disagree, 2 was attached to disagree, 3 was attached to uncertain, 4 was attached to agree and 5 was attached to strongly agree. The unstandardized coefficient (constant or c in our linear regression) was 3.88. The two most significant elements of the developed model were usefulness with 0.618 and the positive aspects of risks with 0.273. Usefulness had a negative 0.020 coefficient while the positive risks had a 0.029 positive coefficient. The ease of use, subjective norm and the negative aspects of risks where not accessed as being significant with 0.016, 0.018 and 0.002 significance respectively. Ease of use had a positive 0.086 coefficient, the subjective norm had a negative 0.120 coefficient and the adverse risks had a positive 0.102 coefficient.

In running the regression analysis for TAM the R Square of the developed model was a far less impressive 0.284 showing the proportion of the variation in the dependent variable (acceptance), which is explained by the independent or explanatory variables, which in this case were ease of use and usefulness. The unstandardized coefficient constant was 0.391 for the independent variable of acceptance of the technology if it was a major means of transacting. Usefulness was again significant with 0.839 with a negative 0.010 coefficient. The ease of use was not significant with 0.007; it had a positive 0.117 coefficient.

7 Conclusion

It appears that the development of electronic mediums of exchange and their proliferation is leading to a more sophisticated verification system. To help in the understanding it was seen that the developed acceptance model was more useful in explaining the issues of acceptance of a verification mark than the previous Technology Acceptance Model however further research is needed to explain the prevailing relationships.

References

[1] Ajzen, I., Fishbein, M. Understanding attitudes and predicting social behaviour. Englewood Cliffs NJ: Prentice Hall, 1980.

[2] Bollen, R., The regulation of Internet banking. Journal of banking and finance law and practice, Vol 12, pp. 5-17, March, 2001

[3] Davis, F. D. Perceived usefulness, perceived ease of use and user acceptance of information technology, MIS Quarterly, vol. 13 (3) pp. 319-340. 1989.

[4] Dean, R., A right to privacy? The Australian Law Journal, Vol 78, pp. 114- 125, February, 2004.

[5] Fishbein, M., Ajzen, I., Belief, attitude, intention and behaviour: An introduction to theory and research: Addison-Wesley, 1975.

Human Perspectives in the Internet Society: Culture, Psychology and Gender, K. Morgan, J. Sanchez, C. A. Brebbia & A Voiskounsky (Editors) © 2004 WIT Press, www.witpress.com, ISBN 1-85312-726-4

[6] Foucault, Discipline and punish: Penguin books, 1975.
[7] Green, E., We need to think straight about electronic payments. Journal of Money, Credit, and Banking, Vol 31, 3, 2, pp. 668-670, Aug 1999.
[8] Hansen, J., In the shadow of big brother. Connect, January 20, pp. A22-A23, 2001.
[9] Ling, S., DBS goes into debit. Straits Times August, pp.21, 2001.
[10] Matlack, C, Djemai, K, Fairlamb, D., A cash-free France? Don't bet the store. Business week, November, pp. 1-2, 2002.
[11] Solomon, E., Electronic Money Flows the moulding of a new financial order: Kluwer Academic Publishers, 1991.
[12] Warren, S. & Brandeis, L., The right to privacy. Harvard law review, Vol. 4, pp. 193-220, 1890.

Human Perspectives in the Internet Society: Culture, Psychology and Gender, K. Morgan, J. Sanchez, C. A. Brebbia & A Voiskounsky (Editors) © 2004 WIT Press, www.witpress.com, ISBN 1-85312-726-4

Section 3
Cyber interactions

Online audits and energy using behavior

K. Tiedemann
BC Hydro and Simon Fraser University, Canada

Abstract

During the past ten years, there has been an increasing realization that reducing household energy use and the resulting harmful emissions are not primarily a technological or engineering problem. Cost effective technologies that could reduce household energy use and emissions are widely available, but they are used by only a minority of households. Inadequate customer information on the nature and benefits of energy-efficient technologies is a key barrier to the greater use of these technologies that can be addressed through online customer information mechanisms. BC Hydro's Home Energy Profile program is a computerized, online self audit that provides customers with detailed information on their energy consumption by end use together with recommendations on how the customer can reduce energy consumption in a cost effective manner. This paper estimates the quantitative impact of the program on homeowner energy use.

1 Introduction

The Home Energy Profile Program was launched in February 2001. The program includes a computerized self-audit that is designed for those in single-family dwellings, duplexes and row houses where the impact of common walls on space conditioning loads is minimal. The customer enters data on a variety of household characteristic and energy use variables into the audit program which then provides an estimate of energy consumption by end use using a whole building computer model. Answers to specific questions also trigger recommendations for a variety of energy saving measures. The main types of information required to complete the audit include location, basic dwelling information (floor area, housing type, age, occupancy), construction (foundation type, insulation, doors, windows), space conditioning and water heating equipment (controls, fuels, usage), appliances and lighting.

Human Perspectives in the Internet Society: Culture, Psychology and Gender, K. Morgan, J. Sanchez, C. A. Brebbia & A Voiskounsky (Editors) © 2004 WIT Press, www.witpress.com, ISBN 1-85312-726-4

The rationale for the Home Energy Profile Program is that providing customers with detailed estimates of their energy consumption by end use together with recommendations on how to save energy will result in those customers taking energy saving actions and significantly reducing their energy consumption. The purpose of this paper is to estimate electricity savings of program participants using a pre/post comparison with a control group and to estimate gross and net energy savings for individual retrofit measures or technologies.

2 Previous research

Over the past twenty years, conditional demand analysis has emerged as the analytical tool of choice for the detailed analysis of household energy consumption. Conditional demand analysis refers to the statistical analysis of energy consumption to estimate energy consumption by end use. It is thus a substitute for direct metering of end use consumption, which is often expensive, difficult and time consuming to employ. Conditional demand estimates also have the advantage that with large samples they be estimated at a disaggregated level, such as geographical area and housing type.

The basic idea behind conditional demand analysis is that total household consumption of electricity is the sum of the consumption of the various end uses plus an error term. Appliance saturation levels are measured by an indicator variable or alternatively by a count of the number of units of the appliance in the household. This term is generally multiplied by an indicator variable for the use of electricity for that end use. For example, water heating as an end use is relevant only if the home has electric rather than natural gas or oil water heating. In the simplest models the regression coefficient for a variable is the unit energy consumption.

There is a large and growing literature that uses conditional demand analysis to estimate energy consumption by end use in residential dwellings. Recent papers include Barnes et al. [1], Branch [2], Dubin and Hensen [3], Dubin and McFadden [4], Haas et al. [5], Leth-Petersen [6], Madlener [7], Parti and Parti [8], Poyer and Williams [9] and Reilly and Shankle [10].

Much of this literature uses a combined thermodynamic-behavioral approach. Basic thermodynamic relationships are used to provide the basic modeling framework, but this framework is modified to incorporate the effects of usage rates and control strategies. Individual end use energy consumption levels can be modeled as functions of relevant physical and behavioral variables.

3 Data and preliminary analysis

In order to collect information for the impact evaluation of the Home Energy Profile Program, a detailed telephone survey was conducted with 100 program participants (who participated in the program during its first month of operation which was February 2001) and 100 control group customers (who were neighbors of participants).

Human Perspectives in the Internet Society: Culture, Psychology and Gender, K. Morgan, J. Sanchez, C. A. Brebbia & A Voiskounsky (Editors) © 2004 WIT Press, www.witpress.com, ISBN 1-85312-726-4

The survey collected basic information on customers, asked about their awareness and sources of awareness of energy efficiency, examined energy efficiency actions taken by customers and the reasons for those actions, examined the role of the program in encouraging energy efficient actions and asked about customer satisfaction. Customers were also asked for permission to link their survey responses to their billing histories for further analysis. Survey questions relevant to the present report included the following. (1) Area of conditioned space changes to area of conditioned space, occupancy and changes in occupancy. (2) Fuels used for space heating and water heating. (3) Energy efficient actions undertaken including the installation of additional insulation, additional draft proofing, new double paned or triple paned windows, high efficiency water heater, low flow shower heads, faucet aerators and compact fluorescent lamps.

After the survey was fielded, the resulting data was cleaned and entered into a database. For those respondents who agreed to the linking of their survey responses to their billing files, the survey results were reviewed to determine whether there had been significant changes in the area of heated space or changes in occupancy during the period to be covered by the analysis. The purpose here was to limit the analysis to houses where the change in energy consumption could realistically be attributed to either retrofit measures or changes in weather. For the participant group, this left some 68 homes available for subsequent analysis and for the control group this left some 63 homes available for subsequent analysis.

Billing analysis for participant and control homes was then conducted using weather normalized consumption for the pre-program period (April 2000 to March 2001) and the post-program period (April 2001 to March 2002). This analysis was done separately for electrically heated and non-electrically heated houses, on the assumption that the main impact on consumption would be on the space heating load.

Savings for electrically heated participant homes and for non-electrically heated participant homes were then estimated using the double deflation method, as shown in Table 1, where savings equals (pre-program consumption minus post-program consumption for participants) minus (pre-program consumption minus post-program consumption for control group members). Using this method helps to control for natural changes in consumption and other exogenous changes and increases the validity of the resulting savings estimates.

For electrically heated homes, participants experienced a decrease in consumption of 398 kWh per year while controls experienced an increase in consumption of 275 kWh per year. The net effect is a savings estimate of 673 kWh per year for participants with electrically heated houses. For non-electrically heated homes, participants experienced an increase in consumption of 97 kWh per year while controls experienced an increase in consumption of 159 kWh per year. The net effect is a savings estimate of 62 kWh per year for participants with electrically heated houses.

Human Perspectives in the Internet Society: Culture, Psychology and Gender, K. Morgan, J. Sanchez, C. A. Brebbia & A Voiskounsky (Editors) © 2004 WIT Press, www.witpress.com, ISBN 1-85312-726-4

Table 1: Energy savings for participants.

	Participants (kWh/year)	Controls (kWh/year)	Savings (kWh/year)
Pre/post change for electrically heated homes	398	-275	673
Pre/post change for non-electrically heated homes	-97	-159	62

We can gain a preliminary insight into the sources of these energy savings by comparing changes in electricity consumption for those program participants who did and did not undertake various measures. Table 2 compares changes in pre-program minus post-program electricity consumption for those program participants who installed and who did not install five key residential energy conservation measures. These measures include: additional insulation; draft proofing; double paned or triple paned windows; high efficiency water heaters; and compact fluorescent lamps. For additional insulation, draft proofing and windows, the change must be in a dwelling where the main space hearing fuel is electricity to be relevant. There are energy savings when measures are installed in non-electrically heated homes, but since information on alternative heating fuels such as natural gas or fuel consumption was not available, these savings could not be estimated. Similarly, for high efficiency water heating, the change must be in a dwelling where the main water heating fuel is electricity. For compact fluorescent lamps, all dwellings are appropriate.

Table 2: Participant change in consumption.

Efficient Measure Installed	Installed Measure (kWh /year)	Did Not Install (kWh /year)
Insulation	1290	293
Draft proofing	682	295
Windows	1131	289
Water heater	444	351
Compact fluorescent lamps	377	352

4 Regression models

Conditional demand models were used to provide amore rigorous analysis of measure savings. The conditional demand models were estimated using ordinary least squares regression. Ordinary least squares regression involves choosing the regression parameters so as to minimise the sum of squares of the error terms. The basic idea of least squares regression is to choose the parameters to minimise the sum of squares of the errors. The rationale for using minimum least squared error as the criterion for choosing parameter values makes intuitive

Human Perspectives in the Internet Society: Culture, Psychology and Gender, K. Morgan, J. Sanchez, C. A. Brebbia & A Voiskounsky (Editors) © 2004 WIT Press, www.witpress.com, ISBN 1-85312-726-4

sense since large errors are more important than are small errors. In the usual framework, the regression model is given by

$$y_t = x'_t\beta + \varepsilon_t, \tag{1}$$

where $\varepsilon_t \sim N(0, \sigma^2)$ and $t = 1,2, \dots T$.

Here, y_t is the dependent variable at observation, x_t is a k×1 vector of independent variables at observation t, β is a k×1 vector of parameters assumed constant for all observations and T is the number of observations. In other words, (1) is a set of T equations where the value of y_t at time t is a linear function of k variables, $x_{1t}, x_{2t}, \dots, x_{kt}$.

It is convenient for what follows to write equation (1) in matrix form as follows

$$y = X'\beta + \varepsilon, \tag{2}$$

where y is a T×1 vector, X is a k×T matrix, β is a k×1 vector, and ε is a T×1 vector.

We assume that X is a non-stochastic matrix of full rank $k \leq T$ that satisfies the regularity condition $\lim_{T\to\infty} (X'X/T) = Q$, where Q is a finite and non-singular matrix. We use E for the expectation operator and note that the Eε is 0 since the expectation of each of its components is zero. Then we define the sum of the squared errors as S and note that the variance of the errors is the expectation of S

$$S \equiv \varepsilon'\varepsilon = (y - X'\beta)'(y - X'\beta) \text{ and } E\varepsilon\varepsilon' = \sigma^2 I. \tag{3}$$

The ordinary least squares estimators of the vector of parameters β^* and the variance of the errors σ^{2*} are found by minimizing the sum of the squared errors

$$\partial S/\partial\beta = -2X'y + 2X'X\beta^* = 0. \tag{4}$$

Solving (4) for β^* the estimated value of β yields the following expression

$$\beta^* = (X'X)^{-1} X'y. \tag{5}$$

The ordinary least squares estimate of the variance of the errors σ^2 is used to estimate confidence intervals and conduct statistical tests and is given by the following expression

$$\sigma^{2*} = \varepsilon^{*\prime}\varepsilon^* / (T - k) \text{ where } \varepsilon^* = y - X\beta^*. \tag{6}$$

The estimate of σ^2 is used to estimate standard errors, to construct confidence intervals and to conduct hypotheses tests for the parameters.

Human Perspectives in the Internet Society: Culture, Psychology and Gender, K. Morgan, J. Sanchez, C. A. Brebbia & A Voiskounsky (Editors) © 2004 WIT Press, www.witpress.com, ISBN 1-85312-726-4

5 Gross measure savings

To estimate the impact of individual measures on energy consumption, we use a modified form of the conditional demand approach (CDA). Suppose that initially separate CDA equations are developed for the pre-program and the post-program periods using weather normalized data to remove the effect of weather differences between the periods. If the post-program equation is subtracted from the pre-program equation, the resulting equation is an equation in differences, in which any terms constant between the two periods cancel. This leaves a model in which the change in consumption is a function just of changes in retrofit actions.

Formally, the individual customer change in weather normalized consumption is modeled as a function of change in insulation, change in draft proofing, change in windows, change in water heating and change in use of compact fluorescent lamps. The change variables are dummy variables that take on the value "0" if there is no change and the value "1" if there is a change in the relevant retrofit technology.

$$\Delta kWh = \beta_1 + \beta_2\Delta in + \beta_3\Delta draft + \beta 4\Delta win + \beta_5\Delta wat + \beta_6 CFL + \varepsilon \quad (7)$$

Heteroscedasticity exist if the error terms are not constant across household observations, but, for example, are larger for larger dwellings. To deal with possible heteroscedasticity in the residuals, two models were estimated. The first model has the change in consumption per dwelling as the outcome variable. The second model has the change in consumption per square foot as the outcome variable.

Results for the two regression models are shown in Table 3. Model 1 has change in electricity consumption per dwelling as the outcome or dependent variable. Model 2 has change in electricity consumption per square foot as the outcome variable. Standard errors are shown in parentheses.

Table 3: Regression results for energy savings.

Efficient Measure Installed	Model 1 (kWh per dwelling)	Model 2 (kWh per square foot)
Insulation	1062 (475)	0.679 (0.268)
Draft proofing	334 (333)	0.204 (0.188)
Windows	587 (475)	0.287 (0.269)
Water heater	473 (445)	0.213 (0.251)
CFL	226 (222)	0.064 (0.125)
Adjusted R-squared	0.12	0.11

Human Perspectives in the Internet Society: Culture, Psychology and Gender, K. Morgan, J. Sanchez, C. A. Brebbia & A Voiskounsky (Editors) © 2004 WIT Press, www.witpress.com, ISBN 1-85312-726-4

The results from these regression models can be used to estimate the impact of the various measures on electricity consumption as shown in Table 4. For Model 1, the regression coefficients directly provide the required estimates of the impact on the outcome variable (change in consumption per dwelling). For Model 2, the regression coefficients are multiplied by 1902 (the average square footage of participant dwellings).

Table 4: Gross impacts of measures.

Efficient Measure Installed	Model 1: (kWh per dwelling)	Model 2: (kWh per dwelling)
Insulation	1062	1291
Draft proofing	334	388
Windows	587	546
Water heater	473	405
CFL	226	122

6 Net measure savings

In order to assess the net impact of the program, participants were asked how important the completion of the Home Energy Profile was in their decision to make retrofit changes to their home. Using a scale of one to five, where one is not at all important and five is very important, participants rated the importance of the Home Energy Profile in undertaking various retrofits as shown in Table 5.

Table 5: Attribution rate or score.

	(5)	(4)	(3)	(2)	(1)	Score
Weight	1.00	0.75	0.50	0.25	0.00	-
Insulation	40%	40%	20%	-	-	0.80
Draft proofing	15%	30%	25%	10%	15%	0.51
Windows	-	14%	14%	43%	29%	0.28
Water heater	17%	33%	17%	-	17%	0.58
CFL	20%	28%	17%	11%	11%	0.52

A weighted score was then calculated using the following weights: a score of five has weight of 1.00, a score of four has weight of 0.75, a score of three has weight of 0.5, a score of two has weight of 0.25, and a score of 1 has weight of 0.00. The weighted average of the scores is then the attribution rate. We can express this in terms of the familiar free rider rate, where the free rider rate is the share of participants who would have undertaken the measure in the absence of the program. The weighted average of the scores is then equal to one minus the free rider rates for each type of retrofit. In other words, one minus the free rider rate is the attribution rate. These scores state the following findings: the shares of gross savings for each retrofit attributable to the program are as follows:

Human Perspectives in the Internet Society: Culture, Psychology and Gender, K. Morgan, J. Sanchez, C. A. Brebbia & A Voiskounsky (Editors) © 2004 WIT Press, www.witpress.com, ISBN 1-85312-726-4

insulation 80%; draft proofing 51%; windows 28%; water heaters 58%; and CFLs 52%.

Table 6 provides estimates of net energy savings for the two sets of gross savings estimates. Note that for each model and for each retrofit measure, net savings are just the product of gross savings and the attribution rate. For Model 1, estimated net savings per year are 850 kWh for insulation, 170 kWh for draft proofing, 164 kWh for windows, 274 kWh for water heaters and 118 kWh for CFLs. For Model 2, estimated net savings per year are 1033 kWh for insulation, 198 kWh for draft proofing, 153 kWh for windows, 235 kWh for water heaters and 63 kWh for CFLs.

Table 6: Estimated net impact of measures.

	Gross Saving Model 1	Gross Savings Model 2	(1- FR)	Net Savings Model 1	Net Savings Model 2
Insulation	1062	1291	0.80	850	1033
Draft proofing	334	388	0.51	170	198
Windows	587	546	0.28	164	153
Water heater	473	405	0.58	274	235
CFL	226	122	0.52	118	63

7 Conclusions

BC Hydro launched the Home Energy Profile in January 2001. The program is a computerized, internet-based self-audit that is designed for those in single family dwellings, but also provides valid results for those living in row houses or town houses where the impact of common walls is minimal. Customers enter data on a wide range of variables into the audit program, which merges this information with their energy billing and weather files, undertakes a simplified whole-building simulation, estimates consumption by end use and provides recommendations on retrofits.

In this study we have analysed the impact of BC Hydro's Home Energy Profile Program on energy consumption of a cross-section of program participants. The analysis indicates that online household energy audits are an effective method of changing residential energy use. Using weather normalised billing data, gross estimates of savings were made applying a pre/post comparison with a comparison group. This difference-of-differences methodology is designed to control for extraneous factors that might affect energy consumption. Gross energy savings are estimated at 673 kWh per year for electrically heated participants and 62 kWh per year for non-electrically heated participants.

Estimates of the impact of individual measures was undertaken by using a modified form of the conditional demand approach to estimate gross savings and by using survey data to estimate net impacts. Two models were estimated: the first model using change in consumption per dwelling as the outcome variable

Human Perspectives in the Internet Society: Culture, Psychology and Gender, K. Morgan, J. Sanchez, C. A. Brebbia & A Voiskounsky (Editors) © 2004 WIT Press, www.witpress.com, ISBN 1-85312-726-4

and the second model using change in consumption per square foot as the outcome variable. For Model 1, estimated net savings per year are 850 kWh for insulation, 170 kWh for draft proofing, 164 kWh for windows, 274 kWh for water heaters and 118 kWh for CFLs. For Model 2, estimated net savings are 1033 kWh year for insulation, 198 kWh for draft proofing, 153 kWh for windows, 235 kWh for water heaters and 63 kWh for CFLs. These are significant levels of electricity savings.

References

[1] Barnes, R., Gillingham, R. and Hagemann, R. "The Short-Run Demand for Natural Gas," *The Energy Journal,* Vol. 3, No. 1, 1982.

[2] Branch, E.R., "Short-Run Income Elasticity of Demand for Electricity Using Consumer Expenditure Survey Data," *The Energy Journal,* Vol. 14, No. 4, 1993.

[3] Dubin, J.A. and Henson, S.E. "An Engineering/ Econometric Analysis of Seasonal Energy Demand and Conservation in the Pacific Northwest," *Journal of Business and Economic Statistics,* Vol. 6, No. 1, 1988.

[4] Dubin, J.A. and McFadden, D.L., "An Econometric Analysis of Residential Appliance Holdings and Consumption," *Econometrica,* Vol. 52, No. 2, 1984.

[5] Haas, R., Biermayr, P., Zoechling, J. and Auer, H., "Impacts on Electricity Consumption of Household Policy in Austria: A Comparison of Time Series and Cross Section Analysis," *Energy Policy,* Vol. 13, 1998.

[6] Leth-Petersen, S. "Micro Econometric Modelling of Household Energy Use: Testing for Dependence between Electricity and Natural Gas," *The Energy Journal,* Vol. 23, No. 4, 2002.

[7] Madlener, R. "Econometric Analysis of Residential Energy Demand: A Survey," *The Journal of Economic Literature,* Vol. II, No. 2, 1996.

[8] Parti, M. and Parti, C. "The Total and Appliance-Specific Demand for Electricity in the Household Sector," *Bell Journal of Economics,* Vol. 11, No. 1, 1980.

[9] Poyer, D.A. and Williams, M., "Residential Energy Demand: Additional Empirical Evidence by Minority Household Type," *Energy Economics,* Vol. 15, No. 2, 1993.

[10] Reilly, J.M. and Shankle, S.A., "Auxiliary Heating in the Residential Sector," *Energy Economics,* Vol. 10, No. 1, 1988.

Human Perspectives in the Internet Society: Culture, Psychology and Gender, K. Morgan, J. Sanchez, C. A. Brebbia & A Voiskounsky (Editors) © 2004 WIT Press, www.witpress.com, ISBN 1-85312-726-4

Cohesion in online groups

P. Rogers & M. Lea
Dept. Psychology, University of Manchester, UK

Abstract

Groups are traditionally defined in terms of the interpersonal bonds that exist between group members and thus cohesion is based on the strength of those bonds. The transition of this definition of the group onto online groups leads to attempts to emulate face to face behaviour through presentation of group member pictures, video and detailed personal descriptions. However, this can be problematic due to reduced bandwidth and individual cues necessary for supporting interpersonal behaviour. A social identity approach to groups, in contrast, defines the group in terms of group members' cognitive representation of the group identity, rather than interpersonal bonds. From this perspective cohesion is defined in terms of the strength and salience of the group identity and is not dependent on the transference of interpersonal cues, or constrained by group size. Indeed, interpersonal information can act to the detriment of group cohesion. This counter-intuitive approach to cohesion in online groups has a number of implications in terms of group development and group behaviour in online groups. Two longitudinal field studies of computer-mediated collaborative learning groups investigated these issues. Cohesion in the groups was achieved through the application of this approach to both the design of the group tasks and communication environment, and results showed amongst other things, that cohesion was determined by identification with the group, and that this identification was associated with increased accountability, decreased conflict and, furthermore, positively influenced group productivity (measured by the group mark) through group member prototypicality. This paper discusses the theoretical approach outlined here, the specifics of the two longitudinal studies and the wider implications of this approach to online groups.
Keywords: social identity, cohesion, online groups, cmc, prototypicality, group performance.

Human Perspectives in the Internet Society: Culture, Psychology and Gender, K. Morgan, J. Sanchez, C. A. Brebbia & A Voiskounsky (Editors) © 2004 WIT Press, www.witpress.com, ISBN 1-85312-726-4

1 Introduction

Computer-mediated, or online technologies enable group communication that spans traditional geographical and temporal boundaries. Individuals are brought together in work teams, project groups or collaborative learning groups to work collectively via technologies such as asynchronous electronic bulletin boards and synchronous chat facilities. However, despite the many and often discussed advantages that computer-mediated technologies can bring to group communication, the nature of the medium can also lead to difficulties for the effective working of the group. The absence from the relatively anonymous text-based communications of non-verbal cues and other such interpersonal information results in an environment that is markedly different from traditional face-to-face group communication, and can have significant implications for group dynamics. For example, it has been suggested that social influence and thus cohesion in online groups suffers because of the lack of available interpersonal cues [1].

Cohesiveness, which describes a property of the group as a whole, is traditionally conceptualised in terms of interpersonal attraction or bonds between group members, and involves an aggregation of these bonds [2, 3] Moreover, cohesiveness defined in these terms is reported to be positively associated with, and a key element of, group performance and effectiveness [4, 5]. From this perspective, therefore, in order to ensure effective online groups, these groups should be cohesive and to achieve this interpersonal bonds between group members should be supported. Indeed, Greenberg [6] suggests that text based communication is inadequate and that individuals in a group workspace should have at least a voice channel. He goes on to say that, "Electronic virtual workspaces must emulate the affordances of physical workspaces if they are to support a group's natural way of working together" (p. 246). Attempts to emulate face-to-face behaviour, or at least increase interpersonal behaviour, in the computer medium include provision of photographs, video and other individuating information. It is assumed that to support group processes, the focus should be on the interpersonal level, i.e. supporting interpersonal communication between individuals within the group, and the relative anonymity offered by computer-mediated communication should be reduced to a minimum.

An alternative perspective to group cohesion, however, is provided by a social identity approach to groups [7, 8]. This approach suggests that there are two broad classes of identity which can define the self: personal identity, which comprises idiosyncratic personal relationships and traits; and social identity, which defines the self in terms of particular group memberships. Similarly, a distinction is made between personal attraction, or liking based upon interpersonal bonds, and social attraction, which is defined as inter-individual liking based upon perceptions of self and others not in terms of individuality, but of identity related group prototypes. If self-definition is determined by a group identity, group cohesion will not be determined by interpersonal bonds, but by concepts such as the level of group identification and perceptions of group prototypicality. In other words, from a social identity perspective, a group is

Human Perspectives in the Internet Society: Culture, Psychology and Gender, K. Morgan, J. Sanchez, C. A. Brebbia & A Voiskounsky (Editors) © 2004 WIT Press, www.witpress.com, ISBN 1-85312-726-4

defined in terms of the group identity that exists as individuals' cognitive representations and it is this group identity that provides the 'social glue' or sense of belongingness that holds the group together. Furthermore, associated with the group identity are norms which govern group behaviour, and adherence to these norms is, to a large extent, determined by the level of group identification, i.e. the degree to which one identifies with the group. For example, motivation to work for the group should be intrinsically linked to group identification [10].

The social identity approach to groups has a significant advantage over traditional perspectives when considering computer-mediated groups. The information required to convey a social identity is minimal and can be as little as a group name, and so can easily be transmitted to a number of group members through text-based technologies. Even this small amount of information can carry with it norms and behaviours associated with that identity and can foster feelings of group belongingness. This is in stark contrast to that necessary for the transmission of interpersonal cues or information. Furthermore, at any one time either a personal or particular social identity can be prominent or salient [9] and so interpersonal information can in fact detract from the development of a strong social identity. A number of laboratory studies have demonstrated that a reduction of interpersonal cues through anonymity in computer-mediated communication can be harnessed to raise social identity salience of the communication group and overcome the often-cited drawback of computer-mediated interaction at a distance [11, 12, 13].

1.1 Research domain

This paper investigates the social identity approach to online groups in two field studies of collaborative learning students. Students were based at either the University of Manchester or the University of Amsterdam, and in each cohort ten groups consisting of 2 or 3 students from each University participated. Groups collaborated for five weeks to produce a single group report on a given topic. All communication was via a web-based conferencing software, WebBoard, which enabled synchronous chat as well as email and discussion board functionality. Groups were required to communicate during a one and half hour class each week, but were also expected to continue communications outside of this allocated class time. Indeed, in order to complete the assignment, groups found it necessary to communicate extensively over the five week period. Although groups were given some specific tasks to complete each week, they were free to organise themselves as they saw fit. At the end of each week participants completed self-report questionnaires, which measured items such as cohesion, identification, prototypicality, interpersonal liking and accountability on 9-point scales. There was some variation, however, in the content of questionnaires from week to week and between cohorts. The objective performance measure was taken to be the group grade received for the group assignment.

Human Perspectives in the Internet Society: Culture, Psychology and Gender, K. Morgan, J. Sanchez, C. A. Brebbia & A Voiskounsky (Editors) © 2004 WIT Press, www.witpress.com, ISBN 1-85312-726-4

1.2 Research interventions

A number of interventions to the design of the task, instructions and web environment in which students collaborated ensured that the identity of the collaborating group was salient throughout the collaborative period. This included an emphasis on the group rather than individual responsibilities, a completely anonymous initial group meeting (to facilitate sole focus on the group) and an intergroup comparison phase to aid ingroup-definition. In addition the web environments through which groups collaborated were collectivised (as distinct from personalised) throughout the collaborative period. This was achieved with the use of distinct group colours, icons and reflective descriptions focusing on the group, rather than on individual group members. All these interventions were designed to enhance the salience of the collaborating group over and above alternative identities, e.g. nationality, university affiliation as well as personal identity. It was predicted that this would ensure that group members identified with the collaborating group, and consequently saw group members in terms of prototypical, or representative group characteristics, rather than focusing on interpersonal factors.

2 Results

Identification with the collaborating group was measured in both cohorts at weeks 1, 2, 4 and 5. Cohesion was also measured during these times, but only in cohort one. Figure one demonstrates that identification with the group and cohesion increased over time.

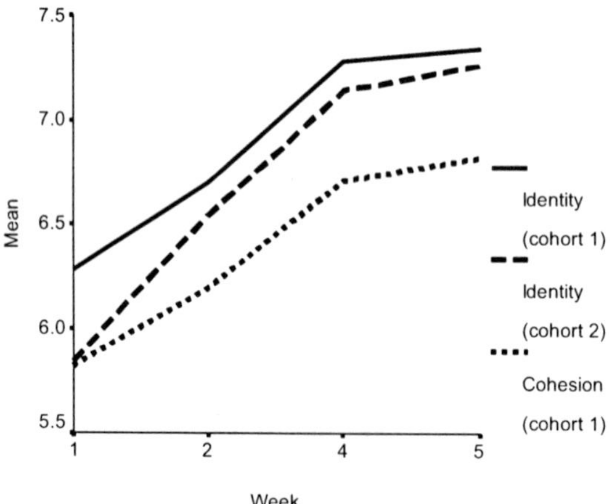

Figure 1: Group identification and cohesion over time.

To confirm that cohesion was based upon group level, rather than interpersonal level perceptions, multiple regression predicted cohesion by group

Human Perspectives in the Internet Society: Culture, Psychology and Gender, K. Morgan, J. Sanchez, C. A. Brebbia & A Voiskounsky (Editors) © 2004 WIT Press, www.witpress.com, ISBN 1-85312-726-4

identification, prototypicality and interpersonal liking. Table 1 displays the results of these regressions at time 2 and time 4 for cohort 1 (prototypicality and interpersonal liking were only measured at these times). Group effects were also investigated, but none were significant. At both times, cohesion was significantly predicted by group identification, rather than other measures, although this was more pronounced during week 2. Group members identified with the collaborating group and thus perceived the group to be cohesive. Interpersonal bonds were therefore not necessary for the group to become cohesive.

Table 1: Regressions predicting cohesion at weeks 2 and 4, *p<0.01.

	Week 2		Week 4	
IV	B	β	B	β
Group Identification	0.98*	0.93	0.46*	0.34
Prototypicality	-0.05	-0.03	0.41	0.28
Interpersonal liking	0.11	0.09	0.33	0.29
R^2	0.90		0.66	

The next question is what effect, if any, does this formulation of cohesion have on group performance, as measured by the final group product? Initial correlation analyses revealed no significant effects of cohesion on the final group product. However, group identification based prototypicality had some positive association with group performance.

This issue was further investigated with path analysis using LISREL 8.54 [14]. The social identity approach posits that identification with a salient social identity, involves a shift away from individual personal identities and towards the perception of the self and others to representatives of the social category. This process assimilates the self and others in terms of the ingroup prototype and encompasses the norms and goals of the group. It was therefore predicted that identification with the group increased prototypicality in the group, which subsequently led to improvements in group performance. Table 2 presents the input correlation matrix for the path analysis.

Table 2: Correlations and descriptives for the LISREL input variables, *p<0.01.

	Group id wk2	Group id wk4	Proto wk2	Proto wk4	Group Mark
Group id wk2	1.00				
Group id wk4	0.57*	1.00			
Proto wk2	0.55*	0.34*	1.00		
Proto wk4	0.45*	0.59*	0.62*	1.00	
Group mark	0.07	0.20	0.37*	0.30	1.00
Mean	6.69	7.28	6.61	6.85	69.09
SD	1.69	1.21	1.26	1.12	6.18

Human Perspectives in the Internet Society: Culture, Psychology and Gender, K. Morgan, J. Sanchez, C. A. Brebbia & A Voiskounsky (Editors) © 2004 WIT Press, www.witpress.com, ISBN 1-85312-726-4

The proposed model is shown in Figure 2. Analysis of the model fit criteria indicated that the model fit the data [$\chi^2(4) = 4.14$, $p = 0.39$, RMSEA = 0.03; AGFI = 0.86; standardised RMR = 0.05] (for a discussion of these fit criteria see Brown and Cudeck [15]). The paths from group identification to prototypicality are significant, as are the longitudinal paths. However, the path from prototypicality at week 4 to group performance is non-significant, as is the path from prototypicality at week 2 to group performance, although this later path is near to an acceptable level. If the model is re-specified, omitting the path from prototypicality at week 4 to group performance, however, then the model remains a good fit [$\chi^2(5) = 4.26$, $p = 0.52$, RMSEA = 0.00; AGFI = 0.89; standardised RMR = 0.05] and the path from prototypicality at week 2 to group performance is stronger and significant ($\beta = 0.28$, $p<0.01$). It seems, therefore, that prototypicality had a greater effect on group performance during the early, rather than later stages of the group development.

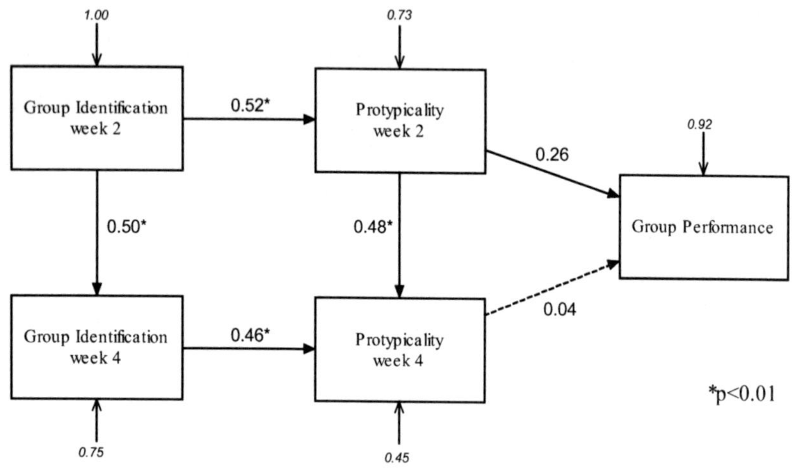

Figure 2: Model of group identification, prototypicality and performance.

This above model was contrasted with alternative models which suggest that social identity based cohesion improved group performance, or that increased interpersonal liking within the group improved performance. If the prototypicality measures in Figure 2 were replaced by cohesion, then the model was a reasonable fit [$\chi^2(4) = 5.00$, $p = 0.29$, RMSEA = 0.08; AGFI = 0.85; standardised RMR = 0.06], but the paths from cohesion at week 2 and 4 were both non-significant and near zero (week 2: $\beta = -0.03$, ns; week 4: $\beta = -0.01$, ns). Removing one or other of these paths had no effect on the effect of cohesion on group performance. Similarly, the model was also adjusted to replace the prototypicality measures with interpersonal liking measures. In this instance the model did not fit the data fit [$\chi^2(4) = 6.07$, $p = 0.19$, RMSEA = 0.11;

Human Perspectives in the Internet Society: Culture, Psychology and Gender, K. Morgan, J. Sanchez, C. A. Brebbia & A Voiskounsky (Editors) © 2004 WIT Press, www.witpress.com, ISBN 1-85312-726-4

AGFI = 0.80; standardised RMR = 0.07], although all but the paths from interpersonal liking to group performance were significant. The path analysis therefore demonstrated that it was prototypicality that influenced group performance rather than cohesion. Both cohesion and prototypicality were grounded in group identification and are therefore related constructs (correlation between cohesion and prototypicality week 2, r=0.53, p<0.01; week 4, r=0.70, p<0.01). However, where cohesion is a perception of group unity as a whole, prototypicality takes into account the relative impact of each group member as representative of the group, and reflects a perception of a group of 'team players'. This will be expanded upon in the discussion below.

Thus far, the results have focused on the constructs investigated during cohort one and have demonstrated the crucial nature of group identification in both group definition and behaviour. This theme was continued during cohort two and although there is not space to go into details here, some brief observations are possible. For example, group identification was associated with increased posts to the discussion board (week 2: r=0.35, p<0.05; week 4: r=0.34, p<0.05; week 5: r=0.33, p<0.05), and efficacy (week 1: r=0.59, p<0.01; week 2: r=0.65, p<0.01; week 4: r=0.64, p<0.01; week 5: r=0.75, p<0.01). It was also correlated with conflict resolution measures (week 2: r=0.42, p<0.01); reduced task and personal conflict (week 4: r=-0.36, p<0.05; r=-0.44, p<0.01, respectively); and with increased feelings of accountability (week 1: r=0.54, p<0.01; week 2: r=0.77, p<0.01; week 4: r=0.80, p<0.01; week 5: r=0.54, p<0.01). Furthermore, in both cohorts, group identification and prototypicality were shown to be instrumental in intragroup leadership emergence and support [16].

3 Discussion

This paper has presented an approach to computer-mediated groups that is theory led and thus amounts to more than mere provision of group communication tools. Furthermore, the approach is counter-intuitive, claiming that rather than attempting to emulate face to face interaction in the computer medium, interactions that are appropriate to the medium should be encouraged. It is then possible to use the anonymous nature of computer-mediated communication to the advantage of collaborating groups rather than trying to overcome it. This is achieved through a re-conceptualisation of the group from one based upon interpersonal bonds, to one based upon a shared social, or group, identity. From this perspective, group cohesion is based upon the group identity, but it is this identity and perception of the group members' in terms of this identity, rather than cohesion per se, that determines subsequent group behaviour. In addition to the results described above, anecdotal evidence from the field study cohorts provides further demonstrations of the strength and nature of a salient group identity. For example, in cohort two, one (all female) group was allocated the group name 'Pink' and consequently their collaborative web environment was coloured pink. Throughout the collaborative period, this group referred to themselves as the 'Pink ladies' and arranged to all be dressed in pink for the final video-conferencing session, in which they presented their work to the rest of

Human Perspectives in the Internet Society: Culture, Psychology and Gender, K. Morgan, J. Sanchez, C. A. Brebbia & A Voiskounsky (Editors) © 2004 WIT Press, www.witpress.com, ISBN 1-85312-726-4

the groups. This further demonstrates that the shared identity, based as it was initially on a colour, had significant behavioural implications for the group.

Group identification, although instrumental in much group behaviour, did not have a direct impact on group performance. Simply because an individual identifies with a particular group, does not guarantee group success. However, perceived prototypicality in the group did positively affect group performance, although only at the earlier stages of group development. This demonstrates that it is important, not only for each individual group member to be working for the group, but that they perceive that other members of the group are acting in the same way, i.e. demonstrate the characteristics of 'team players'. It is suggested that this is particularly important in small distributed groups working in a computer medium where it is not always clear what the other group members are doing. Identification with the salient group and prototypicality are closely related constructs, i.e. as a shared social identity and therefore individual identification with the group is primed at the beginning of the collaborative period, prototypicality emerges as a consequence of this identification. In addition, prototypicality can also affect subsequent levels of identification with the group. These two constructs of identification and prototypicality differ, however, in a number of ways. Firstly, prototypicality is more context dependent than group identification and is subsequently more likely to be sensitive to comparative context (e.g. intergroup comparisons); and secondly, prototypicality is concerned with the position of the individual group member relative to other group members, whereas group identification reflects the extent to which the group as a category is integrated into the self [17]. Within the framework of a shared social identity, prototypicality therefore encompasses the norms and perceptions of the whole group and can have a significant effect on the output performance of the group.

The central premise of this paper is that the group should be defined in terms of a shared group identity rather than interpersonal bonds between individual group members. Furthermore, the emphasis at all times should be on the shared social identity rather than alternative category memberships or personal identities. However, it should be made clear that it is not the position that groups should consist of homogenous group members who show no intragroup differentiation. Instead, it is argued that when the focus is on the shared group identity, intragroup differentiation takes place that is based upon group prototypicality. Therefore, individual group members can take on different roles and demonstrate individual talents, but it must be perceived that these are for the benefit of the group rather than the individual. In addition, friendships and interpersonal bonds between group members will develop over time and are not discouraged. These are natural developments. However, it should not be the role of the design process to increase the salience of personal identities as this would detract from the goal of the group. This is particularly important during the early stages of the group development when a group identity has not been established. This is in contrast to traditional 'ice-breaking' tasks where the personal identity is made salient during the initial group meeting and then personalising tasks continue the attempt to foster interpersonal bonds.

Human Perspectives in the Internet Society: Culture, Psychology and Gender, K. Morgan, J. Sanchez, C. A. Brebbia & A Voiskounsky (Editors) © 2004 WIT Press, www.witpress.com, ISBN 1-85312-726-4

The results of this research presented above have been specifically addressed to collaborative learning groups using computer-mediated communication. However, many of the implications are relevant, not only to learning groups, but to any group communicating via CMC technologies, e.g. distributed research groups or project groups. If the nature of the group is re-conceptualised from one based upon interpersonal bonds to one based upon a shared social identity, the salient group identity can ensure a cohesive group whose members are motivated to work for the group due to their shared identity. This is in contrast to groups that consist of individuals whose salient identity may be, for example, personal, departmental, organisational or national, and can have significant impact on group behaviour and performance. In focusing on the group's commonalities, rather than differences, it is hoped that the group can become more successful and efficient.

Acknowledgement

Financial support for this paper was provided by a project grant from the UK EPSRC (Multimedia and Networking Applications Programme, GR/M25933).

References

[1] Kiesler, S., Siegel, J. & McGuire, T.W. (1984). Social psychological aspects of computer-mediated communication. *American Psychologist, 39*, 1123-1134.

[2] Cartwright, D. (1968). The nature of group cohesiveness. In D. Cartwright and A. Zander (Eds.), *Group dynamics: research and theory*, pp. 91-109. Tavistock: London.

[3] Yang, H. & Tang, H. (2004). Team structure and team performance in IS development: a social network perspective. *Information and Management, 41* (3), 335-349.

[4] Beal, D., Cohen, R., Burke, M. & McLendon, C. (2003). Cohesion and performance in groups: A meta-analytic clarification of construct relations. *Journal of Applied Psychology, 88* (6), 989-1004.

[5] Chang, A. & Bordia, P. (2001). A multidimensional approach to the group cohesion – group performance relationship. *Small Group Research, 32* (4), 379-405.

[6] Greenberg, S. (1998). Collaborative interfaces for the Web. In J. Ratner, C. Forsyth & E. Grose (Eds.), *Human factors and Web development*. Lawrence Erlbaum: New Jersey.

[7] Hogg, M. A. & Abrams, D. (1988). *Social Identifications: A social psychology of intergroup relations and group processes*. London: Routledge.

[8] Turner, J. C. (1984). Social Identification and psychological group formation. In H. Tajfel (Ed.), *The social dimension: European developments in social psychology* (Vol. 2, pp. 518-538). Cambridge University Press: Cambridge.

Human Perspectives in the Internet Society: Culture, Psychology and Gender, K. Morgan, J. Sanchez, C. A. Brebbia & A Voiskounsky (Editors) © 2004 WIT Press, www.witpress.com, ISBN 1-85312-726-4

[9] Turner, J. C.(1987). *Rediscovering the social group: a self-categorization theory.* Basil Blackwell: Oxford.

[10] Haslam, S. A. (2001). Psychology in Organizations: The Social Identity Approach. Sage: London.

[11] Rogers, P. & Lea, M. (manuscript in preparation) Modelling anonymity processes in computer-mediated groups.

[12] Lea, M., Spears, R. & De Groot, D. (2001). Knowing me, knowing you: Effects of visual anonymity on self-categorization, stereotyping and attraction in computer-mediated groups. *Personality and Social Psychology Bulletin, 27* (5), 526-537.

[13] Spears, R. & Lea, M. (1994). Panacea or panopticon? The hidden power in computer-mediated communication. *Communication Research, 21*, 427-459.

[14] Jöreskog, K. G. & Sörbom, D. (1999). *LISREL 8.3*. Scientific Software Inc.: Chicago.

[15] Brown, Browne, M. & Cudeck, R. (1993). Alternative ways of assessing model fit. In K. Bollen & J. Long (Eds.), *Testing Structural Equation Models*. Sage: London.

[16] Rogers, P. & Lea, M. (under review). Cognitive and Strategic Processes in Prototypicality Based Leadership Emergence and Evaluation. *Journal of Personality and Social Psychology.*

[17] Jetten, J., Spears, R. & Manstead, A. (1997). Distinctiveness threat and prototypicality: combined effects on intergroup discrimination and collective self-esteem. *European Journal of Social Psychology, 27,* 635-657.

Human Perspectives in the Internet Society: Culture, Psychology and Gender, K. Morgan, J. Sanchez, C. A. Brebbia & A Voiskounsky (Editors) © 2004 WIT Press, www.witpress.com, ISBN 1-85312-726-4

Section 4
New interaction methods

Do short texts imply small thoughts? An investigation of the semantic networks associated with restricted and non-restricted text production

G. B. Svendsen[1], J. A. K. Johnsen[2] & B. Evjemo[1]
[1]*Telenor R&D, Tromsø, Norway*
[2]*Norwegian Centre for Telemedicine, Tromsø, Norway*

Abstract

Short Messaging System (SMS) and similar technologies restrict the amount of text that can be utilized in communication. The present study aimed to investigate how the restricting aspects of such technologies affect the time used to reproduce a message, and the mental processing of the content of that message. The results show no differences in time spent writing. However, a reaction time task indicates that participants with restricted text space, compared to non-restricted participants, have a wider range of story-related concepts readily available in working memory. Areas of future research are outlined.
Keywords: SMS, message analysis, memory, mental processing.

1 Introduction

The use of the SMS text messaging system has increased dramatically the last years. For instance, in Norway a country with population of about 4,5 mill, 515 137 000 SMS messages were sent in 1999 and 2 540 759 000 in 2002 [1], representing a fivefold increase over three years. An obvious characteristic of SMS is the constraint it places on the amount of text the user can put into the message. An SMS has a maximum of 160 characters. Thus the average length of a SMS message has been reported to be about six words [2], and between 71 and 123 characters [3]. This is in contrast to email and word–processing where one study [4] reports that an average e-mail contains about 700 words and is significantly shorter than word-processed text that contain about 1000.

Human Perspectives in the Internet Society: Culture, Psychology and Gender, K. Morgan, J. Sanchez, C. A. Brebbia & A Voiskounsky (Editors) © 2004 WIT Press, www.witpress.com, ISBN 1-85312-726-4

While the impact of SMS messaging has been assessed in relation to many aspects of private life, for instance micro coordination [5], gift giving [6], and building relationships [5], as far as we know, the effects of reduced text space per se have not been investigated. Thus the purpose of this paper is to explore if a reduction in usable text space, i.e. number of characters that can be used to write a message, have any effect on the time it takes to compose a message and how it influences the manner in which the writer thinks about the message he or she produces.

These questions are relevant for the design of messaging systems, and for our understanding of the impact of these systems at large. For instance, if subjects spend more time producing a short message than a long message about the same subject matter, it can be argued that user interfaces demanding short text input, forces the user to expend excess mental effort. On a broader scale, two arguments are feasible; that putting constraints on textual expressions leads to reduced reflection, or that constraints on expression lead to more thorough reflection on the subject matter. Which, if any, of these hypotheses are supported have relevance for how we assess the widespread use of short text messaging. Is it another step towards an "amusing ourselves to death" society [7], or just another technology that contributes to the "death of distance" [8]?

2 Method

In order to investigate these questions an experiment was conducted.

2.1 Participants

Forty participants aged between 31 and 61 (mean age 46.3) were recruited from a large corporation. 33 participants were male, 7 were female. Females were distributed evenly in the two experimental conditions. The participants were employed in several areas, spanning management, sales, research, maintenance, and clerical work. Thus, despite coming from the same corporation the participants comprised a heterogeneous group. As a compensation for their partaking, participants were included in a lottery with a total value of about $100.

2.2 Design

The participants' main task was to read a short story and write a summary of it. The experiment had two conditions, a short text group (ST) and a long text group (LT). In the ST group the summary or message could not exceed 80 characters. In the LT group, there was no restriction on message length. There was no time limit on the production of the summary, and the short story was displayed on screen as the participants wrote the summaries. The 80-character limit was selected to approximate the mean SMS message length when sent by phone [3].

The story read by the participants had 70 words, 395 characters (with space), and spanned five and a half lines. The story described a happy boy walking home from school on a warm and beautiful summer day. At home, the house was decorated for celebration. A party was held, including speeches about his bright future (a Norwegian tradition). His grades were also announced, and they were all average. He was applauded and felt at home and happy.

It is hard to obtain a good measure of how much the participants have considered or deliberated a story. In the present study a semantic network paradigm was employed for this purpose. In this paradigm, reaction time (RT) to a stimulus is utilized as an indication of the activation and availability of a given concept in consciousness [9]. Low RT signifies that a concept is readily available and/or activated; while high RT signifies that the concept is less activated and/or available. Thus, by using concepts that are on differing distance from the core of the story as stimulus material, differences in RT between the conditions would signify that the conditions have invoked different thought patterns in the participants.

Two classes of concepts were used: Concepts that were close to the story core (CC), and concepts that were far removed from the core (RC). Close to the core concepts were concepts that could be found in the story, concepts that were closely linked to he episodes in the story, and concepts that were indicative of the caring family described therein. Examples include "school", "summer" and "love". Removed from the core concepts included concepts that were indicative of the small anomaly in the story (big celebration and average grades) and concepts that had no obvious relation to the story. Examples include "denial" and "truck". In total, 30 concepts were employed, with 15 in each concept class.

With regards to the CC concepts it is hypothesized that there will be no difference in RT since the concepts will be activated in both conditions more or less equally. However, the condition that gives rise to most thorough analysis of the story is expected to result in lowest RT on the RC concepts. The reason is twofold. First, a more thorough analysis of the story would probably activate concepts that have to do with the story's anomaly, thus lowering the RT to the anomaly concepts. Second, thinking through the story will make it clearer what is and what is not a part of it, thus making the RT to the non related items shorter [10].

The design is factorial with the fixed factor, condition, with levels ST and LT and one repeated measure factor, concept type, with levels CC and RC. A significant interaction between the factors would indicate different levels of text analysis in the two conditions.

2.3 Procedure and material

The participants were randomly assigned to the two experimental conditions when arriving at the laboratory. They were then informed about the experimental procedure by the research assistant running the experiment.

A trial version of Inquisit was used to run the experiment [11]. The program was run on a Hewlet Pacard Omnibook 500 laptop computer, with a 256 MB ram, a 600 MHz processor and a 15 inch LCD color display. Participants used the keyboard when responding. For the RT trails, the CRTL key was labeled 'Yes' and the ALT key was labeled 'No' (both keys left side of keyboard).

Human Perspectives in the Internet Society: Culture, Psychology and Gender, K. Morgan, J. Sanchez, C. A. Brebbia & A Voiskounsky (Editors) © 2004 WIT Press, www.witpress.com, ISBN 1-85312-726-4

The experiment consisted of three parts. First, the participants were told to read through a short story. Second, after finishing reading the story they were prompted to write a summary of the story. In the small text condition they were informed that the summary could not be over 80 characters, and that characters over 80 would not be entered or stored. In the large text condition subjects were not informed of any limitations with respect to length. This difference was further emphasized by physically reducing the size of the text input window in the small space condition. Third, after finishing the summaries the participants were told that the short story they had just read had in fact been part of a longer story, and that they were to make judgments whether words that would appear on the screen had been part of, or could have been part of, the story. The participants were requested to make their decisions as fast as possible, and within 3000 milliseconds. Responses were given using the 'Yes' and 'No' labeled keys. The stimuli words were presented centered on screen, in font Courier New, size 49, and random ordering. Before this task, the subjects completed a training session where they were asked to decide whether the words they were presented described fruits or not. After completing the task the subjects were thanked for their participation and asked not to tell anybody what had transpired in the experiment.

Table 1: Mean number of characters and mean time to completion in seconds in the two conditions. Standard deviation in parenthesis.

Condition	#Characters	Time to completion
Short Text	76.3 (6.6)	236.8 (136.9)
Long Text	193.4 (69.4)	207.6 (161.7)

3 Results

Five participants were removed from the data analysis because they had ignored the instruction and made no effort to keep their message under 80 characters. Thus, the total number of participants were reduced to 35, with 20 participants in the LT condition and 15 in the ST condition.

The mean length of the text in characters and the mean time to produce the text in the two groups are presented in Table 1.

The difference between mean text lengths in the two conditions is highly significant as shown by a t-test ($p < .00001$, $t = 6.49$, $df = 33$), while the difference in time to produce text is not significant. Restricting text length thus had the desired effect. Also, the *SD* of the ST condition was about a tenth of the *SD* in the LT condition, signifying a ceiling effect. However, as reported, the reduction in text length had no effect on the time it took to complete the task. In fact, the mean time to complete the task is slightly longer in the ST condition than in the LT condition, indicating that the subjects in the ST condition expended more mental effort to produce the short text. This is in line with casual

Human Perspectives in the Internet Society: Culture, Psychology and Gender, K. Morgan, J. Sanchez, C. A. Brebbia & A Voiskounsky (Editors) © 2004 WIT Press, www.witpress.com, ISBN 1-85312-726-4

observations made throughout the experiment. Subjects in the ST condition appeared to have more difficulty completing the task.

3.1 Reaction time to concept types

No difference was found in RT between 'Yes' (M = 1300.94 ms, SD = 467.76) or 'No' (M = 1269.92 ms, SD = 456.32) responses across concept types.

Figure 1 shows the mean reaction times to the two sets of concepts in the two groups. As can be seen, the ST group has lower reaction times to the concepts that are removed from the story core. A repeated measures ANOVA shows no main effects, but a significant interaction ($p < .05$, $F = 4.3$, $df = 1,33$). This indicates that a restriction on text length leads to a more thorough mental processing of the text.

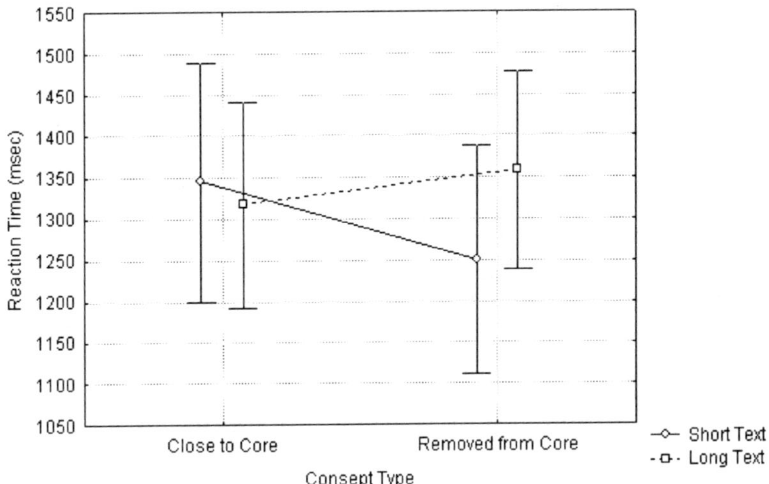

Figure 1: Mean reaction time in the four conditions. Vertical bars denote 95% confidence interval.

4 Conclusion

There is no indication that short text conditions lead to less consideration of the subject matter. On the contrary, forced limitation of text length appears to require more effort and a more thorough mental processing of the subject matter. This result ties in with studies showing that user-interface induced effort leads to more deliberate problem solving [12].

5 Further research

As the methodology utilized here is strictly experimental, the external validity of the results is questionable. Further, the lack of communication between

Human Perspectives in the Internet Society: Culture, Psychology and Gender, K. Morgan, J. Sanchez, C. A. Brebbia & A Voiskounsky (Editors) © 2004 WIT Press, www.witpress.com, ISBN 1-85312-726-4

individuals in our tasks negates a straightforward link to SMS or similar technologies (for instance IM). To extend the relevance of the present results, interaction between participants needs to be included.

It is tempting to suggest that the effects observed in this study may also apply to the perception of the recipient of the message. In other words, when a person has a limited number of characters available to her/him, it becomes more important for this person to judge the recipient of the message in order to ensure that her/his message is effectively conveyed. Thus, people communicating through similarly restricted media might consider in more detail the attributes, values, and attitudes of their communication partners (or be more motivated to do so). This, again, might throw light on the popularity of lightweight communication technologies for relationship building and maintenance. RT paradigms, similar to the one utilized in this study, may prove useful for investigating these matters.

References

[1] Statistical Yearbook of Norway www.ssb.no/aarbok/tab/t-101250-519.html.

[2] Ling, R. The Socio-Linguistics of SMS: An Analysis of SMS use by a Random Sample of Norwegians. In *Front Stage/Back Stage: Mobile communication and the Renegotiation of the Social Sphere,* Conference Proceedings, eds. R. Ling & P. Pedersen, Grimstad, Norway, 22-24 June, 2003.

[3] Grinter, R. & Eldridge, M. y do tngrs luv 2 txt msg? *Proc. of the ECSCW '01.* Kluwer Academic Publishers: Dordrecht, The Netherlands, pp. 219-238, 2001.

[4] Beisenbach-Lucas, S. & Weasenforth, D. E-mail and word processing in the ESL classroom: How the medium affects the message. *Language Learning and Technology,* **5**, pp. 135-165, 2001.

[5] Ling, R., and Yttri, B. Hyper-coordination via mobile phones in Norway. In *Perpetual contact: Mobile communication, private talk, public performance,* eds. J.E. Katz & M. Aakhus, Cambridge University Press: Cambridge, pp. 139-169, 2002.

[6] Taylor, A.S. & Harper, R. Age-old practices in the "New World": A study of gift giving between teenage mobile phone users. *Proc.of the CHI 2002, CHI Letters*, **4**, pp. 439-446.

[7] Postman, N. *Amusing ourselves to death: Public discourse in the age of show business*. Viking Press: New York, 1986.

[8] Cairncross, F. *The death of distance: The trendspotter's guide to new communications*. Harward Business School Press: Boston, USA, 1997.

[9] Higgins, E. T. Knowledge activation: Accessibility, applicability, and salience. *Social Psychology: Handbook of Basic Principles,* eds. E. T. Higgins & A. W. Kruglanski, Guilford Press: New York, pp. 133-168, 1996.

Human Perspectives in the Internet Society: Culture, Psychology and Gender, K. Morgan, J. Sanchez, C. A. Brebbia & A Voiskounsky (Editors) © 2004 WIT Press, www.witpress.com, ISBN 1-85312-726-4

[10] Glass, A. L. & Holyoak, K. J. Alternative conceptions of semantic memory. Cognition, **3**, pp. 313-339, 1975.

[11] Inquisit 1.33 [Computer software]. Millisecond Software: Seattle, WA, USA, 2002.

[12] O'Hara, K.P & Payne, S.J. Planning and the user interface: The effects of lockout time and error recovery cost. *International Journal of Human-Computer Studies*, **50**, pp. 41-59, 1999.

Human Perspectives in the Internet Society: Culture, Psychology and Gender, K. Morgan, J. Sanchez, C. A. Brebbia & A Voiskounsky (Editors) © 2004 WIT Press, www.witpress.com, ISBN 1-85312-726-4

ICT – the solution of communication hurdles in the modern family?

E. Mauritzson-Sandberg & T. Nordmark
Department of Human Work Sciences,
Luleå University of Technology, Sweden

Abstract

The daily life situation for the family has changed drastically over the last few decades and during the same period of time the development within the area of information and communication technology (ICT) has, more or less, exploded. In this paper the two different development curves are combined in order to study the impact of new ICT applications on the daily life situation of the families of today. The two studies presented in this paper focuses primarily on the communication within families with children. The first study aims at mapping the patterns of communication within targeted families and their attitudes to, and need for, different ICT applications. In the second, trial set-ups of different ICT applications are evaluated. The results show that, although the families were assessing themselves as positive to, and experienced in using, ICT the response was moderate. The main reason for this was the lack of time to learn new ways of communicating within the family even though in the long-run it could be the real time-saver.
Keywords: information and communication technology, ICT, family, communication, coordination.

1 A new and different situation for the modern family

The situation for families of today has drastically changed during the last decades. Earlier, a majority of women were stay-at-home mothers. Nowadays, the economic reality, more or less, requires both parents to work outside the home. In the 1960s about 70 per cent of the women in Sweden were stay-at-home mothers while the corresponding figure in the 1980s had decreased to 20 per cent [1]. Valerie Frissen [2] labelled the part of life when fulltime work

Human Perspectives in the Internet Society: Culture, Psychology and Gender, K. Morgan, J. Sanchez, C. A. Brebbia & A Voiskounsky (Editors) © 2004 WIT Press, www.witpress.com, ISBN 1-85312-726-4

has to be matched with pre-scholars as "the rush hour of life". With this she points at how hard this part of the life could be with a large amount of stress from trying to match parents' work hours with children's school and leisure activities. Frissen [2] inquired in his study if ICT can be a solution for the problems families of today face in matching parents' work hours with children's school and leisure activities, and if so, might the result be more time for other activities within the families? All parents have probably sometime felt that there never is any time left when all household cores are taken care of. The following story meritorious manifests this dilemma:

"It is in the beginning of the day and during shortest possible time all family members have to get out of their beds and everyone has to be in time for their specific activities. You make breakfast, get clothes for the children, take a shower, pack the schoolbags for the children, make sandwiches for the picnic, or see to that the kids have money for their school travels. Then you try to get the car to start, leave the kids at their day care or schools, and rush away to get to work on schedule. Somewhere between 3 to 5 pm it is time to pick up the children, go shopping, make dinner, clean the table, make the laundry, pick up and leave the children on different leisure activities, and attend a meeting at your children's school. All this at the same time as you try to give time to, notice, and show interest in each child. Then it is time for "the go to bed procedure" with tooth brushing, fairytale reading and getting the children to go to sleep. Around 9 a clock pm you throw yourself in the couch to, in a more or less mentally absent condition, try to understand what the television newsreader is talking about." (translated from Plantin [3]).

2 The fast development of ICT

The development in the information and communication technology area is tremendously fast. Cellular phones have changed from being dreadfully large in size with clumsy batteries to be incredibly small and tiny, though, at times at the expense of their usability. Personal computers have gone from being a rather rare private appliance to be an, more or less, indispensability in every home. The Swedish Institute for Transport and Communications Analysis showed in their annually report, "*Facts about information and communication technology in Sweden 2002*", that about 65 per cent of the Swedes have access to a personal computer as well as to a mobile phone. Furthermore, that about 50 per cent of the Swedes are connected to the Internet although the percentage of the elderly (above the age of 65 years) is much lower. However, in the ages of 25 to 44 years old were most of families with children belong the corresponding per cent is about 70 regarding access to a mobile phone, about 80 regarding a personal computer, and about 70 regarding Internet connection [4]. A hypothesis is that the noted increase in access to mobile phones, among other things, also has boosted the daily communication between parents in families with children in order to improve the logistics of their every day life.

Human Perspectives in the Internet Society: Culture, Psychology and Gender, K. Morgan, J. Sanchez, C. A. Brebbia & A Voiskounsky (Editors) © 2004 WIT Press, www.witpress.com, ISBN 1-85312-726-4

3 Study 1

3.1 Respondents, material, and procedure

The families varied in configuration from having one child to three children. The ages of the children varied between 4 months of age to 21 years of age. In one family the parents were divorced and lived in separate households. The parents were in the ages between 28 and 46 years. All, except from one, were in full time work. Each of the parents was interviewed for about 45 to 75 minutes. The interview was composed of three different parts. The first part consisted of questions of sociodemographics such as what technical devices the person used for communication and with which frequency. The aim of the second part was to create a map of the subjects' communication patterns. During the interview the interviewer drew a map of who the subject communicated with, in which way, and what the purpose of the communication was. After the map was created the subject was asked to look at it, reflect over its correctness and to disclose how satisfied he or she was with it. When a subject was not fully satisfied the question was asked if he or she could suggest how it actually should be. In the third, and last, part of the interview scenarios of possible ICT solutions were presented. These were assessed by the subjects by answering two questions. The questions were about interest in the scenario in question and interest in buying such an ICT application. The idea behind this was that interest is a necessary concept for acceptance but not enough. The question about buying has of course its limits in that no cost could be set in this stage of the project. The assumption was therefore that the cost would be comparable to other similar functions that are available today.

3.2 Coordination

All of the interviewed parents mentioned that they communicated by phone about the logistics of everyday life activities. Naturally, within those families where parents had high job demands and children with lots of leisure activities the need for an effective intra-family communication was larger.

The intra-family communication most often was about who should be responsible for dinner, who should pick up the children from their day care and schools, and who should be responsible for the leisure activities in the evening. These questions were, of course, dependent on family configurations but all had these daily contacts. One mother said: *"Since we got the mobile phones we don't plan our days as well as before and lot of the calls we make shouldn't need to be done."* At the same as she is somewhat critical to the new ways of communicating she also acknowledges the easy way of connecting with other family members.

Another interesting area concerns the question of who should be responsible for initiating the intra-family communication as well as who is responsible for bringing agreed decisions to a conclusion. Most often, in reality the mothers had the main responsibility for initiating intra-family communication and bringing

Human Perspectives in the Internet Society: Culture, Psychology and Gender, K. Morgan, J. Sanchez, C. A. Brebbia & A Voiskounsky (Editors) © 2004 WIT Press, www.witpress.com, ISBN 1-85312-726-4

agreed decisions to a conclusion although several of the families stated a fifty/fifty share. Actually, it was quite rare that the father had the responsibility. In line with this, Orth-Gomér [5] showed that male managers had one peak in their stress curve in the middle of the day while female managers had one in the middle of the day and one in the evening when the unpaid work at home begins. The fact that the mothers more often are responsible for initiating the intra-family communication as well as for bringing agreed decisions to a conclusion is an interesting finding regarding the development of ICT applications since they are the ones most benefiting from it. Earlier research has also shown that women have another approach to technology then men [6]. Women tend to see technologies as a pure tool meant to ease up their lives and not as a good thing just by itself or as a tool for entertainment such as, for instance, computer gaming. Concerning computer games users of this are, more or less, only men. Aune [6] categorize users of personal computers into three different groups depending on kind of relation to the computer. In the first category the personal computer is perceived as a work tool, in the second both as a work and a leisure tool, and in the third the using in itself is in foci. Among these, women are most likely to be found in the first. Women do not use the personal computer just for fun or entertainment and therefore the usefulness becomes central.

To finalize, although the respondents in this study seemed rather satisfied with the intra-family communication within their families they were open for improvements. One such suggested improvement was ideas about a calendar possible to synchronize between family members. Out of this, an ICT application was developed and tried out by 13 families.

4 Study 2

4.1 Test pilots and procedure

Thirteen families with children volunteered for the trial set-up. The families consisted of two parents in the ages between 25 and 48 years. There was between two and three children in each family. The ages of the children varied between 1 and 20 years of age. Each parent, or test pilot, was asked to judge their family's interest in new ICT applications and their competence in using them. The results show that all families were highly interested in, and experienced with, using ICT. On a 7-point graphical scale the average of interest and experience were 5.6 and 5.4, respectively. The ICT applications used for the trial set-up were possible to reach from the family's own homepages and they were protected by individual user names and passwords.

4.2 Material

The trial set-up originally consisted of four different ICT applications but only two of them, the Bulletin Board and the Shopping List, were applicable to the problems described by the families in Study 1. On the Bulletin Board it was possible to post notes of activities to bring to a conclusion. The notes could be

Human Perspectives in the Internet Society: Culture, Psychology and Gender, K. Morgan, J. Sanchez, C. A. Brebbia & A Voiskounsky (Editors) © 2004 WIT Press, www.witpress.com, ISBN 1-85312-726-4

sent to the mobile phones used within the families and they were possible to reach from any personal computer connected to the Internet. The Shopping List was a complement to the Bulletin Board. Items that were to be shopped could be typed in onto the list and then picked up by the mobile phone.

4.3 Evaluation of the bulletin board

The Bulletin Board was used by all test pilots and it was the application that got the most positive reactions and, hence, perceived as the most useful. However, there were also some drawbacks such as, for instance, the placement of the personal computer within the home as well as the necessity of always having the computer running. *"The computer isn't accessible all 24 hour of the day like the fridge door is",* in other words, it is easier to put notes on the fridge door than to go to the computer, warm it up, and start using it. Another thing that was criticized was that it was impossible to send a note just to one single family member. All notes sent reached all the members of the family. Finally, some responses to the trial set-up:

- *Useful but it would be better if the note could be sent to a specific person.*
- *It was useful in that the other family member could get the notes via SMS.*
- *The best thing is that the notes could be sent by SMS.*
- *The idea with the Bulletin Board is good but it becomes somewhat crowded when the notes are placed over each other. We miss the opportunity to prioritize the importance of the notes*
- *To hard to use it is much easier to write notes on paper or make a phone call.*

4.4 Evaluation of the shopping list

The Shopping List was a complement to the Bulletin Board and it was introduced in the middle of the test. The response to this application was quite negative. It seemed difficult to use and there were problems with connecting the list with the mobile phone. This was supposed to be done with the help of a WAP service but it didn't really work. Some responses from the families were:

- *Didn't really get it to work.*
- *Good idea. A little bit tricky to distribute the list to the cellular phone.*
- *Hard to let go of old routines (paper end pen).*
- *Perfect, easy to use and really useful with the handheld computer were you can draw a line over the things that you already have picked.*
- *Haven't used and can't see the usefulness of this solutions.*

4.5 Further trial set-ups with improved equipment

Two of the families were given the opportunity to try out improved versions of the Bulletin Board and the Shopping List. The improvements consisted of a

Human Perspectives in the Internet Society: Culture, Psychology and Gender, K. Morgan, J. Sanchez, C. A. Brebbia & A Voiskounsky (Editors) © 2004 WIT Press, www.witpress.com, ISBN 1-85312-726-4

handheld computer. One of the families seemed very satisfied with the improvements while the other was more negative. The former perceived the improved version as easier to use and that the graphics as better while the latter thought that the only thing that had happened was that there was an additional applicant to worry about. Although the response was somewhat negative it probably is important with which equipment the applications are tried out.

4.6 Time as a limit

An important issue is what the families refer to as lack of time. When the families described why they did not use the solutions more frequent they referred to lack of time" *Takes to long time, - It takes time to make a new technology a part of everyday life, - Lack of time"*. This is of course of interest when doing user tests. Maybe the test period should had been over a longer period of time than the 6 weeks this test run. Moreover, the test period was scheduled in late spring and it could be that this time of the year is the busiest and, hence, there was no time for learning the new technology. Although these solutions were created for saving time they were more perceived as consuming time.

5 Discussion

First and foremost, the results of the above presented studies show that the families that participated had a huge interest in, and were quit experienced with using, ICT. Moreover, that the everyday life of the families of today seemed to be quite stressful and that they had some problems with the logistic communication within their families. The Bulletin Board and the Shopping List were designed to solve these problems. However, the participating families were not overwhelmingly enthusiastic about more ICT applications and the disparity between the designers' point of view and end-users are still obvious. The Shopping List is a good example of what is called user unfriendliness. It is also clear that it is not common that people use ICT just for the fun.

In only one case the placement of the personal computer could be considered as central while it in all others was in the bedroom, or the children room, which clearly hindered its use. And ease of use and usefulness is central aspects in designing new ICT applications. It is also of importance to further study if users really are interested in additional applications or if existing ones could be redesigned to include new inventions.

As mentioned the time aspect seems critical in adjusting to new technologies both in general and in more specific cases like this. This problem could of course be a symptom of this specific test set-up but probably it also tells us a lot of how the situation in everyday life is.

In every part of human life were communication is done over distance it is important to consider what the social consequences might be. Maybe some part of the resistance against ICT might be traced back to the human need for factual meetings rather than just meetings in virtual environment?

Human Perspectives in the Internet Society: Culture, Psychology and Gender, K. Morgan, J. Sanchez, C. A. Brebbia & A Voiskounsky (Editors) © 2004 WIT Press, www.witpress.com, ISBN 1-85312-726-4

References

[1] Bäck-Wiklund, M., Bergsten, B., *Det moderna föräldraskapet : en studie av familj och kön i förändring, (The modern parenthood : a study of family and gender in change)*, Natur och kultur, Stockholm, 1997.

[2] Frissen, V., ICTs in the rush hour of life, *Information Society*, Jan-Mar2000, Vol. 16, Issue 1 pp. 65-75.

[3] Plantin, L., *Män, familjeliv och föräldraskap, (Men, family life and parenthood)* Boréa, Umeå, 2001.

[4] Swedish Institute for Transport and Communication Analysis, *Facts about information and communication technology in Sweden 2002*, Fälth & Hässler, Värnamo, 2002.

[5] Orth-Gomér, K., Kvinnors stress, sociala miljö och hälsa i ett livsperspektiv (Chapter 5). *Psykosocial miljö och stress, (Psychosocial environment and stress)* ed Theorell, T., Studentlitteratur, Lund, 2003.

[6] Aune, M., The computer in everyday life: Patterns of domestication of new technology, *Making technology our own? Domesticating technology into everyday life*, ed. Lie, M., Sörensen, K.H., Scandinavian University Press, Oslo, 1996.

Human Perspectives in the Internet Society: Culture, Psychology and Gender, K. Morgan, J. Sanchez, C. A. Brebbia & A Voiskounsky (Editors) © 2004 WIT Press, www.witpress.com, ISBN 1-85312-726-4

Section 5
Applied psychological uses for computers

An expert system supporting diagnosis in clinical psychology

R. Spiegel[1] & Y. P. Nenh[2]
[1]*Department of Experimental Psychology and Wolfson College, University of Cambridge, UK*
[2]*Department of Computing, Goldsmiths College, University of London, UK*

Abstract

We introduce an expert system prototype that is meant to support psychologists in finding out what disorders their clients might have. The expert system provides a user interface that permits the psychologist to enter a large variety of symptoms. The symptoms are linked to a database where records of these symptoms/symptom combinations as well as their underlying disorders are stored. The system provides fuzzy rather than deterministic feedback, i.e. instead of suggesting only one diagnosis it indicates all possible diagnoses and estimates the risk for each possible diagnosis individually. The system is not meant to replace psychologists, but rather to support them in generating hypotheses at an early stage of diagnosis.
Keywords: expert system, database, clinical psychology, user interface, symptom classification.

1 Introduction

Early career psychologists often find it challenging to diagnose disorders. What makes this task particularly difficult is the fact that many disorders show a large overlap in terms of their symptoms, e.g. there can be significant weight loss in an eating disorder such as anorexia nervosa, but the same can apply to an affective disorder such as major depression. Current diagnostic manuals such as DSM IV (*Diagnostic and Statistical Manual of Mental Disorders*) [1] or ICD 10 (*International Statistical Classification of Diseases and Related Health Problems, 10th Revision*) [2] are books listing a large amount of symptoms

Human Perspectives in the Internet Society: Culture, Psychology and Gender, K. Morgan, J. Sanchez, C. A. Brebbia & A Voiskounsky (Editors) © 2004 WIT Press, www.witpress.com, ISBN 1-85312-726-4

assigned to disorders. Due to the aforementioned symptom overlap, however, this format makes it difficult to establish a diagnosis, as the symptoms of different disorders constantly need to be compared with each other until a diagnosis can be formed. Another problem with using book-format is the fact that disorders are described on separate pages, and going back and forth to compare symptoms and symptom combinations can take a considerable amount of time.

An alternative solution would be an automated system that would permit the psychologist to enter symptoms and to get feedback from a database listing possible disorders. Such a system would mimic an expert's behaviour, in this case a clinical psychologist searching for symptoms/symptom combinations and underlying disorders in a diagnostic manual. Rather than manually applying this procedure by referring to the aforementioned manuals in book-format, this system would search through the entire database of symptoms and disorders. This would have a couple of advantages:

First, the automatic search would be much faster than a manual search. Second, this system would be far more reliable than a human expert, provided the symptoms are entered correctly into the database. The human expert might make an error in the large number of listed symptoms/symptom combinations. Third, novel research findings about symptoms and underlying disorders can be updated more easily in a database than in a book. Finally, the graphical user interface in the automated version allows the psychologist to enter symptoms by simply clicking on symptoms that are present and by getting immediate feedback. This saves time over writing down symptoms during the surgery and later assigning these symptoms to an underlying disorder. Moreover, an electronic record of the symptoms can be stored in the system and is immediately accessible to other healthcare professionals through the database. This is advantageous over making manual records of symptoms, which would have to be entered into a database later. All these examples save valuable time that can be spent on the care for the client. Before going into technical details, we would like to give a general introduction on expert systems and support this introduction by practical examples from our system.

1.1 Introduction to expert systems

The purpose of an expert system is to simulate professional practices of a human expert. In our example, the human expert would be a *clinical psychologist* and the professional practices would be *considering symptoms and symptom combinations to diagnose an underlying mental disorder*. A more formal definition is provided by Jackson [3]: "An expert system is a computer program that represents and reasons with knowledge of some specialist subject with a view to solving problems or giving advice." Because our system is applied by a clinical psychologist, the justification for this system is to improve productivity by supporting the psychologist in the early stages of diagnosing a mental disorder. To be of practical use, expert systems should be quick and reliable in performing the particular task they specialise in. Expert systems are very specialised and restricted to a particular area, e.g. an expert system simulating a

Human Perspectives in the Internet Society: Culture, Psychology and Gender, K. Morgan, J. Sanchez, C. A. Brebbia & A Voiskounsky (Editors) © 2004 WIT Press, www.witpress.com, ISBN 1-85312-726-4

broker could not be applied to diagnose mental disorders. The specialised area is called *Knowledge Base* (Jackson [3]) and has been developed after careful study of the human expert, i.e. it usually contains knowledge provided by the human expert. In our case, this knowledge was provided by the careful study of diagnostic manuals. Moreover, the first author was both a computing professional and a psychologist with detailed education in clinical psychology. Other psychologists and healthcare professionals were also asked for advice. The knowledge gained from the human expert can be implemented into the system by a set of if-then rules (Alter [4]): "If certain conditions are true, then certain conclusions should be drawn." According to Alter [4], an ideal expert system should contain the following components:

- A *user interface* that lets the user enter facts and receive feedback. In our case this is a graphical user interface where the psychologist (user) can enter symptoms (facts) and get an estimated diagnosis of likely disorders (feedback).
- A *database* where facts (in our case: symptoms and diagnosis) are stored.
- A *knowledge base* that makes use of *if-then* rules. These rules were provided by an expert (psychologist).
- An *inference engine* that links the rules from the knowledge base with the facts from the database (in our case symptoms) to infer a result (in our case: a diagnosis) or to give alternative feedback (e.g. you have not specified any symptoms yet). The inference engine also makes use of *if-then* rules.
- An *explanation* offered to users who want to know how the inference engine draws conclusions (in our case: the reason why a diagnosis was made).

1.2 Introduction to diagnosis in clinical psychology

Clinical psychologists often refer to the two most widely accepted diagnostic manuals [1,2] when forming a diagnosis. There are a range of different disorders such as Generalised Anxiety Disorder, Obsessive-compulsive Disorder, Post-traumatic Stress Disorder, Borderline-type Personality Disorder, Anorexia Nervosa, Bulimia Nervosa, Acute Schizophrenia-like Psychotic Disorder, etc.

Possible causes of mental disorders can be organic, i.e. when a somatic illness such as a brain tumour is responsible for a mental disorder. Alternative causes could be reactive (e.g. someone suffering from depression due to the death of a loved family member) or endogenous (when the underlying cause is unknown). It is important to realise that the diagnosis can be the same irrespective of the underlying cause, e.g. someone can suffer from a major depression due to a change of neurotransmitter activity in the brain or due to an event that has no organic cause, such as the death of a loved one. Several authors have tried to define mental disorders. One example is that abnormal can be

Human Perspectives in the Internet Society: Culture, Psychology and Gender, K. Morgan, J. Sanchez, C. A. Brebbia & A Voiskounsky (Editors) © 2004 WIT Press, www.witpress.com, ISBN 1-85312-726-4

defined as "deviating from the norm or average" according to Gross et al. [5]. On the other hand, clinical psychologists usually avoid to classify clients into categories such as normal or abnormal. Rather, they assume that there is a continuous difference between people with and without a disorder, and differences may exist in terms of the degree specific symptoms are present. For a discussion see Davison and Neale [6] or Baumann and Perrez [7]. In order for something to be considered as deviating from the average it usually has to persist for a certain amount of time. If something is very transient, it might not be considered a mental disorder. One example would be a football supporter who feels depressed after his/her favourite team lost the cup finals. Although this person might show symptoms of depression right after the match, these symptoms might not persist in the same intensity for several weeks. Consequently, it would be wrong to assign a mental disorder to this person. An expert system simulating diagnosis in clinical psychology should therefore also consider the duration of these symptoms.

Another feature of diagnosis in clinical psychology is that the statistical manuals usually pre-classify disorders into specific categories, e.g. ICD 10 has groups such as *Schizophrenia, schizotypal and delusional disorders* or *Mood disorders*. DSM IV has categories such as *Eating disorders* or *Anxiety disorders*. This makes it easier for a clinical psychologist who might suspect that their client has an eating disorder. S/he can use one category when comparing different eating disorders. Having given an introduction to diagnosis in clinical psychology, we will now refer to the implementation of the system.

2 Implementation of the expert system

What follows is a detailed explanation of how the earlier mentioned five components (User Interface, Database, Knowledge Base, Inference Engine, Explanation) were implemented. At this stage, the expert system has the form of a prototype that certainly needs further testing and possible elaboration.

2.1 The graphical user interface

The interface was created in html code and PHP was used to connect the interface with the database. One reason for selecting html is that it can be viewed in any web-browser. Therefore, it should be accessible in health care institutions all around the world. This should also apply to institutions that have difficulties to afford the latest computing equipment. In order to access the expert system, the user (in our case a clinical psychologist) has to log onto the password-protected system. Once the user is logged on, s/he will receive an overview with a description about the purpose of the system and how it can be used. Based on the earlier mentioned diagnostic manuals [1,2], the symptoms are divided into categories, such as mood related symptoms, eating related symptoms or anxiety related symptoms. Each category is highlighted and once the psychologist clicks on a category, a list of symptoms appears on the screen. An example of three symptoms that appear in the category *mood-related symptoms* can be found in Figure 1.

Feeling sad or blue

☐ YES ☐ NO

Loss of interest or pleasure in usual activities

☐ YES ☐ NO

Fatigue or loss of energy

☐ YES ☐ NO

Figure 1: Example of symptom display on the interface.

In addition to the list of symptoms, the interface offers other features such as a Body Mass Calculator. The Body Mass Index BMI (kg/m^2) gives a numerical guideline whether a person's weight is within the normal range or not. The BMI adds to eating-related symptoms when diagnosing an eating disorder. It is calculated automatically when the psychologist enters the client's height and weight. JavaScript was used to implement the function that calculated the BMI.

Bipolar Disorder

High risk
1
2
3
4
5
Low risk

Figure 2: Graphical representation of risk for a specific disorder, e.g. bipolar.

Having entered all symptoms, the psychologist clicks on the submit button and the form with all indicated symptoms is submitted to the database. What happens to the submitted form in the database will be described later, but referring to the interface, the psychologists receives immediate feedback about a possible diagnosis. The psychologist is reminded that the system only performs an estimate and no final diagnosis. Moreover, the diagnosis is formulated in

Human Perspectives in the Internet Society: Culture, Psychology and Gender, K. Morgan, J. Sanchez, C. A. Brebbia & A Voiskounsky (Editors) © 2004 WIT Press, www.witpress.com, ISBN 1-85312-726-4

terms of risks but not as a final answer, e.g. *based on the symptoms, there is a high risk that the client suffers from a bipolar disorder (=manic depression). 8 symptoms matched the description of a bipolar disorder*. Moreover, a graphical representation on a scale from 1 (high risk) to 5 (low risk) can be obtained for the risk assessment of different disorders (Figure 2 displays an example). This enables a quick visual comparison between a range of possible diagnoses. A numerical representation is also available.

Furthermore, the interface allows the psychologist to enter any additional information in text format. This information will be stored in the database and can be used to exchange with other health professionals who are involved in the care for the client.

2.2 The database

Postgres was used as the database management system. Postgres is a relational database management system with the advantage that it can be extended to handle rules and objects similar to those in object oriented programming languages. Detailed information on Postgres can be found in [8]. After the psychologist clicks on the submit button, a connection to the database is established and the form with the client's symptoms is sent to the database. This database already contains information about all symptoms and all disorders, i.e. for each possible disorder, a list of symptoms is stored. Using the symptoms the psychologist indicated on the form, a query is created to find out how many of these symptoms overlap with the symptoms listed for each disorder. The number of overlapping symptoms indicates how well the symptoms on the submitted form match with each possible diagnosis. What has to be further considered is that occasionally some symptoms are better diagnostic features for a particular disorder than other symptoms, e.g. the symptom *low mood for at least 2 weeks* is a more important diagnostic feature for depression than the symptoms *fatigue or loss of energy*. Consequently, symptoms can have a different weighting for the same disorder (in this case depression). Alternatively, the same symptoms might differ in the way they match with a particular disorder, e.g. the symptom *excessive exercise* applies to both anorexia and bulimia nervosa, but it is a better indicator for anorexia nervosa, so it should be rated higher when the database searches through the symptom list describing anorexia nervosa. Instead of summing up the mere number of symptoms, it is therefore necessary to calculate the sum of weighted symptoms with respect to a disorder. The weighting is closely related to the knowledge base, which is based on experts estimating how the symptoms can be related to the disorder.

2.3 The knowledge base

The knowledge base is typically inspired by verbal reports from experts stating how they apply their knowledge to carry out a particular task. Subsequently, this knowledge is translated into a set of rules that can be programmed. It has to be kept in mind, however, that a real diagnosis in clinical psychology might be more complex than the set of rules that are eventually implemented into the expert system. According to Jackson [3] "few experts will provide a well-articulated sequence of steps that is guaranteed to terminate with success in all situations", so this expert system should only be seen as a tool to support the psychologist rather than as a tool that replaces expert knowledge. Real expert knowledge might consist of a large number of implicit skills and experiences that experts are not able to fully verbalise.

One example of translating expert knowledge into a knowledge base are the symptoms of depression (Gross et al. [5]), which is defined by persistent low mood for a duration of at least two weeks, plus five of the following symptoms:

- Significant weight loss or gain.
- Inability to sleep or difficulties staying asleep.
- Loss of energy or fatigue.
- Agitation, restlessness or irritability.
- Loss of pleasure or interest in usual activities.
- Pessimism or hopelessness.
- Recurrent thoughts of suicide, death or suicide attempts.

These symptoms of depression can be translated into a set of rules quite easily, but it gets more complex when symptoms have to be weighted. This is because there is hardly any quantitative measurement that would allow to weigh symptoms in a way that would be translatable into expert systems. Few psychologists know exactly how to weigh the symptom *exercise excessively* in anorexia nervosa as compared with bulimia nervosa. Even though clients with anorexia nervosa might be more likely to have this symptom, not all psychologists might agree in terms of the weighting that this symptom should be given. Although we relied on advice from psychologists, any future elaboration of this system will need to rely on further expert advice. After the symptoms have been translated into rules, these can be implemented. This happens in the inference engine.

2.4 The inference engine

The inference engine interacts with the previously mentioned components in the following way: when the symptoms are clicked and the form is submitted to the database, the database will proceed with this information because each symptom is stored as a fact in the database. Moreover, each fact is attached to rules in the inference engine. These rules were previously generated based on the information from the knowledge base. What follows are two examples of a rule in text format:

IF the weighted amount of anorexia nervosa-related symptoms is larger than or equal to 14, there is a high risk of anorexia nervosa. IF the weighted amount is smaller than 14 but larger than or equal to 10, there is a medium risk of anorexia nervosa. IF the weighted amount is smaller than 10 but larger than/equal to 5 there is a small risk. ELSE there is no risk of anorexia nervosa.

Human Perspectives in the Internet Society: Culture, Psychology and Gender, K. Morgan, J. Sanchez, C. A. Brebbia & A Voiskounsky (Editors) © 2004 WIT Press, www.witpress.com, ISBN 1-85312-726-4

An alternative rule would be:

IF there are 4 or more symptoms related to bulimia AND including the symptom "binge and purge" AND the body mass index is less than 18 THEN there is a high risk of bulimia nervosa.

PHP was applied to implement the rules and SQL SELECT statements were applied to calculate the sum of the weighted symptoms.

2.5 The explanation

Once the final results have been calculated by the inference engine, stored in the database, and sent back to the user interface, it would be good to have more than the mere output of the disorder. A confidence rating indicating how much the user can rely on this diagnosis would certainly be useful. This is partly provided in the earlier mentioned risk estimate (Figure 2), but could also give more detailed feedback, e.g. the exact number of symptoms which suggested a particular disorder. For example: there were 5 symptoms related to depression and 2 symptoms related to a Bipolar disorder (=manic depression).

3 System evaluation

Having implemented an expert system it is certainly necessary to test whether it works. There are different techniques to perform an evaluation. One is to test reliability, i.e. whether the system implementation is flawless. For example: are all the calculations performed in the correct way? Though only a prototype at this stage, the system was thoroughly tested and no error could be found. More specialised types of reliability are the concepts of *retest reliability* and *inter-rater reliability*. The former tests whether the diagnosis is the same if the same psychologist enters the same symptoms at 2 independent points of measurement. The latter tests whether two psychologists end up with the same diagnosis when entering symptoms for the same client. Whilst *retest reliability* was tested and is fulfilled in 100 percent of the cases, our prototypical system is still evaluated in terms of *inter-rater reliability*. It has to be said, though, that retest reliability is much easier to test in our case. If the system is correctly implemented then it will always give the same diagnosis provided the same values are entered at different times. This is because the underlying system will perform the same operations and therefore obviously output the same results. Inter-rater reliability, on the other hand, requires a detailed case study with different clinical psychologists who interact with the same client. This in turn requires a large research budget to carry out the evaluation. Another important technique is to determine *validity*, i.e. does the system really provide a valid diagnosis given the symptoms. This is an important test, because in case the symptom weighting or the rules in the inference engine are incorrect, the system will not provide a valid diagnosis. We performed two tests to cross-validate our prototypical system. In the first test, an expert with training in clinical psychology was asked to indicate what symptoms would be expected for a person with a particular disorder (e.g. a bipolar disorder). This expert then had to answer the questions related to the symptoms (of which a subset is shown in Figure 1). The expert was told to answer the questions in a way that the diagnostic result would indicate a high risk for a bipolar disorder and low risks for any other disorder. This case of cross-validation worked surprisingly well and the expert succeeded in this task. The second test was to generate a random answer pattern for the questions. If this expert system works, then a random answer pattern should not indicate any high risk for any disorder. This test also succeeded, but it remains to be said that these tests are case studies and need to be more extensive once this system leaves the prototypical stage. Cross-validation will become a more challenging task once more symptoms/disorders will be entered into the database.

4 Conclusions

The results of our prototypical system suggest that it seems possible to implement a large scale project of this expert system. It remains to be said, though, that this requires advice from more experts and probably a large administrative team that is responsible for entering the symptoms into the database. Entering the thousands of disorders/symptoms as well as more extensive validity checks will necessary. As mentioned before, this system would be able to support clinical psychologists at an early stage of diagnosis. As encouraging as our initial results might be, the present system should by no means be over-interpreted in a way that it might be able to replace clinical psychologists. If one considers this system as a support tool, however, then it might be beneficial. Though electronic versions of diagnostic manuals exist (such as the electronic version of DSM IV, Pies [9]), these are computer aided versions that help the psychologist search electronically rather than manually, but do not contain expert system features. As a result, we believe that an automated expert system similar to our prototype could be a useful addition to current diagnostic manuals. Our prototype was predominantly based on a classical approach, where rules are used to represent expert knowledge. The idea of having an expert system supporting diagnosis could probably be further extended with ideas from other computational approaches. One group of candidates might be models implementing analogical reasoning, as psychologists might often see analogies between clients who suffer from the same disorder. The analogies between clients in terms of behaviour, expression and other symptoms might further enhance the applicability of our system. Error-based learning would be possible if the database stores the combinations of symptoms and the suggested diagnosis, the psychologist verifies or alters the diagnosis and feeds it back into the database. The more people were diagnosed with this system, the more would the database be able to learn about symptom combinations and the resulting diagnoses. Consequently, the system would be able to make analogies between the symptoms/disorders of previous and new clients. These analogy-making processes might also help when attempting to

Human Perspectives in the Internet Society: Culture, Psychology and Gender, K. Morgan, J. Sanchez, C. A. Brebbia & A Voiskounsky (Editors) © 2004 WIT Press, www.witpress.com, ISBN 1-85312-726-4

diagnose disorders with the automated system. Various analogy-making models that could be adapted for this purpose are described by Hofstadter [10], Mitchell [11] as well as Spiegel and McLaren [12].

References

[1] *Diagnostic and Statistical Manual of Mental Disorders - Fourth Edition (DSM-IV)*, American Psychiatric Association, Washington D.C., 1994.

[2] *International Statistical Classification of Diseases and Related Health Problems,* 10th Revision, Chapter 5: Mental Disorders, Geneva, World Health Organization, 1992.

[3] Jackson, P. *Introduction to expert systems*, Addison-Wesley: Harlow, UK, 1999.

[4] Alter, S. *Information Systems*, Prentice Hall: Upper Saddle River, NJ, 2002.

[5] Gross, R., Mcilveen, R., Coolican, H., Russel, J. & Clamp, A. *Psychology: A new introduction*. Hodder and Stoughton General: London, 2000.

[6] Davison, G.C. & Neale, J.M. *Abnormal Psychology*. Wiley: New York, 1998.

[7] Baumann, U. & Perrez, M. *Lehrbuch Klinische Psychologie: Grundlagen, Diagnostik, Aetiologie*. Huber: Bern, 1990.

[8] Postgres: http://db.cs.berkeley.edu//postgres-v4r2/postgres.faq.

[9] Electronic version of DSM IV according to R. Pies: http://www.mhsource.com/expert/exp1052101a.html.

[10] Hofstadter, D. *Fluid Concepts and Creative Analogies*. Basic Books: New York, 1995.

[11] Mitchell, M. Analogy-Making as Perception: A Computer Model. MIT-Press: Cambridge MA, 1993.

[12] Spiegel, R. & McLaren, I.P.L. Abstract and associatively-based representations in human sequence learning. *Philosophical Transactions of the Royal Society, (Biological Sciences)*, **358**, pp. 1277-1283, 2003.

Human Perspectives in the Internet Society: Culture, Psychology and Gender, K. Morgan, J. Sanchez, C. A. Brebbia & A Voiskounsky (Editors) © 2004 WIT Press, www.witpress.com, ISBN 1-85312-726-4

Skills in computer use, self-efficacy and self-concept

E. Makri-Botsari[1], F. Paraskeva[2], E. Koumbias[3], A. Dendaki[3] & P. Panaikas[3]
[1]*School of Pedagogy and Educational Technology*
[2]*Department of Technology Education & Digital Systems, University of Piraeus*
[3]*Faculty of Primary Education, University of Athens*

Abstract

In today's information society knowing information technology is a critical factor for academic and professional education. The judgments of the individual about his/her competence in computer use can influence their goals and future plans concerning professional career and success. The continuously increasing rates of change in all aspects of contemporary life (technological, economic and social), as well as the production, distribution, exchange and diffusion of an enormous volume of information, facilitate collaborations while, at the same time, they increase competition and the standards set by the individual for him/herself making it hard to maintain a positive perception for his/her competence or adequacy in various domains. The purpose of the present study is to investigate the relations between computer self-efficacy and self-concept. The results of the study reveal a positive relationship between the aforementioned variables.
Keywords: self-concept, self-efficacy, computer self-efficacy, academic and professional education, career.

1 Introduction

Academic self-concept and academic self-efficacy have been estimated as unique factors that contribute to academic achievement or performance [3,20]. Academic self-concept and academic self-efficacy refer to the individuals' self-

Human Perspectives in the Internet Society: Culture, Psychology and Gender, K. Morgan, J. Sanchez, C. A. Brebbia & A Voiskounsky (Editors) © 2004 WIT Press, www.witpress.com, ISBN 1-85312-726-4

concept and self-efficacy beliefs that are formed specifically toward academic domains. More specifically, academic self-concept refers to the individuals' knowledge and perceptions about themselves in achievement situations [2]. Academic self-concept incorporates attitudes, feelings and perceptions relative to one's intellectual or academic skills, and represents a mixture of self-beliefs and self-feelings regarding general academic performance [11]. Academic self-concept has been found to be predictive of overall grade performance suggesting that a student's belief about his/her general academic capabilities is related to his/her overall academic performance [11].

Academic self-efficacy is more related to one's ability to succeed in a given specific subject [3]. Bandura defined self-efficacy as a person's "judgments of [his or her] capabilities to organize and execute courses of action required to attain designated types of performances". Research has generally shown self-efficacy to be a stronger predictor of subject-specific academic performance and goals than more global measures such as self-esteem or self-concept [1,11]. Further, other studies have found that self-efficacy is not necessarily fixed, but can be attenuated or increased by performance on a previous task. Past performance can affect current feelings about self-efficacy about a given subject.

Both constructs received much attention from educational researchers because of their purported influence on students' academic functioning. Numerous studies have reported how positive self-concept or self-efficacy facilitated students' academic engagement, goal-setting, task choice, persistence and effort, motivation, strategy use, performance and achievement, and even career selection etc.

In today's information society becoming proficient with information technology is a critical factor in academic, personal and career development. A seminal study found that undergraduate students who possessed a low sense of self-efficacy in computer use, thus displaying little interest in acquiring information technologies competencies. Individuals increasing their interest in information technology, can acquire skills, expand the range of career choices and use the computer as a problem-solving tool [17].

People's beliefs about their self-efficacy influence academic motivation, ambitions, interest in intellectual skills, and their effort for academic performance and achievement [1,17]. A strong sense of efficacy creates interests in self-regulated learning environments and it could develop conditions for lifelong leaning programs. A strong sense of efficacy in basic education learners may lead students to develop competence and skills for further social and economic stability [17].

Similar studies point out that lack of self-efficacy with regard to knowledge of information technology could prevent academic and professional development, pointing out that the self- efficacy in computer use and competence constitutes a prognostic indicator of future activities and occupational interests in information technologies [17]. Further development (professional, economic, personal) depends on the interaction with the information technology.

Human Perspectives in the Internet Society: Culture, Psychology and Gender, K. Morgan, J. Sanchez, C. A. Brebbia & A Voiskounsky (Editors) © 2004 WIT Press, www.witpress.com, ISBN 1-85312-726-4

2 Computer self-efficacy

Computer self-efficacy refers to a judgment of one's capability to use a computer [5]. It has been described that individuals base self-efficacy judgments on four main sources of information and the same is considered in Information technologies courses. Individuals evaluate the contributions of these sources of information, regarding their capabilities, and perform their behavior of interest. Individuals who perceive themselves capable of performing certain tasks or activities are defined as high in self-efficacy and are more likely to attempt and execute these tasks and activities. People who perceive themselves as less capable are less likely to attempt and execute these tasks and activities, and are defined as lower in self-efficacy [1].

These four sources of information are described below at declining order of influence [1]:

- The students develop the more important source of computer self-efficacy, from their *enactive mastery experience*, realising computer exercises and laboratorial activities that are related to the computers that require comprehension of material (hardware) and software (software) in the computer.
- Students *observe the successes and failures of others (vicarious experience)*. They constitute models in which they compare their own performance from related standards (successes or failures). In a similar way, the professors shape/demonstrate behaviors that are related to computer activities, and consequently the students constitute models of comparison of their self-efficacy.
- Self-efficacy information is delivered through *verbal persuasion*. Students receive reinforcements or exhortations from instructors and/or fellow students that encourage and support their computer skill and/or competent development.
- Students may acquire self-efficacy information from *physiological reactions*. For example the anxiety of fear prior to an in-class computer exercise might be a sign that they would not do well. On the other hand, a lack of these reactions could be perceived as a sign of computer competence [17].

3 Information technology and relevant computer self-efficacy research

The Computer Self-Efficacy (CSE) construct has been used in order to examine the decision of individual to use the information technology, the software training and performance and the relationship between experience and academic performance [10,17]. Researchers have examined the connection between CSE and several other behaviors of interest to educators. For example, research has found evidence of a positive relationship between CSE and registration in

Human Perspectives in the Internet Society: Culture, Psychology and Gender, K. Morgan, J. Sanchez, C. A. Brebbia & A Voiskounsky (Editors) © 2004 WIT Press, www.witpress.com, ISBN 1-85312-726-4

college-level computer courses, decisions to use computers and performance in software training etc [4,7].

Several research studies have investigated the relationship of CSE to computer training and other individual and situational variables of interest to educators. Some of these studies are briefly summarized below:

In a study of the effects of a training method on CSE and performance with computer software, individuals performed higher CSE when skills were delivered via a behavioral model, than what they provided with an interactive tutorial [7]. Significant increases in student CSE were found following completion of an undergraduate course in computers and information processing where they received both lecture and laboratory instruction [18]. Comparing two training models: (a) behavior and (b) traditional lecture, Compeau and Higgins tried to examine computer self-efficacy, outcome expectations, and performance. Word processing and spreadsheet applications were used. The behaviour model was more effective than the traditional lecture for training the spreadsheet application. For the word processing application no significant difference was found in the training models. Results concluded CSE had a strong influence on performance in both models [4].

Significant increases in CSE were found for students receiving standard classroom instruction in an introductory computer science course, but no significant increase in CSE was found for students who received additional verbal persuasion [15]. In another research, Smith-Weber (2000) investigated the relationship of CSE and the impact of computer technology education. Pre and post tests of the four sources revealed CSE was significantly related to mastery experiences and affective states. In addition, overall perceptions of CSE increased after computer technology education [17].

Zhang and Espinoza examined the relationship between self-efficacy, attitudes toward computers, and desire to learn computer skills. Attitudes toward computers were correlated with CSE, and attitudes about the usefulness of computers predicted desire to learn computer skills. CSE was a strong predictor of willingness to learn advanced computer skills [19].

The relationship of computer experience to CSE has also been investigated by Karsten and Roth [10]. Individuals with prior computer experience are more likely to evidence higher levels of CSE than individuals without such experience. This research also showed that the perceptions of students of their competence of computer use were progressively increased as result of their training. The measurement of the CSE influences the factors that are related to the training providing practical interest in the instructors. Results showed that the measurement of self-efficacy in computer use constitutes a practical vehicle for the evaluation of educational process [10].

The influence of CSE, outcome expectations, affect, and anxiety on computer usage was developed by Compeau and Higgins [5]. Using data collected over a one-year (business subscribers), a significant relationship was found between CSE and outcome expectations. CSE also had a positive influence on affect, anxiety, and computer use [17].

Human Perspectives in the Internet Society: Culture, Psychology and Gender, K. Morgan, J. Sanchez, C. A. Brebbia & A Voiskounsky (Editors) © 2004 WIT Press, www.witpress.com, ISBN 1-85312-726-4

From another study of Joo et al. (2000) founded that the student's self-efficacy in regarding self-learning, has positive correlation with their self-concept, so much in the conventional teaching and also in the teaching that is based on the Internet. Self-efficacy in Internet use was a prognostic indicator of achievement of students when the evaluation based on the Internet tests, but not on the written tests [9].

4 The method

The sample of the study consisted of 175 students from the University of Piraeus [Department of Technology Education and Digital Systems]. Of these 175 students, 91 were first-year students and 84 were fourth year students.

For the purposes of this study, the following measures were used:
- Self-Perception Profile for College Students by Neemann and Harter [13]. From his scale only three subscales were used taping academic self-perception, job competence and self-esteem.
- Computer Self-Efficacy Scale by Murphy et al. [12]. This scale was developed to measure individuals' perceptions of their capabilities regarding specific computer knowledge and skills. Items represent beginning moderate and advanced skills.

Table 1: Pearson *r* correlation coefficients between self-concept and computer self-efficacy.

Construct	Beginning skills	Advanced skills	File & software skills
Self-perception of academic competence	.266**(175)	.353**(175)	.217**(175)
Self-perception of job competence	.168 (110)	.246**(110)	.103 (110)
Self-esteem	.261** (175)	.279**(175)	.185* (175)

Note: * Correlation is significant 0.05 level (2-tailed).
** Correlation is significant at the 0.01 level (2-tailed).
Numbers in parentheses are the sample size.

5 Results

The Pearson r correlations between self-perception, self-esteem and CSE are presented in Table 1. The data in Table 1 indicate that higher levels of self-perception of academic competence and self-esteem are associated with higher

Human Perspectives in the Internet Society: Culture, Psychology and Gender, K. Morgan, J. Sanchez, C. A. Brebbia & A Voiskounsky (Editors) © 2004 WIT Press, www.witpress.com, ISBN 1-85312-726-4

levels of CSE across all skills. In contrast, only the advanced skills in computer use are associated with higher levels of job competence.

In order to investigate whether perceived self-efficacy in computer use changes from first to fourth year of study we performed a t-test. The results in Table 2 indicate that CSE increases with increasing year of study.

Table 2: Relationship between CSE and year of study.

		Levene's Test		t-test						
		F	*Sig.*	*t*	*df*	*p*	Mean diff.	Std. error diff.	95% Confidence interval of the difference: Lower	Upper
Beginning skills	Eva	1.358	.245	-2.612	173	.010	-.2380	.09112	-.41785	-.05817
	Evna			-2.621	173.000	.010	-.2380	.09082	-.41727	-.05876
Advanced skills	Eva	.067	.797	-2.246	173	.026	-.2451	.10910	-.46040	-.02974
	Evna			-2.243	170.811	.026	-.2451	.10924	-.46070	-.02944
File & software skills	Eva	4.957	.027	-3.158	173	.002	-.3450	.10923	-.56058	-.12938
	Evna			-3.186	169.825	.002	-.3450	.10829	-.55874	-.13121

Note: Eva = equal variances assumed. Evna: equal variances not assumed.

6 Conclusion

The purpose of this study was to investigate the relations between self-concept and computer self-efficacy. This study was designed to find the correlation between self-perception (of academic competence and job competence), self-esteem and computer self-efficacy.

The findings of the study show that the higher the self-perception of academic competence the higher the computer self-efficacy in all its dimensions of the CSE scale (beginning skills, advanced skills, file and software) that were cross-examined. These findings appear to support other studies, according to which the higher self-concept one has the better one's computer self-efficacy is, which means that those students who regard their performance as high also expect that they will succeed in the development of computer skills.

However, as far as self perception of job competence is concerned, the findings revealed statistically significant differences only with regard to advanced skills, which seems to mean that the students who have high self-

Human Perspectives in the Internet Society: Culture, Psychology and Gender, K. Morgan, J. Sanchez, C. A. Brebbia & A Voiskounsky (Editors) © 2004 WIT Press, www.witpress.com, ISBN 1-85312-726-4

perception of job competence believe that they need to possess special skills in computer use. This could be based on the current data of competition in the workplace. Therefore, the students appear to use the manual, to describe the function of peripheral systems, to comprehend the levels of data processing, so that they can eventually solve problems – a necessary property for furthering the development of the their career. While this is not the case with beginning skills, and file and software, the former of which they only consider basic and the latter obviously non-existent, maybe because they are lacking in professional experience. On the other hand, the findings regarding self-esteem and CSE show statistically significant differences and this can be combined with the previous findings referring to self-concept. In particular, since they esteem their self-perception of academic competence to be high, this makes them feel emotionally well so that they consider their CSE high as well.

Considering the variable of year of studies, when comparing the means it was found that there is a clear and statistically significant difference between beginning skills and advanced skills. The difference between the means seems to increase considerably at the final level of skills to file and software. This may account for the fact that the more knowledge and experience one gains the better CSE one possesses for further personal and career development.

The present study aimed at drawing college teachers' attention and interest to the existence of differences between first- and fourth-year students. While the age of the respondents was examined as part of data collection, these findings could be related to the questions of the study, which would be an important parameter for consideration. If, for example, it was found that certain ages within a population (high school level, freshmen) demonstrated low self-efficacy, then ways could be suggested to restore this phenomenon [6,8].

References

[1] Bandura, A. (1997). Self-Efficacy: The Exercise of Control, Freeman, New York.

[2] Bong M. and Skaalvik E. M. (2003) Academic Self-Concept and Self-Efficacy: How Different Are They Really? Educational Psychology Review, Vol. 15, No. 1.

[3] Bong, M., and Clark, R. E. (1999). Comparison between self-concept and self-efficacy in academic motivation research. Educational Psychology 34.

[4] Compeau D.R., Higgins C.A. (1995) Computer self-efficacy: Development of a measure and initial test, MIS Quarterly, 19(2), 189-211.

[5] Compeau, D. R., & Higgins, C. A. (1999). Social cognitive theory and individual reactions to computing technology: A longitudinal study. MIS Quarterly, 23(2), 145-159.

[6] Eachus P., Cassidy S., (1997). Self-efficacy, locus of control and styles of learning as contributing factors in the academic performance of student health professionals, Proceedings of the First Regional Conference of Psychology for Professionals in the Americas, Mexico City.

Human Perspectives in the Internet Society: Culture, Psychology and Gender, K. Morgan, J. Sanchez, C. A. Brebbia & A Voiskounsky (Editors) © 2004 WIT Press, www.witpress.com, ISBN 1-85312-726-4

[7] Gist, M.E. Schwoerer, C. Rosen, B. (1989) Effects of alternative training methods on self-efficacy and performance in computer software training, Journal of Applied Psychology, 74(6), 884-891.

[8] Jablonski D., (2001). Analyzing Computer Self-efficacy of Teachers and Its Effect on Curriculum at Hanoka's High School and Intermediate, Available: http:/hale, pepperdine.edu/ djablons/665.casestudy.htm.

[9] Joo, Y. J., Bong, M., and Choi, H. J. (2000). Self-efficacy for self-regulated learning, academic self-efficacy, and Internet self-efficacy in Web-based instruction. Educational Technology Res. Dev. 48(2): 5–18.

[10] Karsten, R., & Roth, R. M. (1998). The relationship of computer experience and computer self-efficacy to performance in introductory computer literacy courses. Journal of Research on Computing in Education, 31(3), 14-24.

[11] Lent, R.W., Brown, S.D., and Gore, P.A. (1997). Discriminant and predictive validity of academic self-concept, academic self-efficacy, and mathematics-specific self-efficacy. Journal of Counseling Psychology, 44, 3, 307-315.

[12] Murphy, C.A., Coover, D., & Owen, S.V. (1989). Development and validation of the computer self-efficacy scale. Educational and Psychological Measurement, 49, 893-899.

[13] Neemann, J. & Harter, S. (1986). Manual for the Self-Perception Profile for College Students, Denver, CO: University of Denver Press.

[14] Schunk, D. H. (1991). Self-efficacy and academic motivation, Educational Psychology 26: 207–231.

[15] Smith, J.M. (1994). The effects of education on computer self-efficacy, Journal of Industrial Teacher Education, 31 (3), 51-65.

[16] Smith, K.H. (2000). The Self-Concept and Verbal Academic Achievement of Primary and Secondary Student Teachers, University of Melbourne avail. at: http://adt1.lib.unimelb.edu.au/adtroot/public/adt-VU2000.0013/.

[17] Smith, K.H. (2002) Using the social cognitive model to explain vocational interest in information technology, Information Technology, Learning and Performance Journal, Vol. 20, No. 1.

[18] Torkzadeh, G. & Koufteros, X. (1994). Factor validity of a computer self-efficacy scale and the impact of computer training, Educational and Psychological Measurement, 54 (3), 813- 821.

[19] Zhang, Y., & Espinoza, S. (1998). Relationships among computer self-efficacy, attitudes toward computers, and desirability of learning computer skills, Journal of Research on Computing in Education, 30(4), 420-437.

[20] Zimmerman, B. J. (2000). Attaining self-regulation: A social cognitive perspective. In: Boekaerts, M., Pintrich, P. R., and Zeidner, M. (eds.), Handbook of Self-Regulation, JAI. Press, New York, pp. 13–39.

Human Perspectives in the Internet Society: Culture, Psychology and Gender, K. Morgan, J. Sanchez, C. A. Brebbia & A Voiskounsky (Editors) © 2004 WIT Press, www.witpress.com, ISBN 1-85312-726-4

Section 6
Influencing gender roles

Gender issues in the career development of computer science staff

K. Adeboye, V. Flynn & K. Darlington
Faculty of Business Computing and Information Management, South Bank University, London

Abstract

Women form a tiny minority of staff who lecture in Computer Science at universities in the UK. This gender imbalance reduces the scope for women to contribute to research and development and reinforces in students' minds the impression that computing is a male dominated profession. To encourage more women to consider a career in lecturing, research was undertaken on the factors that influenced the careers of a sample of female computer science lecturers. The paper presents the findings of the research and makes recommendations for improving the position of women lecturers.

1 Introduction

Government statistics indicate that women form a very small minority of Computer Science academics at UK universities. There are only ten female Software Engineering professors, for example, compared with 210 males. At senior lecturer/researcher levels, the figures for females and males are 79 and 474 respectively [1]. Although this gender imbalance can be found in other Engineering disciplines, the centrality to computing to social, economic and technological progress makes it particularly worrying. With so few women at universities contributing to research in IT, there is a real risk that the development and application of computing will reflect male interests. The paucity of women lecturers may also reinforce in students' minds the impression that Computing is a 'man's profession', making it difficult to reverse the decline in the numbers of women embarking on careers in Computing [2, 3].

Although steps clearly need to be taken to increase the numbers of women lecturing in Computing subjects, there is very little research to guide

Human Perspectives in the Internet Society: Culture, Psychology and Gender, K. Morgan, J. Sanchez, C. A. Brebbia & A Voiskounsky (Editors) © 2004 WIT Press, www.witpress.com, ISBN 1-85312-726-4

policy-making. A report by Greenfield et al. [3] on the careers of women in Science, Engineering and Technology (SET) makes some useful recommendations but does not focus on Computer Science staff per se nor provide much qualitative data on career development issues. It was to fill this gap in the literature that the research described in the paper was carried out. Semi-structured interviews were conducted with a number of female Computer Science lecturers at various stages in their career. The aims were to find out what had attracted them to a career in lecturing and the factors that had influenced their career development. The results reported here are the first stage in what will be a long-term study of the career development of women Computer Science lecturers at selected universities in the UK and abroad. The next section describes the methodology used in more detail.

2 Methodology

The decision to interview the women was based on the desire to 'see the world through their eyes' and obtain as much qualitative information as possible about their careers. The interview method is particularly well suited to this type of data gathering [5, 6]. Surfing the Web sites of Computer Studies departments of universities located the participants. Where contact details of female members of staff were given, an email was sent requesting their assistance with the research. Care was taken to ensure that those contacted were employed at 'new' (post 1992) and 'traditional' universities and that the universities were situated in different geographical regions.

A stratified random sampling method was adopted to ensure that the research would not only represent the overall population but ensure that participants from both traditional 'red brick' universities and the 'new' universities were fairly reflected in the sample. A sample of 30 women were selected for interview by telephone. The interviews were conducted via telephone because the respondents lived over too wide a geographical area to make face-to-face interviews viable. A schedule was devised to guide the questioning. This sought information on the participants' background, roles and career history; their motivations for pursuing a career lecturing in Computing at university and factors that had helped or hindered their career development. The latter was based on a review of women's literature which reveals the importance of such factors as having a mentor, supportive parents and/or a supportive spouse, self-belief, family friendly employment policies, the ability to network and a willingness to work long, unsocial hours [7,8,9,10,11,12,13]. Assurances were given that the information gathered would be treated in strictest confidence and that no details would be published that could be used to identify participants or their institutions.

3 Results

Of the thirty women contacted, twenty agreed to take part in the research. Seven of these were employed at traditional 'red brick' universities; the remainder at

Human Perspectives in the Internet Society: Culture, Psychology and Gender, K. Morgan, J. Sanchez, C. A. Brebbia & A Voiskounsky (Editors) © 2004 WIT Press, www.witpress.com, ISBN 1-85312-726-4

'new' universities. Although members of the sample occupied positions at all levels of the hierarchy, fourteen were at senior lecturer level and above. This is much higher than the national average but was justified on grounds that there may be more to be learned from examining the careers of women who have been relatively successful [14].

In terms of biographical data, the average age of the women was 47 years. Half were married, the rest were either divorced, single or separated. Fifteen had children but because of the high average age of the participants, most were now grown up. Only six had children under the age of ten. The sample was very well qualified. Twelve held a PhD, seven an MSc. Although most had majored in technical subjects, a number came from Arts backgrounds and had worked in non-computing fields before entering academia. This may help to explain why a large number (14) specialised in the softer areas of Computing such as HCI, E-Commerce, Systems Analysis and Knowledge Management. Only six taught traditional Computer Science subjects such as programming, object oriented methods etc. Half the sample had worked in industry at some point during their career; the other half had only ever worked in academia. Of the latter, two had previously been school teachers the other four had worked in Further Education (FE) colleges.

When asked to describe their roles, most said they spent about 43 per cent of their time on teaching and 19% on course administration. The amount of time devoted to teaching varied according to seniority. Those with departmental responsibilities spent 30% of their time on teaching and 50% on management. The average amount of time allocated to research was 25%, slightly higher than the national average for university lecturers. Differences in the amount of time devoted to research emerged between staff teaching in the new and old universities. Women in the new universities spent 18% of their time on research compared with 32% in older establishments. This might suggest that different factors are important in influencing the careers of staff at different types of institution, i.e. traditional universities place greater emphasis on research than teaching/management and reward those with strong research backgrounds. This could have important implications for the careers of the women since Greenfield (2001) maintains that childrearing responsibilities can limit the amount of time available to spend on research. When asked about this, only one of the interviewees believed that childrearing had a detrimental impact on her research activities and career. However, everyone felt that research was important for career mobility. They were also reluctant to take career breaks. Only three of the mothers had taken more than six months off work following pregnancy.

A key objective of the research was to find out what had attracted the interviewees to a career lecturing in Computer Science. Although obviously interested in research, this is not what had brought them into academia. Only six had followed the traditional researcher career route through Higher Education (HE) and only one said that the desire to carry out research was the main reason for working in HE. For seven of the women it was 'the desire to teach and pass on knowledge". This probably reflects the large number of the sample who had worked exclusively in academia. Although most were mothers and the academic

Human Perspectives in the Internet Society: Culture, Psychology and Gender, K. Morgan, J. Sanchez, C. A. Brebbia & A Voiskounsky (Editors) © 2004 WIT Press, www.witpress.com, ISBN 1-85312-726-4

year suits family commitments, only one of the interviewees sited this as the main reason for wanting to teach. A recurrent theme of the interviews, however, was that teaching and motherhood mixed quite well, particularly where the university provided childcare facilities. As to why the interviewees wanted to teach at universities rather than other educational institutions, the results suggest that Higher Education is perceived to offer better career opportunities and higher status. Those who had worked in schools or Further Education Colleges left usually "for progression".

The statistics quoted at the beginning of the paper on the numbers of women computer lecturers suggest that the interviewees were overly optimistic about career opportunities available. However, they had risen to quite senior positions so the question arises of, to what do they attribute their success? When asked to rate the factors that were important on a scale of 0-5, the overwhelming majority felt that their success was due mainly to self belief/assertiveness. It was the lack of these qualities that was seen as the main constraint on women's career development. The most senior member of the sample put it this way: "I think a key problem is the attitude of women towards men, we value men more highly than ourselves and think we can't do the job." Apart from self-belief, the women felt that a certain amount of luck, the ability to make informal contacts and a supportive spouse or partner were important. These findings are consistent with other studies of women high-fliers which suggest they have a strong belief in their own abilities but also recognise the need to network and gain support to be successful [13].

A factor that emerged as very important in influencing the women's success was their ability to 'make themselves visible'. The careers literature suggests that women often find this difficult and dislike promoting themselves. In the present sample, the interviewees demonstrated no such reservations. They made themselves visible within the university by sitting on departmental and university committees, acting as course or programme directors and assuming external examiner roles. Visibility within the academic community was achieved by editing journals, organising conferences and managing research teams. Although the interviewees shared most women's distaste for organisational politics, it was clear that they recognised the need to engage in politics to advance their career.

Apart from personal factors, there is evidence that institutional differences affected the interviewees' career development. This is suggested by the sharp divisions in their views on the support received from their university. A minority had been promoted several times internally so that they now occupied influential positions. These women had nothing but praise for their institution and their 'supportive male colleagues'. Others were less sanguine. While employment policies were generally considered good, appraisal interviews were felt to be ineffective, particularly as a vehicle for providing feedback on performance and chances of progression. Six of the interviewees definitely felt they had not had the same opportunities as their male colleagues and believed that senior male staff would choose men for key posts 'even when they were clearly less competent'. One of the researchers complained that male supervisors saw female research assistants as 'easy to control'. While she felt this might

Human Perspectives in the Internet Society: Culture, Psychology and Gender, K. Morgan, J. Sanchez, C. A. Brebbia & A Voiskounsky (Editors) © 2004 WIT Press, www.witpress.com, ISBN 1-85312-726-4

actually help women in the initial stages of their career, it was a major impediment later on, when they needed to be seen as having leadership ability.
This observation was made by an interviewee at one of the traditional universities but, overall, no clear differences emerged between the old and new universities in terms of the perception of gender bias or opportunities for career development. The sample included senior staff at both types of institution and their views contained a mixture of both positive and negative comments.

One possible constraint on the career development of the interviewees was the lack of suitable role models and mentors. Less than half the members of the sample had been mentored by a senior colleague. Research on mentoring suggests that individuals who have a mentor are more likely to achieve career success and higher earnings than those who have not been mentored. With so few women occupying senior positions in Computing Departments or within universities, the interviewees found it difficult to obtain the support and guidance they needed. They were obliged to rely on senior male colleagues to act as mentors. While this can work well, studies suggest that it is fraught with problems and can place women in an invidious position.

The lack of appropriate role models and/or mentors may account for the interviewees' modest career ambitions. Although a picture has been built up of a successful group of women, when asked about their long-term ambitions, they did not see themselves occupying the highest echelons of academia. Only five said that by retirement they would like to be a Professor or Chair. One said she might like to become a vice chancellor but quickly qualified this with 'it will never happen'. Many expected to end their careers either at the same level or one grade higher. This suggests that their careers had reached a plateau or the effects of early sex role differentiation are so ingrained, they persist even amongst the most able women.

4 Conclusions

The main objectives of the research were to (a) determine what made a career teaching Computer Science attractive to the women, (b) examine the factors that had influenced their career development in academia. Although the sample was not typical in that it contained a higher than average number of 'senior' staff, the results provide interesting insights into the careers of the women that could be useful in guiding recruitment and career development efforts.

In terms of recruitment efforts, the key finding is that most of the women seem to have demonstrated a strong early commitment to education. Over half had only ever worked in education and were very motivated to teach. While it is important to attract staff with industrial experience, recruitment efforts amongst women should perhaps be directed at those who have already demonstrated an interest in teaching/research as a career. The ideal recruiting ground, of course, is amongst the university's undergraduate and postgraduate Computer Science students. Some female students may have considered a career in academia but been discouraged by the lack of female role models or the paucity of careers guidance. If women staff could be persuaded to discuss career opportunities with

Human Perspectives in the Internet Society: Culture, Psychology and Gender, K. Morgan, J. Sanchez, C. A. Brebbia & A Voiskounsky (Editors) © 2004 WIT Press, www.witpress.com, ISBN 1-85312-726-4

students and to take an active role in mentoring female students, more women might entertain the possibility of a career in lecturing.

The interviewees' accounts of their career experiences in academia suggest that women need to be very proactive in promoting their career if they want to be successful. This appears to be something that they learned over time through trial and error. Although supported by partners and informal networks, the women clearly lacked careers advice and the guidance of a mentor. One solution is for women staff to offer peer and mentoring support to their colleagues, particularly newcomers. There are also external support schemes, however, from which women can benefit. The Athena Project, for example, organises local networks of women in Engineering and there is a nationwide mentoring scheme from which Computer Science lecturers can benefit (and to which, of course, they can contribute) [17].

The research findings suggest that some of the women felt that appraisal interviews failed to provide the feedback needed to improve performance and achieve personal career goals. This suggests that it is important to ensure that those conducting appraisal interviews are trained both in the correct procedures and in managing diversity. UK universities have been criticised for failing to provide adequate HR support. It would appear from the findings that there is a case for closer monitoring of appraisal and also for central HR/Staff Development to become more actively involved in supporting female staff. One way they can do this is by providing careers guidance and support to those in the initial stages of their career and career reviews for those well into their career. Some universities appoint staff development co-ordinators from the academic staff to manage staff development locally. If women Computer Science staff were to assume this role, they would be in a very good position to provide support to female colleagues and ensure that their career development needs are met. As staff development responsibilities demonstrate management abilities, taking on this role may actually benefit the careers of the women.

For many women the key constraint on the career development is family commitments. The findings indicate, however, that the interviewees successfully managed to juggle career and family responsibilities. Indeed, there was quite a strong feeling that lecturing was compatible with motherhood. This is partly because the university calendar fits around the school calendar and partly because lecturing is not a typical 9-5 job, so women have more flexibility to organise their time. A key finding, however, was that the women were reluctant to take a career break because they felt it would adversely affect their chances of promotion. This concern (particularly amongst mothers) could be alleviated if staff were encouraged to keep in touch using mobile computing. Unlike their colleagues in Physics or other 'hard' Engineering subjects, Computer Scientists can frequently dispense with an expensively equipped laboratory. The use of mobile facilities would enable staff to keep in close contact with the university, thereby reducing the impact on their careers of prolonged absences.

One final point from the findings that must be mentioned is the women's areas of specialisation. Many were teaching the 'softer' aspects of Computing and had come from 'non-traditional' backgrounds. Virgo in a study carried out

Human Perspectives in the Internet Society: Culture, Psychology and Gender, K. Morgan, J. Sanchez, C. A. Brebbia & A Voiskounsky (Editors) © 2004 WIT Press, www.witpress.com, ISBN 1-85312-726-4

nearly two decades ago observed that the interpersonal and management skills women possessed could be applied very effectively to the soft areas of Computing and suggested that employers ought to consider this when recruiting for Computing jobs [11]. The findings bear this out and suggest that efforts need to be made to persuade women that Computing is not all bites and bytes but concerns important human and social issues. Two of the interviewees had come into Computing via conversion courses. As these do not require a first degree in Computing and often focus on the softer elements, there may be a case for promoting them to women and perhaps offering scholarships for exceptional candidates.

Most of the initiatives suggested above require changes at institutional level and/or Government support. There is already Government awareness of the need for change, largely due to the work of Greenfield who has drawn attention to the paucity of women lecturing in science subjects. Changes at the institutional level are likely to take a long time to effect, however, because of the small numbers of women who are qualified to teach at this level. If, however, awareness is raised of the importance of recruiting women (and other groups traditionally under-represented within Faculty) then at least steps can be taken that will begin to alter the large gender gap that exists and provide women with the opportunities to fully contribute to the development of computer technology.

References

[1] Department of Trade and Industry http: www.set4.women.gov.uk/ (2003)

[2] *Labour Force Survey* (2000)

[3] Greenfield, S., Peters, J., Lane, N., Rees, T., Samuels, G. *SET Fair: A Report on Women in Science, Engineering and Technology*, DTI, (2002)

[4] Gill, J. and Johnson, P. *Research Methods for Managers*, Sage Publications, (2002).

[5] Easterby-Smith, M, Thorpe, M. and Lowe, A. (1991) Management Research, London: Sage Publications.

[6] Ghauri, P., Gronhaug, K. and Kristianslund, I. (1995) Research Methods in Business studies, New York: Prentice Hall.

[7] Kanter, R.M. *Men and Women of the Corporation*, New York: Basic Books, (1977).

[8] Marshall, J. *Women Managers: travellers in a Male World*, New York: John Wiley, (1984)

[9] Marshall, J. *Women Managers Moving On: Exploring Career and Life Choices*, Routledge: London and New York, (1995).

[10] Riley, S. and Wrench, D. Mentoring among women lawyers, *Journal of Applied Social Psychology*, 15, 374-86, (1985).

[11] Virgo, P. *The Report of the Women into Information Technology Campaign Feasibility Study*, IT Strategy Services.

[12] Warihay, P. D. The climb to the top: is the network the route for women? *Personnel Administrator,* 25, (4), 55-690, (1980).

Human Perspectives in the Internet Society: Culture, Psychology and Gender, K. Morgan, J. Sanchez, C. A. Brebbia & A Voiskounsky (Editors) © 2004 WIT Press, www.witpress.com, ISBN 1-85312-726-4

[13] White, B., Cox, C. and Cooper, C. *Women's Career Development: A study of High Fliers*, Blackwell, (1992)
[14] Dearing Commission Report on the Future of Higher Education
[15] Fagenson, E. A. The Mentor Advantage: Perceived CareerJJob Experiences of Proteges Versus Non-Proteges, *Journal of Organizational Behavior*, 10, 309-320, (1989).
[16] Chao, G. T., Walz, P. M., Gardner, P. D. Formal and Informal Mentorships: A Comparison of Mentoring Functions and Contrast with Non-Mentored Counterparts.
[17] *A Strategy for Women in Science, Engineering and Technology*, Office of Science and Technology,. (2003).

Human Perspectives in the Internet Society: Culture, Psychology and Gender, K. Morgan, J. Sanchez, C. A. Brebbia & A Voiskounsky (Editors) © 2004 WIT Press, www.witpress.com, ISBN 1-85312-726-4

"I don't understand computer programming, because I'm a woman!": negotiating gendered positions in a Norwegian discourse of computing

H. Corneliussen
Department of Humanistic Informatics, University of Bergen, Norway

Abstract

In this article I will discuss how young men and women in Norway perceive the existence of gendered expectations in relation to computers. The male and female students of computing that I have studied, share an understanding of gender and computing – a hegemonic discourse – which creates different expectations to men and women's relations to computers. Men are expected to have more interest, experience and knowledge about computers than women. The discourse affects how men and women understand and present themselves as computer users. But individuals are also free to *negotiate* the discourse, and some describe themselves as being in 'harmony' with the expectations to men and women, while others do not. Whether in harmony or not with the gendered expectations, they are all negotiating the gendered meanings of computers in a Norwegian context.
Keywords: gender and computers, computer education, women's pleasure in computers, discourse.

1 Introduction

It is a common opinion that Norway is a country of gender equality (cf. Skjeie and Teigen [11]). However, very few women choose to study or work with information technology (Corneliussen [5]). One of the problems reported by women within computer education has been related to being a minority in male dominated institutions (Håpnes [7], Stuedahl [12]). Efforts to attract more women to computer education have shown positive results, but do not seem to

Human Perspectives in the Internet Society: Culture, Psychology and Gender, K. Morgan, J. Sanchez, C. A. Brebbia & A Voiskounsky (Editors) © 2004 WIT Press, www.witpress.com, ISBN 1-85312-726-4

have long-lasting effects, and the number of women in the most male dominated areas of computer education is once again decreasing (Computerworld [1]). Although it is true that when women are a small minority, their experiences of the social setting may be negative, the recent decrease in women completing degrees in computer science indicates that the problem not only has to do with the male dominance in numbers. This indicates the importance of investigating other barriers women experience in their relations with computers. We need to find out more about how men and women experience themselves in relation to computers. We need to ask what it means to be a woman working with computers compared to being a man working with computers. A computer is not only a 'dead' object, but also an object interwoven with culture. In order to understand how men and women experience computers, it is necessary to focus on how gender and technology interact and affect each other. In the following we will explore how ideas about gender are interwoven with ideas about computers in the Norwegian culture, and how these ideas affect men and women's personal relations to computers.

1.1 Empirical material and methodology

The empirical material is drawn from my Ph. D. thesis *The power of discourse - the freedom of individuals: Gendered positions in the discourse of computing* (Corneliussen [3]). For three months I observed and interviewed students at the Department of Humanistic Informatics at the University of Bergen on the Western coast of Norway. In Scandinavia, there is a tendency for computer studies within social sciences and the humanities to attract more women then corresponding courses associated with the natural sciences (Corneliussen [5]). As the name indicates, this is a computer course within the humanities, and it has since the latter part of the 90s had between 60 and 70% female students. The students at Humanistic Informatics are trained in technical, practical and theoretical subjects related to ICT. I followed 7 male and 21 female students in a programming course for first term students, in three classes that I was also teaching (Corneliussen [3, 4]).

In line with social constructivist theories, both gender and technology are seen as categories that are not stable or fixed, but are rather constantly (re)constructed in interaction with each other (Corneliussen [3, 4, 6]). I follow Joan W. Scott's insistence that gender should be investigated as a discursive category based on "perceived differences between the sexes" (Scott [10]). Simone de Beauvoir adds the important notion that we all contribute to the construction of gender, through 'what we do about what the world does to us' (de Beauvoir [2], ref. in Moi [9]). It is this dual understanding of gender we will investigate here. The most important analytical concepts in the following discussion are discourse and subject position (Laclau and Mouffe [8]). Discourse refers to a limited and temporarily fixed meaning within one particular area – like the discourse of computing. Subject position refers to a discursive point of identification within a discourse. As we will see, the individual can associate with or negotiate a subject position.

Human Perspectives in the Internet Society: Culture, Psychology and Gender, K. Morgan, J. Sanchez, C. A. Brebbia & A Voiskounsky (Editors) © 2004 WIT Press, www.witpress.com, ISBN 1-85312-726-4

1.2 A hegemonic discourse of computing

In the informants' articulations I found that they all support one particular understanding of gender and computing, which can be seen as a dominating or hegemonic discourse of computing. This discourse has two subject positions, describing some basic expectations towards men and women. Men are expected to have more interest, experience and knowledge about computers than women. Men are expected to be fascinated by the technology, while women are not really expected to be interested in the technology itself. Instead, women are expected to see computers as something useful, practical and something they need to address. Concerning activities, men are associated with computer games, programming and technical tasks, while women are associated with communication, information and writing – tasks that can be described without references to technology.

The hegemonic discourse has a certain power: All the informants refer to this discourse. But the individual's freedom to negotiate a discourse or a subject position is illustrated in their descriptions of their own relations to the computer. They use their own arguments and make their own meaningful connections in order to describe themselves as 'understandable' in relation to computers.

Both men and women use the hegemonic discourse as a frame of reference, but they use it in different ways, and this is what I will illustrate in the main section of this article. By focussing on how the informants position themselves in relation to the hegemonic discourse, it is possible to see a pattern of 7 different positioning strategies; 3 among the men (Corneliussen [6]), and 4 among the women. Women entering computing have to deal with a masculine discourse, which makes women's strategies rather complex to understand. In the following the men's strategies will be treated briefly, before we take a closer look at the strategies found among the women.

2 Positioning strategies among the men

2.1 Rooted in 'a room for men'

The first positioning strategy among the men is articulated by men with a close relationship to computers. They have experience, knowledge and an interest in computers which seem to be in harmony with the hegemonic discourse. They articulate this in relation to the fact that they are men or boys: "… as a boy I have been involved in computing of some form or the other since I was in elementary school" (Jon). It is described as 'natural' to expect that boys have computer skills, and one of the men even thinks "people almost expect that a boy studies computing" (Jon). The men articulating this strategy conform to the expectations towards men in the hegemonic discourse. They are rooted in the 'room' that the discourse opens up for men, and they use these expectations towards men as positive descriptions of themselves.

2.2 Aiming at 'a room for men'

The next group of men cannot exhibit the same harmony with the masculine subject position. However, they aim at 'a room for men' in their positioning

Human Perspectives in the Internet Society: Culture, Psychology and Gender, K. Morgan, J. Sanchez, C. A. Brebbia & A Voiskounsky (Editors) © 2004 WIT Press, www.witpress.com, ISBN 1-85312-726-4

strategy, and they use the masculine subject position as a positive reference for themselves. One of them believes that he can learn tasks on the computer faster because of "the 'taken for granted' assumption that computers-are-something-I-can-handle, because I am a boy…" (Terje). This assumption about men's easy access to computer knowledge becomes a positive force of motivation in his own learning process, and he aims deliberately at gaining access to 'a room for men' by working persistently to learn as much as possible.

One of the other men describes how annoyed he gets when he tries to help the female students: "If I'm explaining something to a female student, or if I say that she has to do this or that in order to solve a problem, she seldom does exactly what I say if she does not understand WHY." (Knut) The women do not take him seriously, because he cannot answer their big 'WHY'. His irritation seems to arise from the women challenging him when he enters the position of a computer competent man – a position that he is not qualified for. But he is also aware of this dilemma himself:

> I think it is good that there are so many women at humanistic informatics, […] If men had been in the majority, you would have to (I feel) pretend all the time that you know more than you actually do, in order not to appear "stupid" (Knut).

He illustrates how he has access to the masculine subject position associated with computer knowledge, without really being qualified. Being associated with this position conceals that he does not have the knowledge that men are expected to have.

The masculine subject position is a goal for the men in this group. They use this position, either by trying to become qualified, or by using the position without being qualified. They illustrate that men are expected to have computer knowledge, but they also illustrate how they as men easily *can* be associated with computer knowledge because of these expectations.

2.3 Outside 'a room for men'

The last positioning strategy found among the men is articulated by one man who does *not* want to be associated with the masculine subject position. Instead he wants to be positioned outside 'the room for men'. In the computer lab, he seemed to be inexperienced with computers. This appearance was further strengthened when he several times spoke of himself as poorly skilled: "I have a PC with a sound board that does not work, that probably tells you how much I have acquired in that area" (Arild). He also refrained from introducing himself as a computer student in front of others, not wanting to be associated with computing. At the end of the term, however, he told me that he had studied computing before. Although I had asked the informants about their computer experience, he had not mentioned this before.

This man clearly did not want to be associated with the hegemonic masculine subject position. He emphasized his lack of knowledge and he kept some of his computing experience hidden. He seems to illustrate how he, as a man, needs an active strategy in order to disqualify himself for the masculine subject position.

Human Perspectives in the Internet Society: Culture, Psychology and Gender, K. Morgan, J. Sanchez, C. A. Brebbia & A Voiskounsky (Editors) © 2004 WIT Press, www.witpress.com, ISBN 1-85312-726-4

The different positioning strategies among the men illustrate that men can position themselves in relation to computing in different ways. However, the positions they describe also illustrate how they use the hegemonic discourse – they identify with it, aim at it or distance themselves from it. The hegemonic discourse gives the guidelines for which qualities or characteristics to emphasize or tone down, in order to associate oneself with or reject the masculine subject position. Even though this position involves some expectations towards computer skills, the connection between men and computer skills is so close, that being a man can function as a sign of computer competence.

3 Positioning strategies among the women

3.1 'A limited room for women'

Moving on to the female students, we remember that the subject position associated with women was described as *limited* in different ways compared to the masculine subject position. The first positioning strategy among the women aims at this 'limited room for women'. To be interested in computers is associated with boys, and is perceived as "boring, masculine and a bit nerdy" (Marit). It is described as 'natural' that women understand less about computers than men do:

> It's quite obvious that the boys have the best understanding of the technical stuff. [...] The fact that the girls don't quite get it and need to have the information spoon-fed is not quite as accepted. It is, after all, men that teach (those topics), or very highly educated women!! (Lillian).

This difference between men and women is described as a general difference: The lack of computer knowledge applies to every woman – except those with higher education. Women with computer skills are not seen as positive role models. Instead they are described as a special category of women that cannot see the particular needs that girls have anymore. It is this gap between women and computer skills they emphasize when they position themselves: "I don't understand computer programming, because I'm a woman!" (Lillian) Because women are not expected to have that kind of knowledge, it is sufficient for this woman to use gender to explain her relation to programming. Being a woman explains her distance to computers as 'natural'.

The women who aim at 'a limited room for women' want to learn to use the computer, but they want a very restricted amount of knowledge. They have a clear opinion of what kind of knowledge they do not want: "I am not going to be an engineer, I'm not going to poke about in a machine at all - I don't understand any of those things .. […] I don't want to understand it. I <u>don't</u> want to learn that" (Lillian). The subject position associated with women in the hegemonic discourse is seen as a valid description of women in general, and they use the expectations about women's limited interest, knowledge, and experience in order to explain their own relation to the technology. They also seem to confirm the expectation that women need to see some kind of usefulness in technology. Usefulness is however a relative concept, and while these women are critical to topics concerning programming and the technical side of computers, many of the other women point to precisely these things when they describe what they have found most interesting to learn about, as we will see in the next positioning strategy.

3.2 'A more open room for women'

The next group of women also start with a limited relation to computers, but they aim at 'a more open room for women', where women have positive relations to computers. "To me it was a conscious decision to enrol in a computer class. I did not want to continue being the illiterate that I felt I'd become" (Marte). Through their own experience at the computer course, these women expand the limited room for women. All of them had earlier experience with computers, but it is as computer students they 'realize' that they actually *can* learn about computers, and that they actually *enjoy* working with computers. These women express a great pleasure in learning more about computers:

> "I started at the bottom when it comes to computer knowledge, really – but I feel that with every new day I master new things [...] It feels like a new world has opened up to me ... and every day I think "How on earth is it possible to walk around and cope without knowing what I know today!??" It has to be a feeling close to something like going from being illiterate to being able to read... I think that I have become addicted to the computer!!!" (Helga).

Many of these women express a surprise that they suddenly have found computing both fun and useful, and many of them describe themselves as 'addicted'. To enter the world where women do not have a natural position is one of the things that seem to fascinate these women the most. Programming is one of the activities that is most exclusively associated with men. One of the women explains that she thinks about programming as a masculine activity, and says:

> "Maybe that is why I want to do programming, because it is so masculine [...] I feel sort of as if I were in a world that's a little bit forbidden. That is probably why I find it especially exciting. [...] I think there is some status symbol connected to it" (Bente).

Programming is an exiting world because it is a forbidden world. Some of the other women find working with hardware most fascinating. In both cases their fascination derives from a feeling of having knowledge in, and authority from, a field dominated by men.

These women appreciate the computer knowledge they have got through the computer course. They are about to create a 'room' where women *are* interested in computers, and in this perspective, they describe themselves as untraditional women. However, in relation to men in the masculine field of computing, they still describe themselves as 'typical women' – in a forbidden world. These women expand the room for women, but they also maintain the borders between

Human Perspectives in the Internet Society: Culture, Psychology and Gender, K. Morgan, J. Sanchez, C. A. Brebbia & A Voiskounsky (Editors) © 2004 WIT Press, www.witpress.com, ISBN 1-85312-726-4

men and women. They emphasize that they do use the computer, but they do not use the computer in the same playful way they associate with boys.

3.3 'A shared room' for men and women

In the third positioning strategy among the women, the goal is 'a shared room' where gender has nothing to do with possibilities or abilities. The women articulating this strategy have a lot of experience with computers. However, they have also experienced being treated in accordance with the expectation that women have limited computer knowledge:

> If I am sitting and trying out something, installing something and sitting poking about a bit, and then a boy comes and says "No, look here, I will show you", then I just get annoyed and say "Excuse me! I can do this just as well as you. Just leave me alone and let me do it." At least they often believe that they know more because they are men, even though I can't see why that's so" (Bjørg).

Even though these women reject the idea that gender has any particular meaning in relation to computers, they still find that gendered expectations are used against them. And they protest against it. Bjørg, who is talking here, claims that gender does not mean anything to her. But at the same time she experiences that gender does mean something, and she fights against it. She believes that what makes the difference is how she behaves when she is confronted with these attitudes – here from a interview together with Sara, who strongly disagrees with her:

> Bjørg: … no boy is allowed to tell me that I am not worth as much as he is, because then I'll tell him what I really think about that.
>
> Sara: Yes, but I think it doesn't matter what you say.
>
> Bjørg: Yes, it does in fact matter what I say, because if I just accept that's the way it is, nothing will happen. But if I put my foot down and say "Hey you, listen, that's not how it is!" Then the person sooner or later, depending on how much you nag and make a fuss about it, will understand …"

Bjørg needs an active strategy – to 'nag and make a fuss' – in order to protest against the meaning that is ascribed to gender. The equal position these women describe does not exist, but has to be created by confronting the exponents of the hegemonic discourse.

Even though these women claim that gender should not matter, they also emphasize that men and women have different relations to the computer:

> "I have a partner […] and every time he passes the study where the computer is, he just has to go into the room and just press a few keys, for instance if he is on his way to the kitchen to get some coffee, he passes the study and just has to go in […] It's like

> 'schwoop' – as if the computer drags him in. It's the same with my brother and my father, and two other men I know. [...] I manage to go passt a computer without having to press some key" (Bjørg)"

Here, men are associated with an unhealthy and uncontrolled relation to computers, in contrast to women. Men and women do different things with the computer. This has nothing to do with abilities or possibilities, but with conscious choices that women make: They just do not care for the same things as men.

This strategy is not about abolishing gender, but about being treated as equals to men. "We are not men. We don't think as men. But we have values that are just as good as men's values, but we have to show that we've got them, and show that we dare to think in a different way..." (Bjørg). These women do *not* consider themselves as 'strangers' in relation to computers. They aim at 'a shared room' of computing which tolerate both a masculine and a feminine subject position. The starting point is however that the hegemonic discourse exists, and that is why they need an active strategy. They need to protest.

3.4 Women in 'a room for men'

In the last positioning strategy, the women position themselves in 'a room for men'. These women also strongly express that men in general have advantages before women: "These thoughts reflect the structure of our society, where masculine values are always treated as better and more serious, yes, more 'human', than female values" (Sara). Perhaps it is this opinion of a general gender inequality that makes them emphasize that they qualify to enter 'a room for men', rather than 'a room for women': "Since I did not have a brother, my sister and I had to fill that 'gap' by learning practical tasks that traditionally often are performed by men." (Lise) They use their experience of performing practical tasks associated with men in order to describe their own relations to the computer.

> Tone: Both Lise and I are atypical women – have managed for years without a man, and become more and more masculine, I think. [...]
>
> Lise: [...] Both of us are raised so that we should know how to saw and ..
>
> Tone: ... different things. My father is a craftsman, and I have worked a lot together with him, and still do.

These women have a tradition for crossing gendered borders, partly because of the absence of men, and partly because the men have brought them along. Performing tasks, operating machines and technical equipment associated with men contributes to their qualification for a positive position in the discourse of computing. They do not reject or protest against the hegemonic discourse, but rather use this as the basis for their articulations. It is within this discourse they define themselves, as women, within 'a room for men'.

Human Perspectives in the Internet Society: Culture, Psychology and Gender, K. Morgan, J. Sanchez, C. A. Brebbia & A Voiskounsky (Editors) © 2004 WIT Press, www.witpress.com, ISBN 1-85312-726-4

4 The power of discourse – the freedom of individuals

Through this short presentation of the different positioning strategies in this group of students we can see how men and women perceive different possibilities. Within these possibilities there are some gendered patterns which seem to open up or restrict their perceptions of themselves as computer users. We could probably find other subject positions and other positioning strategies among other social groups, in other contexts. The tendency shows, however, that it's easier for men to be associated with computer competence. Based on gender, men can easily be ascribed a positive relation to computers. Women on the other hand, have to negotiate in order to be ascribed a positive relation to computers. In this landscape, women are 'the others' – outside the masculine norm. To some of the women this becomes a shelter ("I don't understand computer programming, because I'm a woman!"), while it is more problematic to others, who raise a protest against being excluded. If we compare the strategies among men and women, we can see a greater variation among women's negotiation with the discourse than it is possible to see among the men. The women introduce more new elements in their discursive negotiations than the men, who rather seem to line up in a continuum according to how well they conform to the hegemonic discourse. All the positioning strategies use the hegemonic discourse as a valid frame of reference. It is not necessarily accepted, but it is seen as an existing discourse, as something they meet and have to deal with, and they deal with it in different ways. It is through 'what they do with what the world does to them' they construct their positioning strategies. By negotiating with what they perceive as available subject positions they also contribute to the construction of gender, by proposing that being a man or a woman with a relationship to computers can have other meanings than those described by the hegemonic discourse.

Both in academic discourses and in everyday discourses we refer to myths about gender and computers. These myths have been a rather unclear area, often treated as unsettled questions or as 'fallacies' that simply can be rejected. In my research it has been important to take such myths seriously – not as myths meaning something which is not true, but as cultural stories about the relation between gender and computers. As long as these cultural stories are perceived as a valid frame of reference to men and women who are trying to find their own positions in relation to computers, they also have real effects on real people.

Another point I want to emphasize is the enormous pleasure and joy these women express when they talk about their new relationship to the computer, about the computer in general, about programming or hardware – things that are associated with men in the hegemonic discourse. During the last ten years there have been a number of attempts in Norway to attract women to computer education, not by accentuating women's pleasure in technology, but rather using slogans emphasizing that computing is about communicating with people, a skill specially associated with women. It is as if the stories about women's pleasure in computing are drowned in the hegemonic discourse's claim that 'women do not

Human Perspectives in the Internet Society: Culture, Psychology and Gender, K. Morgan, J. Sanchez, C. A. Brebbia & A Voiskounsky (Editors) © 2004 WIT Press, www.witpress.com, ISBN 1-85312-726-4

care for computers'. One of the challenges for the future is thus to make the stories about pleasure in computing 'stick' to women.

References

[1] Kvinneandelen ved NTNU halvert på ett år. *Computerworld*, 24.10.2003.

[2] Beauvoir, S. d., *Det annet kjønn*, Pax: Oslo, 2000 (1949).

[3] Corneliussen, H., *Diskursens makt - individets frihet: Kjønnede posisjoner i diskursen om data (The power of discourse - the freedom of individuals: Gendered positions in the discourse of computing)* Dr. art. thesis, Dep. of humanistic informatics, University of Bergen, 2002.

[4] Corneliussen, H., The multi-dimensional stories of the gendered users of ICT. *Researching ICTs in context*, A. Morrison, InterMedia Report: Oslo, 3/2002: 161-184, 2002.

[5] Corneliussen, H., Konstruksjoner av kjønn ved høyere IKT-utdanning i Norge. *Kvinneforskning*, **27(3)**: 51-50, 2003.

[6] Corneliussen, H., Male positioning strategies in relation to computing. *He, She and IT Revisited. New Perspectives on Gender in the Information Society*, M. Lie, Gyldendal Akademisk: 103-134, 2003.

[7] Håpnes, T., Hvordan forstå mannsdominansen i datafaget? En dekonstruksjon av fag- og kjønnskultur. *Utdanningskultur og kjønn*, T. Annfelt & G. Imsen, NTNU, Senter for teknologi og samfunn 3/92: Trondheim: 155-183, 1992.

[8] Laclau, E. & C. Mouffe, *Hegemony & socialist strategy. Towards a radical democratic politics*, Verso: London, 1985.

[9] Moi, T., *What is a woman? And other essays*, Oxford University Press: Oxford, 1999.

[10] Scott, J. W., *Gender and the politics of history*, Columbia University Press: New York, 1988.

[11] Skjeie, H. & M. Teigen, *Menn imellom. Mannsdominans og likestillingspolitikk*, Gyldendal akademisk: Oslo, 2003.

[12] Stuedahl, D., Studenten i informatikkstudiet - en rapport om studenters situasjon ved Institutt for informatikk, UiO, Kirke-, utdannings- og forskningsdepartementet, Likestillingssekretariatet: Oslo, 1999.

Human Perspectives in the Internet Society: Culture, Psychology and Gender, K. Morgan, J. Sanchez, C. A. Brebbia & A Voiskounsky (Editors) © 2004 WIT Press, www.witpress.com, ISBN 1-85312-726-4

The role of gender in the outcome of ICT adoption – can nurses be technologists?

F. Bacon & S. Stocking
UWIC Business School, University of Wales Institute, Cardiff, Cardiff, UK
School of Computing, University of Glamorgan, Pontypridd, Mid Glamorgan CF37 1DL, UK

Abstract

The use of computers in the work place has increased in recent years with more and more professions becoming dependent on information and communication technology (ICT).

Research shows that women in general tend to be slow in engaging with computing and there are many records of women's negative experiences with ICT [1]. Women have often been portrayed as passive users [17]. The female perception of ICT tends to be that it is a male dominated area.

Frenkel [9] states that the computer culture is uncomfortable for girls and women, they are ill at ease in a field that seems to encourage "highly focused, almost obsessive behaviour", as the key to success. This study investigates the use of ICT in a female oriented work environment. For the purpose of this research the nursing profession was selected as nursing is a gendered job [6], not only because women make up the vast majority of workers but because of the centrality of care (the socially accepted role of women), to the work they perform [3].

This study shows that nurses as carers find it difficult to transfer any previously acquired information technological skills into their work based information technology needs.

The research was carried out in local hospitals and nursing communities. The method used was survey by questionnaire to ascertain previous knowledge, skills and training in ICT together with nurses' perception of themselves as ICT users.

Human Perspectives in the Internet Society: Culture, Psychology and Gender, K. Morgan, J. Sanchez, C. A. Brebbia & A Voiskounsky (Editors) © 2004 WIT Press, www.witpress.com, ISBN 1-85312-726-4

1 Introduction

Nurses are technologists with extensive technical capabilities and have been for decades. We see them using a huge variety of sophisticated machinery to mediate patient care on a daily basis, from IV therapy in the post war years, ICU in the sixties, to microchip driven IV pumps, blood pressure units and finger thermometers in the nineties as well as many more technological innovations designed to support their role as carer. All of these, nurses have become accustomed to and expert at using. However, a number of case studies show that when it comes to using new technology, especially when it involves administrative and documentation tasks that take the nurse away from the patient, many display the characteristics of the novice use [14, 21, 23]. In other words they exhibit dual personalities when using technology. The 'expert user' comes to the fore when they use technology that supports their role as carers, however the 'novice' is in evidence when the technology, described as 'new' or 'information' is used.

Today, the nursing profession is expected to embrace 'new technology' as part of its professional activity. The term 'nursing informatics' originated by Scholes et al. [15] was derived from the term 'informatics' first coined in the 1970s, and used to refer to the computer milieu. Nursing informatics is described by Suba and McCormick [19] as:

'The use of technology and/or a computer system to...process... and communicate timely data and information in and across health care facilities that administer nursing services and resources, manage the delivery of patient and nursing care...'

Computers and telecommunications are becoming commonplace in healthcare systems. Many hospitals use integrated computer systems to support administrative, financial and clinical functions [2, 7, 11].

Nurses often find themselves required to use computerised systems for the production of detailed plans for the care of hospital inpatients, these systems were introduced in the 1980s and 1990s as part of the Resource Management Initiative. A study carried out by Timmons [23] which involved three hospitals using similar patient care systems, found that user resistance was rife although the systems were not rejected outright, this he called 'resistive compliance'. A reaction typical of those who consider themselves novice users and a form of system failure referred to by Lyytinen and Hirschheim's [12] as *interaction failure*, failure concerned with levels of use and user satisfaction.

The nursing profession has moved towards using evidence based practice (EBP) for example, according to the Strategic Advisory Group for Nursing Information Systems (SAGNIS) nurses are expected to incorporate research-based practice into their professional activities [13]. A key factor in the success of this approach is the use of ICT especially skills needs to interrogate the Internet.

Human Perspectives in the Internet Society: Culture, Psychology and Gender, K. Morgan, J. Sanchez, C. A. Brebbia & A Voiskounsky (Editors) © 2004 WIT Press, www.witpress.com, ISBN 1-85312-726-4

Nurses are expected to be computer literate. They are expected to make effective use of information technology in their profession. Nurse educators are very aware of the impact of ICT has on the health service [24]. Since the introduction of Project 2000 all pre-registration nursing courses must cover ICT. At present the United Kingdom Central Council (UKCC) requires all nursing students to be able to demonstrate the computer skills needed to record, enter, store retrieve and organise data essential for care delivery before their can be put onto the nursing register. It also requires nurses to be able to interpret and utilize data and technology to deliver and enhance patient care.

Despite the attempts of nurse educators and the thrust of government policy, Sinclair and Gardner [16] point out that those entering the profession come from a wide range of educational backgrounds and therefore there is a diversity of previous exposure to and experience of ICT. Regardless of previous experience of ICT researchers find that in general nurses still do not see the use of ICT as central to their work. [21, 23, 25]. They exhibit the behaviour of novice users by denigrating their skills, deploying avoidance tactics or exhibiting compliant resistance. This occurs because they are not able/willing to transfer their ICT skills to their work as carers.

A study by Timmons and Tredoux [22] found that although some of the nurses surveyed had computers at home and had access to the Internet, none had used the Internet in order to find information related to their nursing profession. However, the doctors surveyed all owned computers and all had used the Internet regularly to either communicate with colleagues or retrieve medical information. The survey also found that whilst doctors used the Internet regularly as part of their job, nurses claimed to be 'too busy'. In other words, the doctors had no problem in transferring the skills they had developed previously to the practice of their profession whereas the nurses, with similar exposure to ICT in their training, had not transferred these skills into their work practice.

Why does this happen? As stated earlier, nurses are competent technologists where the technology supports their role as carer.
The answer may lie in the perception nurses have both of new technology and of their chosen profession.

Nursing is the largest female profession in the healthcare service and looks to stay that way in the future with the majority of entrants into the profession being female. (A study carried out by Sinclair and Gardner [16] found that 90% of students on a nursing diploma course were female). This together with its centrality of care (the customary duty of women) makes it an inherently female gendered profession [6]. The role of nurse blurs with that of the ideal woman – self sacrifice, altruism etc. in contrast to the doctors' expertise which is seen as scientific and the result of acquired knowledge [5]. The domestic roots of nursing gave women the authoritative voice on all matters relating to home, hearth and family – the reign of the woman in the private sphere of the home. When nursing moved to the public sphere of hospitals, nurses could not shake off the socially constructed association between the role of the nurse and the role of the woman – and the role of the woman was to care for the sick. So the social foundation of the nursing profession was based on intuition and empathy, the

Human Perspectives in the Internet Society: Culture, Psychology and Gender, K. Morgan, J. Sanchez, C. A. Brebbia & A Voiskounsky (Editors) © 2004 WIT Press, www.witpress.com, ISBN 1-85312-726-4

time-honoured qualities every woman must have making nursing the archetypal female role. This is in direct contrast to the social foundation of the medical profession where the qualities lauded are empiricism and rationality [8].

Historically, medical tasks have always had a higher status than caring tasks, physicians cure (using that which is scientific, objective, technical and masculine) whilst nurses care (using that which is intuitive, empathic, subjective and feminine). This reflects the gender assumptions that have perpetuated the experiences of both clinicians and patients within the health service.

Society perceives technology as masculine and it acquires from this its superior status.

'Technology enters into our sexual identity; femininity is incompatible with technical competence; to feel technically competent is to feel manly. The gendering of men and women into 'masculine' and 'feminine' is a cultural process of immense power. People suffer for disregarding its dictates' (Coburn, 1986,p.12)

It is well known that women are under-represented in computing from qualifications gained through education to working in the industry [10]. Frenkel [9] states that the computer culture is uncomfortable for girls and women, they are ill at ease in a field that seems to encourage "highly focused, almost obsessive behaviour", as the key to success. A study carried out by Wishart and Ward [26] that compared attitudes towards and use of ICT between nurse and teacher training students found that males held consistently more positive attitudes towards computers than females.

This paucity of women in computing Smith [18] suggests is because women accept their lack of technological ability as being predetermined by their gender in the same way that men delight in their supposed superior ability. This then suggests that definitions of what constitutes technology may shift over time according to the gender of the user [25]. This can be seen throughout the history of nursing. Technology no longer considered complex by physicians has been passed to nurses, for example taking temperatures and drawing blood. In fact physicians were keen to teach the necessary skills to nurses in return for being relieved from what they considered tedious or boring tasks [8]. Interesting, today nurses differentiate between the technology they use on the wards to support their patient care referring to it as 'machines' and the new technology they are expected to use for information system applications which they refer to as 'technology' [25].

Nurses want to be valued for what they do. There has been an attempt to address this problem by giving nurses a professional status. However, this professionalism lies within the masculine framework where scientific objectivity, standardized practice and technical know-how are the critical success factors [25]. The dichotomy now facing nurses is whether to align themselves within this professional model or remain within their gendered role of hands-on carers.

Human Perspectives in the Internet Society: Culture, Psychology and Gender, K. Morgan, J. Sanchez, C. A. Brebbia & A Voiskounsky (Editors) © 2004 WIT Press, www.witpress.com, ISBN 1-85312-726-4

Therefore it is likely that they feel that using computers takes them away from the patient and mitigates hands-on care. Also, as feminine culture is associated with caring not science, they are likely to believe computers are not within their realm of capabilities.

2 The study

This research set out to show that nurses as carers find it difficult to transfer any previously acquired technological skills into their work based technology needs and that despite adequate exposure to and training in ICT, nurses refuse to see themselves as expert users. The study was not based in any one institution but used nurses from a number of local hospitals and communities. The work explored the nursing qualifications, ICT training, and nurses own perception of their ICT ability.

This was accomplished through the use of questionnaires designed in two sections. Section A to ascertain the nurses' qualifications and experience, Section B to gain an understanding of their use of ICT and their perception of their ability in the use of ICT.

The sampling methods used were, firstly, snowball sampling, this is commonly used when it is difficult to identify or contact members of the desired population. Using this method we contacted four members of the nursing profession and asked them to identify and contact further members of the profession. Self-selection sampling was then used on all contacts made. That is, questionnaires were distributed and those that selected to take part returned them. 80 questionnaires were distributed and 46 were returned giving a response rate of 58%.

3 Results

From the questionnaires returned:

Gender	**Responses**
female nurses	39 (86%)
male nurses	6 (13%)

These figures support the finding in the literature that approximately 90% of the nursing population is female.

ICT Training	**Females**	**Males**
ICT incorporated as part of their course	13	3
Other ICT training	6	1
Both	6	2
None	14	0

It can be seen that 64% of the females and 100% of males had received ICT some type of training.

Human Perspectives in the Internet Society: Culture, Psychology and Gender, K. Morgan, J. Sanchez, C. A. Brebbia & A Voiskounsky (Editors) © 2004 WIT Press, www.witpress.com, ISBN 1-85312-726-4

ICT Usage	Females	Males
Daily	24	5
Weekly	3	
Monthly	1	
Occasionally	6	1
Never	5	

That is, of the females surveyed, 70% use ICT weekly or daily, and 30% less than this. Interestingly, even though most female nurses use ICT in their job on a regular basis they still did not consider themselves to be experts.

Own perception	Female	Male
Novice	14	
Adequate	25	
Expert		6

However, 87% of the males use ICT weekly or daily, and 13% less than this and all considered themselves to be expert.

Type of ICT related work carried out was looking up blood results in a database, using the patient administrative system (PAS), using the Internet for research, using PowerPoint to prepare presentations, using Word to write letters and reports.

4 Conclusion

This research is a small contribution to the understanding of the role of gender when a gendered profession adopts ICT. The results support many of the findings of the literature review. As a result of wanting to improve their position, nurses have campaigned for professional status. This professionalisation of nursing has forced nurses to embrace new technology in their work and become competent users. It assumes that nurses are comfortable with ICT especially as now it is part of their training. However, the results of the research show that despite the fact that the majority of nurses in the study used ICT on a regular basis, the females still did not consider themselves expert users. They did not see the use of ICT as central to their role as carers and therefore were not concerned with expertise. As discussed by Cockburn [4] 'technical competency is incompatible with femininity' and nursing is a gendered profession. The male nurses surveyed had no such concern. All considered themselves to be expert users.

In contrast to this, the technology female nurses are comfortable with is that which has been delegated to them by doctors and so has become degendered. It would appear from this research that men and women still carry their perceptions of gender behaviour into their place of work. Can Nurses be technologists? Yes they can but only in areas of technology that support their primary role as carers.

Human Perspectives in the Internet Society: Culture, Psychology and Gender, K. Morgan, J. Sanchez, C. A. Brebbia & A Voiskounsky (Editors) © 2004 WIT Press, www.witpress.com, ISBN 1-85312-726-4

References

[1] Adam, A. (1997) 'What should we do with cyberfeminism?' In: R. Lander & A. Adam Women in Computing, Intellect Books, Exeter.

[2] Banta D. & Gelijin A. (1994) The future and health care technology: implications of a system for early identification. World Health Statistics Quarterly 47, 140-148

[3] Brechin, A., Walmsley, J. & Peace S (1988), Care Matters: Concepts, Practice and Research in Health and Social Care, Sage Publications, London

[4] Cockburn C. (1986) Machinery of Dominance: Women, Men and Technical Knowledge, Pluto Press, London

[5] Davies C. (1995) Gender and the Professional Predicament in Nursing Open University Press Buckingham

[6] Davies, C. and Rosser, J. (1986) 'Gendered jobs in the Health Service: A problem for labour process analysis' In: D Knights & H Willmott, Gender and the Labour Process, Gower Publishing Company Ltd., Hampshire

[7] Davison D. &Rhodes D. (1996) The Virtual University. Nursing Standard 10(27): 21-22

[8] Fairman J. & D'Antonio P. (1999) Virtual power: gendering the nurse-technology relationship. Nursing Inquiry 6:178-186

[9] Frenkel, K. A. (1990). Women & computing. Communications of the ACM, 33 (11), 34-46.

[10] Grundy, F. (1999) Women and Computers, Interlect, Exeter

[11] Healy P. (1996) E-mail the nurse. Nursing Standard 10(27), 14

[12] Lyytinen & Hirschheim's (1987) 'Information System Failure: A survey and classification of the empirical literature'. Oxford Surveys in Information Technology Vol. 4. 257- 309.

[13] NHSE (1995) Information Systems for Nurses, Midwives and Health Visitors. National Health Service Executive, department of Health, London.

[14] Phillips K. (2004) Nurses Taking Technology into Their Own Hands. http://www.Nursezone.com

[15] Scholes M., et al. 1983 The Impact of Computers in Nursing: an International Review. North-Holland, Amsterdam

[16] Sinclair M. & Gardner .J (1999) Planning for information technology key skills in nurse education. Journal of Advanced Nursing 30(6):1441-1445

[17] Slyke C. V., Comunale, C., & Belanger, F. (2002), Gender differences in perception of Web-based shopping. Communications of the ACM, Vol 45, No. 8, 82-86

[18] Smith, J. 1997 Different for Girls: How Culture Creates Women, Chatto Press, London

[19] Suba, V.K. & McCormick, K.A. (1996) Essentials of Computers for Nurses. McGraw-Hill Publishing New York.

Human Perspectives in the Internet Society: Culture, Psychology and Gender, K. Morgan, J. Sanchez, C. A. Brebbia & A Voiskounsky (Editors) © 2004 WIT Press, www.witpress.com, ISBN 1-85312-726-4

[20] Suchman, L. & and Jordan, B. (1988). Computerisation and women's knowledge. In: Women, work and computerisation: IFIP conference proceedings, 1988, Amsterdam.

[21] Timmons S. & Miller S.(2002) A comparative case study of resistance to nursing computer systems. Information Technology and Nursing 14(8):2-7

[22] Timmons S. & Tredoux T.(2000) The doctor-nurse computer game Information Technology in Nursing 12(2): 3-7

[23] Timmons S. (2003) Nurses resisting information technology. Nursing Inquiry 10(4): 257-269

[24] Ward R. 1997 Computer networking and the Internet in Nurses Education. Nurse Education Today 17: 178-183

[25] Wilson M. 2002 Making nursing visible. Information Technology & People 15(2) 139-158

[26] Wishart J. & Ward R. (200)2 Individual differences in nurse and teacher training students' attitudes towards and use of I.T. Nurse Education Today 22: 231-240

Human Perspectives in the Internet Society: Culture, Psychology and Gender, K. Morgan, J. Sanchez, C. A. Brebbia & A Voiskounsky (Editors) © 2004 WIT Press, www.witpress.com, ISBN 1-85312-726-4

An outreach venture: bringing computer literacy to rural women in Malaysia

H. Awang[1] & M. Jaffar[2]
[1]*Faculty of Economics and Administration, University of Malaya*
[2]*Foundation for Women's Education & Vocational Training, Malaysia*

Abstract

With each IT/ICT development, the digital divide grows wider between the information "haves" and the "have-nots". In the effort to narrow the gap and to facilitate the adoption of ICT by rural residents, an outreach training course through the Community Communications Development Program was initiated to provide hands-on training in computer literacy to cultivate interest and appreciation in the importance of ICT knowledge and skills.

The training was conducted on-site using a mobile unit equipped with 16 computers and peripherals, and was stationed in a selected area for 5 days. Training was divided into morning and afternoon sessions with 15 trainees per session to provide them with one computer each. The men attended the morning session, and the women the afternoon sessions. They were taught for a total of 16 hours on how to operate a basic computer system, Microsoft Word and the Internet facilitated by 3 trainers. The participants had little or no knowledge on IT/ICT and many had never touched a computer before. At the beginning the women had more fear due to their lack of confidence in handling the so-called sophisticated machine than their male counterparts. Compared to the men, women took a longer time to learn keyboarding skills but they had more patience and stronger learning perseverance. There was no difference between rural men and women in terms of attitude and willingness to learn and use the new technology.
Keywords: gendered digital divide, computer literacy, rural women, mobile training, community communications development program.

1 Introduction

The development in information technology (IT) and the convergence between information and communications technology (ICT) and multimedia has brought

Human Perspectives in the Internet Society: Culture, Psychology and Gender, K. Morgan, J. Sanchez, C. A. Brebbia & A Voiskounsky (Editors) © 2004 WIT Press, www.witpress.com, ISBN 1-85312-726-4

about many changes and new approaches in the way people work, conduct businesses and communicate. With each ICT development, a phenomenon called the 'digital divide' grows wider. The digital divide refers to the disparities between the "haves" and the "have-nots" in terms of the availability of and access to information and technologies. Digital divides exist both within countries and regions and between countries. It transcends locality, race, gender, age, language, culture and religion.

The digital divide affects a large number of the remotest villages which will have no chance of tapping into the global store of knowledge in Malaysia. Thus the digital divide describes the gap caused by various factors, between those who have access and those who do not have access to computer facilities, information literacy or even basic computer literacy skills. Women in general have a lower literacy rate and most are in the deepest part of the divide, so are thus further removed from the information age than men whose poverty they share.

More and more concern is being shown about the impact of those left on the other side of the digital divide because the restrictions will be magnified as the progress of IT enhancement accelerates.

2 ICT development in Malaysia

Malaysia has made an enormous inroad into the digital society to advance its economic and social development. The efforts, included among others, the creation and reinforcement of enabling environments such as a rapid investment expansion on IT infrastructure and the installation and integration of national IT development strategies into its overall economic and social development plans. The use of IT for development poses great expectations and challenges for the country because IT is not simply a series of technological advancement and innovation for enhancing the material well-being of people but may open up a new horizon of human civilisation which promises society further improvement in economic, political, social, cultural and spiritual dimensions.

In terms of the extent of ICT usage, both personal computers (PC) and Internet penetration are showing phenomenal rates of growth from 610,000 and 18,000 subscribers in 1995 to 2.2 million and 1.5 million in 2000, respectively (see Table 1). PC ownership in 2003 was 4.2 million which accounts for 16.7 percent of the total population of 25 million while the number of internet subscribers and internet users increased to 2.1 million and 8.4 million, respectively in 2003. The Malaysian government's pro-IT policy also helps play a big part in taking the campaign forward: for example, the big drive towards computer ownership under the slogan "one home one personal computer", and the songs being aired over national television networks and radio stations, promoting the needs of harnessing IT. Everybody seems to know the word IT.

Access to a computer is known to be associated with higher level of computer literacy (Gattiker and Hlavaka [5]) and, as shown in Table 1, the growing numbers in computer ownership, Internet subscribers and users certainly suggests an increasing level of computer literacy in Malaysia. Expectedly, computers are used mostly for word processing and Internet browsing and the

Human Perspectives in the Internet Society: Culture, Psychology and Gender, K. Morgan, J. Sanchez, C. A. Brebbia & A Voiskounsky (Editors) © 2004 WIT Press, www.witpress.com, ISBN 1-85312-726-4

Internet users in Malaysia are mostly young males and urban dwellers belonging to the middle class and above, working in both public and private sectors.

Table 1: Selected ICT indicators 1995 and 2000.

Indicator	1995	2000
Newspaper circulation per 1000 population	162	159
Telephone lines per 1000 population	161	204
Telephone subscribers	3.33m	4.65m
Personal computers (units installed)	610k	2.2m
Personal computers per 1000 population	29.5	95.7
Mobile phones	873k	5.1m
Number of Internet subscribers	18k	1.5m
Number of Internet users (Source: Eighth Malaysia Plan)	30k	6.0m

Of course there are also many definitions of computer literacy (Mitra [8]; Loyd and Gressard, [7]) with some being either too narrow or too broad. For example, Mitra [8] defined computer literacy as amount of computer knowledge acquired in the past and the length of computer usage, while the measure of computer literacy level by Loyd and Gressard [7] includes the amount of time spent on the computer, computer ownership as well as the number of computer courses taken. In this paper, computer literacy refers to computer experience and use, and computer knowledge acquired through formal or informal training.

3 Gendered digital divide

Why should ICT and IT discriminate against women? One obvious reason is that IT is seen as very hardware based. The computer is a sophisticated machine. The language of technology both reflects and shapes culture contributing to and sustaining gender disparities in relation to participation (Cukier et al. [3]). Research has shown that males dominate in the use of computers (Geissler and Horridge [6]). Even in a situation where male and female are given equal access men are more likely to be the main computer user than women (Becker and Sterling [1]).

The other problem that is faced with the gendered digital divide is the training on use of the technology. Women may have the hardware but they have the most trouble with using the software. It is still widely thought that older people are naturally wary of computers and that women lack the interest to learn. In many cultures, when training is available, it is directed at men only or the emphasis remains upon the male. Computer games were designed by and for males resulting in boys and men getting more computer experience. Women have additional handicaps. It takes time for them to learn keyboarding skills and often at home the husband and children get the right to access the keyboard before them. At a higher level, Busch [2] found that among undergraduate students, not

Human Perspectives in the Internet Society: Culture, Psychology and Gender, K. Morgan, J. Sanchez, C. A. Brebbia & A Voiskounsky (Editors) © 2004 WIT Press, www.witpress.com, ISBN 1-85312-726-4

only had male students had more computer experience in programming and computer games than female students, they also had previously received more encouragement from parents and friends. Furthermore, much of the discourse regarding IT still equates IT with computer science and electronic engineering, which tend to be male dominated. This has the effect of reinforcing and perpetrating the exclusion of women (Cukier et al. [3]).

Recognizing the importance of ICT as a medium for gathering and distributing shared knowledge, gender equity must be embraced in all facets of life if the new IT is to be fully effective. It is important that women have equal access to IT, thus there is a need to address to the pressing need for and possible avenues to turning the digital divide into digital opportunity through digital bridging.

4 Bridging the digital gap

To help promote access to communications and internet connectivity to the rural areas, the Malaysian Communications and Multimedia Commission (MCMC), the regulator for the converging communications and multimedia industry, includes in its mission the Community Communications Development Program (CCDP).

The objective of the CCDP is to increase communication access to network services and facilities to underserved areas that will not only enable the local communities to help narrow the digital divide, but also provide the local economic activities to be marketed via a new medium, that is over the World Wide Web. While the CCDP is fully funded by MCMC, its development and implementation involves a collaborative effort between MCMC, local councils, state governments, and NGO's. The program coverage is nation wide beginning with the state of Perak, which was officially launched sometime in mid 2003 under the Kedai.Kom projects. Kedai is a Malay word for shop and there are altogether 54 Kedai.Kom sites in this state equipped with high powered broadband Internet access via VSAT satellite dish. The sites are selected within a five kilometre range of the nearest town or village with an active community but which lack communications access, and a strong and active Village Development and Security Committee to ensure success and sustainability of the program.

Each Kedai.Kom is provided with 5 PCs, telephone, a printer, and is managed by an operator, selected from among the local entrepreneurs. The operator is required to provide a safe and comfortable shop/premise with constant electricity supply to place the computers and related equipment. All operators are required to attend training on how to manage the Kedai.Kom, conducted by MCMC in collaboration with the service provider and training provider prior to opening their Kedai.Kom. The service providers commissioned by MCMC are Time.Com and Maxis Communications for providing and maintaining the infrastructure and hardware, and The Foundation for Women's Education and Vocational Training, an NGO, for conducting the training of the operators as well as the local residents at their respective villages.

Human Perspectives in the Internet Society: Culture, Psychology and Gender, K. Morgan, J. Sanchez, C. A. Brebbia & A Voiskounsky (Editors) © 2004 WIT Press, www.witpress.com, ISBN 1-85312-726-4

The ultimate objective of the implementation of the CCDP is for the local communities to own the project, thus each Kedai.Kom would be considered a success only if it is fully utilised by them, and service providers, support the project with quick response so that the Internet access is always available. A necessary requirement for this active participation begins with training in computer literacy that cuts across gender and generation.

4.1 Outreach training program

For each of the 54 Kedai.Kom sites, the training for the rural communities consists of various phases over a period of 5 years. This presentation only covers the first phase of the training program which aims at providing exposure to the world of computers and ICT, as well as cultivating interest and appreciation on the importance of ICT knowledge and skills. For each training site, a mobile unit equipped with 16 computers and peripherals is stationed in a selected premise, usually a community hall, for 5 days. Training is conducted in two sessions, 15 participants for the morning and 15 for the afternoon session so at to provide one computer for each person. They are taught on how to operate a basic computer system, Microsoft Word, Internet, E-mail and Homepage with the use of an LCD projector, assisted by 3 trainers, for a total of 16 hours. Participants are awarded a certificate of attendance at the end of the training period.

At the beginning, when registration was on a first come first served basis, there were very few women participants. And even among those who had registered, they would not come at the slightest excuse or they would replace with their schooling sons or daughters at the last minute. Although both men and women had no computer knowledge or experience, and for many of them it was their first close encounter with a computer, the women showed more fear of working with the PC. Compared to the men the women were a shy lot and had much lower confidence in using the computer. Realizing that the problem could be due to the mixing of gender in the same session, the training group was separated accordingly, the morning session for the men and the afternoon session was reserved for women. The timing was perfect because the women would have completed their family duties and house chores by about noon. The learning content for the women was also modified to include cooking recipes, and fashions which appeal to them. The response was very encouraging and through word of mouth both sessions were equally full in terms of attendance and sustainability throughout the five day period.

5 The outcomes

Since the launching of the Kedai.Kom about 1,500 rural folks have received basic training in computer literacy, of which almost half were women. Among the 54 Kedai.Kom operators, 11 are women which make up about 20 percent. From the observations made at the few training sites, consisting of 131 male participants and 120 female participants, it was found that the women were shy at the beginning and took longer time to learn to use the computer than the men,

Human Perspectives in the Internet Society: Culture, Psychology and Gender, K. Morgan, J. Sanchez, C. A. Brebbia & A Voiskounsky (Editors) © 2004 WIT Press, www.witpress.com, ISBN 1-85312-726-4

but they showed stronger learning perseverance and longer concentration span. The participants range from 16 to 65 years with the respective age groups shown in Table 2 and the majority of them had not gone beyond secondary schooling.

At the end of the training, participants were asked to fill an evaluation form which contains, among others, three questions relating to their understanding of the course and competency in using the computer. The participants were provided with a rating scale of 1 to 5, 1 refers to the lowest rating and 5 the highest. The result shown in Table 2 indicates that the participants rate themselves quite high in terms of their understanding of the topics taught, confidence level and interest, as well as their willingness to use the knowledge and skills. There is no significant difference between male and female participants although higher means for the female are observed on two of the questions.

It was also found that the favourite topic among women is the application Microsoft Word where they prepare recipes using the different fonts, Word Art and Clip Art and send it to another fellow participant as an attachment via email. Among the male participants, browsing through the Internet to search for sports websites and news seem to be their favourite part of the course. It is encouraging to see that more than fifty percent of the rural men and women who attended the training are in the age groups 35 years and older, and almost all of them indicated that they would like further training to enhance their knowledge and skills in the use of computers and information technology.

Table 2: Outcomes of computer literacy training.

Variable/question	Male N=131	Female N=120
Age: 16-24 years	35.9 %	29.2 %
25-34	19.8	17.5
35-44	18.3	21.7
45 and above	26.0	31.6
(Rating scale: 1 = lowest, 5 = highest)		
How do you rate your understanding of the topics taught?	4.08	4.16
Has the training increase your interest and confidence in using the computer?	4.20	4.48
How do you rate your willingness to use the knowledge/skills in the future?	4.10	4.06

6 Conclusion

Bringing information access and connectivity to the rural community is the only way to help bridge the digital divide between the information 'have' and the 'have nots'. There is no difference between rural women and men in terms of learning on how to use the technology, given equal opportunity. These rural

Human Perspectives in the Internet Society: Culture, Psychology and Gender, K. Morgan, J. Sanchez, C. A. Brebbia & A Voiskounsky (Editors) © 2004 WIT Press, www.witpress.com, ISBN 1-85312-726-4

women certainly have moved themselves well from kitchens to the keyboards. Although they took longer time to learn keyboarding skills and develop confidence, they showed stronger learning perseverance. IT had helped generate the kind of enthusiasm that money cannot buy.

References

[1] Becker H.J., Sterling C.W., Equity in School and Computer Use: National Data and Neglected Considerations, *Journal of Educational Computing Research*, Vol. 3, No.3, pp.289-311, 1987.

[2] Busch T., Gender differences in self-efficacy and attitudes toward computers, *Journal of Educational Computing Research*, Vol. 12, pp. 147-158, 1995.

[3] Cukier W., Shortt D., Devine I., Gender and Information Technology: Implications of Definitions, *Journal of Information Systems Education*, Vol. 13(1), pp.7-15, 2001.

[4] Eighth Malaysia Plan 2001-2005, Government of Malaysia, pp. 363-378, 2001.

[5] Gattiker U.E., Hlavaka A., Computer attitude and learning performance: Issues for management and training, *Journal of Organisational Behaviour*, Vol. 13, pp. 89-101, 1992.

[6] Geissler J., Horridge P., University students' computer knowledge and commitment to learning, *Journal of Research on Computing in Education*, Vol. 25(3), pp. 347-365, 1993.

[7] Loyd B., Gressard C., The effect of sex, age and computer experience on computer attitudes, *AEDS Journal*, Vol. 18(2), pp.67-76, 1984.

[8] Mitra A., Categories of computer use and their relationships with attitude toward computers, *Journal of Research on Computing in Education*, Vol. 30(3), pp. 281-292, 1998.

Human Perspectives in the Internet Society: Culture, Psychology and Gender, K. Morgan, J. Sanchez, C. A. Brebbia & A Voiskounsky (Editors) © 2004 WIT Press, www.witpress.com, ISBN 1-85312-726-4

Mentoring computer science undergraduates

J. McGrath Cohoon, M. Gonsoulin & J. Layman
University of Virginia, USA

Abstract

We investigated the nature and outcomes of faculty mentoring behaviour at 117 undergraduate computer science programs in the United States. Our data describe who mentors undergraduates, how much, in what way, and why. We also tested the relationship between mentoring and departmental outcomes including mean grade point average, retention in the major, progression to graduate school, and whether the gender balance of enrolment and retention are influenced. Our study found evidence that mentoring has a positive effect on how many of a department's seniors go directly to graduate study and the quality of the programs these students will attend. It also appears that mentoring motivated by the desire for diversity helps retain women in computer science programs.
Keywords: mentoring, women in computer science, gender, grade point average, retention, attrition, progression to graduate school.

1 Introduction

Mentoring is frequently endorsed as an effective method for improving student outcomes. Despite some ambiguity about what effective mentoring entails in an academic setting and how implementation might affect outcomes, there are many who believe that active sponsorship by faculty is a positive force for student academic achievement and retention of under-represented student groups. Their faith has motivated countless individual faculty and departmental or school initiatives, plus several discipline-wide programs that attempt to provide women in computer science (CS) with the benefits of mentoring. For example, the Computing Research Association's Committee on the Status of Women has run two NSF-funded mentoring programs for years. Support for these programs comes from industry, public and private foundation grants, and private donations. The promise and proliferation of these mentoring activities led us to

Human Perspectives in the Internet Society: Culture, Psychology and Gender, K. Morgan, J. Sanchez, C. A. Brebbia & A Voiskounsky (Editors) © 2004 WIT Press, www.witpress.com, ISBN 1-85312-726-4

take a closer look at the nature and outcomes of mentoring in undergraduate computer science programs located in doctoral institutions. Our investigation is based on the assumption that departments where mentoring is a common practice should differ in measurable ways from departments where mentoring is rare.

2 Background

Belief in the value of mentoring is based on more than the many enthusiastic testimonials from participants in mentoring programs. Previous studies in other disciplines have found a variety of positive outcomes. For the most part, this research was conducted at single institutions and targeted only graduate students. The consensus of results indicated that certain mentoring activities were related to positive student outcomes ranging from increased satisfaction to increased productivity or retention in the program or institution. Studies disagree about the importance of matching mentor and protégé by sex, but it appears that this dispute arises from differences in the outcomes that were measured [1]. While it is true that students were more satisfied with same-sex mentors, it is also true that they experienced similar instrumental benefits regardless of their mentor's sex.

An example of the general benefits of mentoring can be seen in one graduate-level single-university study that compared results for men, women, and women in male-dominated disciplines. Survey data obtained from more than 300 students over two points in time show that faculty mentoring increased protégé's academic self-confidence and career commitment [2]. Mentor support was measured as a combination of both affective support, such as sensitivity to students' non-academic commitments, and instrumental support, such as finding financial support. This comprehensive mentoring was positively associated with career commitment for both men and women, including women in male-dominated disciplines. Mentor support also had a particularly positive effect on the academic self-confidence of women in disciplines where the majority of faculty were men.

Another study demonstrated that mentoring of graduate students may have differential effects depending on the nature of the mentoring activities and the context in which they occur. For example, survey responses from almost 200 graduate students at a single university showed that instrumental mentoring had a significant positive effect on student publication records, but affective mentoring did not [3]. Students who reported that their mentors offered instrumental help such as improving writing and presentations, and exploring career options had more publications with their advisors than students whose advisors did not provide this sort of help. This effect held regardless of the discipline. (Nine disciplines were considered – psychology, economics, anthropology, history of consciousness, linguistics, chemistry, biology, earth sciences, and physics.)

Academic success associated with faculty mentoring has also been demonstrated at the undergraduate level. Mentored students in one university's three year study earned .3 of a higher grade point higher average than non-mentored students who entered the study institution at the same time with the

Human Perspectives in the Internet Society: Culture, Psychology and Gender, K. Morgan, J. Sanchez, C. A. Brebbia & A Voiskounsky (Editors) © 2004 WIT Press, www.witpress.com, ISBN 1-85312-726-4

same sex, ethnicity, and high school GPA [1]. Mentored students were also less likely than the comparison group to drop out of their institution.

Student outcomes specifically related to mentoring in the discipline of computer science have not yet been widely reported. Sturm and Moroh [4] included mentoring as one component in a multi-faceted approach to recruiting and retaining women in CS at a single institution. They produced a brochure, seminars, and workshops promoting women's participation in CS, developed undergraduate research projects, and had women faculty teaching at least one section of every lower-level course, all in addition to a program of alumnae mentoring for undergraduate women. Unfortunately, it is not possible to discern what consequences can be attributed to women's participation in the mentoring component of their efforts.

One publication indicates that mentoring may be related to women's retention in undergraduate computer science programs. Departments where many faculty mentored their undergraduate students retained women at comparable rates to men, achieving an equality that is atypical in this discipline [5]. This statewide study of 23 CS departments suggested that faculty mentoring could help ameliorate the disproportionate loss of undergraduate women.

Our current report expands the statewide study of mentoring in computer science by examining one-third of the CS programs at doctoral-level institutions in the United States. We examine the prevalence and nature of mentoring in undergraduate computer science, and investigate the outcomes associated with mentoring of different types. Our findings show that faculty motivations and actions with respect to mentoring can have measurable department-level effects on students' retention and progression in computer science.

3 Methods

We selected departments in Ph.D.-granting institutions that awarded thirty-five or more baccalaureate CS degrees in 1996 or 1997 (according to data available online at the National Science Foundation's WebCASPAR), or that were among the 20 most prestigious computer science programs (according to the National Research Council's 1993 rankings). As a group, these departments capture approximately one third of the USA's computer science bachelor's degrees awarded in recent years.

In spring of 2001, a survey of up to twenty-five faculty in each study department collected information on common mentoring practices, student grade point averages and attrition rates between 1994 and 2000. Participants were selected with a stratified random sample that over-selected female faculty. In most of the study departments, our selection method resulted in the inclusion of all full-time permanent faculty members who taught undergraduates. The overall response rate was 51% from an eligible sample of 1642 faculty members. Every department in the study is represented by at least one respondent, although some respondents chose not to answer all survey questions.

The questionnaire instructions define mentoring as "an out-of-class relationship that may be formal or informal. Office hours might include some

Human Perspectives in the Internet Society: Culture, Psychology and Gender, K. Morgan, J. Sanchez, C. A. Brebbia & A Voiskounsky (Editors) © 2004 WIT Press, www.witpress.com, ISBN 1-85312-726-4

mentoring activities, but mentoring is distinct from academic advising. A mentoring relationship could include, but would not be limited to writing letters of recommendation. Mentoring entails activities such as: involving individual students in professional activities, offering personalized advice to individual students, encouraging individual students, and helping individual students establish careers".

The survey questions relevant to this paper use a five-point scale to measure how often faculty engaged in seven mentoring activities. The scale ranges from never (1), to rarely (2), on occasion (3), often (4), and all the time (5). The mentoring activities were:

- Involve undergraduates in your research
- Publish research with undergraduates as co-authors
- Inform an undergraduate of research opportunities
- Supervise an undergraduate's work that is not course related
- Help students navigate academic rules or requirements
- Encourage students who are shy but competent
- Personally give specific positive feedback to an undergraduate

Two distinct types of mentoring: research mentoring and support mentoring were identified from these different activities. Research mentoring is captured by the first four activities in the list – involving undergrads in research, publishing with undergraduates, informing undergrads of research opportunities, and supervising non-course work. Support mentoring is captured by the last three activities in the list that are more guidance-oriented – help navigating rules, encouraging shy students, giving positive feedback.

Additionally, respondents were asked to indicate whether they made a special effort to mentor particular students. If so, the survey requested that they indicate whether they mentored specific groups on a scale from not at all (1), to slightly (2), moderately (3), substantially (4), and completely (5). The options were:

- student eagerness to learn
- desire to overcome under-representation
- student need
- superior student ability
- personal rapport
- other (please list)

Responses to these survey questions were aggregated to the department level for analyses relating these data to outcome measures.

In order to measure outcomes, each participating institution was asked to provide data enumerating students by sex, academic level, grade point average (GPA), and outcome (persistence, switch to another major, etc.). These data proved particularly hard to come by. When the enrolment and outcome data were available, we used them to calculate rates of attrition from the major for each sex. The formula for the average departmental attrition rate was the six year average of students who switched to a different major, divided by that number plus the 6-year average of students who continued in CS each year. The gendered attrition rate was the male departmental rate minus the female departmental rate.

Human Perspectives in the Internet Society: Culture, Psychology and Gender, K. Morgan, J. Sanchez, C. A. Brebbia & A Voiskounsky (Editors) © 2004 WIT Press, www.witpress.com, ISBN 1-85312-726-4

Thus, a value of zero or greater indicates that women leave the department at equal or lower rates than men, and a negative value indicates greater female attrition than male attrition.

We tested hypotheses predicting that departmental outcomes would vary by the type and amount of mentoring their faculty offered undergraduates. The outcomes we considered were student achievement measured by mean grade point average, rates of attrition to other majors, percent of seniors who progressed directly to graduate school, and the quality of the graduate program students to which students went. Based on the widespread endorsements of mentoring, we expected that more mentoring would be associated with higher GPA, lower attrition, and more students proceeding directly to graduate school, and entrance into higher quality graduate programs. We also expected that mentoring results would be particularly favourable for women students, and might even be associated with higher proportions of female enrolment. As you will see, the reality of outcomes related to mentoring is much less simple than our initial predictions.

Our methods introduced a couple of important limitations. First, in examining the link between mentoring activities and grade point average, our sample size is only thirty institutions. Sample size also meant that analyses including attrition or enrolment measures were limited to the 45 cases that supplied enrolment and disposition data, thus limiting the number of variables we could include at one time. Second, it is worth noting that our study is not necessarily applicable to other fields. Computer science departments provide a unique context that might or might not indicate whether mentoring activities or mentoring with certain goals in mind would produce similar results elsewhere. The findings of this study speak to computer science departments in doctoral institutions and can only be suggestive for other settings.

4 Results

Before reporting on the relationship between mentoring and student achievement, retention, and progression to graduate school, we describe who does what types of mentoring and how often. These descriptive results are based on CS faculty as a whole. They show that men and women faculty members at doctoral institutions are about equally likely to mentor undergraduates, but they sometimes engage in different types of mentoring for different reasons.

Faculty of both sexes mentored a median of 6 undergraduates in an academic year, and devoted a median of two hours per week to their mentoring activities. In most cases, the mentoring relationship was initiated by the student (62%). Occasionally mentoring was part of a formal program (less than 16%). The frequency with which mentoring involved particular activities is shown in Figure 1.

Several aspects of mentoring varied by faculty member sex (16% of faculty in our study were women). Women faculty were more likely than men faculty to engage in support mentoring activities. Women faculty were also more likely than men to initiate a mentoring relationship with an undergraduate student, as

Human Perspectives in the Internet Society: Culture, Psychology and Gender, K. Morgan, J. Sanchez, C. A. Brebbia & A Voiskounsky (Editors) © 2004 WIT Press, www.witpress.com, ISBN 1-85312-726-4

shown in Figure 2. Forty-seven percent of men, but 63% of women faculty, made special effort to mentor particular students. Female faculty were more likely than male faculty to mentor female students, although all faculty members mentored more men than women. The latter fact is not surprising due to the gender composition of most CS programs. At 26% female, mentored students over-represent women, who comprised only 22% of the average doctoral program in our study.

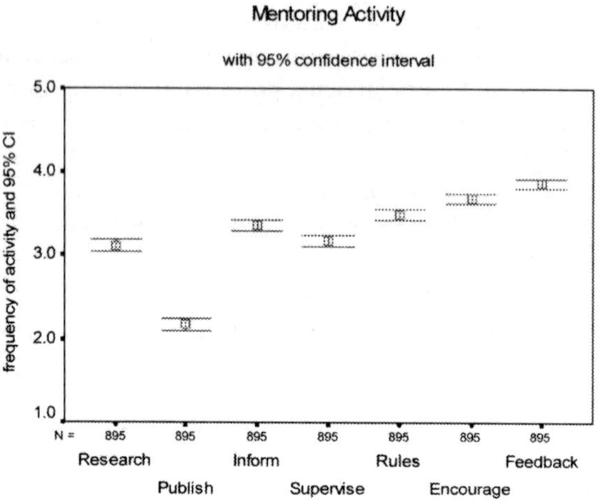

Mentoring Activity

with 95% confidence interval

frequency of activity and 95% CI

N = 895 895 895 895 895 895 895

Research Publish Inform Supervise Rules Encourage Feedback

Figure 1.

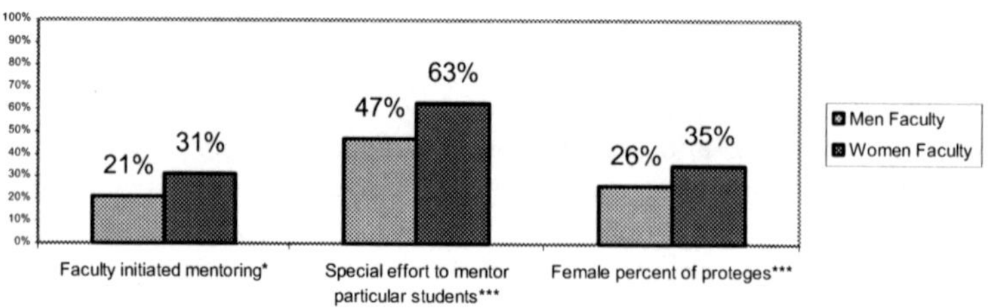

Figure 2.

4.1 Motivation and mentoring

Faculty motivations for putting special effort into mentoring particular students are shown in Table 1. The data show that women were more likely than men to mentor because of student need and personal rapport, but the biggest gender difference in motivation is in diversity. Women were more likely than men to put

Human Perspectives in the Internet Society: Culture, Psychology and Gender, K. Morgan, J. Sanchez, C. A. Brebbia & A Voiskounsky (Editors) © 2004 WIT Press, www.witpress.com, ISBN 1-85312-726-4

special effort into mentoring particular students because they wanted to overcome under-representation.

The way motivation was typically translated into action is measured by Gamma and shown in Table 2. Overall, these relationships were weak, but they showed some additional gender differences in faculty mentoring behaviour. For example, motivation by student eagerness was associated with mentoring for men, but not for women faculty. Thus, despite the fact that student eagerness was the strongest motivation leading women to mentor, we found nothing to predict what the nature of that mentoring would be. Likewise, despite being motivated by rapport, women faculty were not led to any particular mentoring action in response. Only in the case of diversity was women's motivation translated into some of the specific actions we measured. When spurred to action by the desire to overcome under-representation, women informed and encouraged undergraduates. And women were significantly more likely than their male colleagues to take these actions under these conditions.

Table 1.

Faculty Motivation to Mentor

	Eagerness	*Need*	*Ability*	*Rapport*	*Diversity*
Mean	3.93	3.36	3.74	3.28	2.63
Male	3.92	3.12*	3.73	3.22*	2.52**
Female	3.97	3.17*	3.77	3.48*	3.01**

1=not at all 2=slight 3=moderate 4=substantial 5=complete

* Sig difference between men and women at .05

** Sig. difference between men and women at .001

Table 2.

Significant Relationships between Faculty Motivation and Mentoring Activities

	Eagerness			*Need*			*Ability*			*Rapport*			*Diversity*		
		Male	Female		Male	Female		Male	Female		Male	Female		Male	Female
Involve	.18**	.17**		-.22***	-.21***	-.25*	.23***	.23***	.23**						
Publish				-.20***	-.22***		.19***	.21***							
Inform	.15*	.21**		-.12**		-.27**	.22***	.24***		.11*	.14**		.14**	.10*	.32***
Supervise	.15**	.16*		-.13**	-.11*		.24***	.28***		.16**	.17**				
Rules				.25***	.26***					.13**	.13*		.11**	.10*	
Encourage	.24***	.25***		.33***	0.33***	.26*				.16***	.19**		.24***	.20**	.27***
Feedback	.21**	.22**		.29***	.25***	.37***				.23***	.23***		.15**	.12*	

* Sig of Gamma at .05

**Sig. of Gamma at .01

*** Sig. of Gamma at .001

Having described who typically mentors undergraduates, in what way, and why, we turn to findings about outcomes at the department level.

4.2 Research mentoring

Unsurprisingly, faculty engage in research mentoring with undergraduates most often in departments where quality is high – the quality of students, as measured by the median SAT score of incoming freshmen, and the quality of the CS program, as measured by 1993 NRC quality rating. The correlation between research mentoring and median institutional SAT score was 0.46, significant at the .001 level. For the NRC rating, the correlation with research mentoring was 0.27, significant at the .02 level.

Based on published reports about the value of research experiences for undergraduates [6], we expected that research mentoring would have numerous beneficial effects on students in departments where it was a common practice. In particular, we expected a positive association with grades, retention, and student progression to graduate school. We also anticipated that women's enrolment and retention would benefit particularly from research mentoring. As it turned out, not all of our expectations about research mentoring were supported by our data.

There is a significant department-level relationship between research mentoring and one aspect of progression to graduate school. Research mentoring was positively associated with the quality of the graduate program students entered. *The chance that most or all of the students who went directly to graduate school went to top-tier programs was highest in departments where research mentoring was prevalent, even when student quality and program quality were controlled.* The more often faculty involved undergraduates in research, published with undergraduate co-authors, informed undergraduates of research opportunities, and supervised extra work, the more likely it was that students would go to excellent graduate programs, regardless of the quality of their undergraduate program or the general academic quality of students at their institution. (Adjusted R2 = 0.69, significant at .001 level, Beta for research mentoring = 0.19, significant at the .014 level.) The gender composition of the department's faculty had no measurable impact on this relationship.

4.3 Support mentoring

We expected that support mentoring would help students succeed and persist. We also expected that departments where support mentoring was common would enrol women in relatively large portions, would retain women in the CS major, and progress large portions of women to graduate school.

We found evidence that support mentoring had the expected measurable effects only on progression to graduate school. *Departments where it was common for faculty to provide support mentoring sent larger portions of their seniors on to graduate school than did departments where this form of mentoring was uncommon.* Regardless of the quality of students or program, more support mentoring was associated with more students proceeding directly to graduate programs. (Adjusted R2 = 0.24, significant at .001, and Beta for support mentoring was 0.33 when controlling for SAT and NRC rating.) Neither the quality of the graduate programs to which students went nor the gender composition of the faculty had a measurable influence on this relationship.

Human Perspectives in the Internet Society: Culture, Psychology and Gender, K. Morgan, J. Sanchez, C. A. Brebbia & A Voiskounsky (Editors) © 2004 WIT Press, www.witpress.com, ISBN 1-85312-726-4

We also observed an unexpected positive association between support mentoring and attrition from the major. Departments where support mentoring was common were more likely than those where support mentoring was not common to lose students to other majors, even when the median SAT and presence of female faculty were taken into account. This observation suggests that support mentoring was not generally sufficient for overcoming the conditions that led men and women to switch to other majors.

4.4 Motivated but unspecified mentoring

Finally, we considered the possibility that particular mentoring actions are less important to outcomes than are the motivations that underlie the actions. In particular, we tested whether diversity-motivated mentoring had gendered consequences independent of the specific mentoring activities performed. Based upon results from the average CS department, we expected that departments in doctoral institutions would also retain women at comparable rates to men when many faculty mentored students out of a desire for diversity.

Our results were very interesting, but not conclusive. In the 45 doctoral institutions that provided enrolment data, there was a moderately weak correlation between the percent of a department's faculty that mentored for diversity and the gap between male and female attrition rates ($r = 0.24$, significant at .06). When we controlled for the factors significant in the average CS department, there were only 36 degrees of freedom, but the relationship persisted (Beta for diversity mentoring = .23, significant at .05). Furthermore, when research and support mentoring activities were also controlled, the relationship between diversity motivation and gendered attrition rate remained essentially the same but achieved a level of statistical significance (Beta for diversity mentoring =.30, significant at .01). The small number of cases and moderately weak relationship led to these results that wavered between being sufficient and insufficient for confident generalizing to all mid- to large-sized CS departments at doctoral institutions. However, the consistency of the relationship leads us to believe that diversity-motivated mentoring improves the relative retention of undergraduate women in CS at doctoral institutions.

5 Discussion

Mentoring has been associated with positive consequences for the individual students who are lucky enough to receive it. Student-faculty relationships that include activities promoting involvement in computing professions, helping students establish their careers, and providing personalized advice and encouragement could be very beneficial. Student protégés might earn higher grades, persist beyond any doubts or difficulties, and continue on to graduate school, all to a greater extent than students not in mentoring relationships with faculty. Mentoring might even help increase women's participation in computer science. But unless faculty mentoring of undergraduates is a common practice, there would be no evidence of these department level benefits. Isolated efforts of individual faculty would benefit a few students, but the big picture would remain the same – low grades, high attrition, few students proceeding to graduate study, and persistent gender disparity.

Our multi-institution research has two important strengths – benchmarks and evidence of some measurable large-scale outcomes associated with mentoring in CS. It also raises many questions and points to avenues for further exploration that cannot be adequately discussed in the available space. The benchmarks document common mentoring practices and motivations in the United States with special attention to the similarities and differences between men and women faculty. The hypothesis tests of department-level consequences from widespread mentoring showed that mentoring can mean more than its individual successes and failures. Perhaps this greater impact is why women's presence and representation on a faculty demonstrated no measurable association with any of the large-scale outcomes associated with the prevalence of mentoring. As other studies have found, we saw that the material benefits of mentoring do not depend on who does it, only that someone does. Our study might add that some gender-balancing benefits do not depend on the particular forms that mentoring takes, only on the motivation that drives them.

Acknowledgements

This material is based upon work supported by the National Science Foundation under grant number #EIA-0089959. Any opinions, findings, and conclusions or recommendations expressed in this material are those of the authors and do not necessarily reflect the views of the National Science Foundation.

References

[1] T. A. Campbell and D. E. Campbell, "Faculty/Student Mentor Program: Effects on Academic Performance and Retention," *Research in Higher Education*, vol. 38, pp. 727-742, 1997.

[2] B. Ulku-Steiner, B. Kurtz-Costes, and C. R. Kinlaw, "Doctoral Student Experiences in Gender-Balanced and Male-Dominated Graduate Programs," *Journal of Educational Psychology*, vol. XLII, pp. 296-307, 2000.

[3] H. R. Tenenbaum, F. J. Crosby, and M. D. Gliner, "Mentoring relationships in graduate school," *Journal of Vocational Behavior*, vol. 59, pp. 326-341, 2001.

[4] D. Sturm and M. Moroh, "Encouraging Enrollment and Retention of Women in Computer Science Classes," presented at National Educational Computing Conference, Boston, MA, 1994.

[5] J. M. Cohoon, "Toward improving female retention in the computer science major," *Communications of the ACM*, vol. 44, pp. 108-114, 2001.

[6] A. W. Astin and H. S. Astin, "Undergraduate Science Education: The Impact of Different College Environments on the Educational Pipeline in the Sciences. Final Report," California University, Los Angeles ED362404, November 1992 1992.

Human Perspectives in the Internet Society: Culture, Psychology and Gender, K. Morgan, J. Sanchez, C. A. Brebbia & A Voiskounsky (Editors) © 2004 WIT Press, www.witpress.com, ISBN 1-85312-726-4

Gender in information technology: review of a mentoring initiative

C. Armaroli, E. Costantini, F. Guerzoni, C. Malacarne & O. Mich
Center for Scientific and Technological Research (ITC-irst), Italy

Abstract

There is, generally, a lack of women in the science, engineering and information technology research fields at all career levels. This is a worldwide phenomenon that seems related to social and cultural stereotypes. The *Gender and Science ITC-irst* group has investigated those actions that could be proposed to support the female researchers inside ITC-irst in spreading out effective role models and in improving their scientific skills. A first cycle of scientific lectures was organized in the winter 2002-2003. At the same time, a series of mentoring workshops was proposed with the main objective of increasing the experience of ITC-irst female researchers and to grow the self-esteem for all participants. Given the positive results of the first initiatives, the Gender and Science ITC-irst group organized a second series of scientific lectures and mentoring in winter 2003-2004. All the activities were organized whilst paying particular attention to gender issues. This paper describes the second series of activities, and their evaluation.
Keywords: gender issues, information technology, women in science, mentoring, role models.

1 Introduction

A gender difference is present in the way of living the job. Although this difference may enrich the working environment, it is not always perceived as a value. Several studies have shown that women often have difficulties in finding appropriate career models in science and information technology areas, and are under-represented with respect to males at all career levels, with the greatest unbalance at the top of the hierarchy [1-3]. An internal study [4] highlighted a

Human Perspectives in the Internet Society: Culture, Psychology and Gender, K. Morgan, J. Sanchez, C. A. Brebbia & A Voiskounsky (Editors) © 2004 WIT Press, www.witpress.com, ISBN 1-85312-726-4

similar situation in our research institute ITC-irst [5]. Consequently the Gender and Science ITC-irst group [6] decided to experiment with some activities aimed at promoting the presence of women researchers, inspired by previous experiences in the specific fields of women in Engineering and Computer Science [7].

The group started in 2002 with a series of scientific lectures held by experienced international female researchers working in some of the most advanced scientific areas of Computer Science, Information Technology and Microsystems. The principal objective was to encourage female students and researchers by giving them successful examples of research careers experienced by women, in areas close to those of interest to our institute. In the same year the group organized some mentoring workshops [8] connected to the scientific lectures. These mentoring activities, addressed only to women scientists, aimed at increasing the awareness of women scientists of their role within the institute and at contributing to a positive change in the local cultural environment.

After the positive results of both the initiatives, the group planned a new series of scientific lectures and mentoring workshop in the winter of 2003-2004, opening the mentoring workshops to all researchers (female and male). Therefore, the mentoring workshops offered an opportunity to improve one's professional preparation and skills, paying special attention to individual styles and gender peculiarities.

The scientific lectures initiative and its evaluation are described in section 2 of this paper, whereas the description and evaluation of the mentoring workshop activities are reported in section 3. Conclusions and future work of the *Gender and Science ITC-irst* group are presented in section 4.

2 Scientific lectures

2.1 Description of the initiative

Despite considerable progress, women are still severely under-represented, with respect to males, in science, engineering and technology. Although two-fifths of PhDs in the EU are women, in approximately half of the Member States just one woman for every ten men reaches the higher echelons of a university career [9]. In the Eastern and Central European countries women constitute the majority of teaching staff in academies of sciences and in universities, but they tend to be concentrated in the lower academic positions [10]. Influence of social and cultural stereotypes seems to be mainly at the origin of this worldwide phenomenon. However, also the lack of role models, in particular for non-traditional careers as could be those in the Information Technology (IT) field, seems to discourage girl students to follow challenging scientific careers. Say *researcher* to girls and they probably think of a *man* in a white lab coat. If a girl has never met a woman engineer or a software programmer, she might conclude engineering and computer programming were men's work, and turn away from an interesting career.

Important projects have been developed throughout the entire world to promote women participating in scientific and technological studies and jobs,

Human Perspectives in the Internet Society: Culture, Psychology and Gender, K. Morgan, J. Sanchez, C. A. Brebbia & A Voiskounsky (Editors) © 2004 WIT Press, www.witpress.com, ISBN 1-85312-726-4

connecting girls with meaningful role models. The Women of NASA [11] sponsored the educational initiative *Women of the World*. Through this program, online chats were available with the nation's most successful females in a wide range of professions, offering young people anywhere opportunities and experiences to gain insight into their own future choices. This project supported students, parents, and schools in an important learning opportunity to dialogue with USA's most successful female leaders via the World Wide Web and provided a way in which they could dialogue with women typically not accessible to the public. The MIT Department of Electrical Engineering and Computer Science (EECS) organize a *Residential Summer Program* [12] to introduce High School girls to EECS in the summer after 11th grade. The goal of this project is increasing High School girls' interest and confidence in pursuing engineering and computer science. The committee of *Introduce a Girl to Engineering Day* [13], inside the National Engineers Week in the USA, proposes plenty of initiatives: for example, an evening for middle school student girls to help them understand engineering, science & technology. Six female engineers will be the speakers; tours of lab and engineering areas, one-on-one time with female engineer-mentors, etc...

The *Gender and Science ITC-irst* group proposed the first *Women in Science lectures* initiative in 2002, a scientific lecture series held by experienced international female researchers [7]. The speakers were professors at prestigious universities or in charge of research groups in some of the most advanced scientific areas of computer science, information technology and microelectronics. The principal aim of the initiative was to encourage female students and researchers by giving them successful examples of research careers experienced by women, in areas close to those of interest to ITC-irst institute.

Since this first experience obtained positive results [8], the group decided to propose a second series of *Women in Science lectures* for the winter 2003-2004, with a slightly different organization derived from the first series results. First of all, for this second series, the heads of scientific departments inside ITC-irst and other local scientific subjects (university) were involved in drawing up and in the selection of the speaker list. This fact favoured a higher rate of participation and a more effective local relapse. Secondly, a propaedeutic activity for stimulating networking has been organized: young researchers and research managers could meet personally the speakers during individual meeting for showing demos and speaking about their own scientific interests. Thirdly, to give our audience a different *point of view,* a *non-scientific* speaker has also been invited; a journalist who will refer to the present discrimination in the scientific field towards female researchers. Afterwards, she will conduct live her daily radio transmission involving the present people. During the transmission, a local female researcher will be interviewed.

2.2 Evaluation of the initiative

In order to evaluate the 2003-2004 *Women in Science Lectures* series, two aspects have been considered: the participation to the lectures and the networking activity connected with them.

Human Perspectives in the Internet Society: Culture, Psychology and Gender, K. Morgan, J. Sanchez, C. A. Brebbia & A Voiskounsky (Editors) © 2004 WIT Press, www.witpress.com, ISBN 1-85312-726-4

Regarding the participation, a high number of people, internal and external researchers, attended both the lectures so far given. This is definitely the consequence of the higher involvement of the scientific departments in the lecture organization.

Regarding the networking activity, the contact with the speakers both for the *Gender and Science ITC-irst* group and ITC-irst researchers has been positive. The members of *Gender and Science ITC-irst* group, meeting the speakers, could improve their knowledge about the gender theme and get new enthusiasm and ideas for organizing future initiatives. ITC-irst researchers could establish new contacts and reinforce old ones for future projects.

Since the second *Women in Science Lectures* series are not yet concluded, a deeper evaluation will be done only after the last lecture, in September.

The objective of the *Gender and Science* ITC-irst group was to propose alternative models for female scientists' careers, different from the classical male models. The idea was to propose models of female scientists that arrived at the top of the scientific career, realizing a good balance between scientific and private life.

3 Mentoring workshop activities

3.1 Mentoring overview

We think that mentoring activity is one of the strategies to pursue for increasing the presence and the advancement of women in technical-scientific fields. After the success of our first mentoring workshops cycle (2002-2003 [8]), a second cycle has been organised for 2003-2004. The activity had several objectives and is aimed at improving both the skills of the researchers and the quality of the working environment. In fact, awareness of individual capabilities and professional preparation lead at the same time to a consciousness in both male and female researchers about the role of women in the research and may contribute in this way to a less *chilly* climate.

In our case, the most explicit aim is the improvement of personal and professional skills of both junior and senior researchers, so that they can acquire more self-confidence and self-esteem. In fact women who successfully pursue careers in science, despite these challenges, often have to face additional difficulties in their interpersonal relationship and self-esteem [14]. Furthermore, a social environment that attributes familial and care-taking roles to women, as wives and mothers, competes with research demands, so that some times female researchers can feel stuck in their career. In addition, since this activity was open to all research personnel, male and female; it was an occasion to meet new colleagues, who could be interested in participation in similar activities and in discussion on gender issues. Finally, this initiative also has the long-term aim to contribute to a positive change in the local cultural environment, enhancing internal and external visibility of women and giving an example of an environment accessible and approachable by either gender.

Human Perspectives in the Internet Society: Culture, Psychology and Gender, K. Morgan, J. Sanchez, C. A. Brebbia & A Voiskounsky (Editors) © 2004 WIT Press, www.witpress.com, ISBN 1-85312-726-4

3.2 Description of the initiatives

Mentoring is traditionally a relationship in which an experienced person, the mentor, provides support to a less experienced person, the mentee. In the traditional model a personal relationship is established, where the mentor fulfils either or both the technical and psychosocial needs of the mentee. The model followed in our institute is instead a *collective, cross-gender* mentoring.

The *collective* aspect is a consequence of different factors. Firstly, one-to-one relationships require a lot of people to act as mentors and models, as well as a well-built organisation to manage the mentorship; being at the beginning of this kind of initiative we can look at this model only as a possible future goal. Secondly, the proposal of thematic seminars on specific topics seemed to be the most appropriate way to reach our objectives. We decided for an external person as a mentor, being difficult to find a person with such a professional preparation and with the personal wish to take on this role inside our institute.

The choice of a *cross-gender* mentorship is also the result of several factors, but principally we tried a different strategy with respect to our 2002 mentoring experience, when an exclusively female mentor activity was performed (female were in that case both the mentors and the mentees), believing that a more egalitarian environment will benefit men as well as women. However, we are aware that this choice might have some disadvantages (principally the reproduction of the same problems of cross-gender relationships existing in a gender-privileged society). For this reason we always favoured speakers that were sensitive to gender and job topics.

The mentoring initiative has been planned on the basis of the results of our past mentoring activity [8]. The main differences with our past experience (besides the cross-gender character) were: the development of independent activities of seminary cycle *Women in Science* and *Mentoring Workshops*, the organisation of two longer mentoring workshops instead of four (2-hours) seminars, the opportunity of getting feed-backs from the mentors, and the restricted number of participants. We think that in such a way we could grant higher involvement of participants and effectiveness of the meetings. Both seminars were carried out by organisational psychologists and they aimed not only at improving practical skills in the treated topics, but also at reflecting on the possible ways to achieve better results.

The first mentoring seminar focused on the capability of presenting a scientific paper, providing the tools necessary to prepare a paper and to present it in public in a clear and convincing way. The bases of the theoretical aspects of information transfer were given, as well as feedback on the effects of the presentation and tips for improvements.

The second mentoring seminar concerned scientific visibility. In particular, it addressed the issues of constraints and possibilities offered by our belonging contexts. A novelty was introduced in this second seminar: each participant had the possibility to get personal feedback and/or advice from the mentor. In fact, the participants were given two months to communicate with the mentor after the seminar. At the moment results of this telementoring are not available since it is still in progress.

Human Perspectives in the Internet Society: Culture, Psychology and Gender, K. Morgan, J. Sanchez, C. A. Brebbia & A Voiskounsky (Editors) © 2004 WIT Press, www.witpress.com, ISBN 1-85312-726-4

This activity, devoted to the research personnel inside our institute, was promoted inside our job place by means of brochures, a web site and advertisements in the internal journal.

3.3 Evaluation of the mentoring workshops

3.3.1 Workshop participants profile

19 people took part in the first workshop (10 males and 9 females) and 15 in the second workshop (8 males and 7 females), for a total of 34 people (18 males and 16 females). Among researchers that attended the mentoring, the average age was 35. Male participants have been slightly more numerous than females in both initiatives. People age has been partitioned into the following classes:

- 25-30 years (20% of the participants);
- 31-35 years (38%);
- 36-40 years (25%);
- more than 40 years (17%).

Regarding the type of degree and the working experience: 75% of them have a scientific or technical curriculum, whereas 21% humanistic, others did not specify, 29% of the participants have worked less than 3 years in the research field, 38% between 3 and 6 years, 33% more than 6 years, 21% of the participants had a scientific PhD, and 17% are PhD students.

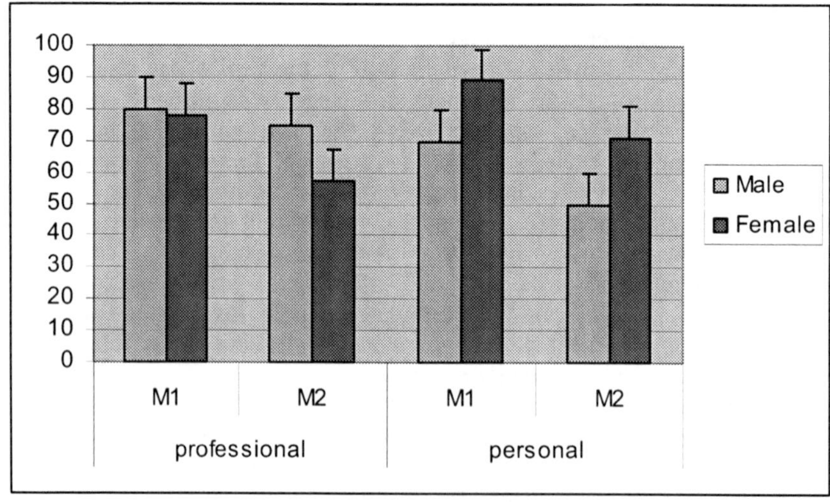

Figure 1: Percentage of *total agreement* for the items *professional* and *personal* growth for each Mentoring (M1 and M2).

3.3.2 Evaluation questionnaire

To evaluate how the participants appreciated the initiative, we asked them to fill out a questionnaire immediately after each of the workshops. All the collected questionnaires were anonymous. The questionnaires included a total number of

16 close-ended questions aimed at evaluating the organisational aspects, the speaker, different aspects of utility (personal awareness, acquisition of new skills, professional growth, etc.) and the overall quality of the workshop. Two last open-ended questions aimed at collecting free comments and suggestions.

The questions evaluating the speaker and the utility required answers on a four-point grading scale of agreement (total agreement, partial agreement, partial disagreement and total disagreement). According to the questionnaire answers, both the two workshops were highly appreciated by participants. On average all the items got positive rates (total or partial agreement on positively expressed items): very few negative answers were recorded, and most of the items got 100% of positive rates. The results on average do not seem to be influenced by sex, age or research experience of participants (averages and standard deviations for all those categories were very similar). Interestingly, there is a trend for women to rate higher utility of the workshop at the personal level rather than at the professional level (see Figure 1); in addition, the "personal level item" is the only one where women are more enthusiastic than men.

4 Conclusion and future work

The mentoring initiatives presented in this paper was carried out at ITC-irst, the Institute for Scientific and Technological Research of Trento, Italy. It consisted in two main activities: a scientific lecture series and a mentoring workshops cycle. The scientific lectures were presented by experienced international female researchers, whereas the mentoring workshops were held by organizational psychologists (one female and one male). All the speakers were sensitive to gender and job issues. The scientific lectures proposed positive role models, with the aim of encouraging female students and researchers to continue in pursuing the scientific career. The mentoring workshops focused on the improvement of both researchers skills and of the working environment. Both the activities obtained positive results and high level of participation and appreciation.

In the near future the *Gender and Science ITC-irst* group is going to propose the following activities:

- a third cycle of *Women in Science* scientific lectures;
- an analysis of the ITC-irst research personnel, focused on the female researchers positions;
- participation in the Gender Action Plan of two European Projects launched under the Sixth Framework Programme.

Acknowledgments

We would like to thank the present Institute director, Mario Zen, for his support in pursuing our activity, and all the colleagues that contributed to the initiatives. Special thanks to Luigina Aiello, our former director, for her encouragement and support to the Gender and Science group initiatives. We are very grateful to Lorenza Ferrario and Anna Perini for their precious contribution to the organisation of the presented initiatives and to this paper.

Human Perspectives in the Internet Society: Culture, Psychology and Gender, K. Morgan, J. Sanchez, C. A. Brebbia & A Voiskounsky (Editors) © 2004 WIT Press, www.witpress.com, ISBN 1-85312-726-4

References

[1] ETAN, Expert Working Group on Women and Science, Policies in the European Union: Promoting excellence through mainstreaming gender equality European Commission 2000. ftp://fpt.cordis.lu/pub/etan/docs/women.pdf.

[2] Wright S. H., Studies on Women Faculty, MIT News Office at the Massachusetts Institute of Technology, Cambridge, Mass. March 2002.

[3] Palomba R., Figlie di Minerva, Franco Angeli Editore, December 2000.

[4] Ferrario L., Mich O., Perini A., Genere e Carriera Scientifica, il caso ITC-irst, ITC-irst internal report, 2001, http://genere.itc.it/GenereScienza.pdf.

[5] ITC-irst Istituto Trentino di Cultura - centro per la ricerca scientifica e tecnologica, http://irst.itc.it.

[6] Genere e Scienza ITC-irst group, http://genere.itc.it.

[7] Armaroli C., Beatrici S., Ferrario L., Mich O. and Perini A, Can Mentoring be used as a Positive Action to Favor the Presence of Women in Science? Proc. of the 13th International Conference on Innovations in Education for Electrical and Information Engineering (EAEEIE 02), York (UK), April 2002.

[8] Mich O., Armaroli C., Beatrici S., Ferrario L., Nardon M. and Perini A., Mentoring for Women in Science: a case study. Proc. of the 14th International Conference on Innovations in Education for Electrical and Information Engineering (EAEEIE 03), Gdansk (Poland), June 2003.

[9] European Commission Directorate-General for Research. She Figures - Women and Science Statistics and Indicators. European Communities, 2003, http://europa.eu.int/comm/research/science-society/pdf/she_figures_2003.pdf.

[10] ENWISE group, Waste of Talents: turning private struggles into a public issue. Women and Science in the Enwise countries European Communities, 2003.

[11] Women of the World project, http://quest.nasa.gov/women/TODTWD97/wow.html.

[12] Women's Technology Program – Massachusetts Institute of Technology, http://wtp.mit.edu/.

[13] Introduce a Girl to Engineering Day, National Engineers Week, USA, http://www.eweek.org/site/News/Eweek/girlsday.shtml.

[14] Chesler N., Chesler M., Gender-Informed Mentoring Strategies for Women Engineering Scholars: On Establishing a Caring Community, Journal of Engineering Education, pp.49-55, January 2002. http://vtb.bme.wisc.edu/images/Chesler_JEE_2002.pdf.

Human Perspectives in the Internet Society: Culture, Psychology and Gender, K. Morgan, J. Sanchez, C. A. Brebbia & A Voiskounsky (Editors) © 2004 WIT Press, www.witpress.com, ISBN 1-85312-726-4

Section 7
Gender and computer behaviour

Gender impact assessment in the Department of Digital Media of Furtwangen University of Applied Sciences, Germany: design of the study and first empirical results

S. Selke, K. Töpsch, P. Pfeiffer, K. Kugele & I. Munder
Centre of Competence TanGenS,
Furtwangen University of Applied Sciences, Germany

Abstract

The study was carried out within the frame of the programme of the Baden-Wuerttembergian Ministry of Science, Research and Arts "Institutionalisation of Women's and Gender Studies at Baden-Wuerttembergian Universities". Its objective is to implement gender studies in research and academic teaching. The Centre of Competence TanGenS (Technology and Gender in Applied Sciences) is moreover interested in investigating gender aspects at Furtwangen University of Applied Sciences (Fachhochschule Furtwangen - FHF). The University as a customer and underlying field specifies topics and methods. We introduce the design and first results of a gender impact assessment as carried out in the department of Digital Media. Cross references to other projects and their empirical results complement the findings.

1 Gender studies at a university of technology, business and media

How do these fit together? Indeed, associations with Furtwangen University of Applied Sciences usually are not centered on gender studies. Nevertheless, since the founding of the Centre of Competence TanGenS (Technology and Gender in Applied Sciences) within the frame of the programme "Institutionalisation of Women's and Gender Studies at Baden-Wuerttembergian Universities" in 2002,

Human Perspectives in the Internet Society: Culture, Psychology and Gender, K. Morgan, J. Sanchez, C. A. Brebbia & A Voiskounsky (Editors) © 2004 WIT Press, www.witpress.com, ISBN 1-85312-726-4

there have been gender studies on very different levels, which fit together like the pieces of a jigsaw puzzle.

Inside the FHF TanGenS is affiliated to the Institute of Applied Research, the research organisation of FHF. Due to the University's orientation along technology and business, the IAF's major fields of research are surface technology, medical technology, environmental technologies and micro systems. By the topics Gender and Culture TanGenS is adding complementary aspects and is integrating women's and gender research in other department of FHF.

2 Implementation and institutionalisation of women's and gender research

After female advisories, appointed by the Ministry of Science, Research and Arts in Baden-Wuerttemberg, had found out that institutionalisation of women's and gender studies in exact sciences and technologies were still in an initial stage at regional level as well as at federal level, it was decided to implement that research perspective at the universities of Baden-Wuerttemberg. Centre of Competences should serve as crystallization points for regional, supra-regional and international co-operation. These Centres of Competence are designed to establish competences in women's and gender research and both, students and university lecturers, should take profit out of it. In practice this means to offer gender-sensitive teaching contents for students as well as provide the teaching professionals with gender relevant information for their classes in the form of empirically verified research results. Only on a basis of reliable data it is possible to sensitise students and academic teachers for gender.

In 2002 and 2003 we offered various gender-sensitive classes such as a practical training "experiencing technology", gender-sensitive classes of physics, career training for women, gender- and culture-sensitive modules in Computer Science in Media and others. There was also carried out a quantitative as well as qualitative survey on "technology and gender" among students. Their results can be found on the TanGenS homepage at http://www.tangens.fh-furtwangen.de.

Since October 2003 these measures are being added by two other activities: a representative online-survey on the students' satisfaction with the study environment including some gender modules as well as a Gender Impact Assessment (GIA) at the department of Digital Media. These measures aim to gather reliable empirical data which will serve as a basis to discuss further activities in gender equality. They are a prerequisite for a sustainable implementation of gender aspects in research and teaching.

3 Field-related conceptualisation of gender research at (FHF)

The idea of the Gender Impact Assessment is to initialise a process of a growing gender sensitation. The basic idea is a) appropriateness to the object, i.e. the questions are original and meaningful primarily for FHF and not only for the scientific community, b) method-triangulation i.e. various quantitative and qualitative survey methods will be used and c) service orientation, i.e. all

Human Perspectives in the Internet Society: Culture, Psychology and Gender, K. Morgan, J. Sanchez, C. A. Brebbia & A Voiskounsky (Editors) © 2004 WIT Press, www.witpress.com, ISBN 1-85312-726-4

projects serve to application and documentation of methods that basically can be transferred to other universities as well. In this approach TanGenS goes far beyond the idea to anchor gender contents in studies and examination regulations. According to the TanGenS' approach, we start with the analysis of the local field. This is to be done by methods which allow an easy transfer to other universities. By this the Centre of Excellence can support the implementation of gender contents on regional and supra-regional levels.

Before introducing the concrete methodology of the GIA as an example of such field-based conceptualising, we will make clear why the connection between gender and technology is worth a closer look.

4 Women and technology - a draught

One cannot deny that the world we are living in has a rather gendered structure. Perception of sex and following performative acts serve for (still) effective reduction of complexity. In everyday knowledge and everyday practice bisexuality is regarded as fact, unchallengeable and existing beyond social life. Everyday representations of gender are experienced in a binary way, are legitimated biologically and mostly experienced in an unproblematic way. Gender herein resembles societal norms - just deviation makes people realize a fundamental principle of standardisation.

Such irritating experiences occur in technology field and technology studies. For a lot of people technology still seems to be connected to an exclusively male connotation. Technical areas are mostly taken by males, technical education and courses of studies span a field characterised by male habits [1, #119]. Women are comparatively seldom able to enter this area and only by passing barriers that refer latently to their sex. Also in the academic programme, gender makes a difference. There are a couple of reasons for it, that point (in a cultural way) to a long established connection between technology and gender, or more precisely, gender blindness. In following overview will help to remind us.

Ontological inequalities: male primacy in technology

Personhood is manhood, gender is womanhood. Quite a chapter of societal and science history can be reduced to this stereotyped blasting composition. The unquestioned equalisation of human nature and maleness (Simone de Beauvoir) finds its expression in the cultural primacy of maleness in the area of technology genesis in the form of technology as a male myth. A deeply rooted connection of maleness and technology has become independent and makes it arduous to sort out all cross connections. Over a long period of time, amalgamation of two social constructions - maleness and technology - have obviously been handed down and has deeply been remembered in habit and therefore in the structures of the field as well as social practice [2, #15, 111]. Taken away from everyday perceptions by a cultural monopoly, these attributions have become self-referential and draw a picture of technology including associated dimensions like technological interest, technological talent, technological affinity, and technological

Human Perspectives in the Internet Society: Culture, Psychology and Gender, K. Morgan, J. Sanchez, C. A. Brebbia & A Voiskounsky (Editors) © 2004 WIT Press, www.witpress.com, ISBN 1-85312-726-4

competence - a picture of maleness without alternatives. These mechanisms get a status of more or less natural regularity which has a specific dialectical charm when thinking of the very dichotomy of nature and technology. For three decades researchers in social sciences are analysing the phenomenon, why women avoid technical fields or how determinants of careers in technical fields do differ in a gender-related way (e.g. Schulte-Florian [4, #373]). Meanwhile sociological research has unmasked technology as well as gender as cultural constructions.

Especially in practice, these findings do have consequences. Thus researchers are asking because of which kind of socialisation effects men and women choose a technological academic programme and with which (technical) previous knowledge they start in their academic field. Practice shows quickly that there's still a gendered distribution of opportunities. A very interesting stage is the period between graduation and the beginning of a professional career. Therefore, in order to influence practical behaviour in the direction towards of more equality it is necessary to understand exactly how diversity at the beginning of the academic programme turns into a multiplicity when entering a professional career, or, to put it another way, how do gendered structures of knowledge acquisition emerge and which are the consequence at an individual level. The Gender Impact Assessment at the Department of Digital Media exactly deals with process of how the students transform a gender-neutral offer of academic classes into individual career opportunities.

Being a University of Technology, Business and Media, FHF focuses on teaching applied knowledge in future areas. Until now the conception of academic study programme largely followed an implicit assumption of neutrality with respect to gender. Institutional knowledge and personal competence are emerging in social connections and, vice versa, are continuously shaping social connections. This is particularly true for future technologies like internet, online media, multimedia etc. which decisively influences the forms of working, communication and living in the future.

The assumption of neutrality however, the starting point of a Gender Impact Assessments (GIA), does not apply to the contents the knowledge. It means that the object of GIA is not gender neutrality of programming languages, project management tools or visual design. In contrast to examining the neutrality of contents of knowledge (which is anyways hard or hardly comparable in an inter-subjective way), we examine the gender neutrality of the transfer of knowledge and the acquisition of competence, that is the interaction between the institutional offer and individual demand, as well as the opportunities to allocate competencies in run of the academic programme. So we are checking the hypothesis, whether opportunities are distributed in an unequal, gendered way; we do not check the hypothesis, whether the contents of teaching are gendered.

Are there gender-specific obstacles, filters or selectivity – autonomous or heteronomous ones- that control participation in a social event called "acquisition of competencies at university"? Is the choice of specialisation, the grading of cognitive performance, choice of co-operation partners in practical training or finally the career opportunities influenced by those?

Human Perspectives in the Internet Society: Culture, Psychology and Gender, K. Morgan, J. Sanchez, C. A. Brebbia & A Voiskounsky (Editors) © 2004 WIT Press, www.witpress.com, ISBN 1-85312-726-4

For answering these questions, first results can be derived from the content analysis of bachelor theses of the last years. In addition to expert interviews, participant observation of seminars and exercises as well as focus groups with students, this sub-project gives a first impression of gender-specific selectivity of the field. Already the analysis of nine group discussions, carried out in 2003, showed a clear trend: there are gender-specific differences in realizing talents and interests, previous knowledge and socialised cognitive interests. Whereas for men the centre of attention seems to be "application", do women prefer "learning". These “Leitbilder” and types of knowledge are realised evidently in a selective way: "Boys implement, but girls design it". This is a statement done in a discussion group, that metaphorically condenses the necessity to set a focus on the content on the one hand, and gender-specific preferences on the other hand.

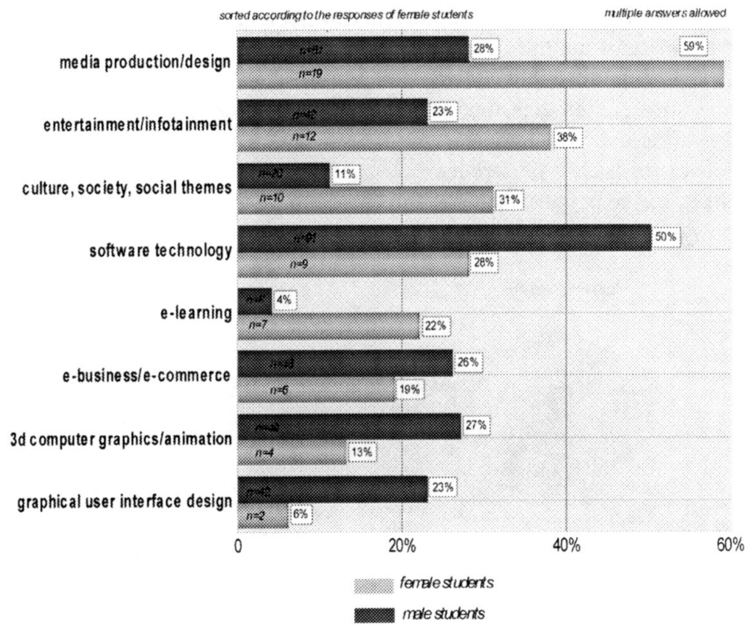

Figure 1: Specialist topics chosen for Bachelor thesis.

How are these differences portrayed in the empirical part? In order to answer this question TanGenS evaluated the abstracts of totally 215 bachelor theses (183 men and 32 women) written between winter term 1997 and summer term 2003. A bachelor thesis is part of the final examination. Aim of the analysis of bachelor theses was to check the neutrality hypothesis, i.e. whether there are gender-specific effects in selecting the seemingly gender-neutral offer of a thesis. The analysis of the diploma theses was based on following premises: 1. students choose topics for their theses in agreement with their individual preferences and focal interest in order to get good results of the examination. 2. They choose

Human Perspectives in the Internet Society: Culture, Psychology and Gender, K. Morgan, J. Sanchez, C. A. Brebbia & A Voiskounsky (Editors) © 2004 WIT Press, www.witpress.com, ISBN 1-85312-726-4

their topics in accordance with their individual professional goals. In the following, the most important results of the analysis are introduced. Because of the small number of cases, in the following text and in the graphics, the absolute values are given additionally.

A first impression of gender-specific differences allows the thematic attribution of bachelor thesis by the "columns" of the department - Technology, Design and Business. Almost all assignments of men (91%; n=166), but only two thirds of women (69%; n=22) can be definitely assigned to the technological area (if more than one coded). An inversion of this perspective evolves in assigning to the design area. Three quarters of the women (75%; n=24) carried out a thesis dealing with creative tasks, but only every other man (57%; n=105) selected such a component. About one third of the students' theses of each sex can be assigned to business. So a focus on business is regarded more seldom as a stepping stone to career, and both, man and women are less interested in it.

The majority of the theses are application oriented. Three quarters of the men (78%; n=141) and one third of the women (66%; n=21) went for this direction. Only one third can be classified as basic research. Interdisciplinary topics were even less attractive. Nevertheless, for almost one quarter of the women's theses we can confirm such a preference (23%; n=7), but only every tenth man (13%, n=21) liked to see beyond the end of his disciplinary noses.

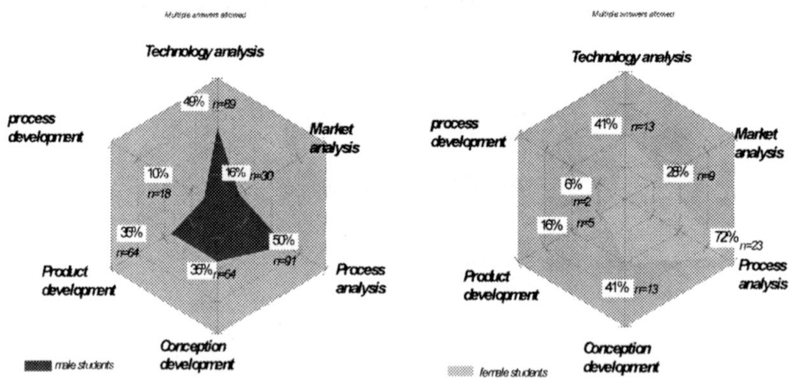

Figure 2: Aim of Bachelor thesis.

However, most gender-specific differences appear most clearly in the choice of areas of specialisation (cf. fig. 1.). Women preferentially decide for design and communication, whereas the men prefer technical areas such as programming. More than half of the women (59%; n=19) but only one quarter of the men (28%; n=51) worked on media production or design. When looking at the areas entertainment and infotainment, we get a similar result. The share of women's' works makes up about one third, the part of men's' theses only one quarter. The men showed least interest to the areas e-learning as well as culture, society and social issues. Whereas almost a quarter of the women (22%; n=6) were interested in e-learning, the proportion of men was negligible (4%; n=8). Only every tenth man was interested in cultural, societal or social topics (11%; n=20), whereas one third of the women did (31%; n=10). Men's' domain is definitely software technology. Every other man decided for this specialisation (n=91), but only a quarter of the women (28%, n=9). Therefore the antagonism is "media design" versus "software programming". Along the axis of preference we are able to locate students, not exclusively, though with a certain possibility.

This first rough impression is deepened by a closer examination of the objectives of the theses (cf. fig. 2). Both, male and female students often deal with the analysis of processes. However, there are clear differences. Whereas only every other man takes such a task, almost three quarters of the women do (72%, n=23) do. Women more often choose a market-analysis or development of concepts, whereas men go more often for technology analysis and product development.

5 Conclusion

Summarizing, we conclude that there are clear preferences and selectivities. Women are more inclined to deal with design, conceptional or communicative-didactical tasks, men prefer programming and application-based development of prototypes or products.

Selectivities, developed in the run of the academic programme, are already perceived outside of the narrow context of a single department. The underlying casualness, how the job market for internships is divided into a male and female sphere ("Would you rather work in a creative or programming area?"), show that employers, with their seismographic talent, do not need any quantitative empirical proof to detect this kind of differentiation.

These first results only deliver a tiny insight in the area "academic programme", its latent and obvious gendered structures, its implementation processes, actions of choice and allocation of opportunities for students. The results of the GIA will be combined with a quantitative survey about the satisfaction with the study environment that will be realised in summer 2004. This spectrum of activities gives evidence of the diversity in implementing the Leitbild "gender". TanGenS is trying hard to introduce gender as a topic in a technology-centred environment, to intensify gender-specific and gender-sensitive educational offers at FHF as well as, in general, to contribute in sensitising students and university lecturers for gender.

References

[1] Brandes, Holger (2001): Der männliche Habitus. Band 1: Männer und sich: Männergruppen und männliche Identitäten. Opladen.

[2] Mooraj, Margrit (2002): Frauen, Männer und Technik. Ingenieurinnen in einem männlich besetzten Berufsfeld. Frankfurt am Main.

[3] Munder, Irmtraud/Tinsel, Iris/Töpsch, Karin (2003): Technikhaltungen, Berufs- und Lebensplanung. Ergebnisse einer schriftlichen Befragung von

Human Perspectives in the Internet Society: Culture, Psychology and Gender, K. Morgan, J. Sanchez, C. A. Brebbia & A Voiskounsky (Editors) © 2004 WIT Press, www.witpress.com, ISBN 1-85312-726-4

StudienanfängerInnen in technischen Studiengängen im Wintersemester 2002/03 an der Fachhochschule Furtwangen. Arbeitsbericht 1 des Kompetenzzentrums TanGenS, Furtwangen.

[4] Schulte-Florian, Gabriele (1999): Determinanten der Karriere. Eine theoretische Analyse unter Berücksichtigung geschlechtsspezifischer Besonderheiten. München.

[5] Tinsel, Iris/Töpsch, Karin (2004): Vom Technikinteresse zum technischen Beruf. Geschlecher- und studiengangsspezifische Analysen zu technikhaltungen und Karriereplanung von StudienanfängerInnen an der FH Furtwangen. Arbeitsbericht 2 des Kompetenzzentrums TanGenS, Furtwangen.

Human Perspectives in the Internet Society: Culture, Psychology and Gender, K. Morgan, J. Sanchez, C. A. Brebbia & A Voiskounsky (Editors) © 2004 WIT Press, www.witpress.com, ISBN 1-85312-726-4

Fair play: gender, digital gaming and educational disadvantage

J. Jenson & S. de Castell
York University and Simon Fraser University

Abstract

Since the spectacular runaway best-seller, "Barbie Fashion Designer" appeared on the shelves in October 1996, selling a half-million copies in its first two months and vanquishing the slash-and-bash market leaders "Doom," "Quake," "Duke Nukem," and "Mortal Kombat," major corporate e-sponsored research campaigns have been launched to identify the differently gendered play patterns of boys and girls and to discover what girls "like best". This astonishing breakthrough into the previously dormant market for computer-based playware for girls ushered in a retooling of technology – a retooling accomplished, however, by affirming rather than challenging received gender stereotypes that preserve girls' historically assigned locations in the gender order. In the field of education, video games have the capacity to capture and hold the attention of players of many different ages, and to "teach" new players the functions and controls of a new game with far greater alacrity and to greater functional effect than schools teach. This paper examines gender and computer game playing, in particular questions of identity, access and playful engagement with these technologies. Because computer-based media are not only central tools for learning and work, and because games and simulations are increasingly being recruited as educational and instructional genres, it is likewise exceedingly important, from an educational equity standpoint, to examine the ways in which rapidly evolving computer game-based learning initiatives threaten to compound and intensify girls' computer disadvantage, a cumulative dis-entitlement from computer-based educational and occupational opportunities.

1 What real girls play

The video game industry is one of the largest entertainment industries in the world, last year (2003) making more money than the Hollywood film industry,

Human Perspectives in the Internet Society: Culture, Psychology and Gender, K. Morgan, J. Sanchez, C. A. Brebbia & A Voiskounsky (Editors) © 2004 WIT Press, www.witpress.com, ISBN 1-85312-726-4

$7 billion U.S. (http://theesa.com/pressroom.html [1]). In the field of education, that video games have the capacity to capture and hold the attention of players of many different ages, and to "teach" new players the functions and controls of a new game with far greater alacrity, and to greater functional effect than schools teach comparably, and even far less complex, skills and knowledge, has not gone un-noticed. Working as we both do in faculties of education, our own studies of gender and computer game playing, examine questions of identity, access, and playful engagement with these technologies from the following premises:

(1) As Henry Jenkins and others have argued for some time, far more boys than girls play computer/video games, and boys' early and sustained exposure to and experience with gaming places them at an advantage with respect to computer competence and confidence when they enter and as they continue their schooling (Jenkins [2], Kafai [3, 4]).

(2) There is a tendency in the literature on girls/women and computer game playing to construct their gaming choices and play styles as distinctly, and essentially "female," characterizing those who choose to play as "liking collaboration," "non-violent" and "easy" computer games (Brunner et al. [5], Glos and Goldin [6], Groppe [7], Orr Vered [8], Schott and Horrell [9], Subrahmanyam and Greenfield [10]). Its worth noticing that the stranglehold these kinds of stereotypical and essentializing identifications and characterizations have had and continue to have on received wisdom, both popular and academic about gender and play interests, styles and preferences by no means originates with video game playing, but is indigenous to the culture of computing more generally, and that this gendered computer culture always already mediates girls' interactions with those technologies, among which game playing is only the most recent subject of attention.

Because computer-based media are now central tools for learning and work, and because games and simulations are increasingly being recruited as educational and instructional genres, it is likewise exceedingly important, from an educational equity standpoint to examine the ways in which rapidly evolving computer **game**-based learning initiatives threaten to compound and intensify girls' computer disadvantage, a cumulative disentitlement from computer-based educational and occupational opportunities. In the U.S., for example, Henry Jenkins and Kurt Squire received $25 million in funding for a collaboration with Microsoft to design playful educational video games. Initially titled the "Games to Teach" project (http://www.educationarcade.org/gtt/ [11]), it has developed in the recent year into the "Education Arcade" (http://www.educationarcade.org/ [12]) and still working on creating discipline- driven computer games (Atwood [13]). In Canada, we are part of a project called SAGE ("Simulations and Advanced Gaming Environments for Education) which just received $3 million to study and build computer games for learning. In educational settings, the tendency has been to presume that technologies are "neutral" tools deployed by educators for ameliorative ends. Video and computer games, however, are far

Human Perspectives in the Internet Society: Culture, Psychology and Gender, K. Morgan, J. Sanchez, C. A. Brebbia & A Voiskounsky (Editors) © 2004 WIT Press, www.witpress.com, ISBN 1-85312-726-4

from neutral and we have seen little evidence of new educational gaming work being informed by attention to girls' perspectives on gaming, their participation in and exclusion from game cultures, and an absence of theoretically adequate and empirically grounded studies of the kinds of games, characters, and overall approaches to 'play' that might better engage and involve girls. A case in point is Jim Gee's recent book on learning in video games, in which he summarily dismisses "gender" from his own consideration of video games and learning (Gee [14]).

This dismissal is typically justified by reference to the recent proliferation of data from large-scale quantative research "studies" reporting that women are playing and buying at least as many computer and video games as men are, and in some cases, reporting that they play *more* often, not less. A recent study by the Pew Internet and American Life Project, for instance reported that 57 percent of female U.S. teenagers play on line (Lenhart et al. [15]), while another study on college gaming finds that "Surprising, slightly more women than men reported playing computer and online games (approximately 60% women compared to 40% men), with about the same number of men and women playing *video* games" (Jones [16]). This study goes on to explain that, "Part of the reason more women than men play computer games may be that video games are generally focused on action and adventure (often violent in nature), while computer games are typically traditional games (e.g. solitaire, board games)." In both of these studies, and indeed in all of the studies we've examined thus far, statistics like these are used to dismiss the question of gender and computer game playing from the outset (it is no longer a "problem" since so many more women are indicating that they are playing). Once gender has been excised as statistically in-significant, there is typically no further gender-based dis-aggregation of data, even when it might seem that statistically relevant distinctions should be made with respect to game preferences and time on the game (c.f. http://www.media-awareness.ca/english/resources/research_documents/studies/video_games/vgc_preferences.cfm [17]), silencing in turn any follow-up research questions about whether and what women/girls are ***actually*** playing, and whether or how their engagement with game play is actually playful at all.

In the initial empirical work that we present here, we find *no reason to believe*, and in fact, *many reasons to disbelieve* the ways in which these large studies are reporting on game play, and good reasons for concern about what of significance is being actively obscured by them.

This process is not without subtlety. A recent study on college student's game play states, for example:

> "Male and female online gamers prefer different types of games, with female gamers preferring quiz, trivia and contest games, while male gamers select action games as their favorite type of online game."

A careful analysis of the kinds of discursive constructions of women as "gamers" illustrates how studies are creatively manufacturing "equal numbers" in order to dismiss gender as a relevant consideration for video game markets. Significant in this case is a slippery discursive shift which constructs women

Human Perspectives in the Internet Society: Culture, Psychology and Gender, K. Morgan, J. Sanchez, C. A. Brebbia & A Voiskounsky (Editors) © 2004 WIT Press, www.witpress.com, ISBN 1-85312-726-4

who play card games as "female gamers". How is playing card games or online board games equivalent to playing a role playing game or first person shooting game? What is accomplished by naming women who play card games or board games on line as "gamers"--- this rhetorical sleight of hand makes possible a significant next move: to disregard gender differences and compile aggregative data on game players as a homogeneous group. And this, indeed, is what typically follows for this same study goes on to report that:

> "People who play online games spend an average of 3 hours per week playing games and an average of 5.4 hours per week playing off line games on their PCs."

With the earlier discursive shift having effectively masked gender, it now becomes possible to refer research findings to "people", instead of to men vs. women) precisely at the points where such a distinction might matter most, for example, in making it evident that, since far more women than men play online card games of 20 minutes or less duration, and far more men play computer and video games which demand upwards of 40 hours to complete, men can be shown in these same data to be playing nearly twice as long as women.

Part of what this kind of reporting is disguising then, is precisely how pervasively video and computer game playing is still the realm of men and boys. Meanwhile, notions of "progress" in the area of gender and technology are continually being bolstered up by a tendency to seek out narratives of redemption in the putting forward of exceptional cases. The BBC, for instance, recently reported on young women gamers playing "Counterstrike." The interviewees in the piece noted that 99% of the people who play Counterstrike are male, and that they created a community to play together because "females that do come into this world feel overpowered or that they are not welcomed. If people just opened their minds and didn't see us as being male or female, it would be much better" (Hermida [18]). What was intriguing about the piece was that women did not compete directly with men in a Counterstrike competition *and* that this fact was an especially "hot topic" for the discussion which is posted following the article.

Moreover, while much has been made in recent years of the fact that computer games have generated more options for female characters and their development, including the much written about success of Lara Croft or of the central role of the female character of Samus in Metroid Prime, it remains the case that female characters account for, according to one source, approximately 16% of available game characters, almost all of whom are highly sexualized. All of this matters greatly when trying to get an accurate picture of what "real girls play".

What video/computer games ***do*** real girls play? Who do they play with? How do they play? And how is it that they themselves are constructing their own game play as different and/or the same as boys/men who play games?

1.1 Solitaire

In our initial talks with girls and young women on the subject of their video game play, we found that besides the usual recitation of the video games and

Human Perspectives in the Internet Society: Culture, Psychology and Gender, K. Morgan, J. Sanchez, C. A. Brebbia & A Voiskounsky (Editors) © 2004 WIT Press, www.witpress.com, ISBN 1-85312-726-4

types of games that they reported playing, (interesting in itself for their remarkable but typically un-remarked on inability even to correctly **name** the games they claim to have played), their own game play was also mediated by whether or not they played alone, who they played against (if anyone), and whether or not they enjoyed competition or considered themselves to be competitive. We found that girls' construction of what they played and for what reasons varied somewhat from individual to individual, but that for nearly all of our pilot subjects (36 in total), if they *did* play video games, they most typically played card games, tetris-like games, gender-appropriate games (like "Sabrina the teenage witch") and online but otherwise traditional board games ***on their own***. In that case, of course, questions of competition and competitiveness can scarcely arise.

Ages of participants in the pilot study ranged from 12-13 and 22-23, with one exception, a woman in her late thirties.

None of the boys reported playing with girls: all reported playing with other boys, and yet **all** of the girls reported playing with boys and only infrequently, with other girls. When girls and young women reported playing games which were decidedly not gender appropriate (like Halo, Vice City, or Diablo II), they *always* reported playing with a male player. While this is just an initial pilot of what will be a much larger study, what we think might be highly significant is whether and how for most women, transgressing gender 'norms' in relation to playing games, occurs most frequently when it is legitimated by male relations (boyfriends, cousins, brothers and fathers) and therefore does not transgress gender stereotypes nor jeopardize a normalized, stereotypical feminine identity which is clearly outside of the masculine culture of video game playing.

Perhaps one reason for this is, again, the masculine culture of computing more generally which positions women and girls as less competent and/or confident in relation to computers. Throughout our interviews, girls and women characterized their own game play as being inadequate and/or less competitive for reasons which make little or no sense in relation to their own lives and experience. One young woman claims that she doesn't play video games anymore because the controls "got too complicated", another claims that her "fingers are too stubby" to work the controls properly to navigate RPG games, and yet another, herself an athlete in a sport requiring exceptional hand-eye coordination, claims that she lacks the hand-eye coordination required for competitive game play. In our previous work on gender and technology we found that young women constructed similar excuses as to why the boys in their classroom tended always to monopolize the best machines – as one young woman put it, "girls have weaker knees" so they couldn't compete with the boys who could "run faster" to get there first (Jenson et al. [19]). These kinds of responses, a species of what we call "magical realism", indicate to us that when girls and women see themselves as competing directly with their masculine counter-parts they tend to side-step the possibility of such gender-inappropriate engagement by discounting themselves as equal-opportunity competitors.

The one and only genre of game which both the young women and girls we interviewed indicated that they played generically was racing games. Racing

Human Perspectives in the Internet Society: Culture, Psychology and Gender, K. Morgan, J. Sanchez, C. A. Brebbia & A Voiskounsky (Editors) © 2004 WIT Press, www.witpress.com, ISBN 1-85312-726-4

games are in an obvious way highly accessible – they all operate on the same general premise, maneuvering an object in a limited space, most typically for a limited amount of time, with simple, familiar and easily intuited controls (which can get be used more complexly but don't have to be) and they most typically (with multiple controllers) can be played with other people. Racing games, uniquely, offer a ubiquitous baseline understanding of 'how to play the game' and while the story line, characters, vehicles and playability might alter, the premise remains the same – driving and/or racing.

One final noteworthy point is that there is a significant generation gap between the girls and young women we interviewed – because the women in their 20's did not, for the most part, currently play video games, their naming and experience of those games was limited to their early preteen and early teenage years. Most young women, for example, indicated that they stopped playing video games around the age of 14 and have not played since and their game playing preferences indicate that. Many are reporting that, unlike boys who play "for fun", girls who continue to play beyond adolescence aren't really, by their own accounts, "playing" at all, they are "de-stressing", relaxing, or passing the time when they are bored---which is surely a very different, and significantly different thing from our invisibly but deeply gendered conceptions of "play". Equally significantly, the games girls report playing or having played are those bundled with the consoles they purchased (e.g. "Duck Hunt"), or else, like Tetris and Solitaire, those readily available free of charge online. Economics intersects here in all-too- familiar ways with gender, and we see that where women *do* purchase games, they do so for their sons, their brothers or their boyfriends. Their rights to and control over their own leisure time are slight relative to their male counterparts, whether men or boys. Finally, we see in subtle and not so subtle ways how girls who in mixed company do not promptly disqualify themselves as credible gamers are invariably ridiculed and their game interests and capabilities undermined and diminished by the boys in whose presence such dangerously inappropriate desires and capabilities are voiced, indicating that it might matter enormously to the validity of game research data in what context and by whom women and girls are asked to speak about their gaming interests, desires and experiences, a point succinctly summed up for us by one young man who explained:

> "If a guy asks another guy, " do you play video games?" he'll pretty much always say yes, because guys know video games are about competing with other guys, and about winning. But if a girl asks a guy if he plays, he'll say no, so she doesn't think he's a social misfit who only likes to stare at a computer screen."

This simple and obvious point about the critical importance of addressivity in computer game research, about who asks what, in what contexts, and for what purposes, seems invariably to be overlooked in both qualitative and quantitative studies of gaming and play. In these and many more respects, we argue, its time for game research to "get real". So what about the girls? What, and how, do "real girls" play?

Human Perspectives in the Internet Society: Culture, Psychology and Gender, K. Morgan, J. Sanchez, C. A. Brebbia & A Voiskounsky (Editors) © 2004 WIT Press, www.witpress.com, ISBN 1-85312-726-4

References

[1] Entertainment Software Association. Online at: http://theesa.com /pressroom.html.

[2] Jenkins, H. (2001). From Barbie to Mortal Combat: Further Reflections. Paper presented at "Playing by the Rules: The Cultural Policy Challenges of Video Games." Chicago, Illinois (October, 2001).

[3] Kafai, Y. (1996). Gender differences in children's constructions of video games. In Patricia M. Greenfield & Rodney R. Cocking (Eds.), *Interacting with video* (p. 39–66). Norwood, NJ: Ablex Publishing Corporation.

[4] Kafai, Y. (1998). Video Game Designs by Girls and Boys: Variability and Consistency of Gender Differences. In H. Jenkins, & J. Cassell (1998) (Eds.), From Barbie to Mortal Kombat (pp. 90-117). Cambridge, MA: MIT Press.

[5] Brunner, C. Bennett, D. & Honey, M. (1998). Girl Games and Technological Desire. In J. Cassell & H. Jenkins (Eds.) *From Barbie to Mortal Kombat: Gender and Computer Games*. Cambridge: MIT Press.

[6] Glos, J. and Goldin, S. (1998). An Interview with Heather Kelly In J. Cassell & H. Jenkins (Eds.) *From Barbie to Mortal Kombat: Gender and Computer Games*. Cambridge: MIT Press.

[7] Groppe, L. (2001). Teen Girl Gaming: The New Paradigm. *Playing by the Rules: The Cultural Policy Challenges of Video Games Conference* (University of Chicago, October 2001), see http://culturalpolicy.uchicago.edu/conf2001/papers/groppe.html

[8] Orr Vered, K. (1998). Blue Group Boys Play Incredible Machine, Girls Play Hopscotch: Social Discourse and Gendered Play at the Computer. In J. Sefton-Green (Ed.) *Digital Diversions: Youth Culture in the Age of Multimedia.* London: UCL Press.

[9] Schott, G. R. & Horrell, K. R. (2001) Girl Gamers and Their Relationship with the Gaming Culture. *Convergence*, 6, 4, p. 36-53.

[10] Subrahmanyam, K. and Greenfield, P. M. (1998). Computer Games for Girls: What Makes Them Play? In J. Cassell & H. Jenkins (Eds.) *From Barbie to Mortal Kombat: Gender and Computer Games*. Cambridge: MIT Press.

[11] Games to Teach. http://www.educationarcade.org/gtt/.

[12] Education Arcade. http://www.educationarcade.org.

[13] Atwood, S. (2004, June). Education Arcade. *Technology Review*. Available on-line at: (http://www.technologyreview.com/articles/atwood 0604.asp?p=1).

[14] Gee, J. (2003). *What Video Games have to Teach us about Learning and Literacy*. New York: Palgrave.

[15] Lenhart, A., Rainie, L. & Lewis, O. (2001). Teenage life online: The rise of the internet-message generation and the Internet's impact on friendships and family relationships. Pew Internet and American Life Project. Available online at: http://www.pewinternet.org.

Human Perspectives in the Internet Society: Culture, Psychology and Gender, K. Morgan, J. Sanchez, C. A. Brebbia & A Voiskounsky (Editors) © 2004 WIT Press, www.witpress.com, ISBN 1-85312-726-4

[16] Jones, S. (2003). Let the games begin: Gaming technology and Entertainment among college students. Pew Internet and American Life Project. Available online at: http://www.pewinternet.org.

[17] Media Awareness Network. http://www.media-awareness.ca/english/resources/research_documents/studies/video_games/vgc_preferences.cfm.

[18] Hermida, A. (2004, Feb. 23). Girl Gamers Strike at the Boys. BBC News World Edition Online. Online at: http://news.bbc.co.uk/2/hi/technology/3496963.stm.

[19] Jenson, J., de Castell, S. & Bryson, M. (2003). Girl Talk: Gender, Equity and Identity Discourses in a School-based Computer Culture. *Women's Studies International Forum, 26* (6), 561-73.

Human Perspectives in the Internet Society: Culture, Psychology and Gender, K. Morgan, J. Sanchez, C. A. Brebbia & A Voiskounsky (Editors) © 2004 WIT Press, www.witpress.com, ISBN 1-85312-726-4

Gender, language and computer-mediated communication

J. Miller & A. Durndell
Department of Psychology, Glasgow Caledonian University, Scotland

Abstract

This research aimed to investigate gender and language in the context of educational computer-mediated interactions. As the use of online discussion groups in campus-based education increases, so does the need to investigate the impact of gender on language and communication styles in this context. It has been claimed that the lack of social context cues in computer-mediated communication (CMC) equalises participation, resulting in a more democratic environment than face-to-face communication. However, gender differences in power and language use have been found online. In total, 197 students (148 females, 49 males) participated in open-ended online discussion as an optional part of their introductory psychology module. Informed consent was sought from the online participants to download the electronic discourse for analysis using Atlas.ti 4.2. Participation and language use were analysed using a combination of quantitative and qualitative methods. A detailed coding scheme was developed during the pilot study that incorporated various linguistic, stylistic, paralinguistic and task variables. This coding scheme was used in subsequent studies and 699 messages from four studies were coded in total. Males and females were similar overall with regard to participation as shown by the total number of posts and mean number of words per post. However, gender-related patterns in language use and interaction styles were found. The results are discussed in relation to previous literature on gender and language in both face-to-face and computer-mediated contexts and in relation to the democratising theories of CMC. The implications of the results for the use of CMC in Higher Education will also be considered.
Keywords: computer-mediated communication, electronic discourse, online discussion groups, gender, language use, qualitative content analysis.

Human Perspectives in the Internet Society: Culture, Psychology and Gender, K. Morgan, J. Sanchez, C. A. Brebbia & A Voiskounsky (Editors) © 2004 WIT Press, www.witpress.com, ISBN 1-85312-726-4

1 Introduction

Asynchronous computer-mediated communication (CMC) refers to text-based communication that takes place over computer networks in delayed time. This includes electronic mail and online discussion forums such as listservs, newsgroups, bulletin boards or asynchronous computer conferences. Online discussion groups allow the exchange of text-based messages surrounding a particular topic. Asynchronous discussion forums are increasingly being incorporated into campus-based Higher Education (HE) courses in order to support peer interaction and cooperative learning. The term computer-supported cooperative learning (CSCL) can be used to cover any form of cooperative learning communication that occurs over a network of computers (McConnell [1]).

It has been claimed that the loss of social context cues, such as gender, in text-based CMC equalises participation, making it a more democratic form of communication, in comparison to traditional face-to-face methods (Sproull and Kiesler [2]). It is proposed that the loss of nonverbal indicators of status and power enable participants, who would otherwise defer speaking turns to higher-status participants in face-to-face interaction, become uninhibited and participate more. For example, it has often been found that males dominate mixed-sex interaction, participating more frequently than females and for longer in public and formal contexts (Coates [3], Tannen [4]).

Furthermore, it has been suggested that under conditions of anonymity males and females may be less likely to feel that they have to project the socially expected qualities corresponding to their gender (Matheson and Zanna [5]). Indeed, early reviews concerning online communication implied that cyberspace was 'a utopian place, where ideas, not social factors, were the key features of these new discourse settings' (Gurak and Eberltoff-Kraske [6]). This makes CMC an attractive option for use in educational contexts, in addition to the benefits of increased time for reflection and the articulation of ideas into words that are shared and built upon through the responses of others (Harasim *et al.* [7]),

The filtering out of cues in CMC is also claimed to result in communication that is less personal, compared to face-to-face interaction (e.g. Sproull and Kiesler [2]) and can lead to increased disinhibited behaviour such as flaming (e.g. swearing and personal insults). However, Joinson [8] notes that disinhibited behaviour can also be in the form of self-disclosure. The lack of social presence that is assumed to characterise CMC is thought to lead to a lack of socioemotional discourse and responsiveness to one another's ideas, relative to face-to-face communication (Sproull and Kiesler [2]). Therefore this suggestion has implications for the use of CMC to support peer interaction in HE and responding to another's ideas is deemed to be an important cognitive skill. Socioemotional content includes use of emoticons, expressions of supporting references, self-references, references to others and self-disclosure (Jaffe *et al.* [9]). However, Walther's [10] social information processing theory assumes that CMC participants are affected by the same internal drive of 'affiliation' as

Human Perspectives in the Internet Society: Culture, Psychology and Gender, K. Morgan, J. Sanchez, C. A. Brebbia & A Voiskounsky (Editors) © 2004 WIT Press, www.witpress.com, ISBN 1-85312-726-4

participants in face-to-face communication and argues that text-based CMC can support socioemotional communication. Gender may influence the expression of socioemotional behaviour online. Males are believed to value status more through the process of gender role socialisation, whereas females are thought to value connection or affiliation, leading to gender-preferential communication styles, differentiated as 'competitive' and 'cooperative' (Coates [3], Tannen [4]). Therefore, females may be more likely than males to express socioemotional responses in CMC such as those described above. However, negative forms that would also qualify as responses to another's ideas, such as expressions of disagreement, are not always included in definitions of socioemotional content.

The Social Identity Explanation of Deindividuated Effects (SIDE) model (Reicher *et al.* [11]) predicts that visual anonymity of the self to others leads to heightened self-awareness and greater adherence to group norms when a social identity is salient. For example, if gender is made a salient social identity in CMC then this could invoke behavioural norms and stereotypes regarding gender appropriate behaviour, influencing expectations and perceptions of CMC users. Similarly, Matheson and Zanna [5] argue that differences in status may actually be accentuated in CMC if cues to gender are available. Low public-awareness levels in CMC are associated with lower social pressures that make the expression of internalised gender biases unacceptable. Therefore, it is possible that CMC could exacerbate existing asymmetrical power differences, or even create them.

Furthermore, cues to gender may not be restricted to usernames and signatures in CMC. Experimental work by Thomson and Murachver [12] found evidence for gender-preferential language in informal CMC and showed that readers of email messages used gender-linked language differences within messages to correctly identify the author's gender. Therefore, if linguistic cues to gender are found in other CMC contexts, this will have implications for the assumption of gender anonymity online and CMC as a gender-free environment.

Gender-related patterns in language style have been reported in Internet discussion groups such as email listservs (e.g. Herring [13], 14]). Similar to face-to-face research, these results suggest that males dominate interaction, which may deter women from participating in CMC or force them to seek women-only groups online. Herring found large differences in language style along the same task-orientated versus socioemotional dimensions as Tannen [4] described. Female postings tended to display features of attenuation, such as hedging, apologising, asking questions and a personal orientation, revealing thoughts and feelings and interacting with and supporting others. On the other hand, male postings were lengthy and/or frequent, adversarial and featured strong assertions, self-promotion, sarcasm and flaming. It is suggested that gender-based communication styles and the power dynamics associated with these styles carry over to electronic environments, despite the loss of overt face-to-face cues to gender [14].

Savicki *et al.* [15] provided some evidence for the gender-related communication styles identified by Herring [14] in their study of Internet discussion groups. Soukup [16] observed traditional masculine and feminine

Human Perspectives in the Internet Society: Culture, Psychology and Gender, K. Morgan, J. Sanchez, C. A. Brebbia & A Voiskounsky (Editors) © 2004 WIT Press, www.witpress.com, ISBN 1-85312-726-4

forms of discourse in Internet chatrooms. However, Yates [17] notes that many studies have failed to replicate these findings. For example, Michaelson and Pohl [18] did not find differences along the supportive/emotional versus adversarial/task-oriented dimensions in their study of an email problem-solving task. Mixed results in terms of gender variations in language use in CMC make in unclear whether CMC moderates or magnifies the gender differences reported in face-to-face research. Perhaps these differences could be attributed to the varying online contexts that have been studied. There is also the extent to which gender can reliably be inferred by researchers from usernames or email addresses. For example, Jaffe *et al.* [9] found that females are more likely to choose a pseudonym to mask their gender when communicating online, which could distort the findings of studies using samples taken directly from the Internet.

The present research is concerned with formal use of CMC on an undergraduate module. This is a context in which gender equality is of major importance. If differences in participation and communication style are found to exist in this context then this will have implications for the increasing use of CMC in HE. Therefore this research aims to investigate the existence of gender-related patterns in participation and language use in educational, mixed-gender, online discussion groups.

2 Method

2.1 Design

The computer-mediated discourse of students using CMC for open-ended discussion of psychological topics was downloaded with informed consent for a qualitative content analysis procedure (Mayring [19]). Qualitative content analysis seeks to conserve some methodological advantages of quantitative content analysis and broaden them to a concept of qualitative procedure. It involves quantitative methods such as defining the unit of analysis and the coding categories and carrying out a check of inter-coder reliability [19]. In the present research, the unit of analysis was at the level of the message, following Rourke *et al.* [20] recommendation. A coding scheme was developed during the initial study that was used to code 699 messages, obtained through four consecutive studies. The coding scheme was extensive and covered 12 linguistic, 8 paralinguistic, 19 stylistic and 19 task codes. A second independent rater coded 20 per cent of the sample and inter-rater reliability was good (Cohen's kappa = 0.9). The results were analysed for overall effects of gender on choice of user identification (real name or pseudonym), quantitative measures of participation (mean number of posts and words per post) and frequencies of coded categories relating to linguistic and stylistic usage (at varying levels of abstraction using Atlas.ti 4.2).

Human Perspectives in the Internet Society: Culture, Psychology and Gender, K. Morgan, J. Sanchez, C. A. Brebbia & A Voiskounsky (Editors) © 2004 WIT Press, www.witpress.com, ISBN 1-85312-726-4

2.2 Participants

The participants were 197 campus-based introductory psychology students (149 females, 48 males) at a Scottish university who had all chosen to take part in the online discussion groups as part of the module. The age range was 17-46 years and the mean age of the sample was 22 years (SD = 6.52).

2.3 Apparatus

The coding list was developed using Atlas.ti 4.2 and mainly consisted of variables coded as potential discriminators of gender in previous studies (e.g. Herring [14]). The coding scheme is listed in Miller [21], along with a full analysis of individual variables. Codes were grouped into eight major code families. These were female language (e.g. self-disclosure, intensifiers), male language (e.g. humour, rhetorical question), task-orientated (e.g. answers question), socioemotional (e.g. references by name), attenuated (e.g. personal opinion, qualifiers), authoritative (e.g. strong assertion, presuppositions), negative socioemotional (e.g. disagreement) and positive socioemotional (e.g. agreement). A full description of these code families and examples is in Miller [21]. Analyses were then conducted on 'supercodes', which are stored queries constructed from combinations of code families using Boolean operators in Atlas.ti 4.2 that are used to search the data and explore patterns of language use.

2.4 Procedure

Students on an introductory psychology module were invited to participate in online discussion groups for extra coursework credit. Students were given instructions on how to access the online forums. They used their real name or matriculation number as a user identification. Ethical clearance permitted access to background details of the students, such as gender. Coding was carried out in Atlas.ti 4.2, as described above. Statistical analyses were carried out using SPSS.

3 Results

A total of 699 postings (538 female, 161 male) were analysed. Table 1 shows the mean number of posts and words per post by gender.

Table 1: Mean number of posts and words by gender.

	Gender	N	M	SD	t
Posts	Male	48	3.35	3.64	-.441
	Female	149	3.61	3.46	
	Total	197	3.55	3.50	
Words per post	Male	48	128.48	89.09	.245
	Female	149	125.23	76.58	
	Total	197	126.03	79.58	

Human Perspectives in the Internet Society: Culture, Psychology and Gender, K. Morgan, J. Sanchez, C. A. Brebbia & A Voiskounsky (Editors) © 2004 WIT Press, www.witpress.com, ISBN 1-85312-726-4

Table 1 shows the online contributions of the 197 participants, in terms of the mean number of posts and words per post. The mean number of posts was 3.55 (SD = 3.50) and words per post was 126.03 (SD = 79.58). Gender was not found to significantly influence the frequency of posts (t = -.441, d.f. = 196, n.s.) or the length of posts (t = .245, d.f. = 196, n.s.).

Table 2: Gender and user id.

	Gives name	Pseudonym	Total
Male	41	7	48
Female	88	61	149
Total	129	68	197

Table 3: Supercode analysis.

Supercode	% of participants		% of postings		x^2
	Male (N=48)	Female (N=149)	Male (N=161)	Female (N=538)	
Attenuated NOT Authoritative	**31%** (N=15)	**64%** (N=96)	**16%** (N=26)	**41%** (N=218)	16.26**
Authoritative NOT Attenuated	**69%** (N=33)	**37%** (N=55)	**40%** (N=64)	**16%** (N=85)	14.88**
Male NOT Female Language	**33%** (N=16)	**12%** (N=18)	**12%** (N=20)	**4%** (N=19)	11.50**
Female NOT Male Language	**33%** (N=16)	**69%** (N=103)	**20%** (N=32)	**44%** (N=235)	19.43**
Male AND Female Language	**73%** (N=35)	**65%** (N=97)	**61%** (N=98)	**46%** (N=246)	1.00
Positive NOT Negative	**35%** (N=17)	**58%** (N=86)	**19%** (N=30)	**35%** (N=190)	7.24*
Negative NOT Positive	**56%** (N=27)	**19%** (N=28)	**27%** (N=44)	**7%** (N=38)	25.32**
Task-Oriented NOT Socioemotional	**56%** (N=27)	**63%** (N=94)	**36%** (N=58)	**30%** (N=161)	0.72
Socioemotional NOT Task-Oriented	**33%** (N=16)	**37%** (N=55)	**16%** (N=25)	**13%** (N=71)	0.21
Task Oriented AND Socioemotional	**65%** (N=31)	**73%** (N=109)	**44%** (N=71)	**52%** (N=279)	1.29

*significant at $p < .01$, **significant at $p < .001$

Table 2 shows the frequencies of male and female participants who chose to give their real name and those who opted for a pseudonym in the form of their matriculation number. Chi-square analysis showed a significant gender difference in the choice of user identification (x^2 = 11.16, d.f. = 1, $p < .01$). Males were more likely to give their real name online in comparison to females.

The electronic discourse was characterised by extensive first person pronoun usage as 87 per cent of all postings analysed contained some form of first person or plural pronouns (e.g. 'I', 'we'). Also, 38 per cent of student contributions directly responded to the ideas of other students by expressing agreement and/or disagreement. Just over a fifth of all postings contained references to own emotions or self-disclosure.

The results of the supercode analysis are shown in Table 3. The supercode queries are listed, as are the corresponding proportions of males and females making each type of contribution, on which chi-square analyses were conducted. The percentages of each type of posting, expressed as a percentage of the total male and female postings are also given in the table. Significantly more females made contributions that were attenuated but not authoritative ($x^2 = 16.26$, d.f. = 1, $p < .001$) and consisted of female language features only ($x^2 = 19.43$, d.f. = 1, $p < .001$) than males. Significantly more males made contributions that were authoritative but not attenuated ($x^2 = 14.88$, d.f. = 1, $p < .001$) and consisted of male language features only ($x^2 = 11.50$, d.f. = 1, $p < .001$) than females. There were no significant gender differences found along the task-orientated versus socioemotional dimensions. However, the socioemotional code family was further divided into positive socioemotional and negative socioemotional families. This revealed that significantly more females engaged in positive socioemotional behaviour than males ($x^2 = 7.24$, d.f. = 1, $p < .01$), whereas significantly more males engaged in negative socioemotional behaviour than females ($x^2 = 25.32$, d.f. = 1, $p < .001$).

4 Discussion

This research investigated participation and language use in educational CMC. As stated in the introduction, males have been found to dominate mixed-sex interaction in both face-to-face (Coates [3]) and computer-mediated contexts (Herring [13, 14]). However, in this study no significant gender differences were found in the frequency and length of posts. Males and females were similar regarding these quantitative measures of participation, supporting democratising theories of CMC (e.g. Sproull and Kiesler [2]). Perhaps equal participation is more likely to be a feature of this context, as opposed to a public online forum, as females may be more motivated to participate in the context of education. Females may also have felt more comfortable participating as they were the majority group and thus may have influenced the overall linguistic norms.

It is also possible that the pseudonymity offered could have been conducive to female participation online. It was found that females were significantly more likely to choose a pseudonym over their real name than males. This suggests that females had a greater wish to appear 'anonymous' than males, which could reflect, as Jaffe *et al.* [9] suggested, an effort to maintain equality of status. Females may experience a lack of confidence or implicit social pressure when participating in mixed-sex interaction that the loss of face-to-face cues and pseudonymity may have reduced, which could in turn explain the equal participation observed online.

The computer-mediated discourse also showed extensive first person pronoun use and over a third of postings expressed agreement or disagreement with other

Human Perspectives in the Internet Society: Culture, Psychology and Gender, K. Morgan, J. Sanchez, C. A. Brebbia & A Voiskounsky (Editors) © 2004 WIT Press, www.witpress.com, ISBN 1-85312-726-4

students. It should be noted that tutors also contributed online and many student postings were in response to questions set by tutors. Just over a fifth of student postings contained references to own emotions or self-disclosure. As these factors are all said to contribute to social presence, this suggests that the computer-mediated context is perhaps not as impersonal as previously claimed (e.g. Sproull and Kiesler [2]) and provides support for social information processing theory (Walther [10]), in that CMC can support socioemotional communication. It is possible that participants, especially females, developed ways of overcoming what could be perceived as an impersonal environment through the development of a norm of explicitly personal writing.

Although no gender differences were found in terms of the amount of participation, the qualitative content analysis revealed gender-related patterns in language use. Females were more likely to make attenuated contributions and use only traditional female language features in their postings, whereas males were more likely to make authoritative postings and use only male language features. These findings support the communication styles identified by Herring [14] to some extent. Females were found to employ personal and emotional forms of language more than males, who in turn used more authoritative language.

However, the results do not support the task-orientated versus socioemotional distinction in relation to gender. Males and females were just as likely to send messages of each type and, more commonly, messages containing both task-orientated and socioemotional content. However, the distinction between these categories was problematic as participants were frequently engaging in task behaviours due to the specific formal purpose, some of which could also be classed as socioemotional behaviour (e.g. requests opinions). Furthermore, the definition stated in the introduction appears to include only positive elements of socioemotional discourse such as expressions of support. However, disagreement and challenging utterances were also categorised as socioemotional discourse in this research, as they also involve references to others and reacting to others. Thus a distinction was made between positive and negative socioemotional behaviour. Gender-related patterns were found as males had a tendency to post negative responses, whereas females were more likely to respond positively to other participants in the online discussion.

The tendency to agree and support, could be interpreted as taking a low-power role in the discussion. Tannen [4] states that women typically use more supportive language patterns, which have the effect of diminishing the power of their own contributions. The issue of the perceived credibility of a contribution that uses personal and attenuated language is worthy of further investigation, as these linguistic forms are often associated with negative stereotyping. Furthermore, the finding that males tend to express disagreement more, whereas females tend to express agreement supports Coates [3] and Tannen [4] that the male style is based on competitiveness and the female style is based on cooperativeness. It could also reflect gender-related learning preferences, as females may prefer to learn through connectedness and cooperativeness, whereas males may prefer a more independent and argumentative learning environment.

Human Perspectives in the Internet Society: Culture, Psychology and Gender, K. Morgan, J. Sanchez, C. A. Brebbia & A Voiskounsky (Editors) © 2004 WIT Press, www.witpress.com, ISBN 1-85312-726-4

It is possible that the gender-related patterns reported here, which are similar to traditional gender role stereotypes, were found as the salience of gender as social category may have invoked norms and stereotypical expectations regarding gender appropriate behaviour (Matheson and Zanna [5], Reicher *et al.* [11]). Gender was made a salient social category to some extent, as some participants used their real name online and the tendency for females to opt for a numerical identification more than males could perhaps have acted as a gender marker in itself. It was also found that some participants revealed their gender in their contributions (e.g. 'as a gay guy', 'as a 19-year old girl').

Finally, the unequal male and female sample sizes were unavoidable in this context as female students often outnumber male students on psychology modules. It is argued that studying gender and CMC in a meaningful context outweighs the potential drawbacks. Future research should investigate the extent to which the gender-related patterns found here can be extrapolated to other educational computer-mediated contexts, for example male-majority courses such as engineering. The relationship between gender identity and expression of that identity in online text-based contexts is also deemed worthy of attention. In conclusion, the results were positive for use of CMC in education in terms of equal participation, however they also suggest that CMC does not guarantee a gender-free environment. Cues to gender were found to exist in the language used by CMC participants and as the work by Thomson and Murachver [12] suggests, CMC users may be able to identify gender based on these cues alone.

References

[1] McConnell, D., *Implementing Computer Supported Cooperative Learning*, Kogan Page: London, 1994.

[2] Sproull, L. & Kiesler, S., Reducing social context cues: Electronic mail in organisational communication. *Management Science*, **32**, pp. 1492-1512, 1986.

[3] Coates, J., *Women, Men and Language*, 2nd edition. Longman: New York, 1993.

[4] Tannen, D., *You Just Don't Understand: Women and Men in Conversation*. Virago Press: London, 1991.

[5] Matheson, K. & Zanna, M. P., Computer-mediated communications: the focus is on me. *Social Science Computer Review*, **8(1)**, pp. 1-12, 1990.

[6] Gurak, L. J. & Ebeltoft-Kraske, L., Letter from the Guest Editors: The rhetorics of gender in computer-mediated communication. *The Information Society*, **15**, pp. 147-149, 1999.

[7] Harasim, L., Hiltz, S. R., Teles, L. & Turoff, M., *Learning Networks – A field guide to teaching and learning online*, MIT Press: Massachusetts, 1995.

[8] Joinson, A. N., Causes and implications of disinhibited behaviour on the Internet (Chapter 3). *Psychology and the Internet*, ed. J. Gackenbach, Academic Press: London, pp. 43-60, 1998.

Human Perspectives in the Internet Society: Culture, Psychology and Gender, K. Morgan, J. Sanchez, C. A. Brebbia & A Voiskounsky (Editors) © 2004 WIT Press, www.witpress.com, ISBN 1-85312-726-4

[9] Jaffe, J. M., Lee, Y. E., Huang, L. & Oshagan, H., Gender identification, interdependence & pseudonyms in CMC: Language patterns in an electronic conference. *The Information Society*, **15**, pp. 221-234, 1999.
[10] Walther, J. B., Interpersonal effect in computer-mediated interaction: A relational perspective. Communication Research, **19(1)**, pp. 50-88, 1992.
[11] Reicher, S. D., Spears, R. & Postmes, T., A social identity model of deindividuation phenomena (Chapter 6). *European Review of Social Psychology – Vol 6*, eds. W. Stroebe & M. Hewstone, Wiley: Chichester, UK, pp. 161-198, 1995.
[12] Thomson, R. & Murachver, T., Predicting gender from electronic discourse. *British Journal of Social Psychology*, **40**, pp. 193-208, 2001.
[13] Herring, S. C., Gender and democracy in computer-mediated communication. *Electronic Journal of Communication* [online], **3(2)**. www.cios.org/www/tocs/EJC.htm, 1993.
[14] Herring, S. C., *Gender differences in computer-mediated communication: bringing familiar baggage to the new frontier* [online]. http://cpsr.org/cpsr/gender/herring.txt, 1994.
[15] Savicki, V., Lingenfelter, D. & Kelley, M., Gender language style and group composition in Internet discussion groups. *Journal of Computer Mediated Communication* [online], **2(3)**. http://www/ascusc.org/jcmc/vol2/issue3/savicki.html, 1996.
[16] Soukup, C., The gendered interactional patterns of computer-mediated chatrooms: a critical ethnographic study. *The Information Society*, **15**, pp. 169-176, 1999.
[17] Yates, S. J., Gender, identity and CMC. *Journal of Computer Assisted Learning*, **13**, pp. 281-290, 1997.
[18] Michaelson, G. & Pohl, M., Gender in email based co-operative problem solving (Chapter 2). *Virtual Gender*, eds. E. Green & A. Adams, Routledge: London, pp. 28-44, 2001.
[19] Mayring, P., Qualitative content analysis. *Forum Qualitative Sozialforschung/Forum: Qualitative Social Research* [online], **1(2)**. http://qualitative-research.net/fqs-e/2-00halt-e.htm, 2000.
[20] Rourke, L., Anderson, T., Garrison, D. R., & Archer, W., Methodological issues in the content analysis of computer conference transcripts. *International Journal of Artificial Intelligence in Education*, **12**, pp. 8-22, 2001.
[21] Miller, J. *Gender, language and interaction styles in online learning environments*. Unpublished Doctoral Dissertation, Glasgow Caledonian University, 2004.

Human Perspectives in the Internet Society: Culture, Psychology and Gender, K. Morgan, J. Sanchez, C. A. Brebbia & A Voiskounsky (Editors) © 2004 WIT Press, www.witpress.com, ISBN 1-85312-726-4

Gender demands on e-learning

R. Meßmer & S. Schmitz
Center of Gender Research in Computer Science and Natural Science, Institute of Computer Science and Social Research, Dep. 1, University of Freiburg, Germany

Abstract

The current debate on gender and e-learning runs the risk of getting trapped in a female-male dichotomy by defining gender-stereotyped styles of learning, communication, and computer literacy. A closer look at the state of the art in this area, however, reveals differences in use and efficiency of new media applied in e-learning scenarios that are too complex to be defined only along the gender border. Learning, working, and communication styles relate to the subjects' personal experiences and their computer literacy; they are context dependant and influenced by the learning environment. However, living in a gender-stereotyped world leads to both gendered cultural and social experiences as well as gendered strategies in learning and dealing with new technologies and new media.

It is a demand on technology itself to reflect this complexity and thus to open its development and constructions for the integration of diverse 'end user demands'. Based on a user-oriented concept we will introduce a set of demands for the construction of e-learning tools that correspond to diversity and gender needs.

We will point up this approach with some examples derived from our work in the "center of gender research in computer science and natural science" (GIN). Our goal is to apply user-oriented demands on the construction of e-learning systems in order to narrow the gender gap in ICT-applications without getting trapped in gender dichotomies.
Keywords: e-learning, gender, diversity, CSCL, group working.

1 Against simplifying research in gender and e-learning

During the last few years e-learning and new media has been a popular and well-supported topic in education and IT market. The constraint to include gender

Human Perspectives in the Internet Society: Culture, Psychology and Gender, K. Morgan, J. Sanchez, C. A. Brebbia & A Voiskounsky (Editors) © 2004 WIT Press, www.witpress.com, ISBN 1-85312-726-4

mainstreaming drew the attention of researchers, developers and designers to the topic of gender aspects and yielded several results concerning differences between men and women in access to and use of new media. However, repeated in several guidelines, abbreviated and pulled out from the specific evaluation constraints these findings bear the risk of reconstructing gender dichotomies (for details see [1]). But gender as well as the construction and perception of technology are fluid and relational processes, generated in social interactions [2, p. 281]. Not only the relevance and performance of gender can vary in different situations, the perception of technology and its symbolic impact is also flexible. Thus users can question and redefine the meaning of artefacts. Discussing the following examples 'computer literacy', 'communication styles' and 'learning strategies', we want to point out why we always have to be cautious not to devise general statements about men and women when they e-learn.

Gendered computer literacy?

Some recent studies concerning computer literacy state that women have less experience with computers than men. Figures about internet users and non-users are presented to confirm the "digital divide" between men and women, e.g. [3, 4, 5]. A closer look on this aspect of computer literacy (there are of course many others) reveals that, while gender is always an influencing factor, there are still many additional intervening aspects to bear in mind. Current surveys on internet usage in Germany, for example, show that the digital divide seems to be a "**generation problem**" to a great extent [6, p. 15]. While there are almost no gender differences between teenagers (the quota of male users exceeds that of female users by only 2%), the gap widens with the rise of age (18 % difference in the group of the 50 to 60 year old users). Internet usage is as well a question of **education**. Where the educational level is low, gender differences are high (14 % females vs. 33 % males regarding persons without vocational training). In contrast, there are only marginal differences in the group of post-graduates (72 % female vs. 77 % male).

Guidelines for implementing e-learning courses for men and women often include the advice to start at a low technical level, as "women face higher technical barriers". A survey on a project where different faculties of the University of Freiburg worked with notebooks in their courses in order to foster mobile learning [7, p. 58] showed that the **discipline** in which e-learning courses are applied has great impact on the motivation of men and women to participate. In musicology and archaeology, there were no or only small differences between the gender relation of the students of the respective discipline and the gender relation of the participants in notebook courses. There were also no differences in the microsystem technology course. In an economics and in a psychological course the participation of women was more than 20 percent lower than the one of men. In this survey a female and a male archaeologist have more in common than a female archaeologist and a female microsystem technology student. In musicology and archaeology, students have not been compelled to use new media in their study, so far. In microsystem technology, both female and male students are familiar with the use of notebooks. In these three disciplines, the

Human Perspectives in the Internet Society: Culture, Psychology and Gender, K. Morgan, J. Sanchez, C. A. Brebbia & A Voiskounsky (Editors) © 2004 WIT Press, www.witpress.com, ISBN 1-85312-726-4

expectations of the students′ computer literacy is equally low or high, which may explain the lack of gender differences. Computer literacy seems to be a "barrier", when computer skills are not part of the curriculum, but are presumed implicitly, as in the psychological and economics course.

Putting communication styles into context

In her analysis of academic mailing lists, Herring [8] found two communication styles, which she assigned to males and females. She characterized the male style as being more aggressive and competitive with put-downs, strong, often contentious assertions, lengthy and frequent postings, self-promotion, and sarcasm. The female style, in contrast, was characterized by two aspects which typically co-occurred: supportiveness and attenuation. Herring stressed that not all or even the majority of users of each sex exhibit the behaviors of each style, but that*"...gender predicts certain online behaviors with greater than chance frequency when considered over aggregate populations of users"* [9, p. 2].

Savicki et al. [10] confirmed Herrings survey only partially. They found obvious gendered styles in homogenous male and female groups or in cases of a majority and a minority of one gender. However, if the **male-female ratio in groups** is balanced, their gendered style is not very distinct, it rises according to the number of people in the group of the opposite sex. The authors also found the effect that the minority – no matter if men or women - adapts its communication style to the style of the majority. Other studies showed that the **level of anonymity** influences the communication style. If the anonymity is high, people tend to resort to gender stereotypes. Thus, communication in huge mailing lists, where people don't know each other, is much more gendered than communication in groups where the number is manageable and people know each other. Postmes et al. [11] found the greatest gender differences in anonymous groups, whereas personal information attenuated the effects. Pohl and Michaelson [12] found no gendered communication styles in mixed-sex email-communication of students. The **level of professionalism** is another influential issue. Gladis We [13] stated that participants perceive online communication in professional contexts as being relatively free of gender cues whereas in social contact there seem to be as many ways of communicating as there are individuals. Cornelius [14] confirms this appraisal and found that expertise can lower gender aspects in communication.

These few examples show that computer mediated communication is "doing gender" within a network of interacting factors which we have to keep in mind when we work in the field of gender and e-learning.

Learning strategies

Do women have learning styles that differ from those men have? The question whether individual learning styles can be defined at all is discussed controversially. There are tendencies rather to speak of diverse strategies that are applied in different situations and in order to fulfill different tasks than of fixed individual styles. Findings concerning the relation between learning styles and gender present no definite results, some surveys found differences, e.g. [15, 16] but a detailed analysis of this field is yet to come. Nevertheless, one finding is

Human Perspectives in the Internet Society: Culture, Psychology and Gender, K. Morgan, J. Sanchez, C. A. Brebbia & A Voiskounsky (Editors) © 2004 WIT Press, www.witpress.com, ISBN 1-85312-726-4

mentioned quite often: More women seem to prefer to work together more often than to work alone. In Frank et al.'s survey [17], university students where interviewed after practice with an e-learning tool. 44 % of the female and only 24 % of the male students considered group working important. Similar results can be found in groups with different age and educational level of the participants, e.g. [5, 18, 19]. As ca. 90 % of all e-learning projects are planned for alone-learners, the e-learning market doesn't serve for all the various learning strategies.

These examples have outlined the trap of redefining gendered stereotypes by explaining the use and efficiency of blended or e-learning scenarios along the border of female/male computer literacy, communication, or learning styles only. Learning and working with ICT is context-dependent, affected by the learning environment and other factors, and relates to a subject's personal experience in learning as well as in interaction with ICT.

2 From gender differences to constructive realism

If we stress pure female/male differences in interaction with e-learning products (or ICT artefacts, in general), we are in danger of maintaining females as a disadvantaged group, always in struggle to acquire male strategies or skills in order to adapt to (male?) technology. Instead of adapting the users to the technology, our approach on gender and ICT aims at adapting technology to the. user-oriented demands. Their inclusion into the development of ICT artefacts is one main research area in our centre GIN "gender research in computer science and natural science". (The centre is supported by a grant from the Ministry of Science, Research, and the Arts of Baden-Württemberg, AZ 24-729.18-1-19/16).

Our concept of constructive realism [20] can help to structure the huge range of aspects in the network of gender and ICT. Here we use it to outline the construction of gender interactions with e-learning and gendered incorporation within e-learning technology on the one hand. On the other, the concept describes the reality of gender diversity in use and efficiency of this technology.

Gender is **constructed** in societal, cultural and power relations and through the interaction of subjects with these relations. To avoid gender stereotypes we have to analyse these constructions with reference to the network of counterpart(ner)s, whether human or technical, with which individuals interact.

Gender constructions are incorporated into technical development itself (e.g. in hardware and software, in content and design of ICT artefacts). A simple explanation is that technical products are for the most part developed by men and therefore suit men's interests and ways of interacting with them more adequately. A more complex explanation, however, again takes the gendered economic and power relations in which the technology is used into account.

With reference to both aspects, the gendered interaction with ICT and the gendered technology itself, and with reference to their mutual interrelations, we emphasize the term co-construction of gender and ICT [21, p. 7].

The term **realism** refers to the fact that we all live in a gendered world. Based on gendered cultural and social experiences, we develop behavioural, learning, or communication strategies. Experience with gendered technologies embedded in gendered societal, cultural, and power relations result in gendered strategies in interaction with ICT in reality. But these strategies cannot simply be divided into male or female traits. As Rommes and Faulkner [1] pointed out, neither women nor men can be treated as a homogenous category. A network of factors and individual differences (e.g. age, class, ethnicity, social and economic status) overlap gender groups. Taking these factors into account, we consequently move from gender to gender diversity.

3 From constructive realism to a constructive approach for technological development

The multifaceted network of gender and e-learning comprises a set of factors which we first group into the three categories interacting in e-learning (see figure 1): the learners, the learning scenarios, and the e-learning systems.

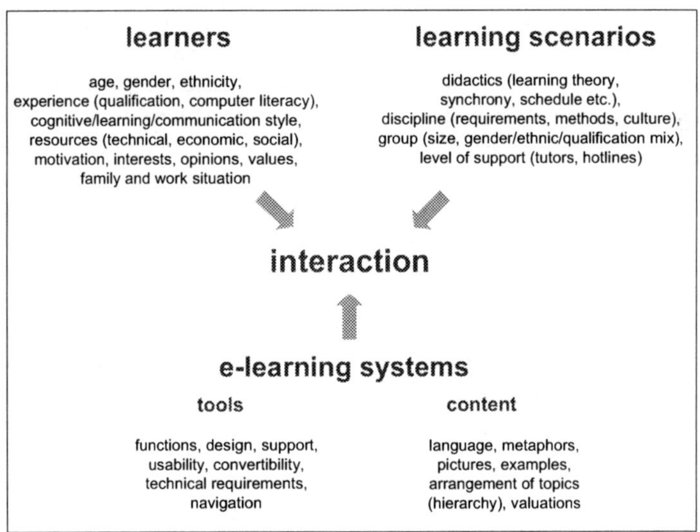

Figure 1: Network of interaction in e-learning.

Learners differing in age, gender, and ethnicity start working in e-learning with a background of diverse academic qualification and with different experiences and skills in computer literacy. They have access to different technical resources (e.g. the computer equipment at their disposal, the programmes they can implement and use, the amount of time they can invest in working with this technology). Learners show a range of cognitive, learning, and communication styles which they have developed during their former learning practice, and which they refer to in e-learning. Moreover, learners vary regarding their motivation, interests, opinions, values, and their family and work responsibilities.

Learning scenarios are as diverse as learners are. Miscellaneous learning concepts and theories form the background for education (e.g. constructivist or behavioural learning theories). Another set of questions refers to the kind of e-learning course: is it a web based training or a blended learning course? Do the learners have to collaborate? What tasks do the users have to solve and how are their performance and efficiency tested? The discipline itself has a great impact as well: which kinds of explicit and implicit skills, behaviour, language, etc. are assumed? Different disciplines are more or less close to technical approaches for e-learning. They provide more or less competence in using ICT facilities, and this holds for teachers and students. E-learning scenarios differ regarding group size and the gender, ethnic, and qualification mix of the participants as well as the level of support that is allocated (tutors, office hours etc.)

The third category refers to the technology of e-learning systems themselves. What functions do they have and how are they designed? Users require different technical skills and different hard- and software equipment. Systems differ concerning aspects of usability as well as the way learners can communicate and navigate. Additionally, it is important to examine the contents presented in the e-learning system. How are they presented and what language, images, and metaphors are used? The way how information is visualized (e.g. in hierarchical orders or in semantic nets) has strong impact on the knowledge retrieval of users [22]. Tools and their combinations in e-learning systems should account for the diversity of learners and learning scenarios in the triangular interaction network. However, current e-learning systems are yet much more invariant.

Our constructive approach for technical development aims to open e-learning technology to diversity. Based on the analysis of inclusions and exclusions in the network of gendered constructions in and through e-learning, we derive a set of diverse user-oriented demands on further technical development. We will then develop e-learning products that are adaptable to these demands and open for participatory and constructive design by their users. Following Cecile Crutzen [23], the integration of users in planning and designing software can help them in gaining computer literacy. Moreover, our systems should also account for diverse communication, navigation and learning styles, and for different learning scenarios. The systems are then to be tested and evaluated in blended/e-learning scenarios in higher education.

3.1 Examples for user-oriented demands on technical development

Technical devices should serve users rather than the other way round. We selected some examples out of the long list of user-oriented demands on technical development which relate to our current concept for technical constructions (see section 3.2).

Decrease of technical barriers and potentiality for diverse learning scenarios
The major challenge for e-learning systems is to parallely facilitate first access and effective use on the one hand and to accompany users throughout learning

Human Perspectives in the Internet Society: Culture, Psychology and Gender, K. Morgan, J. Sanchez, C. A. Brebbia & A Voiskounsky (Editors) © 2004 WIT Press, www.witpress.com, ISBN 1-85312-726-4

with increasing competence on the other (not only during one seminar but also throughout the whole study). In order to promote users starting with minor computer literacy, e-learning systems should not demand huge installations with all available tools in one big programme. Technical barriers can be abolished by simple and intuitive use. A *modular system*, where only those tools needed for the particular learning scenario can be selected, could cater for this. It can also assist different disciplines with particular didactic concepts with particular combinations of e-learning tools. And users even enabled to design small parts of the system gain more competence along with it.

Facilitation of group working

Users who want to write and discuss text material collaboratively or prepare a presentation together, require facilities to visualize the progress of their discussions and work. Current e-learning systems, however, serve individual learners to a greater extent than collaborative working. If we take some of the results on 'learning strategies and group working' in gender research seriously, we have to think about how to promote group working as well as individual learning.

The CSCL (computer supported collaborative system) market has already developed some facilities for group working, e. g., annotation functions for text discussions (for details see: [24]) tools that interleave communication with content management, or text editing functions for the preparation of presentations. These facilities seem to be limited by now, but some of them can be used for adaptation and integration into e-learning systems.

Navigation and presentation of contents

The more complex a thematic area is, the more important is it to visualize the relations between content files. Semantic nets, for example 'topic maps' should be installed in addition to hierarchical presentations of contents in order to account for diverse learning and navigation styles [22]. Additionally, a semantic view that visualizes the relations between contents, facilitates access to a thematic area from different viewpoints and promotes critical thinking.

3.2 Concept for implementation into e-learning products: ModUS = Modular User-oriented Systems

ModUS is a concept for a modular user-oriented CSCL system (Computer Supported Collaborative Learning Systems) based on open-source software [25]. Applying ModUS, learners and teachers do not have to get used to a huge system at the very beginning. Instead, they can combine different tools and use only those they need. More competent users can 'build' more complex and extended versions of their system.

A strong focus of ModUS is set on its efficiency for a particular learning scenario. With ModUS, teachers and students can easily agree upon a selection of tools according to their learning targets and didactic concepts as well as to their preferred learning or communication styles. Thus, ModUS facilitates constructivist approaches on learning. The general aspects of this technical concept are modularity, scalability, and flexibility.

Modularity: The tools of the learning system (e.g. calendar, personal information management, group organization, content management, chat, forum or e-mail), are set up as autonomous modules. They can be combined in a framework and administered on web servers or run as individual applications. Users (learners and/or teachers) can decide on particular combinations of single modules according to the needs of their learning scenario and plug-ins can be extended to arrange special adaptations quite simply. This helps to keep the system slim for 'beginners" instead of getting lost in technical details and learners and teachers can expand the system along with increasing competences and elaborated tasks.

Scalability: The ModUS-server is scalable which means that an individual learner or a workgroup can decide to use e-mail for internal communication whereas the whole seminar can also use chat or forum modules for further discussions. If workgroups with a completely different array of functionalities and different surroundings want to cooperate they can adapt and extend their functionalities according to their cooperation needs. A central unit handles the communication between external and internal data storage and allows de/activation of functionalities.

Flexibility: The modular construction allows access to particular tools via various interfaces. It is possible, for example, to represent the same data with either "normal" HTML interfaces, text editor interfaces, or 3D interfaces. Via interfaces, new tools or tools with different designs can be integrated into the system. Contents can be visualized in hierarchically arranged menus and/or in semantic nets (Topic Maps). Learners can decide which navigation facility is efficiently for her/his individual learning and navigation style. Teachers can decide which presentation may be useful for the display of various viewpoints and for critical knowledge retrieval. Text annotation and text editing facilities can be integrated and facilitate discussions and group working when needed.

Our current work concentrates on the realization of a groupware system that is based on the ModUS concept. The groupware system will then be used and evaluated in interdisciplinary seminars in collaboration with computer science, social sciences and pedagogical science.

4 The interaction of gender and technology: mutual benefits

Many approaches in research on gender and e-learning are necessary: to enter technology and change it for diversity is one. In order to reach this goal, technology and its artefacts have to be revealed as neither being neutral nor fixed. Technology does include more possibilities and chances and is more variable than the existing systems may show.

Our constructive approach has at least two gender issues. It uses interdisciplinary methods of gender research to describe the complex network of co-constructions in gender and e-learning and it aims at narrowing the gender gap in the construction and use of new media. Its goal is to enable users to get actively involved in the construction of new technologies in order to develop solutions that satisfy their individual needs and preferences.

References

[1] Rommes, E. & Faulkner, W., Conclusion (Chapter 7). *Designing Inclusion. The Development of ICT Products to include Women in the Information Society*, eds. E. Rommes, I. von Slooten & E. van Oost, pp. 69-79, 2004. www.sigis-ist.org.

[2] Wajcman, J., Gender in der Technologieforschung. *Wie natürlich ist Geschlecht? Gender und die Konstruktion von Natur und Technik*, eds. U. Pasero & A. Gottburgsen, Westdeutscher Verlag: Wiesbaden, pp. 270-289, 2002.

[3] An Overview of the 2000 Freshman Norms; UCLA Graduate School of Education and Information Studies, Higher Education Research Institute (HERI). http://www.gseis.ucla.edu/heri/00_exec_summary.htm

[4] Sheard, J. & Markham, S., Creating an interest in IT: A gender study. *Proc. of the International Conference on Computers in Education (ICCE 2002)*, Auckland, New Zealand, p. 236, 2002.

[5] Rajagopal, I. & Bojin, N., A Gendered World: Students and Instructional Technologies. *First Monday*, **8(1)**, pp. 1–23, 2003. http://firstmonday.org/issues/issue8_1/rajagopal/index.html

[6] Frauen geben Technik neue Impulse e.V., Initiative D21 & TNS Emnid, (eds.). *Internetnutzung von Frauen und Männern in Deutschland 2003.* Gender Mainstreaming Sonderauswertung des (N)Onliner-Atlas, 2003.

[7] Claus, R., Otto, A. & Schinzel, B., Gender Mainstreaming im diversifizierten Feld einer Hochschule: Bedingungen – Akzeptanz – Strategien. *IIG-Berichte 1/04*, Freiburg, 2004.

[8] Herring, S., Two variants of an electronic message schema. *Computer-mediated communication: Linguistics, social and cross-cultural perspectives*, ed. S. Herring, Benjamins: Amsterdam, pp. 81-106, 1996.

[9] Herring, S., Gender Differences in CMC: Findings and Implications. *The CPSR Newsletter*, **18(1)**, 2000. http://cpsr.org/publications/newsletters/issues/2000/Winter2000/herring.html

[10] Savicki, V., Lingenfelter, D. & Kelley, M., Gender Language Style and Group Composition in Internet Discussion Groups. *Journal of Computer Mediated Communication*, **2(3)**, 1996. http://jcmc.huji.ac.il/vol2/issue3/savicki.html

[11] Postmes, T., Spears, R. & Lea, M., Social identity, normative content and 'deindividuation' in computer-mediated groups. *Social identity: context, commitment and content*, eds. N. Ellemers, R. Spers & B. Doosje, Blackwell: Oxford, pp. 164-265, 1999.

[12] Pohl, M. & Michaelson, G., "I don't think that's an interesting dialogue": Computer-Mediated Communication and Gender. *Women, Work and Computerization: Spinning a Web from Past to Future*, eds. F. Grundy et al., Berlin, Heidelberg and New York, pp. 87-97, 1997.

Human Perspectives in the Internet Society: Culture, Psychology and Gender, K. Morgan, J. Sanchez, C. A. Brebbia & A Voiskounsky (Editors) © 2004 WIT Press, www.witpress.com, ISBN 1-85312-726-4

[13] We, G., Cross-Gender Communication in Cyberspace, Simon Fraser University, 1993. http://www.mith2.umd.edu/WomensStudies/Computing/Articles+ResearchPapers/cross-gender-communication
[14] Cornelius, C., Your mail, you're female. Geschlechtsidentität im Kontext von textbasierter computervermittelter Kommunikation. *Virtuelle Realitäten*, eds. Bente et al., Hogrefe: Göttingen and Seattle, pp. 181-202, 2002.
[15] Witkin, H. et al., Educational Implications of Cognitive Styles. *Review of Educational Research,* **47(1)**, pp. 1-64, 1977.
[16] Belenky et al., *Women's way of knowing. The development of self, voice, and mind*, Basic Books: New York, 1986.
[17] Frank, C. et al., Meeting Students Expectations and Realizing Pedagogical Goals within the Development of a Virtual Learning Environment. *Proc. of the World Conference on E-Learning in Corp., Govt., Health., & Higher Ed.*, pp. 2790-2795, 2002.
[18] Chee Leong, S. & Hawamdeh, S., Gender and learning attitudes in using web-based science lessons. *Information Research* **5(1)**, pp. 1-14, 1999. http://InformationR.net/ir/paper66.html
[19] Martin, S., Internet use in the classroom: The impact of gender. *Social Science Computer Review*, **16(4)**, pp. 411-418, 1998.
[20] Nikoleyczik, K., Remmele, B., Ruiz Ben, E., Schinzel, B., Schmitz, S. & Stingl, B. (submitted), Differences without a cause. Constructive realism as a feminist approach to 'Geschlecht' in computer and natural sciences. *Feminist Theory Special Issue: Feminist Theory and/of Science.*
[21] Van Oost, E., Introduction (Chapter 1). *Designing Inclusion. The development of ICT products to include women in the Information Society*, eds. E. Rommes, I. von Slooten & E. van Oost, pp. 5-11, 2004. www.sigis-ist.org.
[22] Schmidt, K., Von Kriterien zur Konstruktion: Interface Design und Content Management für verteiltes Arbeiten unter Gender Aspekten. Diplomarbeit, Universität Freiburg, 2004.
[23] Crutzen, C., Interactie, en wereld von verschillen. Een visie op informatica vanuit genderstudies. Dissertation, Open Universiteit Niederlande, Heerlen, 2000.
[24] Kienle, A., Integration von Wissensmanagement und kollaborativem Lernen durch technisch unterstützte Kommunikationsprozesse. Lohmar: Eul, pp. 90ff, 2003.
[25] Meßmer, R. et al., ModUS – a Modular User-Oriented CSCL System in Line with Gender Research. *Proc. of E-Learn 2003, World Conference on E-Learning in Corporate, Government, Healthcare, & Higher Education*, Phoenix, Arizona, USA, pp. 2337-2340, 2003.

Human Perspectives in the Internet Society: Culture, Psychology and Gender, K. Morgan, J. Sanchez, C. A. Brebbia & A Voiskounsky (Editors) © 2004 WIT Press, www.witpress.com, ISBN 1-85312-726-4

Instructional technology innovation as transformational learning: female faculty's narratives of experience

K. Campbell
Faculty of Extension, University of Alberta

Abstract

Workplaces are potential learning communities that invite critical reflection on practice that can be shared with others. Higher Education (HE) may be described as a workplace in which instructional development activity may be a form of inquiry in which faculty see "the taken-for-granted with new eyes" [33, p.3], prompting them to critically reflect upon their experiences and practice and leading to a foundational reframing of their core beliefs, assumptions, and values and subsequent actions [31].

Instructional innovation in HE can be personally risky, yet this is the level at which transformational thinking and action occurs and is sustained. The incorporation of instructional technology into teaching practice extends an already complex environment, introducing an unfamiliar realm of expertise. This complexity may be increased for female faculty who already experience some degree of marginalization in HE.

The study on which this paper is based is a feminist project of narrative inquiry informed by the theoretical constructs of transformative learning, and feminist pedagogy in technology-enhanced environments. In this framework narratives of experience can be understood as "statement(s) of belief, of morality" that are values-based, doing social and political work as they are told [19, p.12]. In this study 47 female faculty from Canadian universities participated in research conversations as both method and site for the construction of personal and sociocultural understanding and change.

Comparative analysis of the conversations reveal several interacting themes including psychosocial issues related to female faculty teaching with technology, the role of collaborative design conversations in perspective transformation, and relational practice for action learning.
Keywords: perspectives transformation, narratives of experience, action learning, faculty learning, instructional design.

Human Perspectives in the Internet Society: Culture, Psychology and Gender, K. Morgan, J. Sanchez, C. A. Brebbia & A Voiskounsky (Editors) © 2004 WIT Press, www.witpress.com, ISBN 1-85312-726-4

1 Introduction

While most studies of gender and IT have investigated "possible gender differences in education, computer use, attitudes towards computers, math and sciences…only a few have addressed potential gender differences related to faculty use of and attitudes toward instructional technology in higher education" [40, p.425]. The study referred to in this paper explored the experiences of 47 Canadian female faculty integrating information and communications technologies (ICTs) into the learning environment and suggests that these instructional innovations are adopted if they clearly fit or are aligned with their instructional goals. Further, involvement in a project of instructional development may be an intensely personal process of cognitive and cultural change in which beliefs and values may be realigned. This process is supported and enhanced through a relational process in which these faculty engage in constant collaborative conversations with instructional designers and colleagues. The transformative essence of this critical design narrative may be gender-based.

Workplaces are potential learning communities that invite critical reflection on practice, and support professionals sharing their learning with others [15]. Higher education (HE) may be described as a workplace in which instructional development activity is a form of inquiry in which faculty see "the taken-for-granted with new eyes" [33, p. 3]. For some faculty members, developing technology-based curriculum becomes a "disorienting dilemma" or trigger point that challenges their teaching and learning paradigm, leading to a foundational reframing of their core beliefs, assumptions, and values and subsequent actions [31].

While instructional innovation in HE can be personally risky, this is the level at which transformational thinking and action occurs and is sustained [13]. The incorporation of ICTs into teaching practice increases complexity in an already complex environment, introducing a new realm of expertise. This complexity may be increased for female faculty who already experience some degree of marginalization in HE and in technology-enhanced environments, whether through perception that ICTs are contrary to their beliefs and values, or sociocultural expectations related to women and technology.

The two-year study on which this paper is based is a feminist project of narrative inquiry informed by the theoretical constructs of transformative learning, and feminist pedagogy in technology-enhanced environments [6, 32]. Stories or narratives of experience can be understood as "statement(s) of belief, of morality" that speak of values and…do social and political work as they are told [19, p.12]. Thus, in this study female faculty shared narratives of experience through research conversations as both method and site for the construction of personal and sociocultural understanding and change.

This paper is constructed in 2 main parts: 1) the presentation of the two interrelated theoretical constructs, transformative learning and technology issues related to feminist pedagogy; that frame the 2) selected narrative of experience and transformation. The analysis of the research data is ongoing; at this point interpretive directions are suggested that may be pursued. Additional narratives

Human Perspectives in the Internet Society: Culture, Psychology and Gender, K. Morgan, J. Sanchez, C. A. Brebbia & A Voiskounsky (Editors) © 2004 WIT Press, www.witpress.com, ISBN 1-85312-726-4

and implications for the support of female faculty will be shared during a participant discussion.

2 Theoretical constructs

Faculty involved in instructional development are engaging in a process of both personal and cultural change characterized by active, or action learning. Some research suggests that female faculty generally experience this process under different circumstances and with different expectations than many of their male colleagues: this context potentially increases the personal and professional risks associated with change and innovation.

2.1 Risk factors for female faculty innovators: ICTs as learning catalysts

Female faculty develop their pedagogical values and approaches in an institutional context in which they have historically been marginalized [9, 10, 21, 34]. The typical female faculty member is significantly less likely to occupy a tenured or tenure-track position, at higher ranks is older than her male peers and is less likely to have an authoritative or administrative role in the institution. Academics that are more senior do less teaching possibly because senior faculty are able to obtain course releases through research grants, or for administrative duties [34]. Because of the lower proportion of senior women, female faculty tend to have disproportionately heavier teaching loads than male faculty. As the institution might place less value on activities that are teaching-related, women may get less credit for their time than their more research-oriented male counterparts [1, 26, 22, 34, 35].

Teaching innovation carries added risk when compared to more conventional instruction, for example it is not unusual for student course evaluations to be lower. These evaluations are often used by Faculty Evaluation Committees to help determine faculty pay raises and tenure. Given the higher relative non-tenured proportion female faculty may be proportionately more vulnerable to these risk factors. Developing faculty expertise in teaching innovations has not been well supported in the post-secondary context due, in part, to the historical emphasis of the academy on the scholarship of discovery, the scholarship of integration, and the scholarship of application, which are typically associated with the research rather than the teaching process. Only recently has the scholarship of teaching received increased attention [18]. Western thought, represented in the academic tradition of the classroom lecturer, posits one truth to be discovered and learning as an objective, logical activity of receiving that truth through the Expert. The view of ICTs as delivery vehicles for received knowledge represent this conduit model. But, a view of ICTs as catalysts for faculty learning places emphasis on values-based decisions that align with teaching beliefs and styles, and that are shared, elaborated and reconstructed through relationship, conversation and social negotiation.

The literature on critical feminist teaching in academia [11, 41, 42] aligns the research on preferred teaching styles of female faculty with Kimmel's [27]

Human Perspectives in the Internet Society: Culture, Psychology and Gender, K. Morgan, J. Sanchez, C. A. Brebbia & A Voiskounsky (Editors) © 2004 WIT Press, www.witpress.com, ISBN 1-85312-726-4

proposition that "one mark of a feminist classroom (is) that the personal is not only political but often pedagogical" [27, p.62]. Learners and faculty are encouraged to "seek connections between course content and their own lives, (see) their lives in a larger social perspective...(and) employ experiential activities" that are collaborative, egalitarian and relational, such as discussion seminars and small-group activities [27, p.67]. It is reasonable then to expect, and in fact it has been reported [7], that the technologies employed by female faculty enable a classroom environment that is relational (that is, emphasizing relationships between teacher and students, and among students themselves), experiential (that is, focusing on personal experience rather than abstract knowledge), and non-hierarchical (that is, centered on students rather than the teacher). Learning about the ways that ICTs can support social change may be a way in for faculty struggling to transform learning environments into more participatory and democratic environments.

2.2 Perspective transformation as action learning

Faculty have historically viewed their teaching role as one of transmitting a body of knowledge in their discipline to their students [30]. However, a global shift in emphasis to the learners' experiences suggest a renewal of curriculum and a critical transformation in pedagogy that may enhance the development of students' skills beyond disciplinary knowledge–for example, in skills such as problem-solving and interpersonal and communication skills–and that require instructors to handle more diversity and use more inclusive instructional methods [8, 24, 30, 31]. These changes require education and support and, more importantly, require faculty to modify their personal beliefs about their role as teachers. The development and implementation of innovative models of teaching and learning that meet these challenges is a difficult process that can be transformative at both personal and institutional levels [12, 38].

Proceeding through multiple stages, transformative learning is prompted by a disorienting dilemma or cognitive conflict leading to a change in both worldview and curricular scope [25, 28]. Since admitting uncertainty could be construed as a sign of weakness [36] the incorporation of technology into teaching practice is stressful for academics in that their culture itself resists change. Learning how to use ICTs that support more learning-centered experiences encourages faculty to re-examine core values, expectations, and practices related to teaching and learning. This process of personal transformation also has the potential for grassroots change in institutional policy and practice [5]. The power of this change process lies in sharing experiences and new understandings in a supported learning community.

Mezirow's theory of adult perspective transformative learning [31] can be summarized as a process of acquiring new knowledge while critically examining core beliefs, assumptions, and values. It begins "when we encounter experiences...that fail to fit our expectations and consequently lack meaning for us, or we encounter an anomaly that cannot be given coherence either by learning within existing schemes or by learning new schemes" [31, p.94]. Developing technology-based curriculum may lead faculty to "question their

Human Perspectives in the Internet Society: Culture, Psychology and Gender, K. Morgan, J. Sanchez, C. A. Brebbia & A Voiskounsky (Editors) © 2004 WIT Press, www.witpress.com, ISBN 1-85312-726-4

perspectives, open up new ways of looking at their practice, revise their views; act based on new perspectives" [39, p.3].

As a learning environment, the professional workplace of the University invites critical reflection on practice, and must allow time and space for faculty to collaboratively develop a "more inclusive, differentiated, permeable, and integrated perspective" [52]. Schön [36] defines this sort of activity as inquiry in which constructions of the situation are brought into the open, juxtaposed, and held against alternative accounts or beliefs. In this view, interacting with knowledgeable colleagues, colleagues and instructional designers, is a socialization process that encourages participation in a knowledge community or professional culture. According to Jarvis [23] faculty who actively problematize their practice keep growing and learning, becoming experts in the community from whom novices in turn may learn.

The principles underlying teaching excellence are inherent in the effective use of instructional technology innovations, however HE has failed to make substantial cultural, political, and administrative changes to accommodate the changing nature of instruction. According to Seminoff and Wepner [37] and others [43] measures need to be taken to increase the value of scholarship invested in technology-based projects: as female faculty are strongly invested in teaching and in designing "non-traditional" learning environments these measures may reduce the risk of innovation for these faculty. Innovations present challenges to existing patterns of work and specialization on campuses requiring institutions to work more like close-knit, integrated communities [4]. As female faculty are already marginalized partly by virtue of their teaching role, a collaborative community of practice, in which exposure to premature and summative evaluation is minimized, becomes critical.

3 Narratives of experience

Communities of practice, such as those involving faculty and designers engaged in conversation about teaching in technology-enhanced learning environments, instantiate social reality through the use of language, on the one hand "de-constructing or dissolving meanings" and on the other creating and supporting them [16, p.19]. In other words, to become meaningful, shared and a source of knowledge and understanding, practice must be named. Once named and brought into consciousness, we can be critical of, and reframe or reconstruct, experience.

Gergen [16] points out that discourse influences the ways we create social life together, imbuing events with "coherence, integrity, fullness, and closure" [20]. A narrative structure invests events and memories with moral significance: we are able to understand our actions as purposeful and embedded in our core values. The nature of the instructional design process itself, which was narrative in structure, challenged Susan, an Education professor, to critically confront her beliefs and actions and imagine a transformed practice in which her constructivist goals could frame her pedagogical decisions. Also, in this study faculty were invited to share their narratives of experience both privately and

Human Perspectives in the Internet Society: Culture, Psychology and Gender, K. Morgan, J. Sanchez, C. A. Brebbia & A Voiskounsky (Editors) © 2004 WIT Press, www.witpress.com, ISBN 1-85312-726-4

through a series of community-based conversations; through a forum and in collaborative interpretation and writing of the "data". In sum, the design experience was an action learning process (reflection-in-action), which was further elaborated by the narrative recounting of it.

A comparative, ongoing analysis of the conversations reveal several interacting themes including psychosocial issues related teaching with technology, the role of collaborative design conversations in perspective transformation, and relational practice for action learning, In this short paper, one narrative is chosen that illustrates the experience of a female instructor who began a reluctant journey to "just get a web page" and, through a relational, conversational process that challenged her to connect with her core values, transformed her pedagogy through learning design.

3.1 The collaborative design conversation and perspectives transformation

Initially sceptical about using technology for anything more than a productivity or presentation tool, Susan's growing interest in using technology to create an authentic learning environment is consistent with understanding of the transformative learning that can result from such a project (10:10:03). Part of her reluctance to undertake a course development process was related to her academic status at that time: she was applying for tenure and had an excellent teaching reputation that she did not want to jeopardize, and a developing research program that might be slowed as she made the time commitment to the project. She had been advised by departmental colleagues to "steer clear" of an innovation that would compete with time for writing and publishing, although one outcome of the process was a more fruitful reorientation of her research to issues of technology-based teacher education [17].

Susan recalls her impatience with her instructional designer who asked "lots of questions" directing her to readings "that would help me to think a little bit more about what I had just said. Later, when it came to having to write a philosophy of education for my tenure package, it came so easily to me because I had had to think and read about it so much in the initial part of the project…I remember endlessly asking 'When do I get to make the web page?' Yet that was one time where I had to stop and ask myself questions about what I believed about teaching and learning, which has had so many ramifications".

Susan wanted her students to have specific learning opportunities. Through the design conversation "the first step was to articulate my personal goals…as we (reflected on) my beliefs about teaching and learning, I began to clarify what would be important. My students would need opportunities to learn from real-life authentic problems and practice…I wanted there to be built-in checkpoints for my students to engage in reflection-in-action…and I wanted the learning experiences to be the focus of the course, not the technology.

"It's just been an amazing experience creating (the course)…Not only did I end up having the experience of creating that website for my undergrad course and all the things that have come out of …the new and interesting research areas…But then to have it influence my graduate teaching too…

Human Perspectives in the Internet Society: Culture, Psychology and Gender, K. Morgan, J. Sanchez, C. A. Brebbia & A Voiskounsky (Editors) © 2004 WIT Press, www.witpress.com, ISBN 1-85312-726-4

"In looking back, I can see that so much of what I initially felt as being frustration was…the diamond in the rough, because it turned out to be the most powerful aspect of the whole experience. Everything I've done since then is tied up in asking those big philosophical questions. Whenever anybody has questions about what they can do with technology, I always say, 'You need to start with the design process first'. It's not enough to tell people they need to use technology; you have to have a vision of how it can enhance learning".

Susan came to the process with a traditional, teacher-centered construct of content presentation. But through a series of critical design conversations she developed and was able to articulate a constructivist worldview that now embodies her practice. For example, she is currently developing a comprehensive online, case-based "faculty learning" portal, through which colleagues find teaching resources, connect with peer mentors, participate in problem-solving discussions, and develop collaborative research initiatives related to the scholarship of teaching.

4 Final words

Transformation through innovation potentially has the most impact on other faculty colleagues and instructional practices at the level of the <u>personal</u> [3], a context in which female faculty may prefer to learn and teach. After Albion and Gibson [2], who maintain that individual faculty, sharing innovative teaching methods, can encourage others "to acquire the insights which will enable them to adapt their own practice" (p.1), faculty engagement in a team-supported instructional development process provides a catalyst to change in understanding and practice. Indeed, the sharing of experience with colleagues and designers is a social, relational process of collaborative conversation [14] that supports faculty learning. Personal knowledge based on prior experiences and belief systems is available, and evolves through the social interaction inherent in sharing stories of practice in which we attempt to make our perspectives clear and meaningful to others, and to understand the perspectives they offer in return. This process of social construction challenges us to step outside of our own views and re-evaluate our beliefs about teaching, learning and design. An environment of collaborative conversation, as this one faculty narrative of experience suggests, is one in which female faculty feel comfortable and may prefer, as it subverts notions of status and authority and reduces personal and professional risk.

Currently, the author is investigating implications of gender in the social agency of instructional designers in HE, and exploring the nature of the gendered relationships between faculty and designers related to the transformation of institutional culture vis a vis the scholarship of teaching. It appears that female designers may practice differently than male designers, and that aligning the core values of the designer with the core values of their faculty colleagues impacts the potential for perspective transformation. It also appears that both female <u>and</u> male faculty feel "safer" with female designers as they perceive that the risk of

Human Perspectives in the Internet Society: Culture, Psychology and Gender, K. Morgan, J. Sanchez, C. A. Brebbia & A Voiskounsky (Editors) © 2004 WIT Press, www.witpress.com, ISBN 1-85312-726-4

"not knowing how" is diminished with a woman: conceivably this relates to academic status.

References

[1] Acker, S. (1997). Feminist theory and the study of gender and education. International Review of Education, 33, 419-435.

[2] Albion, P. & Gibson, I. (1998). Designing problem-based learning multimedia for teacher education. Technology and Teacher Education Annual. Retrieved July 12, 2003 at http://www.coe.uh.edu/insite/elec_pub/HTML1998/th_albi.htm

[3] Anderson, T., Varnhagen, S., & Campbell, K. (1998). Faculty adoption of teaching and learning technologies: Contrasting earlier adopters and mainstream faculty. Canadian Journal of Higher Education, 28(2,3), 71-98.

[4] Baldwin, R. (1998, Winter). Technology's impact on faculty life and work. New Directions for Teaching and Learning, 76, 7-21.

[5] Bates, T. (2000). Managing technological change: Strategies for college and university leaders. San Francisco: Jossey-Bass Publications.

[6] Bryson, M., & de Castell, S. (1998). Telling tales out of school: Modernist, critical, and postmodern "true stories" about educational computing. In H. Bromley & M. W. Apple, (Eds.), Education, technology and power: Educational computing as social practice. (65-84). NY: SUNY Press.

[7] Campbell, K., & Varnhagen, S. (2002). When faculty use instructional technologies: Using Clark's delivery model to understand gender differences. Canadian Journal of Higher Education, 32(1), 31-56.

[8] Cranton, P. (1994). Understanding and promoting transformative learning: A guide for educators of adults. San Francisco: Jossey-Bass.

[9] Cumming Speirs, C., Amsel, R., Baines, M.G., & Pickel, J. (1998). Off the track: A profile of nom-tenure track faculty at McGill University. The Canadian Journal of Higher Education, 28(2/3), 1-20.

[10] Dagg, A. I. (1998). Hiring women at Canadian Universities: The subversion of equity. In J. Stalker & S. Prentice, (Eds.). The illusion of inclusion: Women in post-secondary education (108-118). Halifax: Fernwood Publishing.

[11] Davis, Sara N. (1999). Creating a collaborative classroom. In S N. Davis, M. Crawford, & J. Sebrechts, (Eds.). Coming into her own: Educational success in girls and women. (123-138). San Francisco: Jossey-Bass.

[12] Dolence, M., & Norris, D. (1995). Transforming higher education: A vision for learning in the 21st century. Ann Arbor, MI: Society for College and University Planning.

[13] Elrick, Mei-Rei. (1996). Improving instruction in universities: A case study of the Ontario universities' program for instructional development (OUPID). Canadian Journal of Higher Education, 20(2), 61-79.

Human Perspectives in the Internet Society: Culture, Psychology and Gender, K. Morgan, J. Sanchez, C. A. Brebbia & A Voiskounsky (Editors) © 2004 WIT Press, www.witpress.com, ISBN 1-85312-726-4

[14] Feldman, Allan (2000). The role of conversation in collaborative action research. Retrieved May 14, 2000 at http://www-unix.oit.umass.edu/~afeldman/Conversation.html
[15] Foley, G. (2001, July). Emancipatory organizational learning: Research and practice. Keynote address at the Second International Conference on Researching Work and Learning, Calgary, AB.
[16] Gergen, M. (2000). Feminist reconstructions in psychology: Narrative, gender, and performance. Thousand Oaks, CA: Sage Publications.
[17] Gibson, S.E. (2002). Using a problem based, multimedia enhanced approach in learning about teaching. Australian Journal of Educational Technology, 18(3), 394-409.
[18] Glassick, C. E., Huber, M. T., Maeroff, G. I., Boyer, E. L., & Carnegie Foundation for the Advancement of Teaching (1997). Scholarship assessed evaluation of the professoriate (1st Ed.). San Francisco: Jossey-Bass.
[19] Goodson, I. (1995, April). Storying the self: Life politics and the study of the teacher's life and work. Paper presented at the annual meeting of the American Educational Research Association, San Francisco, CA.
[20] Gudmundsdottir, S. (1998, February). What makes a piece of interpretative research narrative? Keynote address: Narrative biographical methods in research on teachers and teaching, University of Oulu, Finland. Retrieved July 14,2003 at http://www.sv.ntnu.no/ped/sigrun/publikasjoner/narroulu.html
[21] Hagedorn, L.S. (1996). Wage equity and female job satisfaction: The role of wage differentials in a job satisfaction causal model. Research in Higher Education, 37(5), 569-598.
[22] Hamrick, F. (1998, April). "I Have Work to Do": Affirmation and marginalization of women full professors. Paper presented at the annual meeting of the American Educational Research Association, San Diego.
[23] Jarvis, P. (1999). The practitioner-researcher: Developing theory from practice. San Francisco, CA: Jossey-Bass.
[24] Kaufman, D. (1995). Preparing faculty as tutors in problem-based learning. In A. W. Wright & Associates (Eds.), Teaching improvement practices: Successful strategies for higher education. Boston: Anker Publishing.
[25] Kegan, R. (2000). What "form" transforms? A constructive-developmental approach to transformative learning. In J. Mezirow (Ed.). Learning as transformation: Critical perspectives on a theory in progress (35-70). San Francisco: Jossey-Bass.
[26] Keim, J. (1998, August). Stressors in academic careers: Male and female perspectives. Paper presented at the annual meeting of the American Psychological Association, San Francisco.
[27] Kimmel, Ellen (1999). Feminist teaching, an emergent practice. In S. N. Davis, M. Crawford, & J. Sebrechts, (Eds.). Coming into her own: Educational success in girls and women. (57-76). San Francisco: Jossey-Bass.

Human Perspectives in the Internet Society: Culture, Psychology and Gender, K. Morgan, J. Sanchez, C. A. Brebbia & A Voiskounsky (Editors) © 2004 WIT Press, www.witpress.com, ISBN 1-85312-726-4

[28] King, K. P. (1999, May). How technology education transforms teachers' perspectives of their profession. Paper presented at the annual meeting of the American Educational Research Association, Montreal, PQ.
[29] Magolda, M. B. Baxter (1992). Knowledge and reasoning in College: Gender-related patterns in students' intellectual development. San Francisco: Jossey-Bass Publishers.
[30] Mentkowski, M. & Associates (2000). Learning that lasts: Integrating learning, development and performance in college and beyond. San Francisco: Jossey-Bass.
[31] Mezirow, J. (2000). Learning to think like an adult: Core concepts of transformation theory. In J. Mezirow (Ed.), Learning as transformation: Critical perspectives on a theory in progress (3-34). San Francisco: Jossey-Bass.
[32] Nawratil, G. (1999). Implications of computer-conferenced learning for feminist pedagogy and women's studies: A review of the literature. Resources for Feminist Research, 27(1/2), 73-107.
[33] Newman, Judith M. (2000, January). Action research: A brief overview. Forum Qualitative Sozialforschung/Forum: Qualitative Social Research.
[34] Park, S.M. (1996). Research, teaching, and service: Why shouldn't women's work count? The Journal of Higher Education, 67(1), 46-84.
[35] Ramsden, P., & Martin, E. (1996). Recognition of good university teaching: Policies from an Australian study. Studies in Higher Education, 21(3), 299-305.
[36] Schön, D. (1987). Educating the reflective practitioner: Toward a new design for teaching and learning in the professions. San Francisco: Jossey-Bass.
[37] Seminoff, N., & Wepner, S. (1997). What should we know about technology-based projects for tenure and promotion. Journal of Research on Computing in Education, 30 (1).
[38] Senge, P. (1990). The fifth discipline. NY: Doubleday.
[39] Sokol, A. V. &. Cranton, P. (1998). Transforming, not training. Adult Learning, 93(3), 14-16.
[40] Spotts, T.H., Bowman, M.A., & Mertz, C. (1997). Gender and use of instructional technologies: A study of university faculty. Higher Education: 34, 421-436.
[41] Tisdell, Elizabeth J. (2000). Feminist pedagogues. In E. Hayes & D. D. Flannery, (Eds.), Women as learners: The significance of gender in adult learning (pp. 155-184). San Francisco: Jossey-Bass.
[42] Weiler, Kathleen (1991). Freire and a feminist pedagogy of difference. Harvard Educational Review, 61(4), 449-474.
[43] Wolcott, L. L. (1997). Tenure, promotion, and distance education: examining the culture of faculty rewards. American Journal of Distance Education, 11(2), 3-18.

Human Perspectives in the Internet Society: Culture, Psychology and Gender, K. Morgan, J. Sanchez, C. A. Brebbia & A Voiskounsky (Editors) © 2004 WIT Press, www.witpress.com, ISBN 1-85312-726-4

Comparative gender differences in faculty job satisfaction at higher education: Taiwan and China

L. C. Tu, P. Bernard, M. Plaisent & L. Maguiraga
Department of Business Administration, Far East College, Taiwan

Abstract

The study examined the IT and gender differences in job satisfaction between Taiwan and China higher education faculty. The data of job satisfaction was obtained from 194 Taiwanese faculty (48 IT faculty) and 211 Chinese faculty at college levels. It is hypothesized that faculty perceptions of job satisfaction affect their attitudes toward the educational reforms. The SPSS v10 software, which included descriptive statistics, analysed the data: t-test, and Pearson correlation coefficient. The mean score of job satisfaction for Taiwanese IT faculty was 13.04, and the mean score for Chinese IT faculty was 10.83. In the total score for job satisfaction, there were no statistically significant IT faculty differences between Taiwanese faculty ($t=-0.802$, $p=0.423$) and Chinese faculty ($t=-0.887$, $p=0.376$) after educational reforms. Moreover, the mean score of job satisfaction for Taiwanese male faculty was 14.57, and the mean score for Chinese female faculty was 12.96. In the total score for job satisfaction, there were no statistically significant gender differences between Taiwanese faculty ($t=-0.649$, $p=0.517$) and Chinese faculty ($t=-0.195$, $p=0.846$) after educational reforms.

1 Introduction

Little research is available on comparing faculty job satisfaction levels between Taiwan and China, especially as the Taiwanese and China governments set different policies during educational reforms.

1.1 Job satisfaction in higher education

Job satisfaction on gender study is a widely researched topic, however, the findings from the present studies are somewhat contradictory. Some studies found no differences between men and women. Some studies found women are

Human Perspectives in the Internet Society: Culture, Psychology and Gender, K. Morgan, J. Sanchez, C. A. Brebbia & A Voiskounsky (Editors) © 2004 WIT Press, www.witpress.com, ISBN 1-85312-726-4

more satisfied than men but some studies found men are more satisfied than women.

1.1.1 Job satisfaction on gender

Al-Yamani and Bu-Gahoos [2] showed the career satisfaction of male and female instructors was positively related to increases in instructor's years of teaching experience, but was significantly related to gender, residence, and qualifications. Similarly, Shapiro and Stern [3] examined the relationship between job satisfaction and sex for professional and non-professional positions. They found that professional and non-professional males' satisfaction with work and promotion was higher than females. In a Southeastern University in the USA, Tang & Talpade [4] found that there were significant positive differences between males and females and those males tended to have higher satisfaction with pay than females. In Riyadh City, the capital of Saudi Arabian, a study of female and male academic department chairpersons from Imam Muhammad Ibn Saud Islamic University, King Saud University, and Girls Colleges, Al-Omar [5] found, first, that there was a significant difference in the present work subscale, with males tending to be more satisfied than females, second, there was a significant difference in the payment, with females being more satisfied than males, third, there was a significant difference in promotions, with higher levels of satisfaction among males, fourth, there was no significant difference between the groups in supervision, co-workers, and the job in general. In Kaduna State, Nigeria, a study of full-time business faculty of higher education (Shinkut [6]) revealed that female faculty were more satisfied than their male counterparts, but the longer the length of service, the lower the job satisfaction. At Washington community college in the USA, in a study of organizational rewards for full-time faculty, female faculty were shown to have job satisfaction related to different factors, which they believe is important to the job. On the other hand, male faculty are influenced by different job factors which produce satisfaction (Hurley [7]). At Pennsylvania State University in the USA, a study of the challenge of workplace diversity of female faculty in six selected colleges Lyimo [8], concluded that female faculty members were satisfied with the supervision, abilities and skills, and interpersonal relationship dimensions of job satisfaction, however, they were found to be neither satisfied nor dissatisfied with the recognition, career advancement, and university policies and practices dimensions of job satisfaction. All of the above studies suggest the importance of job satisfaction in the educational system. Hutton & Jobe [10] also found that women overall were more satisfied than men as community college faculty. Hill [9] also indicated that female faculty in the community college were less satisfied than men in every dimension of work satisfaction. On the other hand, Fedler et al. [11] found that females were more satisfied with colleagues and student quality and males were more satisfied with pay.

2 The Taiwan higher education

The transplanted pre-1945 Republican Chinese higher education was adapted from the U.S. education system of the 1920s (Law [1]) but higher education in

Taiwan replaced China with the Japanese model in 194, therefore, Taiwan displays a close link between higher education growth and national economic planning. Because Taiwan's private-sector economic systems, allowing private colleges and universities to charge fees diversify higher education. Private colleges and universities in Taiwan were subject to curricular, budgetary, and administrative controls by the Ministry of Education (MOE) that were similar to those imposed on the public institutions. Consequently, Taiwan has a high increasing concentration on basic and applied sciences in higher education.

2.1 China higher education

As compared with Taiwan, China restructured higher education into a tripartite system similar to the former Soviet model, with emphasis on educating scientists and technologists. For the construction of a new socialist policy, China has absorbed Marxist thought of the enlightenment tradition and tended towards enlightenment tradition and tended towards egalitarianism to reach high education levels. Private colleges and universities in China were transferred their ownership and administrative powers to the state in the early 1950s. All higher education institutions belonged to and were financed completely by the central government bureaucracy till the early 1980s. Three same transmitting value systems between Taiwan and China are as follows: first, both higher education systems before the 1980s were marked by rigid centralization as a means to limit tertiary institutes, teachers, and student's deviation from plans and procedures outlined by the respective Chinese states. Second, both were marked by politicisation that the ruling political parties' influence on such university affairs as administration, curriculum, and students' extracurricular activities. Third, both states controlled the appointments of the use of the national language as the official medium of instruction, the curriculum, the use of textbooks and teaching references, the establishment of departments and institutes, and the allocation of material and human resources (Law [1]).

2.1.1 The effect of job satisfaction on educational outcomes

Educational reform is a changing structure that might alter the attitudes of instructors. Job satisfaction is also related to faculty abilities, and their perception of administrators' philosophical beliefs.

3 Method

3.1 Participants

The population of interest in this study will be faculty members who are working in both public and private colleges. A total of 300 questionnaires were sent to the Taiwanese faculty members of public and private colleges in the south area of Taiwan. Of the 194 returned responses, the IT faculty response rate was 25% (48 IT faculty and 146 other faculty), and the gender response rate was 64.6% (59 female faculty and 135 male faculty). As compared with Taiwan, a total 420 questionnaires were sent to Chinese faculty members of 17 Normal Universities

Human Perspectives in the Internet Society: Culture, Psychology and Gender, K. Morgan, J. Sanchez, C. A. Brebbia & A Voiskounsky (Editors) © 2004 WIT Press, www.witpress.com, ISBN 1-85312-726-4

and 25 Medical colleges in XuZhou area of China. Of the 303 returned responses, 211 were usable, the IT faculty response rate was 11% (24 IT faculty and 187 other faculty), and the gender response rate was 50% (72 female faculty and 139 male faculty).

3.1.1 Measures

The data was collected by a structured questionnaire that consisted of general characteristics modified by Dr. Suwat for Index Organizational Reactions (IOR). The general characteristics information included the financial rewards (FR), supervision (SU), kind of work (KW), amount of work (AW), physical work condition (PWC), and interactions with colleagues (IWC). A 7-point, 29-item Likert scale was used to measure total job satisfaction. Respondents were asked to rate on the scale where 3=strongly agree, 2=moderately agree, 1=slightly agree 0=not sure, -1=slightly disagree, -2=moderately disagree, -3=strongly disagree.

3.1.1.1 Internal consistency reliability To test for the internal consistency related to questions, alpha reliability coefficients of the modified IOR were developed at similar concepts on the questions. The results ranged from 0.626 to 0.875 and proved reliable for the scale.

3.1.1.1.1 Analysis The collected data were analyzed by the SPSS v10 software that included descriptive statistics: t-test and Pearson correlation coefficient. The t-test calculated the overall job satisfaction according to the department, the gender, and the Pearson correlation coefficient calculated the relationships of job satisfaction and the general characteristics.

4 Results

There are no statistically significant differences between IT faculty and other faculty in job satisfaction between Taiwanese faculty (t=-0.802, p=0.423) and Chinese faculty (t=-0.887, p=0.376) after educational reforms (Table 1).

Table 1: The type of faculty measures with independent samples test.

		Levene's Test for Equality of Variances		t-test for Equality of Means		
		F	Sig.	t	Df	Sig. (2-ailed)
China	Equal variances assumed	3.063	.082	-.887	209	.376
Taiwan	Equal variances assumed	.693	.406	-.802	192	.423

However, other faculty in Taiwan (M=14.60) and in China (M=12.99) tended to have higher satisfaction than IT faculty in Taiwan (M=13.04) and in China

Human Perspectives in the Internet Society: Culture, Psychology and Gender, K. Morgan, J. Sanchez, C. A. Brebbia & A Voiskounsky (Editors) © 2004 WIT Press, www.witpress.com, ISBN 1-85312-726-4

(M=10.83) of the overall satisfaction in Taiwan colleges, but no significantly so (Table 3).

There are no statistically significant gender differences in job satisfaction between Taiwanese faculty (t=-0.649, p=0.517) and Chinese faculty (t=-0.195, p=0.846) after educational reforms (Table 2).

However, male faculty (M=14.57) tended to have higher satisfaction than females (M=13.39) of the overall satisfaction in Taiwan colleges, whereas females (M=12.96) tended to have higher satisfaction than males (M=12.64) in China colleges, but no significantly so (Table 4).

Table 2: The type of faculty measures with descriptive statistics.

	Department	N	Mean	Std. Deviation	Std. Error Mean
China	IT faculty	24	10.83	8.66	1.77
	Other faculty	187	12.99	11.52	.84
Taiwan	IT faculty	48	13.04	12.91	1.86
	Other faculty	146	14.60	11.20	.93

Table 3: The gender measures with independent samples test.

		Levene's Test for Equality of Variances		t-test for Equality of Means		
		F	Sig.	t	df	Sig. (2-ailed)
China	Equal variances assumed	.192	.662	-.195	209	.846
Taiwan	Equal variances assumed	0.019	.891	-.649	192	.517

Table 4: The gender measures with descriptive statistics.

	Gender	N	Mean	Std. Deviation	Std. Error Mean
China	Male	139	12.64	11.51	.98
	Female	72	12.96	10.75	1.27
Taiwan	Male	135	14.57	11.85	1.02
	Female	59	13.39	11.19	1.46

5 Discussion

5.1 Taiwan survey

In correlation finding, Table 5 showed that financial rewards (r=0.664), kind of work (r=0.723), and interactions with colleagues (r=0.697) had high, significant at the .01, correlations with job satisfaction. Similarly, supervision (r=0.597) and physical work conditions (r=0.514) were moderately (still at the .01 level) correlated with job satisfaction. In addition, amount of work (r=0.346) had lower (but still significant) correlations with job satisfaction.

Human Perspectives in the Internet Society: Culture, Psychology and Gender, K. Morgan, J. Sanchez, C. A. Brebbia & A Voiskounsky (Editors) © 2004 WIT Press, www.witpress.com, ISBN 1-85312-726-4

Table 5: Pearson correlations in Taiwan survey between job satisfaction (JS) and dependent variables (DV).

		JS	FR	SU	KW	AW	PWC	IWC
JS	P	1.000	.664**	.597**	.723**	.346**	.514**	.697**
	Sig	.	.000	.000	.000	.000	.000	.000
	N	194	194	194	194	194	194	194
FR	P	.664**	1.000	.174*	.431**	.229**	.277**	.276**
	Sig	.000	.	.015	.000	.001	.000	.000
	N	194	194	194	194	194	194	194
SU	P	.597**	.174*	1.000	.317**	-.071	.202**	.404**
	Sig	.000	.015	.	.000	.324	.005	.000
	N	194	194	194	194	194	194	194
KW	P	.723**	.431**	.317**	1.000	.251**	.350**	.357**
	Sig	.000	.000	.000	.	.000	.000	.000
	N	194	194	194	194	194	194	194
AW	P	.346**	.229**	-.071	.251**	1.000	.101	.147*
	Sig	.000	.001	.324	.000	.	.163	.040
	N	194	194	194	194	194	194	194
PWC	P	.514**	.277**	.202**	.350**	.101	1.000	.235**
	Sig	.000	.000	.005	.000	.163	.	.001
	N	194	194	194	194	194	194	194
IWC	P	.697**	.276**	.404**	.357**	.147*	.235**	1.000
	Sig	.000	.000	.000	.000	.040	.001	.
	N	194	194	194	194	194	194	194

Remarks: ** Correlation is significant at the 0.01 level (2-tailed).
* Correlation is significant at the 0.05 level (2-tailed).
JS present job satisfaction

5.1.1 China survey

Compared with Taiwan, correlation finding of China in Table 6 showed that financial rewards (r=0.663), kind of work (r=0.623), interactions with colleagues (r=0.713) had high significant at the .01, correlations with overall job satisfaction. Similarly, amount of work (r=0.442) and physical work conditions (r=0.58) were moderately (still at the .01 level) correlated with job satisfaction. In addition, Table 4 showed that supervision (r=0.296) had lower (but still significant) correlations with job satisfaction.

5.1.1.1 IT faculty and Genders finding The results of Taiwanese faculty indicated that there were no significant differences in job satisfaction of IT faculty and gender for full-time faculty at higher education; however, the overall mean score males was 14.85 points, indicating higher satisfaction than females, whereas, the overall mean score for IT faculty was 13.04, indicating lower satisfaction than other faculty in Taiwan, but no significantly so. Compared with Taiwan, there were no significant differences for Chinese faculty in job satisfaction of IT faculty and gender, for full-time faculty at higher education at China colleges; however, the overall mean score for females was 12.96 points, indicating higher satisfaction than males in China, whereas, the overall mean

Human Perspectives in the Internet Society: Culture, Psychology and Gender, K. Morgan, J. Sanchez, C. A. Brebbia & A Voiskounsky (Editors) © 2004 WIT Press, www.witpress.com, ISBN 1-85312-726-4

score for IT faculty was 10.83, indicating lower satisfaction than other faculty in China but no significantly so.

6 Conclusion

The status of job satisfaction between Taiwan and China higher education IT faculty and gender members and the factors affecting their satisfaction levels are concerned in this study. In studies in involving the educational reforms, it is quite possible that the participants at college level in Taiwan are not influenced by the reform policies. Specifically, the analysis in the study concludes that the impact of the educational reforms on job satisfaction is not significant difference. Compared with Taiwan, China as a large country faces more complicated issues in educational reforms. Comparatively, China has made even greater efforts to expand compulsory education (Cheng, 1999). He also indicated that decentralization of power from central government to local communities and to the school level is evident. In sum, there were no significant differences in job satisfaction between Taiwanese and Chinese IT faculty and the gender.

Table 6: Pearson correlations in Chinese survey between job satisfaction (JS) and dependent variables (DV).

China		JS	FR	SU	KW	AW	PWC	IWC
JS	P	1	.663**	.296**	.623**	.442**	.580**	.713**
	Sig.	.	.000	.000	.000	.000	.000	.000
	N	211	211	211	211	211	211	211
FR	P	.663**	1	.102	.319**	.238**	.195**	.383**
	Sig.	.000	.	.141	.000	.000	.005	.000
	N	211	211	211	211	211	211	211
SU	P	.296**	.102	1	.019	.107	-.085	.053
	Sig.	.000	.141	.	.781	.123	.218	.440
	N	211	211	211	211	211	211	211
KW	P	.623**	.319**	.019	1	.231**	.353**	.378**
	Sig.	.000	.000	.781	.	.001	.000	.000
	N	211	211	211	211	211	211	211
AW	P	.442**	.238**	.107	.231**	1	.139*	.276**
	Sig.	.000	.000	.123	.001	.	.044	.000
	N	211	211	211	211	211	211	211
PWC	P	.580**	.195**	-.085	.353**	.139*	1	.347**
	Sig.	.000	.005	.218	.000	.044	.	.000
	N	211	211	211	211	211	211	211
IWC	P	.713**	.383**	.053	.378**	.276**	.347**	1
	Sig.	.000	.000	.440	.000	.000	.000	.
	N	211	211	211	211	211	211	211

** Correlation is significant at the 0.01 level (2-tailed).
* Correlation is significant at the 0.05 level (2-tailed).

References

[1] Law, W.W., The role of the state in higher educational reform: mainland China and Taiwan. Comparative Education Review, 39(3), pp. 322-253, 1995.

Human Perspectives in the Internet Society: Culture, Psychology and Gender, K. Morgan, J. Sanchez, C. A. Brebbia & A Voiskounsky (Editors) © 2004 WIT Press, www.witpress.com, ISBN 1-85312-726-4

[2] Al-Yamani, S.A. & Bu-Gahoos, K.A., An analytic study of the career satisfaction (frustration) of mal and female instructors serving in general education in Bahrain (Abstract). Educational Sciences, Jordan, 23(2), pp.269-287, 1996.
[3] Shapiro, H.J. & Stern, L.W., Job satisfaction: male and female, professional and non-professional workers. Personal Journal, 54, pp. 388-389,406-407,1975.
[4] Tang, T.L., & Talpade, M., Sex differences in satisfaction with pay and co-workers: faculty and staff at a public institution of higher education. Public Personnel Management, 28(3), pp. 345-349,1999.
[5] Al-Omar, A.M., Job Satisfaction Among Female and Male Academic Department Chairpersons in Saudi Arabian Institutions of Higher Education, Idaho: Dissertation Abstracts International, pp. 4015A, 1999.
[6] Shinkut, M.B., Job Satisfaction of Full-Time Business Faculty of Higher Education Institutions in Kaduna State, Nigeria, Missouri: Dissertation Abstracts International, pp. 2829A, 1999.
[7] Hurley, J.A., The Effects of Organization Rewards on the Job Satisfaction of Washington Community College Full-Time Faculty, Seattle: Dissertation Abstracts International, pp. 3425A, 1996.
[8] Lyimo, J.G., Meeting the Challenge of Workplace Diversity: an Assessment of the Job Satisfaction of Female Faculty in Selected Colleges at the Pennsylvania State University, Pennsylvania: Dissertation Abstracts International, pp. 4525A, 1998.
[9] Hill, M.D., Some factors affecting job satisfaction of community college faculty in Pennsylvania. Community/Junior College Quarterly of Research and Practice, 7, pp. 303-313, 1983.
[10] Hutton, J.B. & Jobe, M.E., Job satisfaction of community college faculty. Community/Junior College Quarterly of Research and Practice, 9, pp. 317-324,1985.
[11] Fedler, F., Counts, T. & Smith, R.F., Survey compares attitudes of male, female professors. Journalism Educator, 39, pp. 3-8, 1984.

Human Perspectives in the Internet Society: Culture, Psychology and Gender, K. Morgan, J. Sanchez, C. A. Brebbia & A Voiskounsky (Editors) © 2004 WIT Press, www.witpress.com, ISBN 1-85312-726-4

Section 8
Gender stereotypes

Paradoxes in the impact of the Internet on women

J. Morahan-Martin
Department of Psychology, Bryant College, USA

Abstract

The Internet has been used to promote women's causes and has been a tool of women's empowerment while also being used against women's causes and to victimize women. This paper explores the contradictory impact of the Internet on women. It first explores how women have engaged in political activism online to promote women's causes and how this has led to a sense of empowerment on an individual and group level. It then explores how online political activism of hate groups and anti-feminist men's activists has worked against women's interests. Finally, it explores how women's online presence has resulted in their being subject to online harassment.
Keywords: gender, women, Internet, political activism, hate groups, feminism, men's activism, women's activism, online harassment.

1 Introduction

The Internet has empowered women while also being a vehicle of oppression which has served against women's interests. On the positive side, the Internet has been a potent tool that has enhanced women's lives. Online activism has generated worldwide support for women's issues such as violence against women, political oppression, social and economic inequities. Women also have created community and social support online. However, the Internet also has created and amplified problems for women. Hate groups have proliferated online, some specifically targeting women. These online groups can create support for deviant and undesirable behavior, and can legitimize hostile, inappropriate or dangerous behavior, some directed explicitly at women. Women have been targets of online harassment, some because of their online participation and activism.

Human Perspectives in the Internet Society: Culture, Psychology and Gender, K. Morgan, J. Sanchez, C. A. Brebbia & A Voiskounsky (Editors) © 2004 WIT Press, www.witpress.com, ISBN 1-85312-726-4

This paper will explore the contradictory impact of the Internet on women in two areas: activism which has both enhanced and oppressed women; online harassment resulting from women's online presence.

2 Women's political activism

The Internet is changing the face of social and political activism worldwide. Activists' ability to connect directly with other individuals with similar interests and to gain access to resources throughout the world is vastly expanded online. "Because e-mail is near-instantaneous and costs just fractions of a penny, one can communicate very quickly with a lot of people at the speed of word of mouth. Because it is browsable from home, at any hour, it provides a much easier first point of contact between a campaign and interested participants" (Boyd [1], p. 16). Using the Internet for political activism allows activists to bypass traditional media outlets as well as governmental controls or censors. This helps "level the playing field between an entrenched government and corporate and media power and an insurgent citizenry" (Boyd [1], p.17). Activists are not limited by geographical or social boundaries; instead, they have access to a global community. The Internet "allows people to share experiences and ideas and discover that others throughout the world are identifying the same issues. By interacting via the Internet with those others, the individual is no longer an isolated voice but part of a network of like-minded people...(who are) dispersed (geographically) and yet can constitute significant grass roots...movement" (Trendle [2], p.14).

Activists have made use of the Internet's unique ability to transmit information and promote communication in a variety of areas including advocating women's and feminist issues, human rights, peace and environmental causes, political campaigns, and grassroots social causes. As detailed in the next section, these groups have used the many capacities of the Internet to promote their causes in a variety of ways: Providing information, mobilizing advocacy for specific causes, fundraising, and providing social support for members.

2.1 Using the Internet to provide information

Most online activist organizations have some presence on the Web that both gives visibility to the organization and provides information about the organization. Often these sites provide information relevant to its cause. Many also provide links to similar groups. Some sites primarily serve as online information centers. An excellent example is UNIFEM [3], the Web site of the United Nations Development Fund for Women, that serves as "a portal on women, peace and security." It provides information about women's empowerment and gender equity, including UNIFEM's programs to ensure economic empowerment, political participation, women's human rights, and protection of women in armed conflict. Of interest to readers is UNIFEM's work promoting gender equity in IT.

Human Perspectives in the Internet Society: Culture, Psychology and Gender, K. Morgan, J. Sanchez, C. A. Brebbia & A Voiskounsky (Editors) © 2004 WIT Press, www.witpress.com, ISBN 1-85312-726-4

The Internet has also been used by activists to broadcast video footage. Witness, a non profit group founded in 1992, has given video cameras to 150 human rights activist groups throughout the world. These have been used to document and expose social injustices including the systematic rape of girls and women during Sierra Leone's 10 year civil war and sweatshops in New York (Scheeres, [4]). One group, Revolutionary Association of the Women of Afghanistan (RAWA), used the Internet to publish video footage of the atrocities committed by Islamic fundamentalists in Afghanistan. Using miniature camcorders hidden under their burqas, RAWA members documented videos of Taliban atrocities, including amputations, beatings and public executions which was instrumental in focusing international outcry against the Taliban regime and helped in fundraising to build schools and hospitals (Scheers [4]).

The Web also has been used as a resource center. The Women's Studies/Women's Issues Resource Site [5] provides annotated links to more than 500 Web sites, including over 80 activist Web sites for women's issues. Although almost all sites are in English, the focus of this frequently updated archive is international. It provides information on a variety of activist causes including women's health, human rights violations, violence against women, reproductive rights, sexual exploitation and harassment, and legal and policy issues. The Feminist Majority Foundation Online [6] also offers a wealth of information at its site, including relevant news items and the global feminist resources, which lists over 60 international feminist activist groups.

2.2 Grassroots organizing on the Internet: Using the Internet to mobilize forces

The Internet is a highly effective tool for mobilizing both online and offline. Feminist.com provides online action alerts at its site and also provides links to other activist groups. Those who sign up to be on an e-mail list may also be informed of relevant issues. For example, the 25,000 members from 160 countries who are members of the Women's Action Network (WAN) receive regular e-mail updates on human rights violations against women and girls around the world. These are used to prompt members to mobilize public pressure against these abuses by petitions, e-mail campaigns, letter writing and to raise awareness within their own communities of these issues (Equality Now [7]). E-mail campaigns have been successful in some causes. "Claudia Rodriguez in Mexico, who was imprisoned for the homicide of her would-be rapist, was freed after the e-mail activist network Modemmujer sent out Claudia's words to hundreds of women's organizations in Mexico, Latin America, and North America" (Harcourt [8], p.695). Alice Garg, a member of the Bal Rashmi Society in India explains how global support generated by the Internet helped her after she and other colleagues were arrested for their work against human rights violations against women including sexual exploitation, rape, dowry deaths and torture. "The credit for our being able to survive goes in no small measure to…IT. It was through this that we mobilized support for our unequal struggle from all over the world. People and organizations responded in

Human Perspectives in the Internet Society: Culture, Psychology and Gender, K. Morgan, J. Sanchez, C. A. Brebbia & A Voiskounsky (Editors) © 2004 WIT Press, www.witpress.com, ISBN 1-85312-726-4

great numbers and very spontaneously.... We would all have been behind the bars had people not rallied in our support" (Cited in Harcourt [8], p. 695).

The Internet also has been effectively used to have activists meet and demonstrate in real life. The Internet enables large social and political mobilizations to unfold with minimal bureaucracy, hierarchy and cost. This is best illustrated in the anti-war demonstrations preceding the U.S. invasion of Iraq. On March 16 2003, the eve of the U.S. invasion of Iraq, "(a) wave of candlelight vigils, following the sun west across the Earth, involved an estimated 1 million people in more than 6,000 gatherings in 130 countries and every state in the nation (U.S.). This global action was put together in...six days by an organization with only five staff people, MoveOn" (Boyd [1], p. 13). Through its use of the Internet, MoveOn also was able to deliver a petition of 1 million signatures to the UN Security Council and have 200,000 people call representatives in Washington in a single day. These feats were made possible by its mailing list, now over 2,000,000, which has been developed mostly by online word of mouth and a type of Web software called "meeting tool." The software product "meeting tool" allows anyone anywhere to use the Internet to propose a meeting time and place in her or his own neighborhood, and makes it easy for others to sign up. These "meet-ups" are scheduled through use of meetup.com, a free Web service (Boyd [1]).

This model has been adapted by small grassroots groups, with memberships of 5,000-10,000 which "use their use websites to foster self-organizing—putting their organizing kit online and trusting their activist base to run with it" (Boyd [1], p. 14). For example, the Million Mom March site [9] also promotes members to create meet-ups to bring together others interested in promoting gun control. Additionally, the Million Mom March also uses its site to promote its upcoming activities, provide information about joining local chapters, forwarding information about the organization to others, and sign legislative petitions.

2.3 Using the Internet for fundraising

The Internet has been an effective tool for fundraising for activist causes. Almost all activist sites make it possible for users to make direct donations online. Many, like the Million Moms March, use the Internet to sell products for publicity and fundraising. Other fund raising possibilities are being developed that allow a cause to reach a broader market to raise funds. For example, in Jordan, rural Boudouin women were not able to sell their weaving products because the tourist industry had been affected by local conflicts. However, a marketing program was developed to make their handicrafts available over the Web. "As a result, these women have been able to achieve self-reliance and begin assuming significant economic, social and even political roles in their communities" (Noor and Cummings [10]).

Human Perspectives in the Internet Society: Culture, Psychology and Gender, K. Morgan, J. Sanchez, C. A. Brebbia & A Voiskounsky (Editors) © 2004 WIT Press, www.witpress.com, ISBN 1-85312-726-4

2.4 The Internet makes it easier to be an activist

As with non-Internet activism, there are all levels of participation in online activism, but the Internet makes it easier to be aware of issues and participate at whatever level an individual chooses. Some believe that the Internet can stimulate political involvement from individuals who would otherwise not be involved. "Many people are apolitical because they don't feel like they can be part of the process" (Bennett and Fielding, cited in Cyberadvocacy [11]). Even those who might not be able to participate in person can participate online. For example, Wilson-Heuser [12], in a popular magazine, *Mother*, writes of activist opportunities for mothers of young children who are caught between a newly awakened desire to make their children's world better at a time in their lives when they have minimal time. Certainly, being able to participate from home is a benefit to all, but perhaps especially to women trying to juggle the demands of a family and/or work outside the home. Most activist groups use a listserve to inform their members of issues important to group. For example, NARAL, a U.S. advocacy group for reproductive rights, sends frequent alerts to members informing them of relevant issues including upcoming votes and judge appointments. These provide information on how members can contact elected representatives to voice their concern. This allows those who might not have the time to follow related news to be more actively involved with minimal effort, at their convenience, and without leaving their computer. This may be particularly attractive to those who lack time or inclination for more active participation: the five minute activist.

2.5 Enhanced communication between activists and empowerment

The enhanced ability of activists to use the Internet to communicate with others and themselves has been implicit in much of the discussion above. E-mail, list serves, meet-ups, Web sites, discussion groups all allow communication among activists in ways that would not have been possible earlier. Women activists attest to the importance of online communication to their work. Lamis Alshehni, an activist from Yemen, declares, "The Internet has totally revolutionized my work on women's rights…It is the possibility of raising the voice of local Arab women on a global level that has inspired me to network, build coalitions to achieve my goals using the Internet" (cited in Harcourt [8], p. 694). "We exchange information, thoughts and experiences with such a wide audience that could not been imagined a decade ago" concurs Khawar Mumtaz, a Pakistani NGO human rights activist (cited in Harcourt [8], p. 694). Even women in politically divided communities can interact. "The Internet has been a revolution in the communications between women from the two communities of Cyprus, the Greek Cypriots and the Turkish Cypriots (who have not been able to meet in three years)…, but the authorities cannot stop the communication through the Internet" (Economidou, cited in Harcourt [8], p. 694).

And, activists feel empowered. Peggy Antrobus, founder of DAWN (Development Alternatives with Women for a New Era), summarizes the impact of the Internet. "Most of all, (it) has empowered us by giving us the information,

Human Perspectives in the Internet Society: Culture, Psychology and Gender, K. Morgan, J. Sanchez, C. A. Brebbia & A Voiskounsky (Editors) © 2004 WIT Press, www.witpress.com, ISBN 1-85312-726-4

the analysis the sense of solidarity, the experience of shared achievements, the encouragement and moral support that comes from being part of a network, a movement with common goals and visions" (cited in Harcourt [8], p. 695). Wendy Harcourt [8], with the Society for International Development in Italy, explains. "The ferment of activity we see on the Internet by women is a direct and exciting example of how women's place based politics is stretching old boundaries and divides and creating new spaces for women to network, organize and change the world...(W)omen are building up solidarity among groups that share the same goal even if they never meet face to face. In almost revolutionary ways, women's groups are using the Internet as a tool for empowerment changing women's daily lives, their hopes and futures" (p. 697-697).

3 Online hate and men's anti-feminist activist groups

The impact of online activism for women has not been all positive, however. At the same time the Internet is being used to empower women, it is being used to work against women both at the individual and group levels. Activists have worked in anti-feminist and hate groups which have victimized women, especially those in minority groups. Women's online presence also has made them targets of online harassment and stalking. These will be discussed below.

Not all Internet activist groups are promoting social justice. In fact, some explicitly promote hate—some expressly against women and others targeted because of racial, religious, ethnic and/or sexual preference. The Internet can be a powerful tool for hate groups. The Simon Wiesenthal Center (SWC [13]), which monitors online hate sites, has documented "the growing use of the Internet as a key propaganda weapon, marketing tool, and fundraising engine" for both hate groups and terrorists. The same Internet characteristics that allow promotion of social justice causes can be utilized to promote injustice and hate. Hate sites have proliferated on the Internet although the actual number of hate sites online is not known. There was one known hate group in 1995 (Levin [14]). By March 2004, SWC, [13], 2004), estimates there are more than 4,000.

Online men's activist groups have received less attention. Many men's activist organizations are reactionary groups that oppose what they call radical feminism. Although they are separate organizations, many have joined forces in international umbrella groups such as the Mandefender World Ring, Mensactivism.com, and the International Men's Network. Under the rubric of social justice, they advocate for men's rights and against feminism and discrimination against men. Their issues mirror those of women's groups: Sexism, economic, legal and legislature discrimination, violence against men, false charges against men, family rights, reproductive choices for men. They abhor sexist practices and misangony (male hating), which they believe to be the male equivalent to misogyny. However, their anti-feminism is at best venomously misogynous. The names and descriptions of some of the groups listed on and linked from the Anti Feminist Pro Men Page [15] are informative. The Black Mens Anti Feminism site says: "(n)o political correctness allowed!! Devoted to giving black men the credit they deserve!...and to prove how

Human Perspectives in the Internet Society: Culture, Psychology and Gender, K. Morgan, J. Sanchez, C. A. Brebbia & A Voiskounsky (Editors) © 2004 WIT Press, www.witpress.com, ISBN 1-85312-726-4

women's liberation witch destroyed black men, and the black family!!". The Married Mens Militia proclaim this is "where men learn to fight back...offers a lot of practical advice". The Sex-Ploytation site provides "a look at how some women use sex to exploit and oppress men". The Stiff site advertises it is "helping build a better world without viciously deranged feminists." The warning at the end of the list is chilling. "Note: feminist hate mail can expect retaliation."

These groups use the Internet in similar ways as political activist groups. They recruit, raise money, provide information on news, legal activism, upcoming events, have discussion groups. They even post names of favored and disfavored groups. One radical anti-abortion Web site, Christian Gallery, has posted lists of abortion providers that include their home addresses, cars and regular travel information, "with slash marks through the names of those (providers) who have been murdered" (Levin [14], p. 969), and has called for Nuremburg-style trials for abortion providers. Two men's groups, Stand Your Ground.com and Mensactivism.org, have posted a list of companies to boycott. The name of the list is informative: "Companies to avoid doing business with due to male bashing" [16]. It includes mainstream companies in the U.S. and Europe like Ford Motor Company that boycott proponents claim has aired male bashing commercials, "blatant discrimination against men, particularly white men" (Boycott Ford [17]), and has financed feminist causes through the Ford Foundation (a major U.S. Foundation founded with money from the Ford family). "FoMoCo (Ford Motor Company), or more accurately the Ford Foundation, has been monetarily subsidizing misandric (male hating) feminists organizations and other anti-male ultra liberal causes for some time now. Their significant financial grants are one of the prime reasons we are in the mess we are in now" (Luek, in Boycott Ford [17] [author's grammar]).

3.1 Hate speech

Like other activist groups, online hate and male activist groups use the Internet to provide information to foster their goals. They post "how to" manuals of hate groups can include sabotage manuals, oft with legal disclaimers.

In the U.S., free speech rights provide protection for online hate groups. This has encouraged some hate groups from other countries to publish online through U.S. groups. Messages on hate and men's activism sites often ennoble and justify hate. Their messages tend to be "slickly packaged and carefully cloaked in ...euphemisms" (Firstman [18]). "Virtual bigots like to couch hate in lofty terms. Emoting about freedom and racial self-preservation, they allude to a racial holy war and exhort others to join the struggle. Sacrifice becomes the mark of a dedicated racist. Experiences of alienation, disapproval or persecution are thus eased by the inner assurance that one is battling for a cause greater than oneself" (Brown [19]).

For example, the United Kingdom Men's Movement (UKMM [20]) contains a synopsis of major men's rights issues which is written in a semi-academic style. This documents alleged injustices to men in areas such as health, domestic violence, local and national government, media, advertising, family issues,

Human Perspectives in the Internet Society: Culture, Psychology and Gender, K. Morgan, J. Sanchez, C. A. Brebbia & A Voiskounsky (Editors) © 2004 WIT Press, www.witpress.com, ISBN 1-85312-726-4

education, defense, employment, and criminal law. Overall, the appearance of the paper is that of a well written and researched report, with no inflammatory language. However, the agenda becomes clearer when one looks at some of the theses developed in the document.

> > The suicide rate for men is 3.7 times that for women…There is so little attention given to male suicides because men are considered to be the expendable sex (as in the first world war).
>
> > In this era of feminist's demands for equality, they should get it. If men for example pay 75% of the taxes then they must get 75% of the benefits.

After each section, readers are given links to follow through to promote UKMM's agenda. The same style and agenda is used in UKMM's section on human rights for men [21]. This section includes recent cases at the European Court of Human Rights and their submission to the UN Human Rights. Overall, it is striking how these documents parallel many academic documents of the women's rights activists. Its aims, however, consistently are opposed to those of women's rights groups.

3.2 Anonymity and disinhibition

Online anonymity is a key factor to online hate groups. Potok argues that the Internet has allowed a broader exposure to hate groups' messages to "people who in the past would not have gotten near these groups" (cited in Levin [14]). Even before they become members, anonymity allows interested people to privately explore the group's materials. Anonymity also can serve as a protective shield those involved in hate groups; they can threaten someone without repeatedly without being readily identified. Glaser et al.'s research [22] suggests that people might be less willing or able to exercise restraint and therefore act less morally online in part because of perceived online anonymity. This conclusion would be expected given the wealth of research which supports that behavior online can be less inhibited online because of lack of face-to-face contact and anonymity (Joinson [23]).

3.3 Communication and solidarity though online groups

Hate and men's activists groups are not limited to Web pages. Extremists also use the Internet "to access private message boards, e-mail, research, hacking, hidden instructions, listserves…, and chat rooms" (Levin [14], p. 968). Potok argues that "the real extremist action on the Internet is in interactive venues like discussion groups, closed E-lists and person to person e-mail" (cited in Levin [14], p. 965-6). Disinhibition or the loss of inhibition online may foster aggressive and antisocial behaviors on the Internet. Anonymity and lack of face to face communication provide shelter for members to behave online in ways that they would not in real life and this may transfer to their offline life. Online hate and anti-feminist groups can provide a sense of community and a safe haven for members who once felt isolated from others. As with women's online groups,

Human Perspectives in the Internet Society: Culture, Psychology and Gender, K. Morgan, J. Sanchez, C. A. Brebbia & A Voiskounsky (Editors) © 2004 WIT Press, www.witpress.com, ISBN 1-85312-726-4

participants achieve a sense of belonging and solidarity from membership. In these groups, hate mongering beliefs and behaviors usually are the norm. Tolerance and acceptance of these antisocial behaviors and beliefs in online groups validates them. This can lead to unacceptable behaviors offline as well.

4 Online harassment

A second area of concern to women using the Internet is the possibility of being the target of online harassment and stalking. Men as well as women have been victimized online, but women are more likely to be victims (D'Ovidio and Doyle [24]). Further, limited evidence indicates that women who are involved in feminist groups may be singled out for harassment because of their online presence, especially lesbians and anyone who is highly visible (Leiblum and Döring [25]; Kennedy, [26]). Online harassment and stalking is facilitated by online anonymity and disinhibition. "By enabling human interaction without the constraints of physical barriers and with the perception of anonymity, the Internet has become the ideal instrument for individuals who wish to intimidate, threaten or harass others. (Anyone) can use the Internet to send alarming message anywhere, within a matter of moments, under the guise of a fictitious screen name or pseudonym" (D'Ovidio and Doyle [24], p. 10).

The content and methods of harassment and vary. A small scale study of women who had founded and maintained feminist Web sites reports that women had their sites hacked, and had received derogatory insults and threats to their personal safety, including death threats. Some received phone calls and others warnings that the sender knew where she lived. Women were more likely to be harassed if their websites threatened the patriarchal structure; e.g., websites against sexual assault and harassment. Reactions of those who were harassed varied. Most said they were angry; a third said they felt threatened, and some took safety measures online and off. However, all but one continued their Websites (Kennedy [26]).

The impact of cyberharassment has received little study. Many factors come into play: the type and intensity of harassment, whether it extends beyond into real life, the individual involved. Limited evidence indicates that the experience can be terrifying, the victim can feel violated, and suffer psychological disturbance as a result of harassment although there is considerable variation in responses (Kennedy [26], Spitzberg and Hoobler [27], Ybarra [28]).

5 Conclusions

In conclusion, the Internet has been used by activists both for and against women's interests. Both have found the Internet an effective tool to recruit, provide information, raise funds, mobilize action, and provide social support and empowerment. Women's online presence puts them at risk for cyberharassment. Anonymity, lack of face to face interaction and online disinhibition facilitate the expression of antisocial behaviors in hate groups and online harassment.

Human Perspectives in the Internet Society: Culture, Psychology and Gender, K. Morgan, J. Sanchez, C. A. Brebbia & A Voiskounsky (Editors) © 2004 WIT Press, www.witpress.com, ISBN 1-85312-726-4

References

[1] Boyd, A. The Web rewires the movement. *The Nation,* **277(4)**, pp. 13-17, May 4, 2003.

[2] Trendle, G. Cyberspace: A 21st century diwan. *The Middle East*, pp. 14-15, September. 2002.

[3] UNIFEM, www.unifem.org

[4] Scheeres, J. Pics worth a thousand protests. *Wired News*, 2003, October 17. Online. www.wired.com/news/print/0,1294,60828,00.html

[5] Women's Studies/Women's Issues Resource Site, www.research.umbc.edu/~korenman/wmst/links.html

[6] Feminist Majority Foundation Online, www.feminist.org/global/beijing/beijing2.html

[7] Equality Now, http://www.equalitynow.org/english/about/wan_en.html

[8] Harcourt, W. The personal and the political: Women using the Internet. *CyberPsychology and Behavior, 3*, pp. 693-697, 2000.

[9] Million Mom March, www.millionmomsmarch.org

[10] Noor, Queen of Jordan, and Cummings, E. M. Women in the developing world. *CIO Magazine*, Fall/Winter, 2003. Online. www.cio.com/srchive/092203/noor.html?printversion=yes

[11] Cyberadvocacy: How the Internet may help people become more politically involved. *The Futurist, 34(5)*, p. 67, 2002.

[12] Wilson-Heuser, C. (2000, November-December). Online activism: Political power on the Web. *Mothering*, pp. 76-80, November-December 2000.

[13] Simon Wiesenthal Center (SWC). SWC presents digital terrorism and hate 2004 to U.S. Congress. Los Angeles: Author, 2004. Online. www.wiesenthal.com/mailings_swc/swc_mar2304.htm

[14] Levin, B. Cyberhate: A legal and historical analysis of extremists' use of computer networks in America. *The American Behavioral Scientist*, **45**, pp. 958-988, 2002.

[15] Anti Feminist Pro Men Page, www.freewebs.com/antifeminist/

[16] Companies to avoid doing business with due to male bashing. Stand Your Ground.com, Online. http://www.standyourground.com/boyc.php

[17] Boycott Ford for discrimination against men. Mensactivism.org. Online. http://www.mensactivism.org/articles/02/02/11/165238.shtml

[18] Firstman, R. Hate in online America. *Family PC*, pp. 83-88, May 2001.

[19] Brown, S. Virtual hate. *Soujourner, 29 (5)*, pp. 18-21, September 2000.

[20] United Kingdom Men's Movement (UKMM). Synopsis of major men's rights issues. UK: Author. Online. http://www.ukmm.org.uk/issues/synopsis.htm

[21] United Kingdom Men's Movement (UKMM). Human rights for men. UK: Author. Online. www.ukmm.org.uk/camp/hr/hrmen.htm

[22] Glaser, J., Dixit, J., & Green, D.P. Studying hate crime with the Internet. *Journal of Social Issues*, **58(1)**, pp. 177-193, 2002.

Human Perspectives in the Internet Society: Culture, Psychology and Gender, K. Morgan, J. Sanchez, C. A. Brebbia & A Voiskounsky (Editors) © 2004 WIT Press, www.witpress.com, ISBN 1-85312-726-4

[23] Joinson, A. Causes and implication of disinhibited behavior on the Internet. *Psychology and the Internet: intrapersonal, interpersonal, and transpersonal implications*, ed. J. Gackenbach, Academic Press: San Diego: pp. 43-60, 1998.

[24] D'Ovidio, R. and Doyle, J. A study on cyberstalking: Understanding investigative hurdles. *FBI Law Enforcement Bulletin*, **72 (3)**, pp. 9-17, 2000.

[25] Leiblum, S. & Döring, N. Internet sexuality: Known risks and fresh chances for women. *Sex and the Internet: A guidebook for clinicians,* ed. A. Cooper, Brunner-Routledge: New York, pp. 19-45, 2002.

[26] Kennedy, T. An exploratory study of feminist experiences in cyberspace. *CyberPsychology and Behavior,* **3**, pp. 707-719, 2000.

[27] Spitzberg, B. & Hoobler, B. Cyberstalking and the technologies of interpersonal terrorism. *New Media & Society*, **4(1),** pp. 71-92, 2002.

[28] Ybarra, M. Linkages between depressive symptomatology and Internet harassment among young regular Internet users. *CyberPsychology and Behavior,* **7**, pp. 247-257, 2004.

Human Perspectives in the Internet Society: Culture, Psychology and Gender, K. Morgan, J. Sanchez, C. A. Brebbia & A Voiskounsky (Editors) © 2004 WIT Press, www.witpress.com, ISBN 1-85312-726-4

Gender and IT: do stereotypes persist?

C. Lang & T. Hede
School of Information Technology, Swinburne University of Technology, Melbourne, Australia

Abstract

The media depiction of IT users being predominately male was reported by Ware and Stuck in their 1985 paper "Sex-role messages vis-à-vis microcomputer use: a look at pictures". Much has been written in the intervening years about gender and IT, and in a climate of declining proportional representation of women in IT, the effect of media portrayals is recognised as a powerful yet under-investigated influence on career choice. This paper replicates part of Ware and Stuck's study to report whether stereotyping of computer and IT use in teenage magazines persists. Current statistical information on gender and IT enrolments in Australian secondary schools and higher education institutions is presented, as well as the findings of the analysis of pictorial representations of IT use and application in teenage magazines. This Australian study found that pictorial representations in advertisements and articles in computing magazines are gender-balanced and did not find the stereotypical representations that were evident in 1985. However, stereotypes appear to persist in gaming advertisements and the absence of depictions of computer use or advertisements in the most popular girls magazines could be construed as stereotyping of IT as male.
Keywords: information technology (IT), gender stereotypes, media.

1 Introduction

In 1985 Ware and Stuck [18] analysed the pictorial representation of men, women, boys and girls in popular computer magazines and concluded that stereotypical portrayals were evident. Their longitudinal analysis of three personal computer (PC) magazines found that men were depicted twice as often as women, women were overrepresented as clerical workers and sex objects, and that men were more likely to be represented as managers, experts and repair

Human Perspectives in the Internet Society: Culture, Psychology and Gender, K. Morgan, J. Sanchez, C. A. Brebbia & A Voiskounsky (Editors) © 2004 WIT Press, www.witpress.com, ISBN 1-85312-726-4

technicians. Women were more often depicted in a passive role while men were depicted more often in a position of authority. Importantly, only women were shown as sex objects [18]. While they did not make a causal connection between computer magazine portrayals and the reluctance of girls to pursue IT careers, a concern was expressed about continued stereotypical representation of IT as a male domain as a contributing factor to this perceived reluctance. This current study conducted almost twenty years later, analysed pictorial representations in the two most popular computing magazines in Australia. This initial analysis raised questions regarding readership demographics and led to the study being widened to include an analysis of the two most popular teenage-girl magazines. The purpose of replicating Ware and Stuck's methodology was to determine if mass-market magazines are still stereotyping information technology (IT) as a male domain through their pictorial representations in 2003, just as they were in 1985. The influence of stereotypical representation of IT in the media, and its effect on the career choices of young females will be discussed.

The field of IT continues to be more attractive to males than females in 2004, just as it was in 1985, despite many programs in USA [7], Australia [6], and UK [8] that were implemented and funded by governments, universities and various other bodies to reverse or ameliorate the male dominance of the discipline. These programs included advertising and promotional materials to attract females to the discipline, as well as other marketing strategies. Many have targeted females in secondary schools and produced short-term gains in enrolments or perceived changes in attitudes, but none of the programs have grown to be self-sustaining and reversed the current trend, as indicated by the enrolment statistics presented in the next section. The trend of females not embracing IT to the same extent as males is contrary to trends in higher education in general. In most western countries females are the majority on campus, and in recent years, are more than half the new enrolments in previously male-dominated disciplines, such as Medicine, Law and Veterinary Science [2].

Several reasons have been put forward as contributing factors to the gender imbalance of the IT discipline, and stereotypical media representation is one of them. This paper will present an overview of current enrolment statistics in IT in secondary and higher education in Australia as well as discuss the media's influence in perpetrating stereotypes. In presenting the results of this study, some observations will be made regarding the implications of the findings and suggestions for further research.

2 The gender imbalance in IT in Australian education

The proportion of girls studying IT at both tertiary and senior secondary school level in Australia is in decline. The Victorian statistics for the senior secondary school courses named Information Technology show both a decline in numbers of students studying IT (from 64000 in 1994 to 54000 in 2003), and a decline in the proportion of girls enrolled in these subjects [16]. The proportion of girls enrolling in IT courses has declined from 48.1% of the student enrolments in 1994 to 32% in 2003 [16]. In higher education, proportionally fewer females

Human Perspectives in the Internet Society: Culture, Psychology and Gender, K. Morgan, J. Sanchez, C. A. Brebbia & A Voiskounsky (Editors) © 2004 WIT Press, www.witpress.com, ISBN 1-85312-726-4

than males are selecting IT courses, but unlike secondary schools, the actual numbers of girls choosing IT has increased.

The broad classification provided by the Department of Education and Training (DETYA) divides the discipline into the four main areas of Computer Science and Information Systems General (CS & IS Gen) not including Business Data Processing, Computer Science (CS), Information Systems (IS), and CS & IS Other (CS & IS other) [2]. Figure 1 provides a closer look at higher education participation figures in the each of the categories of the discipline over a ten-year period.

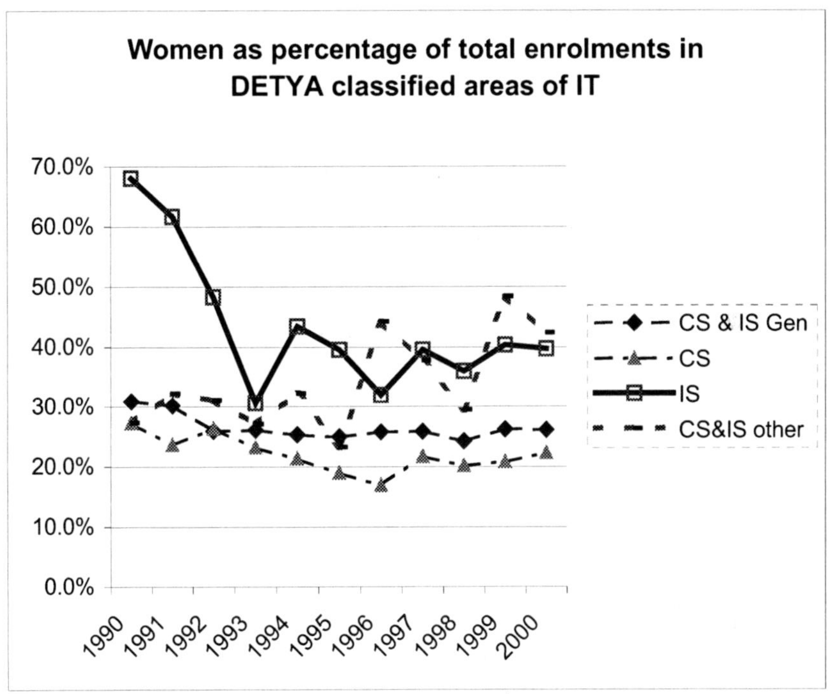

Figure 1: Proportional enrolments of women.

While proportional participation by women has fluctuated within the specialisations of the discipline (Figure 1), men are increasingly attracted to these degree courses at a much greater rate than women. The graph indicates a marked decline in the participation of women in IS yet in reality the actual number of women enrolled almost tripled (927 in 1990 to 2,599 in 2000), but male participation increased at a much greater rate (1,077 in 1990 to 5,625 in 2000). The proportional participation of women in Computer Science (CS) has declined by several percentage points, while in fact once again the number of women have more than doubled (1,084 in 1990 to 2,694 in 2000) [2]. These statistics display a trend of gendered differentiation in enrolment in IT, and raise

Human Perspectives in the Internet Society: Culture, Psychology and Gender, K. Morgan, J. Sanchez, C. A. Brebbia & A Voiskounsky (Editors) © 2004 WIT Press, www.witpress.com, ISBN 1-85312-726-4

the concern that some female secondary school students may be closing doors to potentially rewarding IT careers at an early age. Girls are choosing IT courses in higher education in greater numbers than the past, but still well below the number of boys that are attracted to the discipline.

The reasons why girls are not choosing IT courses to the same extent as boys are not clearly evident. While a direct causal link between pictorial representations of people in IT and career choice cannot be proven, accepting that the media appears to have a great influence on affecting student career choice is gaining currency in the literature [7,8,14] and is a premise assumed by this research. The influence of the media in creating and perpetuating gender stereotypes is discussed in the next section.

3 Media and gender stereotypes

There is a need for more detailed analysis of the factors that encourage an interest in the IT discipline and what part the media play in creating perceptions about the career path by replicating stereotypes. Ware and Stuck found that computer magazines are predominately produced by males, for males, and portray the images of males using, designing and spending their leisure time on computers [18]. Recently Margolis and Fisher concluded that non-computer teenage magazines produced for boys have many more advertisements for computers than those published for the teenage girl market [7]. The effect of these portrayals and the effect of popular film and television characters portraying female lawyers and doctors with equal status and power to their male counterparts ("*Legally Blonde*", "*ER*") on influencing young girls' career choices also needs further investigation. Stewart-Miller claimed that the power of the media is very important in helping young females identify with a sub-culture, and in perpetuating the gendered nature of IT being male [14].

A recent study in the UK of the ICT (Information and Communications Technology) industry concluded that

> "The image of the ICT industry amongst the general public may well be shaped by media influences. The two sectors most commonly mentioned as desirable to work in are portrayed in popular television dramas, such as Ally McBeal, This Life, E.R., Casualty, etc. There is a lack of similar positive role models for the ICT industry on popular media." p. 5 [8].

The same report emphasised the importance of promoting role models of every day people with difficult circumstances who have been successful in IT, to ameliorate common perceptions of IT as a male industry [8]. Susskind [15] suggested that to counteract all existing stereotypes there needs to be affirmative action in portrayals. This USA based research found that "children expect people to act in a stereotypical manner"[15], p. 492, and concluded that to increase "gender flexibility" children need to regularly see both sexes participating in non-traditional roles [15].

Human Perspectives in the Internet Society: Culture, Psychology and Gender, K. Morgan, J. Sanchez, C. A. Brebbia & A Voiskounsky (Editors) © 2004 WIT Press, www.witpress.com, ISBN 1-85312-726-4

Jewell reported in an Australian study that "Females appear to be rejecting involvement in information technology not because of their perception of what it is but because of what it is not" [6], p.301. Their perception of what it is not (personal, human contact etc) is supported by media portrayals of IT being a haven for geeks and nerds [14]. Jewell surveyed five hundred Australian female undergraduates in 2000 about their attitude to IT, and 25% stated that they were misinformed and that with better information they would have chosen IT careers [6]. It is assumed that misinformation came from a variety of sources, including the popular media.

Researchers give argument to the need for aggressive counter-stereotypical marketing by IT bodies, governments and universities to entice more girls study IT [7, 8], but as Susskind concluded, any interventions may be a "drop in a bucket" because stereotyping of gender does not occur "in a vacuum". There is a need for sustained and covert interventions over long time periods [15].

Morrison and Shaffer investigated gender perceptions and the influence of stereotypical portrayals in advertisements [9]. Their "gender-role congruence model" predicted the effectiveness of advertisements based on gender-role orientation of viewers. This research added validity to the argument that IT vendors market to boys and males because they are their major consumers. Newman et al. [11] investigated patterns in children who were considered comfortable with their gender, and how they reacted to computers. This research concluded "Gender constant girls with high levels of gender knowledge liked working with computers less than participants in any other subgroup" [11], p. 337. The authors posited that changing negative attitudes based on gender schemata is a complicated and involved process [11], p. 338. Supporting this position, Bouchard and St-Amant [1] found that girls resist stereotyping to a greater degree than males (44% compared with 88%) and those from families that are inclined to less social conformity, often experience greater success. They recommend that education encourage girls and boys to critically challenge gender assignations and assumptions [1].

These studies support the premise that stereotypical representations influence children's behaviour and choices. There is considerable evidence of stereotypical representations in the media of IT being a male domain [7,14,18]. This is considered a contributing factor to the reasons why girls are not choosing IT to the same extent as boys [6,8]. Our study will investigate whether these stereotypical portrayals are still evident in popular mass-market magazines in 2003.

4 Research design

The methodology defined by Ware and Stuck [18] was replicated as much as possible. This required analysing a selection of computing magazines to count and classify the number of pictorial representations of people and IT presented in both advertisements and articles. There was some deviation from their original methodology as will be explained. A longitudinal analysis of IT magazines was excluded, because the initial two editions analysed were determined to be typical

Human Perspectives in the Internet Society: Culture, Psychology and Gender, K. Morgan, J. Sanchez, C. A. Brebbia & A Voiskounsky (Editors) © 2004 WIT Press, www.witpress.com, ISBN 1-85312-726-4

of the medium, based on the experience of the researchers. After this initial analysis and a discussion about the demographic profile of the typical reader, teenage-girl magazines were added to the study to determine if they contributed to the stereotypical portrayal of IT being a male domain. The researchers had a lack of familiarity with teenage-girl magazines, and so a longitudinal analysis was carried out because it could not be determined if the two initial editions analysed were typical of the medium.

The magazine titles were selected from the readership results for the year ending 2003. This was obtained from the website of a large research survey company in Australia, Roy Morgan Research [12]. The two highest selling magazines marketed for teenage girls were easily identified, as were the most popular personal computer (PC) magazines. The PC magazines reached more than 670,00 readers in 2003, the teenage-girl magazines had a readership of more than one million in the same year. The four magazine titles selected were clearly the most popular of their genre [12].

After an initial analysis of the magazines to classify the categories of portrayals as provided by Ware and Stuck (expert, manager, clerical, teacher, learner, repair technician, game player, sales, sex object), additional "Game Setting" and "Game Character" categories were added to allow a more accurate classification. Several sweeps were taken through each magazine (total pages = 1987). The first to identify pages with IT and human beings (or human body parts). The first researcher then took a second sweep to classify each representation. The second researcher classified each representation without being aware of the first researcher's results. Finally a joint comparison of classifications was undertaken to compare, affirm and deal with discrepancies between the classifications. This will be discussed in more details in the following section.

5 Results

In this section a detailed description of media portrayals in magazines will be presented. Where possible demographic profiles of magazine purchasers will also be provided.

5.1 PC magazines

Australian *PC User* is the highest selling personal computing (PC) magazine in Australia with a reader profile that is 80% male, the majority of whom are in managerial positions, work full time and have a home personal computer [12]. Only seven advertisements or articles pictured people and computers. Of these there were slightly more males depicted than females. Two males and one female were in obvious managerial positions, one female student and one male clerical worker were also depicted. The group depictions showed an apparent Internet savvy family and a group of young upwardly mobile shoppers keenly waiting for a sale to start. The second magazine analysed, *PC World*, is the second highest selling PC magazine in Australia [12]. A readership profile was not available.

Human Perspectives in the Internet Society: Culture, Psychology and Gender, K. Morgan, J. Sanchez, C. A. Brebbia & A Voiskounsky (Editors) © 2004 WIT Press, www.witpress.com, ISBN 1-85312-726-4

This magazine had many more depictions of people than the previous one analysed, and slightly more females than males depicted (by one). Men were depicted in business settings only once more than women, two boys were depicted (game players) and one girl (student). A game advertorial portrayed female combatants with overly accentuated curvaceous body images. On two occasions females could be construed as sex objects (i.e. only there for their smile (keyboard advertisement) or their body (screen shot of female sportswoman) but this was not consensus between the two researchers. Ware and Stuck's definition of sex object is someone who appears to be in the picture for his/her sexual or physical characteristics [18]. One researcher (male) believed this classification could be applied to a young male in an advertisement, the depiction of which was accepted and overlooked by the other researcher (female). After discussion it was agreed that the only agreed sex-object portrayal was the female sportswoman.

5.2 Teenage-girls magazines

Dolly is the highest selling teenage girl magazine in Australia with a readership of 463,000 in 2003 [12]. Six issues were analysed from January 2003 to January 2004. In all issues there were at least three pages of advertisements for ring tones and images for mobile phones, but no depiction of computer use at all. There was one editorial on 'cam girls' which interviewed girls who use web pages for diaries including a warning and story of one who was murdered. Two issues of *Girlfriend*, the second most popular teenage-girl magazine were analysed producing almost identical results. There was however one profile of a young girl who maintained her own web page, but at no time was there a depiction of a girl using or buying a computer or computer part.

6 Discussion

The outcome of this analysis is that males and females are depicted as IT users and buyers in almost equal numbers in PC magazines, and that there is no pictorial representation of IT use in any of the teenage girl magazines. There was repetition of advertisements in the PC magazines. Both PC magazines depicted males and females in positions of power (i.e. managerial, or in control), however only young males were depicted as game players. As previously mentioned, there was a disagreement on the classification of a male in an advertisement being construed as a sex object, indicating the uncritical acceptance of males in computing advertisements by the first researcher (female).

6.1 Game Representations

As noted earlier, additional categories of "Game Character" and "Game Scene" were added to the original Ware & Stuck classifications. In the PC magazines examined, several depictions of computer game characters and computer game settings occurred. Game setting and character depictions were generally militaristic in nature. One advertisement for a computer sound system showed a

Human Perspectives in the Internet Society: Culture, Psychology and Gender, K. Morgan, J. Sanchez, C. A. Brebbia & A Voiskounsky (Editors) © 2004 WIT Press, www.witpress.com, ISBN 1-85312-726-4

squad of soldiers attacking a fortification. One magazine showed a scene from the popular game "*Grand Theft Auto: Vice City*", with the avatar armed with a large pump-action shotgun stalking the city streets. A third depiction had two female soldiers armed with large weapons, dressed in futuristic body armour, with bare midriffs and exaggerated physiques (large breasts, minimal waist).

A number of studies have shown that game preference and console ownership are gender biased toward males [5]. Games remain a largely male-dominated domain, and the media depiction in the magazines sampled would seem to correlate with this perception: the only female game characters present are both armed and sexualised. However, recent data released by the Interactive Digital Software Association in the U.S. has shown that the number of female game players is approaching 39% [10], although many of the games played (such as Hearts and Solitaire) are outside the milieu of the corporate game industry. There was an absence of any IT or console game advertisements in any of the issues of the teenage girl magazines.

6.2 Absence of representation in teenage girl magazines

As noted in the findings, there were only two depictions of IT use in the teenage girl magazines. On a second sweep through these magazines it was noted that their main focus was fashion and popular culture. While there was an absence of depiction of other careers, there is much implication of possibilities. Each of the magazines had at least three pages of advertisements for mobile phone and ring tones, and many of the contests in the magazines had mention of entering via the Internet. This confirms earlier studies that girls use IT almost in equal numbers to boys, but their use is primarily as a communication tool [8, 7, 14]. The teenage-girl magazine cannot be overlooked as a medium to reach girls and raise their awareness of IT as a potential career path.

7 Conclusion

This research replicated the Ware and Stuck research from 1985 to determine if gender bias was still evident in selected print media in 2003. While there was evidence of some stereotypical representations of females in the new category of games, the depiction of males and females in IT magazines was found to be almost equal with no obvious stereotypical representations. Both genders were depicted as users and purchasers. The results of this research imply that there is a more balanced depiction of males and females as users, managers and purchasers of IT products in 2003 than in 1985. This could be a reflection of a more enlightened society as well as a result of equal opportunity laws and policies in advertising. The magazine readership profiles indicate that few girls read PC magazines and in games advertisements, advertisers are responding to a market driven economy. The lack of game playing advertisements in the teenage girl magazines does not reflect the growing popularity of this activity with young girls. The paucity of portrayals of IT use or advertisements in teenage-girl magazines highlights that there is a potential for using this medium to lift the

Human Perspectives in the Internet Society: Culture, Psychology and Gender, K. Morgan, J. Sanchez, C. A. Brebbia & A Voiskounsky (Editors) © 2004 WIT Press, www.witpress.com, ISBN 1-85312-726-4

profile of IT as a career option for young women. It implies that more aggressive advertising could be employed to attract females to the discipline, as recommended by the MORI study in 2001 [8].

This research only scratches the surface of the role of media in influencing future career paths and could be extended to include film and television portrayals. There is a potential for further investigation into the increasing participation of girls in the gaming genre. The title of this paper asks if gender stereotypes persist. The answer from this study is not clear-cut. While there is not the clear stereotypical portrayals that Ware and Stuck found, the stereotypes are portrayed in gaming advertisements, and the absence of IT advertisements or promotion in teenage girl magazines could be construed as a product of stereotyping embedded in society's beliefs that IT is male and not of interest to young girls.

References

[1] Bouchard P. & St-Amant J-C. Gender identities and school success. *Alberta Journal of Educational Research AJER* XLVI /66, p.281, 2000.

[2] DETYA Higher *Education Students Time Series Tables 2000* Commonwealth of Australia, Canberra, 2001.

[3] Gansmo, H., J., Fun and Play: Design, marketing and use of New Media entertainment by and for women and girls, Report *to the European Commission Information Society Technology*, URL: http://www.rcss.ed.ac.uk/sigis/public/displaydoc/full/D08_03, Accessed 30 March 2004.

[4] Interactive Digital Software Association, "Essential Facts About the Computer and Video Game Industry: 2003 Sales, Usage and Demographic Data", 2003, URL: http://www.theesa.com/EF2003.pdf, Accessed 30 March 2004.

[5] Herr, A., ~~Girls~~ Women Just Want to Have Fun – A Study of Adult Female Players of Digital Games, Published in Marinka Copier & Joost Raessens (eds.): *Level Up: Digital Games Research Conference Proceedings.* Utrecht: Universiteit Utrecht, pp270-285, 2003.

[6] Jewell, H., Female involvement in Information Technology degrees: perception, expectation and enrolment. *ACIS Conference Proceedings*, 2001.

[7] Margolis, J. &Fisher, A. *Unlocking the clubhouse: Women in computing.* Cambridge, Massachusetts, USA: The MIT Press. 2002.

[8] MORI (Market & Opinion Research International). Image of ICT for e-Skills NTO. 2001.

[9] Morrison, M.M.& Shaffer, D.R. Gender-role congruence and self-referencing as determinants of advertising effectiveness. *Sex Roles: A journal of research* vol. 49, p.265-276, 2003.

[10] Taylor, T.L., Multiple Pleasures: Women and Online Gaming. *Convergence*, Vol. 9, No.1, 21-46, Spring 2003.

Human Perspectives in the Internet Society: Culture, Psychology and Gender, K. Morgan, J. Sanchez, C. A. Brebbia & A Voiskounsky (Editors) © 2004 WIT Press, www.witpress.com, ISBN 1-85312-726-4

[11] Newman, L.S., Cooper, J. & Ruble, D.N. The interactive effects of knowledge and constancy on gender-stereotyped attitudes. (Gender and Computers, part 2). *Sex Roles: A journal of Research* vol.33, p.325-352, 1995.
[12] Roy Morgan Research Polls, Roy Morgan readership results for the year ending June 2003, Article No. 271, August 25. URL: http://www.roymorgan.com/news/press-releases/2003/271/index.cfm. Accessed 23 December 2003.
[13] SIGCSE Bulletin, *inroads: Women in Computing,* vol.34, no. 2, June, 2002.
[14] Stewart Miller, M., *Cracking the gender code: who rules the wired world.* Pluto Press, Sydney, 2002.
[15] Susskind, J.E. Children's perception of gender-based illusory correlations: enhancing pre-existing relationships between gender and behaviour. *Sex Roles: A Journal of Research* vol. 483 no.12, 2003.
[16] VCAA 2003, Research Branch research.vcaa@edumail.vic.gov.au
[17] Wardle, C & Burton L, 'Programmatic efforts encouraging women to enter the Information Technology workforce' SIGCSE *Bulletin*, vol.34, no.2, pp. 27-31, 2002.
[18] Ware, M.C. & Stuck, M.F., Sex-role messages vis-à-vis microcomputer use: a look at the pictures *Sex Roles,* vol.13 no.3/4, pp. 205-214, 1985.

Magazines used in study:
Dolly ACP Publishing, Sydney, Australia. Editions: 382,388,389,391,392,399.
Girlfriend Pacific Publications, NSW, Australia. Editions: Feb.2003, Jan.2004.
PC User ACP Publishing, Sydney, Australia. Vol.16 No.1.
PC World IDG Communications Pty. Ltd. NSW, Australia. January 2004.

Human Perspectives in the Internet Society: Culture, Psychology and Gender, K. Morgan, J. Sanchez, C. A. Brebbia & A Voiskounsky (Editors) © 2004 WIT Press, www.witpress.com, ISBN 1-85312-726-4

Section 9
Cyber society norms and values

Understanding cultural and national identity in teleworking and electronic communication

Z. Mustafa
University of Science and Technology, Jordan

Abstract

The goal of this research project is to study the computer mediated interactions between teams and individuals from extremely diverse cultural and linguistic backgrounds. In particular, the study aims at determining the sets of activities, behaviors and attitudes that are most conducive to positive or successful computer mediated cross cultural interactions between teams from highly diverse cultural and linguistic backgrounds. The research question is addressed by a project where representative groups from populations of Jordan and Norway interact together in computer mediated environments. The participants are second year students majoring in Computer Science from Jordan University of Science and Technology in Jordan and Bergen University in Norway. The data on which this study is based consists of two parts. The first part was collected through questionnaires measuring technology attitude, personality, and feeling of team cohesion among group members. The second part consists of records of online chatting between the members of the Jordanian and Norwegian teams on predetermined topics. The results suggest that there would appear to be some cultural differences between the subjects from Norway and Jordan. The main difference would appear to be linked with early family life and experience. Obviously this was a preliminary study but the results do suggest that online cultural differences might be linked to differences in family structures and behaviors and not necessarily to differences in education or language.
Keywords: teleworking, electronic communication, cultural diversity, computer attitudes, chatting, foreign language.

1 Introduction

Much of the existing literature on computer based interaction in online distance learning (ODL) and computer supported cooperative working (CSCW) is based on scenarios which involve individuals with a common culture or a common

Human Perspectives in the Internet Society: Culture, Psychology and Gender, K. Morgan, J. Sanchez, C. A. Brebbia & A Voiskounsky (Editors) © 2004 WIT Press, www.witpress.com, ISBN 1-85312-726-4

language. It can be argued that even those studies which have involved cross-cultural interactions, for example the Copernicus projects within the European Union (EU), have enforced what we will call a "Single Language Single Culture" (SLSC) medium. In such SLSC environments participants are restricted to using a computer mediated system in a particular way, which is culturally biased towards the culture of the designers of the system in terms of direction of written text and icons used for actions. Furthermore, participants are usually forced to interact and "think" using a single language which may or may not be their own mother tongue. Such scenarios give native English speakers an advantage, and this is often shown in terms of higher scores and "superior" performance indicators. In comparison, very little research has been performed to investigate the factors involved when the culture and language of collaborators are dramatically different. Investigations into computer mediated interactions between dramatically diverse cultures and languages are felt to be important because as the world becomes increasingly connected by data and communication networks, the future of computer mediated human-human interaction in both education and teleworking will involve collaborations between individuals and teams from increasingly diverse cultural and linguistic backgrounds.

There has been a considerable body of research conducted on learning or acquiring cultures within the fields of psychology, sociology and anthropology. Some of the more recent studies have looked at the role of learning in relation to new technology [9]. These works propose that some of the fundamental tools for cultural indoctrination within a society are the very things found in computer systems. Things such as the use of games, textile patterns and interactive devices. Researchers have recognized that these are the very things that make computing a culture of its own [5] and make computing so addictive to many individuals [8]. Some researchers have even proposed that computing has changed our perceptions of reality and continues to do so [3]. Terms like 'Virtual reality' have now been commonly adopted into western technological cultures, where they would have been quite outside such shared 'cultural reality' only 20 years ago.

Some of the earliest work in the area of designing computer communications technology for undeveloped cultures investigated how different cultures handled technological innovation [9]. These studies found that there was no consistent way in which cultures reacted to changes to technology, but rather each reacted in a unique and unpredictable way, depending on factors such as geographical position, wealth, education, environment and culture. There are more applied suggestions for the design of computer interfaces [9], but these concentrate on rather superficial changes to the medium and do not attempt to support or respect different cultures. In a similar way, some researchers have developed some simple guidelines for the minor changes to the ergonomic design of computer systems required by these populations [11]. More recently researchers in the field of media advertising have investigated the methods of advertising to different emerging cultures. In addition to the research being conducted on how to design effective advertising campaigns, there are companies providing

Human Perspectives in the Internet Society: Culture, Psychology and Gender, K. Morgan, J. Sanchez, C. A. Brebbia & A Voiskounsky (Editors) © 2004 WIT Press, www.witpress.com, ISBN 1-85312-726-4

expertise on the many business issues involved with these emerging cultures and their huge populations of potential customers [2]. The European Union 'Erasmus' program of funding has produced several Masters degree education programs aimed at training business executives on the cultural differences they can expect to find when doing business with emerging countries [6]. In contrast, there is currently little research being conducted into assessing the likely cultural impact of this new technology on the existing ancient cultures of native indigenous peoples. Such a study of the attitudes of indigenous people towards these new mediums and the likely impact of the new technologies would form part of this study.

All the problems that we have discussed with regard to technological change are multiplied when we consider technological introductions into less developed cultures. There are many examples where technological introductions into less advanced cultures have produced social and economic disasters for the indigenous peoples [10]. Thankfully there is now recognition, at least among academics, that when dealing with less technologically developed cultures, there is a vital need to respect the local value belief systems [8]. If this is not done then the consequences can be drastic changes to parts of the social structure. Researchers who have specialized in this area of technological introduction have reported that no aspect of the culture is immune when more advanced technology is introduced into these less technologically advanced societies. Even the political culture is influenced by technology and innovation [8]. In order for the introduction to be successful, seven components have been identified to be vital to effective future development. They are need identification, appropriate resources, correct technology, social conscience, integrity, attitude and problem solving [1]. However, we should not think that the role of new technology is all bad, technology has been shown to break cultural biases that exist in communities [4]. On a more practical level, researchers who have investigated how to change negative attitudes towards technology in less advanced cultures have found that the school teachers attitudes are vital in determining their students own attitudes towards new technology [7]. It is interesting to note that this finding is identical to that reported as the determining factor for computer phobia.

We have reviewed the existing literature on technology and its affects on the development and education of the individual. We have seen that technology has a huge affect on the self-image that each of us possesses and how we interact with the world around us. When our whole environment is pervaded with advanced technology, we need to work not just for communication systems which are easy to use but also communication systems which project a positive self image on users from all cultures who come into contact with them. This issue is the focus of this study, where we will investigate and determine those factors which lead to successful cross-cultural communication using these new technologies.

2 The study

The goal of this project was to study the computer mediated interactions between

Human Perspectives in the Internet Society: Culture, Psychology and Gender, K. Morgan, J. Sanchez, C. A. Brebbia & A Voiskounsky (Editors) © 2004 WIT Press, www.witpress.com, ISBN 1-85312-726-4

teams and individuals from extremely diverse cultural and linguistic backgrounds. In particular, the study aimed to determine the sets of activities, behaviors and attitudes that are most conducive to positive or successful computer mediated cross cultural interactions between teams from highly diverse cultural and linguistic backgrounds. The research questions were to be investigated through a project where representative groups from Jordan and Norway interact together in computer mediated environments. These questions were addressed in a controlled manner which permits the systematic manipulation of the cultural differences represented among the subject populations available. This allows our experimental conditions to closely match the set of real-world situations faced by international commerce and education. First, we identified the sets of characteristics in pre-exposure surveys which we find reported as being associated with positive or successful interactions in the computer based communication. Then, we determined those sets of behaviors and attitudes which were felt by all participants to be directly involved in successful cross cultural computer based interaction.

2.1 Participants

The participants in this study were two groups of second year university students majoring in computer science. They come from two countries which are extremely different linguistically and culturally. The first group consists of 19 students from Jordan University of Science and Technology in Irbid-Jordan. Their mother tongue is Arabic, but they studied English as a foreign language for at least eight years at school. In addition, they have to take one, two, or three courses in English for science and technology at the university level depending on their score in the university English placement test given to all first year students. Moreover, most of their university courses involve a lot of English specially their computer courses in which all the programming is done in English. The second group consists of 11 students from the University of Bergen in Bergen-Norway. Their mother tongue is Norwegian, and they study English as a foreign language for at least 5 years at school. Although some of their textbooks are in English, most of the instruction they receive and all the programming they do is in Norwegian.

It should be mentioned that all the participants reported that they are familiar with using computers since they have to use them for their courses and with Microsoft Hotmail MSN Messenger since they use it for chatting in English in their own time. It is also worth mentioning that the two countries to which the participants belong; Norway and Jordan, are extremely diverse culturally. Jordan is a third world country in the Middle East with Muslim traditional population who speak Arabic, while Norway is a Scandinavian industrial country with Christian or unaffiliated liberal population who speak Norwegian. However, in both countries English is taught and used as a foreign language.

2.2 Design of the experimental method

The experimental method was designed to control observation of interactions

Human Perspectives in the Internet Society: Culture, Psychology and Gender, K. Morgan, J. Sanchez, C. A. Brebbia & A Voiskounsky (Editors) © 2004 WIT Press, www.witpress.com, ISBN 1-85312-726-4

between teams of individuals from diverse linguistic and cultural backgrounds. The participants were given a clear idea about the study and responded to three questionnaires on personality, technology attitudes and team cohesion before they interacted with their counterparts. The interaction between the two teams took place in two computer mediated communication laboratories in which Microsoft Hotmail MSN messenger software was available, and the communication was through chatting in real time.

2.3 Pre-experimental measures

These measures include administering the following questionnaires to the Jordanian and Norwegian participants before they interact with their counterparts.

1. Technology attitudes questionnaire:
This questionnaire is divided into two parts. The first part consists of 22 questions dealing with the participants background and their feelings towards using items which involve technology e.g. computers, cars, stereos etc. The second part consists of 7 questions on early experiences with items involving technology. The items in the two parts require responses on a five-point scale.

2.Personality questionnaire (Thomas Killman's Conflict Inventory):
This questionnaire was designed to investigate how the participants deal with conflict. It consists of 30 items each consisting of two statements from which the participant has to choose the one which best describes his feelings or behavior.

3. Team cohesion questionnaire:
This questionnaire is divided into two parts. The first part consists of 9 items dealing with the participants feelings and their personal involvement with their team. The second part of the questionnaire consists of 9 items dealing with the participants' perception of their team as a whole. The items in the two parts require responses on a five-point scale.

It should be mentioned that all the questionnaires were in English and were piloted on 20 students from Amman University then modified according to the students' responses. The modifications included simplifying the vocabulary used and the scale. The new versions of the questionnaires were piloted again before it was administered to the Jordanian and Norwegian participants prior to their interaction with their counterparts.

2.4 Experimental session measures

Two computer mediated communication laboratories were assigned one at the University of Science and Technology in Jordan and one at the University of Bergen in Norway. These laboratories were equipped for the use of Microsoft Hotmail MSN messenger software. The computer mediated communication using Hotmail MSN messenger in the two laboratories was tested several times

Human Perspectives in the Internet Society: Culture, Psychology and Gender, K. Morgan, J. Sanchez, C. A. Brebbia & A Voiskounsky (Editors) © 2004 WIT Press, www.witpress.com, ISBN 1-85312-726-4

by the researchers and their assistants before the participants used it for online communication. In fact, the researchers themselves used Hotmail MSN messenger to discuss conducting the experiment.

2.5 Conducting the experiment

The computer laboratories in which the experiment was conducted were set in both Jordan and Norway, and the Hotmail MSN messenger software was ready to use. The students in the two countries were assigned special Hotmail accounts and given a special password. The researchers in the two countries and their assistants established the connection and did the invitation for the interaction. Each participant was given a set of instructions on how to proceed in the interaction and the researchers and their assistants provided help when needed. The two teams were divided into twelve groups, eight each consisting of one Jordanian and one Norwegian, and another four each consisting of two Jordanians and two Norwegians.

2.6 Task

Which of the following things do you regard as necessary, which not? Which of them are important for people living in a foreign country? What else might be important for them? Give reasons.

Public schools

Private schools

Free language classes to enable foreigner's children to succeed in school

Right to choose one's own education

Public libraries

Right to choose or change a job

Free radio, TV + press

Radio and TV programs in foreign languages

Free access to information

Privacy of the post

Active and passive right to vote for everyone living in the country

Right to join and found activist groups and political parties

Right to visit and found places to practice religion (churches, mosques etc.)

Subvention of public transport

Right to choose the place to live

Freedom to travel

Human Perspectives in the Internet Society: Culture, Psychology and Gender, K. Morgan, J. Sanchez, C. A. Brebbia & A Voiskounsky (Editors) © 2004 WIT Press, www.witpress.com, ISBN 1-85312-726-4

The interaction lasted among each team members for one hour. The script of the interaction was saved on floppy disks and printed so that the interaction can be analyzed.

3 Data analysis

The data analysis involved applying both qualitative methods and quantitative statistical methods. We analyzed the responses of the Jordanian group and the Norwegian group to the questionnaires on Technology Attitudes, Early Life Experiences, Thomas Killman's Conflict Inventory, and Team Cohesion. The responses of each group were analyzed first separately, and then the responses of the two groups were compared.

The online chats between the Jordanian and Norwegian participants were divided into chat logs each consisting of one utterance which could be a word (e.g. hi), a phrase (e.g. always on time), a sentence (e.g. what is your name?) or more than one sentence. Those chat logs were classified into six types of conversation acts, which are: initiating conversation, passive response, active response, clarification request, no response, and misunderstanding.

A Pearson correlation was performed on the study data using MiniTab Version 13.32. The Jordanian and Norwegian participants' responses to the items used in various questionnaires were correlated with each other, then with the types of conversation acts they used in their online communication. The correlation was performed to the data obtained from the Jordanian subjects separately from that obtained from the Norwegian subjects, then the results were compared.

It should be mentioned that although 30 subjects participated in the study, not all subjects completed all aspects of the questionnaires or online recordings because the participation was voluntary.

4 Results and discussion

The following correlations were found at the 0.05 significance level or better.

4.1 Impact of childhood and family life on later technology attitudes and proficiency

The results showed that childhood experiences affect adult technology attitudes and behavior as can be seen in (Table 1).

The figures in (Table 1) provide a clear evidence of the importance of childhood experiences in forming adult technology attitudes and behavior. It is obvious that those individuals who were given encouragement to explore machines and technology when they were children were significantly more likely to be confident and positive towards technology in adult life. For example, the item (I used to help my family repair equipment when I was a child), from Early Experiences Questionnaire, correlated with (1), (2) and (3) in the table above such that subjects who helped around the home as children were more likely to

Human Perspectives in the Internet Society: Culture, Psychology and Gender, K. Morgan, J. Sanchez, C. A. Brebbia & A Voiskounsky (Editors) © 2004 WIT Press, www.witpress.com, ISBN 1-85312-726-4

have an independent learning style, to enjoy finding out how things work, and to like working with machines in their adulthood. It also correlated with (4) and (5) such that if children were encouraged to help out around the house, they become more independent and competent with technology in their adult life. In addition, it correlated with personality score such that working with one's family when as a child is more likely to make the person a "team player" in later life.

Table 1: Impact of early childhood and family life on later technology attitudes and proficiency.

Technology attitudes and proficiency	Pearson Correlation with early childhood	Probability
1. Independence of learning style	-0.559	0.024
2. I enjoy finding out how things work.	0.477	0.062
3. I like to work with machines.	0.596	0.015
4. I like to repair machines.	0.689	0.003
5. I prefer to use the computer myself rather than have someone else use it for me.	0.689	0.003

Other items which have to do with family encouragement to explore machines include (my family made sure that broken equipment was repaired quickly) which correlated with (4). They also include (I was encouraged to explore how machines worked) which correlated with (3) and (2) such that subjects who were encouraged as children to explore how machines worked are more likely to enjoy finding out how things work as adults.

On the other hand, negative experiences with machines as children are likely to increase negative attitudes towards technology in later life and reduce overall technical ability when the person reaches adulthood. For example the item (I was at least mildly hurt by a machine in my childhood), from Early Experiences Questionnaire, correlated with (I dislike hobbies or activities which involve working with tools or equipment), (I dislike repairing machines) and (computers are too complicated for me to understand), from Technology Attitudes Questionnaire. It is clear that although it is a positive trait to encourage children to explore how machines and technology work it is extremely important that they do not have any negative experiences.

4.2 Self confidence and behavior using new technology

The analysis of the online communication between the Jordanian participants and the Norwegian participants provided a strong evidence that real world personality traits and behaviors were carried over into computer based communications. Although this could be expected, very little work has been done previously to empirically demonstrate that. For example, (Initiating conversations), from the chat logs, correlated with (independence of learning style), (I enjoy finding out how things work) and (I enjoy hobbies or activities which involve doing things in a specific order), from Technology Attitude Questionnaire. It is clear that subjects who initiated most conversations in online communications were also significantly more likely to have more independent learning styles, more interested in finding out how things work and enjoy

Human Perspectives in the Internet Society: Culture, Psychology and Gender, K. Morgan, J. Sanchez, C. A. Brebbia & A Voiskounsky (Editors) © 2004 WIT Press, www.witpress.com, ISBN 1-85312-726-4

hobbies or activities which involve doing things in a specific order. Also (I think computers can help me work better) correlated with (I want to be good at whatever I do). These correlations show that there was good internal consistency (reliability) within the data set. This is a positive indication that the subjects responded honestly and reliably throughout the surveys.

As for the scores from Thomas Killman's Conflict Inventory, it was found that a compromise score correlated with (Technology Attitudes Questionnaire) such that people who take a compromising communication style from the Thomas Killman's Conflict Inventory do not take a computer subject because it will improve their work performance, and further they do not want to be good at whatever they do. This could be indicating that these subjects do not want to be exceptional and, instead, wish to blend into the group. This behavior would match the "compromise" score from the Thomas Killman's Conflict Inventory.

It was also found subjects with a "Competitive" score from the Thomas Killman Conflict Inventory were in the category of "initiating conversation" in their online chats. This would match closely with what would be expected from competitive communicators. On the other hand, subjects with the most passive communication style received the most requests for clarification during online chat communications.

All of these correlations give strong indications that we have a good quality data set with reliable and valid answers.

4.3 Cross cultural differences

The comparison between Jordanian and Norwegian participants' responses to the various questionnaires and the correlations of these responses with their online communications revealed the following cross-cultural differences.

Table 2: Aspects of Norway-Jordan cross-cultural differences in online communications.

Aspects of Norway-Jordan differences	Pearson Correlation	Probability
1. Independent learning styles.	0.332	0.073
2. Taking computing subject because it lead to a better job.	-0.712	0.000
3. Being concerned with damaging the computer.	-0.337	0.069
4. Preferring humans to computers.	-0.622	0.000
5. Being concerned about looking silly when making a mistake while using the computer.	-0.560	0.001
6.Being concerned about looking silly if seen not knowing how to use the computer.	-0.416	0.022
7.Being encouraged to explore how machines worked as a child	-0.561	0.024
8.Initiating conversations in computer based chats.	-0.256	0.263

The data indicates that Jordanian participants had more independent learning styles. It also indicates that Norwegians are more likely to be taking a computing subject because they felt it leads to a better job, they are less concerned with damaging the computer and prefer humans to computers. However, they seem to be more concerned about looking silly if they make a mistake while using the computer or if they were seen not knowing how to use the computer. In addition, the data indicates that Norwegians were less likely to have been encouraged to explore how machines worked when they were children and were less likely to initiate conversations in computer based chats.

5 Conclusion

From these results there would appear to be some cultural differences between the subjects from Norway and Jordan. The main difference would appear to be linked with early family life and experience such that subjects in the Jordan group received more parental encouragement to explore technology and machines in their childhood. This has resulted in more positive attitudes towards technology in later life and more independent behavior in using online communication. Obviously, this was a preliminary study but the results do suggest that online cultural differences might be linked to differences in family structures and behaviors and not necessarily to differences in education or language.

References

[1] Dorsey, S.D. *et al,* The human development spectrum, Social *Indicator Research,* 21**(1)**, pp 93-110, 1989.

[2] Ferraro, G.P., *The Cultural Dimension of International Business*, Prentice Hall, Englewood Cliffs, 1990.

[3] Foster, D. & Meech, J.F., Social dimensions of virtual reality. Simulated and virtual realities: Elements of perception, eds. Carr et al, Taylor & Francis, 1995.

[4] Freedman, K. *et al,* The importance of computer experience, learning processes, and communication patterns in multicultural networking, Educational *Technology Research and Development,* 44 **(1)**, pp. 43-59,1996.

[5] Kafai, Y. & Resnick, M. (eds). *Constructionism in Practice: Designing, Thinking and Learning in a Digital World.* Lawrence Erlbaum, 1996.

[6] Magala, S.J, Cross-Cultural Studies, Msc Erasmus Exchange Program, Erasmu University, Rotterdam, 1998.

[7] Mordi, C. Factors associated with pupils' attitudes towards science in Nigerian primary schools, *Research in Science and Technological Education,* **91**, pp. 39-490, 1991.

[8] Morgan, K., Ethnic Diversity in Computer Based Interactions. Paper presentation, Crossroad in Cultural Studies 2nd Int. Conf., Tempere, Finland, 1998.

[9] Nielsen, J. (ed). *Designing User Interfaces for International Use*. Elsevier, 1990.

[10] Romalis, C. *et al* Sexism, racism, and technological change, *International Journal of Women's Studies, 6* **(3)**, pp. 270-287, 1983.

[11] Wang, Z., Strategies for ergonomics in developing countries. *Ergonomics.* **36 (6)** pp. 597-599. (1993).

Human Perspectives in the Internet Society: Culture, Psychology and Gender, K. Morgan, J. Sanchez, C. A. Brebbia & A Voiskounsky (Editors) © 2004 WIT Press, www.witpress.com, ISBN 1-85312-726-4

Handling paradoxes and uncertainty in virtual networks

J. Aderhold
Innovation Research and Sustainable Resource Management, Chemnitz University of Technology, Germany

Abstract

The euphoria initially experienced by the people in many virtual companies has now evaporated as, in the cold light of day, they are consciously reflecting on the phenomenon. They are turning back to traditional hierarchies although they still believe in values such as flexibility, self-organisation and personal responsibility. Yet the failing of many such virtual cooperations has less to do with the technical problems that are so often observed (although these are an important contributory factor); the greater problem is that many people can only cope with the insecurities of virtual structures to a certain degree, if indeed at all. These are precisely the problems we are going to examine here. We will begin by taking a closer look at the peculiarities of virtual companies – and we will see that they require a lot from everyone involved. Virtual companies develop particular characteristics of their own – characteristics that go hand-in-hand with a great deal of insecurity – that can only be resolved with great difficulty. It is well worth drawing upon the theory of self-organisation to throw some light on the problem here. On the basis of this theory, a four-phase model will be developed to show two things. Firstly, exactly where such insecurities come up and, secondly, how to interact with the insecurities that present themselves.
Keywords: computer, virtual business networks, self-organisation, dynamic, culture.

1 Introduction

With the infiltration of computer technology into our society, the world of computers is becoming an essential part of our everyday lives, both at home and at work [1, 2]. The density of data transfer is increasing in leaps and bounds –

Human Perspectives in the Internet Society: Culture, Psychology and Gender, K. Morgan, J. Sanchez, C. A. Brebbia & A Voiskounsky (Editors) © 2004 WIT Press, www.witpress.com, ISBN 1-85312-726-4

in such a way that any limitations in time or space appear to lose their significance. Additionally, computer based telecommunication has provided us with a new way of transporting data and information, so many more people than previously can be communicatively included in what is going on.

This has generated new room to manoeuvre and there are now more and more ways of interacting with any of the data entered which, consequently, demand new skills. This information overflow on the one hand has provided new data access options that require a greater obligation to select and, on the other hand, has brought about an enormous degree of networking through various technical, physical and social systems (stock exchanges for example, new ways of selling things and internet based discussion groups). These new information technology infrastructures have made possible the sending and transfer of information and data that is almost limitless and independent of time. Once such data has been entered into the network, which is accessible worldwide, it can find its way to, or be called up from, any location.

2 Computers – a blessing or a cause of insecurity?

Against this background it is not surprising that companies respond to these new opportunities by changing their organisational structure as they switch over to these networks. They are putting more and more of their money into being networked (both internally and externally) in order to better cope with the demands for flexibility and innovation in a dynamically changing world [3]. Such networked companies are becoming the central "carriers of information and the global economy" [4]. The victory march of computer technology has at the same time altered the cultural basis of our society [5]. Reality – something that has always been influenced by symbolic values – is being reflected in new ways by virtualisation processes. And this entails a reorganisation of culturally accepted forms of expression. The storage options are unlimited. So, for example, anyone interested in business can now get their information from inexhaustible sources. The marketing strategies of the competition or fine differentiations in customer behaviour can now be processed and strategically exploited for each interest group. Multimedia and pervasive computing create multifunctional machines out of the infrastructure of the PC that can be deployed in almost every communicative or perceptive environment.

2.1 The virtualisation of communication and business

In addition to the immense range of options for the storage and interpretation of information, another factor comes into play: networked computers increase the quantity of people who can be approached, as well as the "speed of connection between individual written communication" [6]. So computerisation of percepti-ons and communications is changing the standard processes and structures in the various systems within our society. In business, changes that are expressed by means of virtualisation are making their mark. According to Lanier [7], we are now involved with a technology, that has come out of computing, that is creating

Human Perspectives in the Internet Society: Culture, Psychology and Gender, K. Morgan, J. Sanchez, C. A. Brebbia & A Voiskounsky (Editors) © 2004 WIT Press, www.witpress.com, ISBN 1-85312-726-4

a new reality within the reality we have always had – and this has the effect of splitting reality. The virtual does not function as an opposite to the real – rather as an exploration of what is possible within the real and the material [8]. Yet computer technology and multimedia options constitute only the preconditions for these changes, they are not at the centre of the changes themselves. It is in fact the virtual technology that has come into being that constitutes the true core of the virtual society [9, 10]. But the stock levels of data and information remain irrelevant for as long as "they do not move into the individual or collective body of knowledge" [11].

2.2 The virtualisation option

Companies concern themselves principally, and more and more, with the opportunities provided by virtual communication. This has come about as an opposite pole to the expanding, growing, merging mega companies. The tried-and-tested organisational and work structures of industry are coming under pressure. People are beginning to call the traditionally valid communication and technical infrastructures into question. The restructuring of social and technical processes, the rapid and precise monitoring of market developments and the permanent search for competent and reliable partner companies should become the only constants in company decision making processes.

Such virtual companies, that are permanently restructuring themselves, set up "network-shaped cooperations for a limited period of time between several legally independent people or organisations for the purposes of fulfilling specific customer contracts" [12]. The new virtual company is now perceived as having no particular location, no fixed offices, no opening times, no organisation chart and no standard product. Virtuality uses coordination structures to handle – 24 hours round the clock – the tasks and projects of teams or individuals that are spread all over the world. This temporarily established combination of tasks comes together only at times when concrete projects need to be handled, when the "best possible know-how in terms of value to the customer can be provided". In terms of organisation, this means that, through the network provided by information technology, company or inter-company cooperations can be put into place that provide an "allocation of parts of the whole work process that is separate from any limitations of time and space" and allow for the creation of expertise in many locations and spheres of action [13].

The first consequences – that affect both the structure and the work of companies within such a cooperation – can now be seen [14]:

- Work on the same project that is staggered over time is made possible by means of data transfer that is not limited by time or distance.
- Particular functions that, until now, have been the preserve of middle management can be replaced by information technology in the form of data flow management. As a result companies can now dispense with several levels of management.
- With telework and telecooperation, it is no longer always necessary for employees to be physically present in a company. A further result of

Human Perspectives in the Internet Society: Culture, Psychology and Gender, K. Morgan, J. Sanchez, C. A. Brebbia & A Voiskounsky (Editors) © 2004 WIT Press, www.witpress.com, ISBN 1-85312-726-4

this is in the setting of time limits on cooperation agreements, which also affects other companies in their use of employees dedicated to particular tasks.

- The frontiers of a company are permanently on the move, depending on the circumstances. Previously fixed combinations are transformed into loose associations and the results of these connections are permanently being reassessed.

On this basis, groups of companies operating in consortium can reconfigure and combine production locations spread all over the world. The value creation chain is thus put into separate packages. The partial solutions and partial steps that have been temporarily found are carried out, in a course of events that passes through various locations, from the idea through the assembly stage to the marketing. This results in virtual companies that only actually exist in the period where the particular product concerned is made. The moment this specific, mutually driven production process ends, the virtual company dissolves and ceases to exist.

3 Virtual networks – a brave new world?

Are virtual companies the solution for companies who wish to successfully respond to the changing requirements of a dynamic marketplace? Davidov and Malone [15] claim that, in the face of ever more aggressive international competition and the anticipated forward thrust of technology, particularly in the area of computers, such a virtual revolution is unavoidable. Furthermore, the expectation is gaining credibility that everyone who does not sufficiently take the challenges of virtualised business into account is going to be left behind by the future development of business and society.

Even before deciding to back the virtual company route, however, those companies who have decided to adopt a wait and see attitude are visibly modifying the formal structure of their organisations. But the consequences of such a transformation are that it is precisely those people who are obliged to make adjustments that are used to drawing upon the routines of a hierarchically structured organisation for their job security [16]. This is difficult for them – and, indeed, also has consequences on the soundness of the virtual structures themselves. It is exactly this transformation from the secure, ordered organisation to the insecure world of virtual networks that brings enormous problems with it. For who is truly in a position to claim that they can still maintain an overview of what is happening from within such complex structures?

3.1 Dynamic response and self organisation

In science we are hearing more and more about a *revolution in thinking*. This revolution acknowledges a change that is taking place in the way we think about nature, how we live together and the world as a whole. We notice phenomena in a great many processes that organise themselves in terms of their own inherent logic. Independent of any initial conditions, environmental conditions and

Human Perspectives in the Internet Society: Culture, Psychology and Gender, K. Morgan, J. Sanchez, C. A. Brebbia & A Voiskounsky (Editors) © 2004 WIT Press, www.witpress.com, ISBN 1-85312-726-4

properties of the components involved, some surprising regulatory principles are generated out of such systems. One suspects that, independent of any primary influences that we already know, the established order is produced within such systems by means of structural patterns that organise themselves. Against this background, a new view of the world – the view of *self-organisation* – has come about [17]. Hermann Haken [18] is making an attempt to capture the primary factors that govern conformity to laws in the creation of order within complex structures by means of the theory of self-organisation. The process of the change in conditions from one stable set of system dynamics to another is termed a phase transfer. Such phase transfers within dynamic systems are well illustrated with the metaphor of a ball in a potential landscape. If the ball is located in a valley its condition is stable. If it moves through changing external parameters or the valley flattens itself, the ball is able to move over a mountain ridge and roll into another valley, i.e. it can take on another stable condition.

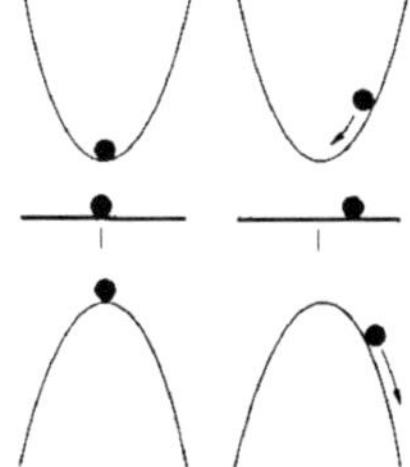

Figure 1: Three modes are presented here to reflect the principles of Haken's potential landscape.

On the mountain ridge, however, the ball is at a point of maximum instability, and it is here that the smallest causes can have the consequence that the ball is diverted towards one direction or another. If, at the same time, the environment is perceived as a changing *potential landscape* (one that incorporates a variety of potential and attractive factors) it then becomes clear that every mountain ridge is made up of various valleys which one can be drawn to (see figure 1).

At the top of the diagram, the ball is in a trough and thus has a stable equilibrium. In the middle, the ball is on an even surface and thus has an indifferent equilibrium. At the bottom, the ball is on an upside-down bowl with, consequently, what we can call an unstable equilibrium. Using the shaping of public opinion as an example, any unpredictable behaviour within a system in unstable situations becomes a lot clearer. And it is precisely here that, at critical moments, only small influences can bring about a U-turn in public opinion. This also demonstrates that rational, well-thought-through arguments often only play a subordinate role in such processes. Such collectively caused phenomena have almost nothing to do with objective criteria; they depend rather more on the subjective opinion that finally asserts itself within the collective environment. It is particularly in the continuously changing value creation frameworks of virtual

Human Perspectives in the Internet Society: Culture, Psychology and Gender, K. Morgan, J. Sanchez, C. A. Brebbia & A Voiskounsky (Editors) © 2004 WIT Press, www.witpress.com, ISBN 1-85312-726-4

networks that strict, rigid processes are the exception rather than the rule. Here we are more concerned with projects or individual cases (see figure 2), where rigid planning strategies are no longer effective. In networks – particularly in networks of project related expertise – the planning and structuring of fixed process sequences as well as the variety and nature of the tasks involved are not fixed.

Case type	Routine	Regular	Project	Individual
Degree of task complexity and variability	Very low	Low	High	Very high
Degree to which tasks can be planned and structured	Very high	High	Low	Very low
Degree of similarity and frequency	Very high, very frequent	High, frequent	Minimal, seldom	Very low
Degree to which process sequences can be fixed	Very high	High	Low	Very low

Figure 2: Process matrix after Nippa [19].

We can assume that each project will recruit new partners – over the total network in different combinations for particular tasks – who, for each case, have to generate a new, specific value creation process within the framework of their own production projects. Any other approach would mean dispensing with specific networking advantages, particularly in obtaining the best possible combination of expertise, as only the best partners should be brought together in such cases. It is only rarely that one can fall back on routines and, indeed, this author has found empirical evidence to indicate that the point in time for the planning of the work or production process is usually fixed shortly before the actual project work of those involved – at the beginning of the project phase and in consultation with a project manager. So it is logical that, in the process of the development of such network cooperations, there are constant challenges that come up – challenges that not only reveal a high degree of complexity, but also a kind of dynamic stability.

3.2 Dynamic response and control

As they have such a spontaneous and informal character, it is not at all easy to set up, to control or even to maintain a virtually structured network. For this reason, the question presents itself as to how contexts can be set up in which the individuals involved are granted the necessary room to manoeuvre. Here we need to say goodbye to the untenable view that structures exist that can be totally calculated and monitored. There is a wealth of preconditions that have to be fulfilled before networks can function. We presume that a characteristic of a suitable infrastructure can be seen in the maintenance and encouragement of informal relationships. Wenger and Snyder [20] describe this cultivation task as a "paradoxical management task". Fundamentally, networks have an informal character and organise themselves, yet they can also be cultivated by special means. The establishment of networked structures serves to improve the total value creation process. The cooperation that is necessary for this is not considered as a collection of functioning units, international affiliates or profit centres and such like, rather as a collection of processes that are dependent on one another – a collection that can be dismantled and reconfigured depending on each newly assigned allocation of work and choice of partners. The effect of this is a decline in the significance of the traditional, growing organisation (see figure 3).

	Traditional company structure		**Virtual network**	
Case type	**Routine**	**Regular**	**Project**	**Individual**
Condition of system	Very stable	Relatively stable	Unstable	Very unstable
Structure of system	Very simple	Simple to complex	Simple to complex	Very complex
Management strategy	Stimulus-response mechanism	Stimul.-response mechanism; rational logical	Rational logical; intuitive, suggestive	Intuitive, suggestive

Figure 3: Classification of systems and management strategy (after [21]).

It can also be noted that, as networks can be reconfigured in response to changing market conditions – and particularly the paradoxes they embrace – they qualify themselves particularly well as dynamically responsive forms of organisation. This factor has even greater significance in virtual company networks, as their strength normally lies in project or individual production programmes. It makes sense for me at this point to take a close look at aspects of dealing with and deploying relationships as a resource – and human resources themselves. It can be seen that the more complex, and dynamically responsive, organisational structures become, the more clearly and significantly do those subjective characteristics come into play that are *not* based on rational, logical ability but rather on personal or social skills and qualities.

4 Cultivating relationships against a background of insecurity

Dispensing with the further institutionalisation of cooperation between companies within a classical management structure is unavoidable in virtual cooperation projects. Any latent or current relationships in the virtual workspace cannot be centrally captured and organised. For anyone who becomes involved in such activities, it is advisable for them to newly define their area of work – right up to the limits of their own company, to distance themselves from any habitual patterns for dealing with things and to define the rules of play of the cooperation together with the other partners. It is of fundamental importance here to have a fully functioning network association, particularly in the creation of virtual ventures. Such a body can only be successful if it can harness both the expertise of

Human Perspectives in the Internet Society: Culture, Psychology and Gender, K. Morgan, J. Sanchez, C. A. Brebbia & A Voiskounsky (Editors) © 2004 WIT Press, www.witpress.com, ISBN 1-85312-726-4

individual key competences, and the networking made possible by information technology – and this not merely to represent a *cooperation of independent companies*. It is essential that this body speaks – on behalf of a dynamic network cooperation consisting of several companies – as if the whole cooperation is only a single company that is producing and marketing that product or service.

As confidence in the constitutional basis of each such network cooperation is so important, it is desirable to re-examine this again and again, even during the "productive" work of the network. Confidence is not something that can simply be promised. All those involved must provide proof of this to one another on an almost daily basis – and this can only come about by means of concrete, relevant activities. Confidence requires, among other things, an expectation that is shared, assured and embraced by everyone involved about how not only the individual actors, but also the complete networked system, will respond to particular disruptions. In fact relationships are always cultivated on the level of separate interactions between individuals. Seen this way, confidence in networks cannot be assessed merely on the basis of organisational or structural success factors; it is reflected much more in primarily personal and relationship-based factors. Yet such relationships are also subject to dynamic change. They must be continuously updated and cultivated alongside the development of the network. Any dynamic changes in the working environment must be recognised early, assessed and integrated into the planning or realisation of the project.

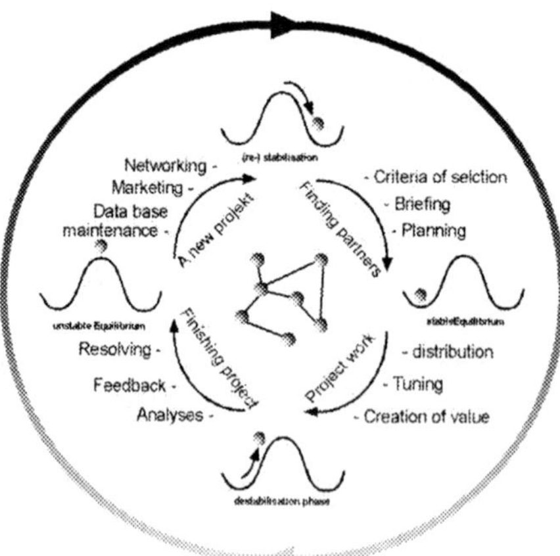

Figure 4: Formation of patterns in networked cooperation structures.

This and other social phenomena need to be known by, and available to, the complete system at all times. A kind of "soft fact management" seems to be obligatory to meet the challenges resulting from the issues argued above [22]. As virtual companies are specially set up to initiate, carry out and conclude projects that are always new, this means that they are constituted differently at various points or periods in time. But in order to be able to see how the turbulent individual sequences link themselves to a dynamically changing unity, it is

Human Perspectives in the Internet Society: Culture, Psychology and Gender, K. Morgan, J. Sanchez, C. A. Brebbia & A Voiskounsky (Editors) © 2004 WIT Press, www.witpress.com, ISBN 1-85312-726-4

necessary to present the important process steps as a model. From the perspective of self-organisation, that has been briefly addressed above, the life cycle of a project can be split into four stages (see figure 4). This model symbolically presents the iterative course of development of a virtual company network:

(1) Finding partners – the "stabilisation phase". When a contract is acquired, the choice of project partners is established by means of specific selection criteria. At a first meeting, or in further meetings, the tasks are defined and allocated. Roles and areas of responsibility are fixed and the project plan is drawn up.

(2) Project work – the "stable equilibrium" phase. The actual value creation takes place at this stage. Following on from the initial consultations and agreements, particular tasks within the project are carried out by the acting parties involved and, finally, the mutually manufactured product is dispatched.

(3) Dissolution – the "destabilisation phase". On completion of the project, or the provision of the service from the network, the value creation process can be analysed. This is done by assessing specific parameters of the value creation process, which is then fed back into the database system so that information about what worked and what didn't work in the cooperation within the virtual organisation is available and can be incorporated in the catalogue of selection criteria.

(4) New project – the "unstable equilibrium phase". This is where levels of insecurity are at their highest. The old project has been concluded and it is not yet clear with whom, and under what new conditions, a new project will be found that can be participated in. It is useful here to have a well-maintained personal network and a reputation that comes across positively.

Each of the stages of cooperation given above reflect different situations that need to take into account, on the one hand, the structures in which the actors involved actually find themselves and, on the other hand, the changes the partners within the network need to make in the way they relate to one another. Particularly in the *finding partners* phase, questions of suitability in terms of ability to cooperate are a constant challenge that is full of inconsistencies.

Many independent developers, programmers, graphic artists and copywriters etc. have tended more and more to handle their cooperatively combined projects and activities through established networks over the last few years. Yet that which, at first glance, has shown itself to be a good little "fighting unit" against large media agencies – and has to a certain degree been able to establish itself – is more and more losing its transparency and in need of either greater control or, indeed, becoming uncontrollable. Internal competition, personal sensitivities, claims to power and unresolved conflicts etc. may lead to the dissatisfaction of all parties concerned. The development of the virtual company can move in a wide variety of different directions, without the actors themselves having access to either the current structure of the association or to the reasons why it is changing, or indeed the perceptions and interpretations of the other partners involved. All the participants within a network have their own perception of the reality of the cooperation – often with unforeseeable consequences on the relationships within the network. A whole range of scenarios are possible in such

Human Perspectives in the Internet Society: Culture, Psychology and Gender, K. Morgan, J. Sanchez, C. A. Brebbia & A Voiskounsky (Editors) © 2004 WIT Press, www.witpress.com, ISBN 1-85312-726-4

a development: the association can dissolve itself, it could lead to the establishment of a company with fixed structures or it is even conceivable that such a unit can merge together and split up at the same time. One of the preconditions for such a project to turn out well is the characteristics of relationships that can only be sketched out here. Factors that support this are transparency in the processes, activities that inspire confidence, the taking on of responsibility and also appropriate network facilitation. Virtual companies are complex and dynamically changing structures. Each intervention that reduces complexity helps the actors to maintain their overview of the project and to remain able to act effectively. As the complexity of networks cannot be reduced by means of traditional structuring and formalisation methods, the choice of reality model that is used, and the degree to which the people involved are willing to interact with the complexity and uncertainty of virtual networks, takes on a new significance here.

References

[1] Bell, D., The Coming of Post-Industrial Society. Basic Books: NY, 1976
[2] Castells, M.: The Network Society, Bd. 1. Blackwell: Oxford, 1996.
[3] Sabel, Ch. & Zeitlin, J., World of Possibilities. Cambridge Mass, 1997.
[4] Castells, M., Materials for an exploratory theory of the network society. British Journal of Sociology, No. 51, pp. 5-24, 2000.
[5] Morley, D. & K. Robins, Spaces of Identity. Global Media, Electronic Landscapes and Cultural Boundaries. Routledge: London, 1995.
[6] Brill, A.: Virtualisierung der Wirtschaft – Grundzüge theoretischer Analyse. Virtuelle Wirtschaft, ed. Brill, A. & M. de Vries. Opl.: WV, pp. 27-52. 1998.
[7] Lanier, J., Virtuelle Realität: Mit dem Computer in die 4. Dimension. gdi impuls 2/90, pp. 3-14, 1990.
[8] Brosziewski, A.,: Virtualität als Modus unternehmerischer Selbstbewertung. Virtuelle Wirtschaft, ed. A. Brill & M. Vries., WV : Opl.. p. 87-100, 1998.
[9] Bühl, A., Die virtuelle Gesellschaft. Westdeutscher Verlag: Opladen, 1997.
[10] Hedberg, B. et al., Virtual Organizations and Beyond. Chichester, 1997.
[11] Klatt, R.,: Wie das Leitbild des 'virtuellen Unternehmens' wirkt. Beispiele aus der Unternehmenspraxis. Arbeit, H.3, Jg. 8, pp. 241-254, 1999.
[12] Gora, W., Vorwort. Auf dem Weg zum virtuellen Unternehmen – Konsequenzen der Dezentralisierung, ed. Gora, W.. FOSSIL-Verlag: Köln, 1996.
[13] Weber, B., Die Fluide Organisation. Haupt: Bern/Stuttgart und Wien. 1996.
[14] Vries, M. de, Das virtuelle Unternehmen. Virtuelle Wirtschaft, ed. A. Brill & M. de Vries, Westdeutscher Verlag: Opladen, pp. 54-86. 1998.
[15] Davidow, W. H. & Malone, M. S.: The Virtual Corporation. NY. 1992.

Human Perspectives in the Internet Society: Culture, Psychology and Gender, K. Morgan, J. Sanchez, C. A. Brebbia & A Voiskounsky (Editors) © 2004 WIT Press, www.witpress.com, ISBN 1-85312-726-4

[16] Drucker, Peter f., Managing Oneself. Harvard Business Review 77 (2), p. 59-77. 1999.
[17] Ulrich, H. & Probst, G. J. B. (ed.), Self-Organization and Management of Social Systems. Springer, Heidelberg/Toronto, 1984.
[18] Haken, H., Synergetics: an introduction. Springer: Berlin 1977
[19] Nippa, M., Anforderungen an das Management prozessorientierter Unternehmen. Prozessmanagement und Reengineering, ed. Nippa, M. & Picot, A., Campus: Frankfurt, 1996.
[20] Wenger, E.C.; Snyder, W.M.: Communities of Practice: Warum sie eine wachsende Rolle spielen. Harvard Business manager 4/2000, pp.55-62.
[21] Kruse, P., Theorie dynamischer Systeme. Stuttgart. 1996.
[22] Meyer, M. et al., Optimization of Social Structure in Business Networks. Journal of Business and Psychology, No. 4, pp. 451-472, 2003.

Human Perspectives in the Internet Society: Culture, Psychology and Gender, K. Morgan, J. Sanchez, C. A. Brebbia & A Voiskounsky (Editors) © 2004 WIT Press, www.witpress.com, ISBN 1-85312-726-4

Relationship of organizational culture with use intensity of the Internet and sales performance: an international empirical investigation

D. A. Karayanni
University of Patras, Department of Business Administration, Patras, Greece

Abstract

This paper addresses the question of why some organizations may successfully involve the Internet in their marketing strategies, whereas others do otherwise. The basic assumption of our study is that a firm's adoption of the Internet may be related to its organizational culture. Thus, this study intends to identify the relationship between a firm's culture and the profitable use of the Internet by its organizational members. Hypotheses stemming from both the organizational culture and the Internet streams of research are tested using correlation and a series of T-tests analyses that were performed upon data selected from 150 business-to-business international organizations with a presence on the World Wide Web. The research results showed that both use intensity and Internet sales are related to distinct culture types. The paper concludes with some fruitful implications for both business managers and academics, concerning necessary modifications of organizational culture towards Internet friendly norms and values.
Keywords: Internet sales, organizational culture, use intensity of the Internet, Internet budget, Web sales, adhocracies, hierarchies.

1 Introduction

Although new to the marketing field, the Internet has been well articulated in contemporary firms' strategies. For example, according to the Forrester Research (2003), inter-organizational e-commerce in North America will exceed $2.7 trillion, by 2004. Notwithstanding that there is a growing consensus about

Human Perspectives in the Internet Society: Culture, Psychology and Gender, K. Morgan, J. Sanchez, C. A. Brebbia & A Voiskounsky (Editors) © 2004 WIT Press, www.witpress.com, ISBN 1-85312-726-4

the benefits of the use of the Internet in their business activities, a few firms report quite disappointing e-business results [1].

Furthermore, a few researchers proclaim that in order for an IT to provide a competitive advantage, it should be closely linked to the strategic objectives of the organization. Indeed, as Senn [2] vividly said: "the advantage of IT depends on its ability to be an 'enabler' of strategy". In the same spirit, both strategy and the inclination towards the adoption of any Information Technology (i.e., the Internet) should be related to an organization's culture [3, 4]. For example, Zammuto and O'Connors [5] suggest that organizational culture may affect the type of an Information Technology's (i.e. the Internet) benefits that a firm seeks, as well as successful implementation of this IT.

The literature often alludes to the constraining effects of an organization's culture as a major barrier to the implementation of a firm's Internet marketing strategy. An organization's culture is built on the shared values and beliefs of its members and manifests itself in the ends the organization seeks (i.e. strategic goals) and the means it uses to attain them (i.e. the use of the Internet). In short, understanding the relationship between an organization's culture with the reception of its organizational members to use the Internet, can provide greater insight into the successful implementation of this strategic IT.

However, inspection of the relevant literature suggests that very little is currently known about these issues. With this study, we start filling this void. More specifically, we examine the relationship of organizational culture with the use of the Internet and sales performance. The organization of the paper is as follows. The next section develops a conceptual framework, together with a number of research hypotheses. The third section is concerned with empirical analysis. A concluding section summarizes the paper.

2 Conceptual framework and hypotheses

2.1 The Internet as a strategic weapon

The Internet is endowed with unique nuances, such as interoperability, interactivity, demmasification and asynchronicity, among others. All of the above characteristics, reflect criteria which Rogers [6] used as criteria for effective communication, that improves addressability, communication frequency and communication quality. The above qualities make the Internet a powerful and multipurpose marketing tool which may be used as: a) an information tool for environmental scanning (gathering of market intelligence), b) an interactive communication tool which improves customer and third parties relationships, c) a promotion tool (i.e., through the WEB sites, or by sending direct e-mail material to the customers), d) a selling tool (audiovisional presentations, direct sales through the WEB, sales leads), e) a distribution tool (in case of services, e.g., software or graphic work), f) a payment tool (electronic payments), g) a market research tool (e.g., market segmentation, new product testing), h) a cooperation facilitator (e.g., between the R&D departments of two

Human Perspectives in the Internet Society: Culture, Psychology and Gender, K. Morgan, J. Sanchez, C. A. Brebbia & A Voiskounsky (Editors) © 2004 WIT Press, www.witpress.com, ISBN 1-85312-726-4

organizations), i) a service tool (e.g., for answering customer queries, routine-service jobs), j) a recruiting tool (efficient personnel recruitment) [7, 8, 9, 10].

As a matter of fact, this multifacet marketing tool may affect organizational effectiveness in many ways. The above potential applications of the Internet enable it to be used for a quite wide range of marketing activities. Below some marketing activities and potential organizational effects are listed, as they have been selected from the germane literature:

- Expansion in new markets locally and globally [8, 11, 12].
- Efficiency improvement (i.e., steming from reductions in transaction, selling, advertising, promotion, service and prospecting costs) [13, 14].
- Enhancement of inter-organizational relationships [15, 16].
- Expansion of business networks (e.g., opportunity networks, virtual networks, co-marketing networks) [16, 17].
- Enhancement of inter-functional communication [9].
- Facilitation of marketing orientation implementation [9, 14].
- Shrinkage of distribution channels [10, 14, 18].
- Empowerment of manufacturers [12, 16].
- Rise of new professions [12]
- Reengineering of the marketing function [12, 13, 16].
- Facilitation of new product development Cycles [11, 13, 14].
- Shorter product life-cycles [11, 14].
- Egalitarianism (i.e., it levels the ground between small and large organizations) [8, 13, 18].
- Empowerment of buyers [13, 19].
- Enhancement of knowledge [17, 19].
- Formation of new advertisement and public relations standards [20].
- Increase of value-added services [21].
- Devaluation of traditional-functioning organizations [20].
- Formation of virtual communities [22].
- Formation of information networks [16, 17, 23].
- Formation of a new identical culture for the users [22].
- Implementation of economies of scope [24].
-

The aforementioned wide range of motives for the use of the Internet proclaims that this is clearly an IT of strategic intent, which has the potential to provide organizations with competitive advantage. Thus, the Internet has the potential to be an 'enabler of strategy', to use Senn's [2] phraseology.

Apart from this major strategic implication, the Internet is 'quasi-public', simple to use, it incurs low set-up and administration costs (cost effective), it creates no switching costs, whilst it creates network externalities by its use. All the above provide it with overwhelming advantages over alternative out-directed information networks, such as Value Added Networks (VANs), EDI systems, Intranets and WANs [17, 25].

Human Perspectives in the Internet Society: Culture, Psychology and Gender, K. Morgan, J. Sanchez, C. A. Brebbia & A Voiskounsky (Editors) © 2004 WIT Press, www.witpress.com, ISBN 1-85312-726-4

2.2 Culture and use of the Internet

Although new to the field of marketing, many marketing scholars have noted the rich potential explanatory power of organizational culture as a predictor of a few marketing issues [26]. Indeed, "the culture of an organization will determine the extent to which it is willing to interact with other organizations and the nature of this interaction" [27]. Organizational culture has been sufficiently operationalized by the Competing Values Model of organizational effectiveness [28]. According to this model, various combinations between uncertainty, ambiguity and goal congruence entail the adoption of different organizational forms (e.g., decision making, directing and controlling), which may be codified under four generic categories, that is, markets, hierarchies, clans and adhocracies [28].

Adhocracies. This culture type is predominantly met in small, entrepreneurial, functionally separate units which are integrated through reciprocal, multiplex and dense ties of long-term relationships, instead of hierarchical authority [29]. Being at the cutting edge of technology innovation, which reflects a strategic orientation similar to the prospector type of Miles and Snow [30], adhocracies should be the first to adopt any new successful communication system, i.e., the use of the Internet in their network orientation efforts. Stated formally, adhocracies should be the most intensive of all four cultural types in using the Internet in their marketing strategies.

Markets. Similarly to adhocracies, they comprise elementary specialized functional units of industrial networks, thus they are highly dependent on external system members for acquiring resources and/or complementing activities which they themselves cannot provide [31, 32]. Nevertheless, what differentiates a market from an adhocracy is determined by the power/dependence balance and their attitude towards the organizations with which they interact, which is competitive in the first instance and cooperative in the second, respectively [33]. Thus, although that they are externally focused, their increased affection towards efficiency and accountability of results, defined as rationality, imply that their strategic orientation fits well with the defender strategy archetype described by Miles and Snow [30]. As a matter of fact, markets would be followers in adopting any new communication technology, such as the Internet, which creates low expectations for the use intensity of the Internet by markets' organizational members in their marketing activities.

Hierarchies. They are characterized by extant formalization, environmental stability, internal focus and increased concern on efficiency control [3, 4]. Their focus on stability and control can best be described by the Miles and Snow's [30] reactor, or the Ruekert and Walker's [34] low cost defender strategic type, thus nurturing low expectations for the use intensity of any new communication technology, such as the Internet.

Human Perspectives in the Internet Society: Culture, Psychology and Gender, K. Morgan, J. Sanchez, C. A. Brebbia & A Voiskounsky (Editors) © 2004 WIT Press, www.witpress.com, ISBN 1-85312-726-4

Clans. They emphasize internally focused values (i.e., clans and bureaucracies) are more likely to adopt an innovation (i.e., in the context of an Advanced Manufacturing Technology) for their productivity (i.e., efficiency) benefits, whereas those emphasizing externally focused values (i.e., adhocracies and markets) are more likely to actively seek both productivity and flexibility benefits [5]. This strategic perspective (regarding the extent to which they develop adaptive capability to respond to the market) is akin on the Miles and Snow's [30] analyzer type, or the Ruekert and Walker's [34] differentiated defender type. Literature on this strategic type implies that organizations are often "second-in" to new product-markets, with the advantage of observing and learning from the new product problems of other firms, often with above the average new product success rates [30]. As a matter of course, clans will be followers in encouraging their organizational members' efforts in using any new marketing tool such as the Internet in their marketing strategies. Synopsising the aforementioned arguments we put forward the following hypotheses:

H1a: Organizations that emphasize adhocracy culture values will have the highest intensity in the use of the Internet, as compared to organizations that emphasize clan, hierarchy, or market culture values.

H1b: Organizations that emphasize hierarchy culture values will have the lowest intensity in the use of the Internet as compared to organizations that emphasize clan, adhocracy, or market culture values.

H1c: Organizations that emphasize clan, or market culture values will have a lower intensity than average, in the use of the Internet, as compared to organizations that emphasize an adhocracy culture value.

2.3 Use intensity of the Internet and sales performance

Delving into the Internet literature we elicit a number of measures for the evaluation of its effectiveness, i.e., duration of time spent on the site, the depth or number of pages assessed, and the number of repeat visits. Notwithstanding, it would be desirable to use an objective function expressed directly in terms of direct sales, or profitability. Thus, we select Web-based sales, in order to measure the performance of organizations' activities on the Internet.

Although new to the marketing field, the Internet literature enumerates a few notable examples of organizations with increased sales on the World Wide Web (e.g. www.amazon.com, www.hanover.com, www.Toys-R.com) [1]. In the same vein, Avlonitis and Karayanni [14] have found that the use of the Internet tools affected both sales and sales relationships. Thus, we anticipate that:

H2a: The marketing budget allocated to the Internet will be related to an organization's sales that are attributed to its World Wide Web site.

Human Perspectives in the Internet Society: Culture, Psychology and Gender, K. Morgan, J. Sanchez, C. A. Brebbia & A Voiskounsky (Editors) © 2004 WIT Press, www.witpress.com, ISBN 1-85312-726-4

H2b: The use of the Internet tools by an organization's members will be related to its sales that are attributed to its World Wide Web site.

3 Empirical analysis

3.1 Sampling and response rate

A random sample of 600 U.S.A., Canadian, European and Asian companies was drawn from the industrial goods and services list of the Google Web directory. Totally 150 organizations responded, producing a response rate of 24.9%, which is quite acceptable, as it compares favourably with response rates obtained in similar large-scale e-mail surveys from executives and managers [14].

3.2 Measures

Organizational culture. The 16-item culture scale was adapted from Deshpande et al. [26]. Crosstabulation analysis which was performed among nationality, size, industry sector and culture type, indicated that there was no meaningful relationship among the above variables.

Use intensity of the Internet. Drawing on the Internet literature we elicit that use intensity of the Internet may be reflected upon the budget that is allocated to it and the intensity of its various services [14]. We built upon this theory and use both the aforementioned measures in order to test our hypotheses.

Use of the Internet tools. The four-item 5-point scale, asking the respondents to cite the extent to which they were using the e-mail, the World Wide Web, the USENET and the File Transfer Protocol (FTP) in their marketing efforts, was adapted from Avlonitis and Karayanni [14].

Internet budget. This was measured by asking the respondents to indicate the percentage of their total marketing budget that the Internet accounted for.

Sales performance. This measure was tapped by asking the respondents to indicate the percentage of their actual sales that their World Wide Web site accounted for.

3.3 Measurement validation

Unidimensionality of the four culture scales, namely, hierarchy, market, clan and adhocracy, was assessed using the EUCLID distance model of multidimensional scaling. This produced an RSQ statistic of .89 (i.e., indicating the proportion of variance of the disparities in the matrix which is accounted for by the corresponding distances in the underlying values), thus indicating quite high explanatory capabilities of the competitive values model to describe respondents

Human Perspectives in the Internet Society: Culture, Psychology and Gender, K. Morgan, J. Sanchez, C. A. Brebbia & A Voiskounsky (Editors) © 2004 WIT Press, www.witpress.com, ISBN 1-85312-726-4

perceptions. Furthermore, reliability analysis produced Cronbach aphas coefficients ranging from 0.64 and 0.79 for the four culture types and the use of the Internet tools scales, indicating very good levels of internal consistency. Table 1 presents the correlations among the variables of the study.

Table 1: Construct correlations.

		Intercorrelations						
	Variables	**1**	**2**	**3**	**4**	**5**	**6**	**7**
1	Use of the Internet tools	1						
2	Internet budget	.287**	1					
3	Clans	- .079	.022	1				
4	Adhocracies	.347**	.074	-.331**	1			
5	Hierarchies	-.182**	-.153	-.254**	-.500**	1		
6	Markets	- .079	.101	-.576**	-.207**	.087	1	
7	Sales performance	.213**	.437**	.019	.043	-.029	-.027	1
	** significance at 0.05							

3.4 Findings

In order to test H1a to H1c we used a series of T-test analyses. To this end, first we calculated the summative index for the four Internet tools scales (min=11, max=33, mean=19.9, st. dev.=4.4), the Internet budget (min=0, max=50, mean=12.2, st. dev.=8.4) and the four culture types. Next, the research respondents were divided into high and low Internet users by a median split, with ties at the median assigned to the high Internet tool users. In the same way, they were divided into high and low Internet budget users. Means of culture, use of Internet tools, the Internet budget and sales performance variables are depicted on Table 2.

Table 2: T-test analysis of the Internet use and Internet budget with the culture and sales performance measures.

Measures								
			Means					
	Number	Coefficient		Internet users		Internet budget		
Scale	**of Items**	**alpha**	**All**	**High**	**Low**	**High**	**Low**	**Std. dev.**
Culture								
Adhocracy	4	0.73	134[a]	146.3	117.8	126.1	133.1	67.2
Clan	4	0.78	124	124.3	120.1	124.2	120.5	68.1
Hierarchy	4	0.64	75[a]	68.5	82.8	72.5	80.1	51.8
Market	4	0.71	92	91.1	94.9	105.5	89.1	56.1
Sales performance								
Web sales	2	0.79	11.5[b]	15.7	8.0	31.9	10.9	3.3
[a] Significant univariate difference between high and low Internet users								
[b] Significant univariate difference between high and low Internet users and high and low Internet budget								

As it is shown on this table, all four types of culture are well represented in the sample. In respect to the Internet tools, three of five measures have significant differences for high and low Internet users – two of four culture scales and the sales performance scales. The two not significant different culture types for high and low Internet users are the clans and the markets. In respect to the Internet budget, only the sales performance variable showed a significant difference. The results in Table 2 are not significantly different by either nationality, or by major industry classifications between consumer and industrial goods and services, or by extent of participation in international business.

Culture. Adhocracy cultures are the most likely, whereas the hierarchical cultures are the least likely to use the Internet, thus supporting H1a and H1b. On the other hand, research results were not significant in respect to markets and clans, thus leading to rejection of H1c. However, they indicate that both markets and clans would be rather among the less intensive users of the Internet.

Sales performance. Finally, the higher sales performers are the more likely to have a higher Internet budget than average and to use the Internet more intensively than average, thus supporting H2a and H2b.

4 Conclusions and implications

Overall research findings supported the initial hypotheses of our study. Specifically, both the Internet budget and the use of the Internet are related to sales attributed to a firm's presence on the World Wide Web. The implication is that CEOs of today should allocate more resources to their Internet departments. It appears that it pays to a firm to show a high commitment to its marketing promotion plans on the World Wide Web (i.e., as expressed in terms of budget allocated to the Internet).

Moreover, we found adhocracies to be the heaviest, whereas the hierarchies to be the lightest Internet users, as anticipated. At the same time, both the market and the clan type culture were unrelated to the use of the Internet tools. As much as the Internet budget is concerned, this was unrelated to all four culture types. The above results, taken together, imply that the culture type of an organization may not influence its top managers' decisions on the resources that are allocated to the Internet. However, it may influence the receptiveness of its organizational members to using this new strategic weapon (i.e. the Internet). It appears that adhocracies enjoy greater benefits from their Internet budgets, as reflected upon greater sales gained from their World Wide Web sites. The implication is that top managers have to align their corporate culture with values adopted from the adhocratic achetype, in order to optimize their Internet marketing strategies and results.

References

[1] Strauss, J., El-Ansary, A. & Frost R., *E-marketing*, p. 4, Prentice-Hall, N. J., 2003.

[2] Senn, J., The myths of strategic systems, *Information Systems Management*, 9, Summer, pp. 7-12, 1992.

Human Perspectives in the Internet Society: Culture, Psychology and Gender, K. Morgan, J. Sanchez, C. A. Brebbia & A Voiskounsky (Editors) © 2004 WIT Press, www.witpress.com, ISBN 1-85312-726-4

[3] Quinn, R. & Rohrbaugh, J., A spatial model of effectiveness criteria: toward a competing values approach to organizational analysis, *Management Science,* 29 (3), pp. 363-377, 1983.

[4] Zammuto, R. F. & Krakower, J. Y., Quantitative and qualitative studies of organizational culture, *Research in Organizational Change and Development,* 5: pp.83-114, 1991.

[5] Zammuto, R. & O'Connor, E., Gaining advanced manufacturing technologies' benefits: the roles of organization design and culture, *Academy of Management Review*, Vol. 17, No 4, pp. 701-728, 1992.

[6] Rogers, M. E., The critical mass in the diffusion of interactive technologies in organizations, Harvard Business School, Boston, MA, pp. 245-263, 1991.

[7] Blattberg, R. & Deighton, J., Interactive marketing: exploiting the age of addressability, *Sloan Management Review*, Fall, pp. 5-15, 1991.

[8] Karayanni, D., The use of the Internet in business-to-business marketing, Work-in-progress, Athens University of Economics and Business, http://www.aueb.gr/karayanni, 1997.

[9] Hoffman, D. & Novak, T., A new marketing paradigm for electronic commerce, *Journal of Marketing*, July, 1996.

[10] Sauer, P., Young, M., & Talarzyk, W. W., The potential impact of emerging communication technologies on distribution channels, *Journal of Direct Marketing*, Aut., pp. 28-38, 1989.

[11] Cronin, B., Overfelt, K., Fouchereaux, K., Manzvanzvike T., Cha M. S. A., The Internet and competitive intelligence: a survey of current practice, *Int. J. of Information Management*, 14, pp. 204-222, 1994.

[12] Samli, C., Wills, J. & Herbig, P., The Information superhighway goes international: implications for industrial sales transactions, *Industrial Marketing Managemen*t, 26, pp. 51-58, 1997.

[13] Sheth, N., Jagdish, & Sisodia, S. R., Feeling the heat - part two, *Marketing Managemen*t, Winder, 4(3), pp. 19-33, 1995.

[14] Avlonitis, G. & Karayanni, D., The Impact of the Internet on business-to-business marketing - examples from American and European companies, *Industrial Marketing Management*, Sep. 28, 5, pp. 441-459, 2000.

[15] Stump, R. & Sriram, V., Employing information technology in purchasing, *Industrial Marketing Management*, 26, pp. 127-136, 1997.

[16] Naude, P. & Holland, C., Business-to-Business relationships, from the book *Relationship Marketing, Theory and Practice*, Paul Chapman Publishing Ltd, 1996.

[17] Cunningham, C. & Tynan, C., Electronic trading, interorganizational systems and the nature of buyer-seller relationships: the need for a network perspective, *Int. J. of Information Management*, 13, pp. 3-28, 1993.

[18] Quelch, A. J. & Klein, R. L., The Internet and international marketing, *Sloan Management Review*, Spring, pp. 60-75, 1996.

Human Perspectives in the Internet Society: Culture, Psychology and Gender, K. Morgan, J. Sanchez, C. A. Brebbia & A Voiskounsky (Editors) © 2004 WIT Press, www.witpress.com, ISBN 1-85312-726-4

[19] Blattberg, R. & Glazer, R., The Marketing in information revolution in the *Marketing Information Revolution*, Blattberg, R., Glazer, R. & Little, J., Boston: Harvard University Press, pp. 9-29, 1993.

[20] Cronin, M. J, *Doing business on the Internet: how the electronic highway is transforming American companies*, New York: Van Nostrand Reinhold, 1994.

[21] Benjamin, R. & Wigand, R., Electronic markets and virtual value chains on the information superhighway, *Sloan Management Review*, Winter, pp. 62-72, 1995.

[22] Armstrong, A. Hagel, J. III, Real profits from virtual communities, *The McKinsey Quarterly,* 3, pp. 127-141, 1995.

[23] Sashittal, H. & Wilemon, D., Integrating technology and marketing: implications for improving customer responsiveness, *Int. Journal of Technology Management*, 9, pp. 691-709, 1994.

[24] Rayport, J. & Sviokla, J., Managing in the marketspace, *Harvard Business Review,* Nov-Dec, pp. 141-150, 1994.

[25] Roche, E., Business value of electronic commerce over interoperable networks, Discussion Paper, National Science Foundation, July, pp. 6-7, Virginia, 1995.

[26] Deshpande, R., Farley, J. & Webster, F., Corporate culture, customer orientation and innovativeness in Japanese Firms: A Quardrad Analysis, *Journal of Marketing*, Jan., Vol. 57, pp. 23-27, 1993.

[27] Morand, D., The role of behavioral formality and informality in the enactment of bureaucratic versus organic organizations, *Academy of Management Review*, Vol. 20, 4, pp. 831-872, 1995.

[28] Williamson, O., Markets and hierarchies: analysis and antitrust implications. New York: Free Press, 1975.

[29] Achrol, R., Changes in the theory of interorganizational relations in marketing: toward a network paradigm *Journal of the Academy of Marketing Science*, 25, pp. 56-71, 1997.

[30] Miles, R. & Snow, C., Fit, failure and the hall of fame, *California Management Review*, 26, Spring, pp. 10-28, 1984.

[31] Ouchi, W, G., Markets, bureaucracies and clans, *Administrative Science Quarterly*, 25, pp. 129-142, 1980.

[32] Anderson, J. C., Hakansson, H. & Johanson, J., Dyadic business relationships within a business network context, *Journal of Marketing*, 58, Oct., pp. 1-15, 1994.

[33] Jarillo, J. C., On strategic networks, *Strategic Management Journal*, 9, Jan-Feb, pp. 31-41, 1988.

[34] Ruekert, R. & Walker, O., Marketing's interaction with other functional units: a conceptual framework and empirical evidence, *Journal of Marketing*, 51, pp. 1-19, 1987.

Human Perspectives in the Internet Society: Culture, Psychology and Gender, K. Morgan, J. Sanchez, C. A. Brebbia & A Voiskounsky (Editors) © 2004 WIT Press, www.witpress.com, ISBN 1-85312-726-4

Architecture between applicational and virtual space

I. Juras
Faculty of Architecture, University of Zagreb, Croatia

Abstract

Architecture was often a field used for the verification of new technological possibilities (innovations) which inspired man's utopian yearning. This yearning can be classified into "external" and "internal". External yearning is the desire for flight through the endless space of the universe; internal yearning is the desire for immersion into virtual space. Both involve intervening into and manipulating man's environment, transforming it in accordance with the degree and range of technical development (architecture is culture), thereby directly confirming the level of civilisation through the house-city organisation. In the creative anticipatory process, architects are immersed in virtual space, with reality as an afterthought, and are subjected to a particular kind of mental gymnastics in their attempts to project themselves into the position of a future end-user, whereby they are forced to view and analyse their own project through the eyes of this end-user. On a second level of projection, the problem which arises is the balancing of potential reality and the desire for a utopian vision, which the architect does not see literally as a picture, but rather something about which the architect hypothesises as an ideal. However, since architecture is not a phenomenon ***per se***, and since the house-city has served humans as a type of refuge in the face of varying climates and other requirements, the pertinent question is what purpose architecture will serve at a point where a synthetically produced human comes into existence. Today, modern man, with all his physiological traits, is steadily becoming out-dated – an archaic and anachronic being, unadjusted to immersion into virtual space because he still uses gravitational pull and the sun's traverse across the sky as a means of guidance. It would seem that this is only a temporary act of media domination over reality and nature.
Keywords: virtual, applicational, space, humankind, architecture, city.

Human Perspectives in the Internet Society: Culture, Psychology and Gender, K. Morgan, J. Sanchez, C. A. Brebbia & A Voiskounsky (Editors) © 2004 WIT Press, www.witpress.com, ISBN 1-85312-726-4

1 Fictitious and actual reality

Technology has always had the task of interpreting the application of systematic learning in the production of targeted products and objects. Only in the 1950s was there any mention of it playing a part in the verification of scientific theory. Theoretical knowledge was supposed to transform into a framework which would enable technology to facilitate the bridging of the gap between science (irrespective of which type of science) and technical development.

Architecture is a more complex issue since it is disputable whether it belongs to the field of technical sciences or to the arts, in view of its utilitarian function. Scholars and scientists unwillingly make concessions and tend to relegate it to the realm of "applied arts", or interpret the theory of architecture under the History of Art and Aesthetics. However, new theoretical research is laying the foundations for an authentic architectonic theory which does not tend towards creating some kind of handbook for the production of syntheses or for the establishment of rules of induction based on which a hypothesis would be generated mechanically.

Another issue is a product of the imprecise terminology used in reality, as well as the "syndrome of inexpressibility" which warns us that a set of signs in one system cannot be applied to another system.

The concept of reality was primarily a philosophical question, but the application of computers has introduced an element of unease into our physical and cultural environment. The question is whether "virtual reality" also includes "fictitious reality". If virtual reality is not reality, then the logical question is what is actual reality? This can be problematized as a type of illusion as in the case of the man in the desert who sees a Fata Morgana [21]. It is quite natural for human beings to see an oasis (or mirage) that does not exist, so this is not divorced from reality, no matter which type of shared experiences we may have.
In order to confirm Polić's claims, it would be useful if this type of reality were verified on the basis of a statistical sample (a survey), which would establish how many people have the same illusion at the same spot. If the majority were not to see the oasis or the mirage of an oasis, then this would lead to the assumption that this reality does not exist, thereby also confirming that the real-reality, the conventional reality of the man in the desert, does not exist either. This ambiguity, or multiple meaning, is also confirmed by Mach's example of the slanting pencil submerged in water, creating an optical illusion that defies the logic of what we expect to see. We are even prepared to confuse this actual reality with "conceptions of reality", as a result of which we accept our conceptions and symbols as being a part of reality [9].

If we do not insist on precision, then we can only talk about the reality created by our senses. We know that even conventional space is inhabited by virtual beings (witches). Or, seen from a religious viewpoint, human beings in conventional space can be influenced, or their behaviour can be predicted, depending on commands received from virtual space.

According to Bergson [5], multiple meaning in reality springs from the complexity of man's individuality, which is caused by the ability of cells in the

Human Perspectives in the Internet Society: Culture, Psychology and Gender, K. Morgan, J. Sanchez, C. A. Brebbia & A Voiskounsky (Editors) © 2004 WIT Press, www.witpress.com, ISBN 1-85312-726-4

organism to merge and separate. This would presume that it is possible to dislocate from a personal existence and that other individuals in the same personalism have a frame (work) for their return (p. 7).

An architect in the process of designing is able to dislocate himself from his personal existence and finds himself in an ecstatic state intermingled with a real sense of fear about not being able to return, which may even lead to a schizophrenic state. It is always possible to keep the framework in mind, or it is predictable, because anything new is always simply a reorganisation of old elements due to the inertia of the spirit.

Cache [6] subscribes to a conventional reality, which generally amounts to the shape of vector types that carry the living meaning to vital points of the physical structure of a city in combination with the configuration of the terrain in a city. He, therefore, differentiates between real-weight vectors and abstract-space vectors (p. 23). Although he eliminates the influence of genius loci, he does not have recourse to apply vectors of shapes readily supplied by and produced in nature. Emigrants from Dalmatia (Croatia) recognise the same space – the ambient of San Pedro, California (USA) and rediscover a reflection of the essential qualities of their earlier lifestyle. This, then, may be what Bergson means by a possible separability of personalism (the emigrant has left a part of himself in his first homeland), but also what is implied by Cache when he talks about the separability of the physical from the abstract vector, in spite of his views on inflection.

One might dispute the assumption that it is in the nature of the human spirit to recognise greater order, physical and atmospheric similarities for objects in its environment than can be found in nature. Similarities are always imbued with imagination that is grounded in similarity-reciprocality. Screams of fear are spontaneous signs of fear, but are not analogous to fear itself. This [14] is why it would better to use the term affinity. After all, how can a representation of virtual space be viewed without prior experience, and all prior experiences are derived from these realities. Not even the "babble of similarity" can offer the imagination a retreat into the turbidity of interrelated emptiness.

2 The rise of a new virtual era

In both virtual and non-virtual space (inverted derivative) the architect, at least in the initial phase of developing an idea, resorts to using a drawing, while all those who use words as a medium needs must translate their thoughts. Words provide but a thin layer and have to increase a thought twofold very much like a façade ([14], p. 94). In view of this, it is more difficult to follow the line of thought during the process of creation, as it does not evolve successively, whereas what is finally expressed in words does.

Baudrillard [3] raises the alarm because of the disappearance of objects and belongings so that virtuality is used to represent a mediated truth of objectivity and authenticity. This marks the advent of a new reality for man. Nothing depends on man any longer, it depends on DNA. Čatić [10] warns that nanotechnology has reached the bounds of the physical world. New theories (the

Human Perspectives in the Internet Society: Culture, Psychology and Gender, K. Morgan, J. Sanchez, C. A. Brebbia & A Voiskounsky (Editors) © 2004 WIT Press, www.witpress.com, ISBN 1-85312-726-4

Selfish Gene Theory) set forth the thesis that genes sustain the human race for the purpose of their own survival [15], so that the sum total of all molecules cannot express spirituality or emotionality. If the human body [16] is only a machine for the survival of genes, then, efficient medical researches necessitate the employment of a variety of machine applications, like computer tomography and magnetic resonance. One should begin to liberate oneself from the misconception that man has a heart and soul [1].

Recent city surveys and plans, whether they represent the entire city or only parts of it, are fragmented pieces, a network of warped surfaces, transparent disjointed or connected structures, stick-like columns of varying shapes made up of a multitude of different material, with larva-like membranes (for now beaches only have sanitary installations), with modular or non-modular, reversible or irreversible structures, etc. The surfaces have a twisted, Escheresque quality to them in the form of a Möbius strip, negating the interior and exterior or inevitably converging as a vortex without a point of departure, but also without a construction of recursive functions.

Pictures are made by using synthetic colours and digital lipstick (M.Troy). New terms are being adopted, like: trans-architecture, trans-modern, trans-culture, but with an underlying reference to virtual reality. Everything is verified by mathematically and algorithmically exploring space, so that the decisive element of a vision is mathematical intuition and algorithmic design, which is outside the experiences within Newton's space. They are created within virtual space defined by axioms, and graphically represented by lamina, and arranged in a series of ideal surfaces [20].

Information becomes a global resource and changes applicable space into information space [23]. The interplay between the virtual and the applicable creates an amalgam of intelligent houses woven from of a net of optical fibres and communication systems.

3 Presence and the tools of illusion(ism)

J. Rajchman [22] starts his discussion on the virtual house by implying that we are switching from a Bauhaus aesthetics of geometrical abstraction to an electronic aesthetics of "free" abstraction. The virtual house does not resemble anything that we know or can see. In view of this, the search for infinite complexity is, in some ways, a type of virtuality in the form of pure fantasy. It is not just a "possibility" of something that can be "realised" but is real and does not have a representational or mimetic relationship with what it actualises. This is of very little significance for architects, if anything, they have to relate to a potential reality, even if it is only utopian space. There is no other way to discuss a house generally, even when discussing a virtual house. Mentioning only virtual space, but not the house, is too indefinite, no matter how literal and not reflective this may be. I.H.Bergson believes that virtual geometry degrades logic [5]. However, Rajchman is aware of the dangers of using a computer when designing or planning, since this may lead to a loss of perception of the scale of architectonic and urban space, unlike designs drawn by hand. Part of this

Human Perspectives in the Internet Society: Culture, Psychology and Gender, K. Morgan, J. Sanchez, C. A. Brebbia & A Voiskounsky (Editors) © 2004 WIT Press, www.witpress.com, ISBN 1-85312-726-4

complex problem is due to the size of the picture produced and the possibility of superimposing groundplan solutions for various floors. The architect's primarily task is to anticipate a house, which presumes that you do not first build a house in order to establish its values, and then, should they be faulty, pull it down.

If there is no perception within a vacuum, then there is no vision outside the vision itself. How can we send out a message and communicate if we do not share similar or identical experiences? The real world is but a fluctuating bundle of sensations, where the conventional division into reality and illusion cannot apply. Objective reality exists, but as an independent phenomenon, whereas the actual manifestation of reality is a product of our senses. Bachelard [2] wrote: "Je suis l'espace ou je suis" (I am the space where I am).

The problem of visualisation is an ever-present problem as there is always a discrepancy between the plan and design of a house and the constructed house. An architect cannot be the photographer of a potential reality, especially not in utopian visions, if he has not first seen the future as a literal picture, but only as an ideal. The destruction of this classical urban model led to the advent of new "rod-like urban design" models. A house now has more façades. The concept of space is futuristic and the psychology of perception is that of P.Modrian. It can only be perceived as a whole if we walk around adding up all of its façades. This has led to the introduction of a new topic - the dimension of time, which led to numerous discussions (Poincaré) on chronophotographic space. No matter how you view it, the initial design or plan was always a substitute for a multidimensional reality. To present the designs of their houses, Le Corbusier, F. L. Wright, O. Wagner, and others used a model of wire geometry which was then arranged on a descriptive construction imitating the central (frontal), biocular and polyocular perspective. The designs of F.L.Wright confirm this in particular; the construction emerges from the groundplan, the foundations are arranged in perspective as proof of their validity. (Edward H. Dohney Ranch, Sierra Madre Mountains, California, 1921., and Charles Ennis House, Los Angeles, California, 1924.)

Le Corbusier believed that the groundplan was the most important contribution for a definition of modern architecture -"plan générateur", as there should be no original assumption. The starting point is a blank sheet of paper. A cross-section view is important when designing a house on sloping ground, whereas the façade is easy to imagine, which is why it was the basis for all naïve, inverse axonometric projections and drawings of medieval towns. According to E. Bacon, these were more projections than the groundplan of an existing city, which had an organic structure and was built on sloping ground.

Be that as it may, the tools of illusion have been used since ancient times to achieve perspective and up until today in computer simulations. Horizontal and vertical lines are arbitrarily defined and Euclid's postulates are no longer valid. A line is the product of man's mind and cannot be touched, felt, smelt or tasted. If we try, we only end up getting our hands dirty. Therefore the rightful place for planning and design is in some imaginary architect's office. There is truth that can be demonstrated, but also conventional truth. (verticals in perspective projections, convergence of two planes…).

Human Perspectives in the Internet Society: Culture, Psychology and Gender, K. Morgan, J. Sanchez, C. A. Brebbia & A Voiskounsky (Editors) © 2004 WIT Press, www.witpress.com, ISBN 1-85312-726-4

4 Concepts of space and their pertinent dimensions

Although Cartesian space is defined by a symmetrical geometrical grid, and Descartes's matrix presumes a three-dimensional expansion of physical reality, these matrices stand in opposition to others in which space is not a general marker of objects and is not founded on data from sensory perception. Space belongs [24] primarily to the realm of thought (Kant) and ideas are first and foremost and, not the experienced object. It is the essence of space and "the dialogue of the spirit with its environment" (Vischer).

Material forms, and not space itself, are the essential elements of architecture (Wölflin). Or, thought, spirit and emotions, are what is important (H. Sögel). Schumacher strongly advocates the importance of spirituality and believes that optical perception is only one of the aspects for identifying space. Motor and tactile perception are important, but everything is governed by invisible stimulation and mystical powers that vibrate through the air, and which can only be registered by nerve endings on the skin. The essence of a spiritual foundation disputes perspective in space, according to which the world is finite (Newton). Space is a field, and not an "empty space" and depends on three dimensions of space and one of time.

When discussing the topic of space, one should be aware of the fact that it goes hand in hand with the topic of dimensions in space, especially when applied to an orthogonal geometrical grid like a matrix. This element is assigned a magical quality because it denotes a transition from a potential reality to architectonic magnitudes regardless of heuristic and nominal dimensions [17]. The grid-like pattern of a picture [8] on television also applies to architecture. We do not necessarily see a grid, just as we do not hear the ticking of a clock when we choose to ignore it. An architect sees in pictures, so the grid-like pattern disappears the closer he is to a final solution. Within the same operation, even in virtual space, it is essential for man to have a sense of orientation which means that two systems of reference should be employed: a visual key and a cognitive map. These maps are not so much cartographical as they are diagrammic. When these are linked to man's lifelong experience they become bio-grammes, which cannot really be defined by space and time, but in an abstract manner. Every space must be drawn in, no matter whether it is real or virtual. Some will read it literally, others reflectively. The former are searching for a vision and needs must be rational as they are aware of the physical qualities of a material, the stability of form, the populousness of space, and architects use a façade as a dividing screen between the interior and exterior. The latter are interested in the idea – the concept of a diversity of shapes, a tension of foam-like quality immersed in a fluid space, puzzles and dream visions. In the former case, dimensions are empirical; in the latter case, they are transcendental or metadimensional. The former accepts form, whereas the latter generates it.

As Peter Eisenman himself states, the Bio-Centre Project in Frankfurt am Main [13] was created through the application of a scientific method. Traditional architecture with its system of spatial hierarchies should be discarded because they are rigid and bar the way to the possibility of a house's further growth.

Human Perspectives in the Internet Society: Culture, Psychology and Gender, K. Morgan, J. Sanchez, C. A. Brebbia & A Voiskounsky (Editors) © 2004 WIT Press, www.witpress.com, ISBN 1-85312-726-4

Eisenman [25] wishes to explore other formal options that open up between biology and architecture. Since traditional biology differs from biology today, so its architecture needs to be divorced from traditional architecture. By abandoning Euclid's geometry and accepting fractal geometry and its dimensions, the form of an architect's house almost resembles the geometrical structure of DNA, that is, its inventory of shapes is closer to virtual architecture.

If one accepts that the virtual lies in the realm of the potential, then our bodies do not need to travel, only our thoughts do. To start with, machines would then be able to create new spaces for body and mind. The extent to which they influence architecture still remains open to discussion and is, as yet, hypothetical. If chips were to create invisible cities, then the following assumption by I.Calvino [7] would be feasible "…a lie resides not in the words, but in the objects themselves". Without a vision and supported only by words, there is no communication. Those who offer visions in the form of words must share the same or a similar experience with those who receive the vision.

On the other hand, a virtual house may perhaps mean a house on a screen in congruence with the paradigm we use when discussing virtual libraries, museums or shopping malls [22]. Architecture is not framed by walls; on the contrary, they hover like information on a screen, which would mean that an unreal picture of reality has been created "…a disembodied mind linked up to all the others in a virtual realm" (Ibid, p. 171).

R. Carpenter believes that the term virtual can be understood as meaning non-spatial, a term for "pure ex-territoriality", but ostensibly each point of the virtual can, but need not, be linked to a point in real space. What interests architects most is whether a system of repetition integrates architecture or architectonic form within the time structure, no matter whether literally or figuratively. In such a case, architecture would be a framework for past and future experiences, that is, it would need to have a plural dimension, and those dimensions would then digitally refashion architecture.

Virtuality has finally liberated itself from Alberti's perspective, but also from all that is specific to a house. Interfusion and diversity of application is best proffered by an empty house, so that a virtual "groundplan" is neither ideal, nor impossible. "Even Leibniz's best of all possible worlds is not a perfect world, but a world with the most virtuality" ([5], p. 175).

One may optimistically conclude that, in spite of everything, it is impossible to design such a house, so there is no reason to surrender to despair and uncertainty.

5 The beginnings of constructing a virtual house

Only one technical equipment has developed, safety features are able to guarantee increased comfort, solar systems can be controlled, better materials have been discovered, the climatic conditions in a house can be controlled and lights can be switched on and off with the help of sensors that react to human body temperature can serious thought be given to the building an "intelligent" or "smart" house. This would increase the quality of life for senior citizens and

Human Perspectives in the Internet Society: Culture, Psychology and Gender, K. Morgan, J. Sanchez, C. A. Brebbia & A Voiskounsky (Editors) © 2004 WIT Press, www.witpress.com, ISBN 1-85312-726-4

those who live on their own. A computer would control heating and conditioning systems, the functioning of the refrigerator and oven and would be mobile-phone activated. A more sophisticated system would be able to produce a breeze or a hurricane force wind, so that we would be able to lie back on the bed in our bedroom and watch the artificial dynamic interplay of light reflected off the water's surface of a pool in front of our living room and onto our ceiling. The artificially produced wind would blow through the curtains, causing an artificial draught that would slam doors shut. The only real example of a house that includes this anticipated virtuality [18] is that by J.Nouvel (Institut du Monde Arabe, in Paris, 1987). The building site of the Helsinki Virtual Village is in the suburbs of Helsinki and the plan is to have a wireless community. It should confirm the latest achievements in the information revolution with trite phrases uttered in reference to the metamorphosis of architecture and urbanism. This has already been done in the Italian village of Colletta di Castelbianco, which has been preserved intact, renovated and networked under the supervision of the architect Giancarlo de Carla. Some architects who are immersed in virtual reality tend to separate it into unit-based systems which they find in the "data supermarket". They are not interested in the changing form and possible picture, but in the idea of fragmenting form within space, which can then, in one particular moment of time, be realised as a para-hologram light projection. The user is linked up to an interactive environment, so that computerised live transmissions are sent out of the pictures and thoughts of the man as he builds "intelligent architecture". A complex house such as this with sophisticated, state-of-the-art software will only be able to house (super) intelligent beings and not people with the physiological and intellectual characteristics and capacities of modern man.

When discussing the virtual, one is filled with a mixed sense of enthusiasm and fear in view of the development of future branches of technology. This has always given rise to the same dilemma: should marginal possibilities be discarded or suppressed and kept far away from any ethical means of authentication? Or should we accept the ethical guide suggested by E.Drexler [12]?

6 The identity of genius loci and home

If form is characteristic trait of space, but also goes beyond it in its own perfection, then it surpasses not only time, but also our mental picture of an interior. This is why it is thought that a space that is being used accepts any type of form, whereas virtual space surpasses it, no matter when it comes into existence. Even when discussing the interpretation of an exterior space that is being utilised, Cache allows for virtuality by reducing it to abstract vector space, that is, to transience. The identity of a place, an important topic when discussing virtual space, is not an inherent trait that man can accept on a permanent basis. What is important is the permanent inter-space between cause and effect. Reality should always be a hollow picture because of possible unexpected events. More often than not, the truth is defined in correlation to the relationship between what

Human Perspectives in the Internet Society: Culture, Psychology and Gender, K. Morgan, J. Sanchez, C. A. Brebbia & A Voiskounsky (Editors) © 2004 WIT Press, www.witpress.com, ISBN 1-85312-726-4

is true and what is false, and not to the relationship between actual applied and virtual space.

"Surfaces of changing curvature are created through automated processes by digital machines" ([6], p. 158). Therefore, there is no indefinitely permanent place created according to preconditioned assumptions, as advocated by Ch. Norberg-Schulz [19].

A place becomes sustainable only when we learn to recognise what can open it up to the new, and not what it is or was. In order to define place, architecture has to satisfy the following three basic images: situation (orthographic map), vector sketch (curvature diagram) and geometrical figures (cone, dihedral, prism, plane), which will form the landscape of any urban composition. The world is no longer a quiet, fenced-in swimming pool filled with water, but the turbulent surface of a running stream that meanders to and fro. Time does not flow, it hesitates, and so the whole of society is turning into a nomadic tribe.

When discussing the spirit of a place [11], one should also mention the importance of feeling at home, which has a marked complexity and multiplicity to it. It is important to mention the following points: the anthropological (with emphasis on the existential dimension), the topofilial (which relates to Bachelard's understanding of space as a place of human warmth and memories) the structural (like the grid of points of a homeland) and the motivational and semantic (the influence of a community on the creation of the referential homeland topos). In a time of change and with a nomadic populace, virtual space, in the Kantian sense, will become devoid of a starry sky above it and lacking moral principles.

7 Man in virtual space

In their work, architects are faced with the interplay of science and technology, even though they use the knowledge of a scientist, whereas scientists use only tools provided by engineers. Everything focuses around which kind of shape and needs a human being will have, and consequently what kind of housing for work and recreation he will want. Evolutionary changes as such are not a primary concern for architects, that is, not until a borderline situation is created between a living being and a machine, especially when newly produced replicators start depending on natural laws. If material production decides on the physiological characteristics of this replicator, then the space will have to be defined without the application of natural laws. This will signify a vital change, followed by the complete disappearance of architects of a profession, which is what has already happened to certain profession in the past.

In all of these deliberations man is only mentioned indirectly. Does this mean that places of hedonistic melancholy and cheerful fatalism [26] will disappear forever? If it is difficult for man to cope with the truth, then he should learn to live with illusions. A new "body space" needs to be created.

This is something that architects find difficult to predict because even in the past they were not able to predict the organisation and appearance of such (groups of) cities in the future. This was done by poets (Marinetti, Mayakovski,

Human Perspectives in the Internet Society: Culture, Psychology and Gender, K. Morgan, J. Sanchez, C. A. Brebbia & A Voiskounsky (Editors) © 2004 WIT Press, www.witpress.com, ISBN 1-85312-726-4

Appolinaire) and painters in their manifests-proclamations in an attempt to find the effusions of the spirit's aspiration towards a new age. Immersed in architectonic form, architects were unable to discard potential realities.

What is confusing is that the closest idea, vision of the geometry of this new space was provided by the Expressionists, in particular a group that committed itself to anthropomorphic expression, like Finsterlin (Dream in Glass), Mendelshon (Musical Sketches), Wijdeveld (Vondel Park), Kiesler (Endless House), and others. Their paintings did not have the lasciviousness of a virtualist, but even without using coloristic diagrams they managed to offer fluidity and freedom of space. In the 1920s Kiesler talked about the infinite dimension of the human body.

Until the production of replicators is complete, in the sense already mentioned, modern man, with the physiological characteristics he has today, will travel the world with the help of optical cables. He will remain in one place while his senses travel. No matter how much electronic technology may extend his central nervous system, this cannot replace the archetypal structure of a house with an archetypal informational solution. The information column cannot help.

8 Afterword

Borderline situations between what is possible and impossible, that is, some kind of indication of natural laws, should be explored or established. All natural laws are valid as long as the law of gravity applies and the sun continues to rise in the same place every morning. It is possible to imagine that some other type of nature can be created, in which the present laws would be either completely or partly unnatural and which would be populated by another species of man, if you can call it that. This would imply that houses and cities would also be completely different.

Maybe this is not necessary.

Baudrillard believes that fantasy is the capturing of a living reality – very much in the same fashion in which Narcissus captured it. Even in this type of nature man has created something that is almost undemonstrable: "You bend over a hologram like God over his creation: only God has the power to walk through walls, through all living things and to find himself in the beyond, on the other side", in the form of immaterial matter ([3], p. 151). Man has acquired divine capabilities and qualities. However, this is but a temporary victory of the media over nature.

References

[1] Armstrong, R., Body Machine. Architectural Design, 11/12, London, p.93, 1998.

[2] Bachelard, G., Poetika prostora, Kultura: Beograd, pp.57-58, 1962.

[3] Baudrillard, J., Simulakrumi i simulacija, Biblioteka Psefizma, Naklada DAGGK: Karlovac, p.151,94,151, 2001.

[4] Bacon, E. N., Design of Cities, Thames and Hudson: London, p.93, 1975.

Human Perspectives in the Internet Society: Culture, Psychology and Gender, K. Morgan, J. Sanchez, C. A. Brebbia & A Voiskounsky (Editors) © 2004 WIT Press, www.witpress.com, ISBN 1-85312-726-4

[5] Bergson, I., Stvaralačka evolucija, Haus: Zabok, p.7,175, 2000.

[6] Cache, B., Pokreti zemlje, Biblioteka Psefizma, Naklada DAGGK: Karlovac, p.23,158, 2000.

[7] Calvino, I., Nevidljivi gradovi, Ceres: Zagreb, p.52, 1988.

[8] Cassierer, E., Ogled o čovjeku, Naprijed: Zagreb, p.75, 1978.

[9] Capra F., Tao fizike, Tipotisak: Zagreb, p.28,75, 1988.

[10] Čatić, I. (2003.), Scijentističko ili kulturologijsko obrazovanje za izazove budućnosti. Proc. Filozofija i tehnika, Hrvatsko filozofsko društvo: Zagreb, p.143, 2003.

[11] Dakić, S., Zavičaj i zavičajnost (predavanje), Motovunska ljetna škola Arhitektonskog fakulteta, p.1, 1993.

[12] Drexler, E., The Coming Era of Nanotechnology, Anchor Books, a division of Random House: New York, p.32, 1986.

[13] Eisenman, P., Bio-Centrum - Frankfurt am Main. Architectural Design, 1/2, London, 1988.

[14] Foucault, M., Riječi i stvari, Golden marketing: Zagreb, 2002.

[15] Gage, S., Intelligent Interactive Architecture. Architectural Design, 11/12, London, p.74, 1998.

[16] Gillian, H., Architecture in `Cybernetic Age' . Architectural Design, 11/12, London, p.53, 1998.

[17] Hamburger, E., Exact and Approximate Dimension, Lotus 37: Milano, p.5, 1983.

[18] Morgan, C. L., Jean Nouvel - The Elements of Architecture, Thames and Hudson: London, 1998.

[19] Norberg Shulz, Ch., Egizistencija, prostor i arhitektura, Gradevinska knjiga: Beograd, p.39, 1975.

[20] Novak, M., Next Babylon, Soft Babylon. Architectural Design, 11/12, London, p.23, 1998.

[21] Polić, M., O virtualnom i stvarnom na primjeru tzv. "virtualne stvarnosti. Proc. Filozofija i tehnika, Hrvatsko filozofsko društvo: Zagreb, p. 255, 2003.

[22] Rajchman, J., Konstrukcije, Biblioteka Psefizma, Naklada DAGGK: Karlovac, p.148,171, 2000.

[23] Romero, Ch., Vortex 2000. Architectural Design, 11/12, London, p.46, 1998.

[24] Van de Ven, C., Space in Architecture, Van Gorocum Assen: The Netherlands, p.117, 1980.

[25] Zaero, A., Peter Eisenman, Croquis 83: Madrid, p.71, 1999.

[26] Žmegač, V., Bečka moderna, Matica hrvatska: Zagreb, p.31, 1998.

Human Perspectives in the Internet Society: Culture, Psychology and Gender, K. Morgan, J. Sanchez, C. A. Brebbia & A Voiskounsky (Editors) © 2004 WIT Press, www.witpress.com, ISBN 1-85312-726-4

Section 10
Threats and challenges to diversity

The role of economic growth in coastal culture: a case-study in Qeshm Island, Persian Gulf

M. Mohebbi & A. S. Mahmoodi
Department of Architecture, Faculty of Fine Arts,
The University of Tehran, Tehran, Iran

Abstract

This paper arises from the quest of reaching a path for economic growth in a port in Qeshm Island located in the Persian Gulf [3]. Currently this port is a town, but in the near future it will become a special economic zone and will play an important role in the economy of the Persian Gulf. We intend to realise its condition and also find a proper way to respect cultural elements while programming and designing for this port. Recently, there has been an attempt to make some investments in the island in order to attract tourists to Qeshm. One possible approach for tourist attraction could be through existing resources on the island, i.e. navigational attractions, which could be appropriate and sustainable. The major task of this study has been to find an answer to this question: "How can we respect cultural values while technology affects our life in this age?"
Keywords: globalisation, coastal culture, Persian Gulf Bridge, dhow, navigation, sea-museum, tribal values, economic growth, respect.

1 Introduction

Culture has production, death and life (Ashouri [2]). It changes in the process of time, but it has the fixed factors, which if considered as the basis in the social and economic development, the primary values of a society will be protected while implementing the local changes.

Culture is also a powerful means of controlling cities, it plays a leading role in urban development strategies based on historic preservation or local "heritage" (Zukin [28]). It is a basic resource for sustainable economic growth (Santagata [24]). In the economic growth of the regions with ancient

Human Perspectives in the Internet Society: Culture, Psychology and Gender, K. Morgan, J. Sanchez, C. A. Brebbia & A Voiskounsky (Editors) © 2004 WIT Press, www.witpress.com, ISBN 1-85312-726-4

background, the shaping of a place is the outcome of power struggles between varies, cultures and fears within the existing social order (Greed [11]). In every growth and development, as the first insight, we should search for the meaning of the region. The meaning is marked out by identity (Graham [10]). It is us who make things mean. Meanings consequently, will always change, from one culture or period to another (Hall [12]). So, the meaning of region where we are studying on, should be discovered and then affect on the final plan. In this sense, many doubts and uncertainties can confound designers' task. How well will her/his work been received by clients and users and will it really satisfy their needs? (Lawson [17]). Users are much important, means natives and we should make a clear communication with them to find what they really need. Communication enables us to identify claims about values (Forester [8]), claims about what natives want to gain, or care about enough to put on the table for discussion.

When a region is studied to be made developed, planners should try to reach the fact of the existence of the region. Then they can design or program considering all details about the region. "Design is a conscious exercise. The unconscious can more than likely never infiltrate a design because the designer makes her/himself aware of every detail" (Bernard [6]), and the meaning of region is the most significant detail, which includes culture as the main consideration. Design at different scales can have a significant influence on the social and cultural relationships (Talebi [25]). In this century, the global commercial forces and technological developments are influencing the cultures of cities. In many people's opinion, development is considered as a threat for identity. But, in this discussion, we try to make a debate about the correlation between the local culture and technology, but in a different way. Technology can affect culture positively, if designers or planners try to find to what extent each of them can affect our life.

1.1 Economic growth and information technology

Social scientists are only now coming to grips with information technology (IT); because it is the main consideration which can be useful in the process of transformation, especially cultural transformation (Henry [13]). It is a fact that we can maximise the usefulness of new information technology in the workplace when we understand culture.

IT is inevitable in the age of globalisation, and technology is only half of what IT is about (Henry [13]). Thanks to IT, planners, investors and ordinary people (Esp. in the developing countries or traditional societies) will be able to achieve better ways to use natural resources. This will end in stable development and progress towards what we call "Social Welfare". The first way to change the current situation and to take advantage of the environmental factor is to promote social welfare. This will end in economic growth by itself. Economic growth can be considered as a direct consequence of IT. We have considered economic growth as the main result of IT in the present study. The latter can lead the society towards better use of environment. This can even happen in a simple

Human Perspectives in the Internet Society: Culture, Psychology and Gender, K. Morgan, J. Sanchez, C. A. Brebbia & A Voiskounsky (Editors) © 2004 WIT Press, www.witpress.com, ISBN 1-85312-726-4

rural area as an economic change. The site is an example of rural areas, which is considered to be developed as a special port.

1.2 Aims

- To respect all values while developing a place.
- To reach proper spaces to consider in this ancient area; which can help us to revive the local values.

1.3 Research methodology (Case-study)

Methodology should be a conversation about everything that could be made to happen (Jones [7]). The methodology of this research includes: 1. Literature Review, 2. Surveying, 3. Field works. The comprehensive plan of this port was first reviewed, then analysed the equipment considered in the plan. Also, we spent more than 2 months in the port and performed several field-works including interviews and filling questionnaires. We analysed the collected data based on the native people's opinion about what we can do to respect the cultural values in the plan. The final section discusses the creation of cultural spaces.

2 The site (the Persian Gulf, Qeshm Island, Loft Port)

Ancient Iranians were the first great navigators of the world. (Nourbakhsh [19]) The Persian Gulf is an area of the world with a seafaring tradition of over 5,000 years in age, it had been considered as the most suitable region for sailing and evolution of human civilisation for its calmness and warm waters" (Amir Ebrahimi [1]). The name of "Qeshm" as the biggest island, is a testimony to Elamites long stay in this area [21]. The island is approximately 120 km long in an east-west direction, and between ten and thirty kilometre wide [22]. Qeshm has a native population of over 85,000, a majority of them are Sunni Moslems. The activities of native people is mainly centred around fishing and shrimp trapping, ship building, palm farming, trade and folk art [23].

Loft is one of the most important towns, which is considered to be developed as a special port in the long-term strategy of the Qeshm development plan. There are three considerable factors in the future development of "Loft": Gavarzin Gas Field, Hara Sea-Forest and The Persian Gulf Bridge, fig. 1.

3 The proposed plan

In the original comprehensive plan prepared for the Qeshm Island, the chapter of "Loft Development", the following subjects were evaluated (Pajouhesh [20]): 60000 square metres is considered for religious-cultural functions, fig. 1. In that classification, "religious" and "cultural" functions have been separated. However, it would have been more appropriate to use the term "cultural" as a major criteria that includes many sub divisions, i.e. "religion". Culture is about different ways of approaching knowledge, different areas which are discussed

Human Perspectives in the Internet Society: Culture, Psychology and Gender, K. Morgan, J. Sanchez, C. A. Brebbia & A Voiskounsky (Editors) © 2004 WIT Press, www.witpress.com, ISBN 1-85312-726-4

while others remain tacit (Veltman [26]). In this context, the ancient culture of navigation is the most considerable factor, which should be evaluated separately.

The coastal bounds have been determined in about 300 metre from the edges of the beach. Also, 50% of this area has been considered for public functions. About 30% of these spaces are located at the perspective of the old context of "Loft", fig. 1. As considered in the comprehensive plan, public functions include hotels, shopping centres and environmental protected parks. This kind of approach to the coastline architecture and urbanism cannot be acceptable. Because public spaces are the primary site of public culture, they are a window into the city's soul (Zukin [28]); and "Loft" port is a city of culture, does not possess an abundance of historic and artistic resources, but is able to generate culture (Santagata [24]). In the present, there is a peerless perspective of the valuable native architecture from the Hara sea-forest side, fig. 2. We should respect this unique view and try to revive the main meaning of dominant elements, which has been forgotten in the visual mind of "Loft" port, along the economic growth. We should define sea bounds by some elements, which are valuable in the aesthetics or functional viewpoint; e.g. definition of some enclosures, which are combined with nature. The nature is a part of heritage; heritage is often envisaged through intangible forms of traditional and popular culture (Graham [10]), but heritage is everything which gives the meaning to a region. As another instance, Definition of some exhibitions (e.g. sea-museum), with using modern architectural technology while respecting traditional forms, can help the designer to revive its rich ancient culture of navigation. In the recent performances of the local organisations, several "Dhow Constructions" were closed under the ignorance of some native craftsmen who earn a livelihood via this craft. The establishment of a "Sea-Museum", can be helpful for the craftsmen. In this museum, they can be active again, this time in the most valuable position, as the reminders of this ancient craft.

The East Side of this site, is considered to program for high residential buildings. fig. 1. This approach is such like the past undertakings in Qeshm City. The present view taken for Qeshm City is basically economic oriented approach. Except for a few buildings, there is not a trace of culture. In such an ancient area (Loft Port), with religious background and cultural marks, planning for high residential buildings can be the worst approach to solve this local problem. Totally, the original decision will be made by the original owners, native people, but not us! In the most important stage of the study, after the evaluation of the comprehensive plan, native people's opinion was asked.

3.1 Constraining problems, probable solution

The proposed bridge in this region with such a valuable cultural background could pose some serious problems. In these new conditions, this town can be a function of the role of the heritage town as tourism capital. If we don't consider coastal culture in a dynamic way, tourism can affect coastal culture negatively. "When the local culture is considered in a more dynamic way, the future is not as a threat for the local culture" (Vogelij [27]). Culture provides the tools to transform the city and to mobilise the population (Belliot [5]); we should try to

Human Perspectives in the Internet Society: Culture, Psychology and Gender, K. Morgan, J. Sanchez, C. A. Brebbia & A Voiskounsky (Editors) © 2004 WIT Press, www.witpress.com, ISBN 1-85312-726-4

find these tools and also, "visible" and "invisible" culture should be considered. Visible culture includes valuable regional architecture as the most considerable factor. But, invisible culture is hidden in the natives' minds. We tried to discover the latter by questionnaires.

3.2 Structure of the questionnaire

The interviewer-administrated questionnaire was used to collect the data on Sea-Culture based on native people's opinions. The questionnaire was prepared based on Sociometry (Using Psychological bases), and "Incomplete Sentences Test" was included at the end. The sampling was a judgement sampling. We had to consider three main groups of clients: "the native sailors, youth and the fixed population of the port." It was intended to have a wide range of opinions. The sample size consisted of 15% of all natives in "Loft" port. Study Group: native sailors (31.8%) and others (68.2%); Target Group: "natives who live in the Loft port"; Alpha: 0.5453; Standard Item Alpha: 0.4907; Age-range: 10-75 years; Mean: 37.8; M/F: ~2/1; Uneducated/educated: ~ 1/2

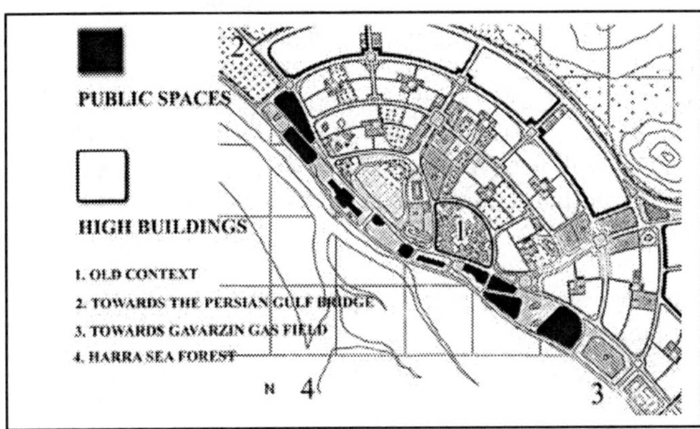

Figure 1: Comprehensive plan of Loft Port, the public spaces considered on sea-bounds.

3.2.1 Results of the questionnaire

A total of 25 questions were given to the natives; however, because of the aims of this article, only five main questions are analysed. The question of whether high technology is good or not, is meaningless (Leamnson [18]). There cannot be a yes/no answer. So, the main part of the questionnaire is provided based on this basically question: "Is technology a change in our culture?" (Frances Higuchi [9]); this part included five Multiple-choice questions. As a result, it is intended to analyse these questions:

1."Does the establishment of "The Persian Gulf Bridge" have any desirable effect on the natives' life?" It is a simple question, but it is very important to find how natives think in this case; because this establishment is very useful for the economy of "Loft" port, but what we can do to create this event in the best way

Human Perspectives in the Internet Society: Culture, Psychology and Gender, K. Morgan, J. Sanchez, C. A. Brebbia & A Voiskounsky (Editors) © 2004 WIT Press, www.witpress.com, ISBN 1-85312-726-4

which natives have a feeling of calmness. After analysing the results, we saw that more than 53.63% of natives think that this event can affect their life negatively (Table 1). In the natives' opinion, the most undesirable result after the establishment of the bridge is "insecurity" (Table 2). The feeling of "insecurity" arises from peoples' mental background. It is such like "Generalised Anxiety"; this anxiety arises from the past unpleasant experiences (Azad [4]). In another questionnaire, which we provided for "Qeshm City", we asked about the economic growth process and its results. More than 63% of the clients believed that "the present process is just the economic growth and we have not been considered as the natives in this process." Qeshm City as an incorrect experience in the neighbourhood can affect the natives' minds negatively. The clients think that this establishment will be a threat for their tribal relations; and their youth become accustomed with the modern manifestations without any knowledge about their historical background. In this condition, cultural growth should be considered along the economic growth. The culture is by our use of things, and what we say, think and feel about them that we give them a meaning (Graham [10]); So, the planners can create culture along while protecting the local values; with the help of local equipment and natives' opinions. It appears that people believe in that the local organisations cannot solve the future problems, which will occur after this link. The first solution to change natives' opinion is the <u>maintenance</u> of the present valuable architectural spaces in this context. It is a step forward. Maintenance in this way, can bring the feeling of security for the natives and, they will believe that they should revere this context as a peerless instance of the coastline architecture in the Persian Gulf, as an important part of the coastal culture.

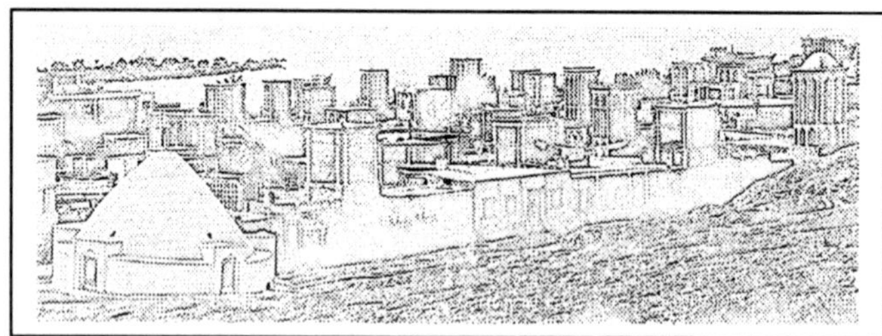

Figure 2: The peerless perspective of "Loft Port" (East Side).

Table 1: The level of desirability of establishment of the Persian Gulf Bridge, based on age groups.

Age group	Desirable	Undesirable	Blank
10-20 (31.57%)	50%	33.33%	16.6%
20-45 (36.74%)	42.86%	57.14%	-
45-75 (31.57%)	51%	30.33%	18.6%

2. Art is an important agent then in transmission of culture. (John and Kneis [15]) But in a city, using of art should be logical; because "A City is not a Work

Human Perspectives in the Internet Society: Culture, Psychology and Gender, K. Morgan, J. Sanchez, C. A. Brebbia & A Voiskounsky (Editors) © 2004 WIT Press, www.witpress.com, ISBN 1-85312-726-4

of Art" (Jacobs [14]). Considering this fact, the museum is a space, which is established based on "Art". In another question, it was asked as a suggestion: "If the establishment of Persian Gulf Bridge has undesirable effect, To what extent, establishment of a sea-museum can improve this condition?" More than 63% of the clients confess that establishing a sea-museum and other similar functions will help protecting the local culture to be alive, after the process of the development. The impact of the museum district is multifold. Its realisation increases the demand for cultural services (Santagata [24]). Sea museums create a social space for the exchange of ideas on which businesses thrive (Zukin [28]); So, considering cultural parks and Eco-museum can be useful in this context, to flourish its economics and revive the tribal values.

3. The other three questions were about sea museum, its location and necessity. The answers showed that the clients approve this kind of programming for this region (Table 3). If we collate group number one by others, will reach these results: Lack of acquaintance between the youth and traditional-cultural values and, inefficient traditional methods, which have been used by local organisations.

The distinction between the approaches is not easy. As a result, modern movements with cultural background can be the best way to develop this region, fig. 3. Also, in people's opinion this approach was been selected. In this point, we reach to the first part of our discussion. If we try to respect heritage and technology through every growth, we can see that the natives will not consider technology as a threat and, the tribal and cultural elements will be shown to the native youth and also, to the visitors of this region.

4 Conclusion

Economic growth and technological development make a new planning for the town, which is considered for this development. This is a critical event when we should work on a town with ancient background. In this condition, there is one brilliant factor, heritage. Heritage means everything and cultural considerations are the most important factors. Town planning is the art and science of ordering the use of land and the character and siting of buildings and communicative routes (Keeble [16]). One major step before making any proposal for a site development should include the search for the appropriate land use of the site. This will require a thorough study about the identity of that site and how could one preserve the major values of that site. If we find the exact and proper function, then planning will go on the right path. In this point, technology and growth cannot be a threat. There are three considerations, which we should notice in the process of such development:

1- The correlation between the spaces and people's faiths.

2- The correlation between the local values and future functions.

3- The analysis of into what extent the future functions and spaces can occur while respecting thc heritage of site.

In this process, we will find the valuable considerations, then our planning can be respectable to natives.

Table 2: The foreseen reasons behind the rejection of the natives for the establishment of the Persian Gulf Bridge, based on age group of 20-45 (the realist age group).

Results Age group	Tribal Reasons	Security	Cultural Values	Unknown
20-45	10.53%	53%	26%	10.47%

Table 3: The level of the native's desirability with the three proposed design approach to construct the museum.

View Age group	Traditional Approach	Modern Approach	Tradition & Modernism	Educated
10-20	33.3%	33.3%	33.3%	83.3%
20-45	28.57%	-	71.42%	85.71%
45-75	44.52%	-	16.6%	34.5%

Figure 3: The different approaches to designing a sea-museum in this ancient site which were asked of natives.

So, technology and identity (culture as the most important factor) have friendly relation. And also, in some cases, technology can help our culture to show itself to the visitors of the place. So, we can use technology and economics to improve our cultural values. Only, we should know how much each of them is worth and also, in what field each of them can affect our lives.

Acknowledgements

Supported by a grant from the "University of Tehran" (Ref. 42/15130), and also a grant from the (NYOIR).

The authors wish to thank Dr. M.R. Mohebbi for revision of the text. We also thank Mr. S. Zoulfaghar Nasab for the statistical analysis and Miss Farkhondeh Saffari for her kind help in the field works. This work is dedicated to the memory of Dr. Nasrin Golijani Moghaddam.

Human Perspectives in the Internet Society: Culture, Psychology and Gender, K. Morgan, J. Sanchez, C. A. Brebbia & A Voiskounsky (Editors) © 2004 WIT Press, www.witpress.com, ISBN 1-85312-726-4

References

[1] Amir Ebrahimi, A., *Persian Gulf*, Humanities Research Centre, Tehran, Iran, 1977.

[2] Ashouri, D., *Definitions and the meaning of culture*, Agah Publication, Tehran, Iran, pp. 3, 2001.

[3] A team of architecture students of the University of Tehran, *The Architecture of Loft Port*, Qeshm Free Area Publication, pp. 16-10-127, 1998.

[4] Azad, H., *Psychopathology*, Be'esat Publication, Tehran, Iran, pp.154-155, 1994.

[5] Belliot, M., Public Culture and Urban Planning, 4th biennial Rotterdam, reports, Parallel Session 6. www.planum.net/4bie/ws6.htm

[6] Bernard Kennif, T., The Clean Street Paradox, *Architectural Research Quarterly*, 6(2), pp.118, 2002.

[7] Christopher Jones, J., *Essays in Design*, John Wiley & Sons Ltd., UK, pp. 246, 1984.

[8] Forester, J., Beyond dialogue to transformative learning, Democratic Dialogues: *Theories and Practices*, ed. S. Esquith, Poznan, The University of Poznan, 1996.

[9] Frances Higuchi, M., Technology - A Change In My Culture?, Hawaii Geographic Alliance, 1999. www2.Hawaii.edu/hga/GAW99/techage.html

[10] Graham, B., Heritage as Knowledge: Capital or Culture?, *Urban Studies*, 39(5-6), pp. 1004-1005, 2002.

[11] Greed H., Clara, *Social Town Planning*, TJ International Ltd., UK, pp. 224, 1999.

[12] Hall, S. (Ed.), Representation: *Cultural Representations and Signifying Practices*, Sage/Open University, pp. 61, 1997.

[13] Henry, M., *I.T. in the Social Sciences*, Blackwell Publishers, Oxford, pp. 9, 1999.

[14] Jacobs, J., A city is not a Work of Art, *Metropolis Values in Conflict*, Wadsworth Publishing Co. Inc. Belmot, California, pp.106-110, 1968.

[15] John, P., Kneis, P., The Scope of Culture, culture, Cultural Studies and Cultural Politics, April 7th/May 1st 2000 www.philjohn.com/papers/pjkd_ga14 .html

[16] Keeble, L., *Principles and Practice of Town and Country Planning*, London, Estates Gazette, pp. 1, 1959 (2nd edition)

[17] Lawson, B., *How designers think*, The Architectural Press Ltd., London, pp. 81, 1980.

[18] Leamnson, R. N., Does Technology Present a New Way of Learning? , *Educational Technology & Society*, 4(1), 2001.

[19] Nourbakhsh, H., Iranians the Pioneers of Navigation in the Persian Gulf, CAIS at SOAS, University of London. www.cais-soas.com/CAIS/ Geography/ Persian Gulf/navigator.htm.

Human Perspectives in the Internet Society: Culture, Psychology and Gender, K. Morgan, J. Sanchez, C. A. Brebbia & A Voiskounsky (Editors) © 2004 WIT Press, www.witpress.com, ISBN 1-85312-726-4

[20] Pajouhesh Me'emari Consulting Engineers, *Comprehensive Plan of "Loft Port"*, Qeshm Free Area Organisation, Volume 13, Tehran, Iran, pp. 9-19-36, 1991.

[21] Qeshm Free Area, The Site of Qeshm Free Area, English Version, Cultural Characteristics. www.qeshm.ir/cultural.asp.

[22] Qeshm Free Area, The Site of Qeshm Free Area, English Version, Historical Places. www.qeshm.ir/historical.asp.

[23] Qeshm Free Area, The Site of Qeshm Free Area, English Version, Occupations. www.qeshm.ir/population.asp.

[24] Santagata, W., Cultural Districts, Property Rights and Sustainable Economic Growth, *International Journal of Urban and Regional Research*, 26(1), pp.9-18-19, 2002.

[25] Talebi, J., Design of Urban Passages and Social Relationships, *proc. of the XXXIAHS World Congress on Housing, Portugal*, September 9-13, 2002.

[26] Veltman, K. H., Why Culture is Important? www. sumscorp.com/articles/art49.htm.

[27] Vogelij, J., Introduction to the exhibition, Content editor and chairman of the board of the 4th Biennial Towns Planners, Culture of Cities Databank. www.planum.net/4bie/documents/vogelij.pdf.

[28] Zukin, S., *The Cultures of Cities*, Blackwell Publishers, Oxford, pp. 1, 11, 13, 259, 1995.

Human Perspectives in the Internet Society: Culture, Psychology and Gender, K. Morgan, J. Sanchez, C. A. Brebbia & A Voiskounsky (Editors) © 2004 WIT Press, www.witpress.com, ISBN 1-85312-726-4

Norms and values in contemporary society: an application to the field of sustainable transportation

J. A. Prades[1], R. Belzile[1], M. Glaus[2], R. Hausler[2], J.-P. Revéret[1] & J. M. Rubio-Ardanaz[1]
[1]*GREIGE. Interdisciplinary Research Group on Environmental Management, University of Quebec in Montreal, Canada*
[2]*Higher Academy of Technology, University of Quebec, Montreal, Canada*

Abstract

The *general objective* of this paper is to have a better discernment of the implications of norms and values in contemporary society. Its *specific objective* is to apply this preliminary theoretical reflection to the critical and practical question of finding a well-founded way to promote sustainable transportation effectively. In this connection, the paper includes two parts, in order to present the setting and the treating of the problem.

1 Setting the problem

1.1 Preliminary considerations and definitions

1.1.1 Norms and values

In behavioral sciences, especially in psychology and sociology, norms are general precepts which, being internalized or accepted by individuals or by social groups, induce conformity in simple actions or in complex judgments. Values are of importance to philosophy, economics and sociology. In philosophy values are part of ethics and aesthetics and give rise to inescapable and fundamental controversy. In economics *the theory of value* is usually equivalent with the *theory of price*. In sociology, the field where we are particularly concerned to, values are constituent facts of social structure. The sociologist does not try to

Human Perspectives in the Internet Society: Culture, Psychology and Gender, K. Morgan, J. Sanchez, C. A. Brebbia & A Voiskounsky (Editors) © 2004 WIT Press, www.witpress.com, ISBN 1-85312-726-4

assess their intrinsic worth, but he treats them as scarce objects of socially conditioned desire [1].

In our sociological perspective, "values" involve desires, and "norms" involve constrained obligations. In this sense, "values" as important as they may be, evoke a kind of wishful thinking and remain frequently ineffectual in practice. On the other hand, "norms" are mainly effective in every day life. As a matter of fact, values are socially significant and meet their real goals when they are in conformity with determinant social norms.

According to Max Weber's celebrated essay on *The Protestant Ethic and the Spirit of Capitalism* [2], the basic values of modern society prioritize socioeconomic aspirations: prosperity for all, profits for business, full employment, good salaries, high level of consumption. These prioritized values did not change since the beginnings of the modern world. In our days, a new emergent society maintains them entirely, while adding two unedited devices: strong respect to the environment and an invading propensity to the massive use of informatics and of new information and communication technologies, in business and in private life.

Unlike of values, that knew some newcomers recently, norms are absolutely unchanged in contemporary society (cybersociety). So in every kind of business, the supreme norm that determines the means leading to the desired goals (socioeconomic values) remains essentially unchanged and undeniable. What is to be done for being successful is to gather societal forces and capital in order to make money and to amass profits. For attaining this goal a unique means (it is an unavoidable social norm) is imperative: each investment must be preceded by a rigorous calculation of feasibility, i.e., of being sure of remunerative commercial and financial returns. Before the first step, every leader must calculate costs and benefits. Put in other words, without a substantial amount of capital no significant project is possible. Without rigorous previous calculation, no capital is available. We face then a clear and decisive vision. In the socioeconomic milieu of modern society, the norm of success, constant and steadfast, involves a few basic stages. (i) To define a set of goals coming in terms with the desires and expectations of the population. (ii) To prepare a detailed project in this connection. (iii) To calculate its costs and benefits. (iv) To make sure that the operation is socially feasible and profitable in commercial and financial terms. (v) To gather together societal forces in order to dispose of the necessary capital for the launching of the project. As Max Weber has said lucidly [3], modern society has leave off the world of magic to dwell in the world of rationality.

1.1.2 Sustainable transportation

We adopt the following definition [4]. "Sustainable mobility is a term that can mean different things to different people. The World Business Center of Sustainable Development defines *sustainable mobility* as the ability to meet the needs of society to move freely, gain access, communicate, trade, and establish relationships without sacrificing other essential human or ecological values today or in future". In agreement of this definition, the promotion of sustainable transportation constitutes the overarching goal of our intellectual work [5].

Human Perspectives in the Internet Society: Culture, Psychology and Gender, K. Morgan, J. Sanchez, C. A. Brebbia & A Voiskounsky (Editors) © 2004 WIT Press, www.witpress.com, ISBN 1-85312-726-4

1.1.3 Norms and values in the field of sustainable transportation

1.1.3.1 ***At the level of values,*** the great majority of specialists agree. The deficiencies of the actual system (pollution, congestion, severe and countless accidents) must be rectified.

1.1.3.2 ***At the level of norms,*** things are quite different. From a sociological, not an axiological point of view, we can state that in the realm of means, most people prioritize mitigation measures involving low costs and only a small minority prioritize substantial innovative measures and high costs. In fact neither of them obtain significant results. Why?

In our view, the real point is not just the calculation of costs. How many billions did the investment on highways, harbors and airports cost in the last century? How many billions do our informatics equipment cost to day? The real point is elsewhere. The failure or the success of socioeconomic endeavor does not depend on costs, but on an accurate preparative work calculating costs and benefits and effectively balancing values and norms, social aspirations and sound management imperatives.

1.1.4 The concept of societal integration

As elaborated in a Durkheim's authoritative piece of work [6], this concept is a basic guideline for our inquiry.

1.1.4.1 ***General principle.*** A sane society, a sane world society, is the highest entity human beings can conceive of. Because they need to be together, humans must collaborate if they want to survive. In the long run, a sane society is not the fruit of endless conflict or of individualistic choices, but the fruit of a definitely integrative endeavor. Contemporary, over-diversified society has therefore but one single option for survival: to promote integration, to find the best ways of sharing individual and social abilities and attainments. In Durkheim's view [7], this vision stems simultaneously from religious, moral, historical and sociological considerations.

1.1.4.2 ***Two constitutive elements.*** Societal integration implies two elements: (i) a coherent combination of *action programs,* ruled by an organizing trustworthy principle and (ii) a convergence of *societal forces* that pursue a common goal, because they can only afford this goal together, and because this collaboration responds to the interests of each of them [8].

We will see below that the assembling of action programs and of societal forces (governments, business, experts, civic associations) that can implement the renewal towards a sustainable transportation system, correspond essentially to the concept of societal integration.

1.2 Provisional conclusion

The above socioeconomic and epistemological reflections help to understand the problems and the queries of the contemporary society [9] in the sustainable transportation issue. There are countless initiatives. The results seem extremely

Human Perspectives in the Internet Society: Culture, Psychology and Gender, K. Morgan, J. Sanchez, C. A. Brebbia & A Voiskounsky (Editors) © 2004 WIT Press, www.witpress.com, ISBN 1-85312-726-4

weak. Either because the remedies are too small and consequently not efficient enough, or because they are not sufficiently prepared in sound managerial skill.

These reflections have lead to a central hypothesis. The move to sustainable transportation requires a plan of action based on huge investment and sound managerial skill, in full agreement to the norms of the contemporary world. How we go about it will be discussed below.

2 Treating the problem

2.1 Delineating specific goals

According to many specialists [10], sustainable transportation must include three complementary measures in order to help millions of people all over the word. (i) To ensure the proliferation of high speed (including short and daily trips) to overcome congestion. (ii) To expand automation and cybernetic control of the transportation system in order to ensure health and security. (iii) To implement energetic sources in order to be done with pollution for the present and future generations.

These values constitute an idea, a kind of basic concept. To put this idea in motion, one needs to design a project. Surely, every project involves an idea. But a project involves moreover numerous essential elements that must be described previously and thoroughly. A concept may be expressed in a few lines of writing. A project needs several pages. The reader will find in following pages a short presentation of our Project.

2.2 Designing the project

The description of our Project includes the following steps. (i) The priorities. (ii) The specific objectives. (iii) The key points. (iv) The characteristics of the work.

2.2.1 Priorities

What is most urgently needed is not endless searching for numerous sustainability measures. What is needed is to set out a comprehensive, coordinated and collaborative Project designed to prepare a new 'world order' in transportation that meets the needs of a vibrant economy for an equitable society and a protected environment [11].

Such a global Project, that has been rarely undertaken before, is nevertheless indispensable for a very fundamental reason. Transportation is a hypercomplex societal system that includes inexhaustible components at economic, social, and regulatory levels. Changes to this system accommodate or upset very different kinds of stakeholders (consumers, investors, public agencies, etc.). It is impossible then, to make significant changes to this system without extremely difficult consensual agreements. These agreements require a very good knowledge of the consequences of these changes, which cannot be acquired simply or spontaneously. Being extremely complex on account of the

Human Perspectives in the Internet Society: Culture, Psychology and Gender, K. Morgan, J. Sanchez, C. A. Brebbia & A Voiskounsky (Editors) © 2004 WIT Press, www.witpress.com, ISBN 1-85312-726-4

multiplicity of the interactions at stake, this knowledge must be the result of a rigorously coordinated global preliminary study.

The essential purpose of this study is not to specify or to complain about the failures of the current transportation system. It is to find a complete, balanced and alternative transportation system that is fully aware of the potential and the limitations of the scientific, technological and regulatory resources of the contemporary world, and invites societal leaders to engage the necessary alternative investment.

2.2.2 Specific objectives

Objective one. To improve our knowledge on best practices concerning the following issues: the ground transportation of people and goods, the ground transportation within cities, between cities and suburbs, and between different cities, the links between ground, and maritime and air transportation.

Objective two. To design a well defined, balanced and optimized combination of efficient transportation modes that are destined to satisfy the growing demand for transportation in the perspective of sustainable development [12].

Objective three. To conceive of and to test the societal receptivity towards the creation of a collective, private and public regulatory coalition, destined to facilitate and to supervise the process of planning, developing and managing this balanced and optimized combination of efficient transportation modes.

Objective four. To demonstrate with facts and figures whether this new transportation system, based on this new regulatory coalition, can or can not satisfy the needs of consumers, investors and public agencies, in a way that is more advantageous than the current transportation system.

Objective five. To submit to consensual agreement the results of this study, in order to test its main findings, to improve them, and to move effectively towards sustainable transportation.

2.2.3 Key points of the preliminary study

In order to attain its specific objectives, the study has to analyze in a systematic manner a large number of key points. Each one of them includes the implementation of detailed analytical reports. These reports end with a coherent set of conclusions, a questionnaire for consulting external experts (to validate these conclusions), and immediate and practical recommendations. Of course, all this work implies a thorough review of the current literature.

It is absolutely necessary to show the complexity and variety of the questions that must be analyzed. A collection of examples follow.

Key point one. The selection of time and space limits.

Report 1. Detailed description and justification. The report presents a global vision of the Project and determines and justifies its main phases (at short, middle and long term) and the convenient places where the Project will be tested. This report considers just the short term and focuses its inquiry on a small suburban North American town that henceforth will be called Middletown (MT).

Human Perspectives in the Internet Society: Culture, Psychology and Gender, K. Morgan, J. Sanchez, C. A. Brebbia & A Voiskounsky (Editors) © 2004 WIT Press, www.witpress.com, ISBN 1-85312-726-4

Key point two. The range of locomotion technologies.

Report 2. The current range of locomotion technologies (for goods and people) in MT. Using advanced data-base and statistical compilations [13], this report analyses two kinds of facts. **First.** The basic data concerning the amount of following current transportation modes: (i) Trains (conventional, light, high-speed). (ii) Cars (conventional, electric, hybrid, neighborhood vehicles). (iii) Trucks (heavy, middle, light, trailers, semi-trailers, conventional or assorted with rail or with fluvial intermodal combinations). (iv) Fluvial fleet. (v) Air connections. **Second.** A detailed picture of the current transportation supply system. (i) Daily miles covered by each transportation mode. (ii) Outstanding regulatory and fiscal measures. (iii) Costs and advantages for transportation consumers. (iv) Degree of satisfaction of consumers, and estimation of their biggest problems (congestion, pollution, accidents, etc,). (v) Global financial input and global financial profitability for private investors and public agencies. (vi) Degree of satisfaction or disapproval of investors in this respect.

Report 3. Conceptual design of an alternative range of goods locomotion technologies for MT. Using simulation techniques, the report presents a picture of a goods transportation supply system, destined to improve productivity and to minimize incoherent daily displacements, thanks to two essential measures. **First**. The distribution of goods founded in three basic principles. (i) A large network of high storied warehouses destined to lay down systematically all goods that come from without and that will be distributed in MT. (ii) These warehouses receive the goods coming from without MT only by an underground or elevated railroad system (no exterior truck can circulate inside the town). (iii) These warehouses distribute the goods by a network of light electric delivery vans. **Second**. The movement of goods (from without to within and from within to within) ordered by a complex data processing console that avoids useless repetition of displacements, and provides the best service.

Report 4. Operational design of the preceding conceptual alternative for goods locomotion technologies. The conceptual alternative has been studied in the report 2. This system must be also defined with all the details that permit the potential investors to put the system in motion. Given the large number of such systems [14], report 4 determines which one offers the best cost effective conditions.

Report 5. Conceptual design of an alternative range of people locomotion technologies in MT. Using simulation techniques, report 4 presents a people transportation supply system designed to satisfy the needs of citizens, to improve productivity and to minimize time-consuming displacements. Two initiatives will be tested. **First**. Building a transportation supply system founded on four complementary principles. (i) An efficient network of stations all over MT, that offer inter city connections, by elevated (or underground) high-speed trains [15]. (ii) The implementation of an efficient network of stations that offer the largest possible quantity of interconnections, by elevated (or underground) light trains. (iii) The proliferation of smart neighborhood electric vehicles [16] designed to access with easy the network of train stations, or to commute between home, station, work, marked or leisure places. (iv) The rational utilization of

Human Perspectives in the Internet Society: Culture, Psychology and Gender, K. Morgan, J. Sanchez, C. A. Brebbia & A Voiskounsky (Editors) © 2004 WIT Press, www.witpress.com, ISBN 1-85312-726-4

conventional automobiles mostly equipped with electric or hybrid engines **Second.** Moving people in MT (from within to without and from within to within) thanks to a complex data processing console that, previously informed of specific needs by a simple telephone call, helps to avoid waste of time and provides the best service. Cars will not disappear. Just change their function in the alternative system.

Report 6. Operational design of the preceding alternative. The conceptual alternative studied in the report 5 indicated three kinds of locomotion systems: high-speed trains, light trains, smart neighborhood electric vehicles, conventional cars equipped with electric or hybrid engines. In order to attain our objectives, report 6 defines each one of these systems with all the details that permit potential investors to put the system into operation in the best cost effective conditions.

Report 7. Current and alternative locomotion technologies in the transportation system. Putting together the results of the preceding reports (2 to 6) report 7 sums up the characteristics of the current and of the alternative supply transportation system, in order to compare their respective costs and advantages [17].

Key point three. The range of information and communication technologies in the transportation supply system.

Report 8. Information and communication technologies in the alternative transportation system. Reports 3 and 5 introduced the concept of new information and communication technologies (ICT). Given that this concept is available in a large variety of modalities, it is necessary to choose the technologies that are best adapted and most cost-effective. Knowing that a massive utilization of ICTs is an important condition for the renewal of business, the objective of report 7 is not to share endless comparisons, but to undertake a systematic exchange with a few important corporations specialized in ICT. (IBM, Global Telematics, Microsoft Research [18]) in order to find the logistics, advertising, e-commerce, selling promotion, and public relations, that are best adapted.

Report 9. Information and communication technologies in the current and in the alternative transportation system. By compiling the results of the report 8, report 9 compares in detail the utilization of ICTs in the current and in the alternative supply transportation system and shows with facts and figures the advantages of the massive introduction of ICTs.

Key point four. The energy sources in the transportation supply system.

Report 10. Energy sources of the current transportation system in MT. Using advanced data base and statistical compilations, this report analyses two kind of facts. **First.** The basic data on energy: (i) the amount of energy sources consumed in the current supply transportation system, in particular for petrol and electrical power, and (ii) the origins, costs, domestic and international conditions, durability and longevity and environmental problems in their production and distribution. **Second.** A detailed picture of the current

Human Perspectives in the Internet Society: Culture, Psychology and Gender, K. Morgan, J. Sanchez, C. A. Brebbia & A Voiskounsky (Editors) © 2004 WIT Press, www.witpress.com, ISBN 1-85312-726-4

transportation supply system based on petrol consumption. (i) Amount of the daily consumption of petrol (ii) Outstanding regulatory and fiscal measures. (iii) Costs and advantages of the daily consumption of petrol for transportation consumers (iv) Degree of satisfaction or disapproval of these consumers. (v) Global financial input and global financial profitability for private investors and public agencies. (vi) Degree of satisfaction or disapproval of these investors and these agencies

Report 11. Energy sources of the alternative transportation system in MT. The alternative supply transportation system proposes a basic shift from petrol to electrical power [19]. Using simulation techniques, report 11 contains two complementary issues. **First.** A conceptual presentation on the needs for electric power in the alternative supply transportation system. **Second.** A detailed picture of the production and utilization of two specific kinds of electric power. (i) The electric power used by trains, produced by central plants and distributed by a large network of cables. (ii) The electric power used by cars, buses and trucks with batteries and other technologies. For economic and environmental reasons, report 11 reviews how central plants can evolve gradually towards renewable and inexhaustible resources, namely by the exploitation of solar energy.

Report 12. Comparative analysis of the utilization of energy sources used in the current and in the alternative transportation system. By compiling the results of the preceding reports (10 and 11), report 12 compares the utilization of energy resources in the current and in the alternative supply transportation system in order to show with facts and figures the numerous and important advantages of the massive introduction of electric power technologies [20].

Key point five. Costs and advantages analysis.

Report 13. Cost analysis. Two elements. **First,** cost analysis is an elementary operation, because it demands a simple alignment of available data. It is also ineluctable, because reorganizing transportation requires huge investment and therefore a good understanding of what is at stake. **Second,** the most important function of cost analysis is to inform stakeholders able to move towards innovation. The knowledge of these costs can discourage a business leader, no doubt. But it can also incite her or him to innovate and to set up the conditions that permit to exceed these costs with remunerative benefits.

Report 14. Advantages analysis. Advantages analysis presents a more arduous task. It requires complex preparatory and imaginative work. Using techniques of simulation, report 14 analyzes the potential advantages of two important components of the alternative supply transportation system. **First**. The creation of a network of warehouses destined to clear definitely the traffic jam in MT. Cost analysis alone can lead to the conclusion that the operation is very high. Advantages analysis helps to prove how this operation can offer profitable returns. **Second**. The combination of new technologies that improve the way of life of millions of commuters that must travel daily. The cost of such an operation is very high indeed. But report 14 calculates also the attraction that these new technologies provide for millions of daily commuters and estimates thereafter their social and economic profitability.

Report 15. Feasibility analysis. Costs and advantages analysis provides the basic elements that lead to major decisions. The feasibility of an idea is conditioned by an important fact: that there are sufficient reasons to convince those that can do it, to do it. Whether or not the proposed project is useful, harmless and profitable, is what stakeholders must be convinced of. Report 15 finds out if the elements involved, will point or not to the proposed alternative.

Key point six. An institutional regulatory coalition in transportation supply.
Report 16. The successful integration of societal forces. This is a complex issue that requires a profound knowledge of the recent evolution of industry and governmental affairs [21]. Three main questions should be dealt in this connection. **First.** A conceptual frame of reference, that following namely the theoretical insights of Durkheim's work [22], designs and justifies the legal, political, social and economic bases of such a regulatory coalition. **Second.** Quantitative estimates. Considering the different situations of the different stakeholders potentially interested to enter in the coalition, quantitative estimates of the cost and the conditions of success for each individual unity, are absolutely indispensable. **Third.** A detailed Delphi consultation [23]. In order to arrive at practical results, the results of previous work must be validated by our panel of critics.

Key point seven. Environmental analysis.
Report 17. The volume of pollution created by the current and the alternative system. Based on extensive knowledge of current literature and simulation techniques, report 17 provides a picture of the volume of pollution of the supply transportation system, the current and the alternative. This comparison is essential for obtaining our objectives.
Report 18. The amount of money saved by the alternative system. The cost and advantages (for customers and for investors) of different transportation technologies has been analyzed previously. One complementary point has to be equally analyzed. The cost of the respective volume of pollution must be calculated in order to provide a valuable argument for sustainable transportation.

Key point eight. Social analysis.
Report 19. Social analysis. Based on a sound knowledge of current literature [24], report 19 organizes different types of inquiries, on the respective advantages of current and alternative supply transportation system. **First.** The interview of goods transportation practitioners, and of daily users of people movers. Their assessment concerns important preferences, as comfort, time spent, price, returns, safety, prestige, etc. **Second.** The interview of qualified members of different public agencies, concerning most particularly the money saved by the alternative system in the matter of pollution.

Key point nine. Local, national and worldwide relations.
Report 20. The geo-political analysis. Report 20 addresses three essential questions. **First.** Interests and resources of investors and corporations. The

Human Perspectives in the Internet Society: Culture, Psychology and Gender, K. Morgan, J. Sanchez, C. A. Brebbia & A Voiskounsky (Editors) © 2004 WIT Press, www.witpress.com, ISBN 1-85312-726-4

planning of an alternative supply transportation system in MT includes large corporations and national business leaders. They have to be invited to participate in the MT plan of innovative work [25]. **Second.** Interests and resources of national public agencies. MT's public authorities do not have the sufficient regulatory power and must negotiate important decisions with the national government. Report 20 has then to investigate the deals that have to be made. **Third** Interests and resources of the world market. A profound change of the supply transportation system in MT is not possible without considering international relations. Such innovative change will surely reverberate in a good part of the world and this dimension has to be taken seriously.

2.2.4 General characteristics of the preliminary study

Some basic indications are submitted for reflection and discussion. Timing: Five years. Budget: One million dollars per year. Sources of funding: A coalition of interested corporations and public agencies. Direction: A qualified management coordinating team. Implementation: A team of qualified specialists invited to prepare and to confront the numerous analytical reports.

3 Concluding remarks

As it is stated above, the primary and immediate purpose of our work is not the direct promotion of social change. Our primary purpose is to ask for collaboration in order to prepare a global study on the societal needs and resources concerning the desired renewal of supply transportation. In this connection, our primary and immediate purpose is not at all of a speculative order. Our purpose is practical in two senses. (1) To give a good idea on the key points that should be attentively considered to face effectively social values according to the requirements of social norms. (2) To prepare a detailed consultation of societal leaders in order to ask them if and how the results of this study can incite to take the pertinent measures.

In brief, what is proposed here is a global, cost effective study, that has never been made before, and that is indispensable to investigate the societal interest and the practical feasibility of the renewal of the current transportation supply system, in order to improve its social, economic and environmental capacities

The every day experience tells us that important societal forces are interested in funding, launching and supervising this study. All other initiatives necessary for the practical pursuit of a sustainable transportation system will follow later, once the analytical results have been sufficiently proved.

References

[1] Mitchell, G.D. Dictionary of Sociology. London. Routledge & Kegan Paul, 1969.

[2] Weber, M., The Protestant Ethic and the Spirit of Capitalism. New York. Scribner. 1930.

Human Perspectives in the Internet Society: Culture, Psychology and Gender, K. Morgan, J. Sanchez, C. A. Brebbia & A Voiskounsky (Editors) © 2004 WIT Press, www.witpress.com, ISBN 1-85312-726-4

[3] Prades, J.A., La sociologie de la religion chez Max Weber. Louvain & Paris. Nauwelaerts. 1969.

[4] World Business Council on Sustainable Development (WBCSD). <www.wbcsd.org>

[5] Prades, J.A., Labriet M. & Waaub, J.-P. Structuring traffic integration. Urban Transport and the Environment in the 21st Century, ed. L. J. Sucharov & C.A. Brebbia, Southampton: WIT Press. 2001.66

[6] Durkheim, É. The Division of Labor in Society. Paris. Alcan.1893.

[7] Durkheim, É. The Elementary Forms of the Religious Life. Paris. Alcan.1912.

[8] Prades, J.A. Durkheim. Paris. Presses Universitaires de France. 1997.

[9] Bartelmus, P. (ed.) Unweiling wealth. On money, Quality of Life and Sustainability. Dordrecht. Kluwer. 2002.

[10] Garrison, W.L. & Ward, J.D. Tomorrow's Transportation : Changing Cities, Economies and Lives. Boston. Artech House. 2000.

[11] Prades, J.A. Global Environmental Change and Contemporary Society. International Sociology.14 (1), p. 7-31. 1999.

[12] Bing, G. Due diligence techniques and analysis: critical questions for business decisions. Westport, Conn. Quorum. 1996.

[13] Transport Statistics. www.ststcan.ca/francais/freepub/50-501-XIF/free_f.htm.

[14] ITT. Innovative Transportation Technologies. < http://faculty.washington .edu/jbs/itrans/ >.

[15] The Baltimore-Washington MAGLEV Project. <www. bwmaglev.com/>.

[16] Advanced Robotic Solutions www.robosoft.fr.

[17] Prades, J.A., Loulou, R & Waaub, J.-P. Stratégies de gestion des gaz à effet de serre. Le cas des transports, Québec: Presses de l'Université du Québec. 1998. < www.er.uqam.ca/nobel/greige2/ges,htm >.

[18] Microsoft Research. http://research.Microsoft.com.

[19] Global Climate & Energy Project. < www.stanford.edu >.

[20] Earth Policy Institute. < www.earth-policy.org >.

[21] Bruchey, S. Public Involvement as an Organizational Development Process. New York & London. Garland. 1990.

[22] Prades, J.A. Durkheim. Paris. Presses Universitaires de France. 1997.

[23] Kenis, D. Improving Group Decisions. Designing and Testing Techniques for Group Decision Support Systems Applying Delphi Techniques. Utrecht. Universiteit Utrecht. 1995.

[24] Sauvé. L. Pour une éducation relative à l'environnement. Montréal. Guérin. 1994.

[25] Porter, M. What is Strategy? Harvard Business Review, 74. 1996.

Human Perspectives in the Internet Society: Culture, Psychology and Gender, K. Morgan, J. Sanchez, C. A. Brebbia & A Voiskounsky (Editors) © 2004 WIT Press, www.witpress.com, ISBN 1-85312-726-4

A study of hospital based social workers in the UK: the importance of verbal communication in this community

J. Harrison, M. Hepworth & P. de Chazal
Department of Information Science, Loughborough University, UK

Abstract

In a study of hospital based social workers in the UK verbal communication within the community was found to be of high octane value. Nine out of ten social workers sought information on a daily basis from their team managers or other social and healthcare professionals. The use of verbal communication is of paramount importance and defined their particular culture, which is practice and not research based.

The study found that the social workers did not think themselves without IT and information searching skills or that they were computer illiterate. The major problem was lack of access to computer facilities and the Internet. These findings were compounded by the fact that the social workers were working in multidisciplinary teams with health professionals who have access to these facilities.

Solutions to empower the social workers and reduce the differential in terms of I.T and information provision with healthcare colleagues included: gaining access to on-site library and information services; negotiating Service Level Agreements; and establishing a new role for Information and Library professionals to identify information management, service delivery and training needs.

However, the drive to implement the technology to improve the use of information in practice must be supported by managers as well as practitioners. If the need to apply technology to promote greater use of information in practice is not acknowledged and applied to this community rapidly, the high octane value of the verbal communication will soon escape, evaporate into thin air and leave the community very much the poorer for this.
Keywords: information needs, information management, social workers, verbal culture.

Human Perspectives in the Internet Society: Culture, Psychology and Gender, K. Morgan, J. Sanchez, C. A. Brebbia & A Voiskounsky (Editors) © 2004 WIT Press, www.witpress.com, ISBN 1-85312-726-4

1 Background to the study

Social workers jointly manage patients in conjunction with other healthcare professionals to provide relevant social care and support services. Social work requires a professional qualification to practise and this can be achieved either through a three year undergraduate course or from a faster postgraduate route. This graduate level entry into a profession is of course typical of many other professions. The higher level of education suggests that social workers should have had exposure and experience of using an academic library. Therefore, the researchers expected that the information needs of the social workers would not be dissimilar to those of medical or nursing professionals.

The social workers in this study were all based in a National Health Service (NHS) Hospital Trust. The requirement to use evidence based practice in health and social care is one that it is currently much emphasised by the UK's Department of Health, as set out in the publication Information for Health [1]. In practice it is demanded by hospital authorities and has become accepted amongst healthcare professionals. Since social care and the NHS is to come together in the NHS Plan [2] it follows that social and health care professionals should have equal access to the knowledge base. It was, however, perceived by management that access to the knowledge base was not equitable between social and health care workers.

2 The research questions

The study reviewed the information needs and provision of library and information services for adult social work teams based in the University Hospitals of Leicester NHS Trust (UHL) UK.

The objectives were to:

- Conduct an information needs analysis of social care professionals based in the Trust.
- Review the perceived gap in library and information service provision for social workers.
- Propose future models of service delivery that are relevant and responsive to user needs and that will support evidence based social care.

3 Methodology

As this study was exploratory in nature, quantitative and qualitative methodological tools were employed in the form of a questionnaire survey followed by focus groups. The questionnaire was used to gather broad population data. Focus groups were chosen to gather rich qualitative data. By continuous cross-checking of the results obtained from the two different data collection methods, a deeper insight was acquired and the quality of the findings was improved. These methods are tried and tested in this field of study, as used by Giltz *et al* [3] and Royle *et al* [4].

Human Perspectives in the Internet Society: Culture, Psychology and Gender, K. Morgan, J. Sanchez, C. A. Brebbia & A Voiskounsky (Editors) © 2004 WIT Press, www.witpress.com, ISBN 1-85312-726-4

All team managers, social workers and community care workers in the Adult Social Work Teams were invited to participate. The questionnaire was intended to elicit the nature and type of information the social workers need in order to carry out their jobs. It also sought to ascertain what information resources and services they would find useful. The questionnaire was anonymous with strict confidentiality being ensured. After piloting, the final version was distributed via the team managers. The data were analysed using SPSS™, a statistical package widely used by social scientists.

Focus groups were arranged by contacting the individual team managers. The purpose of the meeting was explained and an assurance given that confidentiality would be preserved. Permission to tape record the proceedings was sought, and a letter confirming the arrangements was sent to the team managers.

Table 1: Important subject material: general.

Subject	**% respondents rating subject extremely important**
Older people	96%
Community care	93%
Health services	89%
Residential care	86%
Carers and respite care	79%
Medical conditions	79%

4 The information needs of social workers

It was found that the social workers required information on a very wide range of subjects to undertake their everyday practice. However, particular emphasis was placed on the subjects set out in Tables 1 and 2. These reflect the social workers' focus on adult patients.

Table 2: Important subject material: policy/guidelines.

Subject	**% respondents rating subject extremely important**
Departmental Procedures	75%
Best Practice	68%
Developments in Social Work	68%
National Service Frameworks	61%

Human Perspectives in the Internet Society: Culture, Psychology and Gender, K. Morgan, J. Sanchez, C. A. Brebbia & A Voiskounsky (Editors) © 2004 WIT Press, www.witpress.com, ISBN 1-85312-726-4

This information was required to perform their clinical work. There was little evidence for gathering information for educational purposes, or for continuing professional development. Involvement in research was extremely limited, with just 0.4% of the respondents engaged in this activity. These results highlight the client-focused, practice-based work undertaken by the social workers.

5 Types of information required

The wide ranging information needs of the social workers reflected in tables 1 and 2 illustrate that they have both simple and complex requirements.

Examples of straightforward requests for information included:

"I need information on alcohol abuse or perhaps general knowledge on how it affects a person or what sort of stage you would refer to it"

"It would be useful to know if you're discharging somebody to a specific area of the county what nursing would be available there"

"We need to know about cultural issues - being sensitive to cultural issues- and we need to know if there is an allocated worker in the community that I could speak to"

The complex information requirements are illustrated by the following examples:

"If somebody had a stroke (CVA), I think we would know what we're doing operationally in terms of the Community Care Act and our responsibilities but the person you're working with says, *I want to know more about strokes,* and you need to know for instance that the Stoke Association do produce a whole range of very useful leaflets and pamphlets and it would be useful for us to have that quality of data ourselves"

"Well for instance, there's a model of discharge in X area and I need to know about that. I know that there is a model in Y area and buying care from the private sector and you need to understand the rationale behind that"

"I think we do need more information on homelessness, like how a person can access a hostel, and information on how they can find somewhere to live, because sometimes people have come into hospital and they're not allowed to be returned back to where they'd stayed because it's not their accommodation, or they've stayed with a friend - so then we have to contact the Homelessness Service. We could do with more information - that would be good!"

"Maybe it's someone who has a learning disability, or someone who speaks a different language, or somebody who's been deemed mentally unfit to make decisions abut their own future. It's - do you use a team of advocates or are there

Human Perspectives in the Internet Society: Culture, Psychology and Gender, K. Morgan, J. Sanchez, C. A. Brebbia & A Voiskounsky (Editors) © 2004 WIT Press, www.witpress.com, ISBN 1-85312-726-4

different advocates - and how do you contact the more appropriate advocate for that case, how do you get in touch with them, who they are, how do you determine who is the right person to contact in this particular situation or in this particular client's position."

As one social worker summed up, "the information needs for this particular professional group appear to have another dimension that cannot be ignored, that of cost."

"We're expected to (make decisions about best value) because we're made aware when we're putting together care packages that we have to look at prices in those packages. Approval will come at different levels of management depending on how much that care package is going to cost."

Social workers information needs were synthesised by one respondent as:

"You need information, not in depth but you're trying to build up a store of information. You need information on lots of things – quickly and simply."

6 The existing method for obtaining information: verbal communication or "I would ask Jane"

After analysing the responses to the question "what or which resource would you use to find the information" the response was almost always "I would ask Jane" (the Team Manager).

The social workers expressed their needs for different types of information in different circumstances for particular clients or different areas of work. The focus groups engendered rich data where the frustrations of obtaining the most appropriate and timely data were expressed. It emerged that the predominant way of obtaining information was by talking to colleagues. This was easy to do because of the close proximity of the team. Support for team working in decision making is acknowledged in the findings of Cook *et al* [5]. The workplace accommodation in the various hospital locations was at best, small and at worst cramped with several people sharing the same office space. The opportunity to chat or exchange ideas about best practice or best care was readily afforded. Indeed, 89% of the respondents asked for information on a daily basis from their team managers or other social work colleagues. In addition, a high proportion, 65%, also obtained information verbally from other health professionals on a daily basis.

The Social workers reasons for the reliance on the verbal exchange of information were varied and are typified as these:

"The only information I could access at that time was within the team or turning to a manager"

"Well, what we tend to do here is talk about how we carry out interviews and we give each other…on an informal basis… why we do it this way."

These quotations from the Social workers illustrate the '*this is what we've always done'* mode of thinking. This seemed to be accepted by the majority of the respondents. However, frustration and elements of desperation with the existing methods of information exchange were also expressed by several respondents. Their view was that this was not the way information in an evidence-based environment should be exchanged in the 21st Century.

The frustration is illustrated by these quotations:

"You know, if someone has used someone before … or if you've got a manager, you'd ask the manger about it or there have been times when I've been through to the access team in the community to ask"

"It would be good not to be reinventing the wheel all the time and not having to ask all the time"

The researchers concluded that these results strongly suggested that the social workers rely heavily on verbal communication to satisfy their information needs.

7 Existing access to information resources

It became evident when recording and analysing the data in the study that information to support practice was gathered at local and national level both routinely and on an ad hoc basis. Shortage of material was not the problem; despite the lack of research activity in the professional group. It was access to the most appropriate and timely data that presented as a major problem, Blackburn [6].

This lack of access to information tools/resources and IT kit was adroitly and acutely perceived by the social workers and echoes earlier findings of Wilson and Dunn [7].

"I think it would be useful to have access to the Internet….there are a lot of Web sites that are given on articles that you've read, you can look deeper there but at the moment you can't- you're stuck"

"You know the information is out there, but you have no means of access"

This is strikingly demonstrated by the lack of Internet facilities available to the Social workers at the desktop in the workplace. None of the Social workers had access to the internet as shown in Figure 1.

The social workers did not consider themselves to lack the requisite skills to search the Internet to find information as 49% used the Internet at home.

The other major obstacle to providing an information rich environment for the social workers was the lack of access to library and information services available to them on hospital sites. The social workers did not have access to these facilities nor the services of the personnel within them. Most of the social workers had no professional experience of using an information specialist.

Human Perspectives in the Internet Society: Culture, Psychology and Gender, K. Morgan, J. Sanchez, C. A. Brebbia & A Voiskounsky (Editors) © 2004 WIT Press, www.witpress.com, ISBN 1-85312-726-4

This lack of access to facilities was not perceived to be as acute by the majority of respondents, as the group as a whole were not regular library users. This emphasises the poor information environment that the social workers are working in and also exposes the poor information resources coverage available to them. It highlights the lack of investment in information provision by the employers for this group of staff.

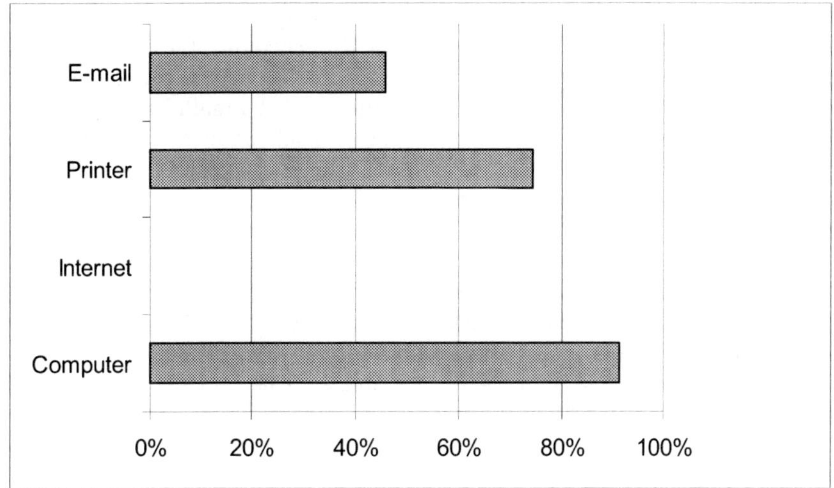

Figure 1: Internet access at work.

Ironically the development of resources for this particular professional group is developing nationally.
eg: www.elsc.org.uk
www.scie.org.uk
www.ex.ac.uk/cebss
www.cswe.org
and internationally www.nyu.edu/socialwork/wwwrsw

However when the question "would you use printed or/and electronic sources if these were readily available" was posed in the focus group setting, respondents said "yes", but that they thought the intense time pressures governing the bulk of social work practice would prevent them from doing so, as illustrated by these examples:

"People don't really do things until they need them- there are so many pressures you're jut dealing with things day to day"

"You're under such pressure – your head's down and you're crashing along. You need space to stand back.

Human Perspectives in the Internet Society: Culture, Psychology and Gender, K. Morgan, J. Sanchez, C. A. Brebbia & A Voiskounsky (Editors) © 2004 WIT Press, www.witpress.com, ISBN 1-85312-726-4

The conclusions from the study data were that there was a severe lack of access to relevant sources and the focus of social workers was almost 100% patient dominated without any time or opportunity to consult the knowledge base.

8 New ways for information provision

This study confirms the perceived gap in library and information library provision for social workers, Harrison *et al* [8]. Therefore for evidence based practice to occur, a cultural shift is required. This is essential if social workers are to be accepted as fully functioning members of the multidisciplinary team and are to be acknowledged as such by their medical and nursing colleagues. A management commitment to lead the cultural change must be acknowledged and acted upon. This change must be managed in a structured way as it may not occur naturally. A number of ways have been identified to help facilitate this change.

These include improved information management, the appointment of an information specialist to work with the social workers and the provision of appropriate skills training. An information specialist would be instrumental in facilitating the necessary culture shift to enable evidence practice to become the norm.

It is concluded that there must be liaison at the earliest opportunity with social care teams to ensure appropriateness of training and to bring about a two –way understanding between the library and social work professionals. A tailored programme would include detailed library orientation, the explanation of library terms and media used and hands–on sessions.

The practice of social work is relatively recent in the patient care field, and this study found a strong verbal culture. This is acknowledged amongst practitioners as the major method for exchanging for exchanging information. Whilst operating in the same arena as clinicians, unlike medicine, the social work discipline does not as yet have the research literature upon which to draw when making practice-based decisions.

Therefore, the verbal exchange of information is of "high octane value "and must not be lost in the improvement of information management skills and the creation of an evidence based practice culture as emphasised in Gerrish and Clayton [9].

A robust I.T infrastructure, enabling easy and rapid access to the knowledge base, underpins the practice of evidence based social work. This is the vital and challenging issue for social services and library management to confront and lead. However, it is essential to preserve the existing verbal culture amongst social workers whilst introducing new methods of working with information. In this environment it is imperative that the process must be managed in an evolutionary way rather than revolutionary.

References

[1] The Secretary of State for Health, *Information for Health,* The Stationary Office: London, 1998

[2] The Secretary of State for Health, *The NHS plan*, The Stationary Office: London, 2000.

[3] Giltz, B., Hasmascu, C.& Sandstrom, H., The focus group: a tool for programme planning, assessment and decision making-an American view. *Health Information and Libraries Journal*, **18(1)**, pp. 30-37, 2001.

[4] Royle, J.A., Blythe, K., Brazil, K., Montemuro, M., Church, A., Cipryk, F., Johnson, T., Assessing the information needs of staff in two long-term care organizations**.** *Educational Gerontology*, **28(3)**, pp. 189-205, 2002.

[5] Cook, G., Gerrish, K.& Clarke, C., Decision making in teams, issues arising from two UK evaluations. *Journal of Inter Professional Care,* **(15)2**, pp. 141-57, 2001.

[6] Blackburn, B., Building bridges: towards integrated library and information services for mental health and social care. *Health Information and Libraries Journal,* **18(4),** pp 203-12,2001.

[7] Wilson, T.D. & Dunn, A.C., Information services in local authority social services departments. *Journal of Librarinship,***8(3)**,pp. 66-74,1976.

[8] Harrison, J., Hepworth, M. & De Chazal, P., NHS and Social care interface: a study of social workers' library and information needs. *Journal of Librarianship and Information Science,* **36(1),** pp. 27-35, 2004

[9] Gerrish, K. & Clayton, J., Promoting evidence-based practice: an organizational approach. *Journal of Nurse Management,* **(12)2,** pp. 114-23, 2004.

Human Perspectives in the Internet Society: Culture, Psychology and Gender, K. Morgan, J. Sanchez, C. A. Brebbia & A Voiskounsky (Editors) © 2004 WIT Press, www.witpress.com, ISBN 1-85312-726-4

ActKM: variety from a complexity perspective

S. Callahan[1] & P. Milne[2]
[1]*IBM Cynefin Centre for Organisational Complexity*
[2]*School of Information Management and Tourism,*
University of Canberra

Abstract

A new framework for communities of practice is required to unite the disjointed approaches currently employed to understand this organisational form. This paper proposes a framework based on complexity theory and applies a model developed by Axelrod and Cohen. A set of mechanisms are explored to understand how a designer might influence variety (of strategies and types) in a community of practice. Four mechanisms are addressed namely: the process of copying strategies and types, copying with error (mutation), recombination of ideas and the role of the physical environment. Understanding these mechanisms a designer can attempt to increase or decrease variety within a community of practice.
Keywords: communities of practice, complexity, knowledge management, variety.

1 Introduction

The communities of practice (CoP) literature are voluminous and disjointed to the point where it has been suggested that a new framework for this organisational form is needed [1]. The research underpinning this paper is examining the culture and impact of a CoP that has developed around the area of public sector knowledge management. The first stage of the research is to respond to this evident lack of a suitable framework.

Any attempt at developing such a framework should prompt both practitioners and researchers to ask a raft of new questions, but more importantly it should help them understand the key processes affecting CoPs using a common language and approach. In a changing and unpredictable environment it would be erroneous to focus the framework on the structure and content of

Human Perspectives in the Internet Society: Culture, Psychology and Gender, K. Morgan, J. Sanchez, C. A. Brebbia & A Voiskounsky (Editors) © 2004 WIT Press, www.witpress.com, ISBN 1-85312-726-4

communities of practice. The most important aspects of the framework will come from investigating relevant processes [2].

This paper develops a new CoP framework by applying a model developed by Axelrod and Cohen [3] which is based on complexity theory. Complexity science is gaining prominence as a way to think about organisations [4-6]. Its applicability is based on the parallels between the basic features of a complex system and modern organisations: many interacting components arranged in networks, non-linear interaction between components, self organisation, positive and negative feedback loops, emergent properties. Stacey [2] illustrates this point in relation to feedback and non linearity:

> "Organizations are clearly feedback systems because every time two humans interact with each other the actions of one person have consequences for the other, leading that other to react in ways that have consequences for the first, requiring in turn a response from the first and so on through time. In this way an action taken by a person in one period of time feeds back to determine, in part at least, the next action of that person."

Communities of practice, in many ways, are a microcosm of an organisation but without the formal hierarchy and rigid bureaucracy. Consequently the arguments for applying complexity theory to organisations pertain equally to communities of practice. Furthermore, many leading thinkers on CoPs allude to the complex nature of communities with references to emergence and self organisation.

> "Asserting that it is learning that gives rise to communities of practice is saying that learning is a source of social structure. But the kind of structure that this refers to is not an object in itself, which can be separated from the process that gives rise to it. Rather it is an emergent structure . . ." [7]

> "Even when a community's actions conform to an external mandate, it is the community – not the mandate – that produces the practice. In this sense, communities of practice are fundamentally self-organizing systems." [8]

Wenger et al. [9] implicitly understand the complex nature of communities to the point where their first principle for a community of practice is, 'design for evolution'. So it is surprising that few authors have systematically applied complexity concepts to a better understanding of communities of practice. Some authors have made contributions to highlight the relationship between complexity and communities [10-12] but none have attempted to directly apply complexity concepts.

Axelrod and Cohen's framework was chosen because its primary intent is to assist managers with a coherent approach to designing interventions using complexity theory. The focus of the framework is on what designers and policy makers can do to make a difference. We have the same objectives for our application of complexity to communities of practice.

Throughout this paper we draw on examples collected using interviews and surveys from a community of practice called ActKM (pronounced Act K. M.).

Human Perspectives in the Internet Society: Culture, Psychology and Gender, K. Morgan, J. Sanchez, C. A. Brebbia & A Voiskounsky (Editors) © 2004 WIT Press, www.witpress.com, ISBN 1-85312-726-4

This community was formed in 1998 with the purpose of building knowledge about public sector knowledge management [13]. It has 890 members who participate in an online discussion forum, meet monthly and convene a yearly conference which attracts approximately 100 attendees. In addition to these formal activities of the community there is considerable informal activity including site visits among members, workplace discussions and spin off collaborations.

2 A complexity perspective of communities

Applying complexity concepts to communities of practice requires the application of new terms in a new context. Axelrod and Cohen [3] provide 12 terms which we will use in describing aspects of CoPs.

- **Strategy,** a conditional action pattern that indicates what to do in which circumstances.
- **Artefact,** a material resource which has definite location and respond to the actions of agents.
- **Agent,** a collection of properties (especially location), strategies, and capabilities for interacting with artefacts and other agents [for example, people].
- **Population,** a collection of agents, or, in some situations, collections of strategies.
- **System,** a larger collection, including one or more populations of agents and possibly also artefacts.
- **Type,** all the agents (or strategies) in a population that have some characteristic in common.
- **Variety,** the diversity of types within a population or system.
- **Interaction pattern,** the recurring regularities of contact among types within a system.
- **Space (physical),** the location in geographical space and time of agents and artefacts.
- **Space (conceptual),** the 'location' in a set of categories structured so that 'nearby' agents will tend to interact.
- **Selection,** processes that lead to an increase or decrease in the frequency of various types of agents or strategies.
- **Success criterion** or **performance measure**, a 'score' used by an agent or designer in attributing credit in the selection of relatively successful (or unsuccessful) strategies or agents.

Using these terms a community of practice can be viewed as a **population** of **agents** consisting of many **types interacting** on a regular and ongoing basis. The **agents select** and apply **strategies** to enhance their position in the population. These strategies are applied in **physical** and **conceptual space** and result in the creation of knowledge and artefacts. Successful agents or strategies are **selected** according to the community's or agent's **success criteria**.

Human Perspectives in the Internet Society: Culture, Psychology and Gender, K. Morgan, J. Sanchez, C. A. Brebbia & A Voiskounsky (Editors) © 2004 WIT Press, www.witpress.com, ISBN 1-85312-726-4

This view of a community of practice has immediate utility in that specific aspects of a community can be explored by a designer for improvement: strategies can be identified, types discerned, variety modified, success criteria articulated. Most importantly new questions emerge when a new framework is introduced.

Axelrod and Cohen focus on three building blocks to explain their framework: variety, interaction and selection. These building blocks are influenced by a range of mechanisms which affect the micro-level interaction among agents (community members) and the macro-level patterns which emerge. In order to manage the scope of this paper we focus here on one building block: variety. Subsequent papers will address interaction and selection.

3 Variety

> "Because communities of practice are voluntary, what makes them successful over time is their ability to generate enough excitement, relevance, and value to attract and engage members. Although many factors, such as management support or an urgent problem, can inspire a community, nothing can substitute for this sense of *aliveness*" [9]

Aliveness is at the core of a successful community of practice. This sense of aliveness is also conveyed by complexity theorists when articulating the difference between order, complexity and chaos. Aliveness occurs at the edge of chaos (complexity) when "… coherent structures that propagated, grew, split apart, recombined in a wonderfully complex way" [14]. The variety of agents, strategies, types, populations and sub-populations significantly influence a community's aliveness.

Variety within a community is reflected by the number of distinct types present. These 'types' might be recognised by members of the community or be a result of analysis by an outside observer. For example, community members might distinguish members who are male or female, and discern people they regard as 'theorists' or 'practitioners'. Regardless of the types recognised by the community there are always more unrecognised types. The types which become apparent to the community are a function of the group's interests, the frameworks adopted by the group and the questions being asked. The types that interest a community designer, however, are those that might affect community behaviour. Consequently male/female ratios might be important while types relating to member height are probably irrelevant.

Variety is an important characteristic in nurturing a community of practice. During a community's life there will be times when new ideas, perspectives and voices will be essential to maintain the liveliness that ultimately attracts and sustains community membership. There will be other times when the community discussion will be awash with concepts and the pace of change is overwhelming. Kauffman [6] calls this phenomena, eternal boiling – a chaotic state where patterns rarely form. Consequently there will be times to encourage diversity while other we should discourage it.

Human Perspectives in the Internet Society: Culture, Psychology and Gender, K. Morgan, J. Sanchez, C. A. Brebbia & A Voiskounsky (Editors) © 2004 WIT Press, www.witpress.com, ISBN 1-85312-726-4

It is misleading to refer to a community of practice as a homogenous entity. Successful communities tend to have a core team who undertake key community roles, an active group who participate in most events, and a peripheral set of members who keep an eye on community development, dipping in and out of activities spasmodically [15]. It makes sense, therefore, to consider variety among these three groups as well as the entire community. For example, the variety of the core team is instrumental in the setting the schedule of events and therefore many of the discussion the community will focus on. ActKM made a point of ensuring that their core team is composed of at least 50% of people from the public sector to guard against private sector interests dramatically re-orienting activities away from public sector issues.

Complex systems are inherently unpredictable which creates a paradox for community designers. On the one hand specific outcomes cannot be predicted yet designers need to increase the chances of success for their community of practice. As a result traditional interventions, which assume discernable and repeatable cause and effect relationships, are typically ineffective [11].

> "Organisms, artifacts, and organizations are all evolved structures. Even when human agents plan and construct with intention, there is more of the blind watchmaker at work than we usually recognize" [6].

Affecting sustainable change in a complex system, like a community of practice, is best done by creating conditions for self organisation which move the system in a general direction rather than driving to achieve specific goals and outcomes. One approach is to provide the conditions for changing variety of types and strategies. Here we examine four mechanisms to affect community variety: simple copying, copying with the introduction of errors, recombining and extinction [3]. A discussion of when variety might be encouraged or discourages then follows.

3.1 Copying

Simply copying of types or strategies reduces variety in a system. When a type or strategy is copied it becomes more likely to be copied again in the future, setting up a positive feedback loop which can result in it dominating within the population. The QWERTY keyboard is a celebrated example. The arrangement of keys on your computer is not the most efficient layout. The QWERTY layout was designed in the 19th Century to slow typists down to avoid typewriters from jamming but the Remington company mass produced typewriters with this keyboard layout [16]. Once typists learnt the QWERTY layout it was easier to stick with this format than adopt more efficient layouts (such as Dvorak). Other companies copied the strategy and the market converged or locked-in ensuring QWERTY dominance. A similar scenario was responsible for VHS ascendancy over Beta in video formats.

Strategies must be visible before they can be copied. Visible strategies can be imitated and an agent's likelihood of imitating a strategy is influenced by a range of factors including, the dominance of the group displaying the strategy, how deeply the strategy has been internalised by agents, how often other people display the strategy and the reputation of those exhibiting the strategy [17].

When strategies are consistently and frequently copied they become norms of the community.

One example from ActKM is how members reinforce the strategy to clearly disclose their name and organisations for which they work. This norm was clearly emphasized when a member, using the pseudonym Gandalf, posted a message in August 2003 which resulted in the following reply by a long-term and respected member, Dave Snowden:

“I'm not really sure about responding to "Gandalf" on the grounds that anonymity is not normally a part of ACT-KM and I'm not sure its (sic) really legitimate to participate in this way - maybe this is an issue for the moderators.” After two more posts as Gandalf and a series of responses from members objecting to the pseudonym, Gandalf revealed his true identity. Interestingly a new member unaware of this norm posted a message closely on the heals of this exchange between Gandalf and Snowden using a pseudonym but then quickly posted a new message saying that he was quickly contacted by a member off the list alerting him to the norm and apologizing for not using his true identity.

Online discussion technique is a highly visible aspect of ActKM and certain approaches to online discussion are frequently imitated. For example, in recent times a group of new members have been posting long, academic posts which have encouraged other similar responses. This strategy has reduced the relative number of practice oriented ‘tips and tricks’ or requests for assistance posts which were once a feature of the online discussion. Not only has the academic style been copied but members have reduced the number of posts that don’t adhere to this style. As a result variety of online discussion type has reduced.

3.2 Copying with error (mutation)

Copying, however, is rarely a perfect process. In most cases errors (mutations) occur. Copying with error increases the variety in a community. Misinterpretation and environmental constraints are two mechanisms which affect mutation.

Misinterpretation can occur accidentally as agents attempt to copy strategies or imitate other types. The availability of case studies might be a source of misinterpretation because the case study cannot hope to capture the entire situation of an implementation. Consequently people who attempt to copy the approach, techniques and tools described in a case study will always copy the strategy with error. The environmental context will also differ, except in the simplest of cases, forcing people to adapt the material. The availability of case study material, therefore, has the potential to increase the number of strategies available to a community, especially if the newly adapted strategies are reported and are added to the community’s artefacts.

The chance for misinterpretation can also be intentionally increased, therefore increasing variety in the system, by communicating ambiguous instructions or by using metaphors or analogies to convey concepts. A community facilitator can issue ambiguous, or even conflicting, instructions to encourage diversity as members attempt to interpret and respond. Metaphor can have a similar effect.

Human Perspectives in the Internet Society: Culture, Psychology and Gender, K. Morgan, J. Sanchez, C. A. Brebbia & A Voiskounsky (Editors) © 2004 WIT Press, www.witpress.com, ISBN 1-85312-726-4

Members of ActKM use metaphor and analogy frequently to help them explain ideas.

In 2003 the New South Wales Knowledge Management (NSWKM) Forum merged with ActKM increasing the membership by 200 people. It was assumed that the addition of NSWKM would have the effect of adding new people of the same type to ActKM, that is, copying types. In fact what resulted by the adding NSWKM was to introduce a range of new types to the community and in particular there were many more people from the private sector and academia.

3.3 Recombining

The recombination process in biology occurs during fertilisation where DNA is recombined to create a new life. Timescales involved in a typical community of practice are too short for us to consider biological recombination as an important mechanism however the combination of ideas, conceptual recombination, plays an important role in community variety. Conceptual recombination occurs when ideas from separate intellectual spheres are combined to create a new strategy, artefact or type. This mechanism increases relative variety and is more likely to result in improvement than mutation because there is less trial and error involved. For example, Charles Darwin's conceptual breakthrough, natural selection, occurred whilst considering the economist and demographer Rev. Thomas Malthus' treatise on population growth. It was the combination of an economic and biological idea that significantly contributed to new thinking – evolution.

The recombination of ideas is well illustrated by the application of ideas posted on ActKM by a primary school principal in Sydney. Over a period of 2 years the school Principal was a lurker on the ActKM discussion forum, collecting ideas which she combined with teaching concepts to develop a knowledge management program for her students. After developing this new approach to student management, the Principal relayed her experience back to ActKM. Her efforts were rewarded when she won the annual ActKM knowledge management prize presented at the yearly ActKM conference.

Recombination creates variety but it is also a product of variety. The likelihood for new combination of ideas increases as new members with different backgrounds interact. It is impossible to say one aspect of the system causes the other. "Real organisms constantly circle and chase one another in an infinitely complex dance of coevolution" [14]. A designer must therefore develop interventions, detect the patterns that form and be ready to nurture desirable patterns and disrupt the undesirable [5].

3.4 Physical environment

The community's physical environment significantly affects diversity. If the physical environment is homogenous and there is only one way to conduct conversations, then variety of members attracted to the community, and the topics discussed, reduces. For example, some members are attracted to online discussion forums while others prefer face to face conversations; some like to

Human Perspectives in the Internet Society: Culture, Psychology and Gender, K. Morgan, J. Sanchez, C. A. Brebbia & A Voiskounsky (Editors) © 2004 WIT Press, www.witpress.com, ISBN 1-85312-726-4

explore the depths of a topic while others enjoy becoming familiar with a range of topics.

3.5 Increasing or decreasing variety

Deciding when to increase or decrease variety is closely linked with the decision to explore new possibilities or exploit the benefits of the current situation [3]. Variety encourages exploration while convergence on a strategy or type assists exploitation. The question is then, 'When should a designer intervene to increase or decrease variety?'

Axelrod and Cohen [3] suggest four heuristics to help designers decide when to encourage variety. Variety should be encouraged when dealing with:

- problems that are long-term or widespread
- problems that provide fast, reliable feedback
- problems with low risk of catastrophe from exploration
- problems that have looming disasters

While these heuristics are useful for general problem solving, a more specific set are needed for communities of practice. The following set of heuristics is by no means exhaustive but form an initial set based on the authors' experience in designing and participating in communities of practice.

We recommend designers should consider increasing variety in a community of practice when:

- the discussion becomes one sided and there is no argument
- there is a long period without new ideas
- the level of excitement wanes and membership stagnates or declines
- the focus of the organisation shifts dramatically away from the interests of the community

We recommend designers should consider reducing variety when:

- the core team is establishing the community and they want to reduce the noise to concentrate on a few important topics
- there is too much noise in the community unrelated to its stated purpose. Getting people back on track.
- there are too many ideas being canvassed in the community making it difficult for members to rally around a concept or practice.

Community variety, at all scales, is an important characteristic of which community designers should remain mindful and, where appropriate, use the mechanism described above to influence. As a designer it is important to remember that command and control approaches are rarely effective in a complex environment. Consequently the designer's role is to modify the environment so that members are attracted to join and participate, useful strategies are selected and copied, and the member variety is appropriate for the community's phase of development.

An intervention can either by applied by an external force, such as forcing members to use a particular online environment, or triggered by the environment and then sustained by the internal workings of the system. The mechanisms discussed in this paper refer primarily to the internal forces that shape the

Human Perspectives in the Internet Society: Culture, Psychology and Gender, K. Morgan, J. Sanchez, C. A. Brebbia & A Voiskounsky (Editors) © 2004 WIT Press, www.witpress.com, ISBN 1-85312-726-4

system. These internal forces are self sustaining and self-organising and while inherently unpredictable, a community designer can intervene in ways to set the system in a direction. The designer, paradoxically, is never in control yet potentially influential in shaping the system.

4 Summary and conclusion

This paper is the first in a series of three which attempts to systematically apply complexity theory to better understand communities of practice. By applying Axelrod and Cohen's framework and focussing on ways to affect variety in a community, a range of new questions and potential new techniques have emerged. The mechanisms of copying, mutation, recombination, plus the affects of the physical environment, are important factors influencing variety of strategies and types in a community of practice. By thinking about variety from a complexity perspectives designers have news ways to influence communities of practice.

From a complexity perspective a designer must adopt a new role. They must be mindful of the patterns emerging in the community and design interventions intended to trigger the internal mechanisms (copying, mutation, recombination). The designer cannot expect specific outcomes from their interventions, rather they need to intervene and monitor, then nurture the desirable patterns while disrupting undesirable effects. The designer should attempt to alter the system in ways that the self organising aspects of the system, such as positive and negative feedback loops, interaction patterns, selection mechanisms and the processes that affect variety, and set the system in an advantageous direction. This paper only explores a small proportion of the total number of mechanisms operating in a complex system by examining how they affect variety. Further work is required to understand how interaction and selection works in a community of practice context. What is the role of barriers? Can members of a community be attracted to form beneficial patterns? How strategies are selected and what is discarded? What is the role of success criteria and how are these criteria determined? The new questions are emerging suggesting that a complexity approach will be a worthwhile pursuit.

References

[1] Henri, F. and Pudelko, B., Understanding and analysing activity and learning in virtual communities. *Journal of Computer Assisted Learning*, **19**, pp. 474-487, 2003.

[2] Stacey, R. D., The Science of Complexity - an Alternative Perspective for Strategic Change Processes. *Strategic Management Journal*, **16(6)**, pp. 477-495, 1995.

[3] Axelrod, R. and Cohen, M. D., *Harnessing Complexity: Organizational Implications of a Scientific Frontier*, Free Press: New York, pp. Pages, 1999.

Human Perspectives in the Internet Society: Culture, Psychology and Gender, K. Morgan, J. Sanchez, C. A. Brebbia & A Voiskounsky (Editors) © 2004 WIT Press, www.witpress.com, ISBN 1-85312-726-4

[4] Holland, J. H., *Hidden Order: How Adaptation Builds Complexity*, Perseus Books: Reading MA, pp. Pages, 1995.
[5] Kurtz, C. and Snowden, D., The New Dynamics of Strategy: Sense-making in a Complex-Complicated World. *IBM Systems Journal*, **42(3)**, pp. 462-483, 2003.
[6] Kauffman, S. A., *At Home in the Universe*, Oxford University Press: New York, pp. Pages, 1995.
[7] Wenger, E., *Community of Practice: Learning, Meaning, Identity*, Cambridge University Press: New York, pp. Pages, 1998.
[8] Wenger, E., "Communities of Practice. Learning as a Social System," vol. 2004: Systems Thinker, 1998.
[9] Wenger, E., McDermott, R., and Snyder, W. M., *Cultivating Communities of Practice: A Guide to Managing Knowledge*, Harvard Business School Press: Boston, pp. Pages, 2002.
[10] Stevenson, B. W. and Hamilton, M., How Does Complexity Inform Community, How Does Community Inform Complexity? *Emergence*, **3(2)**, pp. 57-77, 2002.
[11] Snowden, D., Complex Acts of Knowing: Paradox and Descriptive Self-Awareness. *Journal of Knowledge Management*, **6(2)**, pp. 100-111, 2002.
[12] McElroy, M. W., *The New Knowledge Management: Complexity, Learning, and Sustainable Innovation*, Butterworth-Heinemann, pp. Pages, 2002.
[13] Callahan, S. D., Cultivating a Public Sector Knowledge Management Community of Practice. *Knowledge Networks: Innovation Through Communities of Practice*, ed. P. M. Hildreth and C. Kimble, Idea Group: Hershey PA, 2004.
[14] Waldrop, M. M., *Complexity: The Emerging Science at the Edge of Order and Chaos*, Simon and Schuster: New York, pp. Pages, 1992.
[15] Fontaine, M., Keeping Communities of Practice Afloat: Understanding and Fostering Roles in Communities. *Knowledge Management Review*, **4(4)**, pp. 16-21, 2001.
[16] Gould, S. J., *The panda's thumb: more reflections in natural history*, Norton: New York, pp. Pages, 1980.
[17] Axelrod, R., *The Complexity of Cooperation: Agent-Based Models of Competition and Collaboration*, Princeton University Press: Princeton, New Jersey, pp. Pages, 1997.

Human Perspectives in the Internet Society: Culture, Psychology and Gender, K. Morgan, J. Sanchez, C. A. Brebbia & A Voiskounsky (Editors) © 2004 WIT Press, www.witpress.com, ISBN 1-85312-726-4

Sharing places, enhancing spaces: an investigation into the effects of mobile networking technologies on physical communities

N. Bresnihan & L. Doyle
Disruptive Design Team,
Networks and Telecommunications Research Group,
Trinity College Dublin, Ireland

Abstract

Commentary on the impact of technology in the area of community-building has tended to concentrate on the creation of virtual communities, particularly Internet-based communities. More specifically Jurgen Habermas's concept of the 'Public Sphere', which he defined as "uncoerced conversation oriented towards pragmatic accord", has been enthusiastically claimed by the proponents of online communities. This paper will explore some of the problems with this idea focusing on the deeper philosophical issues which question whether the increasing unsteadiness of the construction of subjectivity online is compatible with the idea of a public sphere which relies on the Enlightenment ideal of the autonomous rational subject as a universal foundation for democracy. The paper will conclude that if the problem with virtual communities is that people are unconnected to their physical surroundings and other network users, the possible solution may be to focus less on cyberspace and more on traditional environments in order to bring proximity and practical cooperation back into the equation. It is suggested that this could be done through the use of mobile communications and wireless networking technologies. The paper will discuss some existing projects in this area and will conclude by advocating a re-examination of the role of physical place in community-building.

Human Perspectives in the Internet Society: Culture, Psychology and Gender, K. Morgan, J. Sanchez, C. A. Brebbia & A Voiskounsky (Editors) © 2004 WIT Press, www.witpress.com, ISBN 1-85312-726-4

1 Introduction

The dramatic decline of civil society during the latter part of the twentieth century has led many to focus on the notion of community and the importance of this notion to the overall health of our societies. In short communities are seen as the building blocks of civil society which, in turn, is seen as the foundation of our democratic institutions. Those who are interested in the relationship between technology and society have naturally looked at whether it is possible for technology to support community-building projects. This paper is particularly concerned with the effects of networking technology on communities and focuses on the importance of the relationships between people and the places that they inhabit to those communities. In order to demonstrate the importance of this relationship it is necessary to look at the shortcomings of communities that do not inhabit the same physical spaces, i.e. virtual communities. After establishing the importance of place we will look at a number of projects that use mobile technologies, wireless networks, and location-aware devices in order to heighten people's awareness of their shared environment including a number of projects that we in the Disruptive Design Team are currently engaged in.

2 Community, communion, and communication

The links between community, civic society, and the health of our democratic institutions have been mapped by many, most notably Robert Putnam in *Bowling Alone* [1] which provides an exhaustively researched account of the collapse of community in the United States. This book definitively shows how we have become disconnected from one another and social structures and the devastating impact of this upon our civic health. While many have blamed technology for this state of affairs (particularly the car for making suburbanisation possible and the television for its privatisation of our leisure time) early commentary on the communication possibilities opened up by the advent of the Internet, and particularly the world wide web, was marked by an adulatory tone conveying the sense of discovery that many have felt on being exposed to the possibility of instant flows of information across vast geographical distances. Putnam himself is cautiously optimistic about the possible effects of telecommunications' technology on the building of social capital:

> "Community, communion, and communication are intimately as well as etymologically related. Communication is a fundamental prerequisite for social and emotional connections. Telecommunications in general and the Internet in particular substantially enhance our ability to communicate; thus it seems reasonable to assume that their net effect will be to enhance community, perhaps even dramatically" [1].

Howard Rheingold, one of the earliest commentators on the potential of the Internet to reverse the decline of traditional communities [2], has defined civil society as "a web of informal relationships that exist independently of government institutions or business organizations, [it] is the social adhesive necessary to hold divergent communities of interest together into democratic societies" [3]. This definition is clear about the relationship between civil society and democracy – one is dependent on the other. In order for democracy to flourish it is essential that its citizens believe that they belong to a greater community. While the concept of community commonly refers to a set of social relationships that operate within specified boundaries or locales, it also has an ideological component, in that it refers to a sense of common character, identity or interests. It is this second aspect of community that has led to optimism that 'virtual communities' can help revitalize civil society. This potential reinvigoration has a theoretical basis in the concept of a renewed public sphere.

3 The Internet and the Public Sphere

In his *The Structural Definition of the Public Sphere*, Jurgen Habermas investigated the notion that there was a historical moment when the discourses of "mixed companies" provided the basis for political action. He formulated these moments/spaces as 'The Public Sphere' which he defined as "uncoerced conversation oriented towards pragmatic accord" [4]. As Craig Calhoun notes "[t]he importance of the public sphere lies in its potential as a mode of social integration. Public discourse (and what Habermas later and more generally calls communicative action) is a possible mode of co-ordination of human life" [5]. In essence what Habermas describes is an idealised 'space' in which rational/critical discussion can lead to the formation of an effective and influential public opinion. Unsurprisingly this concept has been appropriated by those lauding the social potential of the Internet (a search for *Internet + 'Public Sphere'* on Google on March 1st 2004 returned over 48,400 results). Indeed it has been argued that the Internet *is* the public sphere of late capitalism; enabling the kind of communicative possibilities that promise a new level of interactive practice which, in the past, was the foundation of democratising politics.

However, there are a number of problems with this formulation of the Internet as Public Sphere. Firstly, there is the ongoing problem of the digital divide. The technology traditionally needed to engage in these virtual communities, a computer and access to a fixed network infrastructure is simply out of reach for the vast majority of the world's population. Secondly, we have the problem that virtual communities tend to be based purely on communities of interest leading to narrow discussions on mostly predefined topics which, while giving the contributors a *sense* of community, can in fact keep them dislocated from the real world. However while both of these are serious problems *theoretically* they are not impossible to solve. With the right policies and enough money the digital divide could be bridged. Many online communities are not just based on narrow interests they are meeting points for like-minded individuals to talk about a broad range of topics. The more intractable questions arise when we consider the fact that the Internet, after all, is in many ways at the vanguard of a new kind of virtual world. The anonymous sociality of the Internet dramatically increases the unsteadiness of the construction of subjectivity in the online world, encouraging an emerging new individual identity or subject position, one that abandons the

Human Perspectives in the Internet Society: Culture, Psychology and Gender, K. Morgan, J. Sanchez, C. A. Brebbia & A Voiskounsky (Editors) © 2004 WIT Press, www.witpress.com, ISBN 1-85312-726-4

idea of the enlightenment individual with its claims to rationality and autonomy in line with postmodernist theory. Also, unlike older physically determined spaces such as the town hall, the Internet provides a *virtual* community space and as Paul Virilio writes, "What remains of the notion of things `public' when public *images* (in real time) are more important than public *space*?" [6].

Indeed in many ways it is ironic that Habermas' concept of the 'public sphere' has been appropriated by those discussing the democratising effects of the virtual communities enabled by the Internet, knowing that theorist's known antipathy towards the postmodern. Postmodern theorists celebrate heterogeneity as the salient characteristic of our age. Drawing on poststructuralism with its lexicon of 'difference', 'dispersal', 'deference' etc., Lyotard's 'libidinal economy' [7], Deleuze and Guattari's 'rhizomatics' [8] and Vattimo's *il pensiero debole* [9] are all among the postmodern events deeply indebted to the imbrication of distance and divergence. These theorists overtly attack Habermas's position questioning the emancipatory potentials of its model of consensus through rational debate [10]. At issue is the poststructuralist critique of Habermas' Enlightenment ideal of the autonomous rational subject as a universal foundation for democracy.

Therefore any attempt to analyse the implications of the Internet in terms of the extension or replacement of existing institutions is problematic. As Mark Poster has pointed out this tension arises from the fact that our existing political institutions, in the main, have their roots in Enlightenment thought [11]. The notion of democracy itself, a central political ideal, is a distinctly modernist conception. However when dealing with *virtual* communities there is a need to move away from modernist political discourse and the problem, of course, is that there is no adequate postmodern political theory. The very formulation of democracy is premised on the existence of the individual outside history. A postmodern definition, in contrast, would have to allow for the construction of identity within the social and within language.

Thus the postmodern position is limited by the insistence of the constructedness of human identity. In an attempt to avoid the pitfalls of modern political theory, it limits its own scope to define a new political direction. In contrast Habermas sees the public sphere as maintaining the promise of liberalism and the essentially utopian content of the first universalising bourgeois ideology (civil rights, free speech, humanitarianism) against the failure of those ideals to develop in the development of capitalism itself. The inherent contradictions make it hard to believe that the realm of the virtual community represents any extension or refocusing of traditional liberal democracy.

So, despite optimistic predictions, the anonymous sociality that is intrinsic to the Internet seems at odds with traditional theories of democracy. This however is not to deny that the current uses of networking technology are contributing to a *sense* of community and democracy. As Jan Fernback and Brad Thompson have argued: "[I]t seems most likely that the virtual public sphere brought about by CMC [Computer-Mediated Communication] will serve a cathartic role, allowing the public to feel involved rather than to advance actual participation" [12]. Despite this *sense* of sociability the disjunction with

Human Perspectives in the Internet Society: Culture, Psychology and Gender, K. Morgan, J. Sanchez, C. A. Brebbia & A Voiskounsky (Editors) © 2004 WIT Press, www.witpress.com, ISBN 1-85312-726-4

geographically-based neighbourhoods means that the subject becomes unstable, enmeshed in the flows of communication rather than actually taking an active part in their localities and because civil society is a locus for the interaction of the self and the social, if that interaction is diminished so is civil society.

4 Sharing places, enhancing spaces

If the Internet has proved not to be the hoped-for panacea for our lost communities is there *any* way that we can use networking technologies to reinvigorate civil society? One of the problems seems to be that only one aspect of communities is currently being provided for. The sharing of psychological space is amply served by bulletin boards, chat rooms, Usenet, the web, IRC, instant messaging, email, etc., but what of the shared concerns of those who inhabit physical spaces? The Internet brought with it the notion of the 'end of geography'. Space and place were deemed no longer important. According to Nicholas Negroponte "the post-information age will remove the limitations of geography. Digital living will depend less and less on being in a specific place at a specific time" [13]. The problem with this kind of rampant virtuality, based on the eradication of time and space as functional communicative restraints is that it can act to separate people from face-to-face relationships and localities.

So if one of the problems with virtual communities is that they leave people unconnected to their physical surroundings and other network users the possible solution may be to focus less on cyberspace and more on traditional physical environments in order to bring proximity and practical cooperation back into the equation. Fortunately disillusionment with virtual communities comes at a time when we have the technological means to start thinking about the shape of augmented physical spaces. The use of mobile communications and wireless networking has proliferated in the last number of years. Unlike access to fixed networks which tends to be indoors in front of a computer monitor, we now have the opportunity to get people to move outside into their neighbourhoods and to still be online. The question is whether this reintroduction of physical space can make people feel more connected to their communities?

A large part of the blame for the collapse of civil society in the latter half of the twentieth century has been placed firmly on television. Specifically its privatisation of our leisure time has been identified as a root cause of the decline of social involvement. TV ownership and usage has been "linked both in this country and abroad, to reduced contacts with relatives, friends, neighbors. More TV watching meant more time not just at home, but indoors, at the expense of time in the yard, on the street, and visiting in others' homes [1].

Using computer networks to communicate using a stationary workstation has the same effects. McCellan has made this connection: "[R]ather than providing a replacement for a crumbling public realm, virtual communities are actually contributing to its decline. They're another thing keeping people indoors and off the streets." [14]. Virtual communities allow our social ties to be cut off from physical encounters. But what if we could use networking technology to encourage physical contact with people and places?

Human Perspectives in the Internet Society: Culture, Psychology and Gender, K. Morgan, J. Sanchez, C. A. Brebbia & A Voiskounsky (Editors) © 2004 WIT Press, www.witpress.com, ISBN 1-85312-726-4

5 So what's being done?

The upsurge of theoretical work on the importance of community building has recently been matched by practical interventions using new networking technologies. Site specific wireless networks, ad hoc and peer-to-peer networks, personal-area networks, and body-area networks are all available working technologies. Increasing numbers in developed nations are carrying devices capable of both computation and communication. GPS, Wifi triangulation, 3G Phone location finding, and conventional current cell tower locating mean that these devices are becoming location-aware. Soon microchips will be embedded everywhere - from our clothes and accessories to buildings and streets they will enable us to connect to our environment in ways that we cannot yet imagine. But this is merely the enabling technology and it is becoming clear that "[t]he 'killer apps' of tomorrow's mobile infocom industry won't be hardware devices or software programs but social practices." [15].

Already projects like *Upmystreet.com* [16] (postcode level bulletin board and government information service), *Consume.net* [17] and *Nocat* [18] (community WiFi networks) have shown how imaginative applications of technology can open up new possibilities for community infrastructure and communication. Researchers and artists, engineers and social scientists are working on projects that use these technologies to promote community building by encouraging face-to-face interaction through location-based services. Examples include The Wearable Computing Lab at the University of Oregon [19] who use their research into wearable and mobile technologies to encourage and assist collaboration between users. The same urge to use wireless mobile technology to share information among users is the motivation of *Bass-Station* [20] which uses a 1980's boom box as the shell for a locally accessible wireless network which allows people in the proximity to exchange digital information [21]. *The Campiello Project* [22] aims to develop new links between the local communities and visitors in Venice (Italy) and Chania (Crete) by the sharing of local information using a range of networking technologies.

To-date a lot of these projects have taken as their focus the idea of connecting people to people or people to information but the really unique feature of mobile wireless networks, the thing they can do that fixed networks cannot, is that they can enable more meaningful connections between people and places – they promise the end of 'the end of geography'. There is little doubt that the connection of people to the places that they live and work is integral to their sense of belonging and community. The new confluence of wireless, mobile technology and decentralised networking raises the prospect of encouraging both face-to-face interaction and a new identification with the public spaces of our immediate physical surroundings. As those who share common spaces have a common interest in making those spaces better places to inhabit it is hoped that making people more aware of their environment will help to reinvigorate their engagement in their communities. In short, there has been a lot of talk about the use of location-aware devices and the provision of location-based services, what we would like to advocate is the creation of *location-aware people.*

Human Perspectives in the Internet Society: Culture, Psychology and Gender, K. Morgan, J. Sanchez, C. A. Brebbia & A Voiskounsky (Editors) © 2004 WIT Press, www.witpress.com, ISBN 1-85312-726-4

One of the most significant interventions in this area is *Urban Tapestries* [23], a dynamic public authoring platform which allows users to share their experiences of public spaces. Users can add sound maps, content and their own threads, each attached to a physical place, to a database for others to retrieve. Access to the database is provided by mobile and WiFi radio technologies. Threads can be followed as a trail around a city or users can be alerted when an augmented location is nearby. The creators have explicitly identified this project's potential to build community through making its users 'location aware' placing it firmly within the theoretical context which has been outlined here: "The system's ability to engage people with local geography has the potential to encourage greater knowledge of and sense of ownership of an area. This could have the effect of promoting a 'cultural investment' in the environment." [24].

This kind of integration of networks and public spaces particularly appeals to the gaming community. Turning the image of the solitary player hunched over his/her console on its head, *NodeRunner* [25] uses the existing wireless infrastructure in New York to turn the city into a playing board as teams compete to log into as many wireless hotspots as they can and upload photographic proof to their server. Their website encourages competitors to "run the street, enter buildings and galleries, climb up fire-escapes but find more nodes then the other team!" Also bringing the gaming community out onto the streets are UK-based *Blast Theory* [26] who use games to explore how real spaces and virtual spaces are linked and the blurring of the boundaries between them.

What all of these projects have in common is a desire to reaffirm our connectedness to the physical world. Broader movement in this vein include the *Locative Media Lab* [27] and *Headmap* [28]. *Locative Media Lab* explores how digital media being actively used in real places has the potential to influence community. It consists of a syndicate of artists and researchers who host workshops and provide a forum for people interested in the artistic and social applications of mobile technology. *Headmap* is a self-styled distributed think tank which looks at the social implications and applications of location aware devices, augmented social networks, wearable computers, thinking tools and semantic network interfaces. What we can learn from these projects is that with new technology it is possible to augment and transform the physical world. If we can use this ability to re-establish the importance of our locale to our sense of self and community perhaps this will give people an incentive and a forum to interact hence going some way towards rejuvenating our civil society.

6 Disruptive design

It is this interest in people's relationship to their environment that has led to the creation of the Disruptive Design Team in the Networks and Telecommunications Group at Trinity College Dublin. Our projects aim to disrupt people's everyday thoughts and actions, to make them stop and take note of the people around them, the places they're in, and the connections and flows between them. It is intended that by doing so people might be more thoughtful

Human Perspectives in the Internet Society: Culture, Psychology and Gender, K. Morgan, J. Sanchez, C. A. Brebbia & A Voiskounsky (Editors) © 2004 WIT Press, www.witpress.com, ISBN 1-85312-726-4

about their impact on the world around them, that this might go some way towards reconnecting them to their communities.

Inside/Outside is a mobile ad hoc network application designed and created by Katherine Moriwaki. The creation of a hand bag that is capable of collecting digital objects as the wearer moves around the city landscape was undertaken as an experiment in reconnecting people to the urban space:

> "While an ordinary handbag collects physical objects which are often personally invested, Inside/Outside collects digital data about the environment, allowing processes of reflection and action to create personally invested relationships to the city and other individuals in the urban space" [29].

The current prototype is capable of collecting air quality and noise pollution data. Thermo-chromic ink reacts to these levels changing the outward appearance of the bag. When the bag comes within radio range of other bags the collected information can be exchanged giving the users an alternative visualisation of the pollution levels over both the route they have chosen and other routes in the city. It is hoped that the increased awareness of the city environment will lead to increased connectedness to that environment.

Another of our projects *Graffiti Wall* consists of a virtual wall projected on to a real public space. As a public collaborative digital space, it provides a digital meeting ground for participants to 'paint' graffiti using SMS, MMS, e-mail, email image attachments, or a web-based interface. The slogans added to the Graffiti Wall appear in a haphazard fashion and the messages fade with time as real graffiti fades. There is complete freedom of expression, as there would be in a physical environment. Graffiti was specifically chosen over other forms of public expression for a number of reasons. When a piece of graffiti is added to an area, other pieces are added in reply or retort creating a collaborative space whereby people can interact through both pictures and words. However, as well as being elaborate visual displays, these art forms are also objects. As such they are as much artefact as art. As artefacts they are produced to be seen at fixed sites and in specific locales, and an extension of their significance is generated by a dynamic which involves the images taking meaning from their location and the location in turn having a different significance because of the paintings. While on one level, it is primarily the image that it is being used and transformed, on another level it is the physical artefact, fixed in space, which is the subject of activity; taken still further it is the public space in which the artefact is sited that is changed. As such graffiti creates a new type of space; redefining mundane public space as politicised place and thereby helping to reclaim it for the community.

The same impulse, that of making people aware that public space is shared space, informs *Oscillating Windows* [30], an ad hoc network application designed on the principles of enforced cooperation. It consists of two static nodes that control projected images that are displayed on two sides of a large public space. A mobile population of ad hoc nodes associated with the flow of people through the space can lead to the creation of an ad hoc network though which it is possible to make an image oscillate from one static node to the other.

Human Perspectives in the Internet Society: Culture, Psychology and Gender, K. Morgan, J. Sanchez, C. A. Brebbia & A Voiskounsky (Editors) © 2004 WIT Press, www.witpress.com, ISBN 1-85312-726-4

However, the occupiers of the space must form particular patterns in order to create a route for the image. Users can either be instructed to behave in a certain fashion of be allowed to come to their own conclusions about the operation of the project through observation. The users become more aware of their movements through public space and the effects this can have on their environment.

While all these projects are still being developed and tested our interest in them here is based on the premise that by augmenting the local and the physical rather than retreating from it into the global and the virtual we can promote community integration.

7 Conclusion

The underlying concern of this paper is with the purpose and function of technology, the relationship between innovative technologies and emergent values. It is based on the theoretical model of community being the basis of civil society which is in turn is the basis of democracy. In Habermasian terms civil society operates by using the public sphere as an arena for rational/critical debate leading to the formation of a consensus of informed public opinion which can then influence public policy. However in the present communication or media society, the growing commodification of the public sphere is a matter of concern to proponents of the democratic project. The development of the Internet has led some to believe that it could have a role to play in hosting the public sphere of late capitalism. Unfortunately, as we have seen, its tendency to cut some people of from face-to-face interaction and from their local geography encourages a kind of anonymous sociality which renders the basis of democracy, the autonomous rational subject, unstable. It is clear that the importance of the geographical location to communities has been overlooked by those eulogising the 'end of geography' and the 'global village'. The fact of the matter is that an emotional connection to the physical spaces that we inhabit and share is an important element in promoting social interaction. Of course there can be no going back; the poststructuralist knowledge of the world as human construct is undeniable, but that should not of itself breed solipsism. We can acknowledge that the intelligibility of the world depends on our ordering perceptions of it but in order to engage with each other and the world around us we need to acknowledge the world's ontological 'thereness'. The projects that we have looked at are those which are beginning to recognise the significance of a sense of place to our common psyche and their importance lies in their insistence on a *real* world out there which we can interact with and maybe even make better.

References

[1] Putnam, R.D., Bowling Alone: The Collapse and Revival of American Community, Simon & Schuster: New York, p.171, p.124, 2000.

[2] Rheingold, H., The Virtual Community: Homesteading on the Electronic Frontier (Rev. ed.), MIT Press: Cambridge, Mass.; 2000.

Human Perspectives in the Internet Society: Culture, Psychology and Gender, K. Morgan, J. Sanchez, C. A. Brebbia & A Voiskounsky (Editors) © 2004 WIT Press, www.witpress.com, ISBN 1-85312-726-4

[3] Rheingold, H., 'Virtual Communities, Phony Civil Society?', 1998 Online. http://www.rheingold.com/texts/techpolitix/civil.html
[4] Habermas, J., The Structural Transformation of the Public Sphere, An Inquiry into a Category of Bourgeois Society, Polity: Cambridge, 1989.
[5] Calhoun, C., Introduction, Habermas and the Public Sphere, ed. C. Calhoun, MIT Press: Cambridge Mass. and London, p.xi, 1992.
[6] Virilio, P., The Third Interval: A Critical Transition, ed. V. Conley, Rethinking Technologies, U. of Minnesota P.: Minneapolis, p.9 1993.
[7] Lyotard, J.F., Libidinal Economy, Athlone: London, 1993.
[8] Deleuze, G., & Guattari, F., A Thousand Plateau: Capitalism and Schizophrenia, U. of Minnesota P.: Minneapolis, 1987.
[9] Vattimo, G., Il Pensiero Debole, Feltrinelli: Milano, 1988.
[10] Lyotard, J.F., The Postmodern Condition, U. of Minnesota P.: Minneapolis, 1984.
[11] Poster M., CyberDemocracy: Internet and the Public Sphere, 1995, Online. http://www.hnet.uci.edu/mposter/writings/democ.html
[12] Fernback, J. & Thompson, J., Virtual Communities: Abort, Retry, Failure?, 1995, Online. http://www.well.com/user/hlr/texts/VCcivil.html
[13] Negroponte, N., Being Digital, Vintage Books: New York, p.165, 1995.
[14] McCellan, J., Netsurfers, The Observer, p.10, February 13, 1994.
[15] Rheingold, H., Smart Mobs: The Next Social Revolution, Perseus Publishing: Cambridge MA, p.xii, 2003.
[16] http://www.upmystreet.com/
[17] http://www.consume.net/
[18] http://www.nocat.com/
[19] http://www.cs.uoregon.edu/research/wearables/projects.html
[20] http://www.bass-station.net
[21] Wolf, A. & Argo, M. Bass-Station: A Community-Based Information Space, 2003 Online. http://www.bass-station.net/Bass-Station_SIGGRAPH2003.pdf
[22] http://klee.cootech.disco.unimib.it/Campiello/index.html
[23] http://www.proboscis.org.uk/urbantapestries/
[24] Lane, G., Urban Tapestries, 1AD Appliance Design Conference, 6th May 2003, Online. http://www.proboscis.org.uk/urbantapestries/1ad_paper.html
[25] http://www.uncommonprojects.com/noderunner/
[26] http://www.blasttheory.co.uk
[27] http://www.locative.net
[28] http://www.headmap.org/
[29] Moriwaki, K., Inside/Outside: Concept', Online. http://www.kakirine.com
[30] http://www.kakirine.com/

Human Perspectives in the Internet Society: Culture, Psychology and Gender, K. Morgan, J. Sanchez, C. A. Brebbia & A Voiskounsky (Editors) © 2004 WIT Press, www.witpress.com, ISBN 1-85312-726-4

Impediments to development in the border provinces of Iran

H. Shayan
Ferdowsi University of Mashhad, Iran

Abstract

In this study, the conditions of 11 border provinces of Iran including Ardabil, West and East Azarbaijan, Kordestan, Kermanshah, Ilam, Khouzestan, Hormozgan, Sistan & Blouchestan, and Khorassan with respect to certain indicators such as life expectancy, literacy level and birth rate have been explored, using statistical U-, T- and Z-tests as well as correlation coefficients.

The findings indicate that there are significant differences between internal provinces and border provinces, especially Sistan & Blouchestan, Kordestan, Ilam, Kermanshah, West Azarbaijan and Hormozgan with respect to the above-mentioned indicators, differences which have resulted in a negative migration balance. On the other hand, the economic dependence of these provinces on adjacent countries can result in their political-cultural disintegration and consequently in a decline in national identity, power and security.
Keywords: public economic development, migration, life expectancy, standards of living, literacy, border provinces.

1 Introduction

In early 1990s, fourteen republics of the former Soviet Union gained independence. The early reports of the UN's Human Development in this decade published in 1992, identified these republics, especially those with a Muslim population, as countries of low development. Great distance from the capital Moscow and cultural-religious and even ethnic diversity may explain the backwardness of these republics. There is also this possibility that Moscow predicted the separation of these republics. This was not the case in Iran. The current territory of Iran has been for centuries as part of a greater historical land; it has been the home of Islam for over 14 centuries. Therefore, cultural,

Human Perspectives in the Internet Society: Culture, Psychology and Gender, K. Morgan, J. Sanchez, C. A. Brebbia & A Voiskounsky (Editors) © 2004 WIT Press, www.witpress.com, ISBN 1-85312-726-4

especially linguistic, differences, or distance from the capital, could not have played a great role in the development level in various regions.

Russia and Iran, however, have something in common: they have the greatest number of neighbors in the world (Russia with 16 neighbors and Iran with 15 neighbors). They also have the greatest number of manifest and hidden differences with their neighbors [4]. The situation of Iran is more sensitive for the following reasons: the rapid growth of population specially in the border provinces, the transparency of its political stances on the regional and world issues; inability to satisfy the demands of its population in the matters of housing, employment, etc.

In this article, the purpose is to analyze certain fundamental variables affecting human development in border provinces by comparing percentages and using Z score, correlation coefficient, and other tests. The objective is to provide an answer to the question whether distance from the capital has an effect on the level of development. This is made possible by comparing these provinces with other provinces in the country.

2 Birth rate

In 1991 and 1996, birth rate in Iran was estimated to be 28.3 in a thousand [10] and 19.8 in a thousand [8]. Except for Khorassan and East Azarbaijan, birth rate was higher in all peripheral provinces than other provinces in the country. In this five-year period, Booshehr and Ilam showed a positive development since the Z score of birth rate in the two provinces was +0.7 and +1.1 in 1991 and -0.3 and 0 in 1996 respectively.

In four provinces facing a crisis of birth rate, that is, West Azarbaijan, Sistan & Balouchestan, Hormozgan and Kermanshah, the percentage of literacy was the lowest; so was the percentage of urban population, except for Kermanshah province. In these provinces, the average annual growth of population was much higher than that in other provinces of the country in 1986 to 1996.

Based on the T-test, it was confirmed, with 95% accuracy, that there was a significant difference between the peripheral provinces and other provinces in terms of birth rate in 1991, but no such significant difference existed in 1996 (Table 2). Although this is a positive indication, but the effects of high birth rate in non-peripheral provinces such as Chaharmahal Bakhtiyari, Kohkilooyeh-Booyer Ahmad and Lorestan should not be overlooked.

3 Death rate

Since there is no unified mechanism in the country for recording incidences of death, and since the population is distributed over a wide area, death rate statistics are not of much reliability. It is, however, possible to identify the provinces in which death rate is high. Based on available statistics, the provinces with a death rate higher than the average death rate in the country are Ilam, Kermanshah, Kordestan, East and West Azarbaijan. Death rate in Kordestan is almost twice as much as the average death rate in the country.

Human Perspectives in the Internet Society: Culture, Psychology and Gender, K. Morgan, J. Sanchez, C. A. Brebbia & A Voiskounsky (Editors) © 2004 WIT Press, www.witpress.com, ISBN 1-85312-726-4

4 Migration volume

Migration volume may be analyzed in two ways: first, in terms of either the percentage of the population migrated or the percentage of the population residing in a place other than their birth place compared to the total population. Second, in terms of migration balance. According to the first approach, in the whole provinces of the country, the greatest volume of migrants are related to these very provinces, with Tehran having the greatest volume of migrants (Z=+2.9), followed by Kordestan (Z=+1.4), Khoozestan (Z=+1.4), and Ilam, Booshehr, Kermanshah and Khorassan, obtaining the ranks 2 to 9 respectively. According to the second approach, which is more efficient in the analysis of the migration situation, of the eleven provinces under study (except for Khoozestan, which has been receiving migrants because of the return of the people to their homeland with the termination of the war), the provinces of Hormozgan, Sistan & Balouchestan, Ilam, Khorassan and West Azarbaijan have had a relative stability and the other six provinces have exported immigrants. The provinces with the greatest volume of migrants were Booshehr, Ardabil, Kermanshah and East Azarbaijan with a negative balance of 4.3, 3.3, 2.6 and 2.6 percent respectively.

5 Literacy

Except for Khorassan, in all the provinces under study the literacy indicator was lower than that in the other provinces of the country. This is especially true about Sistan & Balouchestan (with the literacy rate of 48.1% and Z=-2.9) and Kordestan (with the literacy rate of 56.9% and Z=-1.7). These two provinces had the lowest ranks among the eleven border provinces with respect to level of development, gross costs per capita and life expectancy (Table 1). Both T and U significance tests show a 99% difference between the border and other provinces. Therefore, priority must be given to the border provinces for promotion of literacy.

6 Urban and rural population

Based on the 1996 census, in all the border provinces under study except for Khoozestan, the level of urbanism is lower than that in other provinces, with Hormozgan having the lowest level (41.8%, Z=-1.1). Therefore, these provinces are expected to have a higher fertility and population growth. What is important is that in the regional plans, considering the structure of the population and economic and security considerations, more emphasis should be placed on agriculture and the resolution of problems in the rural areas. This is especially necessary because the average employment in the industry section in all these provinces (except for Khorassan, where the industry of weaving carpets is very active), is lower than that in other provinces of the country.

According to T and U tests, there is no significant difference between the two groups of provinces with respect to the rate of urbanism. The reason is that there

Human Perspectives in the Internet Society: Culture, Psychology and Gender, K. Morgan, J. Sanchez, C. A. Brebbia & A Voiskounsky (Editors) © 2004 WIT Press, www.witpress.com, ISBN 1-85312-726-4

are provinces with a very low percentage of urbanism among non-peripheral provinces. The standard deviation in these provinces, being 15.3, confirms this. Based on Fisher test, a significant difference between the variances of the two provinces has been proved (Fa=1.46. F0=0.16).

7 Population growth rate

Considering the status of literacy, birth rate and urbanism in these provinces, they are predicted to have a high population growth rate. This is confirmed by a study of annual population rate from 1986-96. For example, the provinces Sistan & Balouchestan, Hormozgan, Khoozestan, Ilam, Kordetsan and West Azarbaijan showed a population growth rate higher than that in other provinces of the country as well as in the provinces of Khorassan, Booshehr and Kermanshah. The figures related to East Azarbaijan (0.8) and Ardabil (1.2) are not valid because of the new administrative divisions and the high rate of migrants' export. Therefore, the provinces that have priority in terms of population growth decrease are those provinces that have a very high birth rate. It should be borne in mind that some non-peripheral provinces that have a high birth rate and a high population growth. For this reason, based on the T-test, there is a significant difference between population growth rates in the two groups of provinces only with an 80 percent accuracy.

8 Gross costs per capita

Based on the 1996 census, the average gross costs per capita in the country was 1899000 Rials. All the border provinces have a lower gross costs per capita. This is especially true about Sistan & Balouchestan, Kordestan and Ilam with 1120000 Rials (Z=-2), 1386000 Rials (Z=-0.85) and 1409000 Rials (Z=-0.76) respectively. Ironically, these three provinces that have a poor status with respect to birth rate, population growth rate and literacy level, also have the first ranks in the country with respect to the dependence ratio along with the provinces of Kermanshah, Hormozgan and Khoozestan. Thus the greatest number of economic problems and pressures exist in the eleven border provinces in general and the 6 above-mentioned provinces in particular.

9 Life expectancy

It was estimated in 1996 that life expectancy in Iran was 69.2 years. Unfortunately, in all the border provinces, life expectancy is lower than that. In Khozestan, for example, where the highest life expectancy is observed, it is 66.9 (Z=-0.97) and in Sistan & Balouchestan, where the lowest life expectancy is observed, it is 61 (Z=-3.4). T and U tests shows a significant difference in life expectancy between the two groups of provinces with a precision of over 99.5%. Since life expectancy is the result of so many other factors, it is of great importance and should be given due consideration.

Human Perspectives in the Internet Society: Culture, Psychology and Gender, K. Morgan, J. Sanchez, C. A. Brebbia & A Voiskounsky (Editors) © 2004 WIT Press, www.witpress.com, ISBN 1-85312-726-4

10 General economic development level

With respect to this variable, the border provinces should be given priority since the provinces Sistan & Balouchestan, Ilam and Kordestan had the lowest indicators and rank. (The indicators were -0.7, -0.68 and -0.57 respectively and the ranks were 24, 23 and 22 respectively in comparison with the 24 provinces of the country). The indicator and rank of the next four provinces are as follows: Kermanshah (-0.32, 17); Hormozgan (-0.13, 16); Booshehr (-0.07, 14), West Azarbaijan (0.15, 11). The significance test has been affected by certain less developed provinces among non-peripheral provinces and the difference has been proved by the T-test with an accuracy level of 85%.

11 Regression analysis of the relationship of variables

Because of the importance of the relationship between the variables, the significance of correlation coefficients in all the provinces of the country was tested. The results are as follows: There are, on the one hand, significant (over 95%) relationships between the variables of literacy and urbanism (r= 0.84); between net percent of migrants and the indicator of development (r=0.52); between population growth and migration balance (r= 0.74), between percentage of urbanism and net percent of migrants with the indicator of development (r=0.81 and r=0.52 respectively). And on the other hand, there are inverse significant relationship between urban population growth and the percentage of literacy (r=-0.7), the percentage of urbanism (r=-0.68), general development (r=-0.61) and between migration balance and percentage of agricultural employment (r=-0.43). This indicates the fact that the main problem in the country is the profound differences between cities and villages and among various provinces. Thus migration from villages to cities in less developed provinces with a low urban population, involves a quantitative change; that is, an increase in the number of the city population, whereas the general development and literacy levels remain low. In fact, in these provinces, the villagers who can no longer stand life in villages rush to cities which have not provided their population with a minimum of standards of living, cities which, however, seem attractive to the newcomers from the province. The important point here is that the economic power of the rural areas in these provinces must be strengthened because one of the major differences between the city and the village is that employment in the city has a higher annual growth, a factor which explains the rush of immigrants to cities [3].

12 Conclusions

To establish justice and because of its geopolitical situation, specially because it is located among such countries as Turkey, Azarbaijan, Iraq, Turkmanistan, Pakistan, Afghanistan and Persian Gulf countries, Iran should treat all its provinces fairly, so that the whole country may function efficiently. If each province functions inefficiently, it affects the country as a whole.

Human Perspectives in the Internet Society: Culture, Psychology and Gender, K. Morgan, J. Sanchez, C. A. Brebbia & A Voiskounsky (Editors) © 2004 WIT Press, www.witpress.com, ISBN 1-85312-726-4

Table 1: Population and economy variables in the border provinces under study.

Province	**Pop. In 1000s**	**Pop. In 1000s**	**Growth rate %**	**Area %**	**Pop. %**	**Birth rate (in 1000s)**	**Urban-ization %**	**Life expectancy**	**Literacy Rate**	**GCPC**	**Mig. Balance**	**Develop. index**
	1996	**1986**	**86-96**	**1996**	**1996**	**1996**	**1996**	**1996**	**1996**	**1996**	**86-96**	**1986**
Ard.	1168	1036	1.2	1.13	1.94	19.8	48.7	65.7	63.2	1652	-3.3	--
E.Azar.	3326	3077	0.8	2.7	5.5	17.1	60.3	66.5	67.5	1652	-2.6	0.33
W.Azar.	2496	1971	2.4	2.3	4.2	30.2	52.7	64.7	61.1	1439	+0.6	0.15
Kord.	1346	1078	2.25	1.7	2.2	21.8	52.4	61.6	56.9	1386.	-1.9	-0.57
Kerm.	1779	1462	1.98	1.45	2.96	23	61.7	65	68.1	1860	-2.6	-0.32
Ilam	488	382	2.5	1.17	0.8	19.8	53	64	67	1409	-0.6	-0.68
Kooz.	3747	2682	3.4	4	6.2	22.2	62.5	66.9	69.2	1781	+3..3	0.42
Boosh.	744	612	1.97	1.55	1.24	18.7	53	66.6	72.5	1493	-3.4	-0.07
Horm.	1062	762	3.38	4	1.8	27.8	41.8	65.9	63.3	1585	-0.3	-0.13
Sist.	1723	1197	3.7	11	2.9	30.8	46.2	61.1	48.1	1120	-0.1	-0.7
Khor.	6448	5280	2	19.4	10.7	18.8	56.6	64.3	73.9	1502	+0.2	0.35
Total	24327	19539	2.22	50.4	40.5	22	55.8	64.5	64.5	1534	--	Neg.
Country	60055	49445	1.96	100	100	19.8	61.3	69.2	72.9	1899	--	

Human Perspectives in the Internet Society: Culture, Psychology and Gender, K. Morgan, J. Sanchez, C. A. Brebbia & A Voiskounsky (Editors) © 2004 WIT Press, www.witpress.com, ISBN 1-85312-726-4

Table 2: Results of significance T- and U-tests (1996).

	Border provinces		Other Provinces								
Variable	Mean	Standard Deviation	Mean	Standard Deviation	T-test	U-Test	T-Acceptance	U-acceptance	T-Acceptance*	U-Acceptance*	F-test
Pop. growth	2.2	0.86	1.8	0.57	1.4	45	80%	-	95%	95%	+
Birth rate	22	4.5	19	3.6	1.9	41	92%	-	98%	99%	+
Urbanization %	53.5	6.2	58.9	15.3	1.1	80	70%	-	95%	90%	-
GCPC	1534	195	1613	253	1.01	65	70%	-	97%	95%	-
Literacy rate	64.5	7.03	72.7	5.7	3.28	33	99.6%	99%	99.9%	99%	+
Life expectancy	64.5	1.84	67.2	2	3.44	34	99.7%	95%	99.9%	99%	-
General Development	-0.12	0.41	0.16	0.65	1.58	56	58%	-	98%	80%	-

*Excluding the three background unborder provinces of Lorestan, Kohkilooyeh & Booyer Ahmad, Chahar Mahal.

Human Perspectives in the Internet Society: Culture, Psychology and Gender, K. Morgan, J. Sanchez, C. A. Brebbia & A Voiskounsky (Editors) © 2004 WIT Press, www.witpress.com, ISBN 1-85312-726-4

A study of the most important variables affecting development in eleven border countries in Iran showed that such provinces should be given priority because based on T and U tests, there is a significant difference between border provinces and other provinces (with the exclusion of three provinces of Chaharmahal Bakhtiyari, Kohkilooyeh-Booyer Ahmad and Lorestan), with respect to the said variables. The provinces of Sistan & Balouchestan, Kordestan, Ilam, Kermanshah, West Azarbaijan, Hormozgan and Booshehr are not in a good position with respect to the variables birth rate, population growth, literacy, gross costs per capita, and life expectancy, and the provinces Ardabil, East Azarbaijan, Kermanshah and Booshehr are not in a good position with respect to migration statistics. Finally, since development is for the people, and is materialized by the people, it is good to remind authorities responsible for development of what Zurick [12] has stated about development: "Go to the people; answers are there."

References

[1] Cullagh, MC. 1975, Data use and Interpretation, Oxford University.

[2] Javan, J. 2001, Geography of population in Iran, Jahad Daneshgahee Publication.

[3] Shayan, H. 2000, "Inter provincial migration in Iran", *The geographer*, Vol. 47, Aligarh University, India. p. 21.

[4] Kamran, H. 2001, "Geographical grounds of outward threats", *Journal of Geographical Research,* Vol. 62. p. 182.

[5] Kalantari, Kh. 2001, "A criticism of methodology of measuring the level of human development", *Journal of Geographical Research,* Vol. 61.

[6] Kourtz, N. 1995 (tr.), An Introduction to statistics in social sciences, translated by Habibollah Teymoori, Nashr Ney, Tehran.

[7] Iran Center for Statistics, 1988, General census of population and housing in 1986, Organization for Budget and Planning.

[8] Iran Center for Statistics, 1997, General census of population and housing in 1996, Organization for Budget and Planning and State Statistical Year Book (1996).

[9] Center for Research and Studies of Architecture and Urbanization, 1991, "Measurement of Industrial Development in Various Regions of the Country".

[10] Moteiee Langroodi, S. 1991, Economic Geography of Iran (Vol. 1), Ferdowsi University of Mashhad. p. 54.

[11] UNDF, 1992, "Human development report", New York, Oxford.

[12] Zurick, D. 1988, "Resource needs and land stress in Rapti zone, Nepal", *Professional Geographer*, America, 40 (4) p. 442.

Human Perspectives in the Internet Society: Culture, Psychology and Gender, K. Morgan, J. Sanchez, C. A. Brebbia & A Voiskounsky (Editors) © 2004 WIT Press, www.witpress.com, ISBN 1-85312-726-4

Section 11
Advertising with an intercultural perspective

Advertising to multi-cultural audiences: promoting energy efficiency in South Africa

K. Tiedemann
BC Hydro and Simon Fraser University, Canada

Abstract

The purpose of this paper is to describe and apply a quantitative framework for the analysis of multi-cultural advertising in the context of the South Africa Efficient Lighting Initiative. The study has four main findings as follows. First, the program's advertising and promotional campaign carefully targeted appropriate messages for separate customer groups. Second, individual advertising vehicles effectively built on the broader national themes of reconciliation and social justice. Third, the advertising program was successful in terms of advertising awareness, reach, coverage, and cost-effectiveness. Fourth, econometric estimates showed significant program impact on sales of efficient lighting products as well as substantial reductions in energy consumption and greenhouse gas emissions.

1 Introduction

There is strong and growing evidence that human activity is having a quantifiable and potentially significant effect on the world's climate, particularly through the production and release of greenhouse gases. The Efficient Lighting Initiative (ELI) is a seven-country program implemented by the International Finance Corporation (in Argentina, the Czech Republic, Hungary, Latvia, Peru, the Philippines and South Africa) aimed at reducing greenhouse gas emissions by accelerating the penetration of energy-efficient lighting technologies through market transformation strategies. ELI is promoting the use of modern and high-quality lighting products to transform domestic lighting markets.

The US$10 million Efficient Lighting Initiative in South Africa is implemented through the joint venture Bonesa, co-funded by the Global Environmental Facility and Eskom. At the time of launch of South Africa ELI,

Human Perspectives in the Internet Society: Culture, Psychology and Gender, K. Morgan, J. Sanchez, C. A. Brebbia & A Voiskounsky (Editors) © 2004 WIT Press, www.witpress.com, ISBN 1-85312-726-4

average lighting efficiency levels were well below those achievable with currently available cost-effective technologies. Promoting energy efficient lighting in South Africa is complicated by the disparities and contrasts in national origin, language, education and income across the program's various target groups. A key challenge for South Africa ELI was to develop and implement a promotional program that could efficiently target the needs of diverse groups while remaining cost effective.

The purpose of this paper is to describe and apply a quantitative framework for the analysis of multi-cultural advertising in the context of the South Africa Efficient Lighting Initiative.

2 Study approach

For this report there are four main issues. First, how effective was the targeting of advertising and promotions? Second, how successfully were the advertising and promotional messages conveyed? Third, how cost effective were alternative advertising and promotional campaigns? Fourth, what was the impact of the program on efficient lighting product sales, energy savings, and greenhouse gas emission reductions?

Several major data sources were used for this study. These included annual surveys of trade allies focusing on product sales by type; in-store product surveys; on-site metering of lighting usage; planning data on lighting technologies; information on electricity system marginal costs for energy and capacity; information on transmission and distribution losses; rates information; and fuel use and emissions by generating facility. Officials at Bonesa and Eskom provided invaluable assistance for this study.

Table 1: Issues, data sources, methodologies.

Study issue	Data sources	Methodologies
Targeting of advertising	Program documents Interviews	Documents review
Impact of advertising	Customer surveys	Cross tabulations
Cost effectiveness of advertising	Trade ally survey Program data	Cost effectiveness analysis
Sales, energy and greenhouse gas emissions impacts	Trade ally survey End use research Emissions by fuel and fuel consumption by generation facility	Regression analysis Algorithms

3 Market summary

South Africa has the most developed and efficient electricity system in Africa. Approximately 95% of the electricity used in South Africa is generated by Eskom, which is one of the ten largest utilities in the world. Eskom also owns

Human Perspectives in the Internet Society: Culture, Psychology and Gender, K. Morgan, J. Sanchez, C. A. Brebbia & A Voiskounsky (Editors) © 2004 WIT Press, www.witpress.com, ISBN 1-85312-726-4

and operates the national transmission system, which is connected to the grids of neighboring countries. Eskom sells electricity to some 381 local distribution companies, to major industrial and commercial customers and to some residential customers. About 89% of Eskom's electricity is produced by burning coal, and this has implications for greenhouse gas emissions and local pollutants.

South Africa has about 11 million residential dwellings, with about two-thirds of these homes electrified. The Government has launched an ambitious program to better house the poorer parts of the population, particularly in rural areas, and to electrify more dwellings. As a result the number of electrified houses and the residential electricity load are both increasing relatively quickly, as indicated in Table 2.

Table 2: Residential electrification.

Year	Number of homes (million)			Share of homes electrified (%)		
	Rural	Urban	Total	Rural	Urban	Total
1997	3.7	5.5	9.2	38.0	74.2	59.7
1998	3.8	5.6	9.4	42.6	76.7	63.0
1999	3.9	5.7	9.6	46.3	79.8	66.3
2000	4.3	6.5	10.8	45.8	74.2	63.0

Source: National Electricity Regulator [5].

Table 3: Household income and lighting use.

LSM	Median monthly income (rand)	Households (thousand)	Share with electric lights (%)	Indoor bulbs per electrified household (number)	Outdoor bulbs per electrified household (number)	Total light points (million)
1	459	1180	3	2	0	0.1
2	619	1190	20	2	0	0.5
3	728	1480	25	3	0	1.1
4	1020	1160	54	4	0	2.5
5	1347	707	88	5	1	3.7
6	1842	597	99	6	1	4.1
7	3951	943	99	10	1	10.3
8	7875	1380	100	19	2	29.0
Total	-	8637	-	-	-	51.3

Source: Eskom Residential Demand Side Management [4].

Lighting makes up at least 10% of the residential electricity load, particularly for lower income consumers, so that encouraging greater use of efficient lighting has significant implications for the size and growth of the residential electricity load. Table 3 shows residential lighting use across Lifestyle Measurement segments for 1998, and is the most comprehensive information available on residential lighting use. The eight Lifestyle Measurement (LSM) segments are essentially based on a composite wealth measure, with LSM 1 to LSM 4 viewed as lower income, LSM 5 and LSM 6 as middle income and LSM 7 and LSM 8 as upper income.

Human Perspectives in the Internet Society: Culture, Psychology and Gender, K. Morgan, J. Sanchez, C. A. Brebbia & A Voiskounsky (Editors) © 2004 WIT Press, www.witpress.com, ISBN 1-85312-726-4

4 Program description

The objective of the South Africa ELI program is to transform South Africa's lighting market through the promotion of energy efficient lamps and luminaires in three broad markets. These markets are emerging market households that are being electrified (some 300,000 homes per year); existing and new mid-to-upper income households (about 5,000,00 homes); and commercial, institutional, and industrial facilities (about 400,000 sites in total). Intended impacts include reduction in energy use, reduction in utility peak load and reduction in greenhouse gas emissions.

During program planning, a number of barriers to increased use of energy efficient lighting were identified. (1) There was initially a problem with the availability of high-quality compact fluorescent lamps (CFLs), with some unbranded CFLs having high failure rates. (2) There was limited consumer awareness of the existence, features and benefits of energy efficient lighting. (3) Prices of CFLs were in the R60-R90 range, well above the acceptable R20-R30 price point according to market research. (4) Only a limited number of sales outlets stocked CFLs and access to these was limited, especially for low-income consumers. (5) There was limited acceptance and knowledge of the nature, features and benefits of energy efficient lamps.

To overcome these barriers, South Africa ELI includes a wide range of activities including advertising and promotions, product testing and labelling, school programs, technology development, and subsidy and direct-install demonstration projects. Unlike the six other ELI programs, product incentives were a major component of the South Africa ELI program. The subsidy program promoted, in particular, high quality, ELI approved CFLs, tri-phosphorous T8 lamps and industrial sectors, and high pressure sodium lamps (HPS).

5 Communication campaigns and themes

The public awareness campaign aimed to build awareness and interest in higher efficiency lighting among South African consumers and included a number of activities including in particular general advertising as summarized below. The South Africa ELI project was initially launched in July 2000 with a major media campaign. This mass media campaign was supported with shopping mall and local media activities in the main centres of the priority regions, including a buy two get one free promotion for CFLs.

There was extensive development of local and national public information brochures, radio spots, media ads, editorials and articles. Local activities included print advertisements in the Sunday Times/City Press, shopping mall and in-store activities, coupons and flyers, booths and displays at exhibitions and trade shows, case studies and local and regional radio and print media campaigns. National activities involved the annual Luminaire Design Competition, outdoor advertising and billboards including the giant CFL at Johannesburg Stadium, mobile and commuter advertising, electronic advertising and national television, media and print campaigns.

Human Perspectives in the Internet Society: Culture, Psychology and Gender, K. Morgan, J. Sanchez, C. A. Brebbia & A Voiskounsky (Editors) © 2004 WIT Press, www.witpress.com, ISBN 1-85312-726-4

Public relations activities involved development of the media strategy, positioning of Bonesa, development of a network of celebrity spokespeople, building on the relationship with the Nelson Mandela Children's Fund (with a portion of CFL sales going to the fund), and building relationships with key stakeholders. Detailed communications themes were developed for the various target audiences as shown in Table 4.

Table 4: Communications themes by target group.

ELI quality logo	Lower income residential (LSM 1-3)	Middle income residential (LSM 4-6)	Upper income residential (LSM 7-8)
ELI logo indicates quality	Yes	Yes	Yes
CFLs as cost-effective, reliable, long-lasting	Yes	Yes	Yes
Monetary and socio-economic benefits of efficient lighting	Yes	Selective	No
Security advantages of efficient lighting	No	No	No
Environmental issues and benefits	Selective	Selective	Selective
Bonesa, light for all	Yes	Yes	Yes
Bonesa as a credible and independent information source	Yes	Yes	Yes

Source: Eskom Residential Demand Side Management [4] and ELI Process Evaluation [3].

6 Television and radio advertising

Although the mass media campaign used a variety of vehicles, television and radio were the most important and to save space we focus on these. The vast majority of South Africans citizens can be reached through either television or radio advertising or both. The major television and radio advertisements are described in Table 5. A detailed review of the television and radio advertising (ELI Process Evaluation, 2003) indicated that the promotional campaign has provided a consistent set of messages and images and accomplished the following. (1) Provided educational value to customers by teaching them about energy efficiency. (2) Served as a marketing tool for ELI, Bonesa, Eskom and other partners. (3) Placed emphasis on working with formerly disadvantaged groups, small business and community groups. (4) Emphasized the themes of national reconciliation and social justice.

7 Advertising awareness

The public awareness campaign has been one of the most successful aspects of the South Africa ELI program. Despite some initial delays in implementation, by

December 2000 there was a high level of program activity. The program has been successful in raising consumer awareness and interest in efficient lighting technologies, especially CFLs, and significant sales levels of CFLs have been achieved. Communicating energy efficiency themes in South Africa represents a unique challenge. The wide variety of cultures and languages, combined with the specific economic and political dynamics of South Africa means that considerable care must be placed on forward media planning, attention to crafting messages for target groups, and ongoing assessment of information and educational activities.

Table 5: Television and radio advertising.

Advertisement	Visuals Summary	Audio Summary
Osram Aircraft Landing (television, 30 seconds)	Dark deserted country road Man working on outdoor sign Wild dog digging Man pull switch to light up street with rows of lights Dog alarmed, candle blows out, glasses shaking Giant airplane landing on lit up country road Osram CFL	Osram – energy efficient lighting Background sounds Energy efficiency initiative brought to you by ElectroWise
Efficient Lighting Initiative (television, 15 seconds)	Woman at window looks out smiling Interracial crowd of people gather and look Giant CFL Bonesa symbol	See the light Join the initiative Enjoy benefits ELI from Bonesa Light for life
Light for life (television, 115 seconds also re-cut in shorter versions)	Bright sun CFLs Female narrator Giant CFL People dancing Mandela Children's Fund Cartoon houses Bonesa quality seal Dawn to dusk Bonesa Symbol	Bonesa partnership between Eskom and GEF CFLs last 10 times longer and use 80% less electricity Nelson Mandela Children's Fund Over lamp life saves 432 kg. coal and 1100 l. water Many areas in home where CFLs can be used
Eskom Bonesa Lighting (television, 15 seconds)	CFLs Eskom symbol Bonesa symbol	Launch of Bonesa ELI Overwhelming public support Better light for all
Corporate Launch (radio, 15 seconds)	Not applicable	Its here. Now To change your life forever The Efficient Lighting Initiative from Bonesa Bonesa. Light for Life

An extensive survey was conducted with key customer groups, using face to face interviews, in the fall of 2001. The residential survey sample (n=520) was stratified into newly electrified (n=220), lower income (n=96) and upper income (n=204) customers. The main purpose of the survey was to understand the awareness and impact of advertising and promotions as well as the interest in and

Human Perspectives in the Internet Society: Culture, Psychology and Gender, K. Morgan, J. Sanchez, C. A. Brebbia & A Voiskounsky (Editors) © 2004 WIT Press, www.witpress.com, ISBN 1-85312-726-4

usage of CFLs. As Table 6 shows, 72% of newly electrified respondents, 79% of low income respondents and 59% of upper income had recently seen or heard advertising for electric lights, lamps or globes. Survey respondents were asked to state the main message of the advertisement with the results shown below.

Table 6: Advertising awareness (unaided awareness).

	Newly electrified	Lower income	Upper income
Recently seen or heard ads for lights, lamps or globes	47	49	50
Saving electricity/lamps that save energy	25	12	36
Cost effective lamps/more economical lamps	15	28	19
More powerful light/brighter light	22	20	16
Safe use of electricity./ don't electrocute yourself	8	13	7
New improved lamps/higher quality lamps	9	7	-
Efficient lighting/high efficiency lamps	6	9	2
Miscellaneous Bonesa roles	-	-	23

Source: Bonesa [2].

8 Media reach and cost effectiveness

The main mass media campaign for South Africa ELI was conducted from April to September 2001. Key components of the media campaign included: print advertising; radio advertising; the initial April/May television campaign; the follow-up July television campaign; and value added media, which is the imputed value of free media coverage in the form of articles and interviews.

Before looking at these results, it is useful to review the relevant terminology. For print, radio and value added activity, the customer base is the population aged 16 and over. For television, the base is the population aged 16 and over with access to television. Coverage refers to the share of the base reached at least once expressed as a percentage of the base. Frequency refers to the average number of exposures per individual reached. Rating points refers to the average number of exposures for those exposed to the advertising times 100. This exposure rating corresponds to the gross rating points (GRP) measure often used in analyzing media buys.

Several features of the data as shown in Table 7 are worth noting. First, the reach of radio advertising is very high at nearly 85% coverage while print advertising reached 48% coverage. Second, the reach of television is also very high, admittedly from a smaller base, with coverage of 71% for the spring

Human Perspectives in the Internet Society: Culture, Psychology and Gender, K. Morgan, J. Sanchez, C. A. Brebbia & A Voiskounsky (Editors) © 2004 WIT Press, www.witpress.com, ISBN 1-85312-726-4

campaign and coverage of 53% for the summer campaign. Third, if a rating of 400 points is thought of as the level needed to achieve break through for an advertising campaign, then South Africa ELI devoted adequate resources to the mass media effort. Fourth, radio appears to be the cheapest medium in terms of rand per rating point, followed by television and then by print. Fifth, value added exposure in the form of articles and interviews was an important vehicle for the program.

Table 7: Media coverage, frequency and cost effectiveness.

	Base (million)	Coverage (%)	Frequency (number)	Rating points	Cost (thousand rand)	Cost per point (rand)
Print	29.0	48	3.9	188	1052	5595
Radio	29.0	85	7.8	662	981	1482
Television (Apr/May)	17.5	71	5.0	353	687	1945
Television (July)	17.7	53	5.0	260	453	1741
Value added	29.0	-	-	-	1377*	-

Source: Bonesa [1]. Note that for value added activity the cost is the imputed value of the media exposure if purchased at commercial rates.

9 Product sales, energy use and greenhouse gas emissions

Incremental product sales, capacity and peak savings are shown in Table 8. Incremental sales were based on detailed econometric modeling of lamp sales. The econometric modeling used an interrupted time-series approach in which sales were modeled as a function of time and a program-related dummy variable. The coefficient on the program-related dummy variable provided an estimate of program impact on sales. Capacity savings were estimated as incremental sales attributable to the program multiplied by unit peak savings while energy savings were estimated as incremental sales attributable to the program multiplied by unit energy savings. Unit peak and energy savings were based on Eskom load research and customer survey data, and include line losses for energy savings and line losses and reserve margin for peak savings.

Table 8: Product sales, energy savings and peak savings.

	Incremental sales (000)	Unit energy savings (kWh)	Unit peak savings (kW)	Total energy savings (GWh)	Total peak savings (MW)
CFL	2968	58	0.045	171	134
T8	33	45	0.015	2	0.51
HPS	7	312	0.067	2	0.5
Total	3008			175	135

Estimates of reductions in emissions were calculated by multiplying emissions factors per kWh of electricity by the number of kWh of electricity produced by each generation facility. In South Africa there is a mix of nuclear,

Human Perspectives in the Internet Society: Culture, Psychology and Gender, K. Morgan, J. Sanchez, C. A. Brebbia & A Voiskounsky (Editors) © 2004 WIT Press, www.witpress.com, ISBN 1-85312-726-4

hydro and coal based thermal generation. Discussions with Eskom system planners indicated that coal based thermal generation was the marginal source of electricity supply, so emissions reduction are based on an assumed reduction in coal use. Table 9 shows the estimated reduction in emissions due to the South Africa ELI program. The program resulted in an estimated annual reduction of 1,401 tonnes of sulfur dioxide, 635 tonnes of nitrous oxides and 154 kilotonnes of carbon dioxide.

Table 9: Annual emissions reductions.

	Total energy savings (Gwh)	Sulfur dioxide (tonnes)	Nitrous oxides (tonnes)	Carbon dioxide (kilotonnes)
CFL	171	1375	623	151
T8	2	10	1	1
HPS	2	16	7	2
Total	175	1401	635	154

10 Conclusions

The US$10 million Efficient Lighting Initiative in South Africa was implemented through the joint venture Bonesa, co-funded by the Global Environmental Facility and Eskom. At the time of launch of the South Africa Efficient Lighting Initiative, average lighting efficiency levels were well below those achievable with currently available cost-effective technologies. Promoting energy efficient lighting in South Africa is complicated by the disparities and contrasts in national origin, language, education and income across the program's various target groups. The purpose of this paper is to describe and apply a quantitative framework for the analysis of multi-cultural advertising in the context of the South Africa Efficient Lighting Initiative.

The study has four main findings as follows. First, the program's advertising and promotional campaign carefully targeted appropriate messages for separate customer groups. Second, individual advertising vehicles effectively built on the broader national themes of reconciliation and social justice and were particularly successful in reaching and informing disadvantaged groups. Third, the advertising program was successful in terms of advertising awareness, reach, coverage, and cost-effectiveness. Fourth, econometric estimates of program impact showed increased sales of some three million energy efficient lamps, reduced energy consumption of 175 GWh, and reduced carbon dioxide emissions of 154 kilotonnes per year.

References

[1] Bonesa (2001). Bonesa Advertising Review.
[2] Bonesa (2002). Report on Phase 1 Research.
[3] ELI Evaluation (2003). South Africa ELI Process Evaluation.
[4] Eskom. (2000). Residential Demand Side Management.
[5] National Electricity Regulator. (2000). Website.

Human Perspectives in the Internet Society: Culture, Psychology and Gender, K. Morgan, J. Sanchez, C. A. Brebbia & A Voiskounsky (Editors) © 2004 WIT Press, www.witpress.com, ISBN 1-85312-726-4

The impact of the homogeneous global advertising on multicultural reality

L. Chilarescu
West University, Romania

Abstract

This paper provides an overview of the main effects of the global homogeneous advertising, which emerged in our country after 1989. This new merger-mania trend, globalization, has been the main worldwide dramatic and significant transformation of the past century. Diverse cultures are becoming visible: new global technology allows this diversity to be declared, acknowledged and shared, allowing for a link of civilizations and societies. However, globalization has also had many negative effects upon humanity. It also submits a perspective on the new tendencies and trends characterizing advertising as a new means of mass education and formation. We shall focus on the relationship between the global corporatism, the global target market and the global market values, on the one hand, and the impact of consumerism and advertising, on the other hand. We shall address the nature of the contemporary capitalism and the impact the market has upon culture and society in general. We shall also approach the intricate relations between globalization, consumption and identity. Above all, the goal of the study is to provide the context and the perspective of the ever-increasing social and cultural impact of the new global advertising system, upon the diverse reality of the world today.
Keywords: globalization, hegemony, corporations, market, consumption, diversity, culture, identity, advertising system.

1 Introduction

1.1 Intention

This essay-study is not the place for a detailed discussion on concrete cultural, economic and political events. Nor is it a thorough and comprehensive analysis of the contemporary advertising system. It tries to provide an overview of some

Human Perspectives in the Internet Society: Culture, Psychology and Gender, K. Morgan, J. Sanchez, C. A. Brebbia & A Voiskounsky (Editors) © 2004 WIT Press, www.witpress.com, ISBN 1-85312-726-4

of the opinions revolving around the matters of globalization, hegemony, corporations, market, consumption, diversity, culture and identity. It is not exhaustive but it tries to present some of the relationships between the above issues in the context of the contemporary Romanian advertising system.

1.2 Motivation

It is commonly agreed that human beings are social beings. We live in social settings, surrounded by other social beings; we cannot even exist as human beings outside society. The system that makes socialization and society work, the system that provides the means of socialization and human interaction is communication. Communication is the main informant of our ideology, of our "cultural sphere of meaning", as Cortese ([1], p. 1) states it.

Everything we know regarding culture, identity and normalcy comes from or is reflected by the mass media and the advertising system, the main "protagonists" in the communication process in the contemporary world. At the same time, part, if not most of what we are, has the same origin.

We define ourselves as human beings based on the information and on its result: the representations we are exposed to. Modern technology has made information and communication global. It reaches nearly every location and informs us about almost everything.

The global media is profoundly and significantly influenced by the advertising system, which is its main sponsor. Furthermore, the global advertising system is indubitably and completely controlled by its generator: the transnational corporations (TNCs). We can easily see that this practice is mostly related to another aspect of communication: the source. This is the one that proposes and produces the message.

There is only one more feature of communication: the receiver. The receiver is the very target of the whole communication process. As receivers, we are informed and formed by it. And we tend to think that we have some control over it, that, we are, too, an active part in the communicational process, not just a passive recipient of the capitalist discourse of the global multinationals.

2 The global world

Globalization is the major trend at the outset of the twenty-first century. We are all experiencing the famous "merger-mania", the joining together on all levels of our lives. We are all integrated and part of the major "Global" world, of the "Global" screen, we are all interconnected.

The continuously advancing technology enables instant personal links between individuals from all part of the world, even the most remote ones. The social and cultural lives of individuals are consequently changing irreversibly. The ideas of space and time are also changing irrevocably. It also enables unbelievable-before economic exchanges and political connections, which lead to major quests for power-attainment.

Globalization is not, as Bart Van Steebnbergen noted, the dreamt and desired "universalism" of philosophers, which was "based on global initiatives and undertakings and on the will to make the world a better place". On the contrary,

Human Perspectives in the Internet Society: Culture, Psychology and Gender, K. Morgan, J. Sanchez, C. A. Brebbia & A Voiskounsky (Editors) © 2004 WIT Press, www.witpress.com, ISBN 1-85312-726-4

it is "what is happening to us all, to global effects that are unintended and unanticipated" ([2], p. 26).

Being global means what "is" and "must be", rather than what "might" or "should be". Globalization expresses the unintended and unpredictable effects of the economic rationalism, of capitalism, of consumerism, manifested on the large, global scale. It "is a story about inexorability, economic logic, natural interest and market forces" (Harris [3], p.1).

2.1 Diversity in the global world

While multinational businesses are springing out and taking over, national and human relationships are gradually forgotten. Respect for the individual uniqueness, for social and cultural diversity becomes incongruous.

Human individuality is at stake because diversity is threatened by the very essence of this process. In the perspective of the cold, economic rationalism, notions such as "community", "cultural identity" and "diversity" seem to be soft and romantic. There is no interest in and respect for human uniqueness, for self-expression when "major", "global" economic reasons are also under consideration. "The ever-increasing transnational flow of commodities, be they material or immaterial, seems to create a set of common cultural denominators which threaten to eradicate local distinctions" (Eriksen [4], p. 2).

Globalization is not only "happening to us all"! It implies new powers, new truths on cultural, social and economic scales, to name just a few. Consequently, it means new issues to be taken into consideration because these new realities are affecting all of us, our lives and our societies.

Therefore, more attention should be paid to its consequences rather than to its overestimated development. Experts on this domain are too focused on the market issues; they are overconsidering the efficiency and profit-increase. It should not be about what we can do for the market (especially to extend the market), but about what the market is doing to us! We should therefore acknowledge and take greater responsibility for the "globalization" ethics, for the morals of the process, which is affecting and changing our "global" world!

2.2 Globalization re-defined

There have been several debates on the grounds, characteristics and effects of globalization. "For some, globalize is what we must do if we wish to be happy; for others 'globalization' is the cause of our unhappiness" (Bauman [5], p. 1). Terms such as "western-ization", "Americanization", homogenization, hegemonization, hybridization, glocalization, expansionism, imperialism, capitalism, continentalisation, marginalization, corporatism, MacWorld, McDonaldization have long and thoroughly been scrutinized by numerous analysts beginning with Ritzer [6] and Barber [7]. Persistence on clarifying these issues would be futile.

To put it shortly, the term globalization is often used to "explain, justify and understand new social, economic and cultural situations and realities in our modern world and, on the other hand, it is never defined, explained or justified as it should be" ([8], p.1).

Human Perspectives in the Internet Society: Culture, Psychology and Gender, K. Morgan, J. Sanchez, C. A. Brebbia & A Voiskounsky (Editors) © 2004 WIT Press, www.witpress.com, ISBN 1-85312-726-4

Economic circumstances, the capitalism and the liberal democracy have the leading word on the world "global" matters. But nothing is restricted to economic circumstances. Its impact is on diverse identities and cultures and it is affecting us all! Although globalization was expectedly beneficial, mutually enriching cultures and diversity through the extended possibility of communication and exchange, its impact has been opposite: it often tried to impose one of these cultures, to impose a homogenic and hegemonic cultural model and discourse ([8], p.1).

2.3 Culture re-defined

Let us define the concept of "culture", because this is yet another overused notion. Many definitions have been suggested; much debate has also been done. We shall consider and make operational the definition stated in a United Nations Document, 2000, called Cultural Diversity and Globalization: "Culture is the sum total of beliefs, myths, knowledge, institutions and practices whereby a society or group affirms its presence in the world and assures its reproduction and persistence through time. In other words, a style of life that takes in the whole existential reality of the persons and communities in a society, and not only arts, folklore and beliefs" ([8], p. 4).

Culture is obviously connected with and based upon diversity! Through the possibility of global communication, the diverse cultures of the world are affected. Specific human beliefs, knowledge and practices are, hence shaped. Internationalism occurs mainly through mass culture and it means importation of foreign media programs.

This theory may be contradicted by fashionable politically correct policies trying to accommodate "multiculturalism". But these attempts are always integrated in and proposed by the hegemonic culture: "recognizing cultural pluralism by accommodating 'multiculturalism' in one way or another – always and inevitably that regime will suppress difference by requiring all cultural groups to negotiate within a public space which is shaped by a particular culture" ([9], p. 3).

Culture is not fixed or predetermined; it does not exist independently, autonomously. But it is a construction and it is also constructing. It coexists, relates and it is part of the global cultural system. Therefore, respect and attention should be paid to its uniqueness.

2.4 Identity and exclusion

Globalization would also imply social exclusion. In fact, Bauman's "warm circle" based upon spontaneous social cohesion, the communal society and the social community is losing grounds [10]. All in favor of rational, economic calculations, of an abstract individual-centered system, of a cold world governed by "efficiency, calculability, an emphasis on quantity (to the detriment of quality), predictability, control and the replacement of human techniques by non-human technology" ([2], p. 31).

This process involves practices of exclusion and rejection; it involves excluded and rejected persons. Bauman's metaphors are very suggestive: Janus' two-faced societies, the door locked on the inside; they are also undeniably expressing the firm, unchangeable "walls" and the impossibility of demolishing them from the outside [5].

Globalization divides and unites, all according to the economic logic. Consumerism, capitalism and market values are the decision-makers. "In a consumer society, people wallow in things, fascinating, enjoyable things. If you define your value by the things you acquire and surround yourself with, being excluded is humiliating. And we live in a world of communication; everyone gets information about everyone else. It's the crime of humiliation!" [5].

2.5 The rule of economic rationalism

Global markets and market values seem to be the only decision-makers on most fields of world matters. Nowadays, global corporations seem to be governing the world. They are not doing it openly or directly; in fact, they are just directing, pressing national governments (which lose autonomy, decision-making and policy-regulation) to rule for them, in their interest. Nation states cease to be effective and lose autonomy in favor of liberal capitalism and global economic management [5].

Consumerism is the reality that binds all the above together. Consumerism is the main interest of the transnational corporations that lead the global world; it is the main message of the mass media and, consequently, of the hegemonic culture. "Economic rationalism defines democracy as something which is meaningful only to those who can participate as consumers – no money means no participation and no choices" ([11] p. 2).

Consumption is not restricted to material products; cultural products are also marketable. They are the issues of mass media and they are responsible for our values, identities and life-styles. The cultural products reflect the cultural values of their producers. Because the media is global and responsible for mass communication, the cultural standards of the global market are globally accepted and worshipped values. Consumerism is the main emphasis of the media discourse. Consequently, it is becoming one of the main values of the global identity.

Owing to globalization, mainly the same cultural and material products are consumed. This is the theory of monoculturalism; it emphasizes the homogenization effect of media imperialism. To be specific, it accounts for the impact of western hegemonic media discourse on the audience; the message of this discourse is consumerism.

It is important to take into consideration the debated idea about the main danger of the globalization process: Globalization is an issue; the power of the capital is the issue. "Economic globalization means [...] the spread of capitalism as a dominant economic model, a capitalism grounded on a consumption culture. Contemporary capitalism has as its defining feature the concept of benefit maximization which means a ceaseless increase in consumption" ([12] p. 6).

Globalization is a product of the urge of the capitalists to expand markets and maximize profits. The world of communications has become a perfect stage for the workings of capitalism with the same main target: that of perpetuating market values [13].

Human Perspectives in the Internet Society: Culture, Psychology and Gender, K. Morgan, J. Sanchez, C. A. Brebbia & A Voiskounsky (Editors) © 2004 WIT Press, www.witpress.com, ISBN 1-85312-726-4

2.6 The advertising system in the mass media

Mass media proposes, promotes and regulates the mass culture. It is the main informant of our ideology, of our culture [1]. Media is considered to be responsible for the production of culture. However, mass media is controlled and regulated by media corporations. No open, direct control of the major TNCs is implemented in the mass media. But, advertising is the discourse of multinationals! It is their switch for culture and media control, it is the very essence of the "global culture".

Of course, officials at the Independent Broadcasting Authority are vehemently denying it: "Even the suggestion that the policy of commercial broadcasting companies is influenced, in some way, by advertisers' requirements, provokes sharp denials" ([14], p.710). Of course, media regulation system does not allow for direct, explicit control.

Because advertising is the "concealed subsidy" of the mass media, it has major decision power. It is effortlessly shaping the mass media, as diverse media compete for their subsidies and, therefore, adapt their programs accordingly to the "marketing needs" of advertisers.

Because TV companies compete for advertising sponsorship, they are selling not their programs, but their audiences. "TV companies therefore seek to make and transmit programmes that produce the audiences advertisers want to reach" ([14], p.717). The desired fragments of the audience are limited groups. In order to reach them, the advertising and the media is representing the reality of those groups, their ideologies and values. This leads to the hegemony and to the homogeneity of the media. But it also leads to its discriminatory nature. The "capitalistically unwanted" segments of the society are excluded from the media programs. Their invisibility proves that the media is a threat for the world diversity and multiculturalism. It also demonstrates Bauman's "crime of humiliation".

Advertising is also influencing the representations of the mass media. It has no interests in portraying the diverse human reality, the problems of unemployment, of homelessness and of underclass. It is presenting the conservative and limited ideology of the middle-to-upper class; it is reinforcing only the ideologies of the capitalism and consumerism [15]. Everything else, every other representation is superficial and stereotypical, yet another proof of the truthfulness of Bauman's "crime of humiliation"!

2.7 Advertising and consumerism

Hence, contemporary world has given advertising a crucial role. As Marx said, in capitalism, everything turns into a commodity. Advertising encourages consumerism by bringing with it both the Discontent and the Salvation. It makes us uncomfortable with ourselves, especially with our bodies; it makes us frustrated, depressed, lonely and unfulfilled. But it also brings the salvation: the product! Consequently, order is reestablished, happiness regained, but all these gained through the products, all for more money gained by producers [16].

Advertising and consuming have become the magic of our contemporary existence, our rituals: "For any society to operate without some form of ritual is

Human Perspectives in the Internet Society: Culture, Psychology and Gender, K. Morgan, J. Sanchez, C. A. Brebbia & A Voiskounsky (Editors) © 2004 WIT Press, www.witpress.com, ISBN 1-85312-726-4

for a society to live without a shared collective memory. While ritual can take a verbal form, it is more effective when tied to material things" [17].

Postmodern consumption is creating a postmodern culture, that of the imperative of the capital and of consumerism. Because of economic inequality, advertising and media are targeting particular audiences and, consequently, generating exclusion. Media is intensifying the effects of globalization, the social division and exclusion based upon the economic logic: "we live in a world of communication; everyone gets information about everyone else. It's the crime of humiliation!" [5].

Because advertising represents only the exclusive reality of some groups, it is a threat to the world diversity and multiculturalism. The images of cultural diversity are only a shallow distraction and a superficial show to mask its homogeneity [18].

2.8 Advertising as decision-making

Advertising, as a tool of capitalism and consumerism, also becomes part of the consumption and production decision-making. "Decisions about production are therefore in the hands of a group occupying a minority position in the society and in no direct way responsible to it" ([19], p. 705). It also implies decision-making about consumption, which should be in the hands of the society as a whole, of the individuals. Moreover, it should be about the needs of the society.

But, it is not the society that controls advertising or production. On the contrary, advertising and production operate to preserve consumption, regardless of the actual specific needs of the society.

As a consequence, consumption of capitalist goods cannot satisfy the human needs. Because these needs remain unsatisfied, "attempt is made, by magic, to associate this consumption with human desires to which it has no real reference. You do not buy an object: you buy social respect, discrimination, health, beauty, success, power to control the environment" ([19], p. 708). No needs are satisfied, or promised to be satisfied. Only social problems are promised to be solved.

This obvious truth does not constitute a drawback for advertising. Quite the opposite, it makes consumption eternal. By not satisfying a need, the quest for its fulfillment is kept alive; desire is also kept alive. "Consumer society proclaims the impossibility of gratification and measures its progress by ever-rising demand. To avoid confusion, it would be better to follow that fateful change in the nature of consumption and get rid of the notion of 'need' altogether, accepting that consumer society and consumerism are not about satisfying needs – not even the more sublime needs of identification, or self-assurance as to the degree of 'adequacy'. The moving spirit of consumer activity is not a set of articulated, let alone fixed, needs, but desire [...] the consuming desire of consuming" ([20], p.184).

2.9 Advertising re-defined

Now, let's see what advertising means. "An advertising is a message that has been called to the attention of a public audience, especially by paid announcement" ([1], p3). It is a cultural system and it also defines the predominant shared meaning system. In fact, advertising is only, or should only

Human Perspectives in the Internet Society: Culture, Psychology and Gender, K. Morgan, J. Sanchez, C. A. Brebbia & A Voiskounsky (Editors) © 2004 WIT Press, www.witpress.com, ISBN 1-85312-726-4

be about constructing commodity signs, but they make the commodity signs possess social status, symbolic meaning and cultural values: "Goods are used in the negotiation of social life, and acts are meaningful 'markers' of social categories. The precise form that this takes is framed by both cultural and economical relations – that is, by social power" ([17], p7). Advertising becomes, consequently a regular part of the culture of the society.

Advertising "is also, in a sense, the official art of modern capitalist society" ([19], p. 704). The advertising images are very powerful and they are immediately internalized. If we tend to analyze language and sounds, we totally take for granted the images [16].

2.10 Discourse of advertising: discourse of TNCs

All these being said, what is the message that the advertising conveys? Advertising ultimately sells our dreams, our normalcies and values, which are associated with certain products. These products are not perfect, but they are said to be better than ever, than anything else, finally, better than yourself. The advertising is transmitting us that these products are beneficial; it is also conveying a complex of inferiority if we do not use the products.

By entering into our dreams, the advertising has gained enormous power. Through this power, they can easily now produce consumers. Because this is what advertising is producing: consumers [16].

In fact, at present, the adverting agents and producers can do almost anything. They are stigmatizing us, stereotyping us, discriminating and, last but not least, reducing us: "Clothes reflect many things (time and place of activity, social status, age, sex, ethnicity, subcultures) but what is produced through the clothing system is not simply the boundaries but the 'meaningful differences' between categories." ([17], p10).

3 Considerations on the Romanian advertising system

This essay study presents some of the main effects of the global homogeneous advertising that emerged in our country after 1989. The major shift recorded in this field was triggered by the privatization of the mass media that followed the Romanian revolution.

During the socialist regime, mass media was public, directed to the Romanian public, to the individuals of the specific society. As advertising was concerned, it was directed to individuals, considered as users with specific necessities that required satisfaction through products. The products were sensible to the specific needs of the individuals, to the specific economic, social and cultural context. The particular ads were unsophisticated and based upon reason and upon words too.

Removal of the socialist system, theoretically considered as the dawn of democracy, was accompanied only by capitalism, consumerism and private interests.

In capitalism, mass media is no longer public, directed to an individualistic, human public; but it is private, controlled by private interests. It is no longer designed for a public, but for a specific audience. As advertising is concerned, it

Human Perspectives in the Internet Society: Culture, Psychology and Gender, K. Morgan, J. Sanchez, C. A. Brebbia & A Voiskounsky (Editors) © 2004 WIT Press, www.witpress.com, ISBN 1-85312-726-4

serves to meet the interests of the producers: to transform the public into consumers and to produce them. The products are there (everywhere). The goal of the advertising system is to create the specific needs of the individuals and the specific economic, social and cultural context for them!

Media and advertising do not address the "capitalistically unwanted" segments of the society. It is not directed to the specific realities of the society: to the minorities or to the underclass. It does not deal with unemployment and homelessness. It is not sensitive to ethnicity, to diversity in social class, status, age, sex, etc. It is only directed to the target audience.

The contemporary "Western" advertising system has become obvious in Romania as a consequence of privatization and, later, of globalization.

Most commercials in Romania are upholding the global advertising discourse because they are assumed, copied and translated global ads (generally for soft drinks, beer, detergents, cosmetics, cars, and so on). These are authentic imported products, but also, TNCs' goods produced in the Romanian subsidiaries: all the commodities that emerged into our market and need consumers!

Recently, Romanian private advertising companies have launched their products on the market. They are designing local commercials for the above products. These ads are very similar to their foreign models, "professional" advertisements, maintaining the "western" discourse, similar in approach, style and expression. But these Romanian advertising agencies also produce commercials for authentic, specific products, which compete with the foreign products (these are also soft drinks, alcoholic drinks, beer, detergents). They are not de-nationalised, global ads, but commercials promoting the Romanian authentic values, myths and life-styles, the authentic Romanian culture.

The above-mentioned argument does not contradict the essence of the "Western" advertising system in Romania. These commercials are not representative for our advertising market because there are only a few, accepted ads in the major global discourse of adverting and they are mainly designed for advertising festivals and only screened for a limited period of time. They cannot be a threat to the main hegemonic discourse of advertising, which is imposing homogeneity, consumerism and the power of capital.

4 Conclusion

We live in the so-called "global informational era". There is information everywhere (better said, misinformation) from most locations in the world, on various topics. We are bombarded with advertising messages all the time. Of course, we do not pay attention to all of them. But we cannot ignore them all, either! Representation in the complex system of advertising discursive formation is everywhere and that is why it should be analyzed properly. The message being of paramount importance, we have to carefully examine it, using reliable semiotic tools.

In addition, we should not take for granted the inflexible and unchanging nature of all the realities discussed above. No reality is predetermined: neither is consumerism, nor is it capitalism and nor is it globalization. Our conclusion is

Human Perspectives in the Internet Society: Culture, Psychology and Gender, K. Morgan, J. Sanchez, C. A. Brebbia & A Voiskounsky (Editors) © 2004 WIT Press, www.witpress.com, ISBN 1-85312-726-4

that they are so powerful because they are seen as fixed and predetermined, part of a preset and inflexible plutocratic reality, because they are not consciously perceived and critically analyzed.

References

[1] Cortese, A., *Provocateur: Images of Women and Minorities in Advertising*, Rowman & Littlefield Publishers: Lanham, pp. 1-45, 1999.

[2] Van Steebnbergen, B., *Towards a Global Culture: Dream or Nightmare?*, Agora débats/jeunesses special issue, pp. 21-31, 2002.

[3] Harris, P., *Globalization: Disrupting the Narrative ("Getting the Bully")*, Science and Society Conference Proceedings, 1996.

[4] Eriksen, T.H., *Globalization and the Politics of Identity*, UN Chronicle, 1999.

[5] Bauman, Z., *Globalization, the Human Consequences*, Polity Press: Oxford, pp. 1-101, 1998.

[6] Ritzer, G., *The McDonaldization of Society*, Pine Forge Press: Thousand Oaks, 1996.

[7] Barber, S., *Jihad versus MacWorld*, Random House: New York, 1995.

[8] *Cultural Diversity and Globalization*, United Nations document for Millennium Forum, 2000.

[9] Kahn, J.S., *Whatever Could/ Should a 'Cultural Politics' Be?*, Science and Society Conference Proceedings, 1996.

[10] Bauman, Z., *Community. Seeking Safety in an insecure world*, Polity Press: Oxford, pp. 7-110 2001.

[11] Litchfield, J., *Art and the Creation of Discursive Spaces in Walyalup/ Freemantle*, Science and Society Conference Proceedings, 1996.

[12] Chiribuca, D., *Notes on Cultural Globalization*, www.wfsf.org.

[13] Herman, E. & McChesney, R., *The Global Media. The New Missionaries of Corporate Capitalism*, Cassell: London, 1997.

[14] Curran, J., The Impact of Advertising on the British Mass Media. *Media Studies. A Reader*, eds. P. Marris & S. Thornham, Edinburgh University Press: Edinburgh, pp. 710-727, 2002.

[15] Qualter, T.H., The Social Role of Advertising. *The Media Studies Reader*, eds. T. O'Sullivan & Y. Jewkes, Oxford University Press: New York, pp. 154-164, 1997.

[16] Documentary: *The Ad and the Id.*

[17] Jhalli, S., *The Codes of Advertising: Fetishism and the Political Economy of Meaning in the Consumer Society*, St. Martin's Press: New York, pp. 1-45, 1987.

[18] Lewis, J., *Cultural Studies – The Basics*, Sage Publications: London, pp.334-379, 2003.

[19] Williams, R., Advertising: The Magic System. *Media Studies. A Reader*, eds. P. Marris & S. Thornham, Edinburgh University Press: Edinburgh, pp. 704-710, 2002.

[20] Bauman, Z., *Society under Siege*, Polity Press: Cambridge, pp.180-201 2003.

Human Perspectives in the Internet Society: Culture, Psychology and Gender, K. Morgan, J. Sanchez, C. A. Brebbia & A Voiskounsky (Editors) © 2004 WIT Press, www.witpress.com, ISBN 1-85312-726-4

Section 12
New learning technologies and paradigms

Current issues in new learning

J. M. Spector
Florida State University, USA

Abstract

A recurrent theme in both the research and popular literature pertains to new learning paradigms and tools. New information and communications technologies and research in cognitive science have prompted much of the discussion about new ways to think about learning. This paper takes a critical look at new approaches to instruction and new methods to support learning. One conclusion is that interest in and emphasis on complex subject matter (e.g., complex and dynamic systems involving things such as crisis management, environmental planning, social policy formulation, etc.) is part of what is new in the world of learning and instruction. What is crucial to progress in improving understanding complex and dynamic systems is the assessment of progress of learning. A framework for assessing learning in and about complex systems is presented along with initial findings with regard to the utility of this methodology.
Keywords: assessment, complexity, expertise, instructional design and technology, learning science, mental models, principles of instruction.

1 Introduction

What has come and will evolve from the many advances in educational research and instructional technologies made in the last twenty years? Responses include:

- New information and communications technologies (ICT) have led to promising computer-supported collaborative learning (CSCL) opportunities.
- New technologies have made it possible to realize life-long learning with learning on-demand, anywhere at any time;
- New technologies have made authentic learning possible by blending learning environments with work environments; and

Human Perspectives in the Internet Society: Culture, Psychology and Gender, K. Morgan, J. Sanchez, C. A. Brebbia & A Voiskounsky (Editors) © 2004 WIT Press, www.witpress.com, ISBN 1-85312-726-4

- New technologies have been used to improve understanding in highly complex problem domains.

The focus here is on the last of these responses with emphasis on the problem of assessing improved understanding. There is a temptation among advocates of educational technology to emphasize new opportunities and potential benefits of new technologies. The assessment issue compels one to ask what improvements in learning can be attributed to new methods and tools. When one asks such questions, one typically encounters pitfalls and serious challenges. Investigating the assessment of learning in complex domains may shed some light on the more serious pitfalls and challenges lurking behind the questions at the beginning of this section. Other fundamental issues such as the problem of identity, the problem of ownership and the problem of verity that are vital to progress are not addressed in this chapter. The argument here is that improved assessment methods appropriate for complex domains are a necessary condition for progress in learning and instruction, but improved assessment is not sufficient. Ensuring that learners, tutors and instructors are the individuals they claim to be is essential. Protecting the intellectual property of individuals and organizations is also essential, as is developing methods to ensure that digital information is accurate and reliable.

2 The varieties of learning experience

As a context for subsequent remarks, it is appropriate to examine what is called learning. Learning is not a single nor a simple thing. Learning is a complex phenomenon. Human learning begins at or before birth and continues until death. It is an ongoing process that may be goal directed – intentional - or that may occur accidentally - non-intentional. Many important lessons are of the latter variety; educational research typically focuses on the former, possibly because one can examine actual outcomes against intended goals. One outcome of recent work in the learning sciences has been the design and deployment of learning environments in which goals are not be made explicit to learners, although the designer has learning goals in mind. The rationale is that non-intentional learning often seems to have a lasting impact on learners; consequently, intentional learning environments ought to be designed to emulate some of the *authenticity* of non-intentional learning, although the evidence to supports this approach is not convincing.

One is inclined to say that learning has occurred when there is an observed and persistent change in the learner. The change may be in the learner's attitudes, beliefs, behavior, mental models, knowledge, or skills. Moreover, if the change does not tend to persist, one is inclined to say that what was learned has been forgotten or that the learning has faded or even that learning failed to occur. Persisting change is essential to learning. Relevant changes may be observed or inferred. It is difficult to directly observe attitudes and mental models, although these are fundamental to understanding. Rather than abandon understanding as an overarching goal of learning and education, it then becomes important to find reliable indicators of improved understanding.

Human Perspectives in the Internet Society: Culture, Psychology and Gender, K. Morgan, J. Sanchez, C. A. Brebbia & A Voiskounsky (Editors) © 2004 WIT Press, www.witpress.com, ISBN 1-85312-726-4

In addition to a product perspective in terms of outcomes, including, there is much discussion about learning processes. The process perspective of intentional learning has focused on the critical roles of language, peers and activity in learning. With regard to activity, it is well established that people learn what they do. As a consequence, much emphasis has been placed on providing learners with opportunities for practice and on providing timely and informative feedback with regard to that practice. Merrill [1] refers to this as the principle of application. With regard to peers, Vygotsky [2] and others argue that peers play a critical role in new learning. Vygotsky's zone of proximal development – a time when children are ready for new learning – is marked by social engagement with other children in relevant activities.

Language is critical to social engagement with peers and is also critical in teacher-student/tutor-learner activities as well as in learning activities involving parents, colleagues, employers, clients and others. Language is an inescapable aspect of learning. Both formal and informal language communities develop around specific activities that become the focus of learning; see Wittgenstein's [3] description of language games. The language used by such communities is flexible and evolves with use and innovation. Some learning is directly associated with learning the language of such communities. Some learning involve insights that occur from linguistic variations and innovations. The richness and variety of language directly contribute to the richness and variety of learning experiences.

When one considers the role of activity, peers and language in learning, regardless of whether it is formal, informal, intentional or non-intentional learning, one is led to the conclusion that learning is filled with variation, that learning is complex, and that there is much that we do not know about learning. The rich variety of learning experiences and our limited knowledge about those experiences has been called the Principle of Uncertainty by Spector [4].

3 Research on learning and instruction

What has research on learning and instruction established? The Principle of Application is well-established and can be found in behavioral, cognitive and constructivist research literature. Merrill [1] identified five principles that are widely accepted by cognitive scientists and instructional designers:

- Principle of Problem Centering – learning is promoted when learners are engaged with meaningful problem solving activities;
- Principle of Activation – learning is promoted when existing relevant knowledge is activated and brought to bear on the problem situation;
- Principle of Demonstration – learning is promoted when new knowledge is demonstrated to learners;
- Principle of Application – learning is promoted when learners practice and apply new knowledge and skills;
- Principle of Integration – learning is promoted when learners are able to make new knowledge and skills a meaningful part of their everyday life.
- Similarly, Spector [4] argued for the following set of basic principles:

Human Perspectives in the Internet Society: Culture, Psychology and Gender, K. Morgan, J. Sanchez, C. A. Brebbia & A Voiskounsky (Editors) © 2004 WIT Press, www.witpress.com, ISBN 1-85312-726-4

- Principle of Change – learning is fundamentally about change;
- Principle of Experience – changes begin with and are based upon experience (similar to Merrill's Principle of Application);
- Principle of Context – meaningful experience is determined by context relative to the individual's situation (also called constructivism);
- Principle of Integration – meaningful integration involves contexts that are multi-faceted and multi-dimensional; and,
- Principle of Uncertainty – learning involves a richly complex set of phenomena about which we know less than we are inclined to believe.

4 Understanding complexity

What makes things complex? Surely what one person finds complex may not be found complex by another. Nevertheless, there are some things inherent in situations and systems that make understanding them particularly challenging for many people with different backgrounds and preparation. Among these things are the following:

- The number of components involved – as the number of components increases, the complexity of the system or situation tends to increase;
- The nature of the relationships among these components – non-linear relationships, delayed effects and fuzziness are particularly problematic for human problem solvers as shown by Dörner [5], Sterman [6] and others.

This is generally consistent with how the system dynamics community identifies factors contributing to complexity. Clearly other factors contribute as well. Some of these involve individual differences, such as differences in backgrounds, differences in preparation in related subject matter, and the relative novelty of the type of problem encountered. The methodology proposed herein attempts to be responsive to differences in types of problems and dynamic situations and systems while being useful in a context that accommodates individual differences. The next section elaborates the assessment methodology.

5 Assessing learning in complex domains

5.1 The problem

Large investments are being made in the area of problem-centered learning, especially when technology is involved in the delivery of instruction. The learning research and educational technology communities have a history of promising that the latest approaches and technologies will significantly improve learning and instruction. Projects are proposed and funded; new instructional paradigms and technologies are implemented in various educational contexts; data are collected and reported; students graduate and researchers get tenure and promotion. Yet there is inadequate evidence to establish to what extent learning has improved, especially in complex domains involving problem-centered instruction and technologically advanced environments.

Have these investments in educational research and technology been worthwhile? Many have probably contributed to improved learning, although the

Human Perspectives in the Internet Society: Culture, Psychology and Gender, K. Morgan, J. Sanchez, C. A. Brebbia & A Voiskounsky (Editors) © 2004 WIT Press, www.witpress.com, ISBN 1-85312-726-4

major finding is typically *no significant difference* according to Russell [7]. Common measures of learning include scores on standardized tests, subjective indications of interest and attitude, and identification/recall of concepts and simple procedures. While such measures only provide indirect evidence of improvement in higher order learning. There have been few direct measures of changes in higher order learning capabilities associated with learner progress from inexperienced beginner to accomplished expert in complex domains. A study conducted at the National Center for Research Evaluation, Standards and Student Testing (CRESST) is an exception; see Herl et al. [8] for details. That study indicated that knowledge mapping methods showed the most promise, but it did not address understanding of dynamic interactions of causal factors in complex domains. The methodology described herein extends knowledge mapping assessment methods significantly as it takes into account understanding dynamic causal relationships in complex problems situations.

In order to provide a context for the problem of assessing progress of learning in complex domains, it is useful to briefly review relatively recent changes in instructional paradigms and educational technology. According to many authors, there has occurred a paradigm shift in learning and instruction in the last 20 years that is commonly and uncritically labeled constructivism. The theoretical foundations for this shift can be traced to a socially-situated learning perspective that draws heavily on the views of Bruner [9], Collins [10], Lave [11], Piaget [12], and Vygotsky [13]. In this perspective, learning is viewed as an active process of knowledge construction in which learners are typically involved with other learners in authentic, problem-solving situations. The need to learn that is created when a group of learners is confronted with a realistic problem provides motivation, promotes interaction, and is likely to result in transfer of learning; for an elaboration see Jonassen et al. [14], Merrill [1] and Spector [15].

Problem-based learning has never been implemented in a pure form such that all concepts to be learned are introduced in an authentic problem-solving context; this is simply not practical nor is it efficient. However, integrating problem-solving activities into the curriculum has firmly established itself as a worthwhile educational practice according to Merrill [1]. Advances in educational technology have evolved with this shift to problem-centered approaches. There have been three broad periods in the modern use of technology to support learning. In the first period (through the 1960's), there was a great deal of enthusiasm for technologies such as radio, programmed texts and television to replace traditional classroom teaching. It is possible to cite success stories and identify some improvements in learning. However, there was a tendency in this first period to focus simply on using a new technology and making it available to support teaching rather than on exploring how specific technologies might be linked to specific learning goals and activities. With the advent of personal computing and networks, a new generation of educational technology came into being that was marked by emphasis on specific technologies in support of particular types of learning requirements (e.g., simulations to support operator training). As a consequence, much was learned in

Human Perspectives in the Internet Society: Culture, Psychology and Gender, K. Morgan, J. Sanchez, C. A. Brebbia & A Voiskounsky (Editors) © 2004 WIT Press, www.witpress.com, ISBN 1-85312-726-4

the last part of the 20th century in the area of effective technology integration. This second generation witnessed some of the same replacement strategies for technology integration that were prevalent earlier, but there was a growing tendency to focus on the process of using specific technologies to support specific learning objectives in this period. Technology in the current third generation of educational technology has evolved to include more powerful and affordable computers, broadband networks and wireless technologies, more powerful and accessible software systems, distributed learning environments, and so on. The current generation of educational technology provides many valuable *affordances* for the problem-centered instructional paradigm. The learning paradigm has appropriately shifted from learning from computers to one better characterized as learning with technology. Consequently, the focus has shifted to larger concerns, including: (a) viewing technology support as part of a larger process of change and innovation, and, (b) using technology to support higher order learning, particularly in complex and less well-defined domains; see Spector and Anderson [16].

In this new generation of educational technology, learning environments and instructional systems are properly viewed as parts of a larger system rather than as isolated places where learning might occur. Moreover, learning is occurring in more dynamic ways than was true in the teacher/system-led instructional paradigm of earlier generations. There are a greater variety of learning activities made possible by technology and this further complicates determining how, when and in which circumstances learning activities promote improved understanding. It is clear that lessons learned in previous generations of educational technology should be taken into account. Simply putting sophisticated technologies into situations involving complex learning activities is not likely to be either efficient or effective. Moreover, what should be studied is not the effect of a particular technology on attitudes, motivation, and simple knowledge tests. Such studies perpetuate a wrongheaded debate about the educational efficacy of media. What should be measured is the impact on learning in terms of improvements in student inquiry processes and other higher order aspects of learning directly relevant to understanding challenging and complex subject matter.

The problem context for this methodology involves learning goals pertaining to understanding complex phenomena and situations. Example problem-solving situations include: diagnosing a medical problem, developing an environmental management policy, and designing a piece for an orbiting spacecraft. In such cases, information is often incomplete, many interrelated factors are involved, and more than one reasonable solution may be possible. Such problems are often avoided in school-based instruction, but the real world is filled with them. Learning in complex problem-solving situations is not directly measurable by a particular solution. Rather, learning is better treated as an ongoing process in which problem-solvers become increasingly expert-like in their problem-solving activities. Measures of learning should be directed at this process and its progress against admittedly difficult to establish standards. The general problem with regard to evaluating problem-centered approaches to learning in these domains is

Human Perspectives in the Internet Society: Culture, Psychology and Gender, K. Morgan, J. Sanchez, C. A. Brebbia & A Voiskounsky (Editors) © 2004 WIT Press, www.witpress.com, ISBN 1-85312-726-4

that there is not a well-established and reliable methodology to determine learning outcomes. As a consequence, previous evaluations have focused on: (1) an analysis of efforts and resources required to successfully implement a particular approach (e.g., cost-benefits); and/or, (2) an analysis of the immediate and easily observed effects reported by those involved in such efforts (e.g., student reactions).

The immediately observable effects often reported are changes in attitudes, which may be relevant to sustaining interest in an area and to promoting change. In general, there is evidence to suggest that problem-centered approaches can have a positive effect on learner attitudes and interests and contribute to improved motivation. However, once again there is only indirect or suggestive evidence of improved learning outcomes by those conducting these kinds of evaluation studies.

Learning outcome measures typically collected for simpler domains (e.g., scores on knowledge tests or performance of steps in a procedure) are only indirectly relevant to higher order problem solving and understanding complex problems. The limitations of these kinds of evaluation are well known. One may perform very well on a knowledge test about disease indicators but still not do well with regard to diagnosing particular cases. Attitude, change agency, cost-benefits, and knowledge measures are relevant in an overall evaluation. However, the critical aspect of improved higher order learning is often overlooked because it is difficult to determine what progress students are making in understanding the complexities involved in more advanced problem-solving areas of science education and domains.

According to the principles described by Merrill [1] and Spector [4], an experiential, problem-centered environment with rich opportunities for collaboration with peers will often be effective. Such an approach has been reflected in the most promising systems developed in the 1990's. However, these collaborations break down when students are asked to derive hypotheses from data or engage in serious reflective discourse (i.e., exemplify higher order thinking). Moreover, well-educated and highly motivated adult learners have difficulty in making strategic decisions about complex systems, as shown by Dörner [5]. In order to show that particular instructional approaches are effective, it is essential to develop and validate a methodology to determine higher order learning outcomes appropriate for these domains. This research builds on research done at CRESST and reported by Herl et al. [8] using knowledge mapping techniques for problem-centered assessments.

5.2 The DEEP methodology

Validating this assessment methodology involves three different domains (engineering design, environmental decision making and medical diagnosis) with different levels of learners. The methodology is based on a view of learning as becoming more like an expert. The methodology, called the Dynamic Evaluation of Enhanced Problem-solving (DEEP), involves:

1. identifying characteristic complex problems;

Human Perspectives in the Internet Society: Culture, Psychology and Gender, K. Morgan, J. Sanchez, C. A. Brebbia & A Voiskounsky (Editors) © 2004 WIT Press, www.witpress.com, ISBN 1-85312-726-4

2. eliciting expert patterns for characteristic problem-solving activities;
3. representing expert patterns in both textual and graphical formats;
4. determining salient features of these representations;
5. establishing measures of similarity in salient features of expert representations;
6. eliciting novice patterns for the same problem-solving activities;
7. representing novice patterns in the same formats used for expert responses;
8. identifying the presence or absence of salient features in novice representations;
9. establishing measures of distance from expert patterns for each salient feature; and,
10. tracking and analyzing changes in learner responses over time and through instructional interventions.

Subjects are provided with a problem scenario relevant to a problem-centered module. They are asked to indicate what they believe may be relevant to a solution, and then they are asked to provide a short description of each item along with a brief explanation why it is relevant. They are also to indicate assumptions about they are making and they are asked to represent their conceptualization of the problem space in terms of: (a) a list of key facts and causal factors influencing the problem situation; (b) documentation of each factor - what it is and how it influences the problem; (c) a graphical depiction of how these factors are linked; (d) annotations of each node and link); and, (e) an indication of other considerations or approaches.

Many examples of medical instructional units constructed around problem solving in the context of patient cases can be found and typically consist of a problem scenario with a patient description, recent history of symptoms and some findings from a physical examination of the patient. The learner is asked to develop a diagnosis and prescribe treatment. The learner's response is then analyzed and compared with a standard solution to the problem. This method builds learner experience in the context of problems but assessments have been aimed at short-term goals, such as an appropriate decision for the specific problem at hand, rather than at longer-term goals involving higher order thinking and an understanding of the dynamic interaction of causal factors that might be involved in apparently similar cases which would warrant different diagnostic procedures or treatments.

Preliminary research suggests that there are noticeable differences in expert and novice responses. Differences include: (1) the number of causal factors taken into consideration; (2) the relationships among the causal factors; and, (3) the depth of response in the annotation of the sample node. The expert response reflects more nodes, more complex interactions among nodes, and a more specific justification for performing the initial test. A pilot test of this methodology involved using annotated causal influence diagrams as the graphical representation of what a person believes about a complex problem scenario. Subjects in the study conducted by Christensen et al. [17] were asked to

Human Perspectives in the Internet Society: Culture, Psychology and Gender, K. Morgan, J. Sanchez, C. A. Brebbia & A Voiskounsky (Editors) © 2004 WIT Press, www.witpress.com, ISBN 1-85312-726-4

indicate the key factors influencing the problem and a solution and to develop a graphical representation of the problem using a modified form of causal influence diagrams.

Another use of this methodology was reported by Seel and colleagues [18] who used the technique to study changes in mental models. Progress of learning was followed for a short period after instruction in this study, which suggests that the basic hypotheses in the DEEP methodology are reasonable.

In order to establish that the DEEP methodology is reliable and robust, it is necessary to determine: (a) whether or not experts in fact exhibit recognizable patterns of responses to complex problem scenarios in the various disciplines studied in this research; (b) that measures of nearness to expert patterns can be reliably derived from novice responses; and, (c) that these measures are likely to change as learning progresses and subjects acquire experience in solving problems in the domain of interest. These constitute the primary goal of this effort.

5.3 Initial findings

Instruments were developed and tested with a small group of intermediate level people in each of the three domains. Instruments included a background survey with basic demographic information, two sample problems for each domain, data collection software for representing problem conceptualizations and associated word processing files for alternative representations, and an open-ended question to collect reflections on the problem solving experience. The problem scenarios were judged sufficiently complex to be likely to evoke noticeable differences among respondents.

Minor adjustments were made to the relevant instruments and then novices (15 per domain) and experts (5 per domain) were given two scenarios in each of three domains: engineering design, environmental decision making and medical diagnosis and asked to represent how they thought about these problems. There does appear to be a pattern to expert responses in all three domains. Experts generally provided more nodes and richer descriptions in their responses than did novices, with one noticeable exception in the engineering domain. One expert respondent there provided only 4 nodes which was fewer than the other experts and many fewer than most novices. However, that expert respondent provided the greatest level of detail in the description of nodes (based on a simple word count). Interpretation of data is continuing on three levels: (1) surface analysis of the response; (2) structural similarity of one response compared with another; and (3) semantic analysis of description of nodes and links. The surface analysis consists of simple counts of nodes and links, the first three nodes created, and the existence of a noticeable pattern in the diagram (e.g., circular, hierachical, spiral, spoke, star, spiral, etc.). These determinations are easily automated and may prove useful in making an initial, fast, and reasonably reliable assessment of a response.

Structural similarity proceeds to analyze one response in comparison with another. In this study, it is the analysis of a novice response with that of another novice or with that of an expert. In a curriculum or evaluation study, the

Human Perspectives in the Internet Society: Culture, Psychology and Gender, K. Morgan, J. Sanchez, C. A. Brebbia & A Voiskounsky (Editors) © 2004 WIT Press, www.witpress.com, ISBN 1-85312-726-4

structural similarity analysis could compare the same subject's responses before and after certain instructional interventions. At this level, the goal is to see if the same or similar nodes are identified and if so whether or not they are linked in the same way. This kind of analysis also lends itself to automation.

The semantic analysis examines the descriptions of nodes and links provided by respondents. As already indicated, such an analysis is notoriously time-consuming and not easily automated. To add to the robustness of findings, a doctoral student is using the same scenarios with Ericsson & Smith's [19] think-aloud protocol analysis methodology to see if similar problem conceptualizations emerge with a different semantic analysis methodology. The reason for including semantic analysis in this study is to determine the extent to which the first two levels of analysis (surface analysis and structural analysis) may reliably predict the third level of analysis.

At this point in the data analysis, expert patterns in problem conceptualizations do exist for the domains and problems studied, and novice patterns are noticeably different from expert patterns in all three levels of analysis for these problem scenarios and the subjects involved. The key hypothesis of whether or not the first two levels of analysis, which lend themselves to automation, will be reliable predictors of the third level of analysis has yet to be determined.

6 Challenges and future directions

The immediate next step is to determine whether or not the data collected thus far supports the important third hypothesis that simpler levels of analysis of problem conceptualizations are predictive of relative level of expertise or mastery. A doctoral dissertation currently underway at Syracuse University should provide important data in this regard. Once this is determined, additional problem scenarios should be examined with different levels of respondents.

In summary, this assessment methodology appears promising and lends itself to automation and use in a variety of contexts ranging from intelligent tutoring systems to program evaluations. Work on the related critical issues for new learning identified at the beginning of this chapter should proceed in parallel so that the potential benefits of new learning can be maximized while minimizing the potential pitfalls.

(This paper was delivered by the author as the keynote address at New Learning 2004 in Skiathos, Greece, on 10 May 2004).

References

[1] Merrill, M. D. First principles of instruction. *Educational Technology Research & Development ,50*(3), pp. 43-59, 2002.

[2] Vygotsky, L.S. *Thought and language*. Cambridge, MA: MIT Press, 1962.

[3] Wittgenstein, L. *Philosophical investigations*. (Tr. G. E. M. Anscombe). Oxford: Basil Blackwell, 1963.

[4] Spector, J. M. A philosophy of instructional design for the 21st century? *Journal of Structural learning and Intelligent Systems 14* (4), pp. 307-318, 2001.

Human Perspectives in the Internet Society: Culture, Psychology and Gender, K. Morgan, J. Sanchez, C. A. Brebbia & A Voiskounsky (Editors) © 2004 WIT Press, www.witpress.com, ISBN 1-85312-726-4

[5] Dörner, D. *The logic of failure: Why things go wrong and what we can do to make them right* (R. Kimber & R. Kimber, Trans.). New York: Metropolitan Books, 1996.
[6] Sterman, J. D. Learning in and about complex systems. *System Dynamics Review, 10*(2-3), pp. 291-330, 1994.
[7] Russell, T. L. *The no significant difference phenomenon.* Raleigh, NC: North Carolina State University, 1999.
[8] Herl, H. E., O'Neil, H. F., Jr., Chung, G. L. W. K., Bianchi, C., Wang, S., Mayer, R., Lee, C. Y., Choi, A., Suen, T., & Tu, A. *Final report for validation of problem solving measures.* CSE Technical Report 501. Los Angeles: CRESST, 1999.
[9] Bruner, J. S. Models of the learner. *Educational Researcher, 14*(6), 5-8, 1985.
[10] Collins, A. Cognitive apprenticeship and instructional technology. In L. Idol & B. F. Jones (Eds.), *Educational values and cognitive instruction: Implications for reform.* Hillsdale, NJ: Erlbaum, 1991.
[11] Lave, J. *Cognition in Practice: Mind, mathematics, and culture in everyday life.* Cambridge, UK: Cambridge University Press, 1988.
[12] Piaget, J. *The science of education and the psychology of the child.* New York: Grossman, 1970.
[13] Vygotsky, L. S. *Mind in society: The development of higher psychological processes.* (M. Cole, V. John-Steiner, S. Scribner & E. Souberman, Editors and Translators). Cambridge, MA: Harvard University Press, 1978.
[14] Jonassen, D. H., Hernandez-Serrano, J. & Choi, I. Integrating constructivism and learning technologies. In J. M. Spector & T. Anderson (Eds.), *Integrated & Holistic Perspectives on Learning, Instruction & Technology* (pp. 103-128). Dordrecht, The Netherlands: Kluwer, 2000.
[15] Spector, J. M. System dynamics and interactive learning environments: Lessons learned and implications for the future. *Simulation and Gaming 31*(3), pp. 457-464, 2000.
[16] Spector, J. M., & Anderson, T. M. (2000). *Integrated & Holistic Perspectives on Learning, Instruction & Technology.* Dordrecht, The Netherlands: Kluwer, 2000.
[17] Christensen, D. L., Spector, J. M., Sioutine, A., & McCormack, D. *Evaluating the impact of system dynamics based learning environments: A preliminary study.* Paper presented at the International System Dynamics Society Conference, Bergen, Norway, August, 2000.
[18] Seel, N., Al-Diban, S., & Blumschein, P. Mental models and instructional planning. In J. M. Spector & T. M. Anderson (Eds.), *Integrated & Holistic Perspectives on Learning, Instruction & Technolog* (pp. 129-158). Dordrecht, The Netherlands: Kluwer, 2000.
[19] Ericsson, K. A., & Smith, J. (Eds.) *Toward a general theory of expertise: Prospects and limits.* New York: Cambridge University Press, 1991.

Human Perspectives in the Internet Society: Culture, Psychology and Gender, K. Morgan, J. Sanchez, C. A. Brebbia & A Voiskounsky (Editors) © 2004 WIT Press, www.witpress.com, ISBN 1-85312-726-4

Burnout and emotional intelligence in Greek employees

E. K. Kondylis, S. Pandelis, M. E. Sfakianakis & D. Prokopiou
Department of Business Administration, University of Piraeus, Greece

Abstract

The concepts of burnout and emotional intelligence are presented in this paper. This research is designed to estimate levels of burnout as measured with the Maslach Burnout Inventory, in relation to levels of emotional intelligence as measured with the Emotional Competence Inventory. Two groups of Greek employees are compared. The first being a group of client service employees in banking, shipping, security systems and insurance companies while the second being a group of insurance consultants who visit clients at their homes. Additionally, levels of burnout and levels of emotional intelligence are compared.

1 Introduction: burnout syndrome

Freudenberger [1] was the first to introduce the term burnout, to describe a specific type of occupational exhaustion that was observed in professions related to medical care. Later, the use of the term was expanded to professions in the field of education until it was finally used for professions related to any services that involved interactions with the public [25, 2, 3, 13].

In the recent years, burnout has become one of the major issues of concern in various professional fields in relation to the rapidly developed research regarding stress and its hazardous consequences both in personal as well as in career life. We may distinguish three types of consequences of burnout [7]: (a) in mental and physical health, (b) in personal relationships and (c) in professional behaviour and performance.

Burnout must be distinguished from occupational stress, as it is considered to be a kind of chronical type of anxiety at work that exceeds the limits of the person's ability to control. According to Maslach [19], burnout is described as a

Human Perspectives in the Internet Society: Culture, Psychology and Gender, K. Morgan, J. Sanchez, C. A. Brebbia & A Voiskounsky (Editors) © 2004 WIT Press, www.witpress.com, ISBN 1-85312-726-4

syndrome of emotional exhaustion, depersonalization and reduced personal accomplishment, which may occur among professionals who work with people in some capacity. As a result of this syndrome, individuals lose their interest and positive feelings for work, colleagues and clients. Additionally, they do not get any satisfaction either from their work or their performance at work and develop a negative image about themselves.

According to Pines and Aronson [22], the long term exposure to emotionally demanding situations leads the individual to a feeling of psychological and physical depletion which generates a loss of the individual's ideals and expectations, something analogous to the grief process.

Burnout was found to be related to difficult work conditions like overloading amounts of work, absence of breaks, ambiguities related to job description and absence of psychological support [4, 5, 9, 20, 24, 23]. Additionally, individual factors were found to influence burnout. Maddi and Kobasa [18], reported a factor which they called hardiness, which is related to (a) the individuals' tendency to invest in their jobs, (b) a feeling of control over their environment and (c) a tendency to perceive difficulties as opportunities rather than threats.

2 Emotional intelligence

Emotional intelligence is generally considered by most current researchers as the individual's ability to perceive, understand, control and make use of feelings. The study of emotional intelligence goes back to Thorndike in 1911 [27], who talked about "social intelligence" as the ability to understand and manipulate men, women, boys and girls, in other words the ability to treat personal relationships in a wise way. It was Gardner in 1983 who used the term "multiple intelligence" which included seven types of intelligence: linguistic, logical, musical, kinesthetic, visual / spatial, interpersonal and intrapersonal.

Salovey and Mayer originally used the term "emotional intelligence" in 1990 [16] and divided it in three areas: (a) appraisal and expression of emotions, (b) utilization of emotions in solving problems and (c) regulation of emotion. Later, in 1995, Goleman associated emotional intelligence with certain social and communication skills related to the understanding and expression of emotions which he divided into personal and social skills and related them to work [11].

According to Goleman's [11] theoretical model, emotional intelligence is the ability: (a) to recognize what you are feeling and be able to manage your feelings before they manage you, (b) to be able to motivate yourself so that you accomplish your goals, be creative and make the best possible use of your skills and (c) to understand how others feel and be able to manage your relationship with them. In other words, emotional intelligence is a combination of self-awareness, management of emotions, motivation, empathy and social skills.

Many researchers in the field of organizational psychology have investigated the effect of emotional intelligence on leadership and occupational performance in general, in the last few years. Results of these works support the view that in fact emotional intelligence is the key to success and well being [12].

Human Perspectives in the Internet Society: Culture, Psychology and Gender, K. Morgan, J. Sanchez, C. A. Brebbia & A Voiskounsky (Editors) © 2004 WIT Press, www.witpress.com, ISBN 1-85312-726-4

3 Aim of the study

This research was designed to study (a) the relationship between levels of burnout and emotional intelligence and (b) differences between two groups of employees working with clients, those working in their own office receiving the clients and those working outside their office visiting clients at their premises.

4 Method: sample and procedure

The sample was taken from big companies established in Athens, which were in the field of banking, insurance, security systems and shipping.

126 individuals participated in the study, 60 men and 66 women ranging from 23 to 59 years of age. 71 employees were the ones who worked in their own offices (client service employees), while 55 were insurance consultants who visit their clients (see Table 1).

Table 1: Age characteristics of the sample.

	N	Age	Age range	Years in position
		Mean/St.d		Mean/St.d
Men	60	37,6 / 8,2	29 - 59	8,1 / 6,2
Women	66	34,3 / 8,5	23 - 59	6,1 / 5,6
Client service	71	34,6/8,3	23-59	6,1-5,4
Insurance advisors	55	37,4 / 8,7	23 - 58	8,3 / 6,4
Overall	126	35,8 / 8,5	23 - 59	7,7 / 5,9

5 Questionnaires

All questionnaires were anonymously answered.

6 Maslach burnout inventory

It is a self-administered Likert-type questionnaire with 22 statements that measures three dimensions of burnout: (a) emotional exhaustion, (b) personal achievements, (c) depersonalization. Answers are given on a scale from 0 (“never”) to 6 (“every day”), which shows the frequency with which situations or reactions are experienced by the respondent at work. High scores on emotional exhaustion and depersonalization, and low scores on personal achievements, correspond to high levels of burnout.

7 Emotional competence inventory

This is a self-administered Likert-type questionnaire of 72 questions answered on a scale from 1(“never”) to 5(“always”) with an additional neutral answer,

Human Perspectives in the Internet Society: Culture, Psychology and Gender, K. Morgan, J. Sanchez, C. A. Brebbia & A Voiskounsky (Editors) © 2004 WIT Press, www.witpress.com, ISBN 1-85312-726-4

which is scored with zero. It measures five different categories of emotional intelligence at work, being self-awareness, self-management, social-awareness, relationship- management and cognitive ability [1].

8 Results

All the statistical analyses were worked out with STAT GRAPHICS PLUS, VERSION 5.1. Comparison of Medians with the Mann-Whitney test showed the following results:

Table 2: Differences of Medians on the dimension of emotional exhaustion between the two groups of female employees and insurance consultants.

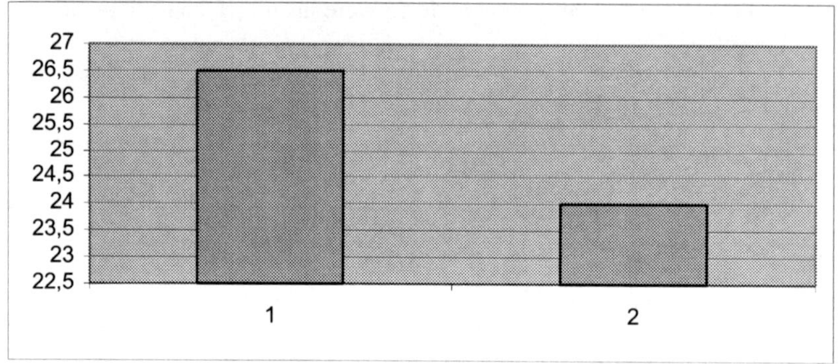

1: Female client service employees
2: Female insurance consultants

Table 3: Differences of Means on the dimension of emotional exhaustion between the two groups of employees for the overall sample.

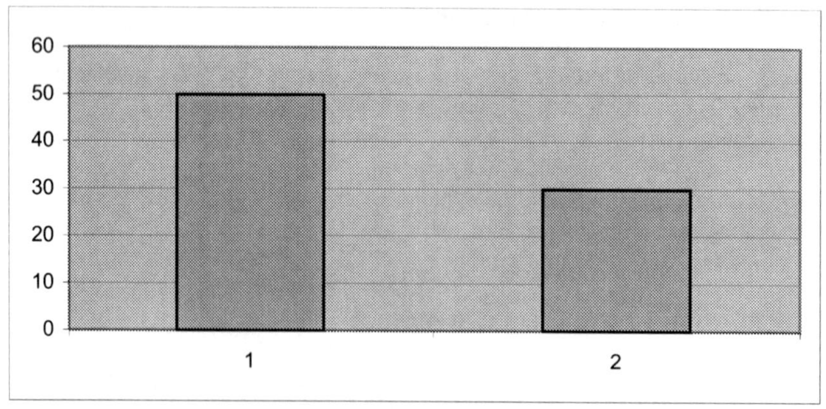

Human Perspectives in the Internet Society: Culture, Psychology and Gender, K. Morgan, J. Sanchez, C. A. Brebbia & A Voiskounsky (Editors) © 2004 WIT Press, www.witpress.com, ISBN 1-85312-726-4

Levels of burnout appeared to be significantly different only for the female population between the groups of client service employees and insurance consultants for the dimension of emotional exhaustion (p< 0,05) and the dimension of depersonalization (p< 0,001) with client service employees showing higher levels of burnout (see Table 2).

A t-test analysis was conducted for the two groups of employees for the overall population which showed that client service employees scored significantly higher on the dimension of emotional exhaustion (t = 2,34, p< 0,02) (see Table 3). There was no significant difference found for any comparison between the groups regarding the levels of emotional intelligence.

A series of Spearman Rank Correlations were conducted which showed the following results:

Table 4: Significant differences between the groups with Spearman Rank Correlation.

Overall client service	EI / EX1	r = - 0 ,47	P< 0,001
Overall client service	EI / EX2	r = 0,33	P< 0,005
Overall client service	EI / Age	r = 0,25	P< 0,05
Overall client service	EX1 / Age	r = - 0,37	P< 0,001
Overall client service	EI / EX2	r = 0,29	P< 0,02
Overall males	EI / EX1	r = - 0,47	P< 0,001
Overall males	EI / EX2	r = 0,33	P< 0,005
Overall males	EI / EX3	r = - 0,36	P< 0,005
Overall males	EI / Age	r = 0,29	P< 0,02
Overall males	EX1 / Age	r = - 0,27	P< 0,01
Overall fem.	EI / EX1	r = - 0,22	P< 0,05
Overall fem.	EI / EX2	r = 0,27	P< 0,02
Overall fem.	EI / EX3	r = - 0,28	P< 0,02
Overall fem.	EI / Age	r = 0,28	P< 0,02
Overall fem.	EX1 / Age	r = - 0,30	P< 0,01

For the sample of client service employees, there is a significant negative correlation between the levels of emotional intelligence (EI) and the dimension of emotional exhaustion (EX1) (r = -0,47, p < 0,001), a significant positive correlation between emotional intelligence and the dimension of personal

Human Perspectives in the Internet Society: Culture, Psychology and Gender, K. Morgan, J. Sanchez, C. A. Brebbia & A Voiskounsky (Editors) © 2004 WIT Press, www.witpress.com, ISBN 1-85312-726-4

accomplishments (EX2) ($r = 0,33$, $p < 0,005$), a significant negative correlation between emotional intelligence and the dimension of depersonalization (EX3) ($r = -0,40$, $p < 0,001$), a significant positive correlation between emotional intelligence and age ($r = 0,25$, $p < 0,05$), and a significant negative correlation between emotional exhaustion and age ($r = -0,37$, $p < 0,001$) (see Table 4).For the sample of insurance advisors, there is a significant positive correlation between emotional intelligence and the dimension personal achievements ($r = 0,29$, $p < 0,02$) (see Table 4).

For the overall male sample, significant negative correlations were found between emotional intelligence and emotional exhaustion ($r = -0,47$, $p < 0,001$) and between emotional intelligence and depersonalization ($r = -0,36$, $p < 0,005$), while a positive significant correlation was found between emotional intelligence and personal achievements ($r = 0,33$, $p < 0,005$). A significant positive correlation was found between age and emotional intelligence ($r = 0,29$, $p < 0,02$) and a significant negative correlation was found between age and emotional exhaustion ($r = -0,27$, $p < 0,01$) (see Table 4).

For the overall female population, significant negative correlations were found between emotional intelligence and the dimensions of emotional exhaustion ($r = -0,22$, $p < 0,05$) and depersonalization ($r = -0,28$, $p < 0,02$), while a significant positive correlation was found between emotional intelligence and personal achievements ($r = 0,27$, $p < 0,02$). A significant positive correlation was found between age and emotional intelligence ($r = 0,28$, $p < 0,02$) and a significant negative correlation was found between age and emotional exhaustion ($r = - 0,30$, $p < 0,01$) (see Table 4).

9 Discussion

Results show that client service employees and insurance advisors do not differ in terms of emotional intelligence.

The group that was found to be at risk, were the female client service employees that scored significantly higher in the dimensions of emotional exhaustion and depersonalization. Therefore, women working in client service positions are more vulnerable to burnout than men are. Furthermore, women insurance advisors are less vulnerable to burnout than women client service employees. Such a result suggests that women working in an office having to deal with clients may experience bigger amounts of stress. It is an interesting issue for further research to investigate the reasons why men are not so vulnerable in such positions. It is also interesting to note that as insurance advisors are moving from place to place to meet their clients plus the fact that they are dealing with one client at a time, seems to create a safer atmosphere to work in.

As age was found to be negatively correlated to emotional exhaustion and depersonalization, earlier findings on this area are verified, suggesting that younger employees are more vulnerable to burnout because they experience bigger stress in their effort to succeed [7].

Human Perspectives in the Internet Society: Culture, Psychology and Gender, K. Morgan, J. Sanchez, C. A. Brebbia & A Voiskounsky (Editors) © 2004 WIT Press, www.witpress.com, ISBN 1-85312-726-4

Emotional intelligence is interestingly found to correlate with lower levels of burnout. This goes along with Maddi and Kobasa's [18] findings on hardiness, as emotional intelligence is closely related to feelings of self-control and self-esteem. Such findings lead to the conclusion that a useful tool for burnout prevention is emotional intelligence training. Organizations may seriously consider the possibility to train their staff accordingly on issues of self-awareness, social skills and stress management. Especially new comers are to benefit more from such a supportive training.

As expectations of one's own performance at work may increase together with the market's pressure for bigger results in productivity, it is important to discriminate between eustress and distress [26]. As burnout may cause mental and physical problems, transform communication to dysfunctional ways of rapport and lead employees to a state of indifference for their career and work [7], it is important to provide employees with opportunities to avoid personal hazards both on psychological and physical levels, which may sometimes be disastrous for the companies themselves.

References

[1] Boyatzis, R., Goleman D. Emotional Competence Inventory (special version for the use at the Weatherhead School of Management).

[2] Byrne, M. (1991) Burnout: investigating the impact of background variables for elementary, intermediate, secondary and university educators. Teaching and Teacher Education, 7, 197-209.

[3] Byrne, M. (1993) Testing for factorial validity and invariance across elementary, intermediate and secondary teachers. Journal of Occupational Psychology, 66, 197-212.

[4] Cherniss, C. (1980) Staff burnout – Job stress in the human services. Beverly Hills: Sage Publications.

[5] Constable, C.J. & Russel, D.W. (1986) The effects of social support and the work environment upon burnout among nurses. Journal of Human Stress, Spring, 22-26.

[6] Cooper, C.L. & Baglioni, A.J. (1988). A structural model approach toward the development of a theory of the link between stress and mental health. British Journal of Medical Psychology, 61, 87-102.

[7] Cordes, C.L. & Dougherty T.W. (1993) A review and an integration of research on job burnout. Academy of Management Review, 18, 621-656.

[8] Cox, T. (1987) Stress. London: MacMillan.

[9] Duxbury, M., Armstrong G., Drew D. and Henly S. (1984) Head nurse leadership style with staff, nurse burnout and job satisfaction in neonatal intensive care units. Nursing Research, 33, 97-101.

[10] Freudenberger, H.J. (1974) Staff burn-out. Journal of social Issues, 30, 159-165.

[11] Goleman, D. (1995) Emotional intelligence, New York: Bantam Books.

[12] Goleman, D. (2002) Primal leadership, Boston Massachusetts: Harvard Business School Press.

Human Perspectives in the Internet Society: Culture, Psychology and Gender, K. Morgan, J. Sanchez, C. A. Brebbia & A Voiskounsky (Editors) © 2004 WIT Press, www.witpress.com, ISBN 1-85312-726-4

[13] Golembiewski, R.T., Munzenrider, R.F. & Stevenson, J.G. (1986) Stress in organizations. Toward a phase model of burnout. New York: Praeger.
[14] Harrison, R.V. (1987) Person – environment fit and job stress. In C.L. Cooper & R. Payne (eds.), Stress at work. Chichester: Wiley.
[15] Kobasa, S.C. Maddi S.R. & Kahn S. (1982) Hardiness and health: A prospective inquiry. Journal of Personality and Social Psychology, 42, 168-177.
[16] Langley, A. (2000) Emotional intelligence – a new evaluation for management development. Career Development International, vol. 5, No 3, 177-183.
[17] Lazarus, R.S. & Folkman S. (1984) Stress, appraisal and coping. New York: Springer – Verlag.
[18] Maddi, S.R. & Kobasa S.C. (1984) The hardy executive. Health under stress. Homewood, Ill.: Dow-Jones-Irvin.
[19] Maslach, C. (1982) Understanding burnout: Definitional issues in analyzing a complex phenomenon. In W. Paine (ed.), Job, stress and burnout. Beverly Hills, CA: Sage.
[20] Maslach, C. & Jackson, S.E. (1984) Burnout in organizational settings. Applied Social Psychology Annual, 5, 133-153.
[21] Maslach, C. & Schaufeli, W.B. (1993) Historical and conceptual development of burnout. In W.B. Schaufeli, C. Maslach & T. Marek (eds.), Professional burnout: recent developments in theory and research. Washington: Taylor & Francis.
[22] Pines, A. & Aronson, E. (1988) Career burnout: Causes and cures. New York: The Free Press.
[23] Roeske, N.C. (1986) Risk factors: Predictable hazards of health care career. In C.D. Scott & J. Hawk (eds.) Heal thyself: the health of health care professionals. New York: Brunner/ Mazel Inc.
[24] Rosenthal, D., Teague M., Retish P., J. & Vessel R. (1983) The relationship between work environment attributes and burnout. Journal of Leisure Research, 15, 125-135.
[25] Schwab, R.L. (1986), Burnout in education. In C. Maslach & S.E. Jackson, Maslach Burnout Inventory Manual (2nd edition). Palo Alto: Consulting Psychologists Press.
[26] Selye, H. (1982) History and present status of the stress concept. In: Goldberger, & Breznitz (Eds.) Handbook of stress. New York, Free Press.
[27] Thorndike, E. (1911) Animal intelligence, New York: MacMillan.
[28] Vachon, M.L.S. (1987) Occupational stress in the care of the critically ill, the dying and the bereaved. New York: Hemisphere Publishing Corporation.

Human Perspectives in the Internet Society: Culture, Psychology and Gender, K. Morgan, J. Sanchez, C. A. Brebbia & A Voiskounsky (Editors) © 2004 WIT Press, www.witpress.com, ISBN 1-85312-726-4

A dynamic web educational assessment system

S. Y. Wu & Z. He
Software Engineering College, Beijing Normal University, Zhuhai (BNUZH)

Abstract

Educational assessment is a mutual dynamic process for both teachers and students. Many assessments in universities usually are one-way and one-time pieces of work. At the end of the semester or teaching period, the student fills in a form, and gives his evaluation to the teacher based on some simple general choice. In such a way, the teachers lose their chances to improve their work during the teaching process. On the other hand, students also don't have much chance to exchange their concern with teachers. This situation is getting worse in the remote teaching system.

To solve the above problems, and to enhance the mutual understanding between teachers and students, a web based evaluation system was built for mutual and dynamic assessment. This system is a Java 2 based system running in Beijing Normal University at Zhuhai Campus now. A multi-layer fuzzy evaluation model is used to handle the assessment criteria group in different layers and from different evaluation groups. The users of the system are categorized into three groups: the teachers, the students and the manager. This system is a sub-system of the management system we developed for Beijing Normal University at Zhuhai Campus. After being used for one semester, most of the users showed their satisfaction to the system.

In this paper, the structure of the assessment system is discussed. The fuzzy evaluation model is shown with an application example. The components used in the system are displayed. We hope this will give a helpful idea to change the traditional assessment process, and to contribute to the quality control of e-learning.
Keywords: DWEAS (Dynamic Web Educational Assessment System), dynamic assessment, remote education.

Human Perspectives in the Internet Society: Culture, Psychology and Gender, K. Morgan, J. Sanchez, C. A. Brebbia & A Voiskounsky (Editors) © 2004 WIT Press, www.witpress.com, ISBN 1-85312-726-4

1 Introduction

In conventional classrooms, the communication between students and teachers usually depends on the character of the teacher. The educational managers at different levels usually only get some evaluation sheets at the end of the class. They have no idea what and how everything going on in the classroom during the teaching process. Only in very special situations will they pay attention to some specific classes. They need a stronger tool to know how the students evaluate their classes, their teachers. The evaluation should not only occur once a semester, but throughout the entire semester.

In network remote education, the evaluation becomes more important. It not only gives evaluation to the teachers, but is a communication tool among teachers and students. Teachers need know the feedback from the students in time. Students need express their concern and opinion on the classes, the lessons and the teachers. The mangers of the education also need know how everything is progressing within classes and lessons.

To meet such requirements, we designed and developed a web based dynamic education assessment system. The evaluation methods and the dynamic evaluation process have proven effective and satisfactory to teachers, students and managers in Beijing Normal University Zhuhai campus (BNUZH) of China.

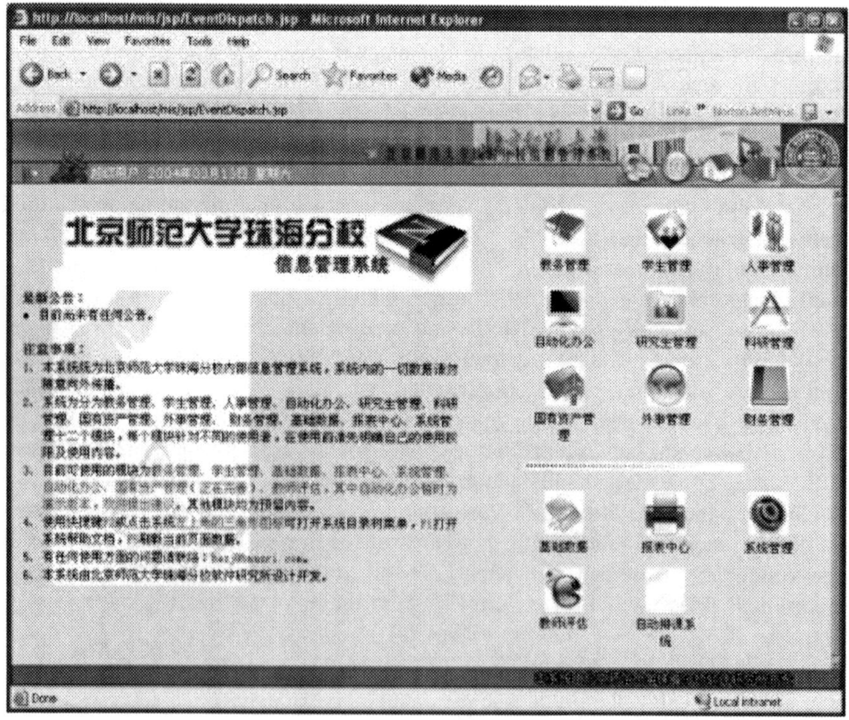

Figure 1: The J2EE based information system of BNUZH.

Human Perspectives in the Internet Society: Culture, Psychology and Gender, K. Morgan, J. Sanchez, C. A. Brebbia & A Voiskounsky (Editors) © 2004 WIT Press, www.witpress.com, ISBN 1-85312-726-4

In this paper, we will show the web based dynamic educational assessment system developed by the Software Research Institute of Beijing Normal University, Zhuhai for BNUZH. In Figure1, the left side icon at the bottom line is the Teacher Assessment Module.

As a search result, we haven't seen much same system built yet.

Table 1: Assessment criteria to teachers.

	Assessment Item	Portion	Type	Assessment Note
1	Overall evaluation of the course	course	Choose	Like very much, like, ok, , not like, hate.
2	Difficulty learning the course	Course	Choose	0k, some heavy, some easy, too heavy, too easy.
3	Difficulty understanding the course	course	Choose	Ok, some hard, some easy, too hard, too easy
4	How are you interested in the course	Course	Choose	Very interested, interested, ok, not interested, boring
5	How important is the course	Course	Choose	Very important, important, ok, not important, forget it
6	Overall evaluation of the teacher	Course	Choose	Good, ok, common, not good, bad
7	What is the teacher's attitude towards the course	Course	Choose	Good, ok, common, not good, bad
8	The clarity and exactness of the course	Course	Choose	Good, ok, common, not good, bad
9	The mutual enhancement between the teacher and the students	Course	Choose	Good, ok, common, not good, bad
10	The combination of theory and practice	Course	Choose	Good, ok, common, not good, bad
11	How the teacher handles the difficult parts of the course	Course	Choose	Good, ok, common, not good, bad
12	How worthwhile is the content of the course?	Course	Choose	Good, ok, common, not good, bad
13	How is the cultivation of the students' ability?	Course	Choose	Good, ok, common, not good, bad
14	Is the course study stimulating	course	Choose	Good, ok, common, not good, bad

Human Perspectives in the Internet Society: Culture, Psychology and Gender, K. Morgan, J. Sanchez, C. A. Brebbia & A Voiskounsky (Editors) © 2004 WIT Press, www.witpress.com, ISBN 1-85312-726-4

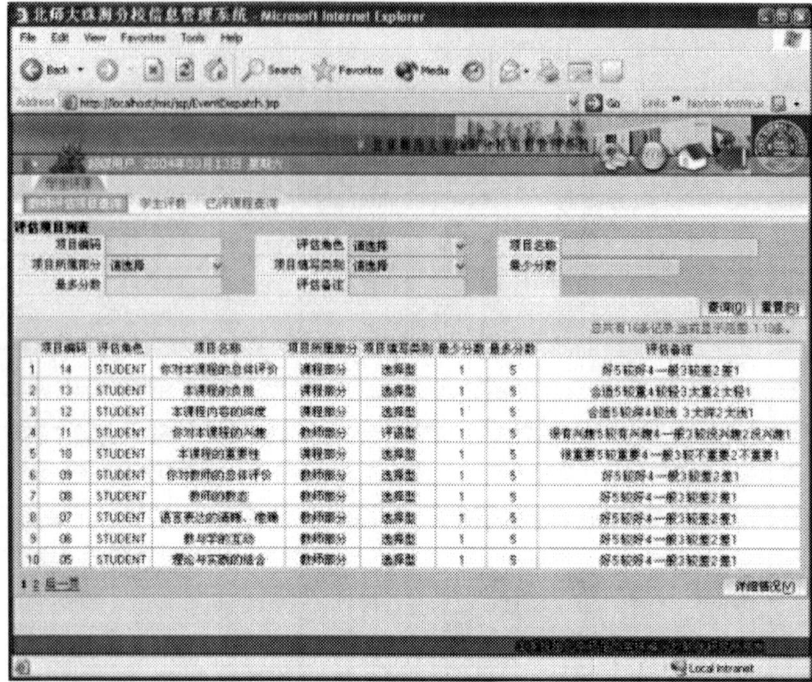

Figure 2: Assessment criteria to teachers.

Figure 3: A student can select one specific course to evaluate.

2 The evaluation model

We used a multilayer comprehensive fuzzy evaluation model to do the evaluation calculation [1]. The evaluation criteria are flexible to choose. The mathematic model can be configured according to the opinion of the user of the DWEAS before the system running. This makes the system easily suited for different colleges.

Also, different parts of the assessment process will set different evaluation criteria for each group. The evaluation criterion for a teacher is different from that of a student. This means a flexible frame for accepting any group of evaluation criteria and giving the correct result is important and necessary in order to set up the correct evaluation system.

3 The dynamic assessment on teachers

It is a three party communication in the educational assessment process. The major mutual assessment is among the teachers and the students. The third party is the management group, who works like a monitor of the other two parties.

As a student, he has right to issue his opinion according to the evaluation strategy defined by the management team. The evaluation strategy includes a time period the student can log in to publish his opinion to a specific course or to a specific teacher following the different assessment criteria, etc.

In BNUZH, we are using following 14 criteria to do the teaching assessment for a specific course taught by a specific teacher. These criteria are displayed in Table 1. The related web page is shown in Figure 2.

Figure 4: Student checks his evaluation result.

Figure 3 is the web page used by a student to evaluate a course teaching by a specific teacher. A student can only choose courses within his registered course list. The education manager can set up the frequency for the student to do evaluation, such as once a week, or a month, etc. Every time the student has to submit a completely filled evaluation page while he is doing his assessment. Otherwise the system will ignore the student's evaluation.

Human Perspectives in the Internet Society: Culture, Psychology and Gender, K. Morgan, J. Sanchez, C. A. Brebbia & A Voiskounsky (Editors) © 2004 WIT Press, www.witpress.com, ISBN 1-85312-726-4

4 The management of the evaluation result

There are lots of data related to evaluation process. In order to efficiently use this data, we designed a view for every different purpose. The student can view the results of his evaluation as shown in Figure 4.

The teacher evaluations can be viewed as the following web page:

Figure 5: View statistics on a teacher's evaluation results.

We can make comparisons between teachers by viewing the distribution of the statistic percentages for all teachers as shown in Figure 6.

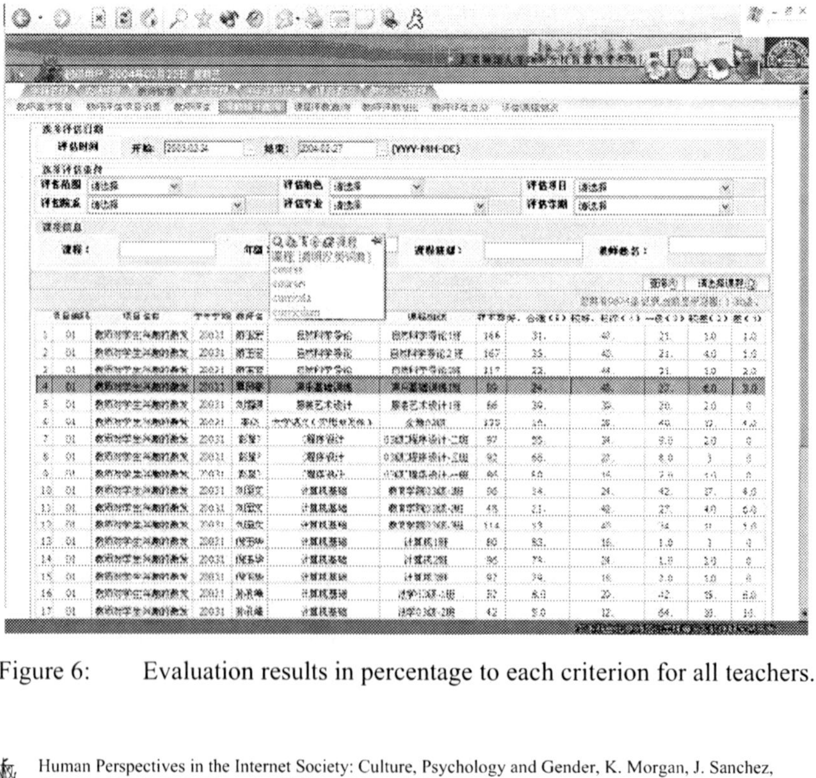

Figure 6: Evaluation results in percentage to each criterion for all teachers.

Human Perspectives in the Internet Society: Culture, Psychology and Gender, K. Morgan, J. Sanchez, C. A. Brebbia & A Voiskounsky (Editors) © 2004 WIT Press, www.witpress.com, ISBN 1-85312-726-4

Figure 7 shows the result to each course as a bar graph and Figure 8 shows the comparison between teachers.

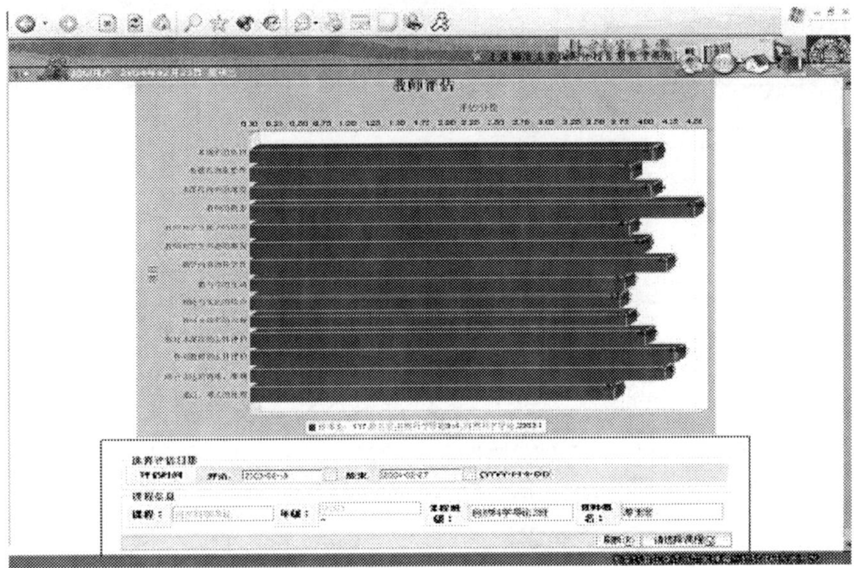

Figure 7: Teacher evaluations for each course with all criteria present.

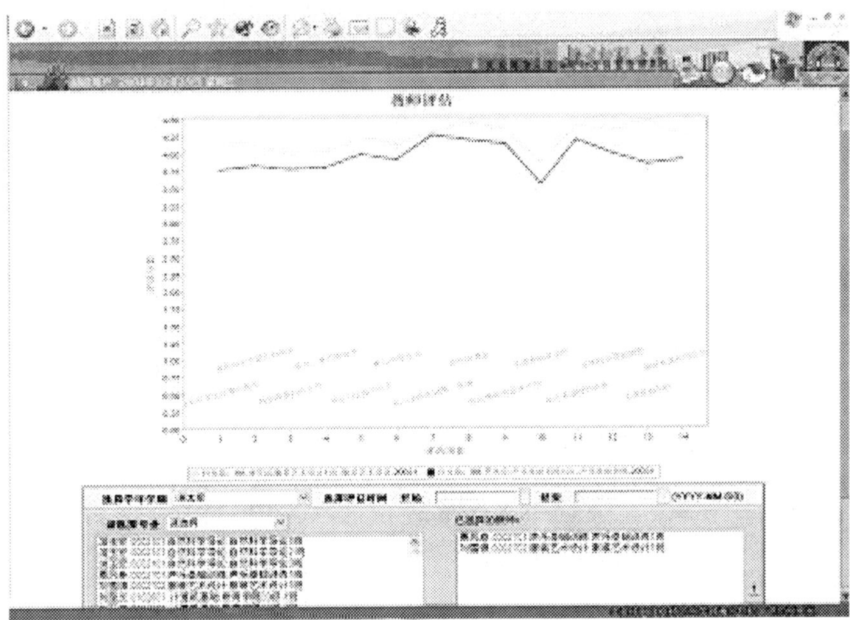

Figure 8: Teacher evaluation comparisons.

Human Perspectives in the Internet Society: Culture, Psychology and Gender, K. Morgan, J. Sanchez, C. A. Brebbia & A Voiskounsky (Editors) © 2004 WIT Press, www.witpress.com, ISBN 1-85312-726-4

Figure 9 shows the evaluation results according to department, a college or a specific course.

Figure 9: Evaluation results for a college or department.

5 Conclusions

Dynamic assessment is important in modern education. It gives the chance for students to show their opinion to a specific course. The educational managers can use it to easily design an effective monitoring system to control the educational quality for each course or teacher. They can view the opinion of the students in time and make adjustments according to feedback and can easily compare the teaching quality among different teachers with different courses.

The dynamic assessment system also enables a flexible and convenient communication between teachers and students in network education. With the more and more remote education, the quality of the remote education is not only worried by the students or education managers, but the potential students from a large amount of people. People always want to know how one course is before he takes it. The dynamic assessment system gives them a right tool to know how the exiting course is under the teaching of the teacher. They can know the opinion from the students who already taken the course.

In all, the web based dynamic educational assessment system provides a wide application field in many educational systems, meets many different requirements, and helps the educational management tremendously in teaching quality control, which has been proven in the education practice at BNUZH.

Human Perspectives in the Internet Society: Culture, Psychology and Gender, K. Morgan, J. Sanchez, C. A. Brebbia & A Voiskounsky (Editors) © 2004 WIT Press, www.witpress.com, ISBN 1-85312-726-4

References

[1] Yuxiang Wu, A Mathematic Model of Multi Layer Comprehensive Evaluation Built with Fuzzy Theory and Its Application, Journal of China Mining Engineering Society, No.5, 1985.

[2] Badrul H. Khan & Rene Vega, Factors to Consider When Evaluating a Web-based Instruction Course: A Survey, Web-based Instruction, 1997.

[3] Jac-Woong Kim & Soon-Jeong Hong, Alternative Approach To The Educational Quality Assurance Model For KNOU, Internet.

[4] Quality on the Line: Benchmarks for Success in Internet-Based Distance Education, Prepared by: The institute for Higher Education Policy, http://www.ihep.com/quality.pdf , April 2000.

[5] The Center for Adult Learning and Educational Credentials American Council on Education, Guiding Principles for Distance Learning in a Learning Society, http://www.acenet.edu/.

[6] Xiao Ling Wang (王孝玲), Theory and Technique of Educational Assessment [M], Shanghai Education Pres, 1999.

[7] Jingbing Zhang (张京彬), Shengquan Yu (余胜泉), Kekang He (何克抗), No Quantified Assessment to Net Education [J], China Remote Education, 2000 (10).

[8] Lynette Gillis, <E-Learning Certification Standards>, http://www.astd.org.

Human Perspectives in the Internet Society: Culture, Psychology and Gender, K. Morgan, J. Sanchez, C. A. Brebbia & A Voiskounsky (Editors) © 2004 WIT Press, www.witpress.com, ISBN 1-85312-726-4

Assessment: the Trojan horse of blended learning

R. Harlev
The Q Group PLC, Israel

Abstract

The Quartet Method, a methodology for EFL implemented by The Q Group PLC, is based on core pedagogical principles that underpin a standards-driven, blended language-learning model. The use of multiple delivery channels creates a learning environment whereby skills and competencies are delivered through channels that suit learners best. This blend of delivery channels creates an effective balance in learning and caters to different learning styles.

Assessing the learning achieved through these different channels, however, is not a simple process. Therefore, The Q Group has developed an online grading tool which enables teachers to reflect on the blended Quartet methodology in assessment as well as in learning and teaching. Just as the different learning components that are parts of the courses range from self-paced learning to teacher-monitored learning, and from individual to group learning, and take place in computer-based environments, face-to-face classrooms, and home or workplace environments, so the Quartet Method grading tool allows for input comprehensively reflecting these aspects of learning.

This paper will present the Quartet Method and its grading tool together with their theoretical underpinnings, and provide a sample case of its use.
Keywords: blended learning, assessment, EFL, methodology, teaching, learning.

1 Overview

The Quartet Method is a blended learning methodology developed and implemented by The Q Group PLC in various learning environments in the world for the teaching of English as a Foreign Language (EFL). These learning environments include both corporate and institutional settings. They include environments for young learners as well as environments for young adults

Human Perspectives in the Internet Society: Culture, Psychology and Gender, K. Morgan, J. Sanchez, C. A. Brebbia & A Voiskounsky (Editors) © 2004 WIT Press, www.witpress.com, ISBN 1-85312-726-4

and adults. This paper will describe the Quartet Method and examine issues of assessment of this blended learning in institutional settings, and will show how assessment can be used as a Trojan horse in blended learning environments.

2 Blended learning: a mosaic of delivery channels

2.1 What is blended learning?

Blended learning is not new. Teachers have always used a blend of materials and teaching techniques in their lessons. In a recent teacher development session which I led in Budapest with EFL teachers, I asked the teachers to list all of the delivery methods they use at the moment. They came up with nearly 30 different methods including frontal, lock-step teaching, collaborative project work, pair work, storytelling, use of audio CDs, class discussions, etc. They were able to connect very naturally to the question. So when I suggested that perhaps using various computer-based delivery methods would just be "adding tools to the toolbox" of teaching, rather than negating what they have been doing all along, the comfort level in the room immediately rose.

So what are we referring to when we use the term "blended learning"? Blended learning has been defined in different ways. The term is most often used to describe learning activities that are delivered through a combination of e-learning and more traditional classroom learning delivery channels. Masie (in Rosette [1]) suggests that blended learning, in general, is a mix of two or more different methods of teaching, and that we, as a species, are blended learners by nature. Good practice in EFL teaching reflects this.

So, then, what makes the Quartet Method unique? First of all, the Quartet Method provides materials which allow teachers to blend delivery channels smoothly, incorporating flexible classroom and computer-based components. More importantly, however, the Quartet Method stipulates conditions for the chosen blend. The blend must reflect diverse delivery channels. Most importantly, these delivery channels themselves are chosen to reflect research-based, core pedagogical principles.

2.2 What are the principles of the Quartet Method?

What principles underpin this core? First of all, the Quartet Method is standards-driven. Learners attain standards through the development of skills and strategies, as well as competencies, in the target language. The method integrates standards of what learners will know; i.e., their skills and strategies, with standards of what they will be able to do; i.e., their competencies in the target language. These standards reflect the domains of understanding (reading and listening), speaking (in both interaction and production) and writing.

2.2.1 Delivery channels are informed by pedagogical objectives

Delivery channels are utilised to do what they do best in language teaching and learning. Each of the skills and strategies, as well as their resulting competencies, is taught through the most appropriate delivery channel. Listening comprehension, for example, and strategies for listening (listening for specific

Human Perspectives in the Internet Society: Culture, Psychology and Gender, K. Morgan, J. Sanchez, C. A. Brebbia & A Voiskounsky (Editors) © 2004 WIT Press, www.witpress.com, ISBN 1-85312-726-4

details, listening for main idea, etc.) are easily taught through activities which are computer-based, allowing learners to listen independently and to pace themselves accordingly. Communicative competencies, however, are built through interaction. Although some synchronous applications lend themselves to authentic interaction, these competencies benefit from face to face interaction, where oral language is aided by facial expression, lip patterns and gesture. Meaning is negotiated immediately, with no mechanical interference or delay. The computer, on the other hand, provides authentic opportunities for accessing information through the Internet, as well as providing an environment in which reading comprehension and reading strategies can be practiced. Course books also contribute by providing printed texts which, in a face to face environment, can serve as both a contextual presentation of a new grammar structure, and subsequently, as a springboard for discussion.

2.2.2 All course materials are theme-based and integrated, using appropriate delivery channels for the materials

By providing integrated course units based on a theme, learners are working on the theme from many different aspects at the same time. While they are participating in a forum on the topic of food, viewing online videos on food in various countries, discussing and exchanging recipes in class and presenting a short session on cooking, they are employing and practicing necessary cognitive skills and strategies as they are building competencies. A theme-based integrated curriculum provides learners with new learning material simultaneously from different angles, allowing them to develop confidence in their newly acquired language and generate new uses of the language while building on what they already know.

2.2.3 Teachers' roles are diverse, and reflect the pedagogical underpinnings of the delivery channels

Fitzpatrick and Davies [2] suggest that a paradigm shift in teacher and learner roles is necessary in light of new pedagogical horizons. Traditionally, the role of the teacher was to impart knowledge to learners. Today, they claim, teachers must act more often as guides and mentors. They describe the multiple roles of the teacher as encompassing that of facilitator, integrator, researcher, designer, collaborator, orchestrator, learner and evaluator.

With all of these new roles, teachers are thrust into a need for crucial decision-making. What materials should they use? What delivery channels are the most appropriate? In the Quartet Method, teachers are guided in their choices by the provision of recommended, but flexible unit "maps", displaying suggested blends for a unit. These recommendations are provided to assist teachers entering this frontier of new roles for the first time, but still leave room for the confident, experienced teacher to make choices appropriate to both her teaching style and her learners' diverse learning styles.

2.2.4 Learning is learner-centred and caters to various learning styles

In all classes, learners possess different learning styles and different learning style preferences. A blended model creates a place for visual, auditory and

Human Perspectives in the Internet Society: Culture, Psychology and Gender, K. Morgan, J. Sanchez, C. A. Brebbia & A Voiskounsky (Editors) © 2004 WIT Press, www.witpress.com, ISBN 1-85312-726-4

kinaesthetic learners, providing activities that allow for the different strengths and preferences of the learners.

2.2.5 There is a blend of individual and group learning that is served by diverse delivery channels

Learning occurs both individually and in social groupings. Cognitive learning theory suggests that learners develop schemata (Gagne [3]) which allow them to activate background knowledge and assimilate new learning. This is an individual process. On the other hand, Vygotsky [4] claims that all knowledge is socially constructed through language. This view underpins a need for social interaction in language learning. Therefore, as part of this socio-cognitive blended learning methodology, the Quartet Method prescribes that learning activities must include a variety of activities which fall along the continuum of individual to group learning.

2.2.6 There is a blend of self-paced and teacher-monitored learning that is served by diverse delivery channels

While the teacher is still responsible for enabling successful learning to take place, the paradigm shift in learning has shifted responsibility for the actual learning to the learner. One outcome of this shift is the necessity to allow more self-pacing in the learning process. The teacher as integrator and evaluator must monitor the learning that is going on and be sure that learners are moving in appropriate directions. With the acceptance of individual learning style preferences, however, comes the acceptance that learners learn at different paces. Activities, therefore, must reflect the entire continuum of self-paced to teacher-monitored learning.

3 Assessment: reflecting the blend

3.1 What is the role of assessment in this new paradigm of learning?

Language teachers have always assessed learners. They have used both formative and summative methods of assessment. They have provided ongoing feedback which helps learners to learn more effectively, and have clarified to learners where they stand in relation to both the material they are expected to have learned and to the achievements of the peers. They have used multiple methods of assessment ranging from closed-ended, discrete item assessment, to contextualised, open-ended writing or speaking assignments.

3.2 How does assessment inform learning and teaching?

Generally, assessment is thought of as reflecting learning and teaching, and forming a third side of the triangle of learning, teaching and assessment. Traditionally, we often refer to teaching as informing learning, and learning as informing assessment. By moulding the way we expect teachers to look at assessment, however, we indirectly impact the way teachers teach and the way learners learn. Assessment begins to inform teaching, and in turn, learning.

Human Perspectives in the Internet Society: Culture, Psychology and Gender, K. Morgan, J. Sanchez, C. A. Brebbia & A Voiskounsky (Editors) © 2004 WIT Press, www.witpress.com, ISBN 1-85312-726-4

Assessment has always been the Trojan horse of any education reform. By stipulating what is to be assessed and what methods are to be implemented, learning and teaching inevitably mould themselves to reflect the assessment.

3.3 What elements of language learning should be reflected in assessment?

In language learning, there are many aspects of the learning which can be assessed. According to Anderson and Krathwohl's [5] revision of Bloom's taxonomy, teachers should aim to assess the factual, conceptual, procedural and metacognitive aspects of learning. This is usually done in language teaching through varied types of assessment including tests, presentations, written assignments, projects and performance tasks, and often through overall portfolio assessment. These types of assessment take place in the classroom, the computer room, the learner's home or workplace.

3.4 How does the learning management system (LMS) aid in assessment in most blended learning courses?

The LMS generally assesses aspects of learning that reflect the computer-based components of the course, and that have closed-ended, single answer question-types. The learner's results are often displayed in fancy reports, but no matter what the display, they still represent only part of the learning that has taken place. They do not represent any of the learning that was assessed outside of the computer environment.

So even though the learner can track his learning, the tracking inevitably displays only part of his learning. This skews the appearance of the assessment. In addition to this, one of two things may happen when teachers prepare their final grades for their learners. In the corporate environment, the computer-displayed assessment may become the final assessment of the course, despite face-to-face encounters where additional learning events take place. In school environments, the teacher may not be able to access her learners' records when she needs to prepare end of term grades, and the online assessment component may not be included in the learners' grades.

3.5 How can the LMS be utilized to reflect a blended learning environment?

Teachers do keep records. Some do it in hand-written grade books, some on electronic spreadsheets and some in school-based administrative systems. The Q Group has developed a tool which allows teachers to input their own grades into the LMS of the Quartet computer-based system, and decide upon criteria for grading and weighting of the criteria. This online grading tool both provides support for the Quartet Method's blend of learning, and creates a need for the teacher to truly utilize a blend of assessment methods and tools to reflect her teaching. This tool is the Trojan horse of blended learning!

Human Perspectives in the Internet Society: Culture, Psychology and Gender, K. Morgan, J. Sanchez, C. A. Brebbia & A Voiskounsky (Editors) © 2004 WIT Press, www.witpress.com, ISBN 1-85312-726-4

4 Sample case: assessing the blend in a high school environment

4.1 Iris' class

Dahlia is a high school EFL teacher in a government school. She teaches Quartet courses using the Quartet Method. One of her classes is a class of 32 tenth graders who are in their seventh year of English studies, and are at a low advanced level. They study English five hours a week, two hours in the computer room, and three hours in the classroom. They also have access to computers after school hours. Some have fast Internet connections and can access their online computer-based lessons and assignments from home, and others can visit the computer lab in the school during the afternoon and evening hours.

In the classroom, Dahlia does many communicative tasks with her students that range from semi-authentic role-plays to authentic interaction on group assignments. They work on literature, reading several short stories and poems during the course of the school year. They have a number of writing assignments, some based on the literature they read, and others based on the themes they are working on in class and on the computer. They are required to produce group projects based on authentic performance tasks.

In the computer lab, the students do computer lessons to practice reading and listening comprehension and improve their use of cognitive learning strategies. They participate in discussion forums and do a number of open-ended online tasks and assignments. All of these aspects of learning, both in the classroom and at the computer enable the learners to develop the competencies they need in English.

4.2 Building the blend

At the beginning of the school year, Dahlia must build the grading criteria for her class. She goes to the computer and opens the grading tool in the LMS of the Quartet system. She is provided with a number of templates suggesting a recommended grading blend for the level of EFL she is teaching. One template includes six criteria together with their suggested weights: computer-based lessons, 20%; computer-based achievement tests, 15%; in-class tests, 15%; writing assignments, 20%; class work, 20%; homework, 10%.

Dahlia had used this suggested template during the previous school year, but this year feels confident enough with the tool to create a blend that she believes will work for her students in reflecting the many faceted aspects of learning in the course. Dahlia agrees with the first four criteria suggested, but would like to include projects and communicative tasks as well. She doesn't see class work and homework as activities in and of themselves, but as settings in which her students do their writing assignments, their projects, or in some cases, their computer-based lessons and activities.

Once Dahlia inputs her criteria and her weighting for each criteria, each time her class does an assessed assignment, she will be able to use the online grade book to input her students' grades. The LMS will automatically calculate the

Human Perspectives in the Internet Society: Culture, Psychology and Gender, K. Morgan, J. Sanchez, C. A. Brebbia & A Voiskounsky (Editors) © 2004 WIT Press, www.witpress.com, ISBN 1-85312-726-4

weighted grades of her students at any point that they decide to check their records when they enter the LMS.

4.3 The Trojan horse of blended learning: the washback effect of assessment on teaching and learning

Changing the way Dahlia related to assessment of her students had a washback effect (Cheng [6]) (sometimes called backwash effect (Hughes [7]) on her teaching and, in turn, on her students' learning. She was forced to think at the beginning of her course about how she wanted her students' to be assessed. This required her to consider in advance all of the aspects of learning that would go during the course that she was preparing to teach. In order to decide on the relative weights of these aspects, she had to weigh their effect on learning and the percentage of time she and her students would spend working on them. Making these decisions in advance impacted on her teaching. She found herself organizing her lessons to reflect the blend she had decided upon. She analysed her teaching in greater depth than in the past, and reflected upon her choices. She was less tempted to make intuitive decisions about students' grades, and when student grades did not reflect her expectations, she was more apt to analyse the reasons why.

An additional benefit of the washback effect of using this tool is that Dahlia's students knew what their grades would be based on from the beginning of the course. Although this may be common practice in tertiary level courses, it is not so in most high schools. Including students in what their grades are based on allows them to be full partners in their learning, taking responsibility where in the past they may have been quick to blame their teacher. Knowing what aspects of their learning are going to be assessed also allows students to make informed choices about their learning.

5 Conclusion

In a blended learning methodology, assessment must reflect the blend just as teaching and learning do. By providing a tool inherent to the methodology, the Quartet Method encourages teachers to be more reflective about their teaching, to think about their assessment choices in advance and to implement assessment that is consistent with teaching and learning.

References

[1] Masie, E., Blended Learning: The Magic is in the Mix. In Rossett, A. (ed). *The ASTD E-Learning Handbook*. McGraw-Hill: New York, 2002.

[2] Fitzpatrick, A. & Davies, G., (eds). The Impact of Information and Communications Technologies on the Teaching of Foreign Languages and on the Role of Teachers of Foreign Languages: a report commissioned by the Directorate General of Education and Culture of the European Commission. www.icc-europe.com/ICT_in_FLT_Final_report_Jan2003/ICT_in_FLT_in_Europe.pdf

Human Perspectives in the Internet Society: Culture, Psychology and Gender, K. Morgan, J. Sanchez, C. A. Brebbia & A Voiskounsky (Editors) © 2004 WIT Press, www.witpress.com, ISBN 1-85312-726-4

[3] Gagne, R. M., Instructional technology: The research field. *Journal of Instructional Development*, 8(3), pp. 7 – 14, 1986.

[4] Vygotsky, L. *Mind in society: The development of higher psychological processes* (M. Cole, V. John-Steiner, S. Scribner & E. Souberman, Eds and Trans.). Harvard University Press: Cambridge, MA, 1978.

[5] Anderson, L.W., & Krathwohl, D.R., *A taxonomy for learning, teaching, and assessing: A revision of Bloom's taxonomy of educational objectives.* Longman: New York, 2001.

[6] Cheng, L., Changing assessment: washback on teacher perceptions and actions. *Teaching and Teacher Education*, 15, 253-271, 1999.

[7] Hughes, A., Testing for Language Teachers. Cambridge University Press: Cambridge, 1989.

Human Perspectives in the Internet Society: Culture, Psychology and Gender, K. Morgan, J. Sanchez, C. A. Brebbia & A Voiskounsky (Editors) © 2004 WIT Press, www.witpress.com, ISBN 1-85312-726-4

Computer-assisted vs. traditional homework: results of a pilot research project

L. Hassler, L. Dennis, H. Ng, C. Johnson, D. Ossont,
G. Ogawa & C. Nahmias
Florida State University, USA

Abstract

The CAPA pilot research project tested the effectiveness of computer-assisted homework assignments as a complement to teacher led instruction in high school physics at three suburban high schools in Florida during the first nine-week grading period of the semester beginning in January 2004. The study involved three physics teachers (one per school), nine high school physics classes populated by 219 students. The project consisted of a randomized experimental design, with CAPA homework assignments as the treatment and traditional homework assignments (on paper and hand-graded) as the control. Classes of students were randomly assigned to treatment and control groups. The effectiveness of CAPA homework compared with traditional homework was assessed through (1) pre- and post-test gains on physics test items accepted by the physics education research community, (2) responses to a student satisfaction survey and (3) differences in accuracy between initial responses and final responses for the treatment group. Pre- and post-test results for students at each of the three sites indicated there were no significant differences between the treatment and control groups. Further, student responses to a satisfaction survey indicated that students preferred more traditional homework assignments. For students using CAPA at each of the three sites, accuracy of responses improved significantly from the first attempt to the final attempt. The improved performance is attributed to the immediate feedback provided to students regarding the accuracy of their initial answers. Key insights gleaned from the pilot research project will improve the quality of the yearlong research project planned for the 2004-2005 school year.
Keywords: computer-assisted instruction, CAPA, immediate feedback, high school physics instruction, homework.

Human Perspectives in the Internet Society: Culture, Psychology and Gender, K. Morgan, J. Sanchez, C. A. Brebbia & A Voiskounsky (Editors) © 2004 WIT Press, www.witpress.com, ISBN 1-85312-726-4

1 Introduction

During the last decade, significant efforts have been undertaken to reform science instruction through web-based approaches. One such effort is CAPA (Computerized-Assisted Personalized Approach) developed at Michigan State University (see http://capa4.lite.msu.edu/homepage[cej3]. This web-based homework system offers the following features:

- Students receive individualized assignments, made possible through randomization of certain elements necessary to reach a solution.
- Students receive immediate and accurate *corrective* feedback; that is, students are informed about whether or not their submission was accurate.
- Instructors can set the number of times a student can attempt to get the right answer; this feature encourages students to fix their own mistakes and may cause them to spend more time working on physics assignments.
- Students have access to both quantitative and qualitative problems.
- Students can access the homework site from any computer via the Internet, allowing them to submit work and receive immediate feedback on their homework.
- Instructors can access an extensive library of pre-programmed and reliable problems, thereby enabling them to devise quality homework assignments with a minimum of preparation; instructors can also devise their own problems for the system.
- The web-based system grades assignments and records homework scores, thereby freeing instructors to spend more time planning instruction and offering one-on-one help to students during office hours [1].

To date, research on the effectiveness of CAPA has focused on the university level. However, CAPA has the potential to be a valuable instructional tool in grades K-12, particularly in science and mathematics. The purpose of this pilot project is to begin research at the secondary level, specifically in high school physics instruction, to determine whether this instructional tool can boost student achievement.

Several pedagogical innovations in physics have been developed in an attempt to facilitate conceptual understanding in large physics courses. For example, Mazur's [2] ConcepTests allow the instructor to integrate his or her lecture with multiple-choice questions that allow students to reflect on their understanding of concepts just covered by the instructor. McDermott, Schaffer, and the Physics Education Group at the University of Washington-Seattle [3] use Tutorials, a collaborative series of activities that require students to predict what will happen before observing a phenomena and then explain what they actually observed using appropriate physics concepts. Socratic Dialog Inducing Labs [4] revamp the traditional laboratory model in physics instruction by following a method similar to the one described for Tutorials and requiring occasional experiments to help students test the validity of their predictions. Micro-

Human Perspectives in the Internet Society: Culture, Psychology and Gender, K. Morgan, J. Sanchez, C. A. Brebbia & A Voiskounsky (Editors) © 2004 WIT Press, www.witpress.com, ISBN 1-85312-726-4

computer based laboratories [5] allow students to see the effects of their alterations to experimental conditions without having to spend time collecting and graphing data.

While lecture, recitation, and laboratory work are all integral aspects of the physics learning experience, much of a student's physics learning relies on homework problems assigned out of class, usually from the back of their textbook, which students are required to solve independently. The prevailing ideology of the physics community is that 1) homework is an essential part of physics instruction and 2) by practicing problem solving, students will become better problem-solvers. Therefore, efforts to improve homework instructional strategies would seem to be a worthy addition to the innovations in classroom and laboratory instruction described earlier. CAPA's developers report overall success with their use of the system, claiming that student learning is enhanced by providing them with immediate, accurate feedback, and by promoting understanding versus the "plug-and-chug" method of problem solving most often employed by introductory physics students attempting to solve for an unknown variable [6, 7, 8]. What's more, Morrisey et al. [9] have found that the vast majority of students report spending more time on CAPA assignments than on traditional paper-and-pencil assignments.

The characteristics of the CAPA system are consistent with the guidelines for effective high school physics instruction developed by the National Academy of Science [10], particularly in the area of diagnosing student understanding of concepts. According to the Panel for Physics, "Effective teachers are sophisticated diagnosticians of student knowledge, reasoning, and participation" (p. 450), and their collection and analysis of student progress should be ongoing and rely on a variety of sources. The Panel also finds that "coming to understand a concept requires multiple encounters in multiple contexts," and to that end, they recommend several university-developed, computer-based programs that provide student with opportunities to develop conceptual understanding of physics principles. According to the Panel, "it is reasonable to expect that results from [research on these pedagogical methods in] introductory college-level courses should generally apply [to high school physics instruction] (p.457).

The research on Computer-Assisted Instruction (CAI) also points to the potential for CAPA to improve student achievement in physics at the secondary level. CAI "most often refers to drill-and-practice, tutorial, or simulation activities offered either by themselves or as supplements to traditional, teacher-directed instruction" [11]. In a meta-analysis of 42 studies, Bangert-Drowns et al. [12] found that computer-assisted instruction had very beneficial effects on student achievement in secondary schools. However, according to Cotton [11], the best-supported finding in the research literature is that the use of CAI as a *supplement* to traditional teacher-directed instruction produces achievement effects superior to those obtained with traditional instruction *alone*. The results of research comparing the effects of CAI alone with those produced by conventional instruction alone [13], however, are too mixed to support any firm conclusions. Dalton and Hanafin [14] echo this conclusion in their own study, finding that "while both traditional and computer-based delivery systems have

Human Perspectives in the Internet Society: Culture, Psychology and Gender, K. Morgan, J. Sanchez, C. A. Brebbia & A Voiskounsky (Editors) © 2004 WIT Press, www.witpress.com, ISBN 1-85312-726-4

valuable roles in supporting instruction, they are of greatest value when complementing one another" (p.32). The potential for CAPA to boost student achievement in physics at the secondary level, then, seems to lie in the ability of the instructor to successfully integrate the technology into his or her existing physics curriculum.

More recent studies [15] have taken a closer look at feedback and have concluded that while, on average, feedback interventions enhance performance, and in over 33% of the studies analyzed, the effects of feedback were negative. Ilgen and Davis [16] have found that the personality type of the person receiving the feedback has a significant effect on feedback success. Still others have found that limiting feedback to only "outcome" feedback (given on correctness of the answer versus the process) may have a negative impact on learning because the student adopts a trial-and-error approach to arriving at an answer, and thereby shifts his or her focus to getting the right response rather than knowing *why* the response is correct or not. Another relevant feature to the success of feedback is timing. In general, the closer that feedback follows the performance task, the more effective it will be [17], and the more frequent the feedback, the better. While CAPA promises some obvious advantages with regard to providing consistent and timely feedback to students, instructors will have to remain attuned to the impact of that feedback on the learning of individual students with regard to 1) their perceptions about the feedback (i.e., whether they see it as positive or negative) and 2) their approaches to problem-solving based on the feedback (i.e., whether or not they sacrifice process to product).

In summary, prior research into the effectiveness of CAPA for introductory physics instruction at the university level suggests that it holds significant potential for enhancing physics instruction at the secondary level. Furthermore, research on CAI in general suggests that a computer-assisted homework system would have a positive impact on student performance, particularly in science. All of the research and recommendations, however, predicate these successes on the careful administration of the technology, including 1) the integration of the computer-assisted instruction with solid teacher-directed instruction, 2) the ability of the instructor to interpret data and monitor student progress using the program, and 3) the careful monitoring of student responses to the technology (i.e., attitudes and impact on problem-solving and conceptual understanding).

2 Method

In preparation for a yearlong study during the 2004-2005 school year, a CAPA pilot research project was designed to provide initial insights regarding the effectiveness of computer-assisted homework assignments as a complement to teacher-led instruction in high school physics.

2.1 Participants

The pilot research project participants were 218 high school students from nine general and honors physics classes taught by three physics teachers at three

Human Perspectives in the Internet Society: Culture, Psychology and Gender, K. Morgan, J. Sanchez, C. A. Brebbia & A Voiskounsky (Editors) © 2004 WIT Press, www.witpress.com, ISBN 1-85312-726-4

separate schools. Of these students, 98% were juniors and seniors (11th and 12th graders, respectively); 51% male were, 49% female. Three teachers, two male and one female, participated in two training sessions, for a total of four hours, prior to implementation of the project. Consent letters describing the project were sent to parents of all enrolled students. All but four forms were signed by both parent and student, and returned, indicating permission for participation. These four students were eliminated from the study. The three participating high schools were located in Leon County, a semi-urban area of north Florida.

2.2 Research design and procedure

The pilot project employed a randomized experimental design, with LON-CAPA as the treatment and traditional homework (written and hand-graded) as the control. For each teacher, physics classes were randomly assigned to treatment and control groups by the flip of a coin. The nine classes were blocked by type of class (honors versus general) within teacher. Five were randomly assigned to the treatment group (CAPA homework) while four classes were assigned to the control condition (traditional homework). There were a total of 125 participants in the treatment classes and 93 in the control classes.

Each teacher covered a different unit of physics instruction during the pilot research project: Force and Motion, Heat and Temperature, or Energy and Momentum, thereby limiting aspects of the study to within teacher comparisons. Because teachers and schools were not required to follow a uniform schedule or sequence of instruction, a common unit taught by all 3 teachers could not be identified, particularly for a pilot study that began in the middle of the school year (the beginning of the second semester).

For classes in the treatment group, teachers used CAPA for homework assignments. Students without access to computers at home were given homework assignments on paper and the opportunity to enter their responses into the computer at school. For classes in the control group, teachers were instructed to give students the same assignments on paper and grade them by hand.

Teachers selected problems for homework assignments from existing banks of CAPA items, including a bank developed collaboratively by teachers and the FSU Office of Distributed and Distance Learning. As necessary, problems were added during the course of this pilot project to meet the instructional needs of students involved in the project.

2.3 Data collection and analysis

Planned data collection for the pilot research project included:

1. Student performance on physics pre- and post-tests;
2. Student homework completion rate;
3. Student homework accuracy (percent of items correct); and
4. Post-test only student questionnaire regarding the value of homework, computer access and, for treatment students only, their evaluation of CAPA as a learning tool.

As the data collection and analysis phase of the project began, procedural flaws became apparent. At all three schools, the study was shortened from the

Human Perspectives in the Internet Society: Culture, Psychology and Gender, K. Morgan, J. Sanchez, C. A. Brebbia & A Voiskounsky (Editors) © 2004 WIT Press, www.witpress.com, ISBN 1-85312-726-4

original nine-week duration to approximately two weeks to accommodate limited availability of pre- and post-tests for the concepts teachers planned to cover. Students in the treatment groups were not trained in the use of CAPA until after the pilot research project was implemented. One teacher provided a single homework assignment while the other teachers provided two or three. A number of students in both the treatment and control groups chose not to attempt selected problems on the homework assignments while some selected not to attempt the assignment at allIn at least one case, students in the treatment and control groups were assigned different problems.

Limited availability of comparable data for treatment and control groups (diminished further by different topics between schools) and inconsistent application of the treatment raised efficacy issues and resulted in narrowing the analysis of data collected. Questions related to homework completion rates (2) and homework accuracy (3) for treatment vs. control groups were eliminated because the assignments provided to the two groups varied to some extent.

3 Results

While procedural problems limited the scope of data analysis, it was possible to examine several aspects of the effectiveness of computer-assisted homework assignments. Each class in the study took a pre-test in the topics to be covered for that school. The teacher at School A taught motion and force, the teacher at School B taught energy and momentum and the teacher at School C taught thermodynamics. A comparison of the mean of the pre-test scores between the treatment and control groups for each school varied slightly. These differences between the CAPA and traditional homework groups were not significantly different for School A ($t= .137$, $p > .01$), School B ($t= -1.672$, $p >.01$) or School C ($t= -.492$, $p>.01$). In other words, there were no significant differences between the control and treatments groups for each school at the beginning of the study.

A post-test was conducted at the conclusion of instruction at each of the sites. While a comparison of the mean of the post-test scores between the treatment and control groups for each school varied slightly, the differences between the CAPA and traditional homework groups were not significant for School A ($t= 2.482$, $p > .01$), School B ($t= -.336$, $p >.01$) or School C ($t= -2.149$, $p>.01$).

For the treatment group only, students' initial performance on specific problems was compared to their performance after they were allowed multiple tries to succeed on initially missed assigned problems. Table 1 details the results.

The analysis included 125 high school students from three high schools (A, B, and C) who used CAPA during the pilot research project. With an alpha level of .01, there was a significant difference from the initial score to the final score at schools A, B, and C ($\underline{t}$ = 5.361, $\underline{df}$ = 24, $\underline{p}$(two-tailed) = .01; $\underline{t}$ = 12.436, $\underline{df}$ = 73, $\underline{p}$(two-tailed) = .01; $\underline{t}$ = 5.667, $\underline{df}$ = 25, $\underline{p}$(two-tailed) = .01, respectively). The mean improvement scores were 1.520 (SD = 1.418), 4.660 (SD = 3.216), and 2.500 (SD = 2.249), respectively.

Human Perspectives in the Internet Society: Culture, Psychology and Gender, K. Morgan, J. Sanchez, C. A. Brebbia & A Voiskounsky (Editors) © 2004 WIT Press, www.witpress.com, ISBN 1-85312-726-4

Table 1: Mean difference of student performance before and after CAPA homework.

School	N	Mean	Standard Deviation	99% Confidence Interval of the Difference		t	df	p
				Lower	Upper			
A	25	1.520	1.418	.935	2.105	5.361	24	.01
B	74	4.650	3.216	3.904	5.394	12.436	73	.01
C	26	2.500	2.249	1.591	3.409	5.667	25	.01

Table 2: Student Questionnaire: Treatment and Control Group Responses to Items 1-5.

Item	Responses				N
	SA	A	D	SD	
1. The homework assignments helped me learn to solve physics problems.					
Treatment	.9%	47.2%	39.6%	12.3%	106
Control	6.0%	59.5%	31.0%	3.6%	84
2. The homework assignments improved my understanding of physics concepts.					
Treatment	1.9%	40.0%	44.8%	13.3%	105
Control	2.4%	48.8%	40.5%	8.3%	84
3. The homework assignments helped me improve my performance on physics tests.					
Treatment	2.8%	41.5%	47.2%	8.5%	106
Control	8.3%	51.2%	33.3%	7.1%	84
4. The homework assignments have made me more confident in my ability to do physics.					
Treatment	1.9%	25.5%	62.3%	10.4%	106
Control	2.4%	41.7%	48.8%	7.1%	84
5. The homework assignments have increased my enthusiasm for learning physics.					
Treatment	1.9%	16.8%	53.3%	28.0%	107
Control	2.4%	23.8%	56.0%	17.9%	84

For this table: SA = Strongly Agree, A = Agree, D = Disagree, SD = Strongly Disagree.

Human Perspectives in the Internet Society: Culture, Psychology and Gender, K. Morgan, J. Sanchez, C. A. Brebbia & A Voiskounsky (Editors) © 2004 WIT Press, www.witpress.com, ISBN 1-85312-726-4

As indicated in Table 2, student responses to the satisfaction survey indicated that, overall, students in the control group were more satisfied (strongly agree and agree) with the value of their homework assignments than students in the treatment group. The majority of students in both groups, as detailed in Table 3, complete their homework at school. Students in both groups, however, reported better access to a computer at home as well as a relatively infrequent use of computers at school to complete class work or assignments (see Table 4).

Table 3: Student questionnaire: treatment and control group responses to item 6.

Item	At home	At school	At another Location	N
6. I usually do my homework assignments	18%	63%	19%	190

Table 4: Student questionnaire: treatment and control group responses to items 7-9.

Item	Response				N
	Always	Most of the time	Sometimes	Never	
7. When I need a computer at school, one is available					
Treatment	31.2%	50.5%	17.4%	.9%	109
Control	17.9%	53.6%	23.8%	4.8%	84
8. There is a computer at my home that I can use to do class work or assignments					
Treatment	75.2%	15.6%	9.2%	0%	109
Control	78.6%	8.3%	8.3%	4.8%	84
	Very Often	Often	Sometime	Never	N
9. On average, I use a computer at school to do class work or assignments.					
Treatment	5.5%	10.1%	51.4%	33.0%	109
Control	6.0%	8.3%	44.0%	41.7%	84

A number of questions on the satisfaction survey were given only to students in the treatment group. The responses to these questions indicated that most of the students did not like CAPA and did not want to continue using CAPA (see Tables 5 and 6). As detailed in Table 7, while most students did not think using a computer to do their homework assignment was helpful, the

Human Perspectives in the Internet Society: Culture, Psychology and Gender, K. Morgan, J. Sanchez, C. A. Brebbia & A Voiskounsky (Editors) © 2004 WIT Press, www.witpress.com, ISBN 1-85312-726-4

majority of respondents indicated that several features unique to CAPA were very helpful. These included multiple tries to solve problems, getting immediate feedback and not being penalized for a wrong answer.

Table 5: Student questionnaire: treatment only, items 10-13.

	Responses				
Item	SA	A	D	SD	N
10. I liked using CAPA to do my homework assignments	8%	28%	38%	25%	106
11. CAPA helped me learn physics.	2%	34%	50%	14%	104
12. My physics teacher should continue to use CAPA	7%	23%	38%	31%	107
13. CAPA is easy to use	10%	52%	26%	15%	196

Table 6: Student questionnaire: treatment only, Item 14.

Item	CAPA homework	Written homework graded by my teacher	No preference	N
14. I would prefer to have…	18%	63%	19%	106

Table 7: Student questionnaire: treatment only, items 15-18.

Item	Very Helpful	Somewhat Helpful	Not very Helpful	Not at All Helpful	N
15. Doing my homework on a computer is	9%	39%	41%	11%	106
16. Having multiple tries to solve problems is	59%	36%	3%	3%	107
17. Getting immediate feedback on whether my answers are correct is	64%	29%	5%	2%	107
18. Not being penalized for wrong answers is	68%	27%	3%	2%	107

4 Discussion

When mean scores on the pre-test and post-test were compared, there were no significant differences between the performance of students who used CAPA and the performance of those who completed traditional homework assignments. Further study is required to determine the extent to which the procedural concerns influenced this finding. It is suspected that the shortened duration of the study and the students' lack familiarity with the software prior to implementation affected the results. Based on a previous study [14], the teacher's relative lack of experience in integrating CAPA into the existing curriculum may also have influenced these results.

When within student comparisons were made for students using CAPA, a notable result related to its impact on student performance was found. At each of the three sites, the accuracy of students' responses improved significantly from the first attempt to the final attempt. The improved performance is attributed to the immediate feedback provided to students regarding the accuracy of their initial answers. In some cases, students who provided incorrect answers were also provided hints on how to correctly solve the problem. In general, the feedback loop for traditional homework assignments varies greatly across assignments and teachers. The most immediate feedback would result when homework is collected and graded during the class period following the assignment due date. The feedback would be delayed if the teacher collected homework to be graded at a later time. Given an average class size of twenty-five, with five classes per day, teachers would be required to grade 125 problem sets or assignments to provide feedback on the accuracy of students' responses. In some cases, however, traditional homework assignments are collected but not graded. Students may or may not receive credit for completing these assignments. In still other cases, homework assignments ate not collected and students receive no feedback. In the last two scenarios, students do not receive feedback on the understanding of concepts taught until they receive feedback on graded tests.

Responses to the student satisfaction survey indicated that the majority of students were most satisfied with the value of traditional homework and that students who used CAPA preferred traditional homework assignments. These finding are not surprising given students' limited exposure to and experience with CAPA. However, it is important to note that most of the students who used CAPA were very positive about some of its features, such as immediate feedback and multiple trials without penalties for incorrect answers. Responses to the survey also indicate that while students do the majority of their homework at school, they often do not use a computer and may, at times, not have ready access.

Overall, the CAPA pilot research project provided a number of critical insights that will greatly enhance the quality of the study planned for the 2004-2005 school year. High school physics teachers will be provided opportunities to provide input much earlier in the planning process to address the concerns noted above. Teacher experience in using CAPA as an instructional tool this year should increase the likelihood that they will fully integrate CAPA in their physics curriculum. In that the study will span a full year, the impact of teaching the physics topics in various sequences will be eliminated. Finally, valid and reliable pre- and post-tests for each of the topics to be covered can be identified or developed, if needed.

Human Perspectives in the Internet Society: Culture, Psychology and Gender, K. Morgan, J. Sanchez, C. A. Brebbia & A Voiskounsky (Editors) © 2004 WIT Press, www.witpress.com, ISBN 1-85312-726-4

References

[1] Pascarella, A.M., CAPA (Computer-Assisted Personalized Assignments) in a large university setting, *Dissertation Abstracts International,* **63**, p. 2872, 2002.

[2] Mazur, E., *Peer Instruction: A Users Manual*, Prentice Hall: Upper Saddle River, New Jersey, 1997.

[3] McDermott, L.C., Shaffer, P.S. & the Physics Education Group at the University of Washington-Seattle. *Tutorials in Introductory Physics.* Prentice Hall: Upper Saddle River, New Jersey, 2002.

[4] Hake, R., Socratic Pedagogy in the Introductory Physics Laboratory. *The Physics Teacher*, **30**, pp. 546–552, 1992.

[5] Thornton, R.K., & Sokoloff, D.R., Assessing student learning of Newton's laws: The Force and Motion Conceptual Evaluation and the evaluation of active learning laboratory and lecture curricula. *American Journal of Physics,* **66(4)**, pp. 338-352, 1998.

[6] Kashy, E., Sherrill, B.M., Tsai, I., Weinshank, D., Englemann, M., & Morrissey. D.J., CAPA – An integrated computer-assisted personalized assignment system. *American Journal of Physics*, **61(12)**, pp. 1124–1130, 1993.

[7] Kashy, E., Morrissey, D.J., Tsai, I., & Wolfe, S.L., *An Introduction to CAPA: A Versatile Tool for Science Education.* Michigan State University: East Lansing, Michigan, http://capa4.lite.msu.edu/homepage

[8] Kashy, E., Thoennessen, M., Tsai, Y., Davis, N.E., & Wolfe, S.L., Using networked tools to promote student success in large classes. *Journal of Engineering Education*, **87**, pp. 385–390, 1998.

[9] Morrisey, D.J., Kashy, E., & Tsai, I., Using computer-assisted personalized assignments for freshman chemistry. *Journal of Chemical Education*, **72(2)**, pp. 141–146, 1995.

[10] Committee on Programs for Advanced Study of Mathematics and Science in American High Schools, *Learning and Understanding: Improving Advanced Study of Mathematics and Science in U.S. High Schools.* National Academies Press: Washington, DC.

[11] Cotton, K., *Computer-Assisted Instruction.* Northwest Regional Educational Laboratory: Portland, Oregon.

[12] Bangert-Drowns, R.L., Kulik, J.A., & Kulik, C.E., Effectiveness of computer-based education in secondary schools. *Journal of Computer-Based Instruction*, **12(3)**, pp. 59-68, 1985.

[13] Capper, J. & Copple, C., *Computer Use in Education: Research Review and Instructional Implications.* Center for Research into Practice: Washington, DC, 1985.

[14] Dalton, D.W. & Hannafin, M.J., The effects of computer-assisted and traditional mastery methods on computation accuracy and attitudes. *Journal of Educational Research*, **82(1)**, pp. 27-33, 1988.

Human Perspectives in the Internet Society: Culture, Psychology and Gender, K. Morgan, J. Sanchez, C. A. Brebbia & A Voiskounsky (Editors) © 2004 WIT Press, www.witpress.com, ISBN 1-85312-726-4

[15] Kluger, A.N., & DeNisi, A., The effects of feedback interventions on performance: A historical review, a meta-analysis, and a preliminary feedback intervention theory. *Psychology Bulletin*, **119(2)**, pp. 254–284, 996.
[16] Ilgen, D., & Davis, C., Bearing bad news: Reactions to negative feedback. A*pplied Psychology: An International Review*, **49(3)**, pp. 550–565, 2000.
[17] Ilgen, D.R., Fisher, C.D., & Taylor, M.S., Consequences of individual feedback on behavior in organizations. *Journal of Applied Psychology*, **64(4),** pp. 349–371, 1979.

Human Perspectives in the Internet Society: Culture, Psychology and Gender, K. Morgan, J. Sanchez, C. A. Brebbia & A Voiskounsky (Editors) © 2004 WIT Press, www.witpress.com, ISBN 1-85312-726-4

Factors influencing the effectiveness of a web-based learning environment: An assessment from the Malaysia perspective

W.-C. Poon[1], K. L.-T. Low[2] & D. G.-F. Yong[1]
[1]*Faculty of Management, Multimedia University, Malaysia*
[2]*School of Business, Monash University Malaysia, Malaysia*

Abstract

The advancement of computer technology has converged to form a unique revolutionary web-based learning (WBL) and instructional delivery flexibility system methodology. The advent of online technology extends the metaphor for changes in education. Virtual interactive and collaborative learning is the most common mode of transferring knowledge that has expanded exponentially in Malaysia over the last decade into a borderless educational arena. In this vein, this study analyses the effectiveness of WBL by retrospectively assessing the perceptions of various aspects of WBL. Students participating in various courses at eight universities in Malaysia that have been practicing WBL are surveyed. The study indicates that students' behaviour and lecturers' characteristic, interactive application, technology or system, and institutional factors are the five main factors influencing the effectiveness of WBL process. Hybrid WBL is more suitable to be implemented in order to achieve a higher level of effectiveness. Hence, time is needed for us to adapt the changes of the transmission paradigm from the conventional learning to WBL.
Keywords: Web-based learning, effectiveness, personal characteristics, interactive implication.

1 Introduction

Web based learning (WBL) refers to electronic learning (e-learning). E-learning is any form of virtual classroom learning that utilizes a network for delivery, interaction or facilitation [6]. Apart from that, e-learning offers other opportunities and flexibility such as convenience and self-paced learning,

Human Perspectives in the Internet Society: Culture, Psychology and Gender, K. Morgan, J. Sanchez, C. A. Brebbia & A Voiskounsky (Editors) © 2004 WIT Press, www.witpress.com, ISBN 1-85312-726-4

according to their personal schedules. E-learning in Malaysia started with the external degree programs offered by established universities in United Kingdom. This was followed by off-campus programmes that were offered by University Sains Malaysia (USM). The mode of delivery was on print-based because of the absence of the Internet and most of the tuition was conducted via face-to-face session. Reasons for the lack of enthusiasm in WBL during 1980s were firstly due to the low Internet penetration accessibility in Malaysia. Secondly, the attitude of the learners that deemed face to face conventional learning as a mean of building confidence in independent studies. However, during the 1990s, growing awareness of lifelong learning enhances an increasing demand for higher education services and brought about an alternative revolutionary educational environment consequential from the shortage of recruitment in the public universities particular popular among emerging working adults.

Not many relevant researches have been conducted on this area in Malaysia. Therefore, this area of WBL turns out to become an area of interest worthy of our in-depth research. This paper identified the factors influencing the effectiveness of e-learning in Malaysia via the usage of the existing virtual mediated system.

2 Literature review

Three main critical success factors that affect the effectiveness of online learning are technology, instructors' characteristics and students' characteristic [11, 16]. They suggest that students who are lack of necessary basic skills and self-discipline do better in a traditional delivery mode. Besides, Webster and Hackley [17] suggest that student involvement and participation, cognitive engagement, technology self-efficacy (capability to interact with given technology) are part of the successful influential factors of effective WBL. Students who have higher self-efficacy set higher performance goals compare to their peers with lower self-efficacy. Apart from this, students' perceptions of having positive attitude towards e-learning will enhance learning effective. Charp [4] finds that students' characteristic such as active listening and the ability to work independently in the absence of a live instructor become crucial for success. Self-motivation affects the success on WBL for both the learners and programs [15].

Besides, technical support and technological advancement are among the major contributors to the effectiveness of the WBL system. From the technical perspective, the servers and network connection need to be embedded to ensure upload ability, as well as to ascertain accessibility of the learning material are running smoothly in the process. Chang [3] finds out that despite the overall functional framework of WBL portfolio is set up, the WBL portfolio system has not incorporated a complete mechanism for assessment/grading features in auto-management manner, such as browsing record analysis, student assessment, tutors assessment, and peer assessment mechanism. Using electronic sources as a medium enable students' remote accessibility in both asynchronous and real-time modes. Stable server and broad bandwidth is the major key to judge the delivery

Human Perspectives in the Internet Society: Culture, Psychology and Gender, K. Morgan, J. Sanchez, C. A. Brebbia & A Voiskounsky (Editors) © 2004 WIT Press, www.witpress.com, ISBN 1-85312-726-4

efficiency in WBL system. Institutions need broader bandwidth; but confront with high cost of the network systems. On the other hand, studies show that e-learning is an economical and cost-effective mode of instructional delivery [2, 8]. The reason is any additional student's enrol will only incur lower marginal cost.

The availability of interactive application is essential in virtual learning to enhance the communication process. Mason and Weller [12] argue that an online group work activity improves interactive process. More interaction makes learning more interesting to the students [10]. The purpose of communicating online is to sustain the build-up of intellectual discourse and capitalize on distributed knowledge. Meanwhile, Alias and Hussin [1] find that e-learning activities are useful in writing course where students prefer email as a way to stimulate their thinking in the composing process. Apart from that, Hong *et al.* [9] study on University Malaysia Sarawak designates that asynchronous discussion provides a means to exchange view in the virtual learning-teaching process, and for the instructors to monitor the learning process of students. Whilst, Embi *et al.* [7] conduct a survey on National University of Malaysia and find that the respondents favour positively on the set up of E-Group as a tool for virtual communication between lecturers and students.

Also, institutional factor affects the learning effectiveness. Among the issues confronting institutions factor are institutional structure/facilities, which consist of copyright issues, accreditation system, technology, and the availability of virtual digital library. Copyright issues could affect the quality and performance of distance education [13]. Meanwhile, accreditation of the program shows prestige and recognition of the degree. On the other hand, Parker [14] agrees that a well-designed WBL course should include feedback from students as well as experts, and links online resources to other pertinent information.

From the instructor's perspective, to make the success of online facilitation, the facilitator needs to understand the online learners' psyche. Instructor needs to spend time in planning and ensure learners are actively engage in the learning process. A study by Webster and Hackley [17] suggest that three instructors' characteristics that influence learning outcomes are attitude towards technology, teaching style and control of the technology. In addition, Collis [5] strongly agrees that immediate response to the student email or fax questions is important to yield high level of interactivity.

3 Method

Anonymous questionnaires were administered to a total of 500 students randomly who have currently enrolled in at least one internet courses in any of the eight Malaysia universities that have experimenting WBL, namely UNITAR, UNITEN, UPM, UKM, UM, USM, UNIMAS and MMU. The questionnaire set was sent via postage, and e-mail. Section I embraces of questions about demographic characteristics and section II comprises of questions about the learning experience of the respondents. The response rate was 57.4% (287).

Human Perspectives in the Internet Society: Culture, Psychology and Gender, K. Morgan, J. Sanchez, C. A. Brebbia & A Voiskounsky (Editors) © 2004 WIT Press, www.witpress.com, ISBN 1-85312-726-4

Among those, 248 of the respondents are usable with most items adequately responded for analysis, which in turn were finally analyzed.

Respondents are asked to indicate the level of agreement based on Likert scale with '1' indicating strongly disagrees and '4' indicating strongly agree. We hypothesize that in building e-learning system, the effectiveness of WBL delivery courses in local universities would be captured in five factors as survey instrument, namely instructor characteristics, students' behaviour, interactive applications, the effectiveness of technology, and institutional factor.

4 Findings

There are a total of 248 (49.6%) usable surveys. 58.5% are female and 41.5% are male among the respondents. Majority of the students are in the range of 25-29 years of age (42%), 58% are single and 64% have 3-4 children. The survey reports that 67% of those participants are full time employed and 24% are part-time employed, 5% are self-employed, and others are not employed. The majorities (95.5%) of the learners are able to access internet and the learning place is confined to the home or workplace. Almost 30% of respondents do not interact at all with the instructor per week; whilst 60% interact at least once to twice weekly with peers. The relationships between the demographic variables in relation to the effectiveness of learning are tested with one-way analysis of variance (ANOVA). The results show that marital status, internet accessibility, computer literacy, previous experience used/skill of surfing net, and difference employed basis are the demographic variables that significantly influencing learning effectiveness at 5% level (The table of demographic profile of respondents & the significance of the demographic variable with respect to learning effectiveness will be given upon request).

To identify the determinant of the effectiveness of WBL programs, one-way ANOVA is used. Results reveal that all the five factors affect significantly the effectiveness of WBL with $p<0.05$ (Table 1). Students' behaviour has the highest ranking with a mean of 2.94 and a standard deviation of 1.01, follow by technology factor with a mean of 2.784 and a standard deviation of 1.05. Institutions factor and interactive application factors are ranked next with a mean (standard deviation) of 2.718 (0.997) and 2.64 (1.18) respectively, instructor characteristic has the lowest ranking with a mean of 2.541 and a standard deviation of 0.99. Each factor displays with Cronbach's Alpha Coefficient above 0.78, showing the questionnaire (n=248) has attained a rather high reliable level.

Table 1: ANOVA, mean ranking, standard deviation (S.D) and Cronbach's Alpha Coefficients (CAC) of the agreement of the factors affecting the effectiveness of WBL in Malaysia.

Factors	F-value	Sig.	Mean	S.D	CAC
Students' behavior	26.385	0.001*	2.938	1.0162	0.8964
Technology / system	24.619	0.028*	2.784	1.0528	0.8672
Interactive applications	30.814	0.031*	2.638	1.1186	0.7859
Institutions factor	28.710	0.037*	2.718	0.9974	0.8463
Instructors' characteristics	21.957	0.042*	2.541	0.9901	0.8129

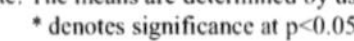

Note: The means are determined by using a 4-point Likert scale from strongly disagree (1) to strongly agree (4).
* denotes significance at $p<0.05$.

Human Perspectives in the Internet Society: Culture, Psychology and Gender, K. Morgan, J. Sanchez, C. A. Brebbia & A Voiskounsky (Editors) © 2004 WIT Press, www.witpress.com, ISBN 1-85312-726-4

4.1 Factor 1: students' behavior and attitude towards virtual education

Students' characteristics factor obtains the highest score of Cronbach Alpha of 0.8964. Among those dimensions that capture learners' perception and learning environment are learners' involvement and participation, students' level of confidence, satisfaction, initiative, motivation and anxiety level, as well as cognitive engagement, past experiences, perceived relative advantage of online delivery and technology self-efficacy. From Table 2, almost all the respondents (93%) perceived time and place flexibility as advantages with means 3.62 and a standard deviation less than 1.0. Learners satisfy with the flexibility system as an effective way to deliver education that fit their tight corporate demanding work schedules.

98% of the respondents, with mean 3.67 and standard deviation 0.5, agree that by actively participating in class activities encourage their learning interest. In fact, about 80% of them feel that it spills higher level of cognitive engagement in the course and builds up higher level of self-confidence. In addition, more than three quarter of the respondents have the learning initiative, motivation, and anxiety level to have the opportunity to get a degree after the course as advantages with means at least 3.0, which motivate them to be more committed in their studies.

Table 2: Percentage, mean and standard deviation of student agreement in Students' behavior and attitude towards virtual education that affect the effectiveness of WBL.

Factor 1: Students' behavior in affecting WBL	Percentages of agreement (%)						
	4	3	2	1	N.R	Mean	S.D.
Satisfaction with time and place flexibility system	79	14	2	0	5	3.62	0.9404
Student involvement & participation	69	29	2	0	0	3.67	0.5135
Cognitive engagement	26	59	9	0	6	2.99	0.9480
Higher level of self-confidence	42	36	18	0	4	3.12	0.9773
Technology self-efficacy (belief capability to interact given technology)	60	23	12	4	1	3.37	0.9173
Students' initiative and motivation	31	53	12	2	2	3.09	0.8299
Students' anxiety level to get a degree	34	43	15	5	3	3.00	0.9847
Total Means	48.71	36.71	10.00	1.571	3.00	3.265	0.9263

Note: The means determined by using 4-point Likert scale rating from strongly agree (4) to strongly disagree (1).

4.2 Factor 2: technology and system

This factor obtains the second highest Cronbach Alpha score of 0.8672 that influence the effectiveness of WBL environment with respect to existing technology and system used in e-learning to capture the reliability, and security of the IT infrastructure, accessibility to information, compatibility of software, information credibility and cost factors. From Table 3, result infers that more than 93% of the respondents perceive the overall framework screen layout and web page design, configuration of colour and overall interface operation are appropriate, attractive and well structure, with high appraisal mean about 3.5 and standard deviation 0.7. Innovative and attractive colour combination of graphics and animations at the websites are useful to attract students surfing diversifies information from the user-friendly environment bona fide. Despite the overall configuration of screen design is appropriate, more than a quarter of the respondents feel that the explanation in portfolio guidance seems to

Human Perspectives in the Internet Society: Culture, Psychology and Gender, K. Morgan, J. Sanchez, C. A. Brebbia & A Voiskounsky (Editors) © 2004 WIT Press, www.witpress.com, ISBN 1-85312-726-4

be comprehensive. The evaluation results reveal that there is still room for improvement.

61% of the respondents strongly perceive easy access to information and 57% perceive information credibility as advantages. The investment of an institution in infrastructure offers high reliability and security of electronic performance support. About 46% of the respondents strongly perceive the institution infrastructure is reliable and secure. Nevertheless, tuition fee of the WBL program is more expensive due to the evolving of Information, Communications and Technology (ICT). More than 40% of the respondents strongly perceive cost of investment in infrastructure to support electronic performance has a negative effect on this subject and has the lowest mean of 1.70. Despite having a rather good system, results reveal that the respondents still encounter technical problems in practical use of WBL, such as experience problem while navigating (85%), internet communication speed (75%) and connection breakdown (77%). Limited bandwidths delay downloading files and creates difficulties in accessing materials online have led to rather time-consuming for browsing the material.

In sum, the major challenge is to develop a system that will facilitate sustainability of student interest to the use of a multidisciplinary approach. The contents of the system should meet the basic features of portfolio. Finally, the technology should always be monitored to reduce the number of breakdowns and upgraded to cater for the needs of WBL.

Table 3: Percentage, mean and standard deviation of student agreement in Technology and System that positively affecting the effectiveness of WBL.

Factor 2: Technology and System that affecting the effectiveness of WBL	Percentages of agreement (%)						
	4	3	2	1	N.R	Mean	S.D.
The screen layout and design is appropriate	55	38	6	0	1	3.46	0.7023
The configuration colour and background is clear and harmonious for the system	58	36	4	1	1	3.49	0.7176
Guidance screen is clear and easy to use	28	44	23	2	3	2.92	0.9285
Easy access to Information	61	24	11	2	2	3.40	0.9101
Information credibility	25	32	25	11	7	2.57	1.1828
IT infrastructure –reliability, and security	46	34	20	0	0	3.26	0.7735
Cost of investment in infrastructure to support electronic performance	7	11	33	43	6	1.70	0.9898
Do not experience problems while navigating	3	12	59	26	0	1.92	0.7061
Rarely disconnected during online tutorial	6	16	40	37	1	1.89	0.8977
Satisfactory with the browsing speed	6	15	44	31	4	1.88	0.9241
Total Means	29.50	26.20	26.50	15.30	2.50	2.6490	1.1343

Note: The means determined by using 4-point Likert scale rating from strongly agree (4) to strongly disagree (1).

4.3 Factor 3: interactive

This factor gains the lowest score of Cronbach Alpha coefficient with 0.7859. 76% of the respondents (mean=3.08) communicate with classmates via web that asynchronous discussions allow no time and space constraint. Moreover, students make the diverse discussion subjects feasible with facilitators and classmate over the availability of interactive application. However, conventional modes of communications are also persisted as a complementary. Sharing knowledge through online discussions is an integral part. More than 70% feel that sharing knowledge through online discussion is a good idea though it is rather time consuming. 93% of them (mean 3.15) feel that discussion enables exchange of ideas and comment. To facilitate discussion, participation marks

Human Perspectives in the Internet Society: Culture, Psychology and Gender, K. Morgan, J. Sanchez, C. A. Brebbia & A Voiskounsky (Editors) © 2004 WIT Press, www.witpress.com, ISBN 1-85312-726-4

could be considered. Good examples of works would be uploaded on the discussion platform, as a benchmark for the student to judge their own works. Due to online presence, slightly more than 50% of the students are much more focused on the quality of learning work.

Besides chat room, classroom forum and workspace are dedicated for students to post questions and to publish their work online. Students are encouraged to participate in the web discussion. Most of them (66%) are invited to ask questions or submit answers. Discussion platform enables articulation of the group assignments and open for commendation within peers. Mutual assessment and feedback mechanism from the instructors and students are welcomed. Majority of the respondents (96%) believes that by browsing their classmates' work allow them to know better about the merits and shortcomings of their works compare to the others. 93% of the respondents feel that the quality of their work can be improved by emulation through the browsing of others' works.

More than 50% of the respondents show high agreement for uploading coursework in the portfolio is being appropriate. But, only 6 per cent of the respondents feel uploading is an easy task. The reason for the low appraisal is probably due to insufficient space and low bandwidth to support the system, and thus display problem during the process of uploading files. In a nutshell, most of the students (84%) show positive feedback in the overall benefit of using this system. Nevertheless, minority of the respondents (5%) has higher interest in browsing peers' feedback of most of their classmate. This is probably due to majority of the working groups do not have ample of time to get acquainting with it.

Table 4: Percentage, mean and standard deviation of student agreement in interactivity that affects the effectiveness of WBL.

Factor 3: Interactivity that affects the effectiveness of WBL	Percentages of agreement (%)						
	4	3	2	1	N.R.	Mean	S. D.
I could have discussion with course mates via web	41	35	19	1	4	3.08	1.0018
Sharing knowledge through online discussions is a good idea	17	61	14	0	8	2.79	0.9979
Sharing knowledge through online discussions is time consuming	15	57	19	0	9	2.69	1.0317
Discussion enables exchange of ideas and comment.	32	61	2	0	5	3.15	0.8804
I would be concentrate on the quality works	12	39	31	12	6	2.39	1.0434
We are invited to ask questions / received answers	14	52	26	1	7	2.65	0.9783
Browsing my classmates' works helps to reflect my shortcoming	71	25	2	0	2	3.63	0.7199
Browsing my classmates' works helps to upgrade the quality	59	34	5	0	2	3.48	0.7717
I browse the peers' feedback of most of my classmates.	5	12	39	41	3	1.75	0.8918
Upload coursework is an appropriate method	10	43	21	17	9	2.28	1.1377
Upload coursework is easy to use.	6	29	21	37	7	1.90	1.0871
Overall, I gain benefit by using this system.	39	45	14	0	2	3.19	0.8250
Total Means	26.75	41.08	17.75	9.083	5.333	2.748	1.1123

Note: The means determined by using 4-point Likert scale rating from strongly agree (4) to strongly disagree (1).

4.4 Factor 4: institutional factor

Issues that may affect students' perception towards WBL from the institutional factors perspective are accreditation, copyright issues, availability of virtual library, and method of delivery course content in this study. Table 5 listed respondent perceptions toward institutional factors. At least 60% of the respondents perceive accreditation, the availability of virtual library, and the method of delivery course content as advantages, with the mean greater than

2.66. To the contrary, more than 60% do not bother the copyright issue of WBL in the institution (mean=2.06). 55% of the students feel that they can easily accessible to the online database information they needed promptly by clicking related link. Almost 70% of the respondents claim that they can easily look for relevant materials, incorporating and digitised all the printed library resources that generating accessibility sharing information to enhance the learning-teaching process at the most convenient virtual environment.

More participants prefer more than one method of delivery. 68% of participants prefer a combination of online learning and traditional classroom mode of delivery to increase learning effectiveness though more costs might be incurred. 38% prefer WBL to classroom face to face sessions in their learning process generally. While, 61% shows greater benefits in favour of face to face delivery. This is because almost 50% of them perceive having discussion face to face is more effective than via online. They perceive the use of technology is frustrating. Furthermore, 56% of them strongly perceive that face-to-face is the complementary for WBL. Some of them (13%) even strongly claim that having discussion face-to-face is more effective than via online.

As regards to students' performance, 28% strongly assent that they learn equally effectively in online environment and classroom base. While 18% indicate better performance in classroom mode of learning. Thus, we conclude that classroom face to face learning mode still appear to be effective.

Table 5: Percentage, mean and standard deviation of student agreement in institutional factor in influencing the effectiveness of WBL.

Factor 4: Institutional factor in influencing the effectiveness of WBL	Percentages of agreement (%)						
	4	3	2	1	N.R.	Mean	S.D.
Accreditation is an important factor for me to determine whether to choose this WBL course	13	53	28	6	0	2.73	0.7635
The availability of virtual library important for me	18	54	13	8	7	2.68	1.0813
The method of delivery course content bother me	16	44	32	6	2	2.66	0.8901
WBL program has its own patent in this institutions bother me	12	17	43	21	7	2.06	1.0714
Easy accessibility by clicking related link in virtual library	19	36	22	21	2	2.49	1.0870
Relevance of materials in virtual library	31	38	28	2	1	2.96	0.8752
I prefer e-learning to face-to-face session	9	29	51	11	0	2.36	0.7979
I prefer face to face classroom delivery mode	13	48	25	14	0	2.60	0.8876
I prefer the combination of classroom mode of delivery and online learning.	26	42	24	8	0	2.86	0.8991
Face-to-face is the complementary for WBL	56	32	10	2	0	3.42	0.7545
I learn equally effective in online environment and classroom base	28	34	23	12	3	2.72	1.0924
I perform better in classroom mode of learning	18	41	34	3	4	2.66	0.9451
Total Mean	21.58	39.00	27.75	9.50	2.167	2.683	0.9888

Note: The means determined by using 4-point Likert scale rating from strongly agree (4) to strongly disagree (1).

4.5 Factor 5: instructors' characteristics

There is a significant relationship between learning effectiveness and the instructors' characteristics, with Cronbach Alpha coefficient of 0.8129. Results (Table 6) report that more than 70% of the students indicate their instructors provide sufficient learning resources online. Slightly more than 30% strongly remark the instructors are friendly and approachable, and feel welcome in seeking advice. Anyway, 43% feel that instructors' availability for appointments is rather unreachable. Thus, instructors should actively solicit interaction to enhance the WBL experience. Nevertheless, at least 73% of them refuse to seek consultation from the instructor as their first choice because the instructors have no enthusiasms to explain via online and the instructors perceive the students have the knowledge of know-how to use the websites at the beginning of the semester. Therefore, training programs should be provided to the instructors and students on how to use various web-based applications. Learning is most proficient with adhere credible active interaction. 85% of them perceive that instructors encourage students interaction is a factor influencing the effectiveness of WBL.

Instructors will not give his opinion unless students' viewpoint is deviated from the correct point (32%). However, majority of them belief it discourages their learning progress. Slightly more than one-third of the respondents say that instructors provide fast feedback from queries. In fact, half of the respondents feel that this is an efficient way in solving emerging problem. Instructor with technical proficiency in handling the technology as a knowledge navigator emerges as an important factor too. 64% of them strongly agree that quality of lecturer would affect the efficient level of teaching-learning process. Anyway, none of them deem that the instructors have insufficient computer skill to handle the web technology efficiently. In a nutshell, the instructor should exhibit interactive teaching styles, encouraging interaction between the students and instructor.

Table 6: Percentage, mean and standard deviation of student agreement in instructor characteristic in influencing the effectiveness of WBL.

Factor 5: Instructors' characteristics in influencing the effectiveness of WBL	Percentages of agreement (%)						
	4	3	2	1	N.R.	Mean	S.D.
Instructors provide sufficient learning resources online.	27	49	15	4	5	2.89	1.0139
Instructors are friendly and approachable to students	31	44	20	2	3	2.98	0.9318
I could easily contact instructor	10	31	34	19	6	2.20	1.0540
Instructors are enthusiastic teaching and explaining via web	3	20	61	12	4	2.06	0.7761
Instructors explain how to use the web-site at the beginning of the semester.	4	10	24	55	7	1.49	0.9155
Instructors encourage student interaction	22	63	14	0	1	3.05	0.6723
Instructors will not give his opinion unless students violate the correct points are an encouraging idea.	5	27	54	12	2	2.21	0.7951
Instructors provide fast feedback about queries rapidly in the discussion forum	7	30	59	2	2	2.38	0.7355
Instructors reply our email queries rapidly.	9	27	43	19	2	2.22	0.9274
Instructors solving emerging problem efficiently.	13	37	45	2	3	2.55	0.8572
Knowledge of instructors in using internet technology affects the efficiency.	21	43	24	12	0	2.73	0.9304
Total Mean	13.82	34.63	35.72	12.63	3.182	2.432	0.9875

Note: The means determined by using 4-point Likert scale rating from strongly agree (4) to strongly disagree (1).

5 Conclusion

The study indicates that student's characteristics are the main factor that influences the effectiveness of online learning process. Besides, the ability to express knowledge via online teaching represents the quality of the instructors implicitly. Hence, the instructors should provide prompt feedback to students' inquiries. A considerable time spend on monitoring the progress in of the asynchronous discussions is crucial. Technical support and technological advancement provide the learning facilities and stable network for interactive applications. The inefficiency in terms of dynamic management functions is yet to be improved. Human resource Management need constantly stay abreast of new and rapid developments in the Knowledge economy. Hence, careful planning is required for sustainability of WBL programs, especially in relation to accreditation issue.

Human Perspectives in the Internet Society: Culture, Psychology and Gender, K. Morgan, J. Sanchez, C. A. Brebbia & A Voiskounsky (Editors) © 2004 WIT Press, www.witpress.com, ISBN 1-85312-726-4

References

[1] Alias, N. and Hussin, S., E-learning at a writing course at Tenaga Nasional University. *A Journal for Teachers as Researchers,* 1(3), 2002.

[2] Ancis J.R., Cultural Competency Training at A Distance: Challenges and Strategies. *Journal of Counselling and Development,* 76 (2), 1998.

[3] Chang, C. C., Study on the Evaluation and Effectiveness Analysis of Web-Based Learning Portfolio. *British Journal of Educational Technology,* 32(4), pp.435-458, 2001.

[4] Charp, S., Online Learning. *The Journal*, 29(8), pp.8-10, 2002.

[5] Collis, B. Anticipating the Impact of Multimedia in Education: Lesson from the literature. *Computer in Adult Education and Training,* 2(2), pp.136-149, 1995.

[6] DeSantis, C.J., How is it different from traditional learning, 1999. Online: http://www.elearners.com/services/faq/q2c.asp [2002, July 18].

[7] Embi, A.M., Yamat, H and Zolkepeli, H., Trainees' Perception towards a web-based online course. *VirTEC Journal,* 1(1), pp.33-39, 2001.

[8] Hall, B., and LeCavalier, J., E-Learning Across the Enterprise: The Benchmarking Study of Best Practices, 2000. Online: http://www.brandon-hall.com/elacenbenstu.html [2002, June 14].

[9] Hong, K.S., Lai, K.W. & Holton, D., Web based learning environments: Observations from a Web based course in a Malaysian context. *Australian Journal of Educational Technology*, 17(3), pp.223-243, 2001.

[10] Lau, S. and Fitri S.M., Online learning is it meant for science courses? *The Internet and Higher Education,* 5(2), pp.109-118, 2002.

[11] Leidner, D.E. and Jarvenpaa, S.L., The Use of Information Technology to Enhance Management School Education: A theoretical View. *MIS Quarterly,* 19(3), pp.265-91, 1995.

[12] Mason, R. & Weller, M., Factors affecting students' satisfaction on a web course. *Australian journal of Educational Technology,* 16(2), pp.173-200, 2000.

[13] McIsaac, M.S. and Rowe, J., Ownership and access: Copyright and Intellectual Property in the on-line environment. *New Directions for Community Colleges*, 99, pp. 83-92, 1997.

[14] Parker, A., A distance education how-to manual: Recommendations from the field. *Educational Technology Review,* 8, pp. 7-10, 1997.

[15] Sherry, L., Lawyer-Brook, D. & Black, L., Evaluation of the Boulder Valley Internet Project: A theory-based approach to evaluation design. *Journal of interactive Learning Research,* 8(2), pp. 199-234, 1997.

[16] Volery, T. and Lord, D., Critical Success Factors in Online Education. *The International Journal of Educational Management,* 14(5), pp. 216-223, 2000.

[17] Webster, J. and Hackley, P., Teaching Effectiveness in Technology-mediated Distance Learning. *Academy of Management Journal,* 40(6), pp.1282-309, 1997.

Human Perspectives in the Internet Society: Culture, Psychology and Gender, K. Morgan, J. Sanchez, C. A. Brebbia & A Voiskounsky (Editors) © 2004 WIT Press, www.witpress.com, ISBN 1-85312-726-4

Oracle 9iAS Portal as a platform for Geographic Information Science distance and flexible learning at the University of the South Pacific

P. Sharma[1], M. Govorov[2], Y. Khmelevsky[3] & S. Dhanjal[3]
[1]*Department of Mathematics and Computer Science, University of the South Pacific, Fiji Islands*
[2]*GIS Unit, Department of Geography, University of the South Pacific, Fiji Islands*
[3]*Department of Computing Science, University College of the Cariboo (UCC), Canada*

Abstract

Providing Geographic Information Systems (GIS) courses over the Distance and Flexible Learning (DFL) in the University of the South Pacific has been until now an area where little concentration has focussed. The USP is an international University serving 12 countries where the majority of students are studying through the DFL mode. Many large universities and educational centres are already effectively using different DFL eLearning solutions as a type of eBusiness. The GIS Unit and the Computing Science Department at the USP have developed a prototype for GIS education for the DFL mode, based on GeoMedia Web Map Server and Oracle 9iAS Portal, which provides a comprehensive way to store and deliver structured and unstructured information from a single point of access on the web.

The purpose of this article is to analyse the specifics of the n-tier architecture of spatial data management within the Web-Portals as an interface for the GIS eLearning. This paper outlines features of development and the content of a GIS Web Portal for distance education in a constrained net environment, and accompanying issues for integration of GIS tools within geodatabase client-server architectures of corporative Web solutions.

Keywords: GIS, eLearning, eBusiness, GIS portal, Web Map server, integration, security control, Internet file system.

Human Perspectives in the Internet Society: Culture, Psychology and Gender, K. Morgan, J. Sanchez, C. A. Brebbia & A Voiskounsky (Editors) © 2004 WIT Press, www.witpress.com, ISBN 1-85312-726-4

1 Project background

The University of the South Pacific (USP) is a regional university owned collectively by the governments of the Cook Islands, Fiji, Kiribati, Marshall Islands, Nauru, Niue, Samoa, Solomon Islands, Tokelau, Tonga, Tuvalu and Vanuatu (see http://www.usp.ac.fj). The architecture of the USP through the region is designed in a hierarchical way. The main Laucala Campus is in Fiji, second one is in Vanuatu, and there are eleven centres, each in every USP country member. The majority of the students are studying through the DFL mode.

In the early 90's, when it had been realized that Pacific Islanders had to leave the Region to seek for GIS education, the USP set out to establish a GIS program. As part of the Geography Department at the USP, the GIS Unit is offering a GIS Certificate and Diploma program. The academic position was assumed by the USP and commitment was made to support various developmental projects in the region through the University's teaching and research programme.

For the past five years, the Geography Department at the USP has included basic and intermediate GIS and introductory Remote Sensing (RS) courses within its undergraduate curriculum. As a result, more undergraduate students and regional GIS users have received basic GIS/RS training. Today the GIS programme is expanding rapidly. Four courses are currently offered. Classroom-based GIS/RS courses are offered in main campus. The number of students taking GIS courses has increased significantly during the last few years. The demands are much higher than the resources (staff, and the workstations in the GIS/RS Lab) currently available at the GIS Unit. In 2000, the introductory GIS courses were offered in all USP member countries by distance education. Different types of DFL delivery are used for conducting the courses for non-in-campus students.

There are a few types of Distance Learning such as classroom-based (summer school), visiting instructor-led training, videotape or satellite video-based training, and computer-aided learning. Last one can be eLearning from a live Internet connection; offline learning delivered by CD-ROM or via pre-download data and mobile professionals or mLearning [1].

Classroom-based, satellite video-based training, and primary eLearning have been used for GIS DFL education in the Department. GIS/RS Summer schools are in demand among the USP students, but it requires additional staffing. Pre-packaged video-based course material was supported by video conferencing through the University's high-speed satellite network. Satellite video-conference training is expensive and more appropriate for lecture delivery. Learning from videotape and course books have lack of contact between a lecturer and auditorium, and appropriate mostly for lectures. ELearning form is best for practical and laboratories GIS DFL.

Comprehensive GIS eLearning has to deliver on-line lectures, practical labs, tests, and assignment submissions; give the possibility for live interactions between instructor and student, or even among the students, and provide tools for

Human Perspectives in the Internet Society: Culture, Psychology and Gender, K. Morgan, J. Sanchez, C. A. Brebbia & A Voiskounsky (Editors) © 2004 WIT Press, www.witpress.com, ISBN 1-85312-726-4

visualization and analysis of spatial data. This approach is much more flexible in comparison with distance teaching via satellite broadcasting. Looking from the other angle, this approach can offer the same possibilities as satellite broadcasting by using satellite equipment and special video coding methods for real-video transfer within the integrated system.

2 GIS Web Portal for USP DFL

Taking into consideration the multifunctional nature of GIS eLearning and teaching, the GIS Web Portal has to be developed to serve these services. A Web Portal is: a web site or service that offers a broad array of resources and services through web applications; provides a single point of entry for retrieving web service; offers a mix of content and services information from (some of which may be provided by partners or other third parties) with a large, diverse, target audience.

The GIS Web Portal for USP DFL has to be developed to satisfy the following requirements:

- Develop professional GIS/RS levels of proficiency in teaching and research in the Geography, and Mathematics and Computer Science Departments (MCSD) at the USP. Reduce demands on in-campus education in Suva and increase the number of students in GIS and Computer Science courses under the same capacity of the existing GIS Unit and MCSD.
- Separate common lectures information and real-life presentations from individual tasks, labs and assignment in the same Portal environment under different access rights;
- Support practical teaching and testing in GIS, Geography and Computer Science through the Internet use among USP campuses and centres;
- Support live-maps and spatial database/datasets on-line. Support integrated multi-user interface for spatial and non-spatial information;
- Manage administration by supervisor or groups of supervisors remotely from the Internet;
- Allow simple customisation;
- Support private accounts with spatial data for individual students, and highest levels of security for test and examination information;
- Keep lectures, demonstrations, labs, and assignments as archival resources and store of all information (audio, video, files, and documents) in the database environment with very flexible search tools;
- Keep and use FAQ's, discussion groups, e-mail course activities and support information within the same environment and within the same database system.

Main constrains for development of the Portal in the USP environment are: low network speed bandwidth from/to USP, poor hardware equipping in some university centres, and frequent staff turnover that can effect maintenance of the Portal. Intranet/Internet connection and videoconference are provided from the main USP campus to other centres through a satellite network. The bandwidth of this network is one Mbps, but practically we have very slow network connection amongst various USP centres.

Human Perspectives in the Internet Society: Culture, Psychology and Gender, K. Morgan, J. Sanchez, C. A. Brebbia & A Voiskounsky (Editors) © 2004 WIT Press, www.witpress.com, ISBN 1-85312-726-4

The GIS Web Portal was decided to implement within integrated environment by using two industrial solutions such as Oracle 9i Application Server (AS) Portal within GeoMedia Web Map Server (GWM) from Intergraph. Factors such as the software availability were considered to reach this decision. Thus, Oracle 9i/8i Server and Oracle 9iAS Portal SW are available in the MCSD and the Department has access to technical support information and Oracle technical library, which are necessary for the project. GeoMedia Pro and GWM are available in the GIS Unit as a part of its Registered Research Laboratory program membership from Intergraph. The Unit has the license for research and education purposes. Secondly, these two solutions offer the possibilities to integrate their components and build GIS Web Portal with required functionalities.

3 Methodology of building GIS Web Portal

There are two strategies to create a web based information system for a particular application. The first choice is to build a system by using client/server or n-tier development within J2EE, JSP/Servlets, Java Applets, ASP, etc technologies; the second choice is employing one or few of the industrial portal products. In case of educational institution like USP, there is no special programmer support group and movement of staff is high, the best strategy is to utilize existing solutions. One solution has to be responsible for spatial data handling, and second one can be fully functional web portal, which enables dynamic integration of spatial data application component. The portal has to have the ability to manage enterprise applications and content resources in conjunction with governing enterprise access to the resources under management [2].

An architectural model for GIS DFL Portal can be based on n-tier design, which can be leveraging all of advance features the Oracle 9iAS Portal environment. Such architecture provides user access to data resources and GIS services through the Web interface and at the same time provides better data and service management and protection via legacy RDBMS. The middle tier is developed using servlets that encapsulate the business logic and provide flow control. Database interface is separated into a back-end tier that allows all database changes to be addressed in one place. It also allows the developer to easily reuse data related programming elements and provides a single access point for implementing connection pooling.

Several deployment components of Oracle 9iAS Portal were considered from the point of view to complying with the requirements for the GIS DFL Portal development. These are application development support, static content publication and customisation, integration of structured and unstructured information, control of user environmental characteristics, security control, administration of the components, and ability for dynamic application integration.

Java2 Enterprise Edition (J2EE) development practices and standards can be deployed for Oracle Portal web based application development

Human Perspectives in the Internet Society: Culture, Psychology and Gender, K. Morgan, J. Sanchez, C. A. Brebbia & A Voiskounsky (Editors) © 2004 WIT Press, www.witpress.com, ISBN 1-85312-726-4

and customisation. Other technologies such as .net also can be used, but has some limitations.

The Portal administrators have the capability to customize the user experience through built-in functionality by managing: templates, navigation pages, styles, categories and perspectives, links, tabs, content. Development and customisation of web site and organization of data is made simpler through portlets. A page inside a Portal is divided into regions; and inside these regions portlets are contained. Portlets constitute a structure that contains the information from different sources. This feature aids a lot during development of website but is particularly useful during maintenance of website when little to large changes are required and this feature allows changes to be made easily. Since the unit of information access is the portlet, GIS users can be given access to information such as map viewing while course coordinator can have access to student user owned folders to assess their work submissions.

Oracle Portal has ability to store and provide structured and unstructured information. The structured data can be broken down into logical entities and stored in database tables. The unstructured data cannot be logically subdivided and can be stored in columns as BLOBs data-types. The Portal can host and manage static content as web pages through portlets, including documents, spreadsheets, web pages, and presentations. Portal users and administrators have the ability to upload and manage single and multiple files, including their directory structures through the Oracle Internet File System (see section 5.3).

Once a web site is made available on a network or Internet, security becomes a major concern. The Oracle Portal deploys a comprehensive security structure in place that controls access to content from unprivileged users. This issue is discussed in detail in section 5.2.

The Oracle Portal offers range of tools for administration of the different components that make up the Portal. Administration can be made through web interface.

The Oracle Portal has a structure in place for integration external (for the Portal) applications such as GeoMedia Web Map into one access point. GWM can provide tools necessary to generate a map from the Web Map Server that can be provided to a client for viewing using a Web browser [3]. Users on the client sites will be able to work with the map interactively and dynamically (see section 5.1 for more detail).

4 Contents of GIS Portal for USP DFL

Traditional classroom-based geo-information science teaching at the USP includes PowerPoint lecture presentations and computer-based practical exercises with using local spatial data and GIS/RS software. The course' content that can to be shared with students should be same for classroom-based and on-line learning.

The prototype of GIS Portal for teaching GE308 "Advanced GIS" course was implemented at first. Oracle Portal technology and GWM were used to implement GIS Portal with the individual pages for each student and pages for each instructor as an administrator. User has to login to own the main page. On the main page, there are tabs, which would hold links to the common content for all students and instructors, e.g. course information, lecture materials, labs and spatial data download; and to individual information e.g. submissions of assignments, marks for assignments and instructor comments. The main GIS Course Page was divided into three regions: First region contains the course content, the second holds submission folders and the third region presents links to external web map applications.

Main page (Figure 1) contains the following tabs, folders and links:

- Course Information tab shows course related information: outline, overview, objectives, resources, schedule, evaluation and polices of the course, and explanation how to navigate and work within the Portal etc. The HTML page with this information is integrated into the tab as a portlet with the link into the same window. Course information also can be downloaded as a PDF file from this tab.

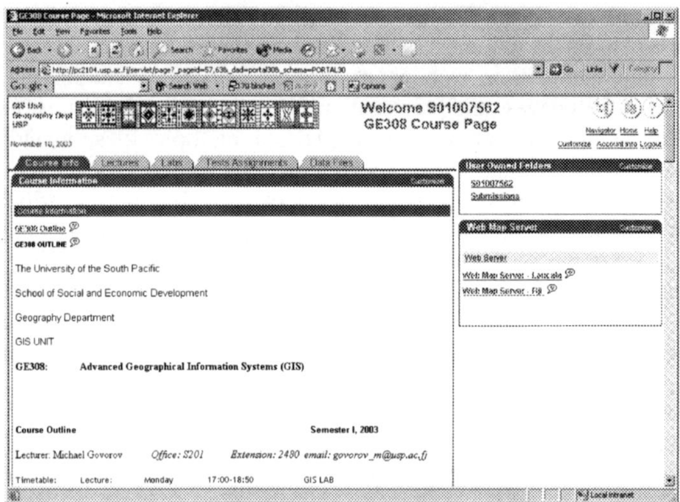

Figure 1: Student main page.

- Lecture Materials tab holds the links to the lecture notes, which are prepared as HTML and/or downloadable PowerPoint or PDF files. The lecture HTML files were linked from the Lecture category as portlet provider and integrated into the tab portlet, while the links pointed to their actual location in the Lectures folder. Since there were a number of lecture files that can be viewed, the type of links was chosen to open lecture content within new window and since the files were HTML files, they would display without any pre-processing. This was made mainly for users who do not have installed software to display files in special formats e.g. PDF. The enhanced version of the Portal may contain links to multimedia files with recorded lecture presentations.

- Lab Materials tab holds the links to the course session files. The laboratory hand-notes are prepared as HTML and downloadable PDF files. Course administrator may prepare and put the current lab files in the Lab folder and create links weekly. The students would view links and open the files during their lab sessions. The lab files were configured to open up in new window in HTML. This material can be supplemented with pre-recorded lab explanations in the next version of the Portal.
- GIS Data Files tab holds the links to the downloadable files and/or folders with spatial and attributive data; e.g. map layers for the lab session course work and assignments. The data files could be opened in external GIS applications like GeoMedia, MapInfo, or ArcGIS.
- Student Submissions folders are for student work submissions to course coordinator. Each student has owned content area for storing files (assignments results) that are to be submitted to course coordinator. A region within the main page was developed that could hold the link to student folder. A student owned folder exists in a content area, which belongs to the student. A student would only view his/her owned folder. For the course coordinator, access control settings are configured in such a way that he/she would have access to all students' folders and would find it easier to download their submission files from one place and access them.
- Results of Assignments links – where student may see individual results of his/her assignments and tests.

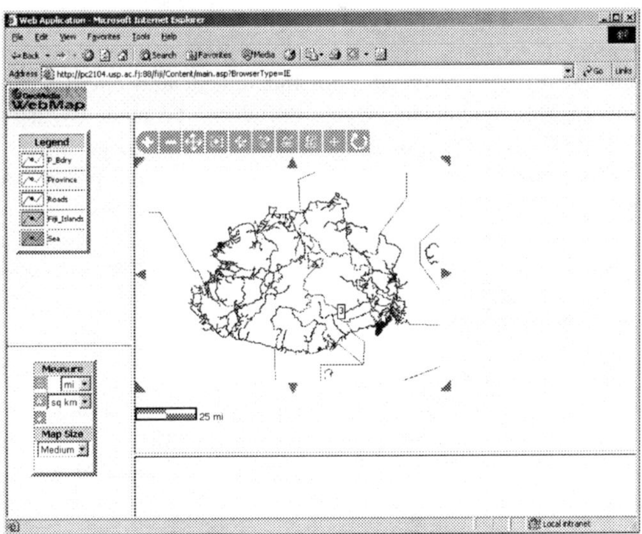

Figure 2: Map view.

- View Maps links allow students to view and work with map files over the web using GWM (Figure 2). Upon applying on any link, an interactive web map

Human Perspectives in the Internet Society: Culture, Psychology and Gender, K. Morgan, J. Sanchez, C. A. Brebbia & A Voiskounsky (Editors) © 2004 WIT Press, www.witpress.com, ISBN 1-85312-726-4

would open up in a new browser window. Functionalities of GWM allow cartographic visualization and simple spatial analysis only (These capabilities are available in all existing commercial GIS Web mapping software). Some lab assignments can be carried out by using GWM only; but more comprehensive assignments still require the installations of full functional GIS/RS software on LAN and/or individual computers.

Since students can belong to either of the courses, each student has a separate account inside of the portal, which would login the students to their course page by default. Student may make simple customization of own folders. Instructors have similar main page, but with more information and higher rights for customisations and changes of student content within Portal Content Area Builder page. The content of the Portal is easily extendable and updateable. An instructor may create new folders, tabs or links, and change their contents during the semester, on an as-needed basis, with little customisation efforts.

5 Implementation issues

5.1 Integration of Oracle Portal and GeoMedia Web Map

The Oracle Portal has a structure in place for integrating external applications into one access point for the Portal. There are three ways for the integration: native J2EE applications using Oracle's Portal Development Kit; certified portlet integration for Oracle 9iAS Portal; and using URL integration [2].

GeoMedia Web Map utilizes the ActiveCGM (Active Computer Graphics Metafile) format to generate client display and employs the technology of Active Server Pages (ASP) or java servlets for medium or thin clients. Integration of GeoMedia Web Map within the Oracle Portal can be made by using Oracle's PDK for the J2EE application or URL integration. For the prototype version of the GIS Portal, GeoMedia Web Map solution based on ASP technology was utilized. To host external applications that have not been developed using J2EE, URL based portlets are integrated into the Oracle 9iAS Portal application framework through registration and configuration through the Oracle PDK.

5.2 Security control for staff and student access

A great feature of Oracle 9iAS Portal is its integrated security. The Oracle 9iAS, as host of the Portal, provides full securing control within Portal by leveraging the capabilities of the Oracle 9i Application Server, Single-Sign-On (SSO) and the Oracle Internet Directory (OID) in addition to management of privileges users and group management. SSO and OID of the Portal guarantees appropriate user authentication and authorization. Security principles to authenticate and authorize users for accessing Oracle Portal content through Oracle 9iAS are as follows [4]:

- Users with URL access have access to public portal content;
- Portal determines if the user is authenticated at login time;
- Oracle portal security determines if the resource being access is protected;

Human Perspectives in the Internet Society: Culture, Psychology and Gender, K. Morgan, J. Sanchez, C. A. Brebbia & A Voiskounsky (Editors) © 2004 WIT Press, www.witpress.com, ISBN 1-85312-726-4

- If the resource is protected, portal security determines if the user is authorized to access the resource;
- User access is granted or denied.

Oracle Portal allows security at the item or component level. All created components in Oracle Portal have an access tab, enabling to specify privileges for a user or a group of users. This feature helps students and staff to control access rights to information. Student user group is not allowed to have access permissions to any folders that contain information on the course, e.g. to Lecture Materials tab etc. Student users are provided with user-owned folder and there is security access control to prevent other student user in accessing these folders, but at the same time allowing course coordinator to access information for student work assessment. Security settings can vary for each item [5].

External applications not registered as Oracle 9iAS SSO partner applications such as GeoMedia Web Map can be hosted through Oracle 9iAS Portal while utilizing an external authentication repository through custom integration.

5.3 IFS for file storage and management

File System within Database (FSDB) is relatively new idea for data file management. FSDB raises the possibility for any file to be created, reviewed, corrected, approved, and finally published with appropriate access restrictions for user groups or simple users into DBMS [6]. At the same time, FSDB can be replicated by standard replication procedures of any sophisticated modern DBMS. The protocol servers that are included, for example, with the Oracle Internet File System (IFS) allow the FSDB to provide support for all common industry standard protocols trough the Internet or application server and within the enterprise network [7]. By using the File System within DBMS, the organization can be confident, that spatial content is secure and accessible from a central location, especially if we use additional encryption for the stored data.

Oracle Internet File System was used to store and manage the spatial data files, files with student assignment and respective submissions. A FSDB provides a powerful and secure tool for the storing and managing files. When, for example, a spatial file is moved to the FSDB for storage, FSDB stores the file into a special repository database object. When the students open the file on the FSDB drive, FSDB retrieves the data into logical format that the GIS software or GIS Application Server can read, update and process as a simple spatial file. FSDB is a tool that enables students to share files on a standard Intranet network and over the Internet, or through an Application Server.

Once files have been stored in the repository, access to them is tightly controlled by the security mechanism built into the repository [7]. A FSDB secures GIS and stores files in a DBMS. The FSDB uses authentication mechanism to get access into a DBMS or repository of FSDB, regardless of the protocol or tool being used to access a file. Newest versions of FSDB have more sophisticated authentication mechanisms, such as SSO servers, Internet Directory or LDAP server's utilization.

Human Perspectives in the Internet Society: Culture, Psychology and Gender, K. Morgan, J. Sanchez, C. A. Brebbia & A Voiskounsky (Editors) © 2004 WIT Press, www.witpress.com, ISBN 1-85312-726-4

6 Conclusion

Oracle 9iAS Portal provides a comprehensive administration feature that caters the needs of today's e-business organizations. This paper describes how these features were utilized for offering GIS web based course through DFL mode at the University of the South Pacific. GIS Portal based on Oracle 9iAS offers huge advantages to staff members as administrators, and students for learning GIS/RS related course.

Course coordinator would find it easier to develop and maintain static and dynamic content of GIS/RS website through adding and removing components within page, tabs, regions, portlets and external application integration with GIS/RS solutions. As a Portal administrator, course coordinator may create and edit users or groups, grant and revoke privileges and controls access at folders, pages and application level. Monitoring is another feature, which course coordinator can use to see who is logging in course Portal, when they are logging in, how frequently they are logging in etc. As a marker, course coordinator can access individual student submission folder and make assessment of assignments. Course coordinator also can have live-interaction with students via aggregation of FAQ, discussion groups, live or pre-recorded video presentations as portlets (these features are not implemented in this project).

The use of Portal technology to provide GIS/RS course on the web is convenient for students residing outside the campus, as well as for on-campus students. This solution gives possibility to integrate all teaching and learning recourses in the same environment; keep and manage these recourses in the same database system. Oracle9iAS allows single point to access, aggregate and search information [5]. A total course for distance students over the web can include all major aspects of the course provided on-campus. Students have possibilities not only to use the GIS Portal content and recourses, but also make a customisation within their working environment (working with files in conventional way, but managed and protected by Oracle DBMS). Part of the GIS/RS courses can be learned by remote users through the web browser since web browser may be the only software available to them. Work with the spatial data can be done through the integration external Web Map Server (e.g. GWM) that was implemented in this project, or via use of dynamic portlets. Second option may provide more functionality for spatial analysis, but required programming development (last feature is not implemented in the current version).

This paper describe only prototype version of the GIS Portal based on Oracle 9iAS Portal and GeoMedia Web Map Server.

The current work was initially motivated in search of the best solution for GIS/RS on-line distance mode education at the University of the South Pacific USPNet. The authors are grateful to USP Research Committee for the financial support of this research.

References

[1] Offline Learning: Serving the Mobile Professional, An IDC Executive Brief, 2002.

[2] Dwight de Vera, Utilizing Oracle 9iAS Portal to Deploy Internet Facing Applications, www.innovative-consult.com, 2001.
[3] Developing Web Solutions with GeoMedia Web Map Technology. Intergraph Corporation, 2002.
[4] Delivering Complete Business Intelligence with the Oracle 9iAS Portal, www.innovative-consult.com, 2002.
[5] ORACLE 9i Application Server, an Oracle White Paper, Oracle Corporation, 2002.
[6] Oracle Internet File System: Technical White Paper, Installation Guide, Release 9.0.1.1.0 for Microsoft Windows NT/2000", Oracle, 2001
[7] Security and the Oracle Internet File System, Oracle Internet File System: Technical White Paper, 2000.

Human Perspectives in the Internet Society: Culture, Psychology and Gender, K. Morgan, J. Sanchez, C. A. Brebbia & A Voiskounsky (Editors) © 2004 WIT Press, www.witpress.com, ISBN 1-85312-726-4

Data-driven modelling of learner's cognitive style in educational hypermedia

S. Fragos[1], T. Mitchell[2], S. Chen[2] & L. K. Stergioulas[2]
[1]*Department of Communication Systems,*
Department of Management Science, Lancaster University, UK
[2]*Department of Information Systems and Computing,*
Brunel University, UK

Abstract

In this paper we propose a framework for modelling the user behaviour in hypermedia systems. This involves the design of time-based features and the selection of the most useful ones that can give the best classification and prediction. The process of variable selection involves a sensitivity analysis via neural network bootstrapping, which aims at maximising the model's classification performance and generalisation ability. The goal of this study is to model and assess the learners' holist/analytic cognitive styles based on the navigational trail recorded while they navigate through learning hypermedia content. The method is generic in nature and therefore applicable to a wide range of behaviour-analysis applications.
Keywords: user modelling, hypermedia systems, features engineering, data reduction, feature design standardisation, neural networks, Principal Component Analysis, audit trail analysis.

1 Introduction

The proliferation of internet-based and networked information systems brought forward the need for obtaining increasingly larger amounts of information on the user's background activities for the purposes of Auditing/Control or improvement of the process or even the system. The need for analysing the user's behaviour in organisations and business environments has recently become more and more imperative. The security-related [1], [2], [3], educational and commercial [4], [5] uses of internal/external customers' behaviour are three

Human Perspectives in the Internet Society: Culture, Psychology and Gender, K. Morgan, J. Sanchez, C. A. Brebbia & A Voiskounsky (Editors) © 2004 WIT Press, www.witpress.com, ISBN 1-85312-726-4

of the most important areas in which the need for modelling the system's user activities has proven to be extremely valuable. Setting aside the special context of each of these areas, the user invariably performs actions via a keyboard or a mouse, navigating through a hypermedia system for a specific purpose. The trail of these actions is directly related to the "ground truth" of what the user wants to do, - which means that it can be interpreted as meaningful conceptual information - while at the same time this trail can be recorded, processed, and classified.

The recordable user activity trail in hypermedia systems can be split into many separate (single) actions which correspond to the various "*interaction components or parts*" of the hypermedia system, which can be viewed or processed by the user at any one time. Such "*components*" can be applications, files, queries, screen menus/buttons or web pages. In this respect, during their interaction with the system the users leave behind "traces", which are simply the mouse clicks or keyboard key-press activities. By encoding all these activities in a manner that facilitates classification or user profiling, we can define new variables, which can then be used in the development of an intelligent, data-driven system for user modelling. Furthermore, time-based features can be designed in a generic form, since the concepts of both "access time" and "interaction parts" are equally applicable in most cases.

A lot of research has been carried out in the field of educational hypermedia systems (EHS) [6], [7], [8]. This study is concerned with the communication module of the EHS, which is focused on the interaction between the user and the system. Our method can be useful either in designing and selecting appropriate system parameters or as a classification and prediction tool for Intelligent Tutoring Systems.

Riding and Cheema [6] made a distinction between two types of learners in terms of cognitive style in an educational computing environment. The first group of learners, referred to as *wholists*, have the ability to view ideas as complete wholes, but struggle to separate these ideas into discrete parts, preferring an external structure to be imposed [8]. On the other hand, the second group of learners, *analysts,* are able to comprehend ideas in parts, preferring to impose their own structure [7]. The purpose of this study is to identify patterns in navigation behaviour of students in order to classify or discriminate the learners in respect of their cognitive styles.

2 The e-learning prototype and experimental set-up

The navigation data used in this study data were generated from the interaction of 46 computer-science students who were taking a course on "Computation and Algorithms" with an educational web site, which serves as an on-line tutorial. In this e-learning environment the learner could access 56 web pages, each with appropriate educational content. The learners were given up to 1 hour to complete their exploration through the site. The web pages were considered as the "interaction parts" of the system and all instances of access to them (usually via a mouse click) were recorded. In this way, the learner's activity was recorded

Human Perspectives in the Internet Society: Culture, Psychology and Gender, K. Morgan, J. Sanchez, C. A. Brebbia & A Voiskounsky (Editors) © 2004 WIT Press, www.witpress.com, ISBN 1-85312-726-4

into an audit trail file, which logs the time when a web page is accessed. The educational content (of the web pages) was hierarchically structured comprising six Chapters, plus four other web pages: (1) Home/starting page, (2) Site map, (3) Site index and (4) Site menu. These have a special role in inferring additional indications about cognitive styles.

The activity on the web pages is encoded accordingly to the six-chapter breakdown of the educational content and is illustrated in Figure 1 (chapters are depicted with different colours).

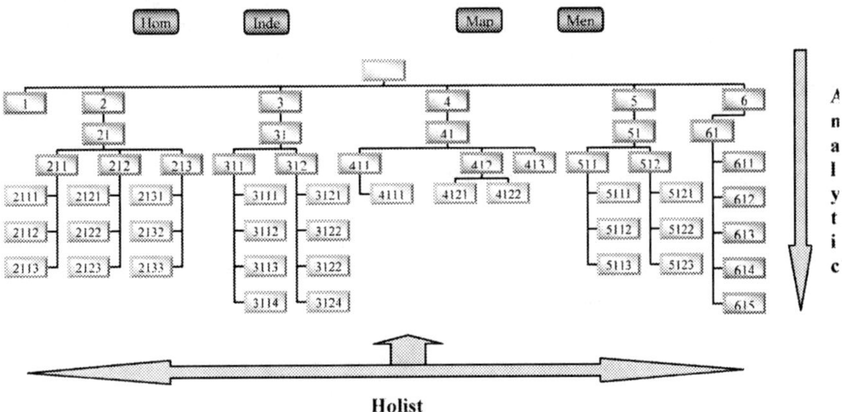

Figure 1: Navigation map.

According to the EHS literature, the problem of identification and analysis of the learner's cognitive style appears to be related to the way in which users navigate through the educational content. In our case, we might expect analysts to follow a top-down, (or depth-first) navigation behaviour, since research has shown such behaviour [14]. On the other hand, wholists might be expected to follow a more "breadth-first" approach.

The navigation paths of students were examined and classified into 3 classes according to the number of the top-down movements performed per branch. The cognitive styles of the students were also identified using Riding and Cheema's [6] Cognitive Styles Analysis (CSA). Though the wholist-analyst (W-A) cognitive style dimension is a continuous one, users were categorised into discrete classes as wholist, intermediate, or analyst. As a first insight, in preliminary analysis the W-A and "depth" scores (derived from the CSA and navigation data set respectively) were found to very similar. Taking this fact into account, the subsequent analysis goes further to identify the patterns which can contribute to correct classification in agreement with Riding's W-A theory. Although the classification involves 3 classes, the focus here is on achieving reliably good performance for the 2 extreme classes (wholist-analyst), which delineate the distinct nature of the learners' cognitive styles. The intermediate class (interpreted as being between wholist and analytic behaviour) can be considered to be ambiguously classified and therefore highly unpredictable.

Human Perspectives in the Internet Society: Culture, Psychology and Gender, K. Morgan, J. Sanchez, C. A. Brebbia & A Voiskounsky (Editors) © 2004 WIT Press, www.witpress.com, ISBN 1-85312-726-4

3 Feature design

In order to classify users with our proposed method, it is necessary to derive features from the mass of data available. Features are meaningful and analysable data chunks that model the situation in hand, in this case the navigation through hypermedia. Working on the structure depicted in Figure 1, features can be designed taking into account two categorising dimensions. The first dimension concerns the aggregation/granularity level of the "interaction parts" (web content in our case). In this way, features are designed for different levels of granularity of interaction components or parts: 1. Individual web pages; 2. Educational chapter (comprised of a number of linked web pages); and 3. Entire record of user's activity

Since the above interaction parts reflect the (educational) content of the system, these features possess a special meaning and represent context-related knowledge that is indispensable for the task of cognitive style classification. In this study, the webpage-based or chapter-based features can provide two different types of context-related information and thus two separate capabilities for discriminating between cognitive styles. More general features based on the overall user activity (for instance the total duration of the experiment for each user) can provide further insight as to the learner's behaviour as a whole.

The second dimension relates to time-based categorisation. Features were extracted from the raw navigational log data and divided in three categories, related to time attributes such as: 1. Access duration (reading or browsing time); 2. User's intensity/frequency of navigating activity (frequency of hits); 3. Chronological order of accessing/visiting or browsing interaction parts

Table 1: Categorisation of features in two dimensions.

	Duration based	Frequency based	Order based	Sum
Webpage-based features	56	56	110	222
Chapter-based features*	7	7	14	28
Features based on overall activity	1	4	-	5
Total	64	67	124	255

* Home, map, index and menu web pages are considered to be one group, represented artificially as Chapter 7.

This time-related dimension allows identification of the degree to which the user is concentrated on or interested in specific "interaction parts". It is obvious that high value of a feature means that the learner lingered in the specific interaction part for a long period of time or generated a large number of hits. Similarly, the earliest he visits a specific web page, the more interested he may be in the content of this web page. Table 1 categorises the derived 255 features in terms of these two dimensions.

As a pre-processing step, the features are normalized so as the maximum and minimum values are equal to 1 and 0 respectively. This is considered to be necessary for two 1. Homogeneity of features and 2. Better suitability of input

Human Perspectives in the Internet Society: Culture, Psychology and Gender, K. Morgan, J. Sanchez, C. A. Brebbia & A Voiskounsky (Editors) © 2004 WIT Press, www.witpress.com, ISBN 1-85312-726-4

features for further processing by a neural network (i.e. smaller values of weights and better adaptation).

4 Architecture of the proposed data analysis system

The high-level architecture of the proposed data analysis system includes a user behaviour pattern generation stage, where the key features of the user (user model) are extracted, and a user classification stage.

The proposed data processing method for user profiling is a hybrid of statistical and self-learning (neural computation) methods comprising four processing stages, three stages of feature engineering and one for the selection of the best user model. To have a model of the user's cognitive style behaviour based only on a relatively small set of features, the method uses Principal Component decomposition and sensitivity analysis to reduce the dimensionality of the input data and provide a simple behavioural model. The resulting user model will thus be a compact, robust behavioural model (user representation in terms of a small number of parameters/features). Given this model, the data analysis system will be able to generate a behavioural pattern for each user and then characterise/classify the user's cognitive style by employing the derived neural network model. More specifically, the method involves the following four stages:

1. Principal Component Analysis and extraction of Principal Component (PC) Scores
2. Sensitivity Analysis of Principal Component Scores
3. Sensitivity Analysis of Selected Features
4. Sensitivity Analysis to define the best model

5 Reduced data representation using PCA

The aim of the proposed methodology is to identify patterns of user behaviour that can lead to a robust classification and prediction model. The number of features that were originally generated is inevitably high; this is typically due to large numbers of time-related parameters, and "interaction groups" (many navigational goals or user groups). Many of the features generated from navigation data are redundant and add noise to the modelling process, which in practical terms translates to lower modelling performance and slower computation times. This makes the need for data reduction not only useful, but necessary. Principal Component Analysis (PCA) is a well known linear-correlation method that has been used mainly for data reduction purposes, while also capable of coping with multi-collinearity problems.

The principal components are derived by the eigenvectors of the features covariance matrix. In our experiment 95% of the total variance is retained, represented by the first 34 principal components. The components can be rotated using the VARIMAX method [10] by maximizing the cross-covariance. This rotation is a necessary step in order to achieve maximization of the variance in

Human Perspectives in the Internet Society: Culture, Psychology and Gender, K. Morgan, J. Sanchez, C. A. Brebbia & A Voiskounsky (Editors) © 2004 WIT Press, www.witpress.com, ISBN 1-85312-726-4

each loading and thus a greater differentiation between principal components in terms of their feature composition.

Principal Component Analysis here serves to transform the input of the self-learning classifier (user model) to avoid over-fitting or noise-induced errors. The original features will then be either selected or discarded using a sensitivity-analysis boot-strapping method.

6 The sensitivity analysis method

Sensitivity analysis is performed on Principal Component vectors or features in order to reduce the number of components by identifying the sensitive (important) components/features with respect to the cognitive style. Sensitivity analysis for the selection of the sensitive components or features is in our case performed using a neural network, which here effectively provides the user model. The neural network model used here has one hidden layer with 8 nodes and the acceptable training error is set at 0.03. The training of the neural network is supervised in terms of three target classes: Analytic, Intermediate, and Holist. Thus, the classification target vector takes three discrete values which are 0 for Analytic, .5 for Intermediate and 1 for Holist cognitive style.

The estimation of the sensitivity (relevance with respect to the cognitive style) of the resulting Principal Components or features is achieved via bootstrapping of the neural network model, as in the following steps:

1. Perform Sensitivity Analysis on inputs which can be Principal Components Scores or features (from now on we call them both "variables" to avoid confusion).
2. Remove the redundant variables from the data representation - keep only the variables that exhibit significantly high sensitivity at the classifier's output, while at the same time achieving a sufficiently small generalisation error.
3. Select the best model that (a) minimises the classification error and (b) achieves maximum generalisation performance.

Bootstrapping involves generating randomly and automatically a multitude of training/validation set combinations from the available data (assuming data is available for large number of users) and performing the training and classification success rate analysis. Here a cross-validation arrangement is used, where the total population of instances/samples (in our case users) is randomly divided to two thirds, which form the training set, and one third, which serves the validation set. It is important for the subsequent process of best model selection to have a sufficiently large number of samples in the validation set.

A random variable is added to the feature set as a gauge of zero sensitivity. This sensitivity analysis process identifies a small number of significant variables, significant in the sense that their variance is significantly higher than that of the added random variable (i.e. highly correlated with user's behaviour).

Human Perspectives in the Internet Society: Culture, Psychology and Gender, K. Morgan, J. Sanchez, C. A. Brebbia & A Voiskounsky (Editors) © 2004 WIT Press, www.witpress.com, ISBN 1-85312-726-4

It should be noted that not all trained models are of the same "quality". The generalisation performance of the trained models is the main criterion of their usefulness. Our aim is to select several trained models with sufficiently low generalisation error from the original dataset. The selection of 100 models (out of 1500 validation sets randomly created) with a satisfactory low generalisation error seems to be sufficient. The threshold under which the error can be considered as low is equal to the smallest error amongst the first 20 models randomly selected. In cases where the instances of such low error are fewer than 100 (a rare occurrence), the best 100 models out of 1500 are selected.

For each successful (in the sense of high generalisation) model, we run a simulation where to each variable (feature or Principal Component Score) of an input vector we assign a range of regularly spaced values from 0 to 1 (10 values from 0 to 1 with step 0.1). Then the variance of the classifier's output can be calculated with respect to these values. This procedure is repeated exhaustively for every variable (including the random variable) for all the input vectors (in both training and testing sets) and the mean (average of 10 values) variance over all outputs is calculated. The final sensitivity value for each variable is then calculated as the average variance over all 100 (successful) models, as derived from this simulation:

$S = V/M$, where
V is the average variance over all successful models and
M is the average of all models' mean outputs.

The variance is here divided by the average of all outputs over all models, so that any distortions that might occur due to differences in the magnitudes in the output values are eliminated. The variables with sensitivity lower than that of the random variable, or sufficiently close to it (e.g. within 10% of its value), are excluded from further analysis.

7 Sensitivity analysis of PC Scores

Overfitting in neural networks is a major problem, which should be tackled if it is to achieve sufficient generalisation and low output variance. Causes of overfitting are large numbers of input variables, as well as multicollinearity problems [11], [12]. Since the number of our original features is very large (compared to the training set), a smaller number of Principal Component Scores can be used as inputs to the neural network (instead of the original features) to overcome this problem.

Sensitivity analysis performed on the PC Scores provided a set of sensitive PCs. The number of the selected significant components (with the highest sensitivity) is 15. Thresholding the product $p = \mathbf{D}^T\mathbf{z}$ of the respective 15 loadings (**D**) and the significance weighting vector **z** (degree of correlation of features with cognitive style) gives the final set of key features, ranked in order of significance. 112 features with high sensitivity (above 0.1) are selected. The purpose of this intermediate process is to offer more reliable results and avoid overfitting.

Human Perspectives in the Internet Society: Culture, Psychology and Gender, K. Morgan, J. Sanchez, C. A. Brebbia & A Voiskounsky (Editors) © 2004 WIT Press, www.witpress.com, ISBN 1-85312-726-4

8 Sensitivity analysis of reduced feature set

The 112 features derived from the previous process were fed subsequently to a similar sensitivity analysis system. Following the same procedure, 27 features are finally extracted (as highly sensitive to the cognitive style). The above features appear to have similarly high sensitivity to the output and they can be considered as the most discriminating in terms of the cognitive styles. Frequency features, especially those corresponding to Chapter 2, seem to offer high discrimination capability.

Table 2: Categorisation of final features.

	Duration based	Frequency based	Order based	Sum
Webpage-based	6	11	3	20
Chapter-based *	1	3	2	6
Overall activity based		1		1
Total	7	15	5	27

9 Defining the best model

The sensitivity analysis process is now repeated for the final set of features, but without the generalisation restriction. Training and cross-validation is performed again using the bootstrapped dataset that comprises only the selected features. A cross-validation procedure is carried out with 100 random validation sets and the overall performance of the 100 models is calculated. The overall performance of all resulting (trained) models is compared and the best model (in terms of maximum classification and generalisation performance) is chosen as the most suitable user model.

The criteria for selecting the best model are (in order of importance):

1. A minimum acceptable (at least 15%) Generalisation Error for the two extreme classes (W, A).
2. Fewer misclassification cases in all three classes.
3. Lower Generalisation Error in all three classes.
4. Larger number of instances belonging to the two extreme classes in the test set.

The selection of best model was decided mainly on the low generalisation error for the two extreme classes (W, A). The second criterion mainly accounts for the misclassification of students belonging to the intermediate class. The students of this class were expected to be more frequently misclassified due to the ambivalent nature of their cognitive style. However, since the selected model is capable of discriminating successfully the two extreme classes, it appears to also provide a method to assign intermediate-class students to one of the other classes in a sensible, satisfactory way. Therefore it can stand in a complementary way next to the W-A test method, helping the expert to verify students' cognitive styles or consider classification alternatives.

In table 3, the average performance of the 100 models with final features and the best model performance are shown. The first row shows the average performance of 100 randomly selected models based on the whole initial set of features.

Table 3: Generalisation performance of neural-network user models.

	Analytic (0)	Intermediate (.5)	Holist (1)
All features	54%	30%	61%
Final Features	81%	27%	84%
Best Model	100%	98%	100%

The second row shows the average performance after the third (final) sensitivity analysis stage. Since 81-84% of students who belong to the holist – analytic classes can be classified accurately, it would be reasonable to conclude that there is indeed an identifiable pattern in the learner's cognitive style behaviour. Thus, the developed model can be used to validate and give an interpretation of cognitive styles. Comparing this performance to that of the first row which is after the first sensitivity analysis stage where all features are taken into account (by means of Principal Components), it is easily recognisable that the contribution of the data selection/reduction stages to performance is extremely important.

The best model appears to have a higher performance in the intermediate class as well and this is a direct consequence of the third criterion. However, any deviation in this class will be in favour of one of the other 2 classes, which might show the capacity of the method to improve on the W-A test results.

10 Conclusions

This paper presented a new method for cognitive style classification, which involves feature design together with statistical feature reduction and sensitivity analysis. It achieves satisfactory performance in classification by combining techniques of feature engineering and supervised learning.

The use of Principal Component Analysis reduces the effects of feature noise and multicollinearity at the first place and ensures that only the features that are most critical to the classification process are selected. The performance is shown to increase dramatically after the elimination of redundant features, enhancing the method's robustness. The features finally selected and the resulting model can provide meaningful, interpretable information to supervisors, tutors or learners in terms of cognitive style classification. The best model gives an overall classification performance of 91% for all classes and 100% for the two extreme ones (WA).

However, more simulations should be carried out in the future to prove the validity of the model over a long term period. Future work can build on the proposed model and address the challenge of developing an embedded audit module that runs in real time. Thus the presented work can lead to the development of online systems, which can monitor the user behaviour dynamically. For example, it can be employed to provide navigation assistance to the learner or critical information to the system supervisor/tutor in terms of the

Human Perspectives in the Internet Society: Culture, Psychology and Gender, K. Morgan, J. Sanchez, C. A. Brebbia & A Voiskounsky (Editors) © 2004 WIT Press, www.witpress.com, ISBN 1-85312-726-4

learning goal – with deviation from desired status acting as a prediction and quality pointer.

Acknowledgement

The authors are grateful for the support of the EPSRC (Grant number: GR/R57737/01) for funding this project.

References

[1] Zhu, D., Premkumar, G., Zhang, X. & Chu, C.H., Data mining for network intrusion detection: A comparison of alternative methods. *Decision Sciences*, **32**, pp. 635-660, 2001.

[2] Lam, K.Y., Hui, L. & Chung, S.L., Multivariate data analysis software for enhancing system security. *J. Systems Software*, **31**, pp. 267-275, 1995.

[3] Denning, D.E., An intrusion-detection model. *IEEE Trans. Soft. Eng.*, **13**, pp. 222-232, 1987.

[4] Silverman, B., Bachann, M. & Al-Akharas, K., Implications of buyer decision theory for design of e-commerce websites. *Human –Computer Studies*, **55**, pp. 815-844, 2001.

[5] Stephanova, M. & Thomas, L.C., PHAB scores: proportional hazards analysis behavioural scores. *Journal of the Operational Research Society*, **52**, pp. 1007 –1016, 2001.

[6] Riding, R.J. & Cheema, I., Cognitive styles: an overview and integration. *Educational Psychology*, **11**, pp. 193-215, 1991.

[7] Liu, M. & Reed, W.M., The effect of hypermedia assisted instruction on second-language learning through a semantic-network-based approach. *Journal of Educational Computing Research*, **12(2)**, pp. 159–175, 1995.

[8] Chen, S. & Macredie, R.D., Cognitive Styles and Hypermedia Navigation: Development of a Learning Model. *Journal of the American Society for Information Science and Technology*, **53**, pp. 3-15, 2002.

[9] Efron, B., *The Jackknife, the Bootstrap and Other Resampling Plans*, Philadelphia: SIAM, 1982.

[10] Kaiser, H. F., The varimax criterion for analytic rotation in factor analysis. *Psychometrica,* **23***,* pp. 187-200, 1958.

[11] Hurvich, C.M. & Tsai, C.-L., Regression and time series model selection in small samples. *Biometrika*, **76(2)**, pp. 297-307, 1989.

[12] Sarle, W.S., Stopped training and other remedies for overfitting. *Proc. of the 27th Symposium on the Interface of Computing Science and Statistics*, pp. 352-360, 1995.

[13] Fragos, S., Stergioulas, L.K. & Xydeas, C.S., Classification of decision-behaviour patterns in multivariate computer log data using ICA, in *KES'03, Lecture Notes in Computer Science: Artificial Intelligence*, Springer-Verlag, Vol. 2, pp. 73-79, 2003.

[14] Ford, N. & Chen, S. Y. (2000) Individual Differences, Hypermedia Navigation and Learning: An Empirical Study. Journal of Educational Multimedia and Hypermedia. 9(4), 281-311.

Human Perspectives in the Internet Society: Culture, Psychology and Gender, K. Morgan, J. Sanchez, C. A. Brebbia & A Voiskounsky (Editors) © 2004 WIT Press, www.witpress.com, ISBN 1-85312-726-4

Section 13
E-business

Concepts, methods, standards and technologies to promote e-business interoperability in a large enterprise

T. Vitvar
Department of Informatics in Transport and Telecommunications, Czech Technical University in Prague, Czech Republic

Abstract

We discuss how strategy, vision, technology, development approach, current trends over the Internet, and customer specifications were balanced together to achieve the e-business solution implemented in a large, European-oriented enterprise. First, we discuss the key discriminators for the future of a distribution and supply chain over the Internet. Accordingly, we describe corporate e-business concepts as the initial proposal for interoperability of the company's and customers' resources. It draws up specifications, boundaries and directives that must be obeyed to achieve comprehensive integration of the enterprise with its business partners in all countries. We propose an incremental development approach, which consists of a number of phases (sub-projects) conforming to the enterprise structure, as well as the lifecycle of each sub-project with respect to the organization of e-business development team and roles of analysts, architects, and developers. Moreover, typical e-business infrastructure based on SAP R/3 Internet Transaction Server is shown as well as its integration into the corporate IT infrastructure. We also describe B2B interoperability standards, such as BMEcat and OpenTrans, and their adoption in automated interoperability between customers' and enterprise's ERP systems. In conclusion, we show an example of e-business ordering process from the enterprise and customer point of view, and the essential back-office activities within the process.
Keywords: SAP R/3, OpenTrans, BMEcat, e-business concepts, e-business process, e-business infrastructure.

Human Perspectives in the Internet Society: Culture, Psychology and Gender, K. Morgan, J. Sanchez, C. A. Brebbia & A Voiskounsky (Editors) © 2004 WIT Press, www.witpress.com, ISBN 1-85312-726-4

1 Why do we need e-business?

With the head office in Germany and manufacturing in Denmark, Germany, Austria, the Czech Republic, Poland and China, nkt cables is the European market-orientated energy and data cable enterprise. Its activity is to develop and manufacture voltage, communication and data cables as well as cables accessories. Among the others, nkt cables intends to extend its selling and procurement activities by opening new channels for its business partners over the Internet. Initial concepts have been identified to form up nkt cables e-Business vision, and answer questions that come into everybody's mind when we only start thinking about such innovation.

Almost everybody today acknowledges that the Internet, being an open and fast medium, will lead us to an open economy where information like pricing strategies, product specifications, delivery performances, creditworthiness of a customer, customers purchase history, supplier and customer satisfaction scores will be available at a mouse-click distance for anybody and anywhere. We also see that the original role models for businesses in the distribution and supply chain will change because of the Internet. In this new economy, businesses can only exist if they can clearly show how and where they are adding value to the final product or service and that service, information and availability are the key discriminators for all customers.

Major drivers pushing every company towards this new economy deal with customer convenience requiring comfortable, easier and cheaper way to gather, choose, order, pay and ship products to their doorsteps. In addition, new trends over the Internet are becoming more and more important, such as interoperability of business partners (B2B), growing number of e-business services (e.g. e-commerce, web ordering services) or on-line competing suppliers (i.e. e-marketplace). All such new activities are nowadays supported by modern technology platforms and standards being the essential and stable e-business background for both, customers as well as enterprises (e.g. ERP interoperability platforms, interchange message standards – BMEcat, OpenTrans, etc.).

2 Corporate e-business concepts

Corporate e-business concepts are the essential part of enterprise information strategy, and are initial proposals for interoperability of company's and customers' resources. Several concepts have been identified forming the e-business vision, such as development approach, structure of development team, and e-business infrastructure with respect to existing electronic services trends over the Internet, modern technology platforms and standards, and domains of company's selling activities. Accordingly, proposed e-business solution exploits SAP R/3 technology, BMEcat and OpenTrans standards, supports interoperability strategies such as web ordering as well as Business to Business, and acts as a comprehensive, corporate and transparent e-business solution as a part of e-European cables market and industry. Following picture shows global e-business architecture as it is proposed in e-business concepts.

Human Perspectives in the Internet Society: Culture, Psychology and Gender, K. Morgan, J. Sanchez, C. A. Brebbia & A Voiskounsky (Editors) © 2004 WIT Press, www.witpress.com, ISBN 1-85312-726-4

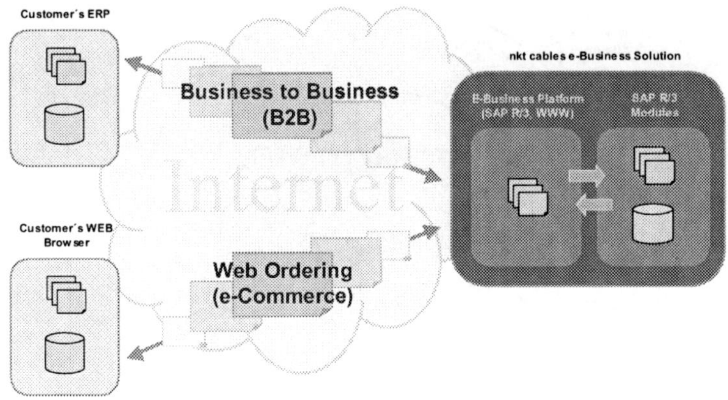

Figure 1: Global e-business architecture.

2.1 Development approach

Essential part of e-business concepts relates to the development approach. Its major idea is to divide the complex project into phases each representing one increment moving the system forward towards the vision. Within each phase, improved e-business solution is delivered in all countries promoting experience together with core implementations gathered from prior phases. All phases are represented by pilot solution development and delivery in the first, most appropriate country, which is then followed by solution roll-outs in subsequent countries. Moreover, standard project lifecycle procedures as well as other enterprise standards and policies are respected.

Phase I – Local Web Ordering solution has been introduced as a preliminary phase in order to achieve corporate e-business solution successively. This phase is focused on the Web Ordering System which delivers underlying e-business infrastructure of SAP R/3 Internet Transaction Server in each country. Customers, who access e-Business services over the Internet using the web browser, are allowed to submit orders from both, ordinary as well as consignment stocks, check products availability on stocks, check orders statuses and their transaction information.

Phase II – Corporate Web Ordering System obeys the enterprise “One Company Approach” and accordingly promotes local e-business sites to one, compact and comprehensive solution at group level. Particular tasks deal with the integration of all locally implemented solutions so that customers are served and treated within one transparent European enterprise.

Phase III is focused on Business to Business solution at both, local and corporate levels. Customers exploit e-Business services on-line over direct interconnection of ERP systems. In addition, enterprise services and products appear on electronic market places in order to compete with others and clearly show their added value.

The following picture depicts incremental development approach, its phases as they were proposed by the IT organization.

Human Perspectives in the Internet Society: Culture, Psychology and Gender, K. Morgan, J. Sanchez, C. A. Brebbia & A Voiskounsky (Editors) © 2004 WIT Press, www.witpress.com, ISBN 1-85312-726-4

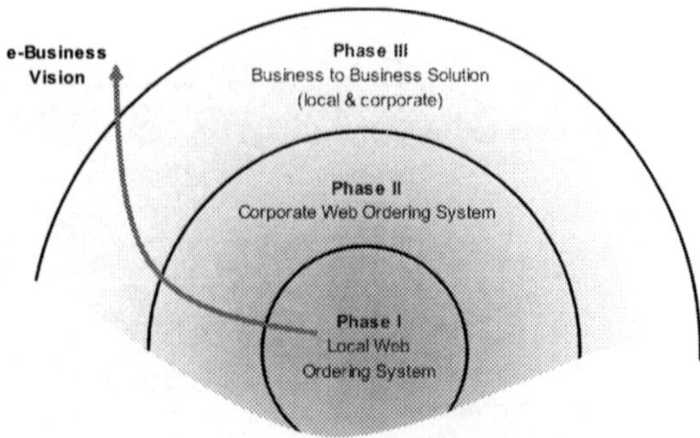

Figure 2: Incremental development approach.

Following scope of methodology stages has been identified as methodology for all phases of e-business project. In particular, the methodology stages can be amended according to a phase requirements.

1. State of the Art and Requirements Analysis – business process and concepts, software, hardware, functions, and organizational aspects,
2. Design – design of function and process architectures as well as software and hardware architectures,
3. Customization/Modification – customization and/or modification of standard SAP components according to the design,
4. Implementation – installation and configuration of system components, testing functionality,
5. Production and Maintenance – technical, functional and organizational maintenance of production e-business environment.

2.2 Structure of development team

Following is the typical e-business team structure for a phase of the project.

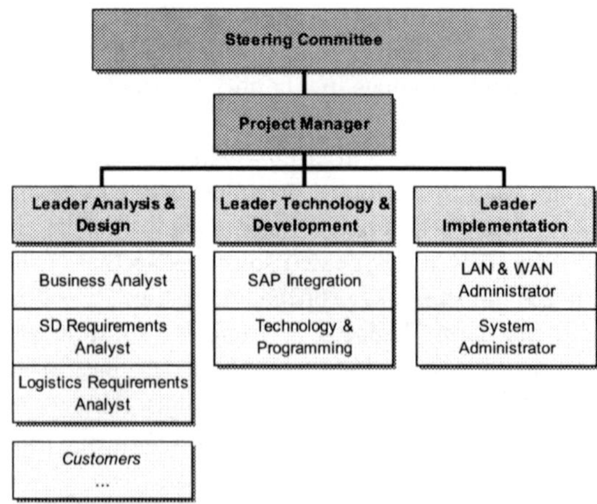

Figure 3: Development team structure.

Human Perspectives in the Internet Society: Culture, Psychology and Gender, K. Morgan, J. Sanchez, C. A. Brebbia & A Voiskounsky (Editors) © 2004 WIT Press, www.witpress.com, ISBN 1-85312-726-4

Another important part of e-business concepts deals with a structure of a development team. It has been approved, analytical and design project tasks will be in charge of internal IT professionals and business people who are aware of business processes and technical infrastructure of the company. Consequently, development team is composed of all, IT professionals as well as business people from particular country of interest, and a selected external vendor. Internal team members are responsible for requirements analysis and conceptual design proposals to be used by a vendor to process further tasks on development, implementation and maintenance.

Steering committee members approve outcomes, deliverables and financial proposals to ensure e-business consistency with other activities, visions, and approaches of the enterprise. It consists of members such as IT Director and responsible board of management representative.

Project manager coordinates the project in order to achieve vision concepts, meet deadlines and financial boundaries. He or she respects directives from Steering Committee and ensures its adoption to underlying development issues.

Analysis and design team involves IT and business analyst professionals, sales, delivery and procurement representatives as well as logistic people. IT analysts gather requirements from business professionals and build integrated design proposals. In order to meet particular customers' requirements, selected key customers are also asked to participate in the project to submit feedbacks and acknowledgements.

Technology and development team members are responsible for technical issues of the project regarding e-business platform, its security, seamless integration into the existing IT infrastructure and continuity with ERP system maintenance and development.

Implementation team members perform tasks concerning e-business system secure connectivity to the Internet, configuration of operating systems and further activities such as administration, monitoring and maintenance.

2.3 E-business infrastructure

Typical e-business infrastructure is depicted in Figure 4: at the enterprise side, it is built on the SAP R/3 technology, such as the Internet Transaction Server (ITS) and Internet Application Components (IAC). ITS is a key-component of SAP R/3 e-business infrastructure which enhances SAP accessibility towards the Internet. ITS uses already implemented application logic in the SAP system and acts only as a component building the client-side content using the Internet web-compliant technologies.

ITS consists of two major building blocks, so-called WGate and AGate components. WGate component is integrated into the web server using its standard API interface. It captures requests from web-clients and passes them over to the AGate server. Subsequently, AGate server executes these requests by calling IAC components and builds web pages using HTML Business Templates. Both, WGate and AGate servers can reside on the same machine as well as on different machines running different operating systems, such as Linux or Windows. Since a big amount of data is being transmitted between WGate and

Human Perspectives in the Internet Society: Culture, Psychology and Gender, K. Morgan, J. Sanchez, C. A. Brebbia & A Voiskounsky (Editors) © 2004 WIT Press, www.witpress.com, ISBN 1-85312-726-4

AGate servers, it is suggested that both machines are connected via a line of a higher capacity (100Mbps is a minimum). To increase the security, a firewall can be placed between the WGate and AGate machines as well as secure connection over SSL is always established for internet users to access the site.

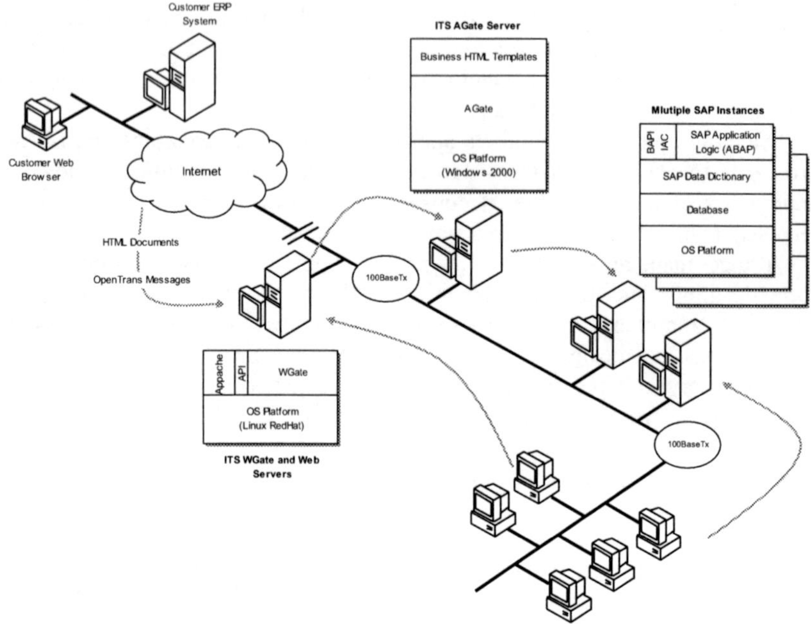

Figure 4: Typical e-business infrastructure.

Internet Application Components (IAC) are standard SAP components built in ABAP which implement e-Business functionality. Such components are IAC On-line Shop, IAC Product Catalogue, IAC Order Creation etc. Moreover, IAC components can be customized to fulfill particular e-Business requirements.

Customer who accesses the e-business site has a choice. He or she can connect to the web server using a web browser and submit requests manually. In this case, the customer provides his or her user identification and a password when logging on to the system. If ERP systems are directly interconnected, all transactions between customers and target ERP system are automatically triggered on submitting ordinary customers' requests in their home systems (e.g. standard order, consignment fill-up and issue orders, pay orders etc.).

2.4 E-business interoperability standards

One of the most discussed e-business requirements is Business to Business direct interoperability between customer's and company's ERP systems. A customer may operate on any kind of ERP system which may have nothing common with the company IT strategy involving SAP R/3 system. Thus, common interface for

Human Perspectives in the Internet Society: Culture, Psychology and Gender, K. Morgan, J. Sanchez, C. A. Brebbia & A Voiskounsky (Editors) © 2004 WIT Press, www.witpress.com, ISBN 1-85312-726-4

communication between both systems should be proposed independently on underlying technology. Since major e-business activities deal with sales and procurement transactions, standards of OpenTrans and BMEcat specifications were chosen for such purposes. We briefly introduce both standards and its adoption in our e-business solution.

2.4.1 BMEcat

BMEcat is a standard for data transfer of electronic product catalogues involving a number of companies in its development, namely Alcatel, Audi, BMW, American Express etc. It has an extensive coverage of multi-media product data and catalogue structures, and it is designed for use of standardised product classification systems.

So that we could adopt BMEcat specifications in our e-business solution, company product catalogue structures must be amended to obey mandatory BMEcat fields and data types. Consequently, mediator system is designed, providing conversion between internal product catalogue and standard BMEcat structures. As a result, any part of company's product catalogue can be exported and provided for use of a customer. If a customer provides his or her product catalogue in BMEcat format, it is imported into the SAP system so that customer materials numbers are available for sales and procurement people.

2.4.2 OpenTrans

OpenTrans initiative defines standards for business transactions and documents, and is managed by German and international enterprises under the direction of Fraunhofer IAO. OpenTrans is XML-based standard defining a number of transaction formats such as Quotation, Order, Invoice, Dispatch Notification etc. Moreover, it is compatible with BMEcat specifications.

Business analysts in cooperation with IT analysts perform an analysis of selected OpenTrans transactions structures in contrast with existing business processes implemented in e-business solution. As a result, documentation is created describing in detail an interface to e-business system captured in OpenTrans format. Such documentation is then provided to a customer, who is interested in building of automated B2B communication on the level of ERP systems. Certain functions are also created in e-business system to process OpenTrans requests and generate OpenTrans replies on result. Such functions operate on existing underlying SAP R/3 structures and processes.

3 Example of e-business ordering process

Implemented e-business solution allows customers to process their requests over the Internet with a minimal involvement of company's back-office activities. E-business is an additional mechanism to existing methods, such as ordering products or enquiring information over the phone, fax or by e-mail. However, certain constraints exist which allows particular processes to be controlled or monitored. In cables industry, when a customer orders a cable, he or she also specifies a length of the cable as well as packaging units. Existing cables on a

Human Perspectives in the Internet Society: Culture, Psychology and Gender, K. Morgan, J. Sanchez, C. A. Brebbia & A Voiskounsky (Editors) © 2004 WIT Press, www.witpress.com, ISBN 1-85312-726-4

stock might be cut into pieces which in turn could cause disorder in sales people daily work. We show an example of ordering process implemented in e-business solution including essential back-office activities in order to avoid inconsistency in stock and sales people effort. Following is the description of a typical sales ordering process implemented in e-business solution over the Web.

1. Customer is required to provide his/her username and password in order to login to the system. If authentication fails, customer is not allowed to process any further actions.
2. If customer is authenticated, he/she selects a stock in a form of a product catalogue assigned to this customer in underlying SAP system.
3. Customer is allowed to search and browse products in the product catalogue according to a name as well as both, internal product/material id or a customer product/material id.
4. For each product that the customer adds to basket, he/she is allowed to select from available packaging units of the product as well as specify individual length for that product. Customer also specifies number of packages.
5. Customer processes quotation on all products in the basket and specifies required delivery date, that he/she wants products to be delivered. Customer receives quotation result showing the expected delivery date and expected price for each product in the basket. Such delivery date may differ from requested delivery date specified by the customer.
6. If quotation results are satisfactory for the customer, he/she submits the order and receives the order confirmation. Customer is also allowed to specify an extra delivery address at this stage. By default, standard delivery address from customer master record in SAP system is used.
7. Order check is performed on each submitted order according to the following rules:
    a. If product is on the stock and requested length matches the length of the product on the stock within the tolerance of –0+3%, standard order processing is allowed automatically, thus subsequent functions of SAP system are performed. In this case, product is dispatched and delivered at suggested delivery date.
    b. If product is not on the stock, or product is on the stock, however requested length requires this product to be cut (requested length doesn't match any length of a product on the stock within the tolerance of –0+3%), such order receives frozen status. Responsible sales person is aware of such order and performs further actions.
        i. If requirements are satisfactory, sales person allows its further standard processing, thus subsequent functions of SAP system are performed. In this case, production/purchasing/cutting order is created, and consequent actions follow in SAP system.
        ii. If requirements are not satisfactory, sales person contacts the customer and negotiates further conditions with him/her. In this case, sales person can submit the order manually to the SAP system, after conditions are understood by both sides.

Human Perspectives in the Internet Society: Culture, Psychology and Gender, K. Morgan, J. Sanchez, C. A. Brebbia & A Voiskounsky (Editors) © 2004 WIT Press, www.witpress.com, ISBN 1-85312-726-4

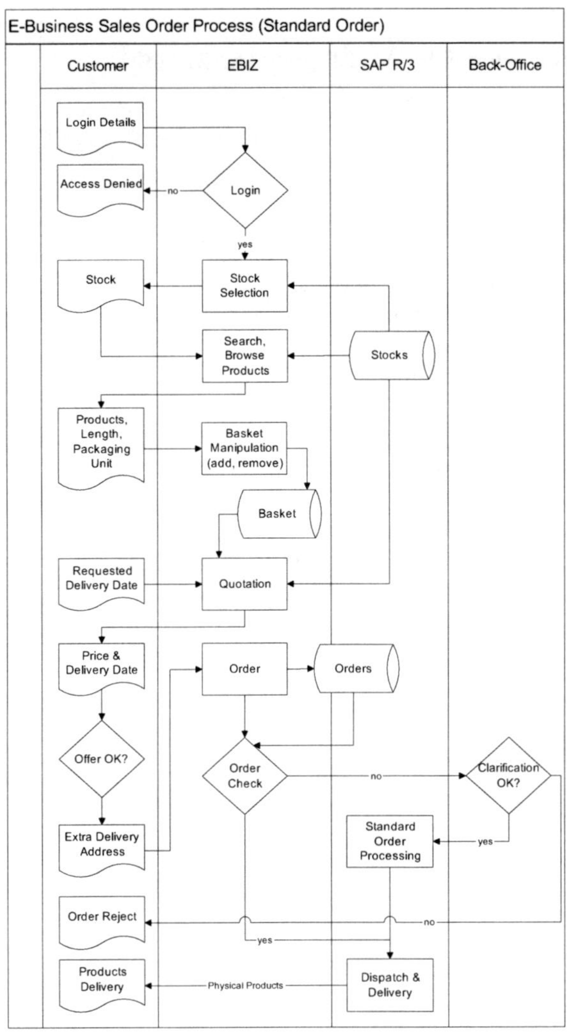

Figure 5: E-business ordering process example.

4 Conclusion

E-business concepts were created to cover fundamental issues of e-business to be implemented in a large, European-oriented enterprise. Some of applied e-business concepts have been shown on a typical example of ordering process over the Web. We sincerely hope that above offers give you some ideas and building blocks to improve and enhance your e-business development practice.

Human Perspectives in the Internet Society: Culture, Psychology and Gender, K. Morgan, J. Sanchez, C. A. Brebbia & A Voiskounsky (Editors) © 2004 WIT Press, www.witpress.com, ISBN 1-85312-726-4

Acknowledgment

This work was supported by AV ČR grant IAA2124301.

References

[1] Fraunhofer IAO, University of Essen BLI, *Specification BMEcat version 1.2.* 2001, www.bmecat.org.

[2] Fraunhofer IAO, University of Essen BLI, *Spezifikation OpenTrans version 1.0.* 2001, www.opentrans.org.

[3] Vitvar T., Stoepker C., *e-Business Concepts in a Large European-oriented Enterprise*, Technology & Prosperity, April 2003.

[4] Arthur M. Langer, *Analysis and Design of Information Systems, Second Edition.* Springer, 2001.

[5] Mario Perez, Alexander Hildenbrand, Bernd Matzke, Peter Zencke, *The SAP R/3 on the Internet.* ADDISON-WESLEY, 1999.

[6] Jiří Voříšek, *Strategické řízení informačního systému a systémová integrace*. Management Press, 1999.

[7] David S. Linthicum, *B2B Application Integration: e-Business-Enable Your Enterprise*. ADDISON-WESLEY, 2001.

Human Perspectives in the Internet Society: Culture, Psychology and Gender, K. Morgan, J. Sanchez, C. A. Brebbia & A Voiskounsky (Editors) © 2004 WIT Press, www.witpress.com, ISBN 1-85312-726-4

E-business security in international perspective

N. L. Karmakar
School of Management, University of Western Sydney, Australia

Abstract

Security is a key barrier for reaping the full benefits of e-Business in an organisation. The term 'e-Business' is used in academic and business circles very frequently since the beginning of the new century. This is not just about commercial transactions over the Web, it is the overall strategy of redefining old business models using new technology to maximise customer value and profits. E-Commerce, an application of e-Business can be used to create virtual global trading collaborations among customers, suppliers, distributors and financial institutions. This radical shift in business paradigm is creating a huge market in cyberspace. The new world of e-Business has been the source of wealth creation for some developed countries, the USA in particular. It is projected that the USA will have up to $7 trillion in online trade by 2006. In spite of this huge potential, it has some set backs that have questioned the reliability of the Web. In 2001, online fraud losses were more than $700 million, or 1.14% of the total online sales of $61.8 billion. The new technology is constantly developing to keep e-Business applications over the Internet safe and secured. The purpose of this paper is to explore major e-Business security issues from an international perspective. With the rising importance of e-Business, security will become an even more pressing concern.
Keywords: cryptography, cybercrime, digital economy, e-commerce, ethics, Internet, law, privacy.

'Do not figure on opponents not attacking; worry about your own lack of preparation'.
-----Book of the Five Rings

1 Introduction

Security issues in cyberspace to undertake e-Business are attracting attention in industries and governments around the globe. E-Business Security is related to

Human Perspectives in the Internet Society: Culture, Psychology and Gender, K. Morgan, J. Sanchez, C. A. Brebbia & A Voiskounsky (Editors) © 2004 WIT Press, www.witpress.com, ISBN 1-85312-726-4

Internet security which is not about protecting hardware, it is about protecting information. The field of security in cyberspace focuses on designing measures that can enforce security policies, especially in the presence of malicious attack.

The Internet is the fastest growing, most user-friendly, and most commercially popular technology to date. This is based on an open network architecture, so information can be transferred freely and efficiently. While this greatly facilitates the development of e-Business applications, it also raises many security concerns. The Internet is the playground for hackers and lawbreakers. Fortunately, by using modern cryptographic techniques, we can make e-Business applications over the Internet safe and secure [1].

In this paper we have introduced some of the issues and measures taken to secure a website or network. Within a business framework, management develops a set of policies and procedures aimed at securing the network from external and internal threats [2]. The Internet is the source of digital economy and globalisation and thus gives rise to new threats to security, privacy, and ethics [3].

2 Security in general

In general, *security* is "the quality or state of being secure – to be free from danger" [4]. It means to be protected from adversaries-from those who would do harm, intestinally or otherwise. A successful organisation should have the multiple layers of security in place to protect its operations, such as *Physical Security*, *Personal Security*, *Operations Security*, *Communications Security*, *Network Security* and *Information Security* [5].

To protect the information and its related systems from danger, such tools as policy, awareness, training and education and technology are necessary. In short, security relates to controlling one's environment for protection of data [6].

3 E-Business and e-commerce in a nutshell

E-Business is an integration of all the business processes required to buy and sell goods and services over the electronic platform known as the Internet. This is not a new concept: rather it is an evolution of traditional business practices taking advantage of the new technologies of the Internet age to enhance efficiency and productivity. IBM defines e-Business as "a secure, flexible and integrated approach to delivering differentiated business value by combining the systems and processes that run core business operations with the simplicity and reach made possible by Internet technology" [7]. It is vital to remember that e-Business is much more than e-Commerce which is defined as 'buying and selling over digital media' [8].

4 What is e-Business security?

E-Business Security may be defined as the *policies*, *procedures*, *practices*, and *technology* that must be in place to undertake business electronically via

Human Perspectives in the Internet Society: Culture, Psychology and Gender, K. Morgan, J. Sanchez, C. A. Brebbia & A Voiskounsky (Editors) © 2004 WIT Press, www.witpress.com, ISBN 1-85312-726-4

networks with a reasonable assurance of safety. This assurance applies to all online activities, transmissions, and storage. It also applies to business partners, customers, regulators, insurers, or others who might be at risk in the event of a breach of that organisation's security. Ultimately, it may be court that is called on to decide whether reasonable security existed at the time of the breach [9].

With the advent of e-Business and increased use of the Internet, security has been a frequent headline in the news media. Many businesses and individuals alike routinely send sensitive data across the Internet. These data must be protected because network-enabled e-Business requires a high level of security in order to be successful. Unfortunately, the Internet was not originally designed to be a highly secure system. The good news is that a number of technologies have been developed to increase the security of the Internet and Web [10].

5 Privacy concerns in e-Business

Security and *privacy* are said to be two of the biggest challenges regarding e-Business. In reality, both are major concerns for any computerised environment including businesses, education, government and individuals. Privacy can be defined as 'the ability to manage information about oneself' [10]. The issue of privacy has become one of the hottest topics in e-Business security at the beginning of the twenty-first century. Many organisations are collecting, swapping, and selling personal information as a commodity and many individuals are aware of these practices and looking to governments for protection of their privacy. The ability to collect information as an individual, combine facts from separate sources, and merge it with other information has resulted in databases of information that were previously impossible to set up [5].

6 Ethics in e-Business

Due to the explosion of e-Business new industries are emerging and new business models are being invented. The new business environment includes new legal and ethical problems that the business people in the digital economy must be acquainted with in order to handle them properly and operate effectively. Ethics is a branch of philosophy that deals with what is considered to be right and wrong. *Ethics* has assumed a new dimension of importance as e-Business open-up a new spectrum of unregulated activities. Business people need guidelines as to what behaviours are reasonable under any given set of circumstances. E-Business is so new that the legal, ethical, and other public policy issues that are necessary for e-Business existence is still evolving [11].

7 Security threats in e-Business

There are many security threats in e-Business which face several challenges that are inherently not as challenging in traditional business. In [12], Kou lists the

Human Perspectives in the Internet Society: Culture, Psychology and Gender, K. Morgan, J. Sanchez, C. A. Brebbia & A Voiskounsky (Editors) © 2004 WIT Press, www.witpress.com, ISBN 1-85312-726-4

potential threats and attacks to which commercial activities in networked environments may be vulnerable:

- Accessing unauthorised network resources
- Destroying information and network resources
- Altering, inserting, or modifying information
- Disclosing information to unauthorised people
- Causing networking services disruption or interruption
- Stealing information and network resources
- Denying services received, and denying information sent or received
- Claiming to have provided services that have not been administered and/or claiming to have sent or received information not given.

E-Business applications and technologies must address these security issues. It is helpful to break the threats into two categories- '*threats to data*' and '*threat to systems*'. Since the Internet is a network of networks, data that are transmitted via the Internet typically pass through a number of networks in order to reach their destination. At any point during the transmission, the data are subject to being intercepted. Once unauthorised individuals access the data, they are subject to misuse or alteration. The implications of intercepting data such as credit card numbers are obvious. However, other types of business data are equally important. For example, an organisation is subject to potential damage if its competitors could get access to sensitive e-mail correspondences.

As the Internet is an open network, it invites easily security threats related to systems. In theory, unless security measures are implemented, any computer on the Internet can access any server on the Internet. As a result, organisations must be careful to secure their systems against unauthorised access. Organisations that fail to take the proper precautions risk potential theft or loss of valuable data. An additional threat to systems comes from viruses that propagate across the Internet. Even if access to servers is restricted, those with access may mistakenly transmit dangerous viruses [10].

In a 2001 survey, 538 security professionals in US corporations on the risk of doing e-Business published by the Computer Security Institute and the FBI's Computer Intrusion Squad were asked "What security breaches or espionage occurred in your company in the past year?". Ninety three percent of the respondents reported computer viruses. These and other threats are summarised in Table 1 [13].

The total projected losses for 2001 due to security breaches were US$377.8 million (up from US$265.6 million in 2000) and losses from financial fraud are rising. The highest single loss (theft of proprietary information) in the 2002 CSI/FBI survey was US$50 million (up from US$10 million in 1997); the average loss was US$4.6 million. The report states that the credit card information is the single most commonly traded financial instrument for attackers [14]. In 2003, 75% of the survey respondents of 530 acknowledged financial losses, but only 47% could quantify the losses [15]. For both individuals and organisations, credit card fraud is really scary [16]. There are however, some threats that US corporations rarely consider as top priority, while managers in other areas of the world must take them into consideration. Political

Human Perspectives in the Internet Society: Culture, Psychology and Gender, K. Morgan, J. Sanchez, C. A. Brebbia & A Voiskounsky (Editors) © 2004 WIT Press, www.witpress.com, ISBN 1-85312-726-4

unrest and regional instability are two examples. Other examples of unique threats include natural disasters in areas prone to those, or civil unrest in other areas, all of which can cause business interruption.

Table 1: Computer Security Institute/FBI 2001 survey of security threats.

Security Breaches	**% Of Respondents** *(approx.)*
Computer virus	93
Insider abuse of Net Access	90
Unauthorised access by insiders	64
Laptop theft	61
System penetration	40
Theft of proprietary information	24
Sabotage	19
Financial Fraud	11
Telecom eavesdropping	11
Telecom Fraud	11
Active wiretap	3

Around the globe, security threats and concerns are similar. For example, a survey of security directors in an Asian corporation revealed that their top ten security issues were similar to those of their US counterparts [17].

7.1 Global trend in general

Senior representatives of more than 3,600 companies in 50 countries were interviewed during 'Global Economic Crime Survey 2003' by the PricewaterhouseCoopers [18]. The economic crime remains a significant threat with 37% respondents report significant economic crimes during the previous two years and the average loss per company was US$2,199,930. The survey has identified that the gravest concerns for the future are asset misappropriation – the most visible of economic crimes and cybercrime. Looking forward over the next five years, 35% of companies expect their greatest economic crime risk to be asset misappropriation and 31% cybercrime. The cybercrime is still seen as a key risk for the future in North America (38%) and Western Europe (37%).

In '*2001 Global e.fr@ud. Survey*' [19], KPMG Forensic & Litigation Services practices surveyed the world's largest companies on the topics of e-fraud and security related issues in the world of e-Commerce in the following 12 countries:

Region	**Countries**
Asia Pacific	Australia, Hong Kong, India
Europe, Middle East and Africa (EMEA)	Belgium, Denmark, Germany, Italy, South Africa, Switzerland, United Kingdom
Americas	Canada, United States

Human Perspectives in the Internet Society: Culture, Psychology and Gender, K. Morgan, J. Sanchez, C. A. Brebbia & A Voiskounsky (Editors) © 2004 WIT Press, www.witpress.com, ISBN 1-85312-726-4

In total, 1,253 completed questionnaires were included in the survey findings, although KPMG sent questionnaires on e-Commerce & e.fr@ud to more than 14,000 CEOs, CIOs, and other senior executives of the largest public and private companies of those countries. Hackers, Poor implementation of security policies, and the lack of employee awareness were identified by survey participants as the greatest to their e-Commerce systems and the responses were consistent for all participating countries. Survey respondents suggested also that security of their e-Commerce system could be most improved by the following:

- ✓ Regular system penetration testing (authorized hacking)
- ✓ Use of software specifically designed for security issues in an e-Commerce environment
- ✓ Increased use of encryption technology

In response to their views on public perception about e-Commerce security, 88% of respondents feel that the public perceives the traditional, more established "bricks and mortar" businesses as being more secure than e-Commerce based dot.com, companies. The participants identified concerns about the security and privacy of information and a lack of familiarity with technology as being the most important preventing the consumers from engaging in e-Commerce transactions.

In Australia, losses from computer crime have more than doubled in one year according to the '*2003 Australian Computer Crime and Security Survey*' [20]. The huge losses, around AUS$ 11.8 million (US$ 9.1 million) over the 214 organizations surveyed, have stemmed primarily from financial fraud (AUS$ 3.52 million), laptop theft (AUS$ 2.25 million), virus, worm and Trojan infection (AUS$ 2.23 million) and insider abuse of resources (AUS$ 1.27 million). External attacks against computer networks are becoming more common in Australia.

8 Cyber-terrorism

Cyber-terrorism is the use of computers and the Internet to launch attacks and horrible acts that may directly harm or kill people [21]. Computer systems control airline traffic and transportation systems, water, oil pipelines, and energy. Therefore, disruptions in any one of these systems could cause loss of life or widespread chaos [9].

Internet population is huge, from about 50 million Internet users in 1997, there could be as many as 750 million by 2007 [22]. Growth in the number of users, online services, and devices connected to the Internet has made more computer crimes possible, profitable, and low-risk. The first half of 2002 saw a 28% increase in Internet attacks, and almost 2000, 000 of them were successful [23].

Fifty or more new computer viruses are created each week [24]. Using evidence from sophisticated malware hacker attacks, the FBI estimated that losses by US businesses had exceeded US$7 billion in 2001 [25]. This estimate does not include the costs of fraud or damages by disgruntled employees.

Human Perspectives in the Internet Society: Culture, Psychology and Gender, K. Morgan, J. Sanchez, C. A. Brebbia & A Voiskounsky (Editors) © 2004 WIT Press, www.witpress.com, ISBN 1-85312-726-4

8.1 Recent events

- UK customers of the US Bank MBNA are being targeted by an e-mail scam. Some of its customers have been sent fraudulent e-mails asking them for their online bank details. MBNA is just the latest of the High Street banks affected by the scam, known as *phishing*. It comes with a variety of subject lines such as "MBNA's Official Notice, "Attention all MBNA users" and "Official Notice for all users of MBNA." The message says the bank is putting in a new security system to "help you avoid frequently fraud transactions and to keep your investments in safety". It then advises people to reactivate their account by clicking on a link in the message. Any customers who tries to login through this fake page is very likely to have their personal bank information or identity stolen and relayed directly to the spammers [26].
- The sixth variation of the worm known as **SoBig.F** was transmitted in August 2003 through a pornographic website. It infected more than 145,260 computers worldwide, jamming with useless e-mails. Bill Gates believes that software is still not strong enough to connect devices together and there are too many viruses and security devices [27].
- A mass-mailing virus 'MyDoom' is dominating news headlines. The virus, which experts say is the fastest spreading e-mail worm in history, has left hundreds of thousands computers vulnerable to hackers and spammers. MyDoom causes no apparent damage to computers. However it leaves behind a program that could allow hackers to steal passwords or files that tracks keystrokes. It has three variants such as, MyDoom.A, My Doom.B & My Doom.C. The original MyDoom.A worm shut down its target, American Software Company 'SCO' by bombarding it with information requests. The third variant, MyDoom.C or Doomjuice, is similar to the MyDoom.B worm, which was designed to overload Microsoft's website using same technique. The economic fallout has been estimated at US$ 26.1 billion. The hunt for the creators has proved fruitless, but the focus is on Russia, where it first appeared. Microsoft and SCO have offered US$500,000 reward for information leading to the prosecution of the creators of the virus [28, 29].

9 Key dimensions of e-Business security

There are six key dimensions of e-Business security:

- *Integrity* - the ability to ensure that information displayed on a Web site, or sent or received via the Internet has not been altered in any way by an unauthorised party.
- *Nonrepudiation* – the ability to ensure that e-Business participants do not deny (repudiate) their online actions.
- *Authenticity* – refers to the ability to verify an individual or business's identity.

- *Confidentiality* – determines whether information shared online, such as through e-mail communication or an order process, can be viewed by anyone other than the intended recipient.
- *Privacy* - deals with the use of information shared during an online transaction. Consumers want to limit the extent to which their personal information can be divulged to other organizations, while merchants want to protect such information from falling into the wrong hands.
- *Availability* – determine whether a web site is accessible and operational at any given moment.

E-Business security is technology designed to protect these six dimensions, when any one of them is compromised, it is a security issue.

10 Encryption technology

Encryption provides the key to providing greater security, and various organisations are considering policies on cryptography. Encryption is the process of transforming plain text or data into *Cipher text* that cannot be read by anyone outside of the sender and the receiver. The purpose of encryption is (a) to secure stored information and (b) to secure information transmission. Encryption can provide four of the six dimensions of e-Business security:

- ➢ *Message integrity* – provided assurance that the message has not been altered.
- ➢ *Nonrepudiation* – provided the user from denying he or she sent the message
- ➢ *Authentication* – provides verification of the identity of the person (or machine) sending the message.
- ➢ *Confidentiality* – gives that others did not read the message.

There are a variety of different forms of encryption technology currently in use. They are

- ✓ Symmetric key encryption
- ✓ Public key cryptography
- ✓ Public key encryption using digital signatures and hash digests
- ✓ Digital envelope
- ✓ Digital certificates and public key infrastructure

Privacy of network communication is ensured by encryption. There is one other method that will facilitate higher levels of security in organisations undertaking e-Business using the Web or other networks. This is the implementation of *firewalls* and proxies within the system servers. Firewalls are an effective means of shielding private, secure, internal networks from nonsecure external networks. For example, firewalls are usually installed between an intranet and the Internet in order to prevent attack from the Internet. Like other security technology, they must be implemented correctly and in accordance with the overall security policy [30].

Security in e-Commerce generally employs procedures such as authentication, ensuring confidentiality, and the use of the cryptography to communicate over open systems [31]. As more and more businesses go online, confidential files are increasingly exposed to the risk of infiltration [32].

Security and disaster recovery planning go hand in hand. A firm's solid reputation can be destroyed in a single day on the Internet. It is important to think through various disaster scenarios and have a plan for addressing each one [8].

11 E-Business privacy policy

It is important to develop a clear, concise, easily accessible privacy policy on an e-Business web site; the law varies significantly among countries worldwide with respect to protection of citizens' privacy. This is why many consumers fear Web-based shopping. But the European Union (EC) has adopted strict privacy laws. Although these legal principles apply only in the EU, their effect is far reaching. This is because the directive also prohibits the transfer of data from the EU to countries which do not have adequate data protection laws. Conversely, the import of data from such countries may also trigger the requirement of the importer to abide by the EU directive. This is one of the factors putting pressure on countries such as Australia to improve their privacy protection laws. In terms of e-mail generally, the tragic events of 9/11(11 September 2001) in New York have led to government increasing their powers to monitor e-mail traffic around the world consequently diluting privacy.

Many of the threats to privacy are not new. Many privacy organisations are fighting for setting standards on the Internet, but as the Internet does not belong to anyone in particular it is not possible to enforce standards. New standards evolve slowly and need to bring advantages to the user in order to be accepted [33]. For this reason, ethical and legal controls are an important part of e-Business security. However, the law is slow to evolve due to the global nature of e-Business. Again the technology involving the Internet is evolving rapidly. Although legal protection is necessary and desirable, trust and confidence in e-Business must be reassured again and again through robust security technologies and ethical standards.

Many organisations take ethics seriously and produce a document guiding the behaviour of its members or employees. Some corporations require new employees to read its code of ethics and sign a promise to abide by it.

12 E-Business security plan

Security is a combination of technical, administrative, and physical controls. A security plan identifies and organises the security activities. The plan is both a description of the current situation and a plan for improvement. A security plan must state the organization's policy on security [34].

A security plan is a very comprehensive document; its creation typically requires the involvement of key information technology personnel as well as end users and management. In order to minimize security threats, e-Business firms must develop a coherent corporate policy that takes into account the nature of the

Human Perspectives in the Internet Society: Culture, Psychology and Gender, K. Morgan, J. Sanchez, C. A. Brebbia & A Voiskounsky (Editors) © 2004 WIT Press, www.witpress.com, ISBN 1-85312-726-4

risks, the information assets that need protecting, and the procedures and technologies required to address the risk, as well as implementation and auditing mechanisms. Public laws and active enforcement of cybercrime statutes are also required to both raise the costs of illegal behaviour on the Internet and guard against corporate abuse of information [35].

13 Conclusions

Recent advances in IT have been and continue to be a driving force in business innovation in general and e-Business in particular. The flow of information over the Internet must be safe and secure so that consumers can take part in e-Business without hesitation. In general, Internet security for building secure e-Business Systems is a growing concern. Contemporary security issues and technologies have been discussed. Most of the countries are not fully prepared to face security challenges. It will take time to develop a uniform cyber law to safeguard e-Business worldwide.

With the emergence of Homeland Security initiatives in 2002 and the National Strategy to secure cyberspace in 2003(both in the USA), the demand for trained information security professionals far exceeds the supply. Securing cyberspace is an extraordinary difficult challenge to undertake e-Business. Despite security breaches e-Business is growing. It will never be possible to eradicate crimes in cyberspace completely, but new evolving security technologies along with policy, procedures and law should keep threats as minimum as possible or manageable. Security breaches will remain a formidable and costly issue which can be countered by effective controls, a strong culture of prevention and deterrence and assertive action when cases arise.

Acknowledgements

The author expresses his gratitude to the Research Management and Training, College of Law and Business, University of Western Sydney for supporting this research partly under the CLAB Research Activity Support Scheme. He remembers the loving support of his children Indira & Bikram and wife Mitra during the preparation of the manuscript.

References

[1] Chan, H., Raymond, L., Dillon, T, & Chang, E., E-Commerce: Fundamentals and Applications, John Wiley & Sons. 2001

[2] Chaudhury, A., & Kuilboer, J., E-Business and e-Commerce Infrastructure: Technologies Supporting the e-Business Initiative, McGraw-Hill/Irwin, 2002.

[3] Karmakar, N. L., Digital Security, Privacy & Law in Cyberspace: A Global Overview, Proceedings of the e-society 2003: IADIS International Conference, Lisbon, Portugal, June 3-6, Vol.1, pp 528-535, 2003.

Human Perspectives in the Internet Society: Culture, Psychology and Gender, K. Morgan, J. Sanchez, C. A. Brebbia & A Voiskounsky (Editors) © 2004 WIT Press, www.witpress.com, ISBN 1-85312-726-4

[4] Webster, M, "security," available from the World Wide Web http//www.m-w.com/cgi-bin/dictionary, 1 February 2002.

[5] Whiteman, M.E. & Mattford, H.J., Principles of Information Security, Thomson. 2003.

[6] Hoffman, D., Novak, T. P., & Peralta, M., Building consumer trust online, Communications of the ACM **42(4)**, pp.80-85, 1999.

[7] Alter, S., Information Systems: The Foundation of E-Business, 4th edition, Prentice Hall, pp. 6, 2002.

[8] Kalakota, R., & Robinson, M., e-Business 2.0 – Roadmap for Success, Addison-Wesley, 2001.

[9] Volonino, L., & Robinson, S., R., *Principles and Practice of Information Security*, Prentice Hall, 2004.

[10] Van Slyke, C., and Belanger, F., *E-Business Technologies: Supporting the Net-Enhanced Organization*, John Wiley & Sons. 2003.

[11] Turban, E. et al., Electronic Commerce: A Managerial Perspective, Prentice Hall, 2002.

[12] Kou, W., Networking Security and Standards, Kluwer Academic Publishers, 1997.

[13] Computer Security Institute, 2001 Computer Crime and Security Survey, http://www.gocsi.com/forms/fbi/pdf.html, July 2001.

[14] Computer Security Institute, 2002 CSI/FBIComputer Crime and Security Survey, http://www.gocsi.com/forms/fbi/pdf.html, Spring 2002.

[15] Computer Security Institute, 2003 CSI/FBI Computer Crime and Security Survey, http://i.cmpnet.com/gocsi/db_area/pdfs/fbi/FBI2003.pdf, 2003.

[16] McNurlin, B. C. & Sprague, Jr., *Information Systems Management in Practice* (6th ed), Prentice Hall, 2004.

[17] Source: The Threat from the Net, Asian Business **36(11)**, pp. 34.

[18] PricewaterhouseCoopers, economic crime survey 2003, available at http://www.pwc.com/extweb/insights.nsf/docid/662DCF05C90F69E6802 56D6E0052125A 2003.

[19] KPMG, 2001 Global e.fr@d.survey, available at http://www.aic.gov.au/research/fraud/surveys.html, 2001.

[20] Gray, P., Australian computer crime losses double, Survey at http://www.zdnet.com.au/news/security/0,2000061744,20274402,00.htm, 12May 2003.

[21] Dasgupta, P, **Cyber** Terrorism**,** The *Statesman* (India), May 24, 2002.

[22] Turban E, McLean, E, and Wetherbe, J., Information Technology for Management: Transforming Business in the Digital Economy (3rd Edition). John Wiley & Sons, 2002.

[23] Barbara, M., Internet Attacks On Companies Up 28 Percent Report Says, *The Washington* Post, P. E5, July 8, 2002.

[24] Vise, D. A., & Daniel E., FBI Warns of Cyber-Attack Threat: U.S. 'Very Concerned' About Vulnerability of Infrastructure, *The Washington* Post, P. A16, March 21, 2001.

[25] Fonseca, B., IT Security Under the Gun, *IT World*, March 12, 2001. http://www.itworld.com/Sec/3832/itwnws010312security/

Human Perspectives in the Internet Society: Culture, Psychology and Gender, K. Morgan, J. Sanchez, C. A. Brebbia & A Voiskounsky (Editors) © 2004 WIT Press, www.witpress.com, ISBN 1-85312-726-4

[26] BBC News World Edition, E-mail scam hits MBNA customers, http://news.bbc.co.uk/2/hi/technology/3518411.stm?headline=E-mail~scam~hits~MBNA~customers, accessed on February 25, 2004.

[27] IT Today, Gates says software needs better security, The Australian, Tuesday, September 2, pp. 37, 2003.

[28] Mills, K., Net virus in the back door, *The Australian*, Wednesday, February 2004.

[29] AFP, Hackers hit website as virus continues to spread, *The Sydney Morning Herald*, pp. 4, Monday, February 2, 2004.

[30] Goldman, J. E. & Rawles, P. T, Applied *Data Communications: A Business Oriented Approach,* Wiley, 2004.

[31] Awad, E., Electronic Commerce: From Vision to Fulfillment, Prentice Hall, New Jersey, 2002.

[32] Besserglik, B., Spotlight turned on cyber crime, The Australian IT/Cutting Edge (The Australian) Tuesday, pp.3, May 16, 2000.

[33] Amor, E., The E-Business Revolution: Living and Working in an Interconnected World, Prentice Hall PTR, 2000.

[34] Pfleeger, C. P. and Pfleeger, S. L., *Security in Computing* (3rd ed), Prentice Hall, PTR, 2003.

[35] Laudon, K. C. and Traver, C. G., E-Commerce*: business, technology, society*, Addison Wesley, 2002.

Human Perspectives in the Internet Society: Culture, Psychology and Gender, K. Morgan, J. Sanchez, C. A. Brebbia & A Voiskounsky (Editors) © 2004 WIT Press, www.witpress.com, ISBN 1-85312-726-4

The impact of the World Wide Web on South African businesses

A. M. Singh
University of Kwazulu-Natal, South Africa

Abstract

In the 1960's, Alvin Toffler predicted in his book "Future Shock", that there would come a time when people would be able to shop from the comfort of one's office or home, and that computers would free them from their offices giving them more time for recreation. For many this was considered wishful thinking. However, a mere three decades later, these predictions have become a reality. At the click of a button, consumers can order items ranging from flowers to computers and even customised motor vehicles and have them delivered wherever they want. The Internet and more especially the World Wide Web have heralded a new era in shopping. Online shopping has taken off in the United States, the United Kingdom and parts of the Far East. However, it has not seen the same success in Third World Developing countries. This study examines the impact of the World Wide Web on South African businesses. In addressing this topic, a non-probability purposive sample was drawn from South African companies with a web presence. Seventy nine companies responded. The companies ranged from small to large enterprises and operated in a number of different industries.

The results showed that the Web had a significant impact on cost saving, improvements in customer service, and some companies achieved additional revenue from Web sales.

This study revealed that although making significant contributions, the World Wide Web was not being utilised to its full potential due to a number of obstacles identified from the study. In order to overcome these obstacles, it was recommended that businesses needed to segment their markets more effectively, identify and serve untapped niches and support the online business, offline.
Keywords: South Africa, e-commerce, business impact of web, value, cost saving, customer service, income generation.

Human Perspectives in the Internet Society: Culture, Psychology and Gender, K. Morgan, J. Sanchez, C. A. Brebbia & A Voiskounsky (Editors) © 2004 WIT Press, www.witpress.com, ISBN 1-85312-726-4

1 Introduction

E-commerce is the use of interconnected networks to do business using web technologies [1]. E-business "has caused companies to either radically restructure their conventional means of doing business, or at least consider the adoption of E-business in their future" [2]. E-business is changing organisational structures [3]. The impact of the Internet on business is phenomenal. "There are those on the net, those who are thinking about going on the net, and those who are probably going out of business" [2]. These statements especially the latter, creates new challenges for organisations.

According to Moodley [4], the traditional "bricks and mortar" business, is rapidly being replaced by "clicks and mortar" business, referring to business being conducted at a click of the mouse. Radebe [5] was of the opinion that businesses that did not get on the net and have a net presence, would be out of business within three years. This is a controversial statement in the South African context, especially since there have been no major closures of businesses that have not developed a Web presence. Furthermore, the converse is true in that many dot.com businesses have gone out of business. The corner store located in a middle to low income suburb, could not possibly face closure if the majority of its market is computer illiterate, and do not own computers. This is evidenced by the fact that only 6.8% of the South African population are Internet users [6]. Microsoft SA have been responsible for the development of digital villages and Internet kiosks would be opened for the lower income groups to have access to the Internet [7]. This initiative would still have little effect on the small corner store as a large portion, that is, 45% of the South African population are illiterate [8]. Why then should businesses be on the net?

According to Oke [9], the United States Commerce Department reported that one third of its nation's 1996 real economic growth came from information technologies. It has been projected that the United States business-to-business market will generate more than $6 trillion in online trade by 2005 [10]. South African online spending is much less than the United States. In 2001 South African consumers spent R162 million on Internet purchases and, business-to-business transactions amounted to around R3.9 billion in 2000 [11,12]. The South African spending pales in relation to the American figures. However, this could be due to the fact that geographically, the United States market is much larger, and more people have access to computers and the Internet. Businesses do not need to limit themselves to local markets since they are now able to exploit millions of potential overseas customers. Based on these figures, businesses should not be asking if we should be on the net, but when? [2].

2 The business value of the World Wide Web

The World Wide Web (WWW) has tremendous potential and exposes new business opportunities for organisations. Figure 1 summarizes the tangible benefits for businesses being online [13]. This diagram served as the basis of

Human Perspectives in the Internet Society: Culture, Psychology and Gender, K. Morgan, J. Sanchez, C. A. Brebbia & A Voiskounsky (Editors) © 2004 WIT Press, www.witpress.com, ISBN 1-85312-726-4

this study and the survey was developed according to the dimensions presented in the diagram.

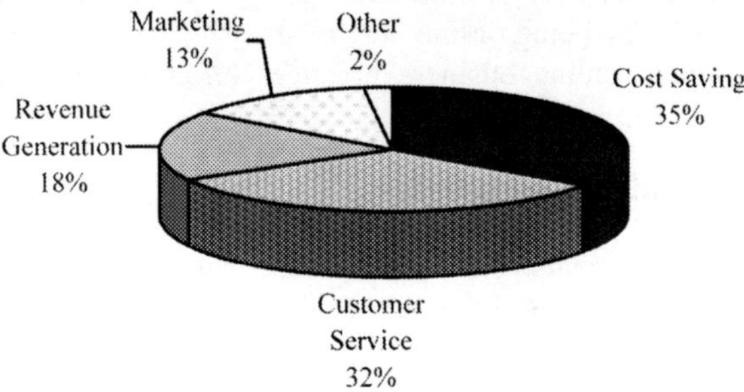

Figure 1: Value generated by the WWW for America's top 100 companies.

Cost saving which is the objective of every organisation has improved due to businesses being online. This is possible due to the use of e-mail which is cheaper than postal and fax services. Furthermore, web pages are capable of carrying detailed information. Therefore, organisations can reduce the cost of printing brochures and the excessive costs of advertising using traditional media. Customer service which is normally limited to working hours is available 24 hours a day seven days a week all year. Websites provide the consumer with detailed product information, troubleshooting, alternate uses and frequently asked questions. The Internet generates revenues from existing and new consumers and other businesses. The Web makes marketing communications more effective than static media such as newspapers and magazines in that, web pages can include sound, graphics and animation and allow for interaction. Furthermore, as a marketing tool the Web is cheaper than television and radio.

Other benefits of being online include among others: instantaneous communication with prospects, customers and employees; global access to customers and business partners; always open allowing for business to continue after hours; reaching highly desirable markets who are computer literate, have access to the Internet and possess disposable income; reaching wider specialised markets such as collectors of rare butterflies, procuring raw materials from cheaper sources; and providing customised goods and services to customers as and where they want it [13, 14, 15, 16].

It is evident that businesses have experienced immense benefits by being online, but is this trend the same in a developing country such as South Africa?

3 Methodology

3.1 Aims and objectives

The aim of this study was to determine whether the WWW had a positive or negative impact on South African companies. Some of the objectives of this

Human Perspectives in the Internet Society: Culture, Psychology and Gender, K. Morgan, J. Sanchez, C. A. Brebbia & A Voiskounsky (Editors) © 2004 WIT Press, www.witpress.com, ISBN 1-85312-726-4

study were to determine whether: South African businesses experienced similar benefits to America's top 100 companies with regards to cost saving, customer service, revenue generation and marketing; the extent to which companies experienced benefits by being online; any relationships existed between industry and benefits gained; online business practices differed from offline business practices.

3.2 Sampling technique and sample size

Due to work commitments, and limited time and financial resources, non-probability sampling was used for this study. According to Zikmund [17], a researcher selects a sample based on his/her judgement of the characteristics of the sample members. If the researcher believes that a subject can add value to the study then that subject should be selected. Initially the South African Top 100 companies were considered to make up the sample. However, this would have excluded small and medium enterprises. In order to get a breadth of knowledge, the researcher consulted a web directory and selected 60 companies of each type, that is, small, medium and large enterprises, that the researcher felt would add value to the study. Some of the top 100 companies fell into the sample.

The use of this approach may affect the accuracy of results and conclusions [18]. Nevertheless, the researcher used this approach to gain invaluable information highlighting some of the trends in the South African context.

It is evident that although contributing to a broad knowledge base, the results of this study cannot be generalised to be representative of the total population.

3.3 Research instrument

A questionnaire consisting of open and closed ended questions, rating and ranking scales was mailed to 180 South African businesses with a Web presence. The questionnaire was pre-tested among a group of MBA students. The responses were consistent and the time taken to answer questions did not exceed 20 minutes.

4 Results

4.1 Sample description

One hundred and eighty questionnaires were administered, only 79 were returned representing a return of 44%, in contrast to the norm of 30% this was an excellent response rate [18]. Of the companies that responded, 22% were small companies, 27% were medium companies and 51% were large companies. A number of different industries were represented in the sample as depicted in Figure 2.

It is evident from Figure 2, that no single industry dominated this sample. The largest group (26.6%) was drawn from the retail sector. The manufacturing

Human Perspectives in the Internet Society: Culture, Psychology and Gender, K. Morgan, J. Sanchez, C. A. Brebbia & A Voiskounsky (Editors) © 2004 WIT Press, www.witpress.com, ISBN 1-85312-726-4

sector comprised 25.3%, education comprised 22.8% followed by computers and technology forming 16.5% of the sample. The lowest number of responses was obtained from the financial sector which made up 8.9% of the sample.

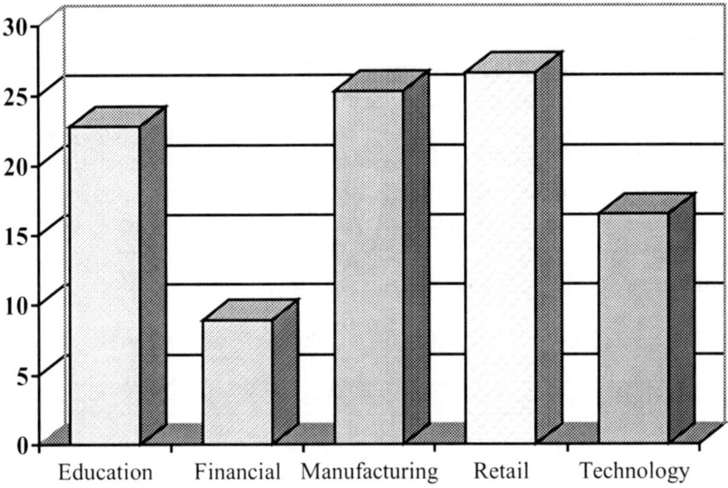

Figure 2: Industries within which responding companies operated.

4.2 Reasons for using the World Wide Web

The reasons for using the WWW included cost saving, customer service, marketing, income generation amongst others (Table 1).

Table 1: Reasons for using the World Wide Web.

Variable	Minimum	Maximum	Mean	Standard Deviation
Cost Saving	1	5	3.924	1.662
Customer Service	2	5	3.734	0.812
Marketing	1	5	3.430	1.009
Income Generation	0	4	1.570	0.957
Other	0	5	0.949	0.876

It is evident that the results of this study were very closely linked to the value that the WWW generated for America's top 100 companies as depicted in Figure1. Cost saving was the main reason for using the Web (0 = 3.924), with the mean tending towards the maximum. Customer service (0 = 3.734), was ranked second. The fact that customer service did not rank below 2 suggests that it was a very important reason for businesses using the Web. Marketing (0 = 3.430), also tended towards the maximum showing it to be an important reason for businesses using the Web. Revenue generation tended towards the minimum,

Human Perspectives in the Internet Society: Culture, Psychology and Gender, K. Morgan, J. Sanchez, C. A. Brebbia & A Voiskounsky (Editors) © 2004 WIT Press, www.witpress.com, ISBN 1-85312-726-4

and did not receive a rank of 5 suggesting that organisations were not using the Internet to its full potential for income generation. Other reasons were not specified.

4.3 Impact of the Web on businesses

4.3.1 Cost saving

Table 2 illustrates the cost saving impact of the Web. Cost savings were average and very low on the itemised rating scale. The majority of companies (81%) experienced very low, cost savings in the 0-9% category. Only 19% of the companies achieved average cost savings of 20-29%. None of the companies achieved above average cost savings although cost saving was ranked as the most important reason for conducting business on the Internet (Table 1). Cost savings were attributed to, in descending order of ranking, reductions in communication, printing, advertising and overhead costs.

Table 2: Cost savings achieved by companies.

Variable	Frequency	Percent
Cost Saving		
0-9%	64	81
20-29%	15	19
Total	79	100%

According to Roberts [15], with e-mail, it is possible to send more detailed information anywhere in the world for less than the price of a fax. This is supported by Ciraolo [19], according to whom it is cheaper to send a 10 page e-mail than it is to send it by overnight courier or express mail. Sending e-mail anywhere in the world costs no more than a local call to one's Internet Service Provider.

4.3.2 Customer service

It is evident from Table.3 that 93.7% of the companies achieved below average (19% and lower) improvements in customer service, with 78.5% achieving 0-9% and 15.2% achieving 10-19% improvements. Only 7.4% of the companies achieved above average (30% and greater) improvements with 1.3% achieving 30-39% improvements and 6.1% improving customer service by 40% and more. It is evident from Table.3 that 93.7% of the companies achieved below average improvements in customer service, with 78.5% achieving 0-9% and 15.2% achieving 10-19% improvements. Only 7.4% achieved above average improvements with 1.3% achieving 30-39% improvements and 6.1% improving customer service by 40% and more. Although the statistics suggest that customer service improvements were minimal, it must be emphasised that there was an improvement in customer service due to having a Web presence. Improvements in customer service was attributed to, in descending order of ranking, cheap means of regular communication, having a frequently asked

Human Perspectives in the Internet Society: Culture, Psychology and Gender, K. Morgan, J. Sanchez, C. A. Brebbia & A Voiskounsky (Editors) © 2004 WIT Press, www.witpress.com, ISBN 1-85312-726-4

questions page, providing detailed online information and the ability to provide instant feedback.

Table 3: Improvements in customer service.

Variable	Frequency	Percent
Customer Service		
0-9%	62	78.5
10-19%	12	15.2
30-39%	1	1.3
>40%	4	6.1
Total	79	100%

According to Parker [7] the goal of every business should be to fine tune the buyer-seller relationship. Due to the low cost of e-mail, buyers and sellers can "talk" to each other more often and at minimal cost. The masses of information that can be contained on frequently asked questions pages makes it possible for consumers to get 24 hour customer service from a company.

4.3.3 Income generation

Table 4 clearly illustrates that the World Wide Web is generating additional income for all the companies in the sample. However, only 17.7% experienced between 20 and 29% additional revenues from web sales.

Table 4: Additional income generated by Web sales.

Variable	Frequency	Percent
Income Generation		
0-9%	65	82.3
20-29%	14	17.7
Total	79	100%

According to Scholtz [20], Kulula.com an online airline generated almost all its income from online ticket sales and has been profitable from day one.

4.3.4 Overall impression of Internet business

Managers were asked to rate their overall impression of having a Web presence. The majority of respondents (60.7%) found the Internet's impact acceptable, followed by 22.8% who were satisfied and two managers (2.5%) were very satisfied. Ten managers (12.7%) were extremely dissatisfied, whilst 1.3% were dissatisfied. Cumulatively, the impact of the Internet tended towards the positive end of the scale with 86% of the respondents reflecting varying degrees of satisfaction.

4.3.5 Obstacles to the optimal utilisation of the Web

It is evident from the results that the World Wide Web has benefited South African businesses. However, the results were not optimal. The respondents were asked an open ended question to identify the obstacles that impeded the impact of the Web on businesses. Some of the responses included consumer

Human Perspectives in the Internet Society: Culture, Psychology and Gender, K. Morgan, J. Sanchez, C. A. Brebbia & A Voiskounsky (Editors) © 2004 WIT Press, www.witpress.com, ISBN 1-85312-726-4

fear, consumer literacy, poor market segmentation, untapped market niches, lack of advertising support, and poor site appearance.

5 Recommendations

In order to achieve optimal utilisation of the World Wide Web, businesses need to address the obstacles that were identified by the respondents in this study.

5.1 Fear

The greatest fear that customers have is the risk involved with transacting online. Businesses need to develop awareness programmes to promote the use of the web. This can be done through Internet Service Providers (ISP). ISP's could be paid to make users aware of the benefits of e-commerce. Advertising and promotions should revolve around the benefits of e-commerce, the ease of using the Internet and advertising the safety of transacting online.

5.2 Literacy

For too long South Africa has run a mixed economy, that is, first and third world. In order to compete in the global economy, the country has to move forward and become a first world economy. Literacy and computer literacy are the social responsibility of the State. Businesses and human rights groups need to canvass government support for developing an electronic society. However, simply making people literate and computer literate will get them online, but does not promise sales.

5.3 Segmentation

Market segments need to be properly researched. Research should focus on biographical data, such as, age, gender, income, level of computer literacy, frequency of usage of the Internet, and willingness to purchase online. Businesses need to clearly identify the target market, and determine the attractiveness of that market. If the market is both attractive and has growth potential, then only should the business go online.

5.4 Untapped niches

Businesses need to identify untapped niches that can be exploited for example, the academic market is a highly lucrative and attractive online market, yet it remains unexploited. Book sellers, computer sales, banks and stationers could offer free training to employees of institutions like Universities, Colleges and Government Departments. Besides providing a "community service", companies can sell their web sites at training sessions.

5.5 Advertising

Promotion and advertising should be done offline, directing traffic to online e-commerce sites. Online advertising and promotion should be kept to a minimum. Businesses need to use traditional advertising to create an awareness and to attract international business online. Savings due to online trade should be given back as price savings to consumers.

5.6 Site appearance

Web masters need to develop user friendly sites that are attractive and free of clutter, loads quickly, contain useful and reliable information, are secure, and have simple addresses. Furthermore, web design should support the image of the business and convey the values that make the business successful.

6 Conclusion

It is evident from this study that the World Wide Web has had a positive impact on South African businesses, especially with regards cost savings, improved customer service and additional revenues due to online sales. It is also clear that although most managers were satisfied with the impact of the Web that there were obstacles that limited the impact and that strategies needed to be implemented to overcome the obstacles. No study is complete without identifying its limitations. As evidenced in this study, the small sample size makes it impossible to generalise the results to all South African businesses. However, the results have clearly identified trends that leave room for further research and debate.

References

[1] O'Brien, J.A. 2000. Introduction to Information Systems. Essentials for the Internetworked Enterprise. ed. 9. Boston: Irwin McGraw Hill.

[2] The Net Imperative. The Economist, July 1999. [Online]. Available at http://www.crab.rutgers.edu/~goertzel/economistnetbusiness.htmhttp://www.crab.rutgers.edu/~goertzel/economistnetbusiness.htm (Accessed: February 2004).

[3] Lucas, H.C. Jr. 2000. Information Technology for Management. Boston: Irwin McGraw Hill.

[4] Moodley, L. 2000. Strategic Use of E-Commerce. Presented at the E-Commerce Seminar. Durban.

[5] Radebe, S. 2000. Improving Customer Service with E-Commerce. Presented at the E-Commerce Seminar. Durban.

[6] Internet Usage Statistics for Africa. 2004. [Online]. Available at www.internetworldstats.com/stats1.htm. (Accessed: January 2004).

[7] Parker, D. 17 February 2000. Online Trade at Risk. Security fears hamper developing e-commerce. The Daily News, p.18.

[8] Aitchison, J.J.W. 1998. A Review of Adult Basic Education and Training in South Africa. [Online]. Available at www.fsu.edu/~/vadca/engli sh/adeas.html. (Accessed: July 2000).

Human Perspectives in the Internet Society: Culture, Psychology and Gender, K. Morgan, J. Sanchez, C. A. Brebbia & A Voiskounsky (Editors) © 2004 WIT Press, www.witpress.com, ISBN 1-85312-726-4

[9] Oke, T.E. 1997. The Future of Internet Trading. [Online]. Available at www.doc.ic.ac.uk /~oao97/article2/ (Accessed: July 2000).

[10] World Research Internet Transaction Survey Results. 1998. [Online]. Available at www. survey.com/tranresults.html (Accessed: August 1999)

[11] South African online sales remain small. 2002. [Online]. Available at www.nua.ie/surveys/index.cgi?f=vs&art_id=905357994&rel=true (Accessed: January 2004).

[12] Vergnani, L. 2000. Cybershopping meets your local deli. The Money Standard, 2(2), p. 49-51.

[13] Gow, K. 1997. Risk v Opportunity. The Premier 100 Supplement to Computerworld, February. p.24.

[14] Benefits of Using the Internet. 2000. [Online]. Available at www.apexit.com/benefits.html (Accessed: December 2000).

[15] Roberts, B. 1996. Manufacturers Get Wired. Companies find Web especially useful for B-toB Activity. Web Week. 2(17). p. 196.

[16] Graham, J.R. 2000. The Internet and its Effect on Your Business. [Online]. Available at www.achrnews.com/cda/..s/bnp_features_item/0.1338,2659,00.html (Accessed: December 2000).

[17] Zikmund, W.G. 2000. Sampling Designs and Sampling Procedures. [Online]. Available at www.iusb.edu/~mlee/ch_12/00/sld017.htm

[18] Welman, J.C. & Kruger, S.J. 1999. Research Methodology for the Business and Administrative Sciences. Cape Town: Oxford University Press.

[19] Ciraolo, M. 1985. Low Cost E-Mail. What electronic mail can do for you. Digital Antic, 4(4), p. 45.

[20] Scholtz, C. 2003. The Trials and Tribulations of an Online Airline. Presented at the 5th World Wide Web Applications Conference. Durban.

Human Perspectives in the Internet Society: Culture, Psychology and Gender, K. Morgan, J. Sanchez, C. A. Brebbia & A Voiskounsky (Editors) © 2004 WIT Press, www.witpress.com, ISBN 1-85312-726-4

Multi-analyses electronic payment system

M. Madhoushi[1] & E. Mohebi[2]
[1]*Department of Management, University of Mazandaran, Iran*
[2]*Department of Industrial Engineering,*
Mazandaran University of Science and Technology, Iran

Abstract

This paper is an overview of electronic payment methods and analyses and compares some types of electronic payment systems which can be grouped into three broad classes: traditional money transactions, digital currency and credit–debit payments. Such payment systems have a number of requirements: e.g. security, acceptability, convenience, cost, anonymity, control, traceability and control of encryption methods. It also evaluates their advantages and disadvantages to the customer, the merchant, the e-payment service provider and the financial institution. These systems employ cryptography to provide security, however many consumers are still reluctant to purchase over the Internet because they are concerned about hackers accessing their financial information.
Keywords: electronic commerce, security, electronic payment system (EPS), digital currency, credit-debit payments.

1 Introduction

Electronic payment systems are an essential part of electronic commerce and electronic business and are greatly important for their further development. However, traditional ways of paying for goods and services do not work properly over the Internet. Existing payment systems for the offline world, such as credit cards, are widely accepted as a means of payment on the Internet; however users don't see in them enough of reliability, trust, security, etc [1].The existing payment systems are also far from ideal for merchants, because of the high transaction costs, fraudulent activity and the multiple parties involved in payment processing [2]. These systems need to strike a good balance between a numbers of deferent issues [3], [4]. The Internet was originally used by individual academics, universities and government agencies (particularly in the military) for research and development purposes. Since the commercialization of

Human Perspectives in the Internet Society: Culture, Psychology and Gender, K. Morgan, J. Sanchez, C. A. Brebbia & A Voiskounsky (Editors) © 2004 WIT Press, www.witpress.com, ISBN 1-85312-726-4

the Internet in 1993, this group has been joined by companies of all sizes, wishing to advertise and trade goods and services both locally and globally. Yet, despite this enthusiasm and rapid growth, the Internet has been recognized as a difficult place to do serious business (see, for example, Poon and Swatman [5]). A major problem, however, is the lack of an integrated financial transaction system suitable for an open electronic marketplace such as the Internet. How the consumer will pay for goods and services and how the provider will receive the payment securely over the Internet are issues which are being seen as some of the most important success factors for Internet commerce. To overcome these problems, many individuals and organizations have been developing financial transaction systems for the Internet which are becoming known as Internet payment systems (IPS).This paper describes the mode of operation of a broad range of e-payment systems available today in order to provide a comparative evaluation from viewpoint of the users [6, 7, 8, 9, 10].

2 Literature of the issue

2.1 Background

2.1.1 E-commerce

E-commerce is a general concept covering any business transaction executed electronically between parties such as companies (business-to-business - B2B), companies and consumers (business-to-consumer - B2C), consumers and consumers (C2C), business and the public sector, and between consumers and the public sector.

2.1.2 Electronic payment systems

The first C2C payment systems were developed in 1999 in USA. The biggest and the most popular e-payment system is Pay Pal. In autumn 2000 Pay Pal broadened its scope of business activity to some European countries. Currently it offers services worldwide. In June 2001 Pay Hound Limited launched the first European C2C payments system, developed specifically for the customers in UK [11]. The problems of electronic payment systems that we are facing at the present moment can be described as a failure to address user requirements and needs in the design and deployment of the systems. It can be suggested that in the design of electronic payment systems not only technological but also user-related factors should be taken into account. Even if there are good technical solutions, but they are not accepted by end users or vendors, the whole system would fail. The existing works that discuss the requirements for electronic payment systems don't provide rationalization for selection of the chosen requirements.

2.2 Types of Internet payment systems

2.2.1 Traditional money transactions

Currently, debit cards are spread widely and deposit transfer via the Internet appears to be coming soon [12]. On-line payment by credit card is already available at many commercial web sites today;

Human Perspectives in the Internet Society: Culture, Psychology and Gender, K. Morgan, J. Sanchez, C. A. Brebbia & A Voiskounsky (Editors) © 2004 WIT Press, www.witpress.com, ISBN 1-85312-726-4

- SET

IBM, Netscape, GTE, CyberCash, MasterCard, Microsoft and Visa have cooperatively developed the Secure Electronic Transactions Protocol (SET) for securing on-line transactions. This protocol will facilitate credit card transactions on the Internet.

- PCT

The Private Communication Technology (PCT) protocol, defined by Microsoft, provides privacy between two communicating applications, and authenticates at least one of the two to the other.

- iKP

iKP is an IBM proposal for a family of public key protocols supporting secure presentation of credit card information [13].

- First Virtual's InfoCommerce System

In this system the credit card information is given to First Virtual via phone only when the account is opened.

2.2.2 Credit-debit payments

In payment mechanisms that use the credit-debit model, including CMU's NetBill, First Virtual's InfoCommerce system, and USC-ISI's NetCheque System [14], customers are registered with accounts on payment servers and authorize charges against those accounts. This payment method is by definition not anonymous. An important advantage of the credit-debit model is its auditability. Once a payment has been deposited, the owner of the debited account can determine who authorized the payment.

- Millicent

Millicent [15] aims at small-scale commercial transactions over electronic networks.

- NetCheque

NetCheque is a distributed accounting service supporting the credit-debit model of payment.

- UEPS

UEPS, the Universal Electronic Payment System [16], is an electronic fund transfer product based on off-line operation.

Others

There are many systems in this category e.g. First Virtual Holdings, FSTC's Electronic Check project, Net-Bill.

2.2.3 Digital currency

Developments in cryptography have brought a new kind of money: the *digital currency* (e.g. the DigiCash system [17], the CAFE project [18]. The digital money, an encoded string of digits, can be carried on a smart-card, or stored on a computer disk. Like a traveler's check, a digital coin is a floating claim on a bank or other financial institution that is not linked to any particular account. One cardholder can make a payment to another without bank involvement, by

Human Perspectives in the Internet Society: Culture, Psychology and Gender, K. Morgan, J. Sanchez, C. A. Brebbia & A Voiskounsky (Editors) © 2004 WIT Press, www.witpress.com, ISBN 1-85312-726-4

placing both cards in a 'digital wallet' that moves coins from one card to the other.

- ***DigiCash***

  The DigiCash system involves the creation of 'electronic coins' in the form of digitally signed numbers in exchange for real money from the user's bank account.

- ***NetCash***

  NetCash is an electronic currency service that supports real-time electronic payments with some provision of anonymity across multiple administrative domains on an unsecured network.

- ***CAFE***

  CAFE provides a high security of all parties concerned without being forced to trust other parties (so-called multi-party security).

- ***Mondex***

  The Mondex system is based on a tamper-proof smart card that holds the cash (in multiple currencies) and the software to make and receive payments.

- ***Brands' off-line electronic cash system***

  In this system a tamper-resistant smart card, issued by the bank and trusted by the user, controls a counter that represents the amount of electronic cash carried by the user [19].

- ***Others***

  Other systems in this category are currently in test or actually in use (e.g. Chipknip and Chipper in the Netherlands)

3 Research methodology and design

The research which this paper describes was intended to identify common effectiveness criteria for Internet payment systems. But before these criteria could be identified, it was necessary to define two subsidiary objectives:

- What are the Criteria to compare, according to each party involved in an Internet payment system?

- Who are the main parties involved with Internet payment systems?

3.1 The identification of effectiveness indicators for IPS

The main reason given was that success factors for IPS primarily depend on customers' needs, so that some effectiveness indicators for IPS providers and financial institutions also depend on consumers' effectiveness indicators. The effectiveness indicators produced as a result of the research [20] include:

- **Ability to allow refunds:** merchants should be able to refund payments to clients if necessary.

Human Perspectives in the Internet Society: Culture, Psychology and Gender, K. Morgan, J. Sanchez, C. A. Brebbia & A Voiskounsky (Editors) © 2004 WIT Press, www.witpress.com, ISBN 1-85312-726-4

- **Ability to support both on-line and off-line activity**: allows more flexibility to operate the system even when the network breaks down.
- **Acceptability: IPS** must be accepted at a wide variety of stores and banks.
- **Accountability:** transactions must be accountable.
- **Anonymity:** the ability to conceal the identity of the payee.
- **Authentication:** the ability to authenticate the users of the system.
- **Customer support:** the IPS should be able to assist customers electronically at minimum cost and throughout the day.
- **Duration of transaction process:** the time it takes to approve the payment (transaction delay must be minimized as far as possible.
- **Ease of use (convenience)**: the IPS must be as convenient as cash to use on any occasion. Its software must also be easy to use (user-friendly).
- **Exchangeability (also known as fungibility):** funds must be easily exchangeable between parties.
- **Flexibility:** the ability to allow different kinds of IPS.
- **Functionality:** the need to increase the functionality of systems to gain competitive advantage over competitors.
- **Irrefutability:** the ability to ensure that the payments cannot be refuted or disproved.
- **Legal certainty:** payments made using an IPS must be legally accepted.
- **Low fixed costs:** costs (including set-up cost, equipment cost and infrastructure cost) must be reasonably low for consumers and merchants.
- **Low transaction cost:** cost of the transaction itself must be as low as possible (zero transaction cost is desirable if possible (just like a cash transaction).
- **Portability (remote access):** the ability to allow consumers to make payments from a variety of locations using a range of different interface devices.
- **Privacy:** the ability to maintain public confidence to ensure customer privacy.
- **Profitability (cost-effectiveness):** implementing the IPS must be profitable and cost-effective, especially from the merchant's perspective.
- **Regulatory framework:** the system must be able to operate in a regulatory framework that the regulators understand and can enforce.
- **Reliability (trustworthiness):** the IPS must be reliable, so that merchants and consumers will have confidence in using the system.
- **Responsibility:** the IPS must be responsible for any fraud, data security, or data privacy.
- **Scalability:** the ability to decentralize the system as much as possible to avoid bottlenecks.
- **Security:** the ability to protect the details of transactions and customers from internal and external fraud/criminal usage.
- **Traceability:** the ability to trace back the transaction, particularly in the case of illegal activities.
- **Transferability:** the ability to transfer value between customers.

Human Perspectives in the Internet Society: Culture, Psychology and Gender, K. Morgan, J. Sanchez, C. A. Brebbia & A Voiskounsky (Editors) © 2004 WIT Press, www.witpress.com, ISBN 1-85312-726-4

- **Universality:** a global standard interface (allow use anywhere around the world).
- **Unobtrusiveness:** the ability to integrate the system into the user's daily life.

According to the responses [21], some characteristics are perceived as more important than others. Characteristics of primary importance are: ***applicability, traceability, trust, security, convertibility, ease of use*** *and* ***reliability***. Lower level of importance was attributed to anonymity and efficiency. The survey illustrated that characteristics of anonymity and support for small payments are perceived by users as unimportant, in contrast to the numerous works that treat them as crucial issues and motivate building whole systems around these characteristics.

3.2 Main parties

According to viewpoint (*Tae-Hwan Shon*, *Paula M.C. Swatman*,), The first result of them survey had led to the identification of six principal roles for those directly involved with IPS [22]:

- Financial Institutions (including bank and non-bank financial institutions).
- IPS Providers (Manufacturers).
- Merchants (vendors).
- Consumers.
- Regulators.
- Network providers

This paper briefly describes the different types of main parties in at least two sets of parties (with broadly similar interests within each set) will need to participate: ***customers*** and ***merchants*** on the one hand, and ***financial institutions*** and ***regulators*** and **IPS Providers** and **Network providers** on the other hand. Arbitrators may be needed in case of a dispute.

At present, the consumer group is the key success factor for IPS success. Effectiveness indicators for IPS vary depending on a number of factors, such as what consumers are looking for and what kinds of payments are being made.

4 The criteria from the viewpoints of users

4.1 Concerns of customers and merchants

1. *Security*
   - Three Levels of Security:

   Digital Signatures- Server Authentication- Factor User Authentication

2. *Acceptability*
3. *Convenience*

4. *Cost*
5. Privacy
6. *Durability*
7. *Immediate control*

4.2 From the viewpoints of *financial institutions* & *regulators* and IPS providers and network providers

8. Traceability
9. Control over the *spread of encryption* mechanisms
10. Transaction cost

Other Criteria:

11. Transaction Size
12. Ability to build up the customers purchasing pattern
13. Availability
14. Reliability
15. On-line and off-line
16. Use of dedicated tamper-resistance hardware versus software only

5 Multi analysis of the criteria

The possibility that a large share of the economy transactions will be carried on a new medium raises a lot of regulatory and public concerns described above. Many of those concerns appear contradictory and conflicting, not all the properties of an ideal system can be accomplished at the same time.

Privacy versus traceability

A conflict exists between the wish for privacy and anonymity and the possibility and desire of regulators and intermediaries to be able to trace any transaction in the economy. Traditional intermediaries (credit card companies, banks, etc.) emphasize the desire by consumers to be able to trace their own transactions themselves. Their systems have a low level of anonymity and serve more the objectives of the credit service bureau than those of consumers.

Hardware versus software

A dedicated hardware solution might look to be the ideal technical solution in many senses, but raises some economical and technical issues. On the one hand, the smart card, a tamper resistant piece of hardware with security functions, can help to solve the double spending problem in an off-line environment.

Transparency versus explicitness

On the one hand users may want transparent money transaction algorithms, the real money transactions are hidden from the user. But on the other hand the users

Human Perspectives in the Internet Society: Culture, Psychology and Gender, K. Morgan, J. Sanchez, C. A. Brebbia & A Voiskounsky (Editors) © 2004 WIT Press, www.witpress.com, ISBN 1-85312-726-4

want to be in the control-loop of all the money transactions. They want to be sure that they only pay what they have asked for and they do not want to spend any money without being notified. Monitoring Customer Purchasing Pattern Privacy advocates are concerned with the use of e-payment systems to assemble details of a customer's purchasing profile across many different merchants. In the case of electronic checks, access to the ACH is needed, so that the merchant cannot offer e-checks themselves. A service provider is required who, therefore, has access to the customer's account number.

Online versus offline

Offline payments involve no contact with a third party during payment the transaction involves only the payer and payee. The obvious problem with offline payments is that it is difficult to prevent payers from spending more money than they actually possess. Online payments involve an authorization server (usually as part of the issuer or acquirer) in each payment. Online systems obviously require more communication. In general, they are considered more secure than offline systems. Most proposed Internet payment systems are online. All proposed payment systems based on electronic hardware, including Mondex and CAFE (Conditional Access for Europe), are offline systems. Mondex is the only system that enables offline transferability: The payee can use the amount received to make a new payment himself, without having to go to the bank in between. CAFE is the only system that provides strong payer anonymity and untraceability. CAFE also provides loss tolerance, which allows the payer to recover from coin losses (but at the expense of some anonymity in case of loss). Mondex and CAFE are multicurrency purses capable of handling different currencies simultaneously. All these systems can be used for Internet payments, Instead of tamper-resistant hardware, offline authorization could be given via preauthorization.

6 Summary

To talk about importance of user-related factors of electronic payment systems we have to take into account that users' perception of payment systems is perception of a complex system with numerous parameters. From the way users perceive and feel about them they make difference in acceptance of the systems, provided that there is more than one system available. Thus, user acceptance of electronic payment systems on mass scale depends greatly on users' attitudes; feasible technological solutions are not the only important issues, but these systems will be perceived in a complex of facets. Issues of **Convertibility, Security, and Applicability** rise with seriousness not by themselves but also because they influence users and their subsequent decision to use payment systems. In relation to variable of anonymity, designers can face a choice: should they design a system that is not anonymous, provided that most of the users do not really feel need for anonymity and may never face consequences of misuse of their private information, or should they deliver a maximally anonymous

Human Perspectives in the Internet Society: Culture, Psychology and Gender, K. Morgan, J. Sanchez, C. A. Brebbia & A Voiskounsky (Editors) © 2004 WIT Press, www.witpress.com, ISBN 1-85312-726-4

solution, thinking that users do not really understand the problem and indeed should be protected in spite of incomprehension? There is also a trade-off: when aiming to provide full anonymity that is possible with the available technology, the resulting systems may fall short on other issues, e.g. being hard to operate or inefficient. Another result derived about small payments is that there might be a significant probability that users may not understand the real need of small payments that is emerging in the Internet industry, or they don't feel need for them simply because they are used getting things for free. However business models that are based on giving out free information and other commodities cannot stay for too long, now we are observing shifts from this direction. Small payments and micro payments will certainly find their place in various applications on the Internet.

7 Conclusion

First: there are a wide variety of electronic payment systems available and payment methods must offer requirements of the user's acceptance. an important conclusion can be made that it makes sense to be more specific in targeting payment systems for various context of use. This has implications that different systems should be designed for various applications and contexts, and there will not be one solution that covers all the requirements. For example, there may be cases when anonymity or convertibility is not highly important in relation to other characteristics. Thus user acceptance implies that people are willing to use a system for payments especially if there is more than one payment system available. Acceptance is dependent on:

-Perception of manifestation of characteristics of payment systems· - Specific applications for payment system for different contexts of use

Second: This survey was a necessary step needed to find out user needs and to guide further design of electronic payment systems with high user acceptance. These results are currently subject to a more detailed analysis. Although survey could identify some problems with defining important characteristics of payment systems, further research will have to employ other techniques for finding dimensions of user acceptance and its relations to characteristics, and validate them. This can be case studies or field research. The next step will be to develop guidelines and principles for design of user-accepted electronic payment systems.

References

[1] Wayner, P., (eds.) Digital Cash: Commerce on the Net, Morgan Kaufmann Publishers, 1997.

[2] Abrazhevich D., Electronic Payment Systems: Issues of User Acceptance, Samenwerkings Organ Brabantse Universiteiten (SOBU), Technical University of Eindhoven (TUE), pp. 1-7, 2001.

Human Perspectives in the Internet Society: Culture, Psychology and Gender, K. Morgan, J. Sanchez, C. A. Brebbia & A Voiskounsky (Editors) © 2004 WIT Press, www.witpress.com, ISBN 1-85312-726-4

[3] Bellare, M., Variety Cash: a Multi-purpose Electronic Payment System (Extended Abstract), Proceedings of the 3rd Usenix Workshop on Electronic Commerce, eds. J. Garry, C. Jutla, M. Yung, 1998.

[4] Tygar, D., Atomicity in electronic commerce. Proc. Fifteenth Annual ACM Symposium on Principles of Distributed Computing, Philadelphia, pp. 8-26, May 1996.

[5] Poon, S. and Swatman, P.M.C., The Internet for small businesses: an enabling infrastructure for competitiveness, Proceedings of the Fifth Internet Society Conference, Ed. C. Kilnam, Hawaii: USA, pp. 221-31. , 1995. Poon, S. and Swatman, P.M.C., Electronic networking among small business in Australia: an exploratory study. Proceedings of the Ninth International Conference on EDI-IOS, Eds., P.M.C Swatman, et al., Bled: Slovenia, pp. 446-60, 1996. Poon, S. and Swatman, P.M.C., Internet-based small business communications: seven Australian cases. Proceedings of the 1997 PACIS Conference, Brisbane: Australia, 1997.

[6] Furche, A. and G. Wrightson, Computer Money: A Systematic Overview of Electronic Payment Systems, Morgan Kaufman Pubs.: Los Altos, CA, 1996.

[7] O'Mahony, D., M. Pierce and H. Tewari, Electronic Payment Systems, Attach House Pubs. Norwood MA, 1997.

[8] Vartanian, T.P., R.H. Lei dig, R.H. and L. Bureau, 21st Century Money Banking and Commerce, Fried, Frank, Harris, Shriver & Jacobson Pubs.: New York, NY, 1998.

[9] Wright David, Comparative evaluation of electronic payment systems, INFOR Journal, University of Ottawa, Feb 2002.

[10] Asokan, N. & P. A. Jansen & M., Steiner & M., Waidner, The State of the Art in Electronic Payment Systems, IBM Zurich Research Laboratory, IEEE, September , pp. 28 – 35, 1997.

[11] Hnatyuk Yuri, et al, Money Mover: Electronic Payment System, User System Interaction Programmer, Eindhoven University of Technology: Eindhoven, Netherlands, pp. 1-4, 2002. http://usis ql.ipo.tue.nl/momo

[12] White L.H., The technology revolution and monetary evolution. The future of money in the information age, Cato Institute's 14th Annual Monetary Conference, Washington D.C., May 23, 1996 (see also: http://www.cato.org/moneyconf/14mc-7.html

[13] Bellare, M., Relations among notions of security for public-key encryption schemes: Advances in Cryptology, Crypto 98 Proceedings, eds., A. Desai, D. Pointcheval and P. Rogaway, Springer-Verlag, 1998.

[14] Medvinsky, G. and Neuman, B.C., Requirements for Network Payment: The NetCheque TM Perspective. Proceedings of the IEEE Comp, Con'95, San Francisco, 1995. ftp://prospero.isi.edu/pub/papers/security/

[15] Glassman S. et al., the Millicent Protocol for Inexpensive Electronic Commerce. Proceedings of the 4th International World Wide Web Conference, December, 1995. (see also: http://www.research.digital.com:80/SRC/millicent/

Human Perspectives in the Internet Society: Culture, Psychology and Gender, K. Morgan, J. Sanchez, C. A. Brebbia & A Voiskounsky (Editors) © 2004 WIT Press, www.witpress.com, ISBN 1-85312-726-4

[16] Anderson R.J.: "UEPS - a second generation electronic wallet", Computer Security - ESORICS 92, Springer LNCS v 648, pp 411-418. (see also ftp://ftp.cl.cam.uk/users/rja14/ smartcards PS. Z)

[17] Chaum D., Achieving electronic privacy", Scientific American, pp 96-101, August 1992, (see also: http://digicash.support.nl/publish/sciam.html

[18] Boly, J. P. et al., The ESPRIT Project CAFÉ: High Security Digital Payment Systems- ESORICS '94, LNCS 875, Springer-Verlag, Berlin, pp.217-230, 1994. http://www.informatik and Mondex; http://www.mondex.com.

[19] Brands, S., Untraceable Off-line Cash in Wallet with Observers," Lecture Notes in Computer Science, 773, pp. 302-318, 1994.

[20] Shon, Tae-Hwan and Paula, M.C. Swatman, Copyright MCB UP Limited,1998.

[21] Abrazhevich D., Electronic Payment Systems: Issues of User Acceptance, Samenwerkings Organ Brabantse Universiteiten (SOBU), Technical University of Eindhoven (TUE), pp. 1-7, 2001.

[22] Shon Tae-Hwan and Swatman Paula M.C., Identifying effectiveness criteria for Internet payment systems. Internet Research. Copyright MCB UP Limited, Bradford: Vol. 8, Iss.3; pg.202-222, 1998.

Human Perspectives in the Internet Society: Culture, Psychology and Gender, K. Morgan, J. Sanchez, C. A. Brebbia & A Voiskounsky (Editors) © 2004 WIT Press, www.witpress.com, ISBN 1-85312-726-4

Interoperable and flexible digital signatures for e-government and e-commerce

H. Baier & M. Ruppert
Darmstadt Center of IT Security and FlexSecure Ltd., Alexanderstr. 10, D 64283 Darmstadt

Abstract

The paper at hand presents the concept of a flexible and interoperable public key infrastructure, the so called FlexiPKI. We show how this concept and its realization enables long term security in e-government and e-commerce. As a proof of concept, we describe the implementation of the FlexiPKI concept at the root certification authority in Germany.
Keywords: cryptography, digital signatures, e-government, public key infrastructure, Java Cryptography Architecture.

1 Introduction

As of today public key infrastructures become more and more popular because of their fundamental role to achieve security goals like authenticity, integrity, non-repudiation, and confidentiality in open user groups. The security of public key infrastructures mainly depends on the security of digital signatures.

The main purpose of a public key infrastructure (PKI) is to bind a public key to an entity of the infrastructure. The binding is put into practice by a certification authority (CA), which plays the role of a trusted third party. The CA digitally signs a data structure, which contains besides some other data the name of the entity and the corresponding public key. The data structure together with the CA signature is called a *certificate*. Once, the CA signatures become invalid, the whole infrastructure collapses. All online applications like e-commerce, online banking, or e-government are no longer secure.

In 2001, based on the European Digital Signature Directive [1], European countries established a new German Digital Signature Act [2] to support the further development of e-government and e-commerce. In Germany, the Regulatory

Human Perspectives in the Internet Society: Culture, Psychology and Gender, K. Morgan, J. Sanchez, C. A. Brebbia & A Voiskounsky (Editors) © 2004 WIT Press, www.witpress.com, ISBN 1-85312-726-4

Authority for Telecommunications and Posts (RegTP) operates the root certification authority (RCA) in conformance with the Digital Signature Act. Currently, the RegTP is installing a new RCA-software. In order to reduce the total cost of ownership and to ensure long-time security, the main design criteria of the software are interoperability and flexibility of the underlying cryptographic primitive.

The contribution of the paper at hand is as follows: First, in Section 2 we describe in detail general requirements for high security digital signatures as needed in the context of e-government and e-commerce. We are not aware of any comparable catalogue of requirements. Next, in Section 3 we describe our concept of an interoperable and flexible public key infrastructure. It is interoperable as our implementation respects all common certificate profiles (such as PKIX [3] and ISIS-MTT [4]). It is flexible for two reasons. First, it is based on the Java Cryptography Architecture (JCA), a Java based framework for cryptographic algorithms. The JCA only delivers the cryptographic interfaces, not their implementation. The implementation is done within a cryptographic service provider (CSP). Second, our approach makes use of the FlexiProvider [5], which is a CSP for the JCA. Currently, the FlexiProvider comprises independent digital signature schemes like RSA, elliptic curve based signatures, and number field cryptographic schemes. Therefore, our PKI is flexible with respect to the underlying mathematical problem. This concept is called the FlexiPKI [6]. We show that our concept of the FlexiPKI meets the requirements of Section 2.

As a proof of concept we show in Section 4, that the new RCA will make use of the concept of FlexiPKI. We therefore consider our concept of FlexiPKI as a best practice solution. The RCA will be able to support RSA, DSA, and the elliptic curve digital signature algorithms. We conclude that our approach is superior to common approaches in the past. Finally, in Section 5 we discuss future developments of our concept.

2 Requirements on digital signatures for e-government use

In this section we describe the requirements, which we impose on digital signatures for use in applications for e-government or e-commerce. First of all, we have to stress that non-repudiation plays a crucial role to establish digital signatures. Non-repudiation of a digital signature has to be provable for a long time. For instance, the German Digital Signature Act enforces qualified certificates to be verifiable for over 30 years [2]. In Section 2.1 we therefore present requirements to ensure long term security.

In addition, e-government or e-commerce applications will be in use by most of the population. A PKI in this context has to operate for millions of people. For example, the CA must produce millions of certificates or must answer millions of requests about the validity of certificates in a relatively short time. We discuss in Section 2.2 the requirements for such a scalable PKI.

Finally, certificates should be used by a broad variety of applications. The certificates thus have to be interoperable. In Section 2.3 we describe common profiles to ensure interoperability.

Human Perspectives in the Internet Society: Culture, Psychology and Gender, K. Morgan, J. Sanchez, C. A. Brebbia & A Voiskounsky (Editors) © 2004 WIT Press, www.witpress.com, ISBN 1-85312-726-4

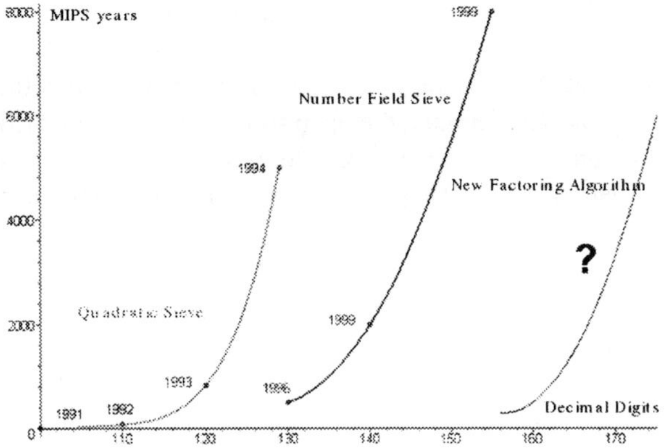

Figure 1: Time to factor an RSA-modulus.

2.1 Long term security

In order to ensure long term security, we have to take various aspects into account. In this section we present the most important ones. First, the underlying cryptographic algorithm has to be secure for a long time. As there is currently no such algorithm available, long term security is achieved by the ability to use different cryptographic algorithms. We present our approach to this problem in Section 2.1.1. Second, we have to make use of a secure hardware, which actually generates a digital signature. However, this hardware often depends on the cryptographic algorithm in use. Once we switch from one algorithm to another one, we have to switch the hardware, too. This results in growing costs. We turn to the problem of appropriate signature hardware in Section 2.1.2. Finally, even if a signature is valid from a mathematical point of view, it is not clear if the signature will be accepted. The decision of acceptance is dependent on the underlying validity model. Different validity models have been proposed in the past. We discuss them in Section 2.1.3 and explain our choice.

2.1.1 Cryptographic algorithms

We discuss our approach to ensure long term security at the level of the cryptographic algorithm. Each public key algorithm, which is appropriate for use in practice, relies on a difficult mathematical problem. The most popular algorithm is the RSA algorithm. As of today RSA is attacked by solving the factoring problem. However, we do not know how difficult the factoring problem actually is. In the past, different factoring methods have been found, which resulted in a significant speed up in the time to factor an RSA modulus, respectively. This is shown in Figure 1.

As a result, we have to be able to use different public key algorithms. Good candidates are the Digital Signature Algorithm (DSA [7]) and the Elliptic Curve

Human Perspectives in the Internet Society: Culture, Psychology and Gender, K. Morgan, J. Sanchez, C. A. Brebbia & A Voiskounsky (Editors) © 2004 WIT Press, www.witpress.com, ISBN 1-85312-726-4

Digital Signature Algorithm (ECDSA [8]). Analogously we have to consider different hash functions.

However, in order to be usable, these algorithms have to be efficiently implemented. Our cryptographic library, the open source FlexiProvider [5], fulfills these requirements. When we proclaim the paradigm of flexibility of the cryptographic algorithm we mean the ability to flexibly choose the cryptographic algorithm.

2.1.2 Signature hardware

The generation of qualified digital signatures enforces the use of special hardware. This hardware has to be evaluated on the basis of ITSEC [9] or the Common Criteria [10]. However, as of today, only smart cards are successfully evaluated. Thus only hardware with restricted resources is available. For this reason, smart cards are often developed for one special use case. A good example is the use of RSA with at most 1024 bit modulus size. This contradicts the paradigm of flexibility as explained in Section 2.1.1.

We therefore propose to be able to easily integrate state of the art cryptographic hardware. Then the total costs of the PKI will be reduced. This becomes more evident once a cryptographic algorithm is broken.

2.1.3 Validity models

We now turn to the problem of an appropriate validity model. This means the following: The validation of a digital signature first involves a mathematical operation. The result is either `true` or `false`. The validation makes use of the public key of the signer. If the mathematical validation outputs `false`, the digital signature will not be accepted. However, even if the output is `true`, the signature may be rejected. The acceptance of the signature depends on validity of the corresponding public key. Its validity is defined within the underlying validity model.

In all, three different validity models have been proposed: The shell model, the hybrid model, and the chain model. Before we turn to these validity models, we first have to explain the notation of a certificate chain. A PKI has one common trusted anchor: the certificate of the root certification authority. Often a root certification authority issues certificates to further certification authorities. Each such CA is called a second step CA. A second step CA may issue certificates to end users or to further CAs, that is to third step CAs. A certificate chain is a chain from an end user certificate to the common trusted root CA certificate.

The shell model requires *all* certificates in the certificate chain to be valid at the signature *validation* time. However, certificates are valid for at most five years. Once one of the certificates in the certificate chain becomes invalid, all signatures will be rejected. Thus in the context of long term validation, this is not a good choice.

Next, we turn to the hybrid model. It is called the modified shell model, too. The hybrid model requires *all* certificates in the certificate chain to be valid at the signature *generation* time. Thus a valid signature stays valid forever. In order to achieve long term validation, this seems to be an acceptable choice to us. However, we prefer the following chain model.

Human Perspectives in the Internet Society: Culture, Psychology and Gender, K. Morgan, J. Sanchez, C. A. Brebbia & A Voiskounsky (Editors) © 2004 WIT Press, www.witpress.com, ISBN 1-85312-726-4

In the chain model a signature is valid, if the signer possesses a valid certificate at signature generation time. In the context of a signature generated by an end user, this means that the end user certificate has to be valid at the signature generation time. In the context of a signature for a certificate this means, that the issuer's certificate has to be valid at the certificate production time. To us this seems to be the best choice.

The answer, if a public key is valid or not at a fixed time, is given by the directory services or the revocation services of a PKI. The validity model is part of the certification policies. All models are in use in practice. Thus a flexible PKI should be able to switch from one validity model to another one.

2.2 Bulk generation of digital signatures

E-government applications address the whole population. A PKI for e-government thus has to operate for millions of people. The CA, for instance, has to be able to generate millions of certificates in a relatively short time, say some weeks. However, certificate generation is not the most requested service of a PKI. The directory and revocation services must answer millions of queries about the validity of a certificate, again in a relatively short time. Often, the Online Certificate Status Protocol (OCSP [11]) is used for status queries. The OCSP answers must be signed digitally. Thus a scalable PKI has to be able to address this feature.

In practice, bulk generation of qualified digital signatures is a rather difficult problem for two reasons. First, the German Digital Signature Act only allows to issue qualified certificates to natural persons. Second, it understands a qualified signature as a declaration of intention. As a consequence it is a strong demand that the signer actually sees what he is going to sign before his approval. At a first glance this contradicts the requirements for bulk generation of digital signatures. However, workarounds to solve this problem exist [12].

2.3 Interoperability

A certificate is used within a PKI application to ensure that a given public key actually belongs to its supposed owner. As of today, a lot of different use cases are known. In general, different use cases require different certificate fields (the so-called extension fields). Extension fields may be defined by everybody. In this context it is very important that the PKI application is able to interpret all extension fields. If this holds for the certificates generated by a CA, then we call the certificates *interoperable*.

In the past, different working groups have written down various profiles for qualified certificates. The main task of a certificate profile is to ensure interoperability. The most important profiles are the PKIX profile [3] and the ISIS-MTT SigG-Profile [4]. We prefer ISIS-MTT for the following reasons.

First of all, the ISIS-MTT SigG-Profile addresses all technical requirements of the *German Digital Signature Act* (SigG) and the *Ordinance on Digital Signatures* (SigV). Although this is closely related to SigG, ISIS-MTT will be adopted by

Human Perspectives in the Internet Society: Culture, Psychology and Gender, K. Morgan, J. Sanchez, C. A. Brebbia & A Voiskounsky (Editors) © 2004 WIT Press, www.witpress.com, ISBN 1-85312-726-4

most European countries. Second, this standard profiles in detail the IETF standards (for example the RFCs of the PKIX and S/MIME working groups). Thus ISIS-MTT is a standard optimization of PKIX for practical use. Third, in contrast to PKIX it is in conformance with the technical specifications of the European Telecommunications Standards Institute [13]. Finally, it restricts the possible implementation alternatives in order to promote interoperability as well as to reduce the costs of implementation and conformity tests.

3 The concept of FlexiPKI

In this section we present our concept of the flexible Public Key Infrastructure, which we abbreviate as FlexiPKI. We show that our FlexiPKI meets the requirements of Section 2.

The main parts of the FlexiPKI are the FlexiProvider and the trustcenter software FlexiTrust. As stated above the FlexiProvider [5] implements various different cryptographic algorithms. Sample schemes are symmetric block ciphers (e.g. AES, 3-DES, Twofish), hash functions (e.g. SHA-1, RIPEMD-160), and digital signature algorithms (e.g. RSA, DSA, ECDSA). A large variety of cryptographic schemes ensures the long term security on the level of the cryptographic algorithm as required in Section 2.1.1.

FlexiTrust is the trustcenter software of the FlexiPKI. Its design and workflow arises from practical experience. We describe it in Section 3.1. The core task of a PKI is the generation of certificates. We come to this area in Section 3.2.

3.1 Design and workflow

We shortly describe the design and workflow of FlexiTrust. FlexiTrust establishes at least three main components for certificate application processing. It consists of a number of modules to fit perfectly to almost every existing environment. The modules are a result of various projects over the last few years. The demands on the certification processes in different application contexts have been put into practice, respectively.

The three core components of FlexiTrust are:

- Registration authority (RA).
- Certification authority (CA).
- Infrastructure services (IS).

The core components and their relationships are given in Figure 2. Let us first describe the registration module. Its main task is to process the registration and application requests. Import of registration data is put into practice using strong authentication. The RA component is scalable: It offers both individual request processing and bulk processing using databases or XML interfaces. The bulk processing is important in context of bulk rollout of certificates as required in Section 2.2. Processing and access rules can individually be defined for all request types.

Human Perspectives in the Internet Society: Culture, Psychology and Gender, K. Morgan, J. Sanchez, C. A. Brebbia & A Voiskounsky (Editors) © 2004 WIT Press, www.witpress.com, ISBN 1-85312-726-4

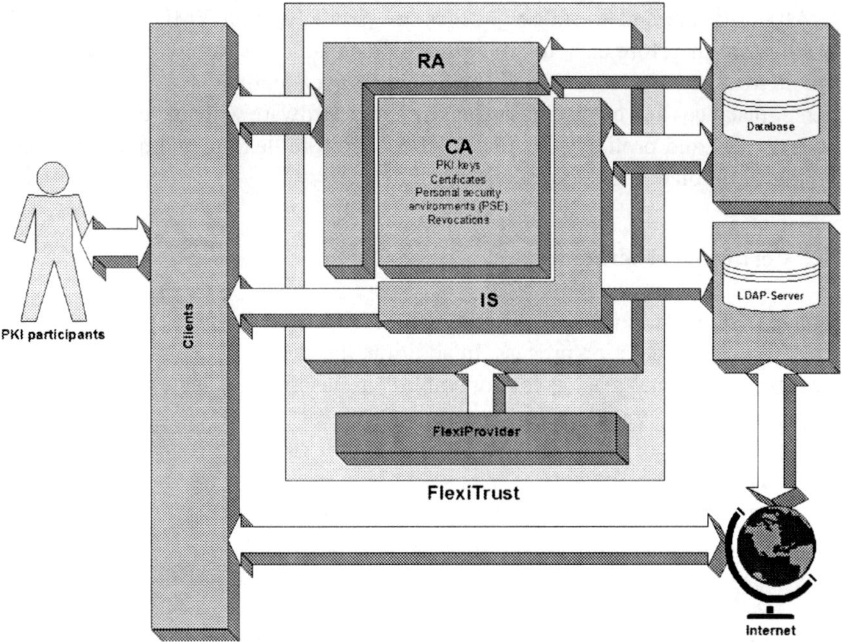

Figure 2: FlexiTrust core design.

We next turn to the CA module. It supports both signing with smartcards and hardware security modules. The CA module is compatible with smartcards and hardware security modules of various suppliers and thus meets the requirement of Section 2.1.2. Furthermore, the CA module allows the two common ways of smartcard personalization. First, it allows both key *and* certificate generation at the certification authority. In this case the module allows to load additional applications on the smartcard. Second, the CA module supports signature token delegation, that is the key generation takes place at the smartcard supplier on the smartcard itself. The CA only handles the certification request (PKCS#10). In this case it is important to use strong authentication (for instance using PKI methods or shared secrets). Last but not least, the visualization of the data to be signed and an interactive signature confirmation are implemented.

Finally, we describe the IS module. Roughly speaking the IS module is responsible for the whole PKI workflow besides registration and certification, that is it handles the whole certificate life cycle after its generation. The IS module handles different secure interfaces to a number of well known PKI services. For instance, the IS module may establish a secure connection to the directory or status information services. These services are not necessarily part of the core components of FlexiTrust, as for these directory services a lot of solutions are available. FlexiPKI supports all validity models presented in Section 2.1.3.

Human Perspectives in the Internet Society: Culture, Psychology and Gender, K. Morgan, J. Sanchez, C. A. Brebbia & A Voiskounsky (Editors) © 2004 WIT Press, www.witpress.com, ISBN 1-85312-726-4

All certificate and workflow profiles are defined within XML structures. The profiles are therefore easy to configure and available for further processing. The whole trustcenter solution has the ability to independently host a number of trustcenter instances and hierarchies using the same hardware with exclusive roll based access rules and profiles. The FlexiPKI is therefore flexible and able to process bulk generation of digital signatures.

3.2 Certificate generation

The requirements of the European Signature Directive [1] affects the workflow of the certificate generation process. In addition, the existence of special profiles for qualified certificates ensures interoperability as described in Section 2.3. The most important security requirements are:

1. Key pairs are unique.
2. The hardware for storage and usage of the private key has to be evaluated on basis of the Common Criteria [10] or ITSEC [9].
3. No copy out of this environment is allowed.
4. The private key token has to be handed over to the certificate owner in a secure manner. The owner gives a receipt.
5. Key and identity will be assigned for about 30 years and the assignment can be verified in the entire period. Thus certificates and all corresponding data have to be stored and be available for a long time. If necessary, this requires re-signatures and time stamping over the data.
6. Every qualified certificate identifies exactly one natural person.
7. A certificate is valid only, if the responsible trustcenter declares the certificate as valid.

The trustcenter software FlexiTrust meets these requirements. It is in conformance with the ISIS-MTT profile and thus guarantees interoperability.

We mention a common problem in the context of certificate generation. As mentioned above, qualified certificates are issued to a natural person. However, often this person does not sign himself, but he delegates the signature process to other persons. From a technical point of view it is not possible to assign such signatures to its signer. Thus a special workflow has to be established to ensure such an assignment.

Typically delegated signatures are used within trustcenter processes. The owner and responsible person for the root or CA keys will never use these keys himself. The delegation is then established by separation of functions.

4 Best practice and proof-of-concept

In this section we describe, how we put into practice our concept of the FlexiPKI. To our mind, the project serves as a best practice example for an interoperable and flexible PKI. In addition, it is a best practice for the cooperation between a research group (Darmstadt University of Technology) and industry (FlexSecure Ltd.).

Human Perspectives in the Internet Society: Culture, Psychology and Gender, K. Morgan, J. Sanchez, C. A. Brebbia & A Voiskounsky (Editors) © 2004 WIT Press, www.witpress.com, ISBN 1-85312-726-4

In the first quarter of 2003, the German Regulatory Authority for Telecommunications and Posts (RegTP) published a call for tender to replace the old root certification authority (RCA) system. T-Systems, a leading provider of information and communications technology services, and FlexSecure, a spin off of Darmstadt University of Technology, submitted a joint offer. The key point of our proposal was the use of FlexiPKI and FlexiTrust within the new RCA instance. Our consortium won the contest.

The customer pointed out that the choice of FlexiTrust was well founded in its ability to establish fail safe concepts and to be updated to new security requirements with almost no effort to enable longterm security. In less than nine months the new solution was specified, adapted to the special needs of the RCA, evaluated and installed.

It was designed to carry out the requirements of the RegTP as well as the requirements of ISIS-MTT. The practical experience during the specification and implementation period ended up in redesigned parts of the ISIS-MTT profiles. For example, a new certificate extension `Validity Model` (http://www.informatik.tu-darmstadt.de/TI/Forschung/FlexiPKI/validitymodel/index.html) was defined to be able to identify the underlying validity model without reading the certification policy.

An entire Common Criteria protection profile meeting the requirements of the German Digital Signature Act had to be specified during the evaluation process with respect to high security achievements as well as basic rules to establish delegated bulk signatures for OCSP services and signature renewal. As a result, the current version of FlexiTrust 3.0 Release 0347 is evaluated according to the Common Criteria, Evaluation Assurance Level (EAL) 3+ high. We point out that FlexiTrust is the only available trustcenter software with such an evaluation.

The development of FlexiTrust started 1999 at Darmstadt University of Technology. The design of FlexiTrust was object oriented ([6]). Two main design criteria determined the development: First, the demand on best integration practice in existing environments. A fundamental basis for this demand is interoperability. Second, the paradigm of long term security based on the flexible use of cryptographic schemes.

5 Forecast

We mention future developments of our FlexiPKI concept. First, as soon as new qualified signature tokens like TCOS 3.0 will be available, FlexiTrust will be re-evaluated. The new evaluation enables signatures with different cryptographic algorithms. Again we point out that this feature is indispensable for the needs of e-government and e-commerce.

Second, we integrate the concept of a fail safe PKI as proposed by Maseberg [14]. Roughly speaking, the fail safe concept is based on a redundant second PKI in the background. Once the operational PKI collapses, the second PKI will stand in to ensure security.

Human Perspectives in the Internet Society: Culture, Psychology and Gender, K. Morgan, J. Sanchez, C. A. Brebbia & A Voiskounsky (Editors) © 2004 WIT Press, www.witpress.com, ISBN 1-85312-726-4

References

[1] Directive of the European Parliament and of the Council on a Community framework for electronic signatures . Directive 1999/93/EC, 1999.

[2] German Digital Signature Act: Gesetz über Rahmenbedingungen für elektronische Signaturen und zur Änderung weiterer Vorschriften, Bundesgesetzblatt Nr 22, 2001, S876ff.

[3] PKIX: Internet X.509 Public Key Infrastructure Qualified Certificates Profile. RFC3039, 2001.

[4] ISIS-MTT: Common ISIS-MailTrusT Specifications for Interoperable PKI Applications, Optional Profile. SigG-Profile, 2002.

[5] FlexiProvider, A Provider for the Java Cryptography Architecture. http://www.flexiprovider.de, 2004.

[6] Buchmann, J., Ruppert, M. & Tak, M., FlexiPKI - Realisierung einer flexiblen Public-Key Infrastruktur. *P. Horster: Systemsicherheit*, Vieweg, 2000.

[7] FIPS186: Digital Signature Standard. Federal Information Processing Standards Publication 186, 1994.

[8] X9.62 - Public Key Cryptography for the Financial Services Industry: The Elliptic Curve Digital Signature Algorithm (ECDSA). ANSI, 1998.

[9] ITSEC: Information Technology Security Evaluation Criteria. 1991.

[10] Common Criteria for Information Technology Security Evaluation (CC), Version 2.0. ISO/IEC-Standard 15408, 1998.

[11] X.509 Internet Public Key Infrastructure Online Certificate Status Protocol. RFC2560, 1999.

[12] Huehnlein, D. & Knosowski, Y., 1000mal signiert: Aspekte der Massensignatur. *Zeitschrift fuer Kommunikationssicherheit*, **02**, 2003.

[13] ETSI TS 101 862 v1.2.1 (2001-06): Qualified Certificate Profile, Technical Specification. 2001.

[14] Maseberg, S., *Fail-Safe-Konzept für Public-Key-Infrastrukturen*. Ph.D. thesis, Technische Universitt Darmstadt, 2002.

Human Perspectives in the Internet Society: Culture, Psychology and Gender, K. Morgan, J. Sanchez, C. A. Brebbia & A Voiskounsky (Editors) © 2004 WIT Press, www.witpress.com, ISBN 1-85312-726-4

Author Index

WITPRESS

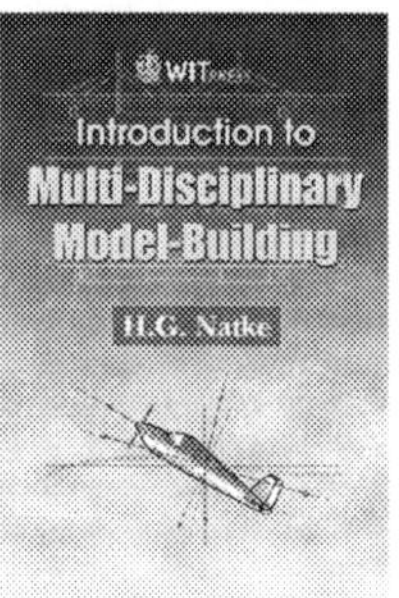

WIT PRESS
Introduction to
Multi-Disciplinary
Model-Building
H.G. Natke

Lightning Source UK Ltd.
Milton Keynes UK
09 December 2009

147258UK00001B/18/A

9 781853 127267